MICHAEL AND NATASHA

The Life and Love of Michael II, the Last of the Romanov Tsars

ROSEMARY AND DONALD CRAWFORD

A LISA DREW BOOK
SCRIBNER

A LISA DREW BOOK/SCRIBNER
1230 Avenue of the Americas
New York, NY 10020

Originally published in Great Britain by Weidenfeld & Nicolson

Manufactured in the United States of America

1 3 5 7 9 10 8 6 4 2

Library of Congress Cataloging-in-Publication Data
Crawford, Rosemary.
Michael and Natasha : the life and love of Michael II,
the last of the Romanov tsars / Rosemary and Donald Crawford.
p. cm.
"A Lisa Drew Book"
1. Mikhail Aleksandrovich, Grand Duke of Russia, 1878–1918.
2. Sheremetevskaya, Nathalie, Countess Brassova, d. 1952.
3. Princes—Russia—Biography. 4. Countesses—Russia—Biography.
5. Romanov, House of. 6. Russia—History—Nicholas, 1894–1917.
I. Crawford, Donald. II. Title.
DK254.M513C73 1997
947.08'0922—dc21
[B] 97-22550
CIP

ISBN 0-684-83430-8

For Roderick, Alastair
and Antonia

My darling, beautiful Natasha, there are not enough words with which I could thank you for all that you are giving me in my life. Our stay here will be always the brightest memory of my whole existence. Don't be sad – with God's help we shall meet again very soon. Please do always believe all my words and my tenderest love to thee, to my darling, dearest star, whom I will never, never leave or abandon. I embrace you and kiss you all over . . .

Please believe that I am all yours. Misha.

Grand Duke Michael Aleksandrovich of Russia writing to Natasha, Copenhagen, August 13, 1909

She's such a cunning, wicked beast that it's disgusting even to talk about her.

Nicholas II on Natasha, after her runaway marriage to Michael, November 21, 1912

Walking in the Liteiny about four o'clock I called on Soloviev, the dealer in rare books and old prints. As I was examining several fine 18th-century French editions in the back of his empty shop, I saw a slender young woman of about thirty come in and take a seat at a table on which an album of prints was laid out. She was a delight to watch. Her whole style revealed a quiet, personal and refined taste. Her chinchilla coat, open at the neck, gave a glimpse of silver-grey taffeta with trimmings of lace. A light fur cap blended with her glistening fair hair. Her pure and aristocratic face is charmingly modelled and she has light velvety eyes. Round her neck a string of superb pearls sparkled in the light. There was a dignified, sinuous and soft gracefulness about her every movement.

Maurice Paléologue, French Ambassador to Russia, February 10, 1916, on first seeing Natasha

She hates you, and does all she can to prevent your name being even mentioned.

Natasha to Michael, about the Empress Alexandra, July 9, 1916

To His Majesty the Emperor Michael: Recent events have forced me to decide irrevocably to take this extreme step. Forgive me if it grieves you and also for no warning – there was no time. Shall always remain a faithful and devoted brother. Now returning to HQ where hope to come back shortly to Tsarskoe Selo. Fervently pray God to help you and our country. Your Nicky.

Telegram from Nicholas II to his brother after abdicating in his favour, March 3, 1917

CONTENTS

List of illustrations ix–xi
Genealogy xii–xiii
Introduction 1

PART I LOVE AND MARRIAGE

1 'That Sinner' 5
2 Darling Floppy 17
3 The Lieutenant's Bride 33
4 An Innocent Abroad 46
5 Scandal in Gatchina 59
6 Pistols at Dawn 67
7 Mistress in Moscow 81
8 A Son is Born 100
9 A Woman Scorned 109
10 A Runaway Marriage 122
11 Exile in Europe 138
12 Mistress of Knebworth 147

PART II WAR AND REVOLUTION

13 Going to War 159
14 Lily-of-the-Valley 170
15 Love and Duty 182
16 Alexandra the Great 195
17 Rival Courts 209
18 War on Two Fronts 221
19 Murder Most Fair 237
20 Palace Plotters 247
21 'Make Yourself Regent' 255
22 Address Unknown 268
23 A Father's Feelings 279

PART III THE LAST EMPEROR

24 Emperor Michael 295
25 Playing for Time 302
26 Retreat to Gatchina 315
27 Citizen Michael 327
28 Prisoner of Perm 341
29 Death in the Woods 353
30 Long Live Michael 364

PART IV THE FINAL TRAGEDY

31 The Death of Hope 381

Acknowledgements 396
Chapter Notes 400
Bibliography 429
Index 434

ILLUSTRATIONS

Between pages 112 and 113

Nicholas II and his brother Grand Duke Michael Aleksandrovich[1]

Michael at a formal meeting of State Council, 1901[2] (detail from painting by Repin)

Grand Duke Michael Aleksandrovich, Blue Cuirassiers[3]

Princess Beatrice of Great Britain and Saxe-Coburg-Gotha ('Baby-Bee')[4]

Princess Patricia of Connaught ('Patsy')[4]

Sergei Mamontov, Natasha's first husband[3]

Lieutenant Vladimir Vladimirovich Wulfert, Blue Cuirassiers[1]

Natasha, photographed by Michael[1]

Michael, Natasha, Grand Duchess Olga, Captain Nikolai Kulikovsky[3]

Michael, Grand Duchess Olga, Wulfert, Natasha, Duke Peter of Oldenburg[1]

The Wulferts at home[1]

Pyramid in a park: Michael, Natasha, Wulfert and others[1]

Close friends: Michael with Wulfert and Natasha[1]

Michael in Copenhagen, photographed by Natasha[1]

Michael's family: Michael, the Dowager Empress Marie Fedorovna, Queen Alexandra of England and Princess Victoria ('Toria')[5]

Natasha's family: Sergei Sheremetevsky, and his three daughters, Olga, Natasha, Vera[1]

Aleksei Matveev, Natasha's brother-in-law and husband of Olga Sheremetevskaya[3]

Michael's estate house at Brasovo, near Orel[1]

1909: Michael at the apartment home of Natasha's parents[1]

Between pages 240 and 241

Michael as colonel of the Chernigov Hussars[1]

Natasha pregnant, photographed at Udinka by Michael[1]

Natasha and her daughter Nathalie ('Tata')[3]

Natasha's birthday portrait, 1911[1]

Michael with his son, George[1]

Michael and Natasha at Brasovo and St Petersburg, and at Brasovo with Michael's adjutant 'Koka' Abakonivich and his wife Maggie, a friend of Natasha[1]

The Getaway Car: Michael and Natasha in his Opel tourer at Bad Kissingen.[1]
Michael, 'the Getaway Man', photographed by Natasha[3]
Honeymoon in Venice[1]
Picnic at Cannes: Natasha, Nicholas Johnson, Grand Duke Andrew Vladimirovich[3]
Michael on the beach at Cannes[1]
Michael and Natasha on the balcony of Hotel du Parc[1]
Lunch table: Michael, Natasha, Grand Duke Andrew, Johnson, Tata, Miss Rata[3]
Skating at St Moritz[3]
Driving in Provence[1]
Putting Jack through his paces[1]
Knebworth garden: Natasha, George, Tata; Natasha's friend Madame Schlieffer and her two children[3]
Going to the ballet: Michael and Natasha, July 1914[3]

Between pages 336 and 337
The Fighting General: Michael in 1915, commanding the Savage Division[3]
Souvenir postcard of Major-General Grand Duke Michael Aleksandrovich[3]
Michael at front-line HQ, 1915[3]
Michael at HQ, Savage Division, 1915[6]
24, Nikolaevskaya Street, Gatchina[3]
Michael at window in Nikolaevskaya Street[3]
Michael and Natasha with Jack, Nikolaevskaya Street[3]
Michael with Jack[3]
Dimitri Abrikosov and Michael, 1915[3]
Studio portrait of Michael and Natasha, 1916[3]
Grand Duke Dimitri and Natasha, Nikolaevskaya Street, 1916[3]
Michael at home, 1916[3]
12, Millionnaya Street, St Petersburg[7]
Korolev Rooms, 3, Siberia Street, Perm, 1918[8]
Prisoner of Perm: last known picture of Michael with Johnson, April 1918, Perm[3]
The Executioners: Myasnikov, with Markov, Kolpashchikov, Ivanchenko, Zhuzhgov
Reunion with Dimitri, 1919[9]
George's last letter to his father, July 1918[3]
Last photograph of George, 1931[3]
Natasha, a woman alone[3]

Sources

[1]School of Slavonic and East European Studies, University of London
[2]Russian National Museum, St Petersburg
[3]Pauline Gray, Leeds Russian Archive, University of Leeds
[4]By kind permission of H.M. Queen Elizabeth II
[5]Print and Photographic Collection, the Royal Library, Copenhagen
[6]Stanley Washburn, *The Russian Campaign*, 1915
[7]The authors
[8]M. Zagulyaev, Perm
[9]Central Archive, Russian Federal Security Service, courtesy Atheneum-Feniks, Moscow, St Petersburg

Maps in text

pages xiv–xv Russia and Europe pre-1918
pages 238–9 Petrograd in 1917–18
page 269 Nicholas II's railway journey, February 28–March 3, 1917

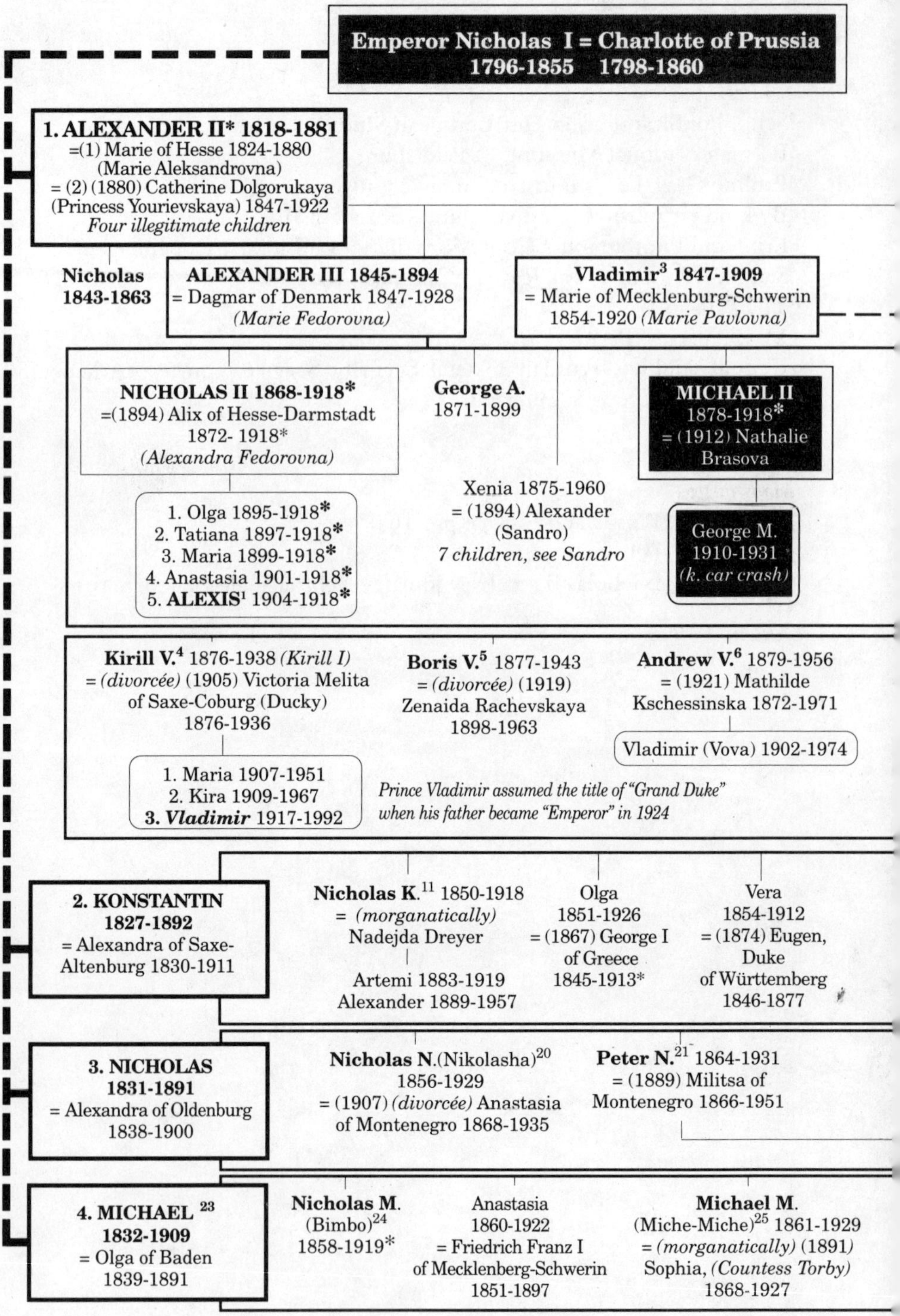

* = murdered; **bold type** = Grand Duke; superior numbering (Alexis[1] to Serge M.[33]) indicates seniority in line of succession at August 1904 on birth of Alexis

DESCENDANTS OF EMPEROR NICHOLAS I

Alexis[7] **1850-1908**

Olga 1882-1960
=(1) (1901) Duke Peter of Oldenburg 1868-1924
=(2) (1916) Col. Nikolai Kulikovsky 1881-1958

1. *Tikhon* 1917-1993
2. *Guri* 1919-1984

Helen 1882-1957
= (1902) Nicholas of Greece 1872-1938

Marina 1906-1968
George, Duke of Kent 1902-1942

Marie 1853-1920
= Alfred, Duke of Edinburgh 1844-1900

One son, four daughters, Marie, Ducky, Alexandra, Beatrice (Baby-Bee)

Serge[8] **1857-1905***
= Elizabeth of Hesse-Darmstadt (Ella) 1864-1918*

Paul[9] **1860-1919***
= (1) Alexandra of Greece 1870-1891

Marie 1890-1958
(Marie Pavlovna jr.)
= (1) (1908) Prince William of Sweden 1884-1965
(diss. 1914)
= (2) (1917) Prince Sergei Putyatin 1893-1966 (*diss.1923*)
1 son, 1918-1919

Prince Lennart of Sweden (b.1910)

Dimitri[10] 1891-1942
= (1926) Audrey Emery of Cincinnatti (1904-1971)
(diss. 1937)

1. Paul Ilyinsky (b. 1928)
= (1) Mary Prince of Memphis *(diss. 1952)*
= (2) Angelika Kauffmann (b. 1932)
Two sons, two dau.

=(2) *(1902) (divorcée)*
Olga Pistolkors 1866-1929
(Princess Paley)

1. Vladimir Paley 1897-1918*
2. Irina 1903-1990
3. Natalia 1905-1981

Konstantin K.[12]
1858-1915
= Elizabeth of Saxe-Altenburg 1865-1927

Dimitri K.[19] 1860-1919*

PRINCES
1. Ioann[13] 1886-1918*
= Helen of Serbia 1884-1962
1 son: Vsevolode 1914-1973
2. Gabriel[14] 1887-1955
3. Konstantin[15] 1891-1918*
4. Oleg[16] 1892-1914 *(k. in action)*
5. Igor[17] 1894-1918*
6. George[18] 1903-1938
And three daughters

1. Marina 1892-1981
2. Roman[22] 1896-1978
3. Nadejda 1898-1988

1. Irina 1895-1970
=(*1914*) Felix Yusupov 1887-1967
2. Andrew[28] 1897-1981
3. Feodor[29] 1898-1968
4. Nikita[30] 1900 -1974
5. Dimitri[31] 1901-1980
6. Rostislav[32] 1902-1978
7. Vassali 1907-1989

Alexander M.(Sandro)[27]
1866-1933
= (1894) Xenia *(see above)*

George M.[26] 1863-1919*
= Maria, 2nd dau. George I of Greece
Two daughters

Serge M.[33]
1869-1918*

Alexis M.
1875-1895

The last son born to a Grand Duke is Paul Ilyinsky, whose father was Grand Duke Dimitri

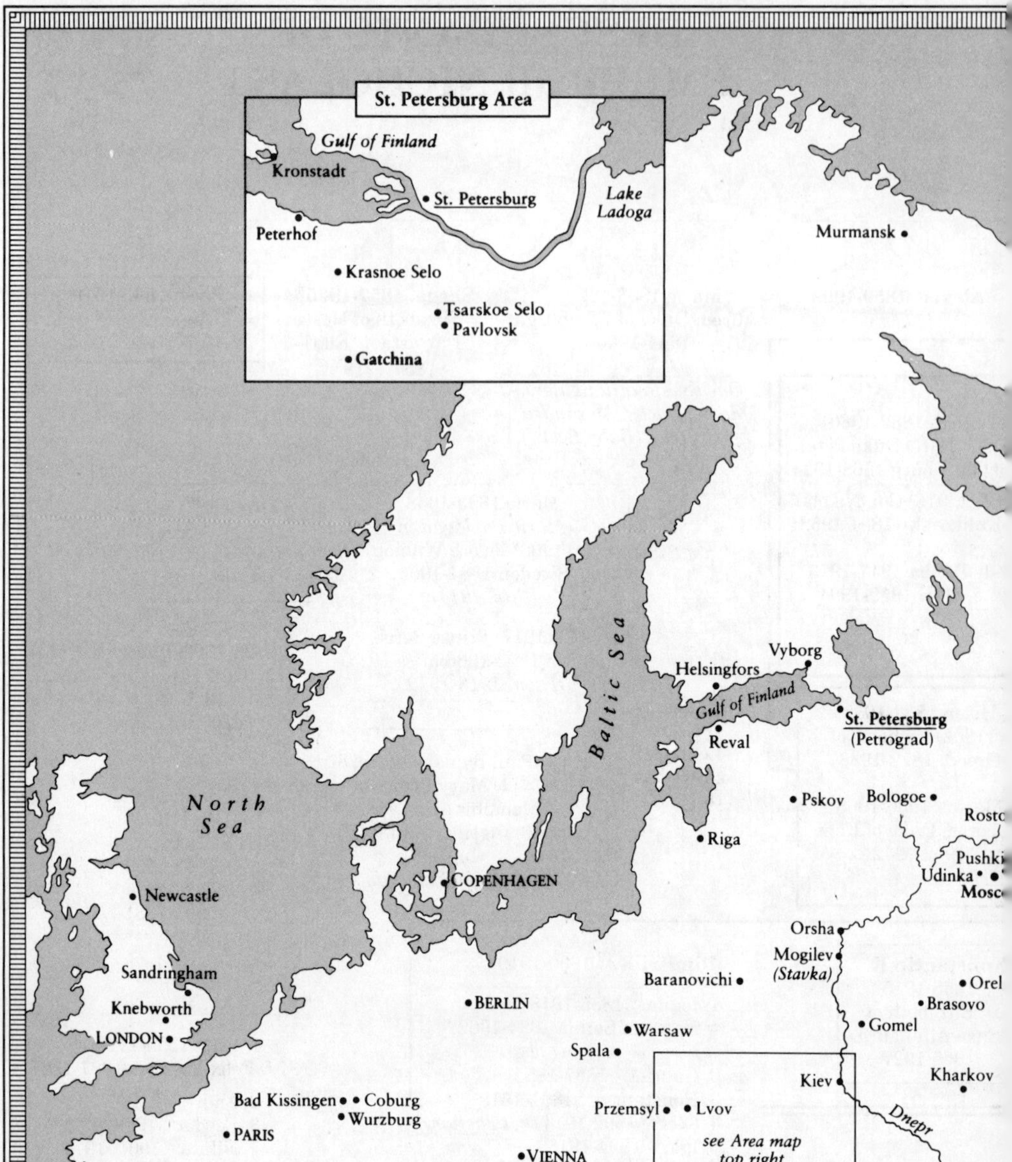
St. Petersburg Area
Gulf of Finland
Kronstadt
St. Petersburg
Lake Ladoga
Peterhof
Krasnoe Selo
Tsarskoe Selo
Pavlovsk
Gatchina
Murmansk
Baltic Sea
North Sea
Helsingfors
Vyborg
Gulf of Finland
Reval
St. Petersburg
(Petrograd)
Pskov
Bologoe
Rosto
Riga
Pushki
Udinka
Mosc
COPENHAGEN
Newcastle
Orsha
Mogilev
(Stavka)
Sandringham
Baranovichi
Orel
Knebworth
BERLIN
Brasovo
LONDON
Warsaw
Gomel
Spala
Kharkov
Kiev
Bad Kissingen
Coburg
Wurzburg
Przemsyl
Lvov
Dnepr
PARIS
see Area map
top right
VIENNA
Dijon
Odessa
Venice
Sebastopol
Ai-Todo
Livadia
Cannes
Constanta
Black Sea
ROME
Constantinople
Sorrento

Distances (in miles) from St Petersburg by rail

Tsarskoe Selo	15	Kiev	936
Peterhof	18	Berlin	1017
Gatchina	29	Perm	1064
Pskov	170	Vienna	1126
Vologda	371	Odessa	1218
Moscow	404	Ekaterinburg	1300
Mogilev	450	Chelyabinsk	1452
Orel	643	Paris	1462
Warsaw	693	London	1745
Brasovo	700	Omsk	1947

INTRODUCTION

The woman who was lying in one of the crowded wards of the Laënnec, a busy Paris charity hospital in the rue de Sevres, was just another dying patient and if the card at the end of her bed bore the name Princess Brasova, it meant little enough to the nurses bustling around her in this January of 1952. Many of the unfortunates who came to the hospital to die protested their dignity and even their once-upon-a-time grandeur.

To the young nurses, the woman was just one more of those sad Russian *émigrés* with whom Paris had been all too familiar in the years since 1918. Once they had money, jewels, and position; more importantly, they had hope. Now that was all a very long time ago – a vanished age – and the world had moved on. There was little enough anyone could do for the woman anyway, save perhaps to ease the pain of the cancer which had taken the life from her face and arms long before it would take the life from her body. Her last address had been an attic at 11 rue Monsieur, only a few streets away from the hospital in the 7th *arrondissement*, on the Left Bank, but when she had become ill and unable any longer to look after herself, the fellow *émigré* who had let her live in the tiny boxroom had brusquely ordered her to leave. But for the hospital, she would have had nowhere to go. She was seventy-one, and death would be a mercy.

She died alone and it seemed forgotten, for when they came to make out her death certificate there was nothing in her pathetic effects to support her claim that she was a princess, merely a faded Russian birth certificate naming her as plain Nathalie Sheremetevskaya. A clerk copied that out, stamped the certificate and duly filed it away.

But the woman who said she was a princess would not be forgotten entirely, for as word spread among the dwindling band of Russian *émigrés* in Paris that the Princess Brasova had died, they did what they could to give her burial the dignity denied her death. They took her to Passy, to lie in the same grave where, twenty years earlier, they had buried her son George, tragically killed on the eve of his twenty-first birthday in a sports car being driven by a fellow student.

They also buried her, by chance, near the grave of Maurice Paléologue, sometime French ambassador to Russia and one of the many men she had once entranced. Indeed, it was Paléologue who, upon seeing her for the first time, had been so overwhelmed by her looks and grace that he went home and wrote about her in his diary, giving a portrait of a young woman who 'was a delight to watch . . . Her pure and aristocratic face is charmingly modelled and she has light velvety eyes . . . There was a dignified, sinuous and soft gracefulness about her every movement.'

When Paléologue wrote about her she was not, of course, just another anonymous old lady but a breathtakingly beautiful woman whose name was known in every court in Europe, though rarely to her credit. Twice-divorced, the mother of an illegitimate child and an outlaw banished from imperial Russia, she was also the woman who, in one of the most remarkable love stories of the age, became wife of the last Emperor of All the Russias – Michael II, brother of the doomed Tsar Nicholas.

PART I

LOVE AND MARRIAGE

DATES

Until February 1918 the Russian 'Julian' calendar differed from the 'Gregorian' in use elsewhere. In the nineteenth century the Russian calendar was twelve days behind, and in the twentieth century, thirteen days behind. As example, January 1, 1910 in Russia was January 14 elsewhere. Throughout this book the Russian calendar is used, unless otherwise stated.

MONEY

It is impossible, because of fluctuating currency values, to give the precise present-day equivalent for monies quoted in the book. Where such figures are given they are those effective at March 1, 1997 as quoted by the Bank of England. The following table may be helpful. The sterling and $ figures in roman type are for average 1910–14; the figures in *italics* are for 1997 equivalent values.

	Russian Rouble	**UK Sterling**	**US Dollar**
1910–1914 *1997 value*	1000	£110 *£4856*	$512 *$8013*
	5000	£550 *£24,282*	$2562 *$40,006*
	20,000	£2200 *£97,130*	$10,250 *$160,264*
	100,000	£11,000 *£485,650*	$51,250 *$801,323*
	1 million	£110,000 ***£4.86 m.***	$512,500 ***$8 m.***

Source: Conversion rates sterling: Bank of England public affairs department; 1997 sterling values @ £1 = £44.15 as average for 1910–1914; £/$ rate calculated at 1.65; £/$ rates for roubles as quoted in *Baedeker's Russia 1914*

ONE

'That Sinner'

Women had long flocked to the Grand Duke Michael Aleksandrovich. When he was a very young man his brother, the Tsar, had been amused to note that on holiday in Denmark his trio of pretty cousins, daughters of the Duke of Cumberland, had hardly been able to keep away from Michael – 'that sinner' – and that 'during walks two of them always hang on his arms'.[1] It was not really surprising.

Celebrating his twenty-ninth birthday on November 22, 1907, Grand Duke Michael seemed possessed of every quality that any woman could desire. He was well over six feet tall, blue-eyed, slim-waisted and still boyishly handsome. He also exuded immense personal charm, was exceptionally kind and good-natured, liked children and dogs, preferred country to court, disliked pomp, and could be very amusing, with a weakness for practical jokes. He spoke French and English fluently, and was a competent musician on piano, flute, balalaika and guitar, composing several of his own pieces. He enjoyed the theatre, ballet and opera and, as a keen military historian, had written several academic papers on the Napoleonic War, published in the journal of the prestigious Imperial Russian Historical Society.[2] Serving as a squadron commander in the élite Guards cavalry regiment, the Blue Cuirassiers, he was also a first-class sportsman, a crack shot, a skilled swordsman, an excellent horseman who won prizes steeplechasing, and was so good with his fists that one American coach regretted that he could not turn prize-fighter.[3] He was also one of the richest young men in the world.

Most people who knew Michael well, liked him enormously. His brother-in-law, Grand Duke Alexander, known in the family as Sandro and married to Michael's elder sister Xenia, wrote approvingly of him that 'he fascinated everybody by the wholehearted simplicity of his manner. A favourite with his family, with his fellow officers and with all his countless friends, he possessed a well-organised mind and would have succeeded in any branch of the service'.[4] His cousin and friend, Prince Nicholas of Greece, observed that 'he was a very keen soldier and a real sportsman; his jovial nature endeared him to all. He was a fine, athletic young man, and went in for physical training, which he practised like a professional gymnast'.[5] Polovtsov, a member of the State Council, and head of the Imperial

Russian Historical Society, judged that Michael 'has an extraordinarily strong will and once he has taken an aim in his sights he will achieve it without haste, and with undeviating firmness'.[6]

As a young man he charmed even Queen Victoria, despite her dislike of the Romanovs in general and of Michael's father in particular. Victoria regarded Tsar Alexander III as a boor, though he was no less unflattering about her, describing her as 'pampered, sentimental, selfish', and a 'nasty, interfering old woman'.[7] Michael met Queen Victoria twice. The first occasion was on a family holiday in the south of France in 1896, when his mother ushered him into the palm-filled Hotel Cimiez at Nice, and introduced him to 'dear Granny'. Later, he went to see Queen Victoria at Balmoral, her Scottish home, and that night, recalling her first meeting with Michael in Nice, she wrote in her diary that he 'is remarkably nice & pleasing & pleasing looking'.[8]

Nevertheless, despite his manifold qualities, the love life of Grand Duke Michael had so far been dogged by misfortune, to put it at its mildest. Over the past five years he had seemed near to marriage three times – once, admittedly, without his being aware of it – and in each instance the result had been turmoil, with two of the three women involved being brought to the edge of a nervous breakdown and the third publicly embarrassed. Two attempts at marriage had failed only because of the vigilance of his brother's secret police, and wisely his last bride-to-be had now fled the country, with the threat of re-arrest if she ever set foot in Russia again. For a man who intended only the best, and who justly prided himself on being more moral than the majority of male Romanovs – 'I'll never be a playboy or a philanderer as many of them were and still are', he would say later[9] – it was an unfortunate record.

Well-meaning though he was, it sometimes seemed as if Grand Duke Michael did little else but write letters of regret. Between 1903 and 1905 he was apologising to Princess Beatrice of Great Britain; in 1906, to Princess Patricia of Connaught; and in 1907 to Alexandra Kossikovskaya, long-time lady-in-waiting to his younger sister Olga. While he could not apologise to everyone, of course, among those who would have expected him to do so were a furious Duchess of Saxe-Coburg-Gotha, an outraged Grand Duchess of Hesse-Darmstadt, an indignant Duke and Duchess of Connaught, a bewildered Buckingham Palace, an enraged Vladimir Kossikovsky, and even the discomfited country priest whom he had bribed to conduct an illegal wedding.

Yet, at his twenty-ninth birthday, there were positive signs that all was by no means lost. Although the secret police continued discreetly to monitor his mail, he was no longer under threat of house arrest and so far as his family was concerned there was a natural hope that the next love affair would end more happily. All's well that ends well.

Certainly, in the first week of December 1907, the members of his immediate family could begin to feel more relaxed about Michael than they had done for a very long time. After a holiday in the Crimea, he returned to his home in the 600-room palace at Gatchina, twenty-nine miles south-west of St Petersburg, looking more cheerful than he had done for many weeks.

A few days later, back on duty with his regiment, Grand Duke Michael Aleksandrovich strolled across from the palace to the riding school of the Blue Cuirassiers. As chance would have it, he was hardly through the doors when he was in trouble again. As he glanced around the *manège* his eye fell on a beautiful young woman who was standing there among a group of officers. Her name, he would discover, was Madame Nathalie Wulfert – Natasha to her friends – a young middle-class divorcée, whose second husband was a lieutenant in the Grand Duke's regiment. Over the next few years the Okhrana, the Tsar's secret police, would come to know her well, as would most of aristocratic Europe.

No one, of course, could know that, as Michael walked across to her, intent on obtaining an introduction. But from that moment, he would never look at another woman again.

Michael was born to marry a royal princess and when he was twenty-three that was exactly what it seemed he would do. His first serious love affair was with the very pretty British-born Princess Beatrice, known in the family as 'Baby-Bee'. They met on holiday in the summer of 1902, and for both of them it appeared to be love at first sight. On the face of it their romance was the perfect royal match.

Because his brother Tsar Nicholas did not then have a son of his own, Michael was heir to the Russian throne, and – ten years younger than Nicholas – might well one day succeed him; since Michael could be Emperor, he needed a wife fit to be Empress. Baby-Bee seemed an ideal choice. She was the youngest daughter of Queen Victoria's second son Alfred, Duke of Edinburgh, and a niece of Britain's King Edward VII; she was also half-Russian, her mother being the sister of Michael's father, Alexander III. There seemed every reason, therefore, to welcome the news that Grand Duke Michael and the very royal Baby-Bee had fallen in love.

Six years younger than Michael, Baby-Bee had been born at Eastwell, in Kent, but at the age of nine she had moved with her family to Coburg in Germany, when her father succeeded as reigning Duke of Saxe-Coburg-Gotha. Although properly part of the German empire forged by Prussia in 1871, the dukedom of Saxe-Coburg-Gotha was effectively a British preserve at the turn of the century, largely because Queen Victoria regarded it as such. Her husband, Prince Albert, had been a Coburger and in consequence she held Saxe-Coburg-Gotha to be sacred to his memory and the inheritance of his children. Baby-Bee's father had taken the dukedom in 1893 and after his death in 1900, when she was sixteen, it passed to her cousin, the Eton-educated and very British Duke of Albany, a grandson of Queen Victoria. Baby-Bee continued to live at Coburg, however, and it was from Coburg that she wrote endlessly to her beloved Michael, believing from his letters that it could not be long before she became his wife, a Grand Duchess, and possibly one day even Empress of Russia.

Michael was in no doubt about his feelings for the girl he called 'Sima'. His first letters to her, in September 1902, were addressed to 'My own darling and beloved Sima'; written in English as were hers to him, they told their own story of his love for her, as well as hers for him. 'I always think of you, my own darling, and wish so terribly to be with you. God only sees how I want you . . .' he wrote on October 1, 1902,[10] and then three weeks later: 'My own precious Sima, Your letters are so full of love and affection for me that it even frightens me sometimes to think that you can care for me in such a way. There is no doubt I love you in just the same way, that's why we understand each other so well . . . my own dear Sima darling, I kiss you many times on your lips.'[11]

Although Baby-Bee was then only seventeen she was not thought too young to marry. Her three elder sisters had each wed at eighteen years of age, and Baby-Bee seemed destined therefore to follow suit. Her eldest sister Marie had married the future king of Romania; the next-born, Victoria Melita, known as 'Ducky', had married Grand Duke Ernst of Hesse-Darmstadt, the brother of Empress Alexandra of Russia; and the third, Alexandra, was wife of the Prince of Hohenlohe-Langenburg. A marriage to Grand Duke Michael Aleksandrovich would therefore round things off nicely for the four 'Coburg girls'.

Unfortunately it was not to be; Michael and Baby-Bee were first cousins, her mother being Michael's aunt. That had not troubled them initially, for marriages between first cousins were not uncommon among royals in Protestant Europe. Baby-Bee's sister Ducky had married her first cousin; so had the Empress Alexandra's sister Irene, the wife of Prince Henry of Prussia, brother of the Kaiser; and so, for that matter, had Queen Victoria herself. But in Orthodox Russia the Church forbade first cousins to wed. Michael's brother, Tsar Nicholas, was sympathetic but firm: there could be no exceptions, and marriage between Michael and Baby-Bee was therefore out of the question.

Baby-Bee was distraught, but there was nothing that could be done about it. Michael was heir to the throne, and as such he could not break Church law or marry without the Tsar's consent. And so in November 1903 he wrote Baby-Bee the most difficult letter he had ever written, breaking off their relationship. He had agonised over it for weeks, but he had no choice in the matter. Afterwards, his elder sister Xenia reported that 'thank goodness, he is generally in better spirits now'.[12]

But that was not the end of it. The family, so united before, now split angrily. Just before Christmas 1903, Xenia received 'a terrible letter' from Baby-Bee's elder sister Ducky, full of complaints about Michael. 'She is trying to show,' judged Xenia, 'that he behaved in an ugly and dishonourable way towards her. And all this after one letter, in which he wrote that, as they could not marry, it would be better to stop writing such letters to each other, and that he hoped they could remain on good terms etc. Lord preserve us from the storm this provoked on their side, it turns out Beatrice is quite ill and has been sent to Egypt, where she cries and grows thinner.'[13]

Three weeks later Xenia was in Cannes, where she joined Ducky and her mother Marie for lunch. Baby-Bee, back from Egypt, was also there, and a shocked Xenia noted that she was no longer the pretty, bright-eyed girl she had known. She was 'pitiful to look at, she has grown so thin, and looks so unwell, poor thing'.[14] In the garden afterwards, Baby-Bee's mother broached again the question of marriage between Michael and her grieving daughter, but 'I could only tell her that Misha cannot marry, for Nicky has told him that definitely, and that he has submitted and looks upon it now as an impossibility . . . Ducky says that Baby-Bee was in such a terrible state they feared she would lose her mind.'[15]

Michael was also still trying to pacify Baby-Bee. On January 1, 1904, he wrote to her: 'Darling Sima, do try and not have that bitter feeling against me, it only worries you and hurts me more than I can say. It seems to me as if you have concluded that you can say anything hard and bitter and that I won't mind, or perhaps you do it on purpose to hurt me . . . Do you understand that I feel very much all you tell me, and can't bear to think you could feel bitter and angry with me, do understand it once and for all, I beg you . . . Your loving friend.'[16]

Baby-Bee was not to be so easily dismissed, and over the next year and longer the recriminations went on until finally, on April 10, 1905, Michael wrote his last letter to her. She was now only 'Dear Sima', as he made plain that there was no point in either of them pursuing a relationship doomed in law.

> *You don't know how it worries me that on account of me you should be worried or unhappy. Please darling girl don't be sad. If I did change the way of writing it was only for the reason that I had no right continuing in the way I wrote before to you. I blame myself and only myself, and feel miserable for having made you unhappy. Now also I feel that my letters only upset and worry you,*

and therefore don't you think it best not to write to you, only Sima always remember that whenever you want my help in anything or simply want to hear from me I will always be ready to do it and help you in anything . . . I will remain your friend forever Sima darling.[17]

It was the end of any hopes remaining in the Baby-Bee camp, though it would be four years before the heartbroken Baby-Bee would have forgotten Michael sufficiently to marry someone else.*

Michael's second serious romance was also doomed from the outset. The new woman in his life was Alexandra Kossikovskaya, known as Dina. She was three years older than Michael and, while no great beauty, she was well-educated, strong-minded and highly intelligent; she was also a 'wonderfully bright conversationalist', and 'exceedingly popular among the younger generation' in smart St Petersburg society.[18] Born in September 1875, in a small town near Orel, her father had then been a provincial but well-connected and ambitious public attorney, Vladimir Kossikovsky.[19] And therein lay the problem: Dina was a commoner, and Grand Dukes were permitted to marry only women of equal rank: royal princesses. The Tsar could waive the law, but like his father he refused to do so, and in recent years two Grand Dukes who had married commoners had been banished from Russia in disgrace.

While heir to the throne, Michael had put duty before love, as in the case of Baby-Bee. But in August 1904 he stepped back one pace from the throne when the Empress Alexandra, after ten years of marriage, at last gave Nicholas a son and heir of his own. Michael was genuinely delighted and jokingly turned up next day in a uniform with the striped epaulette of a reserve officer. 'You see', he grinned at Nicholas, 'I am no longer on the active list.'[20] No longer heir, Michael now felt free to do as he pleased; within the year, what would please him most was to marry the quick-witted Dina.

He had not intended to fall in love with Dina and for a long time he thought of her only as a friend. Michael, it would be said by one contemporary, 'was of a more serious frame of mind than the other members of his family' and because of that he 'found great pleasure in talking with her and discussing many subjects which did not interest those around them'.[21] This initial friendship slowly developed over the months until mutual interest turned into mutual love.

As his sister's lady-in-waiting Dina understood the imperial law as well as anyone else and therefore knew from the outset that she could not marry

* Baby-Bee (1884–1966) married Don Alfonso, Infante of Spain and cousin of Alfonso XIII, in 1909. She returned all Michael's letters to her and they are in the Russian State Archives in Moscow.

Grand Duke Michael. However, Dina wanted to be more than a mistress; prompted by her ambitious father, she persuaded herself that she could become the exception to the rule. Having done so, she set about the task of making Michael believe that marriage to her was not only his right but his duty as a man of honour.

Dina was entitled, of course, to insist on nothing less than marriage. Nevertheless, to be the mistress of a Grand Duke was not necessarily the worst that could befall a woman. And for those in doubt, there was the brilliant example of the prima ballerina *assoluta* Mathilde Kschessinska.* Over the past seventeen years she had been mistress successively to three Grand Dukes, beginning in 1890 with Michael's brother Nicholas, then Tsarevich. Nicholas was twenty-two and the tiny Kschessinska just eighteen. After two years together, they set up home in St Petersburg, at 18 English Prospekt, Nicholas renting in her name the two-storey house then owned by the composer Rimsky-Korsakov; and it was there that they spent much of their time together, leading 'a quiet, retiring life' as Kschessinska would recall afterwards.[22]

But in real life a swan can never be turned into a princess, and in 1894 Nicholas became engaged to Princess Alix of Hesse-Darmstadt and a miserable Kschessinska had to accept the inevitable. In his farewell letter to her, Nicholas wrote: 'Whatever happens to my life my days spent with you will ever remain the happiest memories of my youth.'[23] As consolation, Nicholas also bought from Rimsky-Korsakov the house on English Prospekt and gave it to Kschessinska as his parting gift.[24]

Kschessinska's other consolation was then to become mistress to Grand Duke Serge Mikhailovich, who kept her for the next eight years, before losing her to the boyish Grand Duke Andrew Vladimirovich, seven years younger than Kschessinska. Showered with jewels by all three imperial lovers, and bought houses by each, Kschessinska proved that the role of mistress had its compensations for those who remembered that the bed-chamber was not the route to the bridal chamber.

But Dina was not Kschessinska. At thirty years of age, with more brains than beauty, she knew perfectly well that Michael was the only Grand Duke ever likely to be in love with her. She also had the good fortune to have in him a man of sufficient moral principle to feel that he owed marriage to her, whatever the law might say. Michael's friends urged him to keep her only as a mistress, but he 'scorned such an idea'.[25] With Dina, he had little other choice.

His family were appalled when they learned of the relationship, but did

* The imperial theatres created only two prima ballerinas *assoluta*; the first was the Italian Pierina Legnani in 1893, followed in 1895 by Kschessinska.

nothing about it until Michael wrote to his brother in July 1906 asking for permission to marry her. The letter was couched in terms which suggested that it had been influenced by Dina's lawyer father; it argued that the law, introduced by Alexander III, did not expressly prohibit marriage between a Grand Duke and a commoner for 'it never passed through the Council of State and therefore it is within your exclusive prerogative to annul it altogether, or only for the case in hand'.[26] It was a technical point, of interest only to other lawyers. The Tsar, noting that 'it seems to me that Misha got help from someone else in writing that letter',[27] was in no doubt about his response. While telling him that he wished only 'to see my dear brother happy in his family life', he ruled out any question of a morganatic marriage, warning Michael that 'should you disobey my will, I will have to remove your name from the army and the retinue lists and send you out of the country . . . my decision is irrevocable'.[28]

The Dowager Empress was equally shocked. As she told Nicholas, 'I really don't know what to do – it is unbearable to see him in such distress! Whatever I say to him he explains away in his own way, and keeps on insisting he has no right to act otherwise. I try appealing to his sense of duty, his duty to his country, his obligations, etc., etc. All he says is that that has nothing to do with the case. You must realise and understand what this new tormenting sorrow means to me – day and night I worry over it!'[29]

Since persuasion had failed, the Dowager Empress did not sit idly by. She wrote to Dina dismissing her as lady-in-waiting to Olga, and brusquely told her that it would be best for all if she immediately went abroad and stayed there.[30] She then took Michael off on holiday with her to Denmark, resolved that somehow she must marry him off quickly to a proper wife. A month later came news of Michael's betrothal to Her Royal Highness Princess Patricia of Connaught.

Princess Patricia, known as Patsy, was the daughter of Queen Victoria's third and favourite son Arthur, Duke of Connaught, and she had been born at Buckingham Palace in March 1886, so that she was then just twenty years old, some eight years younger than Michael and eleven years younger than Dina. She was described as 'tall and handsome',[31] which was not the most flattering of judgements, but what counted, at least to the Dowager Empress, was that she was as royal as anyone could be, and that as a niece of King Edward VII, and cousin of Baby-Bee, she was family. Better still, she was not a first cousin.

The news that Patsy was to marry Grand Duke Michael Aleksandrovich appeared on Sunday, September 24, 1906, five days after Michael returned home from Denmark.[32] Since there had been no prior hint of the engagement the announcement was totally unexpected, the first anyone knew of it having come from an agency report wired from St Petersburg the day before.

The author was Guy Beringer, a very senior and respected Reuters correspondent, with enviable connections at the highest levels of the imperial court.[33] His report was therefore to be wholly trusted, and in any case it made excellent sense, for as the London *Observer* pointed out the betrothal reinforced the already close family links between the British royals and the Romanovs. The Tsar was married to a granddaughter of Queen Victoria; Queen Alexandra of England was sister of the Dowager Empress Marie. The *Observer* was also flattering about Michael: 'Like his bride he is exceedingly fond of horses, and has taken part in a good many officers' races. He is also adept at boxing, wrestling, riding, dancing, and swimming. He has always enjoyed the reputation of being a stronger character than the Emperor.'[34]

Like his bride? Patsy was not the only one to blink at that. Within hours of the newspapers landing on British breakfast tables, a flustered Buckingham Palace was issuing denials, prodded by an indignant Connaught family which knew that the reports of a betrothal were wholly baseless.

The official palace denials appeared next morning in the Court Circular published in both *The Times* and *Morning Post*. The terse five-line announcement in *The Times* attempted lofty disdain: 'It is officially stated that there is no foundation for the rumour widely circulated yesterday, on the authority of a telegram from St Petersburg, that a marriage was to take place between the Grand Duke Michael and Princess Patricia of Connaught'. The *Morning Post* said much the same thing.[35]

A bewildered Patsy would never discover how it was that she had been matched publicly with Michael, for it would not occur to her that the blame lay not with a bemused Reuters man or the usual 'reputable sources' on which the agency correspondent had clearly relied, but with the Dowager Empress and Queen Alexandra, who had joined her sister on holiday in Denmark. Desperate that something should be done about Michael, the two sisters appear to have talked each other into believing that hope was fact. The Dowager Empress then said more than she should have done, hence the impression within her entourage that Patsy, who knew nothing about it, and Michael, who did not want to know anything about it, were about to become engaged.

When Michael sailed back to Russia, the rumours of his impending marriage to Princess Patricia sailed back with him. Nevertheless, the authoritative Reuters agency did not deal in mere rumour: the report its correspondent wired from St Petersburg was the result of information provided by a senior court official who clearly believed it to be fact.

Wisely, the Dowager Empress and Queen Alexandra subsequently professed to be as baffled as anyone else, and otherwise remained innocently silent. There was no advantage to confessing that they had simply been trying to remove Michael from the clutches of an ambitious lady-in-waiting.

With the flurry over Patsy ending in embarrassed silence, the best the Dowager Empress could hope for in the immediate future was that Dina, now abroad, would stay there. She was, therefore, 'absolutely furious'[36] to learn in April 1907 that Dina had returned to St Petersburg. Worse was to follow, for in July it was discovered that Michael had found a priest who, for a large sum of money, was prepared to marry them at a church near his estate at Brasovo.[37] The wedding was not to be, for secrecy proved impossible. The priest had to call the banns, and even deep in the countryside, 700 miles from St Petersburg, the Okhrana had its ears. But it was not the end of the matter, for as Michael's sister Xenia noted, 'Dina and her father are trying to catch him at all costs.'[38]

Since a stubborn Michael, and an increasingly agitated Dina, could not wed in Russia, they now planned a runaway marriage in Italy. Michael knew that Dina had been forbidden to follow him abroad, or even to leave the capital, and he told his sister Xenia 'how upset he was by this measure'.[39] Nevertheless he and Dina intended to defy the order. Michael and his sister Olga would leave Russia by train, ostensibly for a holiday in Sorrento; at the same time Dina would travel secretly southwards to the Crimea and take ship from Odessa to Naples. It was a plan which underestimated the extent to which the Tsar would go to stop them.

Dina got only as far as Odessa; there the Okhrana were waiting, stony-faced policemen who took her into custody, shrugging off her furious protests, and then bundled her back on to a train for the 1200-mile return journey to St Petersburg. 'She had her passport ready for going abroad,' Nicholas reported to his mother, 'but as the competent authorities were aware of what was going on she was stopped and asked to go back.'[40] That sounded better than 'arrested', but it amounted to the same thing.

At the Hotel Tramontana in Sorrento a waiting Michael found himself once again outflanked by his family. 'My brother was disconsolate,' Olga recalled. 'He blamed my mother and Nicky. I felt powerless to help him. I sometimes wondered if it had been better for all of us Romanovs to be born without hearts.'[41] There was little that could be done, however, for Nicholas had gone off on a cruise on the imperial yacht *Standart* and the Dowager Empress was on holiday in Denmark.

Dina and her father, outraged by what had happened, sent off a stream of protesting telegrams, to prime minister Peter Stolypin as well as to the Tsar,[42] but they were banging their heads against an imperial wall. As Nicholas told his mother, Michael could expect no indulgence: 'He will have to be categorically forbidden to see her or to go to town at all, under threat of confinement to his home if necessary . . . What a bad impression it all creates and how tiresome it is! Doesn't he really understand what unnecessary trouble he is giving us and how painful it all is for you and me? Still, I do not lose hope that Misha's good sense will prevail in the end – especially when he won't be able to see her at all.'[43]

A 'disconsolate' Michael might have been expected to hurry back to St Petersburg to console his distraught and humiliated bride-to-be, but he did not choose to do so. One reason was that 'Uncle Bertie', King Edward VII, had grandly ordered that a 5600-ton grey-hulled British cruiser, HMS *Minerva*, should be 'placed at his disposal' at Sorrento so that a holidaying Michael could go sailing in the blue waters of the Gulf of Naples.[44] This 'private compliment', as the British First Sea Lord, Admiral Sir John Fisher, delicately put it,[45] involved duty as well as pleasure. A warship with a crew of 422 men had sailed all the way from Malta just so that he could go out for a sail, so sail he did.

On Thursday, August 30, 1907, the six-inch-gunned *Minerva*, dressed overall, fired a twenty-one-gun salute as Grand Duke Michael came aboard to be introduced to Captain Henry J. L. Clarke and his thirty-one officers.[46] That evening he entertained the captain and officers to dinner at the Hotel Tramontana and then hosted a fancy-dress party for them in the hotel grounds.[47] Next morning, Michael returned to the ship with his sister Olga and her husband Duke Peter of Oldenburg, and spent the day on a leisurely eight-hour cruise along the coast.[48]

It seemed to cheer him up, for at the end of the holiday he went on to Denmark to see his mother, who was surprised to find him in 'such a good mood'.[49] The mood appeared to persist, for his mother would write to Nicholas, 'I had a good talk with him, after which I have more hope and my heart is more at peace, for he told me that I can be quite sure he will not do anything against the law'.[50]

Having reported this surprising change of attitude, she was further relieved to find that at the end of his stay in Denmark Michael decided to go on to the Crimea, to stay with his sister Xenia, rather than return directly to St Petersburg, where a distressed Dina was waiting for him, and the Dowager Empress took that as 'a good sign'.[51]

Freed as he had been over the past weeks from the unrelenting pressure of Dina and her father, Michael seems to have decided, somewhat late in the day, that the family battle was no longer worth it. 'Poor Mishken', Xenia wrote in her diary while Michael was with her in the Crimea,[52] but it was poor Dina whose life was left in ruins, for she knew now that there would never again be a chance of capturing Michael.

Dina retreated to England, beaten and blaming the Dowager Empress for the destruction of her life. She would never marry, and never come back to live in Russia, while remaining ever faithful to the memory of the man to whom she would always believe herself betrothed.*

On December 1, 1907, as she was beginning her lifelong exile abroad, Michael returned to Gatchina from his sister's home in the Crimea. A few days later he walked into the Blue Cuirassiers' *manège*. As he would later tell Natasha:

> *I so tenderly remember . . . that afternoon in the riding school when for the first time I saw you and asked 'who's that lady?' and then finally had the courage to come up and be introduced to that unknown lady, and I know that at the same time you were wondering 'who's that new officer?'*[53]

If they had known what would then happen, he said, 'we would have thought "Fantasy" '.[54]

* Dina died destitute in Berlin in 1923, aged forty-eight. In accordance with her wishes her diaries detailing her relationship with Michael until 1907 were then destroyed. On the back of the only surviving photograph of her, in the Hoover Institution, Stanford University, is written: 'The unhappy ex-fiancée of Grand Duke Michael Aleksandrovich'.

TWO

Darling Floppy

Grand Duke Michael Aleksandrovich had lived in Gatchina almost all his life and he would always think of it as home. This was where he had grown up, where he had shot his first bear and where as a young man he continued to live as an officer in the Blue Cuirassiers, the Guards regiment which had its barracks just beyond the palace square.

Set around the glistening waters of the White and Black Lakes, it was part garrison town, part holiday resort for wealthy families who would exchange the summer heat of the capital for the tree-lined boulevards and cool villas of smart Gatchina. In the winter its population was only 18,000; in July and August this would greatly expand, as the trains from St Petersburg pulled into the town's two railway stations and disgorged families, servants, dogs and the mounds of luggage which marked the annual exodus from the capital to their summer *dachas* in and around Gatchina, just an hour or so away by rail. There were evening concerts in the imperial parks, sailing on the wide and sunlit lakes, splendid picnics on the banks of the River Izhora, intimate supper parties, or leisurely dinners at the crowded Restaurant Verevkin on the Lutevskaya.[1] And always and everywhere the delicious murmur of endless gossip about scandals, real or imagined.

Gatchina had been founded on scandal. In the mid-eighteenth century, Catherine the Great had given it and the neighbouring villages to her lover, Grigory Orlov, as reward for helping her to depose, and dispose of, her husband. Orlov then commissioned the famous Italian architect Antonio Rinaldi to build a palace which would be quite unlike any other in St Petersburg or in the imperial estates around the capital. Gatchina was to be built in mellow limestone, but in what the Russians regarded as the 'English style', which meant that it was on austere, simple lines, with walls left in natural stone colour rather than painted yellow, blue, or Venetian red as was the case with the other more classically-styled Romanov palaces. Surrounded by a drawbridged moat, it was said by its detractors to look more like a barracks than a royal palace, though that may have been one of the attractions for the previous Tsar, Alexander III, who retired there for greater security after the assassination of his father in St Petersburg in 1881 and who was the first emperor to make it his home.

Despite its somewhat forbidding appearance, the interior of the central section of the Gatchina Palace was as splendid as any of its baroque or neoclassical rivals, with the same kind of high-ceilinged inter-communicating state rooms richly decorated with the finest paintings, sculpture, mirrors and crystal chandeliers that Romanov money could buy. In one of the galleries there was housed a priceless collection of Chinese porcelain; in the state rooms hung vast tapestries presented by France's Louis XVI. A wide marble staircase embellished with urns of malachite and gold led to rooms separated from each other by great white and gilded doors, with polished floors in which intricate parquetry designs might include as many as eighteen different kinds of wood. And from the tall windows there were views of formal gardens, landscaped parkland, lakes, bridges, pavilions and distant woods of oak, sycamore and silver birch.

Typically, for he eschewed such magnificence, Alexander III preferred to live in one of the adjoining quadrangles known as the Arsenal. There, off a vaulted, low-ceilinged corridor on the monastic-like mezzanine level of the three-storey building, squeezed between the loftier first and third floors, he and his family worked, ate and slept in rooms which had been intended to house not the Emperor of All the Russias but his staff. Alexander III continued to be surrounded by bewigged and liveried footmen, soldiers, court officials and an army of servants of all sorts and descriptions, but in his own quarters, he lived more as squire than as Tsar.

The town of Gatchina, founded in 1796, lay at the door of the palace. It was a graceful place to live; there were houses, painted primrose-yellow, standing in large country-style gardens, elegant apartment buildings, imposing public buildings and two great churches, the first the Cathedral of St Paul and the second the Church of the Intercession of Our Lady, which lay at the head of the main boulevard. But it was the palace which dominated the town as it dominated its daily life. Just five minutes from the Warsaw station and the fast one-hour express line to St Petersburg, the palace and its vast surrounding parkland gave a special character to the town itself, as well as providing social facilities, at least for the privileged garrison officers who could boat on its lakes, stroll in its gardens, take girls for winter sleigh rides, shoot in its woods and on occasion dance in its ballroom.

However, after the premature death of Alexander III in 1894, Gatchina's days as the heart of the empire were over. Only Alexander's youngest son, Michael, continued to live there. The new Tsar, his eldest son Nicholas, returned the court to the Winter Palace in St Petersburg, taking with him the imperial traffic of ministers, ambassadors and officials which had for so many years belonged to Gatchina and choosing as his own country home the more manageable New Palace, thirteen miles away at Tsarskoe Selo.*

* The New Palace later became known as the Alexander Palace; Tsarskoe Selo is now called Pushkin.

Alexander's widow, Marie Fedorovna, forty-seven and now styled Dowager Empress, also moved back to the capital.

Michael's mother, ever metropolitan in her tastes, had always preferred the flamboyant splendour of her beautiful stone-coloured Anichkov Palace on Nevsky Prospekt in St Petersburg, with its white marble staircase lined with green marble columns, reception halls ablaze with silk damask of crimson, turquoise and amber, painted ceilings, glorious blue and pink chandeliers, and a first-floor conservatory filled with enormous palms and guarded by massive beady-eyed frogs, their stone coloured turquoise. Marie had been born Princess Dagmar of Denmark and brought up in a court which of necessity counted pennies, but after marrying Alexander she had not only changed her name but her life-style. Her husband had no time for frivolous society, but he did not deny that society to his diminutive and vivacious wife, who took full advantage of his indulgence. Alexander was a great bearlike figure of a man who could lift his wife effortlessly into the air with only one hand; in turn, Marie could twist him around her little finger.

Beautifully dressed and showered with magnificent jewellery by a doting Alexander, 'Marie Fedorovna considered her chief function was to charm those who came into contact with her; she had every quality needed for doing so and was venerated at court and by the great mass of the people'.[2] She loved dancing and at the lavish imperial balls at the Winter Palace she was 'literally ablaze with diamonds when she entered the ballroom with the Emperor, for on her slender person was displayed all the crown jewels; she was generally dressed in white satin or velvet with the blue ribbon of St Andrew across her shoulder and an enormous diadem, the middle stone of which was a huge pink diamond'.[3]

Alexander would dutifully attend at her side and appear as gracious as he could, but society was her society and it was clear that if he could have done so the Tsar would have left St Petersburg to dance on its own. During the balls it was his lively wife who was the centre of attraction, while her husband stood morosely to one side, fidgeting. 'Sometimes, when the ball had lasted too long to suit him, he would impatiently begin ordering the musicians, one by one, out of the ballroom. Finally, only a solitary drummer would remain on the orchestra stand, too frightened to leave, too frightened to stop playing. If the guests continued to dance the Emperor would turn off the lights as well . . .'[4]

But nothing would stop Marie from dancing. In January 1889, when a planned ball was threatened by the suicide of the Austrian Crown Prince Rudolf and his mistress at Mayerling, protocol demanding that the court go into mourning, the Empress carried on dancing none the less, by simply sending out a substitute set of invitation cards to a *bal noir*, requesting that the guests attend wearing black, a colour which in the event was to set off the dazzling jewels worn to even greater effect.[5] As her youngest daughter Olga would recall, 'she was inherently gay; she loved clothes, jewellery, bright lights around her, in a word, she was made for court life'.[6] The Dowager Empress was thus made for St Petersburg and it was no surprise that she decided to return there, to the Anichkov Palace which had been home to her before Gatchina.

Michael was born in that palace on November 22, 1878, when his grandfather, Alexander II, was still Tsar and living at the Winter Palace, not only with his wife but also with his mistress Catherine Dolgorukaya and their three surviving illegitimate children. The Tsar, aged sixty, waited only forty days after the death of his wife, the Empress Marie Aleksandrovna, on May 28, 1880, before marrying the pretty Catherine, still only thirty-three. Among the last sounds the grey-haired Empress Marie would hear as she lay dying in the palace was the patter of her husband's bastard offspring scampering in the room above her death chamber.[7] Among the last sounds her husband would hear nine months later was the explosion of a terrorist bomb as he was returning to the Winter Palace on Sunday, March 1, 1881. Ambushed as his carriage turned on to the embankment beside the Catherine Canal, the first bomb did only minor damage, but as the Tsar got out to see to the wounded lying in the street, a second bomber ran up and threw another bomb at his feet. Alexander II was ripped apart, his right leg torn away, his left leg shattered, his stomach, chest and face mutilated, but he remained conscious long enough to moan, 'Back to the palace . . . to die there.'[8]

Lifted from the blood-stained snow and placed on a police horse sleigh which had been part of the escort, he was hurried to the palace, a trail of blood marking his passage up the marble staircase to his first-floor study, where he was laid on a couch, one eye closed, the other expressionless. As horrified members of the imperial family rushed to gather around an Emperor now barely recognisable, his new wife burst in, half-dressed, and fell flat on the couch over the body of the Tsar, kissing his hands and screaming his name.[9] The agony would not end for a further forty-five minutes. There was nothing the three doctors summoned to his side could do except finally to pronounce him dead, whereupon the Tsar's young wife gave one shriek and 'dropped on the floor like a felled tree'.[10] From that moment the new Tsar, standing grimly by the window, was Michael's father. As the imperial ensign was being lowered to half-mast above the palace, and a groan arose from the waiting crowds outside, he motioned to his wife and with long strides marched out to his carriage to be driven away down Nevsky Prospekt to the Anichkov Palace escorted by a regiment of scarlet-coated Don Cossacks, 'their red lances shining brightly in the last rays of a crimson March sunset'.[11]

Alexander II, dubbed the 'Tsar-Liberator' because he had freed the peasants from serfdom, had that very morning signed a new constitutional order which would have introduced a measure of representative government into Russia; his murder ensured that the order died with him. His massively-built son, now Alexander III, was not the man to offer concessions to the terrorists who threatened to kill him as they had his father. However, Russia could not afford to lose two Tsars in a row and Alexander III, furious that 'I must retreat now before those skunks',[12] took himself and his family off to the security of Gatchina. It was the only retreat he would make. Once there, he stamped down hard on the anarchists, terrorists, and revolutionaries who thought they could overthrow the Romanovs.*

Thirty-six when he became Tsar, Alexander III did not claim to know what was best for liberal Britain, republican France, or the new thrusting German empire, but he thought he knew what was best for Russia: not muddle-headed constitutional government but the stern hand of a loving father. Under this Alexander, the country would begin to catch up with the industrialised West, the huge bureaucratic machine would begin to tick over more smoothly and Russian prosperity increase as never before.

Favouring peasant dress of blouse and boots, and wearing patched shirts,[13] Alexander had barked the orders in Gatchina which had transmitted his rule from the Baltic to the Pacific, and in so doing he had made Russia respected in every chancellery in Europe and beyond. An intimidating figure, standing six feet four inches tall, his physical strength was as awesome as it was legendary. When, in the midst of a Balkan crisis, the Austrian ambassador was rash enough to hint at a state dinner that his country might mobilise two or three army corps, the Tsar's reaction was to pick up a silver fork, bend it into a knot and toss it contemptuously in the direction of a now discomfited ambassador. 'That,' said Alexander III, 'is what I am going to do to your two or three army corps.'[14]

However, after only thirteen years as Tsar, and at the age of only forty-nine, Alexander III became ill, and although the doctors believed that all that was needed was a long rest and reviving sunshine, the Tsar's condition rapidly deteriorated. He was suffering from a kidney complaint which, long undiagnosed, had developed into nephritis. On October 20, 1894, he died at his holiday home at Livadia, in the Crimea, and at the age of twenty-six his son Nicholas became Emperor.

The death of Alexander III marked the end of an era for Russia. Had

* Among them would be a young student, Aleksandr Ulyanov, hanged in 1888 for attempted assassination. His brother, Vladimir, is better known as Lenin.

he lived his biblical span he would have died in 1915 and the world would have been a very different place. During his reign Russia had remained at peace, and among the tributes to him abroad it would be remarked that 'it is his highest title to the gratitude alike of his own subjects and of mankind that he invariably strove to preserve that peace'.[15] His brand of autocracy might not have saved Russia from revolution in the long term, but the conclusion must be that he would at least have postponed it. With Alexander as Tsar, there would have been little likelihood of Russia drifting into an unnecessary war with Japan in 1904; without the bloodshed and the military disasters of that war, the revolution of 1905 would not have happened as it did. And with Tsar Alexander III growling at Europe from Gatchina, the Balkan crisis in the summer of 1914 might not have ended as it did, in the calamitous bloodbath of the First World War.*

As it was, destiny was to be placed in the hands of Alexander's eldest son Nicholas, a young man unready for the awesome power and responsibilities of the imperial crown.

Because of the ten-year gap in their ages, Michael would share little of his childhood with his eldest brother Nicholas; his chief playmate was his younger sister Olga. The babies of the family, Michael and Olga would remain the closest of friends for many years to come. As she would say, 'he and I had so much in common. We had the same tastes, liked the same people, shared the same interests, and we never quarrelled.'[16]

Michael was 'Misha' to the family, but to Olga he was 'Floppy', the pet name she gave him because of his habit of flopping into chairs with his long legs sprawled about him. It was a name she would continue to use, and sometimes a grown-up Michael trying to look dignified and serious at some official gathering would be disconcerted to hear his sister calling 'Darling Floppy' across some crowded room.[17]

With a father of almost spartan taste, life in those early years at Gatchina was simple enough, made more rigorous by a starched British nanny, Elizabeth Franklin,[18] who brought with her the attitudes thought essential to the proper conduct of the Victorian nursery and to the disciplined upbringing of small children. Regardless of marital status, when addressed in English, all British nannies were styled Mrs and all British governesses were styled Miss. It was thus as Mrs Franklin that the new nanny brought her own form of autocracy to Gatchina.

Whatever she might have thought as she journeyed to her new imperial

* There are many reasons for so saying, but one of them is that the trusted Sergei Witte might well have still been in high office, and there was no man more opposed to the First World War than Witte. He thought it 'madness'. Witte also strenuously opposed the Japanese war; Nicholas, as will be noted, dismissed him as prime minister in 1906.

employment, and to a family which kept up seven palaces and an army of servants, Mrs Franklin was to find at Gatchina that she would have no need to worry about combating the spoiling effects of over-indulgence or excessive opulence. An Emperor who washed in cold water, wore patched clothing and had a boiled egg for breakfast, was not likely to find fault with a nursery regime in which jam on the bread at tea-time was presented as a treat. In the morning there was porridge; for dinner, a mutton cutlet with peas and a baked potato; and only on the most special occasions would there be cake for tea. 'It was', as Olga would still recall several decades later, 'a very plain diet'.[19]

As an approving Mrs Franklin was pleased to note, the plainness extended to the children's bedrooms, furnished with camp beds with one hard, flat pillow and a very thin mattress. There were straight-backed cane chairs, but no armchairs or sofas, and simple wooden desks and tables of the kind which could be found in the most modest household.[20] Yet their childhood could not have been happier; looking back, the days at Gatchina would seem a golden age.

When Olga became old enough for formal lessons, she joined Michael in the dining room which from nine in the morning until three in the afternoon served as makeshift classroom. Their education was entrusted to a series of carefully-selected, private tutors who could provide everything except the companionship of other children. There was Mr Heath, for English, M. Thormeyer for French and the white-whiskered Mr Troitsky who taught them dancing, wore white gloves and who always insisted that a huge pot of fresh flowers be placed on the piano of the accompanist.[21]

On Sundays, and only on Sundays, Michael and Olga could have friends to join them. A carefully-selected band of aristocratic children would board the train at the Warsaw station in St Petersburg to spend the afternoon climbing trees and playing hide-and-seek in the palace, before having tea with the young Grand Duke and Grand Duchess.[22] In its own way it was a carefree life, but only within the park itself and inside the ring of troops who kept ceaseless guard on the palace against any possible terrorist attack. Sometimes Michael and Olga would spot a plainclothes policeman 'darting in and out from behind trees and shrubs',[23] but at least inside the park they had a freedom they could never have outside it.

Michael was not quite sixteen when his father died and it marked the end of his childhood, as it marked the end of an era for Russia. Three months earlier his sister Xenia had married a second cousin, Grand Duke Alexander Mikhailovich and one week after his father's funeral his brother Nicholas married his fiancée, Princess Alix of Hesse-Darmstadt. His other brother George, suffering from tuberculosis, was living in the high air of the

Caucasus in the hope that it would save his life. Michael and Olga, with a distracted mother trying to come to terms with the loss of her husband, moved to the Anichkov Palace, with Gatchina now a place used only for occasional weeks in the summer, though it was Gatchina which Michael would remember as home.

For a young Grand Duke, and a brother of the Tsar, there were few choices in life when it came to deciding his future. Michael could not go into business, or the professions, and accordingly he followed the traditional path into military service. Nicholas had been a Hussar, George had joined the navy before his illness made any career impossible, and Michael opted to be a gunner. After a spell at artillery school, he joined the Horse Guards Artillery, the regiment with which he would serve until he was twenty-three, and his transfer in June, 1902, to the Blue Cuirassiers.[24] In the army he found himself for the first time in his life among young men of his own age, free to make friendships of his own choosing, and to follow his own pursuits. Their interests were also his, for he was already a keen sportsman, more than able to compete with his fellow officers.

Although Michael had grown to stand well over six feet tall, that was only to be expected in a family noted for the height of its menfolk. His father and four uncles were all towering figures, although the tallest Romanov of all was his father's cousin, Grand Duke Nicholas Nikolaevich, at six feet six inches.[25] In contrast, and strikingly so, Nicholas was barely five foot seven inches, a height which encouraged his massive uncles to think that they could browbeat him, as indeed they did. As his brother-in-law Sandro later commented, 'Nicky spent the first ten years of his reign sitting behind a massive desk in the palace, and listening with near awe to the well-rehearsed bellowing of his towering uncles. He dreaded to be left alone with them.'[26]

The small new Tsar took after his tiny mother, not his huge father, and if there was any question of that it would be settled when Nicholas met his British cousin, the young man who one day would be King George V. The Dowager Empress and her sister Queen Alexandra of England looked very like each other, and their sons, Nicholas and George, were so similar in age, size and appearance that they could have been twins; when together, they would on occasion be confused even by members of their own entourages. Since there could never be anything of the Romanovs in Britain's future George V, it is understandable if sometimes the large Romanov uncles looked down on the small Nicholas II and wondered if there was anything of the Romanovs there either.

Michael's twentieth birthday, in November 1898, was an important day: it marked the point when he legally came of age and achieved financial independence, albeit with a trustee appointed to guide and advise him on his affairs for the next five years. The change from minor to manhood was the occasion for considerable official ceremony with a *Te Deum* at an elaborate church service attended by the imperial family, ministers, court and state dignitaries.[27]

In accordance with tradition, the ceremony ended with Michael being beckoned forward by the Tsar to take two solemn oaths: the first to uphold the fundamental laws of succession to the throne and the institutions of the imperial family; the second to pledge his allegiance as a Russian officer. As an ensign stepped forward with the standard of his regiment, Michael took the colours in his left hand, read the two oaths aloud and embraced his brother. He was now, in law, not only a man but a man sworn to give his unquestioning loyalty to his Emperor, and 'to serve His Imperial Majesty, not sparing my life and limb, until the very last drop of my blood'.[28]

Eight months later Michael found himself heir presumptive. His brother George had been found dying beside his overturned motor cycle near his home in the Caucasus, and with his death Michael became the heir to the throne, for although Nicholas had daughters he had as yet no son to succeed him. In eighteenth-century Russia there had been empresses reigning in their own right, but after Paul I succeeded his mother, whom he hated, he ruled that henceforth no woman was eligible to take the crown; that law had been accepted as binding ever since.

Nicholas's wife, who had taken the name Alexandra Fedorovna on her marriage, was now obsessed by her need to produce a male heir. It was already salon gossip that at the moment of birth the Empress was 'in such a state of nervous excitement that those around her were afraid to apprise her of the infant's sex'.[29] The change in the succession brought about by George's death was an unwelcome reminder to her that she had so far failed to give her husband an heir of his own, for six weeks earlier she had been delivered of her third child and once again it had been a girl. Her husband had not given any sign of disappointment when a second girl followed the first, but after the birth of his third daughter, Marie, 'it was noticed that he set off on a long solitary walk', although when he came back he seemed as 'outwardly unruffled as ever'.[30]

When she became pregnant for the fourth time, in the autumn of 1900, it seemed that it might be too late, for Nicholas had fallen gravely ill on holiday in the Crimea and there were fears that he would die. He had intestinal typhus, a disease which in those days could well prove fatal. In that event, Michael would automatically succeed his brother as Emperor. Alexandra refused to accept that, insisting to gathering ministers that even if Nicholas died, the posthumously-born child, if a boy, should be declared Tsar and that in the meantime she should rule Russia as Regent on behalf of her womb. When court minister Baron Frederiks tentatively raised the question of the regency, the ailing Tsar 'sided with his wife'. His response was, 'No, no! Misha will get everything into a mess – he is so easily imposed upon'.[31]

Sergei Witte, destined to become Russia's first prime minister, disagreed. At an impromptu conference in a Yalta hotel he discussed the regency question with interior minister Dimitri Sipyagin, Grand Duke Michael Nikolaevich, governor of the Caucasus, foreign minister Count Vladimir Lamsdorff and Baron Frederiks.[32]

There was no precedent for allowing Alexandra to rule the empire as Regent for a period of several months on the gamble that she would then be delivered of a son. Witte firmly opposed any such idea, insisting that 'the letter of the law should be followed', so that Michael ascended the throne. 'I succeeded in winning over to my side all the members of this improvised conference. It was decided that, in the event of the Emperor's death, we would immediately take an oath of allegiance to Michael Aleksandrovich.'[33]

Dismissed as prime minister in 1906, Witte would date his becoming 'the object of Alexandra's particular enmity' from his stand at Yalta in support of Michael, which she interpreted as 'an underhand intrigue on my part against her'.[34] As it happened, it was all for nothing anyway: the Tsar recovered. And when Alexandra did give birth to her fourth child in the following summer of 1901, the baby was yet another girl, to be named Anastasia.

Witte was impressed by Michael, to whom he had taught political science and economics.[35] Witte had liked, and hoped for much from Nicholas when he succeeded to the throne in 1894, but he came to despise him, making no secret of his preference for Michael. Perhaps sometimes he praised Michael only the better to diminish Nicholas; nevertheless, praise he did.

As heir 'until a son is born' Michael performed his duties with sensible modesty, knowing that anything else would be resented by a brooding Alexandra. In 1901 he represented Russia at the funeral of Queen Victoria in London and was awarded the Order of the Bath. In the following year he returned to London, to represent Russia at the coronation of King Edward VII; although at the last moment the coronation had to be postponed because of the King's illness, Michael was made a Knight of the Garter, a member of Britain's most illustrious order, with his own standard to hang in the chapel at Windsor Castle.

Back home, he continued doing what was required of him, but without appearing to assert himself, as when attending meetings of the Council of State in the Rotunda at the Marie Palace, in the square facing St Isaac's

Cathedral. In this circular room some eighty men at most would gather and in turn-of-the-century Russia it was not thought necessary that there should be more. One room was enough when only one man then dispose of everything.

There exists a portrait of the special formal session of the Council held in March, 1901. There, Michael sat on the right hand of Nicholas, with their uncles Vladimir, Alexis and Serge, the brothers of Alexander III, ranged alongside, wearing full uniform with sashes and gleaming orders. The ministers of the day, in dark navy-blue and gold court dress, were seated facing them in a semicircle.* Whether then, or at those ordinary meetings of the Council he was required to attend, Michael said little; but then, an heir was not expected to hold or express independent views.

Accustomed to the loud voices of Nicholas's huge uncles, only too ready to tell their young nephew Nicholas how to run the country, some ministers misjudged Michael's quiet self-deprecating manner, but Witte did not. One senior courtier observed that Witte, 'never tired of praising his straightforwardness';[36] Grand Duke Konstantin Konstantinovich, a cousin of Michael's father, noted that Witte 'holds a very high opinion of the Heir. The Heir is not well known or appreciated by society; Witte sees in him a clear mind, an unshakeable conviction in his opinions, and a crystalline moral purity. Misha keeps away from affairs of state, does not offer his opinions and, perhaps, hides behind the perception of him as a good-natured unremarkable boy.'[37]

In 1905, as Russia was reeling from yet another battlefield disaster in its eighteen-month war with Japan, Witte was sent to the United States to negotiate a peace treaty. At the conference, brokered by the American president Theodore Roosevelt, Witte brilliantly secured terms so exceptionally favourable that it might have been Russia which had won the war. When he delightedly cabled Tsar Nicholas he received back a grudging and almost resentful telegram which paid no tribute to his extraordinary and unexpected success, but merely demanded that the treaty not be signed until 'the amount fixed for the keep of war prisoners is fixed and ratified by me'.[38] In striking contrast, the telegram from his ex-pupil Michael was generously phrased: 'My heartfelt congratulations on brilliant termination of grandiose work achieved for well-being of dear Fatherland'.[39]

To Witte, that seemed to sum up the two brothers: the younger generous spirited and the other not. One other story Witte liked to recall was from Michael's childhood at Gatchina. Michael and his father were walking in the garden when Tsar Alexander, suddenly put out by his young son's misbehaviour, snatched up a hose and turned it on Michael, drenching him

* The painting by Repin now hangs in the Russian National Museum in St Petersburg.

to the skin. Michael went indoors, saying nothing, and changed his clothes. It was the habit of the Tsar when working on the papers in his study to pause from time to time, to get up from his desk and walk over to the open window in the corner, leaning out over the sill. It refreshed him. This morning it was to refresh him particularly, for waiting for him at the window above was Michael who, upon sighting his father emerging below, tipped a bucket of water over his head, drenching the Emperor of All the Russias no less than he had drenched Michael. It was sweet revenge.

Having changed *his* clothes, the Tsar seemed to take it in good part, chuckling about it as he explained the incident to his astonished valet, who then could not wait to spread the tale. Witte, unable to imagine the Tsar's eldest son Nicholas capable of such defiance, was so impressed that twenty years later he recounted the story in his own memoirs: 'There is very little doubt that none but Michael would have dared to think of such a stratagem and there is no doubt whatsoever that nobody else could have executed it with impunity'.[40]

In so saying, Witte was then, of course, pouring his own bucket of cold water upon another imperial head – praising Michael only in order to debunk Nicholas. But there was more to it than that. The widely-respected correspondent of the London *Daily Telegraph*, Dr E. J. Dillon, recorded him as saying that 'if Alexander III had lived, or if his son Michael had succeeded him or were yet to come to the throne, much might be changed for the better, and Russia's international position strengthened'.[41]

Yet to come to the throne? At the beginning of 1908, though Nicholas was not yet forty and had a son to succeed him, the chances of Michael becoming Emperor were, in fact, greater than they appeared at first sight.

Although Michael ceased to be heir presumptive with the birth of Alexis in 1904, he was named as Regent in the event of Nicholas dying before his son reached manhood. Alexis could not reign in his own right until 1920* and in the interval Nicholas's life could be cut short, by fatal illness, accident, or assassination.

Alexander II was the last Tsar to be killed by terrorists, but there had been frequent attempts on the life of Nicholas, and three years earlier, in February 1905, his uncle and Alexandra's brother-in-law Grand Duke Serge had been blown to pieces by an assassin's bomb while driving across Senate Square inside the Kremlin. His wife Ella, rushing out on hearing the explosion, scrabbled among his remains but of the man who had been the iron-fisted Governor of Moscow little remained but mangled flesh. The blast was so great that one of his bejewelled fingers was found on a rooftop.[42]

* Under Russian law, an Emperor could reign in his own right from the age of sixteen.

In August, 1906, General George Min, the Tsar's equerry and the man who, as commander of the Semenovsky Guards, had played a key role in the quelling of the last stand of the revolutionaries in Moscow nine months earlier, had been gunned down on a railway platform by a woman terrorist.[43] The day before, terrorists had tried to kill Nicholas's new strong-man prime minister Peter Stolypin, lobbing a massive bomb through a ground-floor window of his house in St Petersburg, demolishing the whole front of the building, and killing 25 of the people inside, as well as injuring his two children, one of them, his daughter, being permanently maimed.[44] Stolypin escaped unhurt, but by the end of that month the terrorists appeared set on an even greater prize: the Tsar himself. They failed, the ringleaders being arrested before they could get to him at his summer villa at coastal Peterhof, eighteen miles from the capital; but as Nicholas wrote to his mother afterwards, 'I have been unable to go out riding or even outside the gate, and this at one's own home – at Peterhof, usually so peaceful!'[45]

Assassination could not, therefore, be discounted and should Nicholas be killed, Michael would become Regent for Nicholas's son Alexis – albeit in tandem with his sister-in-law, Alexandra having characteristically ensured that in the manifesto of appointment she was named as co-Regent.[46] With that, Michael had especial reason to pray for his brother's well-being.

However, Alexis's succession was by no means certain. It was a close-kept secret, but little Alexis suffered from the 'bleeding disease' haemophilia, with any bump or bruise a threat to his life. Even if Alexis survived his father, he might not live long, in which case Michael would be Emperor. The dangers to the succession were self-evident, and therefore Michael could not be permitted to jeopardise the throne by a marriage in breach of the imperial statutes. He was more than just a Grand Duke, he was an insurance policy against disaster.

It was for that reason that Michael's idea of marrying Dina had created such alarm, and brought such heavy-handed action against her both by Nicholas and the Dowager Empress. If he married morganatically there was no precedent which would allow his wife to become Empress* and certainly no way in which his children could succeed him on the throne.

When Michael wrote to his brother in July 1906, asking permission to wed Dina, he did not know that two-year-old Alexis was haemophilic, an illustration of the extent to which the disease was kept a secret at Tsarskoe Selo. As he said to Nicholas in promoting his case: 'Thank God, you are well and in perfect health, and so is little Alexis, and besides, you can yet have other children. Even, if God forbid, I'll have to be Regent, my

* Alexander II's second and morganatic wife Catherine Dolgorukaya hoped to have herself proclaimed Empress, but Alexander's assassination ended her ambition; the question was therefore never tested.

marriage will not be in the way'.[47] Not only was little Alexis not in perfect health, but haemophilia ruled out any question of more sons. The succession was not by any means as secure as Michael assumed it to be.

Imperial prestige apart, a morganatic marriage might have mattered less if those following Michael were men of untarnished reputations themselves, with no skeletons in their own cupboards, but that was not the case and most markedly so in respect of those closest to the throne. There were twenty Grand Dukes and twelve imperial princes in the line of succession at the beginning of 1908, but Nicholas needed only to glance at the Grand Dukes who stood immediately behind Michael to know that there was slight comfort to be found there. Among the most senior Grand Dukes it was difficult to find anyone after Michael whose succession to the crown would not produce more questions than answers.

After Alexis and Michael, the succession to the imperial crown stepped immediately sideways, to the brothers of Alexander III and their male descendants. Of these, the senior figure in January, 1908 was Grand Duke Vladimir, who had become, on the birth of Alexis, third-in-line to the throne. Briefly banished by Alexander III after he drunkenly tried to throttle a French actor in an disgraceful scene in a St Petersburg restaurant,[48] he was known to be ambitious both for himself and for his family of three sons. Their grip on the succession was, however, flawed. Vladimir's German-born wife, Grand Duchess Marie, had not converted to Orthodoxy, as required by the imperial statutes[49] and technically that was a bar to his children's rights.

Of his three sons, none inspired great enthusiasm. Kirill, the eldest, had married 'Ducky' – the Grand Duchess Victoria Melita who had first been married to Alexandra's brother Ernst of Hesse; since she was a divorcée, first cousin and non-Orthodox, that marriage breached both Church and imperial laws; accordingly Kirill and 'Ducky' had been banished in 1905 and as yet had not been allowed back into Russia.[50] Alexandra never forgave Kirill for taking her brother's wife; for other reasons she disapproved just as much of the next-in-line, Boris – a disreputable roué involved in a string of scandals; one bride was abandoned by her husband-to-be on the eve of her wedding after she had been 'incautious' with Boris.[51] Of all the Romanovs, Boris was the one more likely to be shot by a husband than by an assassin. The third Vladimir son, Andrew, was living contentedly with the ballet dancer Kschessinska and they had an illegitimate son, 'Vova' – though Vova himself would never be quite sure whether his father was Andrew, who acknowledged him, or Kschessinska's previous lover, Grand Duke Serge Mikhailovich.[52] What mattered, however, was that Andrew would never give up Kschessinska and if he married her it would mean his banishment.

The scene was no brighter further down the line. Vladimir's womanising brother Alexis was living with a French actress in Paris;[53] there too was his other brother Paul, who had married a divorcée commoner and been banished for it.[54] The ninth-in-line to the throne, Paul's son Grand Duke Dimitri, offered more hope but he was still only seventeen; in the event, he, too, would one day be banished, though in his case it would be for murder.[55] Next, at least by birth, was Nicholas Konstantinovich, a nephew of Alexander II, but he had been exiled to Tashkent after a scandalous affair with an American heiress and had married a policeman's daughter.[56] Insisting on calling himself plain 'Nicholas Romanov', and promoting the republican cause, he was regarded as insane.

Taken as a whole, therefore, there were few reasons for the Tsar to feel reassured when he reviewed the list of Grand Dukes nearest to the throne. But whatever the misdeed – morganatic marriage included – no Romanov could be removed against his will from the line of succession. At the time of Kirill's marriage the Tsar wanted to deprive him of his rights to the throne, but Nicholas was advised that he could not do that.*

Five years earlier, after his Uncle Paul had vanished abroad with three million roubles and his divorcée mistress, Nicholas had sent his mother a letter which now seemed depressingly prophetic:

> *How painful and distressing it all is and how ashamed one feels for the sake of our family before the world. What guarantee is there now that Kirill won't start the same sort of thing tomorrow and Boris or Serge Mikhailovich the day after. And, in the end, I fear, a whole colony of members of the Russian Imperial Family will be established in Paris with their semi-legitimate and illegitimate wives! God alone knows what times we are living in, when undisguised selfishness stifles all feelings of conscience, duty or even ordinary decency.*[57]

Nicholas had good grounds for his general pessimism and in time his sister Olga would come to think that he had been right, concluding that: 'too many of us Romanovs had gone to live in a world of self-interest where little mattered except the unending gratification of personal desire and ambition. Nothing proved it better than the appalling marital mess in which the last generation of my family involved themselves. That chain of domestic scandals could not but shock the nation but did any of them care for the impression they created? Never.'[58]

History would show that judgement to be right, for after the little Tsarevich, of the ten Grand Dukes nearest to the throne at the end of 1907,

* Kirill's three-year exile ended in November 1908 when he was allowed to return for the funeral of his uncle Grand Duke Alexis. His father Vladimir died three months later, in February 1909.

six either had been or would be banished and not one had married or would marry in strict compliance with the fundamental laws. But for Nicholas the worst had not yet happened and, with the departure abroad of a beaten Dina, Nicholas and his mother could heave a sigh of relief that at least Michael seemed to have been saved from the kind of fate which had overtaken so many of those behind him.

Madame Wulfert was someone, as yet, of whom they knew nothing.

THREE

The Lieutenant's Bride

Madame Nathalie Wulfert was five foot six inches tall,[1] slender, fair-haired and possessed of deep-set velvety blue eyes which once seen would be rarely forgotten. In 1907 she was twenty-seven, elegant, poised and quite beautiful, with a way of holding herself, a look about her that turned eyes wherever she went. Her taste was impeccable, she had immense charm, she was unquestionably clever and at the dinner table she could converse easily and knowledgeably about books, theatre, ballet and opera. Her friends included the young composer Sergei Rachmaninov and the famed basso Fedor Chaliapin,[2] and she could claim acquaintance with some of the best-known sculptors and painters in Russia.

These were impressive credentials and in her hometown of Moscow they had given her access to the haughtiest salons as well as to the great mansions of the millionaire entrepreneurs who had made their fortunes from railways, textiles and oil as Russia began its rise into the ranks of the leading industrial powers. But Gatchina was not bustling Moscow, it was a small garrison town dominated by swaggering Guards officers and well-bred hostesses interested only in court intrigues, boulevard gossip, and the latest scandal being whispered in the salons of nearby St Petersburg. And what mattered in Gatchina when they considered Madame Wulfert was not her undoubted culture or her refined taste, but that she was a woman about whom there was more than a whiff of scandal.

Moscow was 400 miles away, but Madame Wulfert's reputation had travelled with her. From the moment when, a few months earlier, she had stepped off the St Petersburg express at Gatchina's Warsaw station, she had been the subject of gossip. It quickly became known that she was a divorcée whose marriage had broken up because of her love affair with the man who had brought her back to Gatchina as his bride, along with her four-year-old daughter.

Once unthinkable in Russia, divorce had become more common in recent years. Because of Church law, adultery provided the only practical means of exit from a marriage which had broken down and in such cases it was the accepted practice for all but the most vengeful husbands to present themselves as the guilty party, for it was thought ungentlemanly to expose a woman to the ordeal of humiliating interrogation about her intimate life.

In most instances the evidence presented was a sham, for there were girls willing to be hired for the night and menservants happy to be paid as 'eye-witnesses'.[3]

To more cynical observers it seemed that some younger members of 'the fast set' had begun to regard divorce as simply a means to advancement. 'Many girls marry in haste to get their independence, and look upon their first matrimonial venture as a step to better themselves in the future. It seems very paradoxical, but it is nevertheless a fact that it is far easier for a married woman than for a spinster to find a husband. The breaking off of an engagement creates a scandal, but the severing of matrimonial bonds is becoming quite the usual thing. The most insignificant misunderstanding causes husband and wife to break their marriage vows and go their different ways. Gossips chatter about impending divorces as much as of budding engagements. In Russia a divorced woman does not lose a tithe of her reputation, if no outrageous scandal attaches to her divorce. Should she marry again she returns to society with her new husband and enjoys all of the prerogatives of her new position.'[4]

Yet divorce was not regarded so casually by conventional society, whether in Russia or elsewhere. The uncompromising views of the Dowager Empress, for example, were shared with no less absolute conviction in England by her sister Queen Alexandra, as well as by her daughter-in-law the Empress Alexandra. Their doors were closed firmly in the face of any divorcée, as were those of hostesses, royal or otherwise, who continued to believe, and would go on so believing for half a century more, that divorce was a disgrace which condemned both guilty and innocent parties to the shadows. There were others, however, who took a more liberal view, and in St Petersburg the most prominent of these was the Grand Duchess Marie Pavlovna. In her salons, frequented by the 'fast set', a remarried divorcée with the right husband was as welcome as any,[5] though since her own son Kirill was married to a divorcée, albeit a very royal one, that was not surprising.

In Gatchina, however, views tended to follow the stricter attitudes of the Dowager Empress, not least because she was colonel-in-chief of the Blue Cuirassiers.[6] She took the keenest interest in 'her' regiment and because there were occasions when officers' wives were invited to social events at which she would be present, it followed that wives who had been divorced would not be welcomed, and accordingly that officers were discouraged from bringing such wives into the regiment in the first place. They were an embarrassment.

Natasha may not have understood that when she set off for Gatchina, for she knew nothing of the etiquette in Guards regiments, but by then it was too late. In marrying Wulfert she had married the Blue Cuirassiers, and however beautiful she looked, however loyal and devoted she appeared to her new husband, she would never quite be accepted.

There was also her own family background to provide reason for critical comment, and to count against her. The wives of Guards officers were usually women from the ranks of the aristocracy, or its fringes. Social position counted for a great deal and Guards officers were expected to remember that when they married. In the Blue Cuirassiers they took pride not only in their close connection with the Dowager Empress but in the fact that her son, the Grand Duke Michael Aleksandrovich, was one of their squadron commanders.

There was nothing in Natasha's upbringing which suggested that she would move easily in such imperial circles. Her father, Sergei Aleksandrovich Sheremetevsky, was a lawyer,[7] comfortable enough but by no means rich. Sergei Mamontov, her first husband and father of her child was a musician, a pianist who worked at the Bolshoi Theatre. To be sure, Sergei Mamontov was related to Savva Mamontov, a railway tycoon who had founded the Moscow Private Opera Company,[8] and it was through this connection that Natasha had met and become friendly with so many distinguished composers, opera singers, and artists; however, Savva had been arrested for financial irregularities in 1899 and subsequently had gone spectacularly bankrupt;[9] the Mamontov name had suffered accordingly. She was still friendly with Rachmaninov and Chaliapin, but in a Guards regiment those were not the references they were looking for.

Even without her divorce, and the manner in which it had come about, Natasha would have found it difficult to adjust to life in a Guards regiment and to the narrow world of Gatchina's drawing rooms, with women who in the main scorned intelligent conversation and broad education. A Guards wife could talk happily about horses, children, dogs and servants, but thereafter their talk was enlivened by gossip about friends and enemies. It was such gossip which made their world go round; anything else made them uncomfortable.

Natasha was accustomed to serious conversation. At home in Moscow it had been encouraged, and through her marriage to Mamontov she had mixed with people who took a lively and often noisy interest in the subjects of the day, as well as in their world of the arts. Natasha, the youngest of three daughters, was naturally clever, though not as clever as her elder sister Olga, 'the brains of the family'.[10] Olga would never have adjusted to life as a Guards wife, for she was 'extremely well read, and her circle of friends contained all the intelligentsia of the day'.[11] The very word 'intelligentsia' was anathema in Gatchina's salons.

In imperial Russia everyone was registered in one of five official 'Estates' –

Noble, Merchant, Burgher, Peasant, Cleric – each of which notionally established the holder's social and legal status, although this often had nothing to do with occupation or actual position in society.[12] Many of the so-called peasants who made up eighty per cent of the country had moved into towns and become industrial workers, never to return to the land again; Natasha's father, Sergei Sheremetevsky, was a member of the nobility, the rank which he and in turn Natasha inherited at birth,[13] but as a lawyer and thus as a member of the professional classes he might legally have been registered in any one of the five 'Estates'.

To be noble was not necessarily to be well-bred or well-connected, for the rank could be bestowed for having reached some particular level in the vast administrative machinery which governed Russia day-by-day, and once granted, it was then inherited by subsequent generations. A member of the noble class might be a poor man shunned by society or a revolutionary like Lenin; in contrast, a 'peasant' might own factories and a mansion in Moscow, and believe ardently in the autocratic powers of the Tsar. Sometimes the socially ambitious would argue their way up the official scale and have their legal status changed, but others took a perverse pleasure in remaining as they had been born, flaunting their wealth and position in the face of the peasant stamp inside their passport.[14]

Natasha's 'nobility' meant little, for it was unsupported by great wealth or land, or by aristocratic connections. In other countries she would have been thought a member of the professional middle classes, and that is how, in practice, she was regarded in turn-of-the-century Russia. Natasha's father had built up a sizeable practice in Moscow, employing eleven lawyers in all.[15] He was also for a time a deputy in the Moscow City Duma and a trustee of the Arbat City School.[16] These were not positions of any great distinction, but worthy enough for a man of respectable ambition in local society. If he was never to count himself among the rich, nevertheless he was able to provide his wife and three children with all the advantages which had accrued to the professional classes with Russia's increasing prosperity.

Natasha was born in a rented summer *dacha* at Perovo, on the outskirts of Moscow, on June 27, 1880, some eighteen months after Michael.[17] Her birth date would prove to be a somewhat movable feast, for it would be her good fortune in later life to appear very much younger than she was; she would take full advantage of that, declaring on official forms that she was born not in 1880 but six or even eight years later. Just by looking at her, no one could say otherwise.

Until Natasha was a year old her parents lived on the fashionable Ilinka beside the Kremlin, in an apartment which they rented from Natasha's godfather, a wealthy and prominent Moscow industrialist, Aleksei

Khludov.[18] Natasha's father then bought a modest single-storey wooden house, No. 7 Serebriany Lane, where the family lived until 1893, when Natasha was thirteen. Over the next ten years they moved six times, from one rented apartment to another. They spent a year at 10 Antipevsky Lane and another at 1 Krivo-Nikolsky Lane; in 1896 they moved to 9 Trubnikov Lane and three years later to 10 Mokhovaya Street. In 1900 they were at 14 Volkhonka and two years later at 7 Ostozhenka.[19] Naturally enough, of the eight homes in which Natasha grew up, she would best remember the pretty wooden house on Serebriany Lane, where she had spent most of her childhood.

Fast-changing though Moscow was at the beginning of the century – when it was growing at the same pace as New York – there were still many such wooden houses in quiet, tree-lined sleepy lanes, so much so that one foreign visitor had been surprised at how often it was possible to think oneself 'in the prettiest and most peaceful country retreats one can imagine'.[20]

Despite her family's repeated moves, Natasha's home life was as ordered and comfortable as might be expected of a reasonably successful lawyer. There were maids to help her chain-smoking mother Julia[21] with the housework, a nurse for the children when they were very young, and even a living-in French governess[22] to provide extra polish to the girls' education at an exclusive private day school, though unlike some of their grander acquaintances the Sheremetevskys never quite aspired to one of the more expensive and aloof English governesses whose presence or absence made its own statement about a family's social position. Even so, with a small wooden *dacha* in the picturesque lakeside village of Pushkino, twenty miles north of Moscow, to which the family retired at the height of summer,[23] there was every reason for the Sheremetevskys to hold their heads high in Moscow.

As Natasha turned from an awkward schoolgirl into a strikingly beautiful woman, the Sheremetevsky household found a steady stream of nervous young men knocking on the apartment door. One of these was Dimitri Abrikosov, then a law student at Moscow University. 'There was a friend of my sister, a charming girl, whom I met at that time. Her blue eyes were appealing and my desire to see her became stronger and stronger, but it never went further than holding hands while listening to the Tchaikovsky overture to *Romeo and Juliet*. I did think for a while that she was the only girl who could make me happy . . .'[24] But Abrikosov was 'so young and shy in those days that I had not the courage to express my admiration'. He was 'to suffer a dreadful blow to my dignity when the girl preferred someone else. I must confess I have never forgotten Nathalie with her sad eyes.'[25]

That 'someone else' was Sergei Mamontov, a stockily-built dark-haired young man three years older than Natasha.[26] At first it was thought that he was interested in her elder sister Olga, but clever though she was, Olga could never rival Natasha in looks and when Sergei proposed it was to Natasha, then twenty-one. They were married in 1902.[27]

Natasha's parents were as delighted by this match as they had been by the earlier marriage of their eldest daughter Vera to a solid Moscow businessman. Mamontov was the kind of serious young man who seemed to have prospects in the wider world. A talented pianist, with a slight stutter which seemed only to add to his charm,[28] he had ambitions to be a great conductor. When he married Natasha he was working at the opera company founded by Savva Mamontov; he was a *répétiteur*, one of the accompanists for opera singers at rehearsals, and it would be said later that he knew the scores of thirty-three operas by heart.[29]

The young couple moved into a brand-new apartment at 13 Mansurovsky Lane,[30] off the fashionable Prechistenka, in an area in which many of the richest built themselves handsome mansions. Within a year Natasha had her first child, a girl born on June 2, 1903.[31] She was christened Nathalie, after her mother, but known ever after simply as Tata. At first the marriage was a success, as Natasha met, entertained and became friends with some of the great names associated with the opera company. For a while a young Rachmaninov had been its second conductor; it had launched Chaliapin on his road to fame, and it premièred works by Rimsky-Korsakov.[32]

But husband Sergei was not a frivolous man and the frantic pleasures of society bored him.[33] While Natasha was happy to accept every possible invitation from hostesses eager to entertain the handsome Mamontovs, her husband increasingly seemed to prefer coming straight home after work, rather than going on to supper parties, or dancing into the early hours. Without anything to do in an apartment run by servants, and with a baby entirely cared for by a nurse, Natasha quickly discovered that being mistress of her own home was not the bliss that she had imagined. She was bored and the more she complained to her husband, the more he retreated into his own world.

As his granddaughter would say of him: 'He had been a good and kind husband, but he was of a retiring nature and he could not cope with his wife's outbursts ... He had never enjoyed going to parties and receptions, and now he made the excuse that the pressure of his work precluded attending these functions. It is not really surprising that Natasha started to go out without him ...'[34]

It is also not surprising that in doing so Natasha should find admirers flocking around her, for a beautiful wife without a husband in attendance was bound to be target, and a willing target in some cases, for the handsome and gallant young men who adorned the fashionable salons through which

Moscow society conducted its daily parade. One such, on leave from his regiment, was the blue-eyed and dark-moustached Vladimir Wulfert, who had known Natasha in her school-days.[35] Now she was a celebrated beauty, and he a gauche young man no longer, but a brilliantly-uniformed cavalry officer whose constant attention made him seem infinitely more desirable than the dull, stammering and stolid husband Natasha had left at home.

The start of the break-up of the marriage coincided with an event which made a dark period darker: the 1905 revolution which brought fear and death to the streets of Moscow. For a while the revolution served to divert domestic attention to the more immediate question of simple survival, in a year in which many, not least the Romanovs, thought that their world was coming to an end.

On January 9, 1905, on what history would remember as 'Bloody Sunday', hundreds of men, women and children had been shot down in the square in front of the Winter Palace, when the army opened fire on a mass demonstration of workers marching peacefully to present a petition for civil and political rights to their 'Little Father', the Tsar. The massacre shocked the world and sparked off disorders throughout Russia. By September even the conservative newspapers such as *Novoe Vremya* were defying the censors and demanding reforms. On October 8 the railway workers went on strike in Moscow and within days the disruption had spread across the country – to Kharkov, Odessa and St Petersburg. In the capital, revolutionaries formed a council of workers' deputies, the first Soviet, and from their exile abroad men like Trotsky and Lenin slipped back into Russia believing that their hour had come. There were no newspapers, no banks, no trains, no tramcars, no postal or telegraph services, no bakeries, and even the ballet dancers in St Petersburg went on strike.[36]

When a grudging Tsar was pressured by Witte into conceding an 'October Manifesto', with the creation of an elected Duma to give Russia the semblance of a constitutional monarchy,* Russia pulled back from anarchy. But not yet in Moscow. In December a general strike was called there, and when the authorities attempted to arrest the strike leaders, barricades went up and an armed uprising broke out.

In the Mamontov household minds concentrated on the crisis looming in the streets. And when the shooting came closer and there was the sound of men shouting in the street outside, Natasha and Tata huddled in the bathroom, which had the advantage of having no outside window.[37] But as peace was bloodily restored, with loyal Cossacks and the élite Semenovsky Regiment of the Guard moving into Moscow to clear away the barricades

* After the 1905 'October Manifesto' Witte became prime minister but was sacked six months later, just before the first Duma came into being. He never again held office.

with sword and shot, the battle outdoors was replaced with the battle indoors.

Little Tata, barely more than two years old, would remember: 'there was a lot of conversation between my parents, and as Russians are always inclined to talk at the top of their voices, strains of it percolated to the nursery'.[38] Peace reprieved the Romanovs, but it did not reprieve the Mamontovs, for Natasha had made up her mind and she would not change it however much her husband and family pleaded with her to do so.

Sergei had rescued himself from the closure of the Mamontov opera in 1904 by moving to the Bolshoi, but he could not save himself from the collapse of his marriage. That became inevitable once the dashing Wulfert began to dance attendance. It was a dangerous but exciting liaison, and when Natasha found she could not give it up, she confessed all to her husband. 'Natasha was not, even then nor ever, the sort of person who could live her life in lies and deceit for any length of time',[39] and since also there could never be more than one man in her life, and Mamontov was no longer that man, she braced herself to tell her husband that, although 'she had not meant to fall in love' and that she had 'just thought to amuse herself,'[40] she now wanted a divorce in order to marry Wulfert. Sergei pleaded, but in the end gave in, 'acting the gentleman' by providing her with grounds for divorce. After less than five years as Madame Mamontov, Natasha became Madame Wulfert.

As his name suggests, Vladimir Wulfert was of German descent, and there were many such Germans in Russian society. The Baltic provinces were strongly German and the 'Baltic barons' as they were known were only one manifestation of the powerful German influence which had come to bear in soldiering, banking, the professions, politics and business. In Moscow, one of the richest tycoons was Nikolai von Meck, the first man there to own a motor car; in St Petersburg the minister of the court was Baron Frederiks; in London the Russian ambassador was Count Benckendorff. In the Blue Cuirassiers itself, the regimental colonel was another 'Baltic baron', Colonel Eduard von Schweder.[41]

Some people in polite society used the aristocratic '*von*' when referring to the Wulfert family in Moscow and many years later the pedantic French ambassador Maurice Paléologue would be one of those who remembered Natasha as 'Madame von Wulfert'.[42] However, the Wulferts had no such title and young Wulfert sensibly did not pretend so when he joined the Blue Cuirassiers, for that would have risked ridicule as a poseur. Nevertheless, his acceptance as a Cuirassier was its own evidence of his social standing and, not least, the depth of his pocket, though this was never quite as deep as he would have liked. He had a private income but the Guards had style and it was an expensive business keeping up appearances, and harder still with a new wife and stepchild to support. As Natasha would discover, Wulfert was not as rich as he had appeared to be when he was wooing her in Moscow.

The Blue Cuirassiers, sometimes called the Gatchina Cuirassiers, were formally known as Her Majesty's Life Guard Cuirassier Regiment and had been formed by Peter the Great in 1704. In the officers' mess hung a great oil painting depicting the regiment's attack on the Swedish cavalry at Lesnaya in September 1709, in the Great Northern War, and among its proud possessions were silver bugles decorated with precious stones which had been awarded in the Seven Years War, as well as twenty-two silver bugles for its valour in the Napoleonic war of 1812 and, in particular, at the Battle of Borodino.[43]

The regiment was popularly known as the Blue Cuirassiers because collars, cuffs, epaulettes, braid, piping, and saddle cloths were all blue, in contrast to the yellow of His Majesty's Life Guard Cuirassier Regiment, stationed at Tsarskoe Selo, and known informally as the Yellow Cuirassiers.[44]

Wulfert had spent a fortune in equipping himself as a Gentleman Officer. The full-dress uniform was white, with blue stripes, fastened with hooks rather than buttons, because a gleaming breastplate, the cuirass, was worn over it when in mounted formation. On parade he wore huge white gauntlets, with flaps reaching to the elbows, like a mediaeval knight, and a gilt helmet, crowned with a large golden double-headed eagle with spread wings. Like all dandies in the Guards regiments he bought his uniforms in St Petersburg at Nordenshtrem, the smartest military tailor in Russia, and his full kit included full-dress uniform, frock coats, uniform jackets, tunics, short and long riding breeches and breeches with stripes for parades, drawing rooms and everyday use. At Fokins, he bought his dress sword belt, golden Cuirassier shoulder belts, silver pouch, tricolour sash, gauntlets, broadsword, sabre, epée and his gilded helmet lined with blue silk. They also specialised in a made-to-order forage cap which, slightly crumpled, was considered to be the essence of good taste among the dashing officers of the Guards cavalry.[45] From there he went to Savelev's, for it was thought that their spurs clinked as no others could do.

Wulfert also had to provide at his own cost his regimental horses, any of which had to be inspected by the regimental commander before acceptance to ensure that it 'looked right' and that it did not spoil the appearance of the Cuirassiers. Horses also needed expensive equipment, including huge blue saddle cloths, sewn with gold and with shiny stars in the corners, an officer's field saddle, a sports saddle with flat wings pulled forward in the Italian style, and elegant checked hoods.[46]

With all that, and a wardrobe to which he added full-dress boots, field boots, handmade walking shoes, dress shoes and dancing shoes, a young Guards officer like Wulfert was dressed to kill.

The social life of Guards officers was as lavish as their uniforms and it was one of the reasons why Natasha had looked forward with such eagerness to her new life in Gatchina. She accepted that it would take time to establish herself in a new society, and was well aware of the difficulties she faced over her divorce, but she was determined to show herself as a loyal and devoted wife, and as a hostess to her husband's friends.

In her new apartment at 7 Baggout Street,[47] close by the Warsaw station, she had servants to cook, wait upon her and do the housework; she had also brought from Moscow the nurse who had looked after her daughter Tata. Indeed, among her first memories of Gatchina little Tata would recall an apartment 'always full of good-looking young men in dashing uniforms, who always made a fuss of me'.[48]

There was no apparent shortage of money in the first months of her marriage and Wulfert, unlike her former husband, was a man who enjoyed entertaining as much as she did herself. There were no invitations from Gatchina's hostesses in the first weeks but there were plenty of handsome young bachelor officers only too happy to dine at the Wulfert table and to cast admiring glances at the beautiful hostess whose charm and elegance belied her reputation as a woman who did not quite match the standards required in the regiment. Wulfert might be said to have stolen her from her first husband, but as they sipped their wine in the candlelight and looked across the polished table, the thought occurred that many men would have done exactly that, had they had the same opportunity.

The talk was usually about the regiment, or about the latest play or ballet in St Petersburg. Most officers went there regularly, for while Gatchina could provide its own amusements, there was nothing to match the attractions of the imperial capital or, for that matter, Moscow. Natasha loved Moscow; she was excited by St Petersburg.

Among cosmopolitan Russians there were endless debates about whether Moscow was to be preferred to St Petersburg and it was often the case that people who lived in one despised the other. Moscow was the commercial capital and with eleven railways connecting it with every other part of Russia it was the principal rail junction in the country. Moscow, it was said, was the heart of Russia, St Petersburg the head. Comparisons between the two were likely to produce more heat than light, for in truth Moscow and St Petersburg might have been in two different countries. One was very Russian, the other was foreign, and so much so that many in fashionable society in the imperial capital preferred to speak in French. Going to St

Petersburg from Moscow was like going abroad – or, as one contemporary writer put it, being 'carried to another planet'.[49]

Founded by Peter the Great at the beginning of the eighteenth century, and the capital of imperial Russia since 1712, St Petersburg was the first city in Europe to be designed to a master plan, rather than to grow haphazardly. Before becoming Tsar, Peter the Great had worked incognito as a shipwright in England and Amsterdam and it was the latter which gave him the idea of creating a canal city on the marshy swamps he selected as site for a new Russian capital. Built as a 'window on the West' it is deliberately a European rather than a Russian city, and because the Tsar recruited Italians and not Dutchmen as his architects and designers, the result was more Venice than Amsterdam, with buildings in the warm colours and style of Italy, but on a grander scale than either. Its broad avenues and elegant streets of painted houses, in yellows, reds, greens and blues, were a triumph of Baroque and neoclassical architecture.

In the palaces, mansions, apartments, military barracks, churches, theatres and government offices of imperial Russia, St Petersburg proclaimed itself at every turn as the capital of a great empire. It was intended to impress the world and in that ambition it succeeded brilliantly. Spread over an area of thirty-five square miles and with a population poised to exceed two million, St Petersburg was the largest city in Russia; it was also the largest port, and a major industrial centre – most of Russia's mechanical engineering factories, half its chemical industry and a quarter of its machine-tool capacity was concentrated there. For the privileged rich it offered branches of the best couturiers, perfumeries and jewellers in Paris. On the Morskaya, off St Isaac's Square, could be found court favourite Fabergé and the celebrated goldsmith Bolin, as well as the English bookseller Watkins; on Nevsky Prospekt there were sables and minks at Mertens, hand-painted porcelain at Kornilovs, Cuban cigars at Feiks, and mouth-watering boxes of handmade chocolates at Bormanns.[50]

During the long six months of winter some of the very rich would exchange the bitter cold and swirling snow of St Petersburg for the warmth and sunshine of southern France. From 1898 onwards the luxurious St Petersburg-Cannes express – dubbed 'the train of Grand Dukes' – left the Warsaw station in St Petersburg twice a week, packed with aristocratic Russians. Nevertheless, it was also in the winter that St Petersburg came into its own.

In the 'season', between the beginning of January and Lent, there was no livelier place in all Europe than the capital of imperial Russia, 'cosmopolitan in its leanings but thoroughly Russian in its recklessness'.[51] Two years after 'Bloody Sunday' the lights burned brightly again in St Petersburg, if no longer at the red-and-white Winter Palace.* After 1905 and the revolution which almost brought down the monarchy, Tsar Nicholas II and his suffocating, tight-mouthed wife kept themselves to themselves in the country, in a wing of the New Palace – now coming to be known as the Alexander Palace – in peaceful but heavily-guarded Tsarskoe Selo, fifteen miles away.

The season was lived at an intense pace. Evenings might be spent at a *bal masqué* in one of the many grand palaces to be found in the city, or as a guest in the crimson-and-gilt private theatre in the Yusupovs' princely palace on the Moika, or at a recital followed by supper in some magnificently-furnished mansion. St Petersburg, 'the city that ordered its champagne by the magnum, never by the quart',[52] was an endless round of parties.

For the factory workers in the grim suburbs, and the radicals in their smoke-filled cafés, fashionable St Petersburg offered little that they agreed with and everything they despised. But a society which conversed in French, and believed that it should have its laundering done in Paris or London,[53] listened only to itself.

In Gatchina, the principal event in the 'season' was the winter ball of the Blue Cuirassiers, held in the regimental Assembly Rooms near the palace and with guests from St Petersburg as well as from other Guards regiments. As the first such event that Natasha would attend, she had looked forward to it eagerly. The Wulferts, as did other officers, made up a private party and turned up intent on enjoying themselves.

Among those present was Grand Duke Michael Aleksandrovich, who was obliged on such occasions to remember that he was more Grand Duke than squadron commander. As a regimental officer, Michael was popular and on easy terms with his fellow officers, but because the ball was a semi-public occasion, with many guests drawn from society at large, regimental officers knew that the relationship of fellow officer did not apply. They therefore ignored him unless he spoke first. To stare was vulgar and they studiously avoided any glance, expecting their wives, girlfriends and guests to do likewise.

Natasha, remembering how Grand Duke Michael had introduced himself to her at the riding school, must have wondered if she would meet him again at the ball, but given the immense crush of people there it seemed unlikely. There were many aristocratic society women present and doubtless some were his friends; the party at the Grand Duke's table had been carefully selected and every member would be seeking his attention.

* The Winter Palace is now painted jade green and white.

As the evening would prove, however, Michael had not forgotten his introduction to Natasha and he was not merely wondering whether he would meet her again but determined to do so. Since it was difficult, perhaps impossible, for him to go up to Natasha directly, he recruited the portly and pink-faced regimental commander General Bernov as ally and intermediary. It would have to be done casually but done it would be.[54]

Shortly afterwards the Wulfert party was surprised to look up and find General Bernov, with Grand Duke Michael in his wake. They rose to their feet. Michael greeted those he knew, smiled at those he did not, and turned to Natasha, casually reminding her that he had met her a month earlier. She curtseyed, lowering her head as she did so, and when she looked up again, 'she found him gazing at her very intently'.[55]

That was not to be the end of it. As the ball progressed she found Grand Duke Michael at her table again and this time he invited her to partner him in the *mazurka*.[56] The lively *mazurka*, which can be danced with up to twelve couples, is not for the stately matron, nor for those of a retiring disposition, for it is best done with a little gypsy wildness and a proud toss of the head. Natasha danced the *mazurka* very well and did so with extra verve that night, knowing that all eyes would be upon her.

For a virtually unknown and newly-arrived junior officer's wife to be so honoured was cause enough for notice, but there was greater surprise to come. After the *mazurka* the Grand Duke went back with Natasha to the Wulfert table, took a chair and sprawled among the group of young officers and their wives and girlfriends. He lingered on, leaving only when it became time to join his rightful table for supper, but afterwards he returned again to the Wulferts' and, as Natasha's granddaughter recorded, 'took great care to stay at her side for the rest of the evening'.[57]

It was where he would yearn to be for the rest of his life.

FOUR

An Innocent Abroad

It was galling for Gatchina's stuffier hostesses to have witnessed the attention Grand Duke Michael had paid Madame Wulfert at the ball. Having assured each other that a Moscow divorcée with no family to speak of was not really the kind of woman to fit into Guards society, they had watched tight-lipped as the Tsar's brother led her into the ballroom and then went back to her table. The only comforting thought was that clearly he did not know her background and had therefore assumed that as a regimental wife she would be of impeccable standing. There was satisfaction in so thinking, for assuredly the Grand Duke would now be discreetly warned about Madame Wulfert and there would be no more such unseemly attention. If Madame Wulfert had thought that her evening had been a triumph, her discomfort would be all the greater when she learned that it would bring her no advancement whatsoever. She had been raised up, but only to fall further.

Gatchina was to be disappointed in its hopes of inevitable retribution. Indeed, as the local matrons were compelled to admit, the Wulferts seemed to have become very friendly with the Grand Duke, for his cars emblazoned with the imperial arms were seen parked outside their apartment and he and the Wulferts had been observed driving off together into the country. The Wulferts had also become regular guests at the palace. Gatchina, swallowing its pride, now smiled at Natasha in the street and added her name to its invitation lists.

Natasha's success was dizzying in its speed. The wife of a lieutenant, even one without a blot on her reputation, was expected to know her place and to defer to the wives of senior officers, grateful when one of them condescended to invite her to tea. Now that she and her husband were being included in Grand Duke Michael's circle it was she, and not the senior wives, who seemed in a position to condescend.

This remarkable transformation in the social fortunes of the Wulferts was bound to arouse jealousy and give rise to malicious gossip. Curious eyes could not help but note that it was not Lieutenant Wulfert who commanded the Grand Duke's attention but his beautiful wife. He was obviously greatly attracted to her and made no attempt to hide his admiration. The question therefore was how it would end. Gatchina watched developments and hoped for the worst.

Having divorced her first husband to marry Wulfert and having only just married Wulfert and started a new life with him in Gatchina, Natasha was sensible enough to know that even a breath of further scandal would be fatal to her fortune in the closed society of a garrison town. She was bound to be blamed for any affair. It would be said that the Grand Duke was ensnared by a scheming, unscrupulous and ambitious woman and one too ready to dump her new husband at the first opportunity to advance herself. There would be no mercy for Natasha and in Moscow as well as in St Petersburg there would be many who would take an especial pleasure in watching and helping in her downfall.

Michael had fallen in love with Natasha and for that no one would ever forgive her.

Although the Wulferts' home was an apartment near the railway station and Michael's was the vast Gatchina Palace, it was Vladimir Wulfert who probably lived more comfortably from day to day. Natasha had exceptionally good taste and she also had the gift of making anywhere she lived seem both elegant and welcoming, aims which do not always succeed in being complementary. The palace was enormously grand, but as a home it impressed only those who did not have to live there.

Michael occupied a bachelor suite of three rooms on the same low-ceilinged mezzanine floor of the Arsenal which had been the family quarters in his childhood. He had a bedroom with a single brass bedstead, covered with a white damask bedspread, a sitting room furnished with a button-backed sofa and armchairs, a study with a desk and mahogany desk-chair, and a bathroom with a tin bath, albeit linked to hot-and-cold running water and shelves filled with his shaving tackle and pomades. The rooms were cluttered, as all rooms were in the style of the day, with the walls covered in family photographs and military prints. In the display cabinet in his sitting room there were sets of painted lead soldiers as well as his collection of crystal ornaments and throughout the suite, on side tables and on shelves, there could be found the bric-à-brac to be expected in any apartment occupied by a well-off but not overly fussy young bachelor.*

What his apartment noticeably did not have was a kitchen. When he wanted something, night or day, he ordered whatever it was from the main palace, which was still swarming with uniformed servants, many of them in the dress of the eighteenth-century. For even though the palace no longer had an official place in the business of empire it continued to function much as before, with sailors manning boats on the lake, soldiers on guard at

* Photographs of the rooms, probably taken by Michael, survive in the archives of the Gatchina Palace.

the doors and important functionaries issuing orders to gardeners, footmen, cooks, maids and liveried manservants.

Since Michael was the only member of the imperial family in permanent residence, the impression was that they were all there just for him, which when occasion demanded, they were. Sometimes his mother would return for a few weeks in the summer and then the palace would bustle around the business of luncheon and dinner parties and in opening shutters on rooms closed for most of the year. But otherwise the vast palace primarily served the needs of the people it employed, the kitchens cooking meals for the staff rather than for its imperial master, the maids busy on the cleaning of rooms which from day-to-day only they would walk through.

Modest though his own quarters might be, Michael needed little more. He could entertain whenever he wished in the main palace or under the magnificent painted ceilings of the eighteenth-century Pavilion of Venus in the park. And he was rich enough to buy anything he wanted, or to go anywhere he pleased. Inheritance and savings accumulated by his trustees until he was twenty-five had provided with him with a capital of several million roubles; from the imperial purse he drew an annual allowance of 280,000 gold roubles (£31,000*); in addition he had substantial earnings – rising to another one million roubles a year – from farms and factories owned by him across Russia including, in the Ukraine, the country's largest sugar refinery. His personal assets included a vast country estate at Brasovo, near Orel, as well as another in Poland, then part of the Russian empire.[1]

Some of his wealth was 'invisible' – the use of assets for which he did not have to pay. Apart from having homes in both the Gatchina and Anichkov palaces, the elegant imperial yacht *Zarnitsa* was at his personal disposal, with a crew of 120 men, ten officers and a priest. He also had his own blue-and-gold imperial railway carriage, lavishly furnished; when he wanted to travel by train, it would be hooked on to one of the express trains regularly passing through Gatchina; otherwise a special train would be provided just for him.

His greatest personal extravagance was his growing collection of motor cars, purchased from Britain, America, Germany, France and Italy.[2] But since a Rolls-Royce, for example, carried a price-tag of only 7500 roubles (the equivalent of £825), cost was not a factor. The roads in Russia were generally appalling, but in the immediate environs of St Petersburg they were good enough to allow the pleasure of going out for the day, though long-distance journeys were hazardous and rarely attempted.

* That was substantial money in its time. As can be seen from the Money Table at the beginning of the book, £31,000 converts into March 1997 prices as £1.36 million. With his revenues from his estates and holdings rising to another one million roubles, the equivalent 1997 value of his annual income would soon be around £6 million.

In the summer he might cruise in the *Zarnitsa*, in the Gulf of Finland, or take the train to Brasovo, 700 miles to the south. He also continued to visit Denmark for the regular family reunions there. In the autumn he might spend a week or so hunting on his Polish estate at Otrovo or with his brother on his at Spala.[3]

Nevertheless, when in Gatchina, it was the Wulfert apartment on Baggout Street to which he seemed most drawn as the days went by in 1908. He became a regular guest for dinner and would often turn up in the afternoon for tea. Wulfert might wish that he had been born to the life of Grand Duke Michael but sometimes it seemed as if it was Michael who envied Wulfert.

Although tongues wagged, there was nothing anyone could openly complain about in the first months of the association between Michael and Natasha. He never invited her anywhere without her husband, or without his permission, and while he addressed his letters and notes to Natasha, he was always careful to send his 'regards' to Wulfert. In Russia the polite address in letters is to use the first name and patronymic, leaving out the surname, so that he would write to 'Nathalie Sergeyevna' not to 'Natasha'. He would also use the polite form of 'you', which is *vy*, rather than the familiar one, which is *ty*, since – as with the French *vous* and *tu* – the Russians employed the familiar *ty* only when addressing members of their own family or their most intimate friends.

On April 15, 1908, he sent Natasha a package of photographs which had been taken of them all on one outing into the country and his accompanying postcard could not have been more innocently worded: 'Very grateful to you and Vladimir for your kind wishes. I was so happy to hear from you. I am enclosing the latest but not very good photographs. I hope to see you soon.'[4]

Michael would not only see her soon, but would hardly be off her doorstep over the next few months. If she gave a dinner party he was at the table; if the sun was shining his car would pull up outside and they would all be off on a picnic or a drive in the country. He was attentive, charming, thoughtful, but always correct.

The gossips loved it, though their tales lacked actual evidence of any scandal. Wulfert appeared delighted at finding himself so closely associated with the Grand Duke and since he was always present whenever Natasha was seen with Michael, the Wulferts' entry into his inner circle left Gatchina society with little to do but watch and wait.

Natasha's daughter Tata was nearing her fifth birthday when Grand Duke Michael came into her life. She had spent a year coming to know her stepfather Wulfert, whom she had been told to call 'Uncle Liolocha', and now there was another man in her small world and someone so clearly important that he 'assumed to me the proportions of a legendary figure, rather like St George with his dragon. I imagined him very benevolent, very large, dressed in a toga and a crown, almost with thunder and lightning in his grasp.'[5]

It was this new demigod and not Natasha's second husband who now dominated life in her new home. 'My mother would come rushing in, calling: "Quick, quick, where is my new muslin, we are going for a picnic with the Grand Duke". Or else she would creep into my bedroom late at night with a luscious peach and say that the Grand Duke had specially sent it to me. I would eat the peach and go to sleep, lazily meditating on the omnipotence of Grand Dukes, who produced peaches in the middle of the night.'[6]

Tata was not to wait long before meeting Michael, for he came to tea at the apartment one sunny afternoon. Natasha had made a great fuss about making sure that Tata looked her very best. 'I had been decked out in a white silk smock, which I secretly thought rather plain, my two long straight black plaits were undone, my nails cleaned and I was ushered in . . . a very slim and tall young man, with the thinnest waist and a charming smile, rose from a chair and said: "So that's it, is it? My God, what eyes!" I was completely tongue-tied and speechless, even the gift of a large box of delicious sweets could only produce a very inaudible thank you. Later that day we all went for a drive in the Grand Ducal car; he drove and my mother and I sat in front with him.'[7]

Natasha would, in fact, always insist on sitting in the front with Michael if he was driving, for by now she had also made friends with Michael's younger sister, Grand Duchess Olga and it was Olga who had warned her about Michael's habit of dropping off to sleep at the wheel; on one occasion it had resulted in him somersaulting his car into a ditch, though fortunately neither he nor his sister were injured; nevertheless, Natasha learned that it was wise to sit beside him, ever ready to prod him in the ribs if his eyelids drooped.[8]

Little Tata also had clear memories of Grand Duchess Olga. 'She was a very charming, simple woman, nearly always dressed in a white jersey and a beret. With her usually came a Captain Kulikovsky.' Tata had her own material reasons for remembering Captain Kulikovsky: 'he used to be a marvel at mending toys'. However, she also dimly perceived that Captain Kulikovsky was a man of some mystery and that his relationship to Grand Duchess Olga was the subject of more than usual interest to the adult world around her. 'There was a lot of chat about that, which even percolated to me, though I did not understand what it was all about; gossip of course was rife, especially as she was then married to a Germanic princeling and servants will always talk in front of children, without putting a guard on their tongues . . .'[9]

Tata could not know it, but the chat had been going on a long time and while Gatchina did not dare to show any disapproval, it gossiped about Olga with as much eagerness as about Natasha. Olga was wife of Duke Peter of Oldenburg, but Nikolai Kulikovsky was her lover.

Olga had married Duke Peter seven years earlier, in 1901. He was then thirty-three and she was just nineteen. The marriage had been selfishly arranged by her mother in order to keep her close to home, for otherwise she might well have wed a foreign royal and gone to live abroad. Olga would later complain of her marriage that 'I was just tricked into it'[10] for her engagement was announced without any warning and without her having even an opportunity to refuse. Shocked and dazed to find that she had been betrothed to a man she little knew and liked less, she went home to the Anichkov Palace in St Petersburg, ran to her brother Michael, 'and we wept together'.[11]

The marriage proved even worse than she feared, for Duke Peter was not only a homosexual but a notorious gambler, whose sole motive in marrying Grand Duchess Olga was to acquire her position and, not least, her considerable wealth, a large part of which he spent at the roulette tables in St Petersburg. There was to be immediate evidence of both his sexuality and his addiction to the casino, for he spent the wedding night gambling, while Olga was left to weep alone in her bridal chamber. The shock to Olga was so great, indeed, that her hair fell out and for the next two years she had to wear a wig. Not surprisingly, the marriage was never consummated.[12]

When Michael joined the Blue Cuirassiers in 1902, one of his friends there was Captain Kulikovsky; at a military review the following year he was standing talking to Kulikovsky when Olga called him over and asked if he would introduce them. It was, she said later, 'love at first sight . . . I just told Michael I wanted to meet him and Michael understood. He arranged a luncheon party the very next day.'[13] From that moment Olga and Kulikovsky became almost inseparable, careless of the increasing gossip about their relationship.

As one of the Blue Cuirassier officers would later remark, Olga 'behaved far too freely and independently . . . She began to be seen more and more in Gatchina, where she tended to behave like "an ordinary mortal", shunning all etiquette and pomp. She could occasionally be seen driving through the streets of Gatchina accompanied by Kulikovsky in an ordinary cab. They met in secluded corners of the Gatchina Park, strolling arm-in-arm, as would be normal for any ordinary, commonplace pair of lovers.'[14]

It could not be long before news of the scandal – of an open affair between the married Grand Duchess Olga and an officer in the Blue Cuirassiers – reached the ears of Olga's formidable mother. Appalled that her youngest daughter should have so compromised herself publicly and with an officer in a regiment of which she was colonel-in-chief, the Dowager Empress might easily have compelled Kulikovsky's banishment to some distant outpost of empire. However, since it was scandal and not Olga's marriage vows which concerned the Dowager Empress, a discreet compromise was arranged.

Duke Peter knew about Kulikovsky but had refused Olga a divorce on the grounds that it would damage his family name, for in any divorce it would be Duke Peter who, for the sake of appearances, would be required to be the 'guilty party'. Now he conceded that he would give Olga a divorce but only after sufficient years had elapsed to make it appear 'respectable'; in the meantime, he would appoint Kulikovsky as his personal aide-de-camp and allow him to live in his house, in a *ménage à trois* which was intended to be secret,[15] though in St Petersburg there was never much chance of that.

One of those privy to the arrangement was Michael, not least because he had smoothed Kulikovsky's transfer from the regiment to the household of Duke Peter.[16] He also did more. While Olga and Kulikovsky were quite careless about their relationship in Gatchina, they took more care to conceal their affair when elsewhere, often inviting Michael along as 'camouflage'. To make matters appear even more respectable, Olga would take with her Dina, her lady-in-waiting. It was through this arrangement that Michael and Dina had been thrown together, with ultimately disastrous results, at least for Dina.

Just as Olga had been party to Michael's stormy affair with Dina, so she was to her brother's new relationship, though it was now with a married woman, a divorcée and the wife of a fellow officer. This was a potential scandal of much greater proportions than anything that had gone before and by any reckoning greater than her own. Kulikovsky had not broken up her marriage and her husband had not only accepted the affair but for the sake of appearances had co-operated in promoting it by making her lover his ADC and permitting him to live under his roof. Nevertheless, Olga gave Michael the same kind of support that she had given over Dina. In effect, the foursome of the old days resumed its regular pattern, save that where there had been Dina there was now Natasha.

One of the first pictures taken of Michael and Natasha together was in early May 1908. It shows Natasha sitting demurely on a grassy bank, with a uniformed Michael at her side and behind her are Grand Duchess Olga and her lover Nikolai Kulikovsky. But who is the photographer? The answer is almost certainly Vladimir Wulfert, for it was taken in the days before Wulfert knew of the developing relationship between his wife and Grand Duke Michael. In the photograph Natasha and Michael sit together, but sufficiently apart to be respectable. The body language is intimate, but at the same time guilty, for in the picture only the photographer is unaware of what the others know: that he is there only because the Grand Duke is in love with his wife.

As she sat there, Natasha cannot herself have entirely believed what was happening to her, that within months of her arrival in Gatchina she would find the Tsar's brother at her feet. As a little girl, at her private school in Moscow, she had stared up at the picture of the Tsar on her classroom wall, seeing firstly the bearded and fierce-looking Alexander III, and then, when she was fourteen, a new official portrait of the mild-faced Nicholas II. In church she had prayed to God for both and when she was nineteen she had also bowed her head to pray for Grand Duke Michael, as heir. But the distant imperial family were merely names and faces, important but without personal meaning. Her only possible sight of the Tsar had been in May 1896 when he came to Moscow for his coronation, passing by on a white horse in a long and dazzling procession of troops, bands, princes and gilded carriages bearing the Dowager Empress and then, immediately after her, the new Empress. They came from a different world; now suddenly she was part of it.

Natasha was also falling in love with Michael, but not yet to the extent that she would yield to it. Her head told her there was no future in any relationship with a bachelor Grand Duke who might at any moment go off and marry someone of his own rank, either by choice or because of family pressures. She could never be his wife and the idea of being a mistress was anathema to someone of her bourgeois upbringing. There had been enough shame in her life already and the disgrace of another failed marriage was too awful to contemplate. Morality, convention, duty, common sense and self-preservation were the attributes of what she called 'an honest woman' and she knew she could not throw them over for what might prove merely a summer infatuation.

In August 1908, when Michael went off with his mother on an extended holiday to Denmark, there was opportunity for Natasha to draw breath and decide that on his return she would distance herself from Grand Duke Michael Aleksandrovich. The sensible course was to put him out of her mind and concentrate on her own marriage. It was not the perfect union that she had hoped it would be, but was that because of Wulfert or Grand Duke Michael? Wulfert was a demanding husband, who expected a wife more obedient than Natasha could ever be and there were frequent quarrels over her alleged extravagance and sometimes over Michael. He could not accuse her of infidelity, but Wulfert was a jealous man.

Michael had given Natasha his address in Denmark and insisted that they should write to each other. She promised that she would, but took her time about doing so and then only casually, as if attempting to step back from a relationship which was becoming dangerous. In contrast he wrote to her every few days. His letters and postcards were friendly, innocent, but persistent in their pleas that she should write to him as often as he wrote to her. On September 19 he sent a postcard from Christiana, as he and his mother moved on to join their relatives in Norway: 'I do so much want to know how you two are spending your time . . . Do you go for walks in the park? In my thoughts I am very often in Gatchina . . . Sending you and VV my heartfelt regards.'[17] VV, short for Vladimir Vladimirovich Wulfert, could not take exception to that.

Nor could he complain about the next letter, written five days later, on September 24: 'Yesterday I went to a picture exhibition – I've never seen anything worse, dreadful, the pictures must all have been painted by madmen. I haven't had a card from you for a long time. I'm looking forward to the latest photographs, send me the ones that you don't want to keep, the best must go in your photo album. Neither here nor in Denmark are there any wild flowers in the fields, while in Gatchina I'm sure there are still plenty.'[18] Wulfert would not have understood the reference to flowers, but in Gatchina Michael and Natasha had often gone out to pick flowers together and his mention of 'wild flowers' seems to have been intended as a coded message: that there was no other woman in his life in Norway or Denmark and that Natasha was still the only woman he loved.

Four days later there was another letter, as he was about to leave Norway to return to Denmark. He wrote that although he had left instructions with the Copenhagen post office to forward on his mail to Norway he had received nothing from Natasha, 'not even a single postcard'. That 'makes me very sad and I do not know if you've received my two postcards . . . Do you entertain a lot? What is the weather like? Do you go for walks in the park . . . I know nothing. Don't envy me abroad, it's much better at home. Kindest regards to you, VV and Tata.'[19]

This seems to have ended Natasha's inner struggle, for now at last she started to write to him as constantly as he wrote to her. His answer to her first letter, which he wrote from Hvidore, the house which his mother and Queen Alexandra of England owned jointly in Denmark, reflected his relief at knowing that she had not done what he had feared she might: end the relationship.

She had included a photograph of herself, as he had asked, and it was not as good as he wanted. More confident of himself, he now instructed her to have another one taken, telling her to pose by the Silver Lake in Gatchina and 'to put on your big white hat, not the green one'. He was also flattering: 'you write with such style, I wish I could write as well'. Telling her that he was going on to England 'with my aunt and cousin' he insisted that she write to him there and gave her the address at which he could be reached. It was simple enough: 'England, London, Buckingham Palace'.[20]

Five days later, on October 13, he received another letter from her, 'for which I am passionately grateful'. He promised to 'buy a doll for Tata before leaving here and I'll buy something for you in London ... Kisses to Tata, if I may and to you my heartfelt regards.'[21]

In mentioning his trip to London Michael remarked that 'I know you regard me as an Englishman, but I am in fact Russian through and through, in every respect.* However, I know how difficult it is to make you change your opinion once you've formed one, so I won't even try.'[22] Among the reasons for Natasha's curious observation was her discovery that Michael and his sister Olga wrote to each other in English and that he read the London *Times* regularly.[23] Having badgered Natasha into learning English, she had started to do so. From Buckingham Palace he wrote to say that 'I am glad that you are making progress in English and I will talk to you only in English'.[24]

One advantage of that, though he did not mention it, was that they could then say things to each other which Wulfert would not understand. From London there were no longer 'regards to VV'.

At Tsarskoe Selo, the woman Tsar Nicholas was worrying about was not Natasha but Dina. On his orders the Okhrana were still monitoring correspondence between Michael and Dina, but if they noted the letters to Madame Nathalie Wulfert they were not thought of any consequence. No whisper of Michael's friendship with Natasha had reached either Nicholas or his mother and so their attention remained concentrated on last year's problem: the girl Michael had given up.

When he learned that Michael was going to London from Copenhagen an alarmed Nicholas wrote at once to the Dowager Empress. 'I am afraid "she" is there at the moment,' he wrote. 'Do you think it possible for you to ask Aunt Alix to keep an eye on Misha and not to let him go out for too long a time alone; I am terribly afraid "she" might try to do something decisive and final, which might spoil everything. I know that cor-

* The French ambassador, Maurice Paléologue (*Vol. II, pp. 324–5*) calculated that Michael was only $\frac{1}{128}$th Russian by blood. The rest was German. Although his mother was Danish-born, the Danish royal house was itself of German descent. The *Almanac de Gotha* correctly described the Russian royal family as Holstein-Gottorp-Romanov.

respondence went on between her and Misha the whole time here. Do forgive me, dear Mama, for bothering you with this, but I am so uneasy about it all!'[25]

There had indeed been letters between Michael and Dina, but what the spying Okhrana did not appreciate was that they were the dying spasms of an affair which was over and which would never be brought to life again. Natasha had taken Dina's place and Michael now wanted no one else. He had loved Dina, but it was as nothing to the passion which the very different Natasha aroused in him. She had every quality which he had liked in Dina – intelligence, wide interests and bright conversation – but she had one other which would never be possessed by Dina: she was stunningly beautiful and physically desirable. Michael may have felt guilty about the prim and demanding Dina, but guilt was no longer the force which drove him. Dina was all lady; Natasha was all woman.

Nicholas was therefore wrong in thinking that Michael was going to London to see Dina. The trip, in fact, had been suggested by his aunt, Queen Alexandra, who was also in Denmark with her inseparable middle daughter, the downtrodden and mouselike Princess Victoria. The Dowager Empress and her sister had their own reasons for wanting Michael in London, but when the warning letter arrived from Nicholas it served to remind both sisters that in no circumstances could Dina be allowed to interfere with their plans. The Dowager Empress had been well aware that Dina was in London and had worried about it before the letter from Nicholas, but as she told him, 'I had a talk with Aunt Alix about it and she promised they would never let him go out alone and said that at any rate they would stay only three days in London and then go to Sandringham'.[26]

Dina may well have hoped to see Michael in London, for she knew of his arrival, as did anyone who read the newspapers and if she could have done so, she most certainly would have tried to reach him by letter at Buckingham Palace, hoping that they could meet privately and that their relationship could then somehow be restored and renewed. However, Queen Alexandra arranged matters so that Michael was never in a position to meet anyone not approved by the palace. To make doubly sure that he was not entrapped in some indiscreet rendezvous, the Queen attached to Michael a highly-trained watchdog from the palace's own kennels, the king's equerry, Colonel the Hon. H. C. Legge.[27]

The letter which Michael hoped to get when he arrived at Buckingham Palace was not, of course, from Dina but from Natasha and it was to Natasha he wrote, not to Dina. It was also for Natasha and not for Dina that he went out to find a present, though he confessed that he found it hard to know what to buy. 'There are so many shops one is dazzled . . . and when it comes to choosing I seem to find it difficult.' Nevertheless, he told her that he had bought her knitwear. There was also in his letter a note of jealousy: Natasha had told him that a young officer in her apartment block had gone away and that she was sorry and missed him. 'It seems to me rather suspicious that you are sorry,' Michael replied.[28]

Meanwhile Buckingham Palace kept up its guard against poor Dina, the woman who now presented no threat whatsoever. When Michael went shopping he had Colonel Legge trotting at his heels; from morning to night there was hardly a moment when he was allowed out of sight.

That was true on his first full day in London – Sunday, October 19 – and again on Monday, which Michael spent quietly at the palace with aunt Alexandra and his cousin Princess Victoria in constant attendance, his only venture into the daylight being for a drive in the park with them in the afternoon. On Tuesday evening the Queen took him off to the Garrick Theatre to see *Idols*, and on Wednesday night he was again at the theatre with her, in a box at the Shaftesbury, to see the celebrated actor Mr H. B. Irving in *The Lyons Mail*.[29]

Then, as Queen Alexandra had promised her sister, Michael was whisked to the family's country home at Sandringham, 100 miles from London, in order to reintroduce the girl embarrassingly 'betrothed' to Michael two years earlier. Michael's mother and aunt had not given up in their quest to find him a proper wife and the bride they still had in mind was Patsy, Princess Patricia of Connaught. Sandringham was a means of bringing them together. Indeed, it was the whole reason for Michael being in England, which was why the palace had no intention of allowing Dina to get in the way.

The day before, Patsy, wearing 'a costume of slate-blue cloth and a large hat wreathed with pale yellow and red roses'[30] had been at a charity concert in Belgrave Square, but on Thursday morning she was driven over to Buckingham Palace to join the royal party setting off for Norfolk. Next morning the Court Circular would 'pair' Michael and Patsy by reporting that 'Princess Patricia of Connaught and Grand Duke Michael Aleksandrovich of Russia' had joined the king at Sandringham.[31] Royal watchers who remembered the engagement-that-never-was could only wonder what was now afoot.

At Sandringham, Michael could do nothing to avoid the position in which he found himself. There he was, placed at last by her side, though any idea that the weekend would lead to romance and marriage was never on the cards; nevertheless, Queen Alexandra, like her sister, was becoming desperate about Michael.

Patsy was still there at the weekend, attending morning service at Sandringham's parish church with Michael, but she left early on Monday to return to London. Michael briskly said goodbye to Patsy* and then went off with 'Uncle Bertie', the Queen and daughter Victoria to a hunt breakfast and meet of the Royal Norfolk Fox Hounds at nearby Gayton. That evening he also returned to London and was driven straight to Charing Cross Station, with his British watchdog Colonel Legge still at his heels. He was escorted into a royal saloon attached to the 9 p.m. Continental boat-train, Colonel Legge remaining at his side until Michael was safely aboard the cross-Channel ferry, and thence to the international train which would take him back to St Petersburg.[32]

After ten days in England, Michael returned home without having had even a glimpse of the woman he had so recently tried to marry. The girl he was thinking of on the way home was, in any case, the wife of Lieutenant Wulfert.

* Princess Patricia would not marry until 1919, when she was 33. She became wife of Admiral Sir Alexander Ramsey.

FIVE

Scandal in Gatchina

From the moment that Michael returned to Gatchina in October 1908 there was no turning back for either him or Natasha. The separation had simply confirmed that each loved the other and there was no point in either of them pretending otherwise. Yet that certainty produced its own doubts, for it appeared to be a relationship which could have no future. The greater the joy, the greater the agony.

Later on Natasha would say of the affair which then began that 'those who blame me alone are wrong, for you were also doing everything to make me fall in love with you and achieved that with such perfection ... I so passionately (and I am saying that with great joy) love you and your caresses that I only feel at peace and happy in your arms ... Don't think that I ever have even a momentary flicker of regret about all that has happened, even if it were all harder and more frightening than it is, I would still have no regret so long as I had the joy of seeing you and loving you ...'[1]

Inevitably the rumours about them gathered pace. Michael and Natasha behaved, or thought they were behaving, with the same prudence as before, but because Michael 'could not bear to let her out of his sight for longer than was absolutely necessary',[2] it was impossible for others not to notice that they were entranced with each other and society drew its own conclusions. There was as yet no scandal but there was all the making of one and in the Blue Cuirassiers there was mounting concern that their Grand Duke and a fellow officer were heading on a collision course which would engulf the regiment in the most unsavoury affair. Knowing the gossip and seeing how matters were developing in front of them, the senior officers expected the regimental commander, General Bernov, to act before the situation got beyond control. They were to be disappointed.

Bernov kept quiet, refusing to interfere as he had refused to interfere in the affair between Captain Kulikovsky and the Grand Duchess Olga. As a General of the Royal Household, his senior officers had expected him to haul in young Kulikovsky and order him to behave himself and to warn him that the regiment would not permit him to be the cause of a scandal which could compromise its reputation. Instead, the general chose to say nothing, appearing to be pleased rather than angry that one of his junior officers had succeeded in becoming lover of the Tsar's sister. To the dismay of the other officers, the general took the expansive view that Kulikovsky's 'success' was actually beneficial to the regiment, since it was likely to make it 'even more fashionable'.[3]

This curious reasoning was judged typical of General Bernov, a former Chevalier Garde who was widely regarded within the Blue Cuirassiers as a pompous buffoon. Short and round, he was so corpulent that he had difficulty riding a horse for any length of time and when the regiment went on manoeuvres, a barouche would accompany him as rescue vehicle when he tired.[4]

There were many stories about the absurd Bernov. He was so short-sighted that when out hunting he shot a cat, thinking it to be a lynx; he was still standing proudly over his trophy when the cat's owner arrived and fell weeping over the body. Once, at an army review, he led the Blue Cuirassiers in a charge across the front of the stand filled with watching spectators, including the Tsar who was taking the salute, but Bernov forgot to give the right order, so that only he charged, his bewildered regiment remaining frozen in their original lines.[5]

As regimental commander only Bernov was senior enough to speak to Michael about his developing love affair, but as with Kulikovsky, he chose to keep quiet. What the general's critics could not know was that it had been Michael who had encouraged the relationship between his sister and Kulikovsky and since that affair had the Grand Duke's blessing, there was little that General Bernov could say. Now, faced with a second scandal, it was being said in the officers' mess that 'to please the Grand Duke' he had also decided to 'protect the affair' between Michael and Madame Wulfert.[6]

The general was known to be in awe of the Grand Duke and proud of the keen interest which the Dowager Empress, as colonel-in-chief, took in 'her' regiment. In the Guards, the Blue Cuirassiers were jokingly referred to as *Les petits bleus de Sa Majesté*, for the Dowager Empress was forever paying them visits, dropping in at the regimental hospital to see the sick, turning up at services in the garrison church and talking to troopers in the barracks.[7] General Bernov cultivated this connection and was deferential to the Grand Duke, whom he saw as guarantor of the regiment's favours.

Nevertheless, an affair between Michael and Madame Wulfert could hardly be presented as another 'success' for the regiment's reputation in fashionable society. The Dowager Empress had been angry enough on finding out that one of her officers was seducing her married daughter; she was likely to be enraged on discovering that the wife of another officer had become involved with her son. General Bernov could only pray that she never found out and, since he could not bring himself to say anything to the Grand Duke, there was little he could do but hope that the affair died a natural death and quickly.

One other reason for the general's silence was that, so far, Wulfert himself was silent. He remained, outwardly, the devoted husband, seemingly happily married and making no complaint about the attentions of the Grand Duke to his wife. If he had done so and Michael had persisted nonetheless in seeing Natasha, Wulfert would have been entitled to complain formally to his regimental commander and if that did not settle matters, he could then have written directly to the regiment's colonel-in-chief, the Dowager Empress. Faced with an infuriated Dowager Empress, the hapless Bernov could not have ignored Wulfert and would have been compelled to intervene. The Grand Duke would have had no defence; however popular Michael was with his fellow officers, his rank did not set him above the military code, rather it bound him to it.

But Wulfert did not make any such protest. Flattered to find himself initiated into such high company and thinking that it might lead to his own advancement, he chose to put his head in the sand. When the Grand Duke invited him to be his guest at a function, Wulfert readily accepted and would stand there 'chatting amiably'[8] to the man who was in love with his wife. When Michael arrived at his apartment, it was Wulfert who welcomed him in. When the Grand Duke gave a supper party and seated Natasha next to himself, Wulfert remained affable.

More innocent evidence of Wulfert's public passivity comes from little Tata. As winter came, her memories were of 'tobogganing down gentle slopes ... of building snow fortresses and snowmen and skating in the open'.[9] Michael continued as a regular guest at Baggout Street and 'there was a perpetual stream of visitors, amongst them the Grand Duchess Olga ... I liked her very much, she used to make a fuss of me ... The grown-ups must have had a lovely time. I was always hearing of them going off to the hunt ...'[10]

Tata does not in any of this mention 'Uncle Liolocha', who remains now a shadowy figure, not to be named directly, but included only as one of the 'others' who surrounded Natasha. 'I often went out with my mother and the others, sometimes for long sleigh drives, sometimes to the riding school to watch the officers training their horses for high jumps and often to tea with the Grand Duke in his private quarters in the palace.'[11]

Wulfert was still smiling, but he would not have done if he had been able to read Michael's letters to Natasha. In December 1908, when Wulfert and Natasha went off for Christmas to his parents' home in Moscow, a letter to Natasha followed them, but not to Wulferts' house; instead it was addressed 6 Vozdvizhenka, where Natasha's parents now lived.[12] The letter was not any longer from someone who was merely a friend. It said: 'Come back very soon. I came to the station 15 minutes before the train was due to leave, the others were not there yet. I'm very glad we managed to spend a few moments in the way we had wished...'[13]

A few days later Michael was writing again to Natasha at her parents' home: 'It has been four days since you left and I can really feel your absence, particularly in the evenings. Your cosy flat, usually lit up, was dark and gloomy and I felt sad...'[14]

A crisis was looming. The only question at the beginning of 1909 was when and how it would come about.

Astonishingly Wulfert went on for several months more in his pretence, at least to the outside world, that there was nothing wrong with his marriage, or that he had any cause for complaint against Grand Duke Michael. They continued to appear the best of friends, as Michael's own camera recorded at every event they attended together.

Michael was an avid photographer and his camera tells its own story of his love affair. He took a great many pictures of Natasha and encouraged others to take photographs of himself with her, pasting the results into albums. Over the next five years he would compile fourteen volumes of photographs, each stamped with the year to which it referred or some other identifying title and with most of the photographs numbered and dated. In many of the pictures appears the smiling figure of Natasha, beside the smiling figure of Grand Duke Michael and at her shoulder, the smiling figure of Lieutenant Wulfert.[15]

Sometimes they would all go to St Petersburg by rail in Michael's imperial carriage. Of one such trip there is an intriguing set of photographs, dated Monday, March 23, 1909. In the first, Wulfert is sitting with his arm around Natasha, with Tata on his knee. Natasha, unconsciously, has moved her head away from Wulfert. A few moments later they have swapped places and it is Michael sitting next to Natasha, with Tata bouncing on his knee. Here, Natasha has moved her head towards Michael. They are telling photographs and might well be captioned 'Changing Places'.

On their more public outings it was Moscow which Michael and Natasha preferred to St Petersburg, for if tongues wagged as eagerly there as in the capital, at least there was less chance of courtiers reporting sightings to Tsarskoe Selo or the Anichkov Palace; and after the furore over Dina, Michael was not anxious to provoke further family rows about Natasha.

Natasha had good reason to be in Moscow anyway, since her family lived there, as did Wulfert's. Old friends flocked around her, eager to join her party at races and the theatre. A Grand Duke did much for Natasha's standing in circles which would not ordinarily have met one. In St Petersburg, women stared at Natasha with narrow-eyed disapproval; in

Moscow, among those who had known her from childhood, they looked at her in admiring wonderment.

One of those who remembered seeing Grand Duke Michael, Natasha and Wulfert together at about that time was Michael Bakhrushin. Years later he told Natasha's granddaughter that 'everyone in Moscow knew that the Grand Duke fell in love with Mme Wulfert and that a romance was in progress . . . in Moscow your grandmother was a well-known society figure and I have seen her everywhere, first, when she was married to Lieutenant Wulfert and then when the Grand Duke Michael started to be very evident in their company. The Wulfert couple were always in the Grand Duke's box at all sporting events in Moscow, such as the Concours Hippique, races, etc . . .'[16]

On occasion Wulfert and Natasha went to Moscow on their own, as they had done at Christmas and as they did again on March 26, 1909. Michael volunteered to look after their dog George while they were away. He picked him up from their apartment and took him back to his own quarters at the Gatchina Palace. Late that night he went out with George into the quadrangle, expecting that he would behave as all well-trained dogs should do, 'but it was of little use', he later reported to Natasha. When he and George returned to the apartment, he 'took my valet's leg for a lamppost and then finished off in the red armchair, the result in both cases being very wet. I laughed so much I couldn't kick him. He slept at my feet all night and seemed perfectly pleased with himself.'[17]

That, however, was his careful 'official' letter, which he did not mind if Wulfert read and guessed that he would. There had been rumbles in the Wulfert household about some of his previous letters so now he left out anything likely to be construed as affection. What he wanted to say privately to Natasha he put in a separate letter, addressed to an arranged postbox address. However, he could not be sure that this was foolproof; he had set up a similar system in Gatchina and some of his letters to Natasha had gone astray. 'There is so much I want to say,' he wrote to her in Moscow, 'but unfortunately I don't any longer trust the post. So many times my letters have got lost, but that's half the trouble for I am afraid, in fact it is almost certain, that they were read and it's such a disgusting feeling – to know that other people can read what has been written for one person only. I don't yet know how and when I'll send you this letter, though of course I would like to do it as soon as possible. Don't worry about me, I am well and relatively cheerful. I am troubled and tortured by the thought of your being in Moscow and so far apart from me. I beg you to be careful and please keep doing everything not to annoy him. My Angel, please take care of yourself for my sake.'[18]

Using the familiar 'you' always absent in his 'official' letters, he continued next day: 'From all my heart I hope that everything is all right and quiet, I pray God for it all the time and also for your happiness and health. What bliss and what joy it would be to see you thoroughly happy and perfectly calm – and it is bound to be so! Yesterday I sent you a letter with a card, but I said very little in it, for I am afraid that it might cause some more trouble.'[19]

Natasha also wrote to him and he was overjoyed by her letter four days after she left for Moscow. He answered at once: 'My darling, I can't tell you how happy I was to receive it and to read all those precious things that you are writing in it. Thank you for it all. Your love for me is such joy and I trust you so – it is great happiness. Believe me that I love you infinitely and that I also belong to you with all my heart and wish fervently to see you happy . . . Thank God, everything is still quiet with you, although I still can't be easy . . . Be careful in everything and don't make him angry on any account. I have just read your letter again, oh, it is so full of your love and I am so happy, despite all the hard experiences one has to suffer now.'[20]

One of the 'hard experiences' was that Wulfert had discovered a photograph of Michael in Natasha's possession. Although she made up some excuse for it, the picture was cause for a blazing row. Michael was anxious about that. 'My darling, be careful with my photograph lest something happens again,' he scribbled.[21]

A few days later he was writing his 'official' letter to Natasha to say that 'I hope you and VV will not decline my invitation to come over here in the motor and go shooting. We would then have such a nice and pleasant way of spending two or three days, wouldn't we . . .'[22] Two days later, he was writing privately to say, 'I miss my friend badly'.[23]

Although the position was rapidly becoming impossible, over the next two months Wulfert went on behaving as before, giving no outward sign of his increasing resentment. He continued to be present on social occasions where public discretion was imperative, but there were also days when the cuckolded husband was not thought necessary to appearances, or was simply not available. While Wulfert busied himself on his regimental duties, his senior officer was taking his wife out for afternoon drives, sometimes as before with his sister Olga and Kulikovsky, but often alone now, or with Tata bobbing up and down in the passenger seat.[24]

As spring turned to summer, the Grand Duke introduced Tata to all the mysteries of the great park in which he had spent his own childhood; instead of running about in the confined space of an apartment she could now explore a palace. 'But the biggest thrill of all', she would remember, 'was the boathouse, staffed by a crew of sailors from the royal yacht. There was every conceivable sort of boat there, from a small motor yacht to a Canadian canoe.'[25]

On one occasion at the palace she pattered away on her own and found herself in the throne-room. When a search party came looking for her, they discovered Tata sitting on the crimson-brocaded throne, her feet dangling over the scarlet footstool. 'There were roars of laughter, the loudest from the Grand Duke and I was whisked off it by my mother, who was rather angry and told me I had done something awful. I burst into tears and had to be consoled by the Grand Duke, who promised that he would not tell the Emperor and that everybody would be sworn to secrecy.'[26] Looking back on those childhood days, Tata would 'often think what a lovely time everybody in that set had . . . they had everything: social position, money . . . and they spent their time amusing themselves, devising pleasures to pass the time agreeably'.[27]

In fact, life could not continue that 'agreeably' for the storm was already brewing. Towards the end of May 1909 Wulfert was in his usual place at Natasha's side when the 'set' went to a car rally sponsored by a motoring magazine on the Volkonsky Highway near St Petersburg and later he was also present at a show-jumping event. In mid-June 1909, Michael took Natasha and Wulfert, along with Olga and Duke Peter and the ubiquitous Kulikovsky, to Peterhof to lunch on his imperial yacht *Zarnitsa*.[28]

But the pictures taken that day are the last to show Wulfert as part of the group. His public smile was now through gritted teeth and at home he was becoming increasingly angry about a relationship he could no longer hide from himself. He was also still just a lieutenant; ambition and social-climbing had done nothing but lose him his wife.

He was wholly entitled to be outraged, for Natasha's conduct was deplorable by respectable standards, though it would not perhaps have surprised that shrewd observer the future French ambassador Maurice Paléologue. Years later, after an evening in the company of a much-married princess, he set down in his diary her views on the character of a Russian woman:

> *. . . we are passionate, tender, sensual . . . We are only too ready to worship . . . The frequency of divorce among us is an argument in our favour. When we fall in love with a man, we always think it is for ever . . . We forget quickly and thoroughly . . . To most of us what has happened in the past is dead, or rather has never been . . . When we start on some adventure, we rush into it without even considering where we are going. All our novels end with a catastrophe.*[29]

The catastrophe in Wulfert's case was almost upon him. Tata became aware of the troubles ahead for she remembered that 'almost imperceptibly, a discordant note began to creep into the even tenor of our lives. Voices were frequently raised, doors slammed, my stepfather walked around looking like a thundercloud, my mother looked as if she were often in tears, my nurse sighed and crossed herself more frequently than usual. The Grand Duke was less often mentioned and ceased to come to the house.'[30]

But it was actually very much worse than that. What Tata had forgotten when she wrote about her early days at Gatchina was the violence of the scenes taking place in the apartment and indeed her own hysterics as her stepfather stormed at her mother and threatened her with his revolver, or the occasions when a terrified Natasha locked herself in the nursery after being physically assaulted.[31]

The breaking-point came over Natasha's refusal to share the marital bed. Although Michael and Natasha had agreed that, however passionately they embraced, they would never make love so long as Natasha remained under Wulfert's roof, Natasha had reached the point where now she would not allow her husband to make love to her. It was a clear signal to Wulfert and he was enraged. He therefore took by force what he could not have by consent. There was no such legal concept in those days as marital rape, but rape it was to Natasha.[32] She promptly announced that she was leaving him and going abroad for several weeks. Wulfert protested, but in the face of her scorn and fury, there was little he could do but agree, telling himself that at least she would be away from the influence of the Grand Duke and that when she came back they could start life afresh.

Daughter Tata, now six years of age, remembered only that 'suddenly trunks were dragged out, a feverish activity pervaded the flat, my mother rushed around looking distraught and having collected an elderly cousin of hers, Katya Frolova, presumably as chaperone, we were whisked off to Switzerland'.[33]

In fact, they were going first to Berlin and there would be one more scene, and a public one, before they did so. Natasha, Tata, Katya and the two maids accompanying them, went to Gatchina's Warsaw railway station to catch the international express. Among the small group seeing them off was Michael, who took her a bunch of flowers. As they stood waiting, Wulfert unexpectedly arrived.[34] To the embarrassment of the group on the platform and to the fascinated astonishment of the other waiting passengers, Wulfert began loudly to accuse her of having ruined him by her extravagance and so indebted him that he was now facing court action. As he railed at her Natasha took the flowers in her hand and began to hand them out one by one to the people around her. It was her only response.[35]

The train came in, Natasha and her party climbed aboard and as the express departed Wulfert and Grand Duke Michael were left standing on the platform together. Neither said anything to the other, but both knew that from that moment on only one of them could have Natasha.

SIX

Pistols at Dawn

The international express from St Petersburg to Berlin took twenty-six hours for the 1000-mile journey. On her arrival Natasha went to the Hotel Westminster on Unter den Linden,[1] and three days later she received her first letter from Michael.

> *My dear darling Natasha, My tender one, if you only knew to what extent I suffered for you yesterday when all that unpleasantness began. How disgusting it all was and how out of place on his part and you behaved impeccably and controlled yourself so well, strikingly well. I knew what it meant to you to listen to all that was being said to you. You were so kind and charming at the station . . . you talked to everyone, you thought about everyone, you gave everyone a flower . . .*
>
> *Oh, my dear and charming Natasha. It feels so sad and empty now in our dear Gatchina without you, where every nook and cranny reminds me of you and of the many wonderful moments, hours and days spent together with you. I wanted so much to kiss your hand when the train was leaving, but I did not dare. I still cannot accept that you have gone. I cannot believe that you are no longer here and when I realise that it is so, I feel impossibly sad and desolate. Sleep well and peacefully, my darling. In my thoughts I'm always with you and caressing and comforting you . . .*[2]

Next day he wrote again: 'I am writing this after dinner. It is just the time when I used to be at your place, where I was so happy because of our love for each other. It is less than 48 hours since you left but it seems that it happened long ago and my heart sinks at the thought that you're not here and that I cannot see you, talk to you, caress you. But in my thoughts I'm doing that all the time and every minute . . .' Two days later he was writing again, to reassure her that she should not worry about what was to happen in the future: 'Don't worry, I'll take care of you . . .'[3]

Meanwhile Wulfert was also writing to her in Berlin, though his letters were addressed to the post office, for Natasha had refused to give him her address. Now Wulfert was apologetic, desperately setting out his love for her and believing still that she would come back to him. Natasha was unmoved, writing back a letter which gave him little hope that he had been forgiven or that she felt any love for him:

I believe that such a letter could have been received only by a tenderly-loved and more importantly, tenderly-loving wife. After all that we have been through I believe such a letter is inappropriate. I haven't yet forgotten all the horrors I endured because of you, the sleepless nights and rudeness short of being beaten up. Now that I know you as you really are, whatever you might write will not wipe out the memories of the last days and I still see in my mind's eye your face distorted with fury, a fountain of abuse and accusations . . .

Tell me, why did you shout in front of everyone that you were a beggar, that I had ruined you and you were facing court action because of me and so on. You don't remember all that . . . your letter is pervaded with selfishness, you only write about yourself, about your suffering and not a word about my feelings, just I, I, I . . .[4]

Her letters to Michael were in a very different style. In those she poured out her love and told him that she could not live without him. Overwhelmed by the intensity of her feelings, Michael replied:

My God, you've touched me so . . . Natasha, my darling, my dear Natasha, my tender angel. You do understand also how much I love you, how I belong to you. God willing, everything will work out soon for the best, but please do not fret, don't worry, be patient, cheerful, you must listen to me . . . kissing you endlessly. Your M. PS. In a year, we will be spending this day together. God Bless you.[5]

After a few days in Berlin Natasha had moved on by train to Vevey and into the Hotel d'Angleterre on the shores of Lake Geneva.[6] There she received a letter from him every day, all of them full of his love for her and his joy that she loved him. 'I'm happy because of your love and you must also feel that I love you so much. Farewell my darling star, my enchanting Natasha. Be of good heart. I am yours forever . . .'[7] And then again: 'Oh, Natasha, my darling, my dear, if you only knew how I wish to have you always by my side and if parting from you at all then only to love each other more . . . Never and not for anything, will I ever leave you since I love you so much and you love me too.'[8]

Serious questions had, however, to be faced. Wulfert had yet to be told that she was not coming back to him; he had also to be 'bought off', so that there was no public scandal attached to the break-up of his marriage. Wulfert could make life very awkward for Michael. He could not accuse him of having made love to his wife, for indeed that had not happened, but Michael was certainly vulnerable to complaints that he had behaved improperly and contrary to the honour of a Gentleman Officer. It would be impossible for the two men to remain in the same regiment and equally impossible for them to remain in a town as small as Gatchina, particularly when Natasha returned.

Michael therefore went to see Baron Frederiks, the minister of the court at Tsarskoe Selo, and put the problem to him. Frederiks, at seventy-one, was keeper of all the Romanovs' personal secrets and often he was the man expected discreetly to sort them out; in this instance, Frederiks agreed to help Michael by finding a position in Moscow which he could offer to Wulfert as 'compensation' and which would also be sufficiently attractive to get him out of the regiment. Michael wrote to Natasha to report progress:

> *My conversation with F [*Frederiks*] was a success. He is willing to help us, by calling him and telling him that if he wants a position it will be given and that there is no point in making a scandal. Yes, he really wants to help me in that. I told him that I would write to you about that and ask you if Frederiks can go ahead and proceed, that is, talk to him straightaway, or otherwise should he do it later. If you agree to it being done now, then answer by cable 'Agree now'. But please know that I'm yours forever. I belong to you alone and I love you ardently, deeply and tenderly. May the Lord keep you. I am kissing you endlessly. Your M.*[9]

Two days later, on July 2, he wrote urging her to cable her agreement to the Wulfert proposals because on July 11 Frederiks was going with the Tsar on a state visit to England and would not be back until July 29. If the problem was to be resolved swiftly then the sooner Frederiks talked to Wulfert the better. If Wulfert took the position to be offered 'then I think that you will be free to come back to St Petersburg but it can only be done when, and on the condition, that we are guaranteed that he will not cause us trouble, and here the only person who can help us is F and he will do what he can for us, I'm sure.' He added further reassurance:

> *Please don't worry, my angel, my tender, darling star. I can't even bear the thought that he has rights over you, as you've written. No, you do not belong to him any longer and he must never have sight of you again, since he treats you so basely and took advantage of his power over you when you were alone with him and almost unable to resist. I am appalled. Thank God that you've broken away from him. But this must be final, otherwise it will be even worse and there will never be an end to it. You're mine, entirely mine and I belong to you completely and I'm yours forever.*[10]

Wulfert was not, however, giving up Natasha so easily and there was now also disturbing evidence that he was looking for written proof of Michael's relationship with her. On Monday, June 22, only six days after Natasha went abroad, Wulfert went to Gatchina railway station and attempted to get hold of a letter which Michael had just written to her, claiming to the postal officials that the letter was his and that he needed to have it back. The letter was taken off the train and handed to him, but at that moment the postmaster recognised the handwriting as that of Grand Duke Michael and took it back from him.

A few days later the postmaster felt that he ought to tell Michael about the incident and went to see him at the palace. Michael reported the story to Natasha, adding that 'I did not show my agitation but I was quite shaken by what might have happened if the letter had got into *his* hands'.[11]

Wulfert's next gambit was to pretend that he was ill and write to Natasha asking her to return to take care of him. Natasha wrote to Michael about it and he confirmed to her that Wulfert was, in fact, in perfect health. The ploy, Michael warned, was intended to get Natasha to return then 'to ensure that you never break away again. And he will torture you even worse and more than before, in every way. Therefore, I beg you, do not go back to him. It is too dangerous and you, my tender one, my darling, might fall into such a trap from which you will never escape . . .' He wrote on desperately about his fears, as well as his love.

> *My God, there are no limits to what he will do, he is capable of anything. I am becoming more and more convinced that he is capable of anything to justify his aim – and his aim is to satisfy his selfish ego. He is capable of watching callously as you pine away and die slowly, without trace of pity or true love. Forgive me, for perhaps I have no right to write all that about him. I seem to be at fault myself, but the difference is that I love you, with a pure heart, with every fibre of my entire being. I love you as you are, without interference of any other feeling, it is just one great feeling of love for you and the realisation that I belong to you alone. Can you feel that? Tell me. I know perfectly well how unhappy you are, my angel and for me to have you will be such bliss, to have you by my side, to live with you, to comfort you and love love!*[12]

Natasha had no intention of returning to Wulfert for any reason whatsoever, as she made plain to her husband: 'Each of your letters', she wrote, 'is torture to me. I feel ill after reading them and upset for the rest of the day . . . Your letters torture me as much as you did when I was in Gatchina . . . you are utterly selfish and think only of yourself . . .'[13]

She had also cabled her agreement to Michael about Frederiks summoning Wulfert to offer him a post away from Gatchina. The job was as aide-de-camp to Prince Odoevsky-Maslov in the Kremlin at a salary of 3000 roubles (£330). Just before going abroad with the Tsar, Frederiks reported to Michael that he had discussed the post with Wulfert, but that Wulfert had said he could not decide without first having his wife's consent. In consequence the problem would have to be dealt with after Frederiks's return to Russia on July 29.

Frederiks also reported that Wulfert told him: 'If my wife does not come back to me, then in that case I will shoot myself. I have letters ready for His Majesty and for Grand Duke Michael Aleksandrovich and also letters for others.' Frederiks had replied that 'shooting oneself would be foolish and pointless'.[14] The threat of suicide coupled with 'explanatory letters' clearly intended to be made public, was alarming, but it was also blackmail of the crudest kind. However, Wulfert was saying much the same thing to Natasha, telling her that he could no longer stay in the regiment, that everyone was treating him badly and that his friends had suggested that he shoot himself and could not understand why he had not done so.

'Of course,' Michael assured her, 'that is all made up, because no one would say that.'[15]

Natasha treated Wulfert's suicide threats with contempt. When he wrote to tell her that friends were so frightened for him that Kulikovsky had removed his revolvers from the apartment and hidden them, she refused to be impressed. Kulikovsky had no reason to worry about the guns, she replied. 'Now that I'm gone there is no one to point them at.'[16]

His violence towards her was the issue and she would not let him forget it. What she would also not excuse was the effect of his conduct on little Tata. 'What Tata could see and hear for more than a year could not help affecting her nerves and Nanny has told me she would often come into the nursery and say "they are quarrelling again" . . . nor could it help affecting her when several times I have had to take refuge in the nursery to escape from your revolver, from your rape and your beatings . . . so I can't really blame her for her naughtiness and hysterics . . . my own nerves are in a bad state, although I don't show it . . .'[17]

A month after Natasha left Gatchina her husband went to Moscow and by chance met Natasha's sister Olga. She cabled to Michael that 'he knows all' but that he was 'inclined to be rather peaceful'.[18] That was a relief to both Michael and Natasha, but was it true? Michael was sceptical:

> *I can hardly believe that. My God, how happy I am that you are finishing your life with him. I thank God he freed you. I cannot help being grateful to Him for that. After yesterday's telegram I also breathe more easily . . . Until yesterday morning I did not know where he was and I must say that I was afraid that he would come to me to have it out, or – which would be worse – that he had shot himself. Now I am satisfied that he has done neither and I think he will never do the latter. And why should he, what would be the point?*[19]

Wulfert saw Natasha's sister Olga almost daily while he was in Moscow and his messages to her began to sound convincing. Olga reported him as saying that at first, when he discovered that his wife was in love with Grand

Duke Michael, the shock was so great that 'God only knows what he was going to do to himself or others', but that gradually he had come to accept the position and to regard the whole business as merely 'an unjust misfortune'. Indeed, Olga believed that Wulfert was now willing to give Natasha a divorce and was 'even prepared to take the blame upon himself'. All that he needed, he had told Olga, was to 'know her address abroad so that he can begin proceedings'.[20]

On moving to Switzerland Natasha had written to Wulfert from the Hotel d'Angleterre at Vevey, using the hotel writing paper and envelope. By the time he got her first letter she had moved to the Grand Hotel in the nearby village of Chexbres,[21] while continuing to write to him on Hotel d'Angleterre paper. She made clear, however, that the Vevey hotel was only a postbox and that if he went there he would not find her. Her letters were collected on her behalf and if that was not perfect security it was at least a deterrence against his pursuit.

There is evidence that Wulfert did indeed seek to find her. She later discovered that one of her in-laws was in Switzerland and had spotted her while she was out driving in Montreux; that news went back to Wulfert but it was a false trail for she was in Montreux only for the day, sightseeing with her party.[22]

Although Olga seemed to believe Wulfert's reason for wanting her address, Natasha was not as trusting as her sister. The Wulfert described by Olga was not the husband Natasha knew and she was suspicious that all he was really interested in was finding her whereabouts so that he could set out after her. So far she had not expressly told Wulfert that she was finished with him for ever, but that letter could not be delayed any longer, for Michael had arranged for her to join him secretly in Denmark at the beginning of August and she knew that in doing so she and Michael would become lovers for the first time. It was important to her therefore to make clear to Wulfert that she no longer regarded him as her husband. She could not be wife and mistress at the same time, in conscience if not in law. On Tuesday, July 28, four days before leaving for Denmark, she sent Wulfert a final letter, again on Hotel d'Angleterre paper and posted from Vevey:

I am writing to you for the last time in my life and it's hard to strike that blow. I must tell you that I can't come back to you and I rely on your honour that you will not pursue me and make a scandal for that would not achieve anything and no threats or entreaties can make me change my mind . . .

We are just passing through here and if you fly after me abroad you won't catch me anyway. But I do not intend to hide from you, I simply want you to see reason and not to behave in the kind of outrageous way of which you are capable and of which you yourself would afterwards regret. I cannot go back to the life which I lived for a whole year and I cannot give you any other. You can't make someone love you. I cannot see you in any other light than that in which I see you now – and you, for the satisfaction of your own ego, demand too much from a woman, expecting her to give her entire life against her wish to the man she hates and whose caresses she thinks of with revulsion. You and I are strangers and when everything has been destroyed – both love and respect – one cannot demand or expect a new pure beginning and you know it yourself.

You will never achieve anything by scandal. I cannot live with you and nothing would ever force me to do so against my wish. Believe me, it's hard to write this ... for the sake of the past, please leave me alone and forget me. N.[23]

The night before she wrote that letter, but unknown to her, her husband was seeking out Michael, intent upon a showdown with him. Michael was staying at Peterhof, in the comfortable country-style Alexandra Villa used by his family for summer holidays; he was dressing for dinner when the telephone rang and his valet told him that Wulfert wanted to speak to him. Michael refused but agreed that he would return the call next morning. When he did so, Wulfert insisted on an immediate meeting. Michael hesitated, then told him that he would have to call him back later about that. Writing to Natasha that morning he told her: 'You can imagine how greatly alarmed I am about this ... the trouble is I cannot trust him any longer, I do not know his intention and he is capable of anything ...'[24]

Michael could not be certain what Wulfert would do, but one possibility was that he might shoot Michael and then shoot himself. Was it wise to see Wulfert? Michael decided that it was not and cabled to say so. The response was a letter demanding a meeting.

The next evening Michael returned to Peterhof at 6 p.m., to find that there had been a series of telephone calls from Wulfert and he had barely been given this message when the telephone rang again. It was Wulfert and this time Michael took the call. Wulfert insisted on coming round to see him and Michael yielded. The meeting was fixed for 7 p.m. It took place in the study, the two men facing each other, with Michael somewhat nervous at what might be in store.[25]

Wulfert was in aggressive mood, but fortunately he appeared to be there merely to set out conditions, not resort to immediate violence. 'Natasha has written to me,' he began, 'to say that she is not coming back to me. I certainly do not believe that, since on leaving she promised to come back to me and begin a new life with me. I only let her go abroad on that condition.'

Michael interrupted: 'You cannot begin everything all over again – that is, to believe that Nathalie Sergeyevna will come back to you, when she has written that she will not and that she regards herself as a free woman.'

Wulfert persisted. 'And I am saying to you that she's not free, that she still has a husband who is alive and must be reckoned with. So what are *you* going to do about it?'

There was no point in saying other than the truth. 'I will live with Nathalie Sergeyevna and will never leave her,' Michael replied.

'I will never accept that,' said Wulfert, 'and I offer you three choices: firstly, I will grant a divorce if you promise to leave her; secondly, I will give her a divorce if you marry her; and thirdly, if you wish only to live with her, then I will not accept that and I challenge you to a duel, but certainly not without the Sovereign's knowledge.' Put like that and knowing that Michael could neither marry her nor give her up, the 'three conditions' reduced themselves to the final one.

Duels were illegal, but they were also a recognised way of settling a matter of honour. Grand Duke Michael could not back down, nor simply attempt to ignore such a challenge. Wulfert would make sure that everyone knew that he had done what any officer would have done in his place, in defence of his wife's honour, but that Grand Duke Michael Aleksandrovich had refused to face him and thereby disgraced himself. While it was accepted that duels could be fought only between men of equal rank – a Grand Duke could not fight a lieutenant – that would seem only a technical excuse, for Michael could waive his rank if he chose to do so.

Wulfert left after an hour with the challenge still hanging in the air. 'My darling, how I suffered, if you could only know,' Michael wrote to Natasha.[26]

Although the regiment subsequently hushed up the affair, events moved at stunning speed. Wulfert's challenge might have been only a bluff, intended to embarrass Michael, but it was taken seriously. One official, who would later be entrusted with confidential papers belonging to Michael, wrote of the affair that 'an unprecedented duel was being prepared. An ordinary officer had challenged the Tsar's brother. Seconds were chosen. Pistols were made ready. Suddenly the Grand Duke was summoned to His Majesty . . .'[27]

A furious Nicholas might not have grasped the full story of what was going on but certainly he heard enough – if not from the letter that Wulfert had threatened to send him, then from others – to know that his brother was involved in something which was not to his credit. There was no hesitation on the Tsar's part: Michael was abruptly ordered out of the Blue Cuirassiers and told to remove himself to provincial Orel, 650 miles to the south, as colonel of an ordinary cavalry regiment, the Chernigov Hussars.[28]

Forty-eight hours after Wulfert's challenge, Michael was no longer a Guards officer and the scandal he had hoped to avoid in Gatchina was on the lips of every gossip in town.

The decision that Michael and Natasha would next meet in Denmark came late in the day. At first, thinking that Wulfert might prove reasonable, Michael believed that Natasha would be able to return to St Petersburg after about eight weeks abroad. His mother was due to go off to Copenhagen at the beginning of August and 'I think it would be tactful to go to Denmark for a few days with her, because on August 16 I have to be in Kiev at the Jubilee celebrations of my Bessarabian Regiment [*of which he was colonel-in-chief*]. I will be there for a couple of days, back to Gatchina and then go straight on to manoeuvres on August 28. Could we see each other while I am in Gatchina before the manoeuvres, i.e. between August 18–26 ... provided everything goes well and without trouble and you can come to St Petersburg . . .'[29]

Michael could not, in fact, wait that long. In late July he therefore suggested that Natasha might also travel to Denmark and meet him secretly there, while he was on holiday. She agreed eagerly, but was perhaps disconcerted to learn from him, a few days before her planned departure, that Michael's idea of secrecy went rather further than her own.

'It would be better,' he wrote, 'if you did not stay in Copenhagen, where it would be difficult to come to see you, but in Skodsborg. There is nothing there apart from a hotel which is right by the sea. In front of it is a main road which runs along the coast and behind the railway and whenever you wish you can easily go to town, it only takes three quarters of an hour. There is a large deer park nearby and it will be very easy for me to cycle there. My God, what joy it will be, my darling one, my little star, to see you.'[30]

To see each other would indeed be joy, but not in Skodsborg. Natasha blanched at the idea of being in a place which had 'nothing there' and of spending her days sustained only by the thought that a cycling Michael might be able to pedal out from Copenhagen to see her whenever he could get away. It was good security, perhaps, but a daunting prospect for a woman on her own. She demurred, willing to be discreet but not to hide, and Michael swiftly dropped the idea. In substitute, he suggested the luxurious Hotel d'Angleterre, in the heart of Copenhagen. That sounded more practical and much more agreeable.

Their finalised arrangement was that Natasha would be in Copenhagen a day or so after Michael was due to arrive there with his mother. As she waited there were letters every day, each filled with his love for her. 'From the bottom of my heart I hope that you will have no more troubles and anxieties. I will care for you and protect you from all these ... I do not have a single thing that I would not give to you with joy. All I have is yours ... The only thing I dream about is to have you beside me forever and God willing it will soon be so . . .'[31]

Michael left for Denmark early on Sunday, August 3, 1909 – his last meeting the day before being with some Blue Cuirassiers officers who had just heard about his sudden removal from the regiment and who had come to say goodbye to him.[32] He sailed aboard the *Zarnitsa*; his mother, his sister Olga and her husband Duke Peter, aboard the *Polar Star.* Escorted by the destroyer *Ukraine* they arrived in Copenhagen the following Tuesday morning.[33] Michael would have to leave Denmark on August 13, when he would sail back alone on the *Zarnitsa.*

Natasha also left on Sunday, though it would take her longer to reach Copenhagen. After hugged farewells from Tata and her dancing promises to be very good while in the charge of Mme Frolova, Natasha set off again, with her maid Ayuna, on the last part of her considerable journey across Europe. Once again she caught the Basle express and on reaching the terminus took the overnight sleeper to Frankfurt, changing there into a day train for Berlin.

The journey from Basle to Berlin took almost a day and a half, including the long waits at stations for connections and it was very late in the evening of Monday, August 3, that she and her maid arrived at the Friedrichstrasse *Bahnhof* and the cab which would take them the short distance to the Hotel Adlon at 1 Unter den Linden, on the corner of the Wilhelmstrasse and just beside the Brandenburg Gate. The luxurious 325-room Adlon, opened only two years earlier, had been built to rival the Ritz in Paris and London and to give the German capital a new grand hotel worthy of the German empire,[34] and as soon as she had booked herself in, signing herself as Madame Nathalie Wulfert, Natasha sent off a telegram to Michael in Copenhagen: *Arrived Berlin eleven night, going on soonest possible. If you have time, wire me Adlon own name. Undecided what name to take in D. Am so happy.*[35]

Next morning, she arranged her onward booking to Denmark at the offices of the International Sleeping Car Company in the hotel, relieved to find that she could leave in the early evening on an overnight sleeper express. With the rest of the day to herself, she had a few hours in which to take in the immediate sights of the German capital.

Almost the first sight was one which must momentarily have disconcerted her, for as she stepped out into the sunshine she would at once have found that the majestic Adlon was neighbour to the Russian Embassy,[36] which with its resident Okhrana agents was the one place in Berlin she had most reason to avoid. She knew what had happened to Dina when she set off to join Michael and there was a continuing fear in Natasha's mind that something like that might also happen to her. Apart from that concern, there was her nagging anxiety that somehow Wulfert might come after her.

With relief, therefore, Natasha left that evening for Copenhagen from the Stettin *Bahnhof* on the Chausée-strasse. Until a year or so earlier, the rail journey would have taken seventeen hours, but now a new service was in operation which had cut the time to eleven hours, though it still involved the ferry crossing at Gjedser on Falster Island and the shorter crossing from Orehoved to Masnedsund in Sjaelland, the island on which Copenhagen itself lies. There, in the early morning of Wednesday, August 5, the journey came finally to an end. From her hotel she sent an immediate telegram, addressed to Michael at the Toldboden, the quayside Customs House which acted as postbox for the imperial yachts: *Arrived Hotel d'Angleterre Room 102. Will await you all day impatiently. Natasha.*[37]

She waited several hours. Later she would recall the moment when she first saw him in Copenhagen and her emotions as she travelled to Denmark, longing to see him, fearing that somehow he would not, could not, be there. She stood seemingly for hours, looking down from her room at the square below, searching for him and so pent-up that she could not stop herself crying. Would he never come? Might she never see him at all? Suddenly, her agony turned to 'insane joy when I, all in tears, was standing on the balcony and the door behind me opened and your darling, embarrassed face appeared . . .'[38]

They fell into each other's arms and that day became lovers at last.

The majestic Hotel d'Angleterre has stood on the Kongens Nytorv in the heart of Copenhagen since 1795. Natasha was not, in fact, in room 102 as her telegram claimed, but in the adjoining and magnificent 'Royal Suite', with its vast and classically-furnished drawing room, marble bathroom and luxurious bedroom with a huge canopied bed. Room 102, the smallest room in the hotel and which still today is used as a staff room for guests using the Royal Suite,[39] was occupied by her maid Ayuna and her reference to it is evidence of the caution which she even then knew to be necessary. Should suspicion arise, anyone sent to find out the identity of the woman in room 102 would find the door opened by a blank-faced maid, who knew enough to know nothing.

The Royal Suite and the adjacent room 102 had been booked for Natasha before her arrival, most probably by Michael's long-serving ADC, Captain A. A. Mordvinov, who no doubt also arranged that the bills should be put down to his name. Natasha would, of course, have registered in the hotel on her arrival, but as she made clear in her telegram from Berlin, she had no intention of using her own name. Whatever her pseudonym, Michael needed only to leave a message for room 102, where the faithful Ayuna would be certain to relay it immediately to the lady in the Royal Suite.

The Royal Suite of the Hotel d'Angleterre is located directly above the entrance foyer, with long windows overlooking the square in front. There were then two ways in which a guest could reach it: the first was through the foyer and up the wide sweeping staircase; the second was to slip down the Hovedvagtsgade, the narrow street which ran to the right of the main entrance, and enter the hotel through the tradesman's entrance just below room 102.[40] This allowed entry up one flight of stairs, without passing the scrutiny of the porters or of anyone sitting in the foyer. The side-door approach, to be sure, needed the discreet consent of the head porter, but a generous tip ensured that.

In Copenhagen, Michael and the rest of the imperial family were living aboard their yachts, rather than at Hvidore, for the holiday villa jointly owned by the Dowager Empress and her sister Alexandra was being extensively renovated, but if anything, this made it even more convenient for Michael, since he could reach the hotel from the quayside in a matter of minutes. One other advantage of the arrangement was that he was living on the *Zarnitsa*, not the *Polar Star*, so that he had more freedom than he would have had otherwise. He could escape every night, staying not on his yacht as his mother assumed, but in the Hotel d'Angleterre.

Michael could also sometimes excuse himself from lunch or dinner aboard the *Polar Star.* Meals for guests in the Royal Suite could be taken in the drawing room and there was no need, therefore, for Michael and Natasha to descend to the main restaurant when they were together. What he could not do, however, was to linger over breakfast.

Accordingly, at dawn's early light, the side-door on the Hovedvagtsgade quietly opened and Grand Duke Michael slipped out to hurry back to the Kvæsthsbroen quay where a naval launch could ferry him back to the *Zarnitsa.* An hour or so later he would be aboard the *Polar Star*; when the Dowager Empress emerged after breakfast she would thus have found Michael already waiting for her.

In his time in Copenhagen, Michael played the dutiful role expected of him, without anyone seeming to notice that he was absent more often than present. He escorted his mother to the Amalienborg Palace to visit his sickly uncle, Prince Hans, and dined with his Danish relatives at Bernstorff and the Charlottenlund Palace.[41]

At four o'clock on Saturday afternoon the Dowager Empress, Olga and her husband Duke Peter went off in a royal motor car for a drive into the country and 'Grand Duke Michael', as the Copenhagen newspaper *Politiken* duly recorded, 'followed by bicycle'. What the *Politiken* did not record was his detour on his return, to the side-door of the Angleterre.

On Sunday he joined the imperial party for lunch with the Danish king and queen at Charlottenlund Palace and the following day he was present at lunch at Hvidore, which had been opened for the occasion, when the Danish royals were entertained in return by the Dowager Empress; on Tuesday his mother went to Bernstorff, but he did not; on Wednesday, the day before he was due to return to Russia, a concerned Dowager Empress went again to see her ailing uncle 'whose health has not improved in recent days as hoped' and Michael managed to escape entirely.[42]

Because the Hotel d'Angleterre could be reached easily and quickly from the harbour, Michael might go in and out two or three times a day, arriving sometimes on his borrowed bicycle and sometimes on foot.

Even on Michael's 'duty days' the Dowager Empress did not leave the *Polar Star* until noon and was always back on board by 6 p.m. That gave Michael ample opportunity to slip away every day; what is certain is that, after Natasha arrived in Copenhagen, Michael saw more of the Royal Suite than of the imperial suite. Outside the hotel there was always the risk that they might be spotted; none the less they went out shopping together – Natasha buying armfuls of flowers for the suite – or taking strolls in the parks. In the Hotel d'Angleterre there was less chance of any word of Natasha reaching the ears of the Dowager Empress for hotels of that rank pride themselves on their discretion. Porters, waiters and chambermaids kept their knowledge to themselves. Certainly no word about Natasha escaped the hotel and no word reached the *Polar Star* or Tsarskoe Selo.

Even without discovery those eight precious days had to come to an end for Michael and Natasha and on the morning of Thursday, August 13, came the heartbreaking moment of their parting, she to return to Switzerland via Berlin, he to sail back to Russia on the *Zarnitsa*. He took her in a cab to the railway station, then stood watching until the train disappeared out of sight and he could no longer see Natasha's face under her big white hat staring back at him from her carriage window.

Early that morning, before Natasha left the hotel, Michael had descended into the lobby and written a note to her on the back of a souvenir hotel postcard. Just as the train was departing he put it into her hand and later she read it as she sat alone in her carriage.

> *My darling, beautiful Natasha, there are not enough words with which I could thank you for all that you are giving me in my life. Our stay here will be always the brightest memory of my whole existence. Don't be sad – with God's help we shall meet again very soon. Please do always believe all my words and my tenderest love to thee, to my darling, dearest star, whom I will never, never leave or abandon. I embrace you and kiss you all over . . . Please believe that I am all yours. Misha.*[43]

It said everything that she would have wanted to hear. Natasha would keep that card for the rest of her life.

At three o'clock that afternoon the Danish king and his family all turned up at the Customs House at the harbour to say farewell to Michael, as did the Russian ambassador and his wife. Like all well-schooled royals, Michael smiled, exchanged courtesies and told everyone how much he had enjoyed himself in Copenhagen, which was more true than they could have guessed. Two hours later, farewells over, the Danish royals departed and the curious crowds went with them. At 6 p.m. the *Zarnitsa* weighed anchor and moved slowly out into the harbour and towards the sea.[44]

Next morning Michael wrote a letter which Natasha would also treasure:

I can't express this awful dreadful yearning that fills my soul and heart. My heart is breaking at the thought that I will not see you for a whole month and also because our wonderful life in Copenhagen is over. I feel so clearly that I can't live without you, it's beyond me. I feel such enormous love, such affection, devotion and infinite tenderness.

I could hardly keep my tears back when parting yesterday. I saw you for a long time while the train was pulling away, you were waving a handkerchief and I could see your large white hat . . .

I went back in the same taxi, No. 920, along the same streets that we had driven along only a quarter of an hour earlier and came to the square with our dear hotel . . . I turned and looked long at our two windows with a balcony and crossed myself, praying to God to give us a chance to be there together, one day . . .[45]

SEVEN

Mistress in Moscow

With Michael removed from the Blue Cuirassiers there was never any chance of Wulfert being allowed to remain with the regiment. He had challenged the Tsar's brother, thereby exposing the regiment to scandal, and that could not be tolerated. Shortly after Michael sailed off to Denmark, Frederiks had summoned General Bernov to Tsarskoe Selo and settled Wulfert's fate. Accordingly, Colonel von Schweder called in Wulfert and asked for his resignation on the grounds of his misconduct.[1]

The Blue Cuirassiers, outraged at what had happened, wanted also to punish Natasha. Still thinking that she might return to Gatchina, or that officers might see her in St Petersburg, they held a secret meeting to which their regimental commander General Bernov was not invited. As Bernov had been a Chevalier Garde he was still regarded as an outsider and because he had failed to stop the scandal in its tracks, the regimental officers – excluding the doctor and bandmaster who were not regarded as Gentleman Officers – decided to act without him, regretting now that they had not done so earlier.

They gathered in the dining hall of the regimental assembly rooms, the doors were carefully closed and the mess servants sent away. Their decision was that in future no officer should bow to Natasha on meeting her in the street, no officer should speak to her and no officer should be seen in her company. Wulfert was no longer welcome and the same signal was to be sent to his wife: Madame Wulfert was to be ostracised absolutely, should she return.[2]

The Gentlemen Officers' wives also had to be told that Madame Wulfert was to be removed from society. Socially, she was dead, a non-person no longer to be stared at but looked through, as if she did not exist. It was the cruellest of punishments, but any public scandal involving Grand Duke Michael was bound inevitably to ruin her.

Shortly afterwards, Wulfert wisely contacted Frederiks and told him that he would take the Kremlin post provided that the salary was 5000 roubles (£550) rather than the 3000 roubles originally offered. Michael instructed Frederiks on August 29 to settle at that price 'and to see that he accepts that'.[3] He did. The question now was whether it would suffice to limit the damage already caused.

The original intention in moving Wulfert to the Kremlin had been to avoid a scandal in the capital and in Gatchina, the assumption being that Natasha would return to St Petersburg and that, with all necessary discretion, she would then make her life there with Michael, knowing that her husband was 400 miles away and that she was unlikely ever to see him again.

In turn-of-the-century Russia a wife had no right to live independently from her husband if he chose to prevent her doing so. He had the power to compel her to return to him and if she refused the police could arrest her and take her back to him. In such instances the law allowed separate residence only after a lengthy procedure in which the husband gave testimony, witnesses were questioned, a secret enquiry was conducted – usually by the police – into the couple's relationship and the degree of fault on either side established. In the interval, a wife might obtain a temporary permit to live apart from her husband, but she was not free to leave him permanently without official sanction.

Where a wife was seeking a divorce on the grounds of her husband's adultery, she would be granted legal separation pending the divorce. But if the husband was the innocent party and challenged his wife's application for a legal separation, he could assert his rights over her and insist on her remaining in, or returning to, the marital home.[4]

Michael and Natasha's assumption had been that Wulfert would not oppose, or would be persuaded not to oppose, her application for a legal separation and her residence permit would entitle her to live in the capital. But that was before Wulfert challenged Michael to a duel and the affair became an open scandal. Now the position was that Michael was stationed in Orel, 240 miles south of Moscow; Wulfert had been given an appointment in Moscow; and Moscow was the only place Natasha could be expected to live if she and Michael were to see each other at all – provided, of course, that she could obtain a separate residence permit allowing her to leave Wulfert.

Nicholas had already insisted that Michael should not see Natasha at all; Michael had promised that he would not do so in Orel, in Gatchina, or at his Brasovo estate, but he had glided around the question of a total ban on meeting her;[5] he intended not only to do so, but to set up house with her. The only place he could do that now would be Moscow. But first he had to bring Natasha back into the country.

Natasha was not sure that she would be allowed across the frontier; and when she was not worrying about that, she agonised over whether she would find herself being arrested and taken by the police to her husband. Her imagination tormented her. Remembering Dina, she had few doubts about the extent to which the Tsar would go if he decided that she was a threat to Romanov interests; remembering her husband's face twisted in fury, she knew he was capable of anything.

Yet she had to come back. She was desperate to see Michael, whose letters, full of reassurance for the future, arrived almost daily at the Grand Hotel in Chexbres. 'I'm sustained by the thought of the past wonderful days and about our future life which will be, yes will be; nobody will tear me away from you ... I'm kissing you all over, your entire body, which belongs to me and which I worship so much ... Before you, I have never known and never seen and never will know anyone, apart from you alone, to whom I belong with my entire being.'[6]

After three weeks in Chexbres, Natasha could not any longer bear the separation from Michael. She would return alone and, when she was sure that all was well, she would cable the others to follow her. Having made up her mind, she dashed off her last cable from the post office at Chexbres, in that special non-stop telegraph style which requires the punctuation to be provided by the reader:

> *Thanks for telegram I did not have time to reply have bought ticket for tomorrow evening I am so upset and unhappy without you I kiss you with all my heart may God keep you. Natasha.*[7]

Her return to Russia took her first to Vienna, where she stopped overnight at the Hotel Bristol, with Michael's letters and telegrams waiting for her. She sent off her own telegrams in reply, telling him that she was 'so impatient to see you again very quickly' and as always 'I love you so much my Misha I kiss you with infinite tenderness'.[8] But still she worried about crossing the frontier. Michael was also anxious and accordingly on September 8 he cabled the minister of the court Baron Frederiks: 'Set my mind at rest won't you that the person will be able to cross the frontier freely and that no one will make any difficulties'.[9]

Frederiks proved helpful, replying immediately that 'I don't expect any problems but to make quite certain have cabled the frontier to make the necessary arrangements for free passage'. Michael cabled his thanks, adding that 'I forgot to warn you that the person crosses the frontier at 11 this evening'.[10] He then sent off a reassuring telegram to Natasha, to tell her that all would be well. She was not convinced, as her reply showed: 'Received telegram not reassured. *Enfin qui vivra verra* [Time will tell]. Wire me to arrive 11 p.m. frontier Granitza Vienna train Wagon Lit No. 17. I also rejoice. Natasha.'[11]

Michael replied with another calming telegram, promising her that there was no risk of any embarrassment for Natasha in returning to Russia. He appears to have settled her mind for her last cable before boarding the Warsaw train is more confident: 'Thanks from heart for dear cables and letters I only think of leaving here to meet you very soon your dear letters have so comforted me I kiss your hands in gratitude and tenderness – Natasha.'[12]

The international express from Vienna to Warsaw covered the 244 miles to the border crossing at Granitza in under nine hours and it was there that baggage and passports were checked and passengers changed on to the wide-gauge Russian line. To her vast relief, no one paid any special attention to her. Wulfert had not asked for her arrest; the Tsar had not ordered her to be barred. It was therefore an elated Natasha who settled down for the next leg of the journey to Warsaw, where she changed on to the express which in the next twenty-four hours would bring her to Moscow and to Michael.

She would discover later that her problems were anything but over.

On her arrival, Natasha moved immediately into the elegant National Hotel, opposite the Kremlin. Michael had written to her to say that 'once in Moscow, promise me one thing: if he is there, never go out anywhere on your own and should you see him then only in [your sister] Olga's presence and better still, if some man could be present. Natasha, please promise me that, I beg you . . .'[13]

Michael's pleas were understandable, but unnecessary: Natasha had no intention of seeing her husband, alone or with anyone else. It was deeply unpleasant to think that she could meet him by chance on any day, or that he might come to the hotel to find her, but she was resolved that she would not talk to him, or give him any reason to think that she might change her mind about their marriage.

Happily, there was no immediate confrontation to worry about. Wulfert, it transpired, had gone off on holiday and would not be back until November, when he was due to take up his new post in the Kremlin. Until then, Natasha was free – even to travel abroad again, since her husband was not there to stop her.

The prospect of another holiday abroad tempted both Michael and Natasha. They wanted to be together all the time, without being followed by prying eyes and whispered gossip. Copenhagen had been wonderful, but how much better if they could be in a place where they need not fear discovery. Michael suggested Italy and wrote to his brother for permission to travel there *incognito.* In the circumstances it was a rather transparent plea, but he made it none the less: 'Never before in my life have I been able to travel entirely independently and freely and so all my journeys so far have been of little use and given me no pleasure and so I believe that if I could arrange a trip of my own liking and go wherever I like then such a journey would really give me true pleasure . . .'[14]

Nicholas could hardly believe his eyes. Five days later he wrote to his mother, still on holiday in Copenhagen:

> *A few days ago Misha sent me a letter which amazed me. He begs to be given leave to go to Italy alone. I replied that this year he has been going about enough and must stay with his regiment and gave him a bit of my mind on the subject, ending the letter by saying that next year he will of course be allowed to go where he likes. I hope he has understood at last that one cannot look upon one's duties as an entertainment and that he must set an example to the others.*[15]

By then, Michael had shrugged off the refusal, any momentary disappointment vanishing in the excitement of having found a home for himself and Natasha; it was an eight-room apartment in a large *dacha* near Petrovsky Park and the racecourse. The address was Apartment No. 2 at 36 Petersburg Road.[16] They could move in on November 7. He could hardly wait.

Michael advised Natasha to lease the property in the name of her sister Olga's husband Aleksei Matveev 'in view of the trouble Wulfert could give us if the house was leased in your name. Please talk to Aleksei. He's a practical and thorough man and a lawyer and can also help us with good advice.' His delight could not have been greater at the prospect of the move. 'We are very lucky to have found such a nice comfortable home in the country and yet within easy reach of town,' he told her.[17] Because it was his first home with Natasha, the apartment was better than any palace.

> *I'm glad to think that you are looking for and choosing furniture . . . it's very desirable to leave the hotel as soon as possible and so, my darling, please try to furnish three or four rooms so that we are able to move without delay to our home. First arrange for your own rooms and Tata's – that's priority – and the other half can be finished later and when I come to visit I believe you will allow me to stay with you in your rooms . . . I am so looking forward to our life in our cosy house which we have found for ourselves and which we like so much.*[18]

Over the next days his letters would be full of enthusiasm about the new apartment. 'I urge you to buy the furniture you like ... I know your wonderful taste and besides, I'm so looking forward to moving into our lovely house soon ... Have you chosen the dining room furniture? If not, we could on Saturday go together to Levison', a fashionable store in Moscow, which had been recommended to Michael by officers at Orel. He also told her that she should not fret because of the work still needing to be done at the apartment: 'while it's being renovated a house would seem hopeless and that it would never be ready, but it won't take long now and you must take care of your rooms first so that you can move in as soon as possible'.[19]

Michael's enthusiasm made up for much of his lack of experience in dealing with the furnishings and even the management of a house. Surrounded all his life by servants and by courtiers who dealt with everything, he relished the idea of actually choosing furniture and being involved in the making of a home. Where he was somewhat at a loss was knowing about the money needed to buy things and the cost of day-to-day life.

On one of his first weekends with Natasha, he found that there were urgent household bills to pay and he did not have enough money with him. He was deeply embarrassed, though it was a first lesson in housekeeping which he would never forget.

> *Please, darling Natasha, never feel embarrassed about telling me if you ever need anything. But knowing how hard it is for you to ask me, I'll try to make sure you never have to remind me of it and I'll anticipate these things myself and next week when I come to Moscow I'll have sufficient with me and I promise that never again will it happen the way it did last time when you, my darling, were so upset. If you could know how ashamed I was to find that I had not enough with me to give to you . . . But still, my darling, you shouldn't be so upset, because firstly you should look at these things calmly and secondly, all I do is for you and not for myself.*[20]

Four days later, in writing to her, he stressed that he still remembered about the bills, 'I won't forget to bring the money!'[21]

Even so, it would not be the end of his bafflement about money. He had arranged for her to have a car, and had engaged servants but without really knowing how it was that they got paid. Six weeks later, after they had moved into their home, Natasha would write to him resignedly, as once again she found herself in the unhappy position of worrying about whether her housekeeping money would stretch far enough.

> *You are not used to having anything to do with money and you have no idea of what anything costs. I am not spending on my pleasures, I never go out, I don't give dinner parties, I go to the theatre only twice a month and the money goes on everyday life and in making the house feel like a home, so that you will be pleased and comfortable when are you here . . . Lately, when you have been here, it is I who have paid for everything, for all the motor cars and the chauffeurs and today I must pay 300 for insurance and more than 600 for carpets, so I will be left with only 2,000 from the money you gave me . . .*[22]

She was not really complaining, but she kept her accounts meticulously and was careful with the money given to her for the furnishing and decoration of the house. When she bought something for herself she would tell him and quote the price, as she did when she wrote to say that she had purchased a fur coat, 'a long one', for 800 roubles with a hat for 160 roubles.[23] She was half-apologetic about the expense but 'I couldn't do without...'

Natasha could also chide Michael on his extravagance, as she would on the day when she counted up how much the car he had given her was costing in maintenance and running expenses. Because he did not like the upholstery he wanted that changed; she wrote to say it would be better to sell the car. 'I could easily use cabs instead ... I was shocked to find out that it was so expensive and also because I am a woman they are probably cheating me.'[24]

But the money that Michael was going to need for Natasha would prove to be a sum far in excess of anything that she would have dreamed possible. Questions of money were not going to be about the housekeeping or the car, but about what it was going to cost them to get rid of Wulfert.

The scale of that problem was only dimly perceived in the first weeks, when Michael and Natasha were settling into their new house. It began when Natasha announced that she was pregnant.

The possibility of their having a child was something which Michael and Natasha had discussed before she knew she was pregnant. In early October Michael wrote to her: 'You often ask me whether I'd be happy to have a "little girl with big blue eyes". Of course, my angel, I will be happy and proud to have her but her appearance in this world, because of your sufferings, will give me concern and anxiety and torture. I cannot be happy and at ease that you have to suffer because of me ... I know how much you want to have this little girl and I respect your wish...'[25]

It was to be a matter only of weeks before discussion turned into reality. On October 16 Michael began twelve days' leave and he arranged that he would go by rail in his imperial carriage to St Petersburg and stay in the Hotel de l'Europe.

While Natasha was at the National Hotel in Moscow he would book a separate room there, for the sake of appearances, while spending the night in hers.[26] In St Petersburg he intended that they should share a suite, though for discretion he suggested that she should 'book a suite of two rooms in Hotel Europe overlooking the square, where there is a separate and hence convenient entrance and then it will be easier for me to go in and out without having to go through the main entrance where you always run into somebody. Bring a maid, to help with the luggage and besides – which is more important – it would look proper and right in a hotel.'[27]

The rooms to which he was referring were suite 11, which was well known to young men-about-town. Michael, who normally stayed at the Anichkov Palace on the opposite side of Nevsky Prospekt, learned about suite 11 from his ADCs, who seemed to know more about the management of an affair than he did. They enjoyed a long weekend there, intending to spend the rest of the week driving the 400 miles back to Moscow in one of Michael's stable of cars.

They did not get very far. Some 100 miles from St Petersburg 'at about 3 o'clock in the afternoon of October 26,' as the police report would put it, Michael was involved in an accident in Kresttу District involving a peasant and his seven-year-old son, who were driving in a gig. The sight of the car startled the horse and the little boy was thrown out and injured his face. The local policeman arrived to find a large crowd gathered, more interested in the car than the injuries suffered by the small boy, and insisted that the driver accompany him to the police station. There he discovered that the car, registered as No. 588, belonged to Grand Duke Michael Aleksandrovich. Saluting, he allowed the car to proceed, but then made out a report on the incident.

That evening, the local police also noted that Michael 'was pleased to arrive with a lady in the town of Valdai, where he stayed in Kaurovaya's furnished rooms, due to wear and tear to the engine of his car'. Early in the morning a special train arrived to take Michael and Natasha along the local branch line to Bologoe, thirty miles distant, where he caught an express south to Moscow. 'In accordance with His Imperial Highness's orders the local authorities were not notified of the Grand Duke's brief stay in the town of Valdai.'[28]

However, the Ministry of the Interior received a full report on Michael and 'the lady' and duly filed it, sending a copy to court minister Frederiks at Tsarskoe Selo, marked Top Secret. It would be the beginning of a long relationship between Natasha, the imperial court and the Okhrana, with the report of her night in the furnished rooms at Valdai as only one of hundreds the secret police would assemble in their file marked *Wulfert, Nathalie Sergeyevna.*

Baron Frederiks would also find that his own files on Natasha would grow alarmingly over the next months. The affair would embroil him not only with the Okhrana, but with the Tsar, the prime minister, generals, court officials, policemen, lawyers and ultimately high dignitaries in the church. In the course of it all he would have to deal with threats of murder, questions of arrest, divorce, an illegitimate birth, forged documents, bribes and the sort of uproar which, when he thought about it, had marked much of Michael's previous love life.

What Frederiks could never quite understand was how it was that the Tsar's amiable brother could keep on getting himself into such terrible trouble.

It may be that it was in Kaurovaya's furnished rooms in obscure lakeside

Valdai that Natasha became pregnant, for it was almost exactly nine months later that she would have a child. Whether Valdai or suite 11, what is certain is the intensity of their love-making at that time. 'My God, what great joy it was for both of us to have been together for twelve days and nights! ... Oh Natasha, how accustomed I am and how I adore to sleep in the same bed as you.'[29]

Michael was overjoyed at their love life, never possible in Gatchina, and he told her so repeatedly. He also confessed to his nervousness when he was with her in her suite in Copenhagen, having worried about whether she would find him a good lover. There had been no passion in his relationship with Dina and he had never before had the kind of relationship which he was enjoying with Natasha.

> *Thinking about you, I feel proud that I enjoy the love of such a charming woman as you are ... If you could only know how happy I am and how constantly I think of our latest physical intimacy ...*
>
> *I used to feel so sad and troubled at the thought that there was no intimacy of this kind and I wondered if it might never happen – that's the main reason why in Copenhagen I couldn't experience the joy which I ought to have done. Natasha, perhaps you never noticed that, but now I will reveal to you that I used to suffer dreadfully and torture myself on account of that. And only now have I stopped worrying after I felt how utterly we belong to each other and how thoroughly happy we are together ... It isn't possible to love more than we love each other.*[30]

He was also ever anxious to reassure her that she was much more than a mistress, whatever others might say about her. Their affair, widely talked about, might mean that now 'I will be measured by the same yardstick as any other of my relations, but this I will never accept – I'll never be a playboy or a philanderer as many of them were and still are. I know only one woman to whom I am giving all my love, affection, devotion and tenderness, whom I love and respect as my true wife ... I know that at the beginning it was not right and I had no right to love you while you were not free, but now that awful time is over and you are free and we now have the right to have each other and be happy ...'[31]

Ten days after their holiday together they moved to the new house. Tata had arrived back from Switzerland and was as thrilled as anyone at the prospect: it was 'a darling little house, with a very nice, large nursery with windows giving out onto the garden', she remembered.[32] Michael could also hardly wait to move in. He was 'eagerly looking forward to Saturday', he wrote two days before the move. 'It will be such joy to see you the day after tomorrow. Natashechka, we'll be together again, inseparably together and for the first time in our cosy little house, i.e. completely at home.'[33]

That long weekend was bliss for them both and afterwards he wrote that 'I keep thinking of and remembering the wonderful three days which I spent with you in our dear, cosy little house. It was so nice to be there in every respect . . . Life in it is so joyful, peaceful and so full . . .'[34]

Life was not to be so peaceful thereafter. Wulfert was back in town and demanding Natasha's return. At the same time, he was threatening to murder her.

On arriving in Moscow, Natasha had obtained from the police a temporary permit for separate residence from her husband, pending a decision on her application for a permanent right of separate residence. However, on his return from holiday, Wulfert contested the application, demanding that she be forced to go back to him. He was in a strong position. If the standard procedures were followed and a full enquiry held, Michael would be put in an embarrassing position and there was no certainty that Natasha would succeed in her application.

Wulfert was also becoming violent in his threats. When by chance he met Natasha's brother-in-law Matveev, he told him that if he ran into her in the street he would either kiss her or shoot her 'depending on how he felt at the time'.[35] Mostly, it seemed, he felt like shooting her.

Accordingly, on November 28, 1909, a worried Michael wrote to Baron Frederiks to ask him once more for his help. His letter set out the problem:

> *Two weeks ago Lieutenant Wulfert returned to Moscow. His wife Nathalie Sergeyevna had commissioned a Moscow solicitor to obtain his permission for her separate residence permit, but Lieutenant Wulfert, far from allowing her this, replied that he was never going to stop pursuing her and he even threatened to murder her. Without any scruples whatsoever, he repeats this threat everywhere and has already announced it to her relatives. I trust that this situation is not going to be tolerated and, irrespective of the circumstances in which she has left her husband, the latter must allow her a separate permit.*[36]

Michael told Frederiks he was willing to present a petition to the Tsar; 'on the other hand you might be able to resolve everything on your own authority, for which I will be very grateful to you'. On December 4 Frederiks wrote a reassuring reply, saying that 'while I am in Moscow I will give Wulfert an appropriate reprimand for his inappropriate talk and threats'. He also offered to do what he could to resolve the question of a permit.[37]

A few days later Frederiks found himself caught up yet again in another wearying problem about Michael and Natasha. The Commander of the Moscow Military District, General Pavel Plehve, and Michael's brigade commander, General Stakhovich, were under instructions from the Tsar to keep Michael in Orel and to ensure that Natasha and he did not meet. But they were meeting, in Moscow. What were the two generals to do? They could hardly arrest Michael. The question dropped on Frederiks's desk.

'A situation has arisen', the war minister Vladimir Sukhomlinov told him, 'which is rather difficult for those in command ... the Military Commander is asking for instructions from above as to his course of action from now on, which is why General Plehve has asked for assistance in this delicate situation. Perhaps you will find it possible, while passing through Moscow, to discuss this matter with General Plehve in person.'[38]

Three weeks earlier the general had summoned Michael to Moscow to upbraid him; his 'frequent visits were causing a lot of undesirable talk among his acquaintances', he told Michael. He also reminded him that he was not supposed to leave his post without his 'superiors' permission.'[39]

The interview was unpleasant and the memory of it rankled with Michael. He decided to protest to Nicholas:

> *Since he is my senior commander, I did not think it right to point out to him the impropriety of his allusion to gossip, but, in so far as my service was concerned, I tried to make it very clear to him that I came to Moscow only about three times a month, never remaining there longer than two days at a time and, besides, never leaving the regiment without informing General Stakhovich for whom I often stand in as brigade commander during his absences.*
>
> *I also pointed out that it could not affect my service in any way (and I give you my word of honour that I never neglect my duties) and asked him to determine what in his opinion would not be regarded as frequent visits. General Plehve replied that he expected me to come only in exceptional cases, i.e. when my duties required it.*
>
> *As you can see, I am being put in a very difficult situation: I have honoured your wish that N.S. should not reside here or in the country, but it is not possible for us not to see each other at least once in a while. Moscow is the only place where we can be together and I always go there very privately, if I can put it like this and incognito. On the other hand, I cannot allow General Plehve or anyone else to meddle in my private life, which does not concern anyone but you. Therefore I ask you, when you are passing through Moscow, to make it clear to General Plehve that my private life has nothing to do with him.*[40]

Michael's letter coincided with the letter from the war minister, bringing to a head not only the issue of Natasha's residence permit, but the question of Michael's association with her and his private life in the little house at Petrovsky Park.

The compromise solution which seemed to be appropriate to settle both issues, was that Natasha should be given a right of separate residence from

Wulfert, but with permission only to live in Moscow; she could also have a right to a passport upon application to the imperial authorities. However, the right was not absolute but would 'remain in force until any further instructions might be issued to countermand them'.[41] In short, Natasha was on probation and if Michael's relationship with her, and his visits to Moscow, were to be the subject of any scandal, the right could be withdrawn. Michael could see Natasha, but he was under notice that he had to be exceedingly discreet.

The order was issued in early January 1910 by a senior court official, Baron Aleksei Budberg, on the authority of the Tsar and after the prime minister, Peter Stolypin, had also seen the papers.[42] The decision avoided the procedures which Natasha's original application would have entailed, 'due to the fact that a standard inquiry would have provided the husband with an occasion for making highly undesirable statements which would, in every respect, have been rather unsuitable'.[43]

Wulfert would indeed have had plenty to say; that much was known already, since he was making no secret of his story. At the Kremlin, Prince Odoevsky-Maslov wrote to Michael's ADC Mordvinov that 'Wulfert had told me so many interesting and important things that I find it necessary to let the Baron know about them and . . . it would be best for Wulfert to tell everything to the Baron himself'.[44] That was exactly what Frederiks did not want to happen; there was nothing that Wulfert could tell him that he did not know already. And he was having enough trouble with Natasha as it was.

She was furious. To her the residence order was an outrage; it gave her not a right but only a provisional licence, valid solely in Moscow. Her brother-in-law Matveev was equally indignant, describing the order as 'maltreatment and an abuse of power'.[45] Natasha wrote at once to Michael to protest. 'If the Tsar refused me the identification papers then why don't they say so.'[46] She also suspected that Michael's ADC Mordvinov, who had been instructed to draw up her original petition to the Tsar, had secretly colluded with the imperial court against her.

She was right to be suspicious about Mordvinov. Privy to the affair in Gatchina and to the rendezvous in Copenhagen, he had become increasingly hostile to a woman he now saw as a threat to his master, Michael. Grand Duchess Olga had also decided to distance herself from the affair, fearing that her brother was heading for more trouble than she had expected. Mordvinov knew that and sought her as an ally in his own personal campaign against Natasha. Just after her arrival in Moscow, Mordvinov wrote bitterly to Olga about her. 'Now she has come to Moscow . . . our peace is broken. He is determined to go there . . . I said that I would not accompany him, for I didn't want to serve as a cover. Nothing helped.' He was also angry that Michael, without consulting him, had appointed a young officer, Koka Abakanovich, to his staff, primarily because his fiancée, Maggie, was one of Natasha's friends and 'from her circle'. It will mean, Mordvinov lamented, 'that they will no longer be isolated from society as they are now ... it was a clever plan ... she is now going to be surrounded by allies'.[47]

After that, there was never any hope that Mordvinov would reconcile himself to the affair, or to Natasha. They were enemies and both knew it. After his involvement in the petition to the Tsar, Natasha was so angry with what she saw as his duplicity that she threatened to 'slap his face' the next time she saw him.[48] As she told Michael:

> *Knowing that my husband threatens me with murder because I am living in Moscow, they yet allow me only to live in Moscow, leaving me without papers like some convict under police surveillance. Yet what have I done? And you said that in Russia everything is done in accordance with the law. Here is proof that this is not so. What can I do and who can I apply to for protection?*[49]

Matveev, she would say, emphasised that it was Michael's duty to insist on her rights since he was responsible for her now. He had told her that 'we should stop hiding and that you should openly speak for me and show that you are my protector and that you are able to defend me from such things, since there is no one else I can rely on ... You must immediately, immediately send the paper to F and demand an explanation. You must show them you are not prepared to put up with it and if they do not want you to cause a scandal then they must let me live where I or you wish ... I feel as if I was a dog or a cornered beast and I live without knowing what the next day will bring ...'[50]

Michael was no less angry than Natasha. 'My darling little star, I beg you please don't fret yourself. Please trust me and remember that I will never allow anyone to treat you badly and I will always protect you ... I will demand the papers and will not allow them to wriggle out ... Don't lose heart. I am always by your side whenever you need me and shortly I will be with you all the time ...'[51]

He wrote at once to Frederiks, reminding him that 'I promised that she would not come to Orel and I have kept this promise, so you can imagine my surprise ... I am prepared to regard it as a mere misunderstanding ... please put this matter right and keep your promise.'[52]

Frederiks tried, but the answer which came back to him from Baron Budberg, with copies to the Tsar, was uncompromising. The order, it was made clear to him, had been drawn up 'with the Sovereign's permission ... and can only be countermanded at the Sovereign's will'. Moscow was the only area in which the permit was valid and any variation would require

'His Majesty's permission'; at the same time she was surely better off than before, 'when she could not legitimately reside apart from her husband anywhere at all, without being in danger of police persecution at her husband's first demand'.[53]

Having said that, there was nothing more that Frederiks could do to help. He would sense that things were not likely to improve when Michael confessed to him that Natasha was pregnant.

Natasha was at first thrilled at discovering in December 1909 that she was bearing Michael's baby. Her joy faded only when she remembered that she was still married to Wulfert and that under Russian law he would be deemed the father unless a divorce was finalised before the birth. Because the time between the granting of a divorce and its finalisation was usually not less than nine months, a delay for good and practical reasons, it seemed inevitable therefore that the coming baby would be a Wulfert in law, giving Natasha's husband legal rights over Michael's child. That was too appalling to consider, but it was the reality and it tortured both Michael and Natasha.

While Wulfert did not yet know about her pregnancy, he had told others what he would do if she did have an illegitimate baby. 'I live in fear that my child will be taken and given to an orphanage so that I would never recognise him, as Wulfert has threatened.' Natasha wrote in anguish to Michael.[54]

Her fears about her husband made her worry also about her future with Michael. While she wrote that 'Mishechka, my darling boy . . . I love sitting at my desk among all your photographs and looking at your adored face,'[55] her torment over her position began to dominate her letters to Michael. She loved him desperately, but also feared that he would be forced to give her up, or that one day he would meet and, out of duty if nothing else, marry someone fitted to be his wife. Natasha knew he could never marry her and if he should take a 'proper' wife it would be the end for her. Michael, she knew, would never keep both a wife and a mistress.

Michael tried to reassure her. 'Natasha, you regard me as a child without any views on life, without any principles, without any character and so forth. But my darling, you are wrong. Do you really think that anyone I come across in life can influence me against you and entice me away? As an example, you remind me that I met and fell in love with you and you changed my entire life . . . Yes, it really happened so, but it doesn't mean that it will happen again with someone else . . .'[56]

Nevertheless, he acknowledged her fears about the coming baby. So desperate was Natasha that Wulfert might remove her child that, at one stage, she discussed with Michael the possibility of her having an abortion. Almost immediately she changed her mind. 'I think it is already impossible and I can't bring myself to it. You know, I've already felt some pulsation, always in the same place and sometimes quite strong and besides it could mean that I might deprive myself of children in the future, which would be too painful for me . . .'[57]

It was the threat of Wulfert taking the child which haunted her: 'Could you really allow your son to be taken away and put into an orphanage . . . cold terror grips me when I think about it.' Wulfert was also threatening 'to demand my return to him by court order'.[58] But what she could not understand was how Wulfert could be allowed to behave in such a way when Michael was there to protect her. 'I want to take care of you as of a little child that one wants to protect from all possible danger and pain,' he had written to her.[59] In that case she could not understand why she lived in such fear.

'Unfortunately I know you will do anything for others, but nothing for yourself or for me. To others, this struggle between an officer and a Grand Duke is incomprehensible.' Most people assumed that a Grand Duke could 'easily protect himself against the foul tricks played by an officer upon the woman he loves'.[60]

What Natasha then failed to comprehend, though she would be wiser in the future, was that Michael was not his own master, an all-powerful Grand Duke who could order life as he wished. Her enemy was not merely Wulfert but the Emperor of Russia.

Natasha had thought that a quick divorce might possibly be arranged. 'Usually a divorce takes eight to nine months, but with influence and money it could be accelerated.' Since 'everyone in Moscow knows my story and links your name with mine', she had suggested that Michael ask Frederiks to make the request for an expedited divorce so that it would appear 'impersonal' and confirm that there was no objection on the part of the Tsar. She had also advised him that he should bring 5000 roubles to Moscow 'because we will have to start giving large bribes . . . you will have to give the money directly to the lawyer because I do not want to be involved in that'.[61] At the same time she had warned that they might find that her divorce could prove lengthy – 'for fear that you might marry me they could drag it out and it might take not nine months but three years'.[62]

Believing herself to be the target of a court-inspired conspiracy, she began to think her position hopeless. She also thought that Michael was simply too optimistic, too trusting, to understand what was happening. As she wrote to him in the New Year:

> *I know and believe that so far you still love me, but the influence of those who are around you will certainly one day prevail and triumph, because you are so*

> *weak. But this is not what pains me. Let them influence you. I see that as something inevitable (in the future) but it is unspeakably painful to me that now, when you still love me, that you do not want, or can't prevent, all the dirt and the insults heaped upon my head.*[63]

Alone at home, she was prey to constant fears, alarmed even by trivial upsets, as when he mentioned in a telegram that he had a cold. 'Misha, Misha, if you only knew how much your telegram upset me. I can't tell you, my angel, how concerned I am for your health. Where could you have got that cold? You always seem to be ill when I'm not there. No one looks after you as well as I do and you're always well when you are with me . . . I can't bear the thought that if, God forbid, something really serious might happen to you . . . they will never allow me to come to you.'[64]

A week later she was still despondent, so much so that she wondered if it might not be best to concede defeat.

> *What worries me most is if my husband tries to take my child from me, who will help me then? I hoped so much that they would help to settle everything, so that the child would not bear that name which is so hateful to me and so that he would not have any rights over him. But now, of course, I cannot hope that any longer. It will be better for us if the child had that very name so that he could have a legitimate father and you were not involved. Since they have started making obstacles to prevent us being together they will go on creating difficulties over the divorce, believing as they do that having a divorce can only tie us closer together.*[65]

Her view was entirely logical. So long as she remained married to Wulfert there clearly could be no question of her becoming Michael's wife – of Michael defying his brother and eloping with her to wed in secret, as once he had tried to do with Dina. The fact that Natasha was about to have Michael's child increased, rather than diminished, imperial resistance to any divorce.

It did not help her mood when next day she saw Wulfert for the first time since coming to Moscow. Natasha went to the Bolshoi and from her box in the dress circle she looked down and saw him sitting in the front row. She told Michael:

> *I'm not sure if he saw me, although he was twisting around in our direction all the time, but there were many people in the theatre and in our box, too, but I was sitting bravely at the front and several times it seemed that he was looking straight into my face. It was so disgusting to me that he dared to look at me. I had such an unpleasant revolting feeling that his eyes were all over me and insulted me. Misha, how I hate that man, I can't tell you. He's*

frightfully pale, almost cream and his moustache is so large that it droops down disgustingly.[66]

In an effort to cheer her, Michael went back to Gatchina to collect her pet mongrel Jack, who had been billeted with friends. Natasha had adopted Jack after finding him as a half-starved stray in the street and was overjoyed to see her favourite dog again, even if his first night back with her was a minor disaster. 'He disgraced himself,' she told Michael, 'and made a huge puddle on the sofa in the small bedroom and ruined it. The worst thing is that I put a blanket on the sofa for him and the colours ran, so that now the whole sofa is blue.' Nevertheless, 'I feel so much better now that he is with me . . . he follows me just as he followed you'.[67]

She also felt much better when she learned that Wulfert had agreed to a divorce. After delicate negotiations and a generous payment from Michael's 'bribe fund', Wulfert was to 'act the gentleman' and allow himself to be cited for divorce on the grounds of his infidelity. After all that had gone before, that was an immense relief. Now she could write that 'it's such happiness for me to feel your child under my heart, you can't imagine what it is like . . . I'm thinking about our child with such tenderness . . .'[68]

But would the divorce be in time? If not, Wulfert would still be the legal father. She pressed Michael to write again to Frederiks and impress upon him that her only concern was to prevent Wulfert having rights over her child, for otherwise Frederiks 'might think that all I am after is an illustrious name . . . It would be very unpleasant for me to be thought of as an adventuress. And, of course, that is what they think. However quietly and modestly I live, no matter how clearly my life could prove the opposite, they will always believe all the dirty gossip told about me. Maybe Frederiks will believe your "crystal pure soul", so I beg you . . . to write to him and explain.'[69]

Natasha's petition was lodged with the Moscow Ecclesiastical Consistory on February 19, 1910, when she was four months' pregnant.[70] The first step in divorce proceedings was that the parties were urged to seek reconciliation and if this move failed, or the parties refused, they were summoned to the Consistory for a hearing; thereafter any named witnesses of the alleged adultery were questioned. If the Consistory decided to grant the petition for a divorce, the order had to be approved by the Holy Synod.[71]

Prompted by Michael, Frederiks did what he could to speed up the proceedings. The Church authorities moved, however, at their own pace and a month later they had still not even started the process. Alarmed, Michael wrote to Frederiks again, to 'insist' that the divorce be finalised by the time of the baby's birth. He added: 'I have already told the Sovereign and I repeat it now, that I will not marry N. S. Wulfert and the only reason why I insist on her divorce is that I cannot allow my child to bear V. V. Wulfert's name, or V. V. Wulfert to have any legal rights over my child.'[72] A week later, he decided to write directly to his brother:

If you want to make me happy and reassured, then please fulfil my request. As I already told you the last time I saw you, Nathalie Wulfert is expecting my child in July, which is why I must take steps to ensure that her divorce is finalised by that time, as I cannot countenance that her husband – Lieutenant W. – should have any rights over my child.

In order to avoid disturbing you I was going to write myself to the head of the ecclesiastical court to expedite the divorce, but decided against doing so without your permission. Be so kind, dear Nicky, tell me what to do to speed up Nathalie's divorce, should I write to the head of the Consistory court myself, or will you instruct Frederiks to do so, in which case I will also write to him myself. I ask you please to let me know what you decide.

Let me repeat that I am concerned with Nathalie's divorce only for the sake of the child . . . I have no intention of marrying her, of that I give you my word. I would so like to have some good news to reassure her, otherwise she worries and gets upset the whole time, poor thing, so much so recently that her health has greatly suffered.[73]

Two weeks later, at the end of April, Michael had to dash to London to represent Russia at the funeral of 'Uncle Bertie', King Edward VII, but before leaving he saw his brother at the Anichkov Palace and 'managed to have a word with him' about the divorce. Nicholas promised that he would deal with it as requested 'so there is no need to worry on that score', Michael wrote to Natasha en route to London. 'It will be done.'[74]

As soon as he arrived in London, on Wednesday April 28 (or May 11 in Britain) he went with his mother to Buckingham Palace to the death chamber, whereupon the waiting Archbishop of Canterbury conducted a short family service before 'Uncle Bertie' was placed in his coffin.[75] Michael had liked 'Uncle Bertie' and for the first couple of days his time was taken up in the business of family mourning and formal ceremonies. However, at the weekend, he wrote to Natasha that 'I am thinking of you day and night and the splendour of the court only depresses me and makes me think even more of my darling, tender star of Bethlehem . . .'[76] Still concerned about his own problems, despite his assurances from Nicholas, on that Saturday he also cabled Frederiks from Buckingham Palace: 'If nothing has yet been done, I beg you to deal with it. Absolutely necessary that everything should be finished in one month and that the order to start is given at once. Please help.'[77]

On the following Tuesday he walked behind the gun carriage taking the body of the king to lie in state at Westminster Hall and on Friday he walked again behind the gun carriage at the state funeral. Next morning, at Victoria Station he shook hands with the gathered diplomats and court officials who were there to see him off and then he was on his way home.[78] 'I will be back around 5 p.m. Monday will phone you on 207–31. What joy it will be to hear your tender voice ...' he had cabled Natasha.[79] With his brother's assurance that the necessary orders would be given to push through Natasha's divorce and with his own prompting telegram to Frederiks, he was now confident that all would be well.

Michael was by nature ever an optimist.

EIGHT

A Son is Born

Towards the end of May 1910, with the heat of summer approaching, Michael moved Natasha out of the house on Petersburg Road and into the country, renting from Prince Gorchakov a small estate near Udinka, twenty miles to the west of Moscow.[1] The baby was due in about two months' time and there was still no news of the divorce being finalised. The strain was telling on Natasha and with Michael able to see her only at weekends and not every weekend at that, she was sometimes driven to think that their relationship was doomed. She had risked her reputation, her security, her future, all for a life which could fall apart at any time, leaving her with two children and a name that society despised.

Alone at night she was tortured by fears of what might happen. During the day she busied herself as much as she could within a tight circle of sympathetic friends, among them the Rachmaninovs. Sergei Rachmaninov, married to his cousin Natalya, had gone abroad in 1906 because of the unrest in Russia, completing in Dresden his famous Second Symphony, but in 1908 he had returned to Moscow. The Rachmaninovs had a seven-year-old daughter, Irina, who was the same age as Tata, both having been born in 1903, and they became playmates. 'I used to go to their house to attend dancing classes,' Tata recalled. The first lesson was on November 22, 1909 and Natasha thought it went well; 'very nice girls there . . . afterwards we stayed for tea'.[2]

The long-standing friendship with the Rachmaninovs was strengthened by the fact that Michael had also known Sergei Rachmaninov for many years. In 1904, Rachmaninov had been invited to conduct a season at the Bolshoi Opera in Moscow and the appointment in part was because of Michael's support for him.[3] Michael, of course, did not know then of Natasha and it was a surprise to both when they first met to discover that they should have a friend in common; Rachmaninov and his wife were now of particular importance to them, when so few dared to be friends at all.

Although Natasha kept her head high, the role of mistress was so foreign to her upbringing and nature that there were times when she wondered if she could go on as a woman forced to live in the shadows, abused by society and shaming her family. Her parents had been shocked by her first divorce, bewildered by the break-up of her second marriage and devastated by the fact that she was about to have an illegitimate child. Her behaviour seemed so shameful as to be incomprehensible and they despaired of her future. Natasha's relations with her disapproving father had been so strained that at one point she had written to Michael to say that the name of Sheremetevsky had become 'as unpleasant as my husband's'.[4] Fortunately, over the months, relations between Natasha and her parents improved sufficiently for Michael to become a guest in their apartment on the Vozdvizhenka. He would be included at family occasions, with Natasha's two sisters and their husbands; at these gatherings, Sergei Sheremetevsky 'ignored the origin of the Grand Duke and treated him like a simple mortal'.[5]

Just before moving to Udinka, on Michael's last visit to the Moscow house, he had written asking her not to meet him at the railway station, as she normally did, 'but to wait for me in bed. It will give me such great joy to kiss and caress you while you are still in bed, my dear angel.'[6] A letter from a passionate lover, or from a man who was embarrassed to be seen in public with a mistress seven months' pregnant? Natasha brooded on that and concluded that it was embarrassment, or possibly even shame.

She had already noticed that 'even in front of people who are very close to us, you do not address me as *ty* or as Natasha, but you don't address me at all. It's different when I don't address you as *ty* because I don't want to be accused of undue familiarity. If you like, it's even my duty to see that it does not happen . . .'[7] She also recalled that 'you were embarrassed to walk by my side through the Kursk railway station only because you were afraid you might run into one of your officers or someone from Orel . . . People may say that I have little dignity but I think it is indeed beneath my dignity to be on the run, to hide and generally to be in this preposterous position.'[8]

For a proud woman it was humiliating. She was not prepared to stay out of sight, however much people gossiped or stared at her. When she went to the theatre in Moscow she would insist on sitting in the front row of the box, so that no one could say that she was hiding herself. She knew that the Wulfert family, all living in Moscow, blackened her name at every opportunity; she believed, too, that all those around Michael at Orel also spoke against her, hoping to persuade him to give her up.

In Gatchina, in the Blue Cuirassiers, the gossip about the affair had reached such a pitch that a senior officer whose wife had disregarded a regimental ban on tongue-wagging had been dismissed as a warning to other officers and other wives,[9] though that was not done in deference to Natasha, who remained a non-person, but to protect the reputation of the regiment. After her holiday in the Hotel de l'Europe in St Petersburg she had been told by Michael that 'everyone in town' knew about it and that the gossip might 'create new troubles' and that the best advice was to 'be very circumspect so as not to give anyone cause to accuse us of any indiscretion' which could bring about 'a series of misfortunes'.[10]

That was before she was pregnant, and what greater indiscretion could there be than sight of a swollen mother-to-be? She was torn apart by realising that she could not give him up, while knowing that she could not keep him. 'I am becoming more convinced that there is nothing I can do in life for your happiness,' she said in one letter.[11] By the time she reached the summer home at Udinka she was ready to give up and told him so.

Michael, endlessly trying to reassure her, wrote back hurriedly: 'You have effectively written me a farewell letter – how could you have done that – it's sheer insanity and utter nonsense. You appear to be creating misunderstandings which are not there.'[12]

Natasha persisted. 'You are not the same, Misha, whatever you say to calm me. Deep down you must be aware of it yourself. In Gatchina you were always looking for opportunities to see me and now you go off for walks alone and on your own you seem more cheerful, even picking flowers alone, which is something we used to do together ... I understand and don't blame you, to drag a tired, sick and pregnant woman around is not much fun...'[13]

But doubting him, she never doubted herself. 'I love you as sacredly and passionately and not a fraction less than on that day in Gatchina when I became aware of that...'[14]

Then, on June 15, just a month or so before the birth of her baby, there was a flicker of hope that her divorce might in fact be finalised just in time. Her files were to be sent forward from the Moscow Consistory Court to the Synod in St Petersburg. She cabled Michael asking him to ensure that Frederiks 'sees to their immediate approval by the Synod and their immediate return back to Moscow ... Of course, it should have been done long ago...'[15]

Four days later came encouraging news. Frederiks wired Michael to say, 'I have been informed that there will not be any delay'. Six days later he confirmed that 'the matter which is of interest to Your Highness has been resolved with a favourable outcome. The order has been sent to Moscow.'[16]

A happy Natasha wrote to Michael to tell him 'that I am thinking of you with such tenderness'.[17] There was still a month before her baby was due to be born and all at last seemed well.

As always when Michael came home Natasha recovered her spirits and he returned to Udinka, at the end of June, so that he would be around for the birth of the baby. That summer of 1910 would be remembered as perfection by Tata, once she had become reconciled to the arrival of a stern no-nonsense English governess, Miss Lena. 'For the first time, I began to learn,' said Tata.[18]

But after lessons there were expeditions to the farms around the house and tea in the sunlit peace of the garden. 'Uncle Misha', as Tata now called him, 'would bring a chair into the garden and sit and play his flute; his favourite poodle, Cuckoo, would bear it as long as she could and then join in with unearthly howls, whereupon he would be chased into the house in disgrace.' The household also included a parrot, a number of cats which assumed residency but which were otherwise without name and Michael and Natasha's favourite mongrel Jack. Tata remembered Jack as 'rather ugly, very intelligent, devoted to my mother, whose side he would hardly ever leave and very inclined to show his teeth if one took too many liberties with him'.[19]

Udinka offered a retreat from public scrutiny and that was one of the reasons why Michael and Natasha had moved there, to be themselves, with trusted friends as guests. It was a simple life, 'with a lot of music, more picnics and drives and bathes in the lake'.[20] Tata would go off with her English governess to pick mushrooms; 'my mother, who was an authority on them, would sort them out, some to fry that day for lunch, others to be pickled in vinegar for the winter, others to be salted'.[21]

For Tata, 'Uncle Misha' became this summer 'part of the household'. As she was to remember, 'I soon lost my shyness of him and used to clamber on his knee and follow him about. I was very slightly jealous when he and my mother would kiss lengthily and would try to push him away from her. I am sure they did it on purpose in my presence, as they would roar with laughter when I got angry.'[22]

Michael was at Udinka for Tata's birthday, on June 2. There were fireworks and she was allowed to stay up for dinner, with a menu that would become such a birthday ritual in her childhood that she would still be able to recite it many years later: clear soup with vermicelli, fried fillets of fish, chicken and ice-cream.[23] Some three weeks later, on June 27, Michael was back in time for Natasha's thirtieth birthday, with a party, more fireworks and a rather more elaborate menu at a dinner for which her sisters and closest friends travelled from Moscow. Michael presented her with a mass of presents and decorated her chair with garlands of field marguerites.[24]

Over the following days Michael clicked away endlessly with his camera and his pride in the coming birth of his child shows through in the pictures which he took at Udinka, both before and after the birth. Tata, however, had noticed no change in her mother and would not know that there was anything different about her at all until suddenly 'a subdued bustle pervaded the house . . . my mother was always resting and Uncle Misha was always with her and inclined to be unsociable'.[25]

With the birth imminent, Tata was left behind in the care of Miss Lena and Michael took Natasha to the house in Moscow to ensure better attention than was available in Udinka. Their son was born on July 24. Michael would say later to Natasha, 'I shall never forget the fear for your life that I felt that evening, while I was waiting in the study – and I suffered for you, too. And then, Dr Rakhmanov suddenly walked out of the bedroom and said to me: "Congratulations on a son and heir!" And after that I had the joy of seeing you – yes, it is all so vivid in my memory and so dear, so sacred and precious to my heart. Let God give Baby a happy life and let our boy always bring us joy.'[26]

The baby was named George in memory of Michael's elder brother, who had died in 1899; on Thursday, September 22, 1910, he was christened at the nearest church to their house at Petrovsky Park – the Church of St Basil of Caesarea in Cappadocia – at a service conducted by Father Peter Pospelov,[27] though in accordance with Orthodox rites, which precludes parents from being present, Michael and Natasha waited outside the church.

The godparents were Natasha's brother-in-law Matveev and 'Aunt Maggie', Natasha's closest friend in St Petersburg, Margaret Abakanovich, now wife of Michael's new adjutant Koka. Because 'Aunt Maggie' could not be present, little Tata stood proxy for her, proudly holding her baby brother in her arms.[28] The church, crowded with Natasha's family and friends, watched as Father Pospelov lifted the baby from Tata's arms, pronounced the name George and dipped him bodily into the font. Afterwards, Michael and Natasha led the way to a celebration party. Not surprisingly, no one from his family was present.

The only cloud over that happy day was that little George was still a Wulfert. Three months after receiving the papers from St Petersburg, the Moscow court had still not finalised the divorce.

After the birth of George in July, but before the christening in September, there had still been hope, on Michael's part at least, that something could yet be done about the divorce. Having reassured Natasha until the very last moment that all would be well, he was understandably abashed to find that what had been promised had not been done. When he left Udinka on August 4 he went north to Peterhof hoping to see his brother and somehow put matters right. From there he wrote to Natasha:

> *It was so sad to say goodbye to you yesterday and also to feel that you were displeased with me . . . I always do what I can for you and as for our baby I will also do what has to be done and you must rest assured that everything will work out well . . . Today to my great disappointment I heard that the Sovereign is in Krasnoe for the manoeuvres and will not be back until after*

dinner and I will miss him . . . My darling angel, dear Natashechka, I keep thinking about you all the time with tenderness and love . . .[29]

The next day he wrote that he was still trying to see Nicholas. 'If you could only know how frustrated I am at not having been able to see the Sovereign to talk with him ... You will think again that it's my fault, but please believe that it is not. I am looking for opportunities but so far there have not been any and we've never been left together on our own . . .'[30]

Natasha was unsympathetic. It seemed to her that the damage had been done and she felt let down after all the reassurances that the divorce would be expedited. She also felt that Michael had been almost relieved to get away, pleading duty.

You try to avoid any unpleasant subject, you have distanced yourself . . . I no longer take part in your affairs, you no longer come to me for advice . . . there is a wall between us which you call your duty. 'One should not forget one's duty for love', you wrote, which is not what you were saying not so long ago. And that duty I forgot for your sake, the duty of a wife and an honest woman – that duty was much greater and heavier, but that did not stop me and I will never put anything between us, not even my children.

I am looking at our relationship too deeply, perhaps, but if I ever become aware that I should not have done what I have done you will regret it, but it will be too late. So therefore I entreat you never to put anything between us, for my demands are so minimal and so infrequent . . . I never claimed your attention and was always content with the crumbs which you gave me of your time and splendour . . .[31]

Her misery at her position overwhelmed her. 'Instead of joy I have only sadness and bitterness ... doomed to spend my life alone – Christmas, Easter, birthdays, name days ... You live a life which is so alien to me, always surrounded by the sinister hissing of Mordvinov and company ... You are always so kind to everyone but to me you can sometimes be heartless . . .'[32]

It was not true, but it seemed true and Michael was conscious of that. He knew Natasha was near breaking-point, but he needed time to find out what could be done about the delayed divorce and he also knew that he could not get away from his regimental duties until the autumn. His assurances sounded lame, but they were all he could offer for the time being. Promises now tended to come back in his face. At the christening he had done his best to sound confident, but there was almost no point now in saying anything.

It was painful for him to read her letters, as when she wrote, a week after the christening:

> *I know that you are happy to do everything for me but I also know that 'everything' is so little that in fact you cannot do anything . . . I know I have reached a dreadful emotional stage and am close to a nervous breakdown and I know that you felt uneasy with me and that is why I wanted and still want to leave, since I know that our relationship can only deteriorate! What good is it for you to be with the kind of woman I am now . . . I am exhausted, everything in my soul seems to be killed . . .*[33]

Natasha, alone again in the house on Petrovsky Park, was displaying all the classic symptoms of postnatal depression, but in those days that was not understood. Natasha's condition was thought of merely as 'nerves' and there was enough in her life to make that seem the obvious problem. Michael believed that what was needed was to get her abroad as quickly as possible, in the hope that a prolonged holiday would bring back her health. It was not as easy to get away as he expected, for it was now Natasha who felt she was not free: 'Feeding Baby is too important and I cannot leave now with an easy heart, for instead of enjoying myself I would torture myself. You always put your duties first and now I feel my duties keep me here. The life, well-being and health of the child is a little more important than your soldier games.' Nevertheless, she assured him that she was desperate to have the holiday: 'I do want to go so much and to live quietly together but I keep worrying that something will detain us here . . .'[34]

Something almost did, though it was of an unexpected nature. Natasha was told by her doctor that she might be pregnant again. 'You can imagine how shaken I was,' she wrote to Michael, 'particularly since recently I had joked about it . . . Don't worry, I won't let it happen in any case and Dr Rakhmanov says it would be impossible at this stage and I shouldn't tempt fate once more. If by Tuesday nothing happens he will help me by the most innocent means and he does not allow the possibility that it would be ineffective . . .'[35]

It was also at this point that Wulfert came back to haunt her. He had remained quiet over the summer, but on his return to the house in Moscow she heard ominous rumours that he was planning fresh difficulties, given that he could claim legal rights over her son. Once again, Natasha was alarmed. Once again, Michael tried to reassure her: 'Please, please my angel, don't fret yourself about all that trouble that Wulfert is threatening to make, for somehow the problem has to be (can be) resolved and I promise you that if they won't help me it can always be dealt with by my money . . .'[36]

The money was going to be enormous. But that would be the price of ensuring that little George Wulfert vanished as if he had never been born.

According to George's official birth and baptism certificate, a single document in Russia, Natasha was divorced at the time of his birth,[37] though that was not true. To make it seem true, the finalisation of the divorce was backdated and the original birth and baptism certificate 'doctored'.

To do this the Church authorities had to be pushed into line and, not least, Wulfert had to be persuaded to give his consent. The first was a question of conscience, the second of cash. The date at which both matters were resolved appears to have been in early November, 1910, for it was on November 13 – sixteen weeks after the birth and almost eight weeks after the christening – that Nicholas issued a manifesto in which baby George was given the name of George Mikhailovich with the surname of Brasov; it was an effective acknowledgement that he was the son of Michael, the name of Brasov being taken from Michael's estate at Brasovo and the same name as he himself used as an *incognito*. His rank was acknowledged as 'an hereditary nobleman' – his entitlement from his mother – but there was no title for him.[38] George Mikhailovich Brasov was as much as the Tsar would allow.

Michael had gone abroad with Natasha, leaving the final negotiations with Wulfert in the hands of Natasha's brother-in-law. He had also by then managed to persuade Nicholas to do as he had promised earlier. Nicholas dealt with the Church; Michael dealt with Wulfert.

Moscow society was in no doubt about the settlement agreed between the patient Matveev and a demanding Wulfert. Michael Bakhrushin, who knew Matveev well and had long used him as his own lawyer, recalled that 'it was an open secret in Moscow that [Wulfert] consented to renounce his father's rights on payment of 200,000 roubles'.[39]

This 'ransom money' was an astonishing price to pay, even though Michael could well afford it. It made Wulfert financially independent and under the terms of the original settlement he also had a sinecure as an officer at the Kremlin. Free himself to marry again he would go on to do so, taking as his second wife the daughter of a wealthy Moscow merchant, Petukhov.[40] In time, she would bear him two daughters.

The 'doctoring' of the birth and baptism document took an extraordinarily long time and it would not be for another eighteen months that the final endorsement was put upon it to register it as complete. The delay, in the circumstances, suggests a Church reluctantly dragging its feet on a matter about which it had strong reservations.

To 'doctor' the documents posed serious issues, for what the Church was required to do was to make George, ostensibly the legitimate son of a married woman, into the bastard child of a divorced woman and though that was to correct one falsehood it would be at the price of another.

The Church could move slowly when it wanted to, imperial decree or not, and it was perhaps a measure of the anxieties in the hierarchy of the

Moscow Church that it would not be until 2 December 1911, more than fourteen months after the christening at which he officiated, that Father Pospelov put his name to the official birth and christening certificate and in doing so signed the copy of the imperial decree which had been added to it,[41] which explained some if not all that had happened in the frantic negotiations which preceded it.

The paperwork, however, continued to flow, for in any 'doctoring' there would be yet more tracks to cover in the laborious processes of the Ecclesiastical Authority, whose high officials would be reluctant parties to any such deception. Though prodded by a persistent Matveev and by an impatient Grand Duke, it was not until February 4, 1912, that there came confirmation in the official register, under the hand of two archpriests, that 'these extracts are correct with the books of the Ecclesiastical Archives'.[42]

There was still more, however, and with Matveev no doubt demanding an end to the matter, the Ecclesiastical Authority, two months later, on April 6, 1912, finally put their seal on entry No. 926, though carefully making sure in doing so that they were acting on orders of the Tsar. To the official register was now added their endorsement:

> *By His Majesty's Imperial Decree, the Moscow Ecclesiastical Authority testify that these extracts from the Register of Births collate with the corresponding entry in the authentic Register of Births kept by the Ecclesiastical Authority, which is certified by the following signatures.*
>
> [There followed the signature of Archpriest Afanasi and of the secretary to the Moscow Ecclesiastical Authority.][43]

Matveev was not yet content even with this. It was not until September 1, 1912 – more than two years after George's birth – that he was able to put the matter finally to rest, by having a certified copy of the whole amended document made at the St Petersburg offices of lawyer and friend P. M. Artsybushev, and issued as Registered No. 6382 to a woman calling herself no longer Madame Wulfert but Madame Brasova.[44]

As for Wulfert, Natasha would never mention his name again. The French ambassador Paléologue would later record a comment that a Russian woman's memory is 'like a drawer, to be opened and shut at will'. Natasha shut the drawer on Wulfert. In later years she would say only that when she was very young she had been married to Mamontov and had given birth to a daughter. There was nothing she wanted to remember about her second marriage and so, as her granddaughter puts it, 'she conveniently forgot all about it; it was as if Wulfert had never been'.[45]

NINE

A Woman Scorned

With the settlement of the divorce in the autumn of 1910 and the start of the long process to 'doctor' baby George's birth certificate, Michael was more cheerful and more confident – now with reason – that at last his brother was prepared to accept Natasha as a fixture in his life. In return Michael had assured both Nicholas and his mother that he would not marry her, though neither would he marry anyone else. It was a truce rather than a peace settlement, but it was better than what had gone before.

Three months after George's birth the Dowager Empress had written to Nicholas urging him to be more flexible in dealing with his brother and at the beginning of October Nicholas assured her that he was already being so.

> *Just about a week ago I wrote to Misha in the vein you suggest. Having pointed out to him how difficult and often impossible it was under present conditions to keep one's incognito, I went on to beg him not to travel in the same train with her, saying at the same time that this was not an order, but was given in the spirit of friendly advice. I ended my letter by saying I was sure that, if she loved him as much as he thought she did, she would not want to harm him in any way. I was as gentle as I could be and got a very grateful telegram in reply.*[1]

Ten days later, just before leaving Russia on holiday, Michael wrote to Nicholas, thanking him for granting him permission to go abroad with Natasha and to travel *incognito*. 'You can rest assured', he added, 'that nothing will happen that could produce a bad impression ... if you knew Nathalie Sergeyevna I am sure it would not even occur to you that my trip might cause unpleasant talk. So I ask you again not to worry and not to believe any gossip, as last year when someone told you I had been seen in Moscow in civilian clothes.'[2]

Michael and Natasha travelled separately out of Russia and met up in the Hotel Bristol in Vienna.[3] Natasha, as always when she was with Michael, was once again her cheerful self, happy and contented and excited at the prospect of several weeks of having Michael all to herself. Or almost. For with them, in addition to her personal maid and his valet, came two of Michael's ADCs, Nikolai Wrangel and Captain Mordvinov. The holiday did nothing to improve Natasha's views of either. She called them 'the governesses',[4] a fair enough description given that the two men behaved as if Michael and Natasha were a couple of children who could not be allowed out on their own. They fussed about what could and could not be done and worried endlessly about Michael and Natasha being seen together.

They were certainly a blight in Vienna. Uneasy in the Bristol's elegant restaurant, the impression they gave was of wishing that Natasha took her meals in her room – better still, that she should stay there all the time. In short, they ruined her time there. She would have 'gloomy memories' of the Bristol ever after.

It could not go on like that. So when the party moved on to Rome, to the equally luxurious Quirinale, Michael and Natasha decided to do exactly as they liked,[5] leaving the 'governesses' to fuss at each other. They went on to Venice and Pisa and then to Dijon and Paris.[6] They had a wonderful time, delighting in each other, with all their worries and problems seemingly in the past. As ever, Natasha bloomed when Michael was around. He adored her and showed it; she adored him and showed it no less. Natasha's disappointment was to find, in society-crowded Paris, that Mordvinov was nervously fussing around again, trying to hide her away as he had done in Vienna. It was shaming.

Perhaps because of that, Natasha's old doubts crowded in again after they returned to Russia and Michael had gone back to his regiment at Orel. Suddenly she was alone again, sitting in the little house in Moscow, while he had gone back to a world from which she was excluded, in a town which she was forbidden to enter. Why were they forced to live 240 miles apart and why was it that he seemed not to think it as unbearable as she did?

She protested, because she always said what was on her mind and because 'what I am struggling for is too sacred to allow me to remain indifferent'.[7] Was she to be allowed to come out into the sunshine only in some far-away country, but never in Russia? Was her life to be a few weeks of happiness, then months of loneliness with only weekend glimpses of the man she loved?

> *In Orel you have the same life as you had in Gatchina – races, picnics, hunts, shoots, all this with other people, other women, while I have to sit here hearing about it from all quarters and you expect me never to protest and put up with it all as though it were inevitable. I only blame you for those things that were in your power to spare me and you didn't . . . I am still struggling, but you have killed much in my soul and there isn't much to tie me to life.*[8]

It was dispiriting to read letters like that, for there was precious little Michael could do. He had promised Nicholas that he would not take Natasha to

Orel and he was dependent on his brother's goodwill if he was to avoid more serious obstacles being placed in the way of his relationship with Natasha. Long-term interests required a short-term price and he saw, as Natasha did not, that patience was their best friend. In the meantime he could only despair at Natasha's despair.

Her letters were almost unrelenting in their despondency. She felt, she said, 'like a voice crying in the wilderness ... honestly I do not any longer know if I was or am the most important thing in your life ... Your regiment, your life in Orel and particularly service, service, service, are the most important things in the world to you ...'[9]

A month later, at the end of February 1911, she was still as depressed as ever, 'painfully aware of my loneliness' and desperately missing him.[10] Overwhelmed by hopelessness, she could say things which she knew in her heart were untrue, but which she could not stop herself telling him. 'You only need me for amusement and pleasure. I am used to regarding myself as a plaything in your hands – everything that seemed important in my life – religion, the wish to have a family and children and generally all that fills the life of a woman who is interested in more than merely dressing up and going out – all that is not important any more.'[11]

She could not understand that Michael found it no easier to bear their separation, but had no choice in the matter. He could not walk away from his regiment and he could not avoid the duties which came with his position; besides, if he hoped to win concessions from his brother, he had to be seen to be doing his utmost to comply with his brother's wishes. It was a matter of compromise.

Michael's patience did win two important concessions. In May, 1911, Nicholas agreed that Natasha should have the surname of 'Brasova', so that at least she would be known by the same name as her son. 'I am deeply grateful,' Michael told Nicholas. 'I thoroughly appreciate your affectionate kindness.'[12] At the same time Nicholas conceded that Natasha could stay at Brasovo, previously barred to her. Seventy miles from Orel – although that itself was still out-of-bounds to her – Brasovo was a great deal more convenient for them than Moscow or the estate at Udinka; with the ban lifted, they moved there at once. It would be the first home Natasha ever had which was not rented; she loved it.

Tata retained a clear memory of the exodus to the estate, a night's journey from Moscow. 'Uncle Misha always travelled in his private carriage, which was hooked on to any train which he wanted to take and though Brasovo was not a station proper, the train was stopped there and our carriage unhooked. I was very impressed by the red carpet laid down for his arrival. The house itself was about a couple of miles from the so-called station and we were conveyed there by relays of carriages . . . The coachmen wore black waistcoats, very bright sleeves and peacock feathers in their round hats and the dashing thing to do was to drive up to the house hell-for-leather and stop dead, so that the horses almost sat on their haunches.'[13]

Brasovo, as with most country houses of its kind, was built of wood. The main house, with inlaid polished parquet floors throughout, was of two-storeys with a central tower, reached by a spiral staircase. On either side were single-storey wings, linked to the main house by colonnaded walkways. There were landscaped gardens, with a croquet lawn, swings and fountains.

The estate at Brasovo had originally been purchased by Michael's brother George in 1882 for the immense sum of 4.3 million roubles (£475,000) and had passed to Michael on George's death. It covered 430 square miles and contained nine villages and hamlets. There was a postal and telegraph office in the main village of Brasovo and the estate had its own schools, hospital and churches, two medical dispensaries, an orphanage, an alms-house and a charitable foundation. In the north-west, 184,000 acres were devoted to forestry, though hunting was banned to protect wildlife, such as elk, lynx and bears.

In the rest of the land, crossed by rivers and dotted with lakes, there were extensive farms as well as saw mills, chemical factories producing turpentine, lime, oil, pitch, tar and charcoal, two distilleries, three brickworks, a lime works, twenty-eight mills and a number of craft workshops.[14] Depending on the season the estate employed between 1200 and 2000 workers and under Michael's management its profits each year had increased, taking his estates' income from 125,000 roubles a year to one million roubles[15] (£110,000), or almost four times his annual allowance from the imperial purse.

Apart from tea, coffee, rice and their like, the estate was entirely self-sufficient, producing its own meat, bread and milk. Tata remembered that the bread was of 'infinite variety, from the plain brown loaf to fancy twists, flavoured with poppy seed, caraway seed and saffron'. The bakery also provided sweet iced buns and cakes. 'The cream, milk and butter came from the farm, the cream so thick that a spoon would stand up in it.'[16]

Almost as soon as the move to Brasovo had been completed, Michael had to set off abroad again. In May, his elderly uncle, King Frederick of Denmark, died suddenly on a visit to Hamburg* and Michael hurried off with his mother to the funeral. It was from Copenhagen that Michael then telegraphed to Natasha complaining about the stomach ulcer that had begun to plague him and which periodically would cause him agony over

* He had felt unwell after dinner, and gone for a walk, collapsing in a doorway. It was only after he had been taken to the morgue that he was recognised from his cuff-links.

Tsar Nicholas II and Grand Duke Michael Aleksandrovich, 1909. Michael, formerly heir presumptive, was named as Regent in 1904 in the event of his brother dying before Nicholas's son Alexis reached manhood.

Michael at the formal State Council, 1901. Michael, then heir to the throne, on Nicholas's right hand, flanked by his uncles. (From painting by Repin.)

Grand Duke Michael Aleksandrovich.
The most eligible bachelor in Europe.

Princess Beatrice of Great Britain.
'We feared she would lose her mind.'

Princess Patricia of Connaught.
The bride-to-be who never was.

Husband No.1: Sergei Mamantov.
Piano player, but too dull for Natasha.

Husband no.2: Lieutenant Vladimir Wulfert. Would he shoot himself, or shoot Natasha?

Nathalie Sheremetevskaya ('Natasha').
The most notorious woman in Russia.

May, 1909: The first extant picture of Michael and Natasha together.
A picnic in the woods outside Gatchina. In the background, Michael's sister Grand Duchess Olga, with her lover Captain Nikolai Kulikovsky beside her. Grand Duchess Olga, in her memoirs, would not admit that she had ever met Natasha. Michael and Natasha sit together, yet innocently apart. The photographer? Almost certainly Natasha's second husband Lieutenant Wulfert, unaware that Grand Duke Michael has fallen in love with his wife.

1908: Michael, Grand Duchess Olga, Natasha and Olga's husband Duke Peter, with behind them (centre) Lieutenant Wulfert and (right) 'Koka' Abakanovich, who would be named as Michael's adjutant a year later, to the dismay of Michael's ADC Mordvinov.

At home at 7 Baggout Street. Natasha and Wulfert in the drawing room of their Gatchina apartment. Michael was a frequent visitor throughout 1908 and until the summer of 1909. 'Suddenly he ceased to come,' remembered Natasha's daughter Tata, 'and there were raised voices ...'

Going...

Going...

Gone. As Wulfert disappears from the picture in June, 1909.

(Right) Natasha took this photo of Michael in Copenhagen where they met secretly in August.

Michael's family.
At Hvidore, Denmark, Michael with his mother, the Dowager Empress Marie Fedorovna (seated), widow of Tsar Alexander III, and (left) his aunt Queen Alexandra of England, with her daughter Princess Victoria ('Toria'). This picture was in 1908, when his family knew nothing of Natasha and the girl in their sights was Princess Patricia of Connaught.

Natasha's family.
Natasha's lawyer father, Sergei Sheremetevsky, with his three daughters, (left to right) Olga, Natasha and Vera, the eldest.

Inset: Olga's husband Aleksei Matveev, destined to play a leading role in Michael's life.

The house at Brasovo. The main house on the 430 sq.mile estate near Orel which Michael inherited from his brother George. The estate contained nine villages, factories, farms, a school and clinic.

At home with the Sheremetevskys at 6 Vozdvizhenkan, Moscow.
Michael and Natasha at her parent's apartment in 1909. Matveev (left), sister Olga in foreground, and parents Sergei and Julia behind. Natasha's father pretended not to know who Michael was; at first he was also condemning of the relationship between the Grand Duke and his married daughter.

the years to come. News of it alarmed Natasha, who sent off telegrams insisting that he return immediately. On May 12 she cabled him: 'Am horribly worried ... try to leave tomorrow for St Petersburg without stopping Berlin ... must have reply today without hiding anything I beg you. God bless. I love you. Kiss you tenderly.'[17]

Michael came back in acute discomfort and it would appear that the problem persisted for many days thereafter, for on June 1 there was a sudden announcement from St Petersburg that on the eve of his intended departure for London, to represent Russia at the coronation of his cousin King George V, Grand Duke Michael Aleksandrovich was unable to travel 'for health reasons'.[18] His place had been fixed in the coronation procession, his name had appeared in all the London newspapers and on the programmes being issued by Buckingham Palace. His rakish cousin Grand Duke Boris was hurriedly substituted in his stead.

But with Michael's recovery, life resumed as before. Brasovo was a mecca for a continual stream of guests from Moscow and elsewhere. Natasha's sister Olga and her husband Matveev, her closest schoolfriend Maria Schlieffer, whose two daughters were to become Tata's 'inseparable cronies' in coming years, and the Rachmaninovs were prominent among them, but there were many other of her friends eager for long weekends with Grand Duke Michael Aleksandrovich. For Tata, the 'High Table' at Brasovo seemed ever crowded, with 'rarely less than sixteen to sit down'.[19]

Guests would also be taken off on extravagant picnics, with Sergei, the major-domo at Brasovo, being sent on ahead to set up tables and chairs, servants following to lay out a feast of caviare, smoked salmon, cold game, cold sturgeon, with a vegetable salad and horseradish sauce, 'and if the day was not too hot a fire would soon be built and one would have sizzling hot sausages and potatoes baked in the embers'. Sometimes the servants built bonfires rather than cooking fires and then 'Uncle Misha, followed by the other men, would leap over them'.[20]

It was in that summer that an eight-year-old Tata also came to think of Michael as the father she had never really known in her short life. He took Tata on expeditions into the countryside at Brasovo and would also take her rough-shooting; 'he and I used to go for long walks, a gun under his arm and we would try to spot hawks' which had been raiding the estate's hen-roosts. 'He was an excellent shot'.[21] Tata loved Brasova, as did Natasha; but yet she felt still a prisoner, confined to the estate, and forbidden to go to nearby Orel, the only town of any size in reach. All was well at weekends when Michael was there, but most of the time she was alone. She was, despite herself, still depressed about her position, sometimes thinking of herself as a woman in hiding from the world.

Anxious that she should recover her spirits, Michael insisted on sending her for treatment at Hans Apolant's sanatorium in Bad Kissingen, the fashionable spa town near Frankfurt. Herr Apolant specialised in 'nervous conditions' and after the toll of the past three years Natasha was the first to recognise that she was in need of a rest. The real cure, however, was not a soothing spell in a sanatorium but a resolution of their real problem: that neither Michael nor Natasha could go on living as they had been. Michael was as battered as she was and admitted it in his first letter to her at Bad Kissingen.

> *If I am worried it is only because I feel and see that from the emotional point of view they do not understand me at all, or else they are closing their eyes and refusing to see that I cannot live without you.*
>
> *At this very moment this life is torture for my heart. I cannot, cannot live like this, Natashechka, my charming one. I would like to live at peace with everyone, but if it is not possible (and apparently it isn't) I'll give everything up, leave with you and we'll live together – I don't care where – but just to be together, permanently, inseparably. These are not just words, I'm saying this with conviction and certainty. I'm tired of living here. I have always to live contrary to my views, feelings, aspirations. In any case we'll go abroad in the autumn and from there I'll write back setting out some conditions without which I cannot go on living here. If they are not accepted, then we'll have to stay abroad . . . I want to hear and feel your support – do know that I no longer hesitate . . . we must be very careful in our letters.*[22]

Natasha's reply was more cautious, for she was also beginning to fear that their letters were being intercepted and read and therefore 'it is perhaps best if I do not write certain things'. What she did tell him was what she did not mind anyone knowing: 'I and all my life belongs to you . . . To me you have always been higher, purer than anyone else. It is only on your shoulder that I can rest and be at peace.'[23] That being true, there was nothing that Herr Apolant could do for her.

Since the sanatorium was simply the substitute for an answer and not the answer itself, Natasha spent her time wishing she were back home, while worrying that she might be barred at the frontier. It was a repeat of her fears on her return from Switzerland. 'They' could do anything and what better solution to the embarrassment of Natasha than to allow her to go abroad and then refuse her re-entry.

> *My darling, I'm so afraid at the thought that I might not be allowed back into Russia, that we might be separated, when I think about it I literally pale with horror. What if I never, ever see you again or kiss or embrace you again. You do understand how horrible it would be. I think of nothing else and in my*

> *thoughts and in my dreams I am caressing you as if I was saying goodbye to you forever . . .*[24]

Because of her fears she told him that she would cable him an agreed message once she was safely across the frontier and that if he did not receive it, then 'you immediately leave the country'. She also hinted that she had good reasons, which she 'did not want to disclose', for believing that she would be stopped.[25] These warnings were passages in her letters which she did not mind if 'they' read, for it told them that barring her from re-entry would cause Michael to leave.

Natasha was quite right to be careful. Letters were intercepted and steps were taken and would be taken, to keep her and Michael under surveillance. Natasha sealed her letters with green wax, stamped with the letter 'N', the seals being on the backs of the envelopes at both top corners and over the central flap. Michael did the same with his letters, using red wax, stamped with his arms.[26] It was a deterrence but it was not foolproof and for security they would assume from the summer of 1911 that some things should not be said in their letters.

Nevertheless, they continued to be frank enough about their feelings for each other and in Natasha's case she wrote down whatever she thought, agreeable or not. One of the points she chided Michael about was that he never mentioned little George in his letters. 'This is the child of our love, tenderness and passion and besides he is such an enchanting baby, so easy and quiet and so extraordinarily beautiful. Why you are so indifferent to him I'll never understand . . . I used to think that was not like you but even in this I see that you and I differ so much. I can't tell you how painful it is to me . . .'[27]

Given the extraordinary lengths to which he had gone in fighting for George's rights, the comment stung Michael, who replied at once:

> *Oh, Natasha, my angel, there is only one reason for that. I love you alone so dreadfully much and passionately that I can only think of you alone, particularly when we are apart. But please don't think that I don't love our dear children. I love them tenderly and Baby is so charming and so little that one can't help loving him or looking at him with joy. I couldn't be more happy and content. I am happy that you are such a good and true mother and love your children so much. If it were not so, it would be very sad for me . . . And so please, never think again that I don't love the children, darling Natasha . . .*[28]

If that letter was intercepted and read by the Okhrana the point which might have been the subject of most comment was that it was addressed to 'My darling and charming wife'. Wife was a word that rang alarm bells.

The presence of the 'governesses' on their previous trip abroad had been one of the safeguards against Michael and Natasha deciding on the spur of the moment to get married. Mordvinov, in particular, seemed to think that his role was that of watchdog; whatever the Tsar might have said to Michael's ADCs, there is no doubt that he depended on them to ensure that nothing untoward should occur on trips abroad. In the autumn of 1911 Michael made it clear, however, that they would not be needed on the next trip. He and Natasha would be travelling 'privately', as Count and Madame Brasov* and this time Natasha had put her foot down: 'I am not going abroad with your three governesses,' she wrote from Bad Kissingen. 'You must understand that. Three months each year I want to spend with you in peace and forget that you are a Grand Duke.' She also reminded him how 'Mordvinov poisoned our stay in Paris and ruined even the most cheerful atmosphere'.[29]

Natasha returned to Russia at the end of August, nervous as ever at the frontier, but passing through again without anyone paying any particular attention to her. She was reunited with Michael at the Hotel de l'Europe in St Petersburg – 'book our large suite 11', she asked him from Bad Kissingen.[30] From there she travelled on to Brasovo with Michael. He wound up his duties with the Chernigov Hussars and they went off together, on their long-awaited holiday abroad. Michael having accepted Natasha's complaints about his ADCs, this time Mordvinov and Wrangel stayed behind.

The news that Michael and Natasha would be travelling across Europe free of any guardian ADC had already alarmed Nicholas. If the Okhrana were indeed reading the letters between Michael and Natasha, as both suspected, it may be that he was also aware that on this holiday Natasha intended that the two children should be taken down to the Riviera by her sister Olga and husband. Natasha suggested that to Michael 'so that we can see them and if we want to go out on short trips they can be left behind, but they will be close to us and if something happens we can be there. Besides I do not have anyone to leave them with in Russia.'[31]

This was eminently practical and entirely reasonable, given the time that they intended to be abroad. But it was also suspicious. Michael had given his word that he would not attempt to marry Natasha and Nicholas accepted that; however, he did not trust Natasha. Once abroad, with the children safely out of Russia, Michael might easily be persuaded to stay there and if Nicholas spoke to Mordvinov on that point, he would not have been reassured.

* Abroad they would use the German spelling of 'Brassow'; in Germany, Natasha would use the name Madame von Brassow and in France, Madame de Brassow.

Nicholas did not insist on Mordvinov going with his brother; instead he decided that the Okhrana should be given the task of shadowing Michael on his travels, with orders to prevent any attempt at marriage, by any means necessary, including arrest. In preparation for that surveillance, a Top Secret order was typed out and handed over to the Okhrana's Major-General Gerasimov. It said:

> *The bearer hereof, Major-General of the Gendarme Corps Aleksandr Vasilevich Gerasimov, is commissioned by His Imperial Majesty abroad and is charged with the task of taking all reasonable measures to prevent the marriage of Madame Brasova (Wulfert) to Grand Duke Michael abroad.*
>
> *For the purposes of executing His Imperial Majesty's order, all Russian Embassies, Missions and Consulates abroad shall render Major-General Gerasimov every reasonable assistance that he might need to accomplish the task and, should necessity arise, to put under arrest any persons at the discretion of Major-General Gerasimov.*

The order, dated September 6, 1911, was signed by A. Neratov, Acting Chief of the Ministry of Foreign Affairs.[32] It is not clear, and perhaps it was not clear to Major-General Gerasimov, just how he was to effect 'the arrest' of anyone he suspected of being involved in any runaway marriage. Was he to kidnap Natasha? It would have been difficult, embarrassing and no doubt the cause of a major international incident had he attempted to do so on foreign soil. Natasha was not likely to go quietly and Grand Duke Michael was unlikely to stand by and passively allow the Okhrana to abduct his beloved Natasha.

It was the Paris bureau which was to find itself with the task of preventing any marriage on this holiday, since it was to Paris that Michael and Natasha went first. The Russian church there had been built half-a-century earlier and stood on the rue Daru, just off the Avenue Hoche, not far from the Arc de Triomphe, and if Michael and Natasha hoped to marry in Paris that would be the place they would surely choose. They did indeed go there, but only as ordinary worshippers on Sundays, giving no sign of other intent.

Like innocents abroad, Michael and Natasha went shopping and sightseeing and twice went to Longchamps, Michael dressed in black top hat and frock coat for the big race of the season, the Prix du Conseil Municipal, held on October 8.[33] If they were hatching plans, they were for somewhere else, at some other time.

From Paris, Michael and Natasha went to Cannes, their Opel tourer travelling with them on the train. They booked into the Hotel du Parc, where they would spend the next two months enjoying the autumn sun, going off on drives to Avignon, Grasse and the hilltop villages of Provence.[34] Wherever they went the Okhrana would trail after them, painfully aware that their presence was more than obvious, but unable to do anything but follow orders: *taking all reasonable measures to prevent the marriage of Madame Brasova (Wulfert) to Grand Duke Michael Aleksandrovich abroad . . .*

Fortunately for a relieved Major-General Gerasimov, nothing happened which could give him cause to intervene, or even think that he might have to do so; at the same time the Okhrana had gained experience which would stand them in good stead next time the Grand Duke and Madame Brasova ventured abroad. Or so they thought.

In the autumn of 1911 Michael's two-year 'exile' in Orel came to an end, though by then he would have been happier to stay where he was than go back to the capital. When the question of his return had come up earlier in the year, he had asked his brother for permission to become a brigade commander in Orel, rather than take up an appointment in St Petersburg, where 'as you know yourself, it will be very hard for me to live privately'. A new command at Orel, with Natasha and the family close by at Brasovo, was to be preferred to the limelight of St Petersburg; it would 'enable me to live quietly, as a private individual, in the country, while keeping an official residence in Orel'.[35] Nicholas would not hear of it, insisting that Michael return to public life and command of the Chevalier Gardes, the premier cavalry regiment in the Russian army.[36]

Accordingly, after their holiday abroad, Michael and Natasha in January 1912 found themselves once more in St Petersburg, praying that they might be left in peace, but knowing that it was unlikely. If Nicholas hoped that Natasha would be left behind, he was to be disappointed: where Michael went, she went and he made it clear that he would not be hiding her away. It was a decision greeted with sullen resentment at the imperial court and with dismay by his mother, but Michael took no notice.

He did not get matters entirely his own way. Frederiks was instructed to tell Michael that if he insisted on seeing Natasha in St Petersburg then he could not move into the Anichkov Palace, where he had been born, but would have to live in a modest government apartment at the regiment's headquarters.[37]

Michael took the quarters on offer without complaint and in doing so made clear that in St Petersburg he would see Natasha and his son whatever his mother, or his brother, had to say about it. Officially he lived in the regimental apartment; unofficially, he was to be found more often in Natasha's new apartment, at 16 Liteiny.[38]

It was a vast place of twenty-eight rooms and Natasha had protested at first when he told her about finding it. 'What do I want with 28 rooms, I don't even have the furniture,' she told him. 'To live on my own in an empty house is very depressing.'[39] Nevertheless, she did not argue and tackled the business of turning the echoing apartment into a comfortable home, 'which she furnished with exquisite taste'.[40]

Michael's determination to be seen openly supporting her did not, however, greatly help matters, for 'the whole of society turned its back on her as it had done before. To please the Court no one wanted either to recognise her or to receive her at their home.'[41] Even the Chevalier Gardes, his own regiment, were not prepared to make concessions for their colonel. As with the Blue Cuirassiers the Dowager Empress was colonel-in-chief and it was remembered that she had marked her displeasure with the Cuirassiers over the Wulfert affair by cancelling her usual visits to them. The Chevalier Gardes did not want to find themselves in the same position, so none of the officers ever paid Natasha a visit and none 'would bow to her' if they encountered her in the street.[42]

It was deeply distressing for Michael and the cause of further strain for Natasha, so that once more she began to doubt whether there was any hope for their life together, or indeed whether his sense of duty would not in the end prevail over his love. Again he could only attempt to reassure her: 'I can't live without you,' he wrote. 'I would like to say so much about this but I will refrain since there is a possibility that this letter will be read by somebody else, i.e. fall into strange hands. It hurts me deeply when you start doubting my love, but deep down you can't doubt my readiness to do anything for you ... Yes, my angel Natashechka, you will be convinced of the sincerity of my words ...'[43] Michael had not given up on his hopes of living in peace, but he was moving that way.

In the early summer, in an attempt to ease her situation Michael moved her out of St Petersburg and took her back to Gatchina, a place which he still regarded as home, but which she had left in disgrace, as had he, three years earlier. Nevertheless, they had been happy there once and he oped they could be happy there again. Gatchina was not, however, his first choice. He had hoped to move Natasha to an imperial villa at nearby Lisino; as he pointed out to his brother, 'no one uses the house there at all' and it would make sense to move there 'for it is impossible to remain in town'.[44] Nicholas refused his request; Natasha would never be allowed to live in an imperial property. Given that, Michael had little alternative but Gatchina.

He bought her a villa at 24 Nikolaevskaya Street, intending that this should be their family home, his own apartments at the Gatchina palace clearly being 'off limits', as Natasha herself would have been the first to recognise. The villa was 'a charming, simple, pleasant two-storeyed wooden house, sunk in a verdant garden',[45] but it was also an illusion. Gatchina was not, in fact, the refuge which Michael had hoped it would be. So long as St Petersburg delighted in its slights and backbiting, then there could be no hiding place in Gatchina, which took its lead from the capital and whose salons simply repeated what was being said elsewhere.

For Natasha, back in a town which had given her both love and hatred, it took courage to walk down the streets again and to behave as if she had no cause for shame. There was to be swift evidence that Gatchina, if anything, would be worse than the capital. The Blue Cuirassiers had not forgotten or forgiven her and their regimental ruling that no officer was to acknowledge her in the street or anywhere else was still in force.

One young officer who failed to remember that injunction was unwise enough to go into Natasha's box at the theatre in St Petersburg one evening and keen eyes spotted him. Shortly afterwards a meeting of regimental officers was called to discuss the fate of the young defaulter, Lieutenant Khan-Erivansky. It met in secret, with the doors closed, under the chairmanship of Colonel von Schweder, who set out the charge against the lieutenant, namely that he had appeared in a theatre box 'among a small company which included a certain lady who is well known to you'. He did not need to mention her name.

'In the past,' said the colonel, 'this lady's actions have cast a shadow over this regiment and incurred the displeasure of our most august Honorary Commander, our beloved Empress, onto the regiment. One would have thought that this in itself would be enough to have prompted our officers to sever once and for all contacts with this woman who has blackened the regiment's reputation . . . Gentlemen, there are things which we have no right to forgive and the senior officers of the regiment consider that from now on there is no place for Lieutenant Erivansky in the Cuirassier Regiment.'

The colonel had not finished, however. 'The case necessitates me to warn you yet again that if, contrary to expectations, any one of you has still not as yet broken off all contact with that woman, this should be done immediately. If it comes to my attention that any one of our officers continues to bow to this lady on meeting her, I warn you: this officer will suffer the same fate as Lieutenant Erivansky. You do not have the right to associate with her, nor to greet her, nor even to utter her name in society.'[46]

A young officer, new to the regiment, had sat throughout this meeting in wonderment and when the colonel stood up, bowed to the officers and left, he turned to his neighbour. 'I don't understand', he whispered, 'who is she, this unfortunate lady we are forbidden to know?'

'Madame Brasova,' came the muttered reply.[47]

No officer and no officer's wife looked at Natasha again, or nodded to her in the street and since the Blue Cuirassiers dominated Gatchina society, Natasha was effectively ostracised. Michael was aghast, but there was nothing he could say about it to a regiment which he had been forced to leave because of the same woman.

There was more humiliation when one night she went with friends to the theatre in St Petersburg and again it would be the Blue Cuirassiers who would be involved. In the interval, a drunken officer approached her and in a loud voice began berating her for having 'compromised' the Grand Duke Michael.[48] It was the worst kind of public scene and Natasha, cheeks red, was left fighting back her tears. She could not go on like that; neither, when he found out about it, could Michael, absent on manoeuvres at Krasnoe Selo. It was precisely the kind of disgraceful scene he had feared and the reason why he had wanted to remain in Orel.

Left in peace he would have been happy enough to command the Chevalier Gardes. He enjoyed life in the army and in the officers' mess. One of the high points at Krasnoe Selo that week was a dinner given to celebrate the winning of the King Edward VII Cup at the Stockholm Olympics. The Cup was the centrepiece of the table and Michael laughingly ordered it to be filled with champagne – it held two bottles; he then insisted that Pavel Rodzyanko,* who had won the Cup, should stand up and drink it. 'I lifted the great Cup to my lips,' Rodzyanko would recall. 'Dimly aware of the laughter and cheers of the other officers, I began to drink ... before the Cup was half-empty I fell unconscious to the fumes.'[49]

It was Michael's world, but it was not a world he could continue to accept when it would not accept Natasha. On learning of the scandal in the theatre he wrote to her, begging her to believe that he would not allow this to go on. 'I am full of love for you alone. I love you with my entire being as ardently as it is possible to love ... why would I lie if that is untrue? I know myself that this is not a very good time, but I beg you to be patient until we go abroad ...'[50] Michael had reached the end of the road. He had given his word not to marry Natasha, but the *quid pro quo* was that she should be treated with respect, as the woman he loved and as the mother of his son.

Society, taking its lead from the imperial court, had thought it could treat her with contempt and drive her out of their world. For almost three years she had endured humiliation and insult and nothing he had been able to do had changed any of that.

His contract was therefore broken. He would marry her, because he had been given no other choice.

* A nephew of Mikhail Rodzyanko, sometime President of the State Duma, Pavel Rodzyanko was later to become head of the Irish Free State Cavalry.

TEN

A Runaway Marriage

One lesson the Okhrana learned in their surveillance of Michael and Natasha in 1911 was that they could not hope to follow them in a car. They had tried it, blundering hopelessly in the wake of Michael's grey open Opel tourer, but they were so ludicrously obvious that they decided in the following year to change their tactics. Agents were instructed that they were in future to confine themselves to following the baggage and Grand Duke Michael's staff and servants as they journeyed from place to place by train, whether or not Michael was with them or travelling separately by car.[1] Their object was to prevent his marriage, not watch him going out for a picnic.

When, on September 12, 1912, Michael and Natasha kissed Tata and George goodbye and took the international train to Berlin, their Opel being loaded aboard with the baggage, it was again Major-General Gerasimov who was given the task of ensuring that Michael returned a bachelor. Gerasimov duly went after them, going on arrival directly to the Russian embassy on Unter den Linden to brief the man who was to be in charge of this year's surveillance, Senior Agent Bint.[2]

Michael and Natasha were booked into the Hotel Esplanade, on Bellevue-strasse, near the Potsdam station.[3] The 400-room Esplanade, opened in 1908, was a hotel which in luxury rivalled and in cost exceeded the Adlon,[4] but its particular attraction in their eyes was that it was not next door to the Russian embassy. Natasha was unlikely to forget the shock of walking out of the Adlon three years earlier and finding that 'the enemy' were on her doorstep and it was an experience she did not care to repeat. Michael and Natasha knew that the Okhrana would be keeping an eye on them, but they were disinclined to have them as neighbours.

Although nothing untoward had occurred on their last trip abroad, Bint set about the business of ensuring that Michael and Natasha were kept under as close surveillance as possible, his team of secret policemen trailing them whenever they set foot outside the hotel. Faced with having to answer for any failure and handicapped by the order banning him from following by car, Bint's main hope lay in good intelligence; he knew that any wedding, if it was to have full legal effect in Russia, would have to take place in an Orthodox church; therefore his agents would potentially have three weeks' notice while the necessary banns were called.

Making an arrest on foreign soil – effectively an abduction – would be so dramatic an action that it could be considered only as a policy of ultimate resort; the more practical course was to discover the church in which the banns were being called and then to stop the wedding before it took place by intimidating the priest, or threatening the two formal witnesses required to make a marriage valid. This assumed that the priest would be Russian and that the required witnesses would also be Russian, with interests to protect in Russia and therefore vulnerable to subsequent punishment, but it was a good assumption.

That enforced pause between notice of a marriage and the actual wedding itself gave Senior Agent Bint some grounds for hoping he could intervene, or at least report his findings, before any irreversible damage was done, either to the imperial dynasty, or for that matter, to his own career.

There were no reports as yet of banns being called in the Russian church in Berlin, which was what immediately mattered to Bint. Apparent confirmation that there was no intention of a wedding in Berlin came when on Sunday, September 23, Michael and Natasha left the Esplanade and, repeating the pattern of the year before, took the train once more to Bad Kissingen. The Okhrana duly followed and at the end of that first week in Bad Kissingen Bint reported that Natasha had been admitted for treatment 'at Dr Apolant's sanatorium'.[5] Michael went with her, 'drinking the water and taking baths' as he jovially noted on a postcard to his brother.[6]

It was three weeks later before the bored Okhrana needed to stir themselves again, when they discovered that Natasha had been discharged by the sanatorium and that the Grand Duke was on the move once more. Bint, a practised hand at bribing telegraph clerks and porters, was quickly tipped off on Sunday, October 14, that Grand Duke Michael Aleksandrovich had wired the Esplanade Hotel in Berlin 'asking if they could book tickets for him in a sleeping car from Frankfurt-am-Main to Paris'. Having been told by the hotel that they could do so, the Grand Duke then wired them again, 'asking for four tickets in a sleeper and four first-class tickets to Paris'.[7]

Bint, after making his own arrangements to join the train and having alerted the Paris office to the impending arrival of Grand Duke Michael, was then dismayed to find that almost at once the Grand Duke had cabled the hotel cancelling his own tickets and was loudly declaring to his entourage that his new intention was to drive to Cannes that day, via Switzerland and Italy, leaving his staff to travel separately to Cannes by rail. Given their orders not to follow by car, the Okhrana could only trail the baggage, joining the train which would carry Michael's personal staff and servants.[8]

However, there was no reason to doubt that Michael was going to Cannes. On Sunday, October 14, he sent a second postcard to his brother telling him that 'having now completed my treatment, I am setting out in the car towards Cannes, where I expect to be on Saturday'.[9] That postcard, intended to be read by the Okhrana, or its local informants, seemed to confirm Michael's plans. It was a deliberate feint, but the secret police could not know that.

Next day, Bint was relaxed as he watched Michael and Natasha climb into their chauffeur-driven Opel tourer and disappear sedately from sight. He would be in Cannes before them and that was where attention now focused. There was a pretty, cream-and-blue Russian church on the Boulevard Alexander III at Cannes, built in 1894 and dedicated to the memory of Michael's father; there was also a grander church at nearby Nice, built on the site of the house where Michael's uncle Nicholas had died in 1863;* these were now the most obvious places for any attempted marriage. Agents dashed south from Paris and a week later reported that Michael and Natasha had indeed arrived in Cannes and were at the Hotel du Parc.[10] Settling down to watch them, the Okhrana would not know for some weeks that they were wasting their time: unbeknown to them, in the seven days in which Michael and Natasha were assumed to be driving from Bad Kissingen to Cannes they had married secretly in Vienna.

The Okhrana would subsequently attempt and partially succeed in putting the pieces together, but by then it was too late for anything except desperate excuses and protests that Senior Agent Bint could not have known about the marriage because he was bound by the instructions given by Major-General Gerasimov and 'as the guard did not follow the Grand Duke in an automobile they could not know anything'.[11] Since Michael was in Cannes, it was left to a rattled Paris office to explain what had gone wrong, which they did first by way of telegram No. 382, sent to Okhrana headquarters in St Petersburg on December 4, 1912, and then by an embarrassed explanation, set out in report No. 1638, despatched from Paris on December 17, marked 'Absolutely Confidential' and signed by a cringing A. Krasilnikov, who ended his sorry tale by 'begging Your Excellency to accept an assurance of my deep respect and sincere faithfulness'.[12]

The embarrassed Okhrana was initially baffled as to how the marriage had taken place without their knowledge. Spurred on by an angry St Petersburg, their agents found the church in Vienna, gained sight of the marriage register and identified the hotel to which Michael and Natasha had gone just before their wedding. However, the final report suppressed the fact that the marriage register recorded the banns being called on the three Sundays preceding the marriage, the Okhrana bureaus in Berlin, Vienna and Paris

* Grand Duke Nicholas, elder brother of Alexander III, died of tuberculosis, aged twenty. His fiancée was Princess Dagmar of Denmark, who then became engaged to Alexander.

hoping thereby to avoid some awkward questions about their lack of diligence. Instead, they covered up their own failings by pretending that the wedding had been a last-minute affair, arranged 'unexpectedly' and that it had taken place only because the Grand Duke 'suddenly changed his mind' about travelling to Paris by rail.[13]

The report not only deliberately misled in that respect, but was also careless in some of its essential dates. It dated the marriage as being on October 17, instead of 16, and it also wrongly dated the arrival of Michael and Natasha in Cannes, giving it as October 21, instead of two days later.[14] What mattered, of course, was not that a flustered Okhrana muddled up some of the details afterwards, but that Grand Duke Michael had made fools of them. The trip to Berlin had been a decoy; the stay in Bad Kissingen had been a diversion. While Senior Agent Bint and his men had been watching the Esplanade and standing idly by while Natasha completed her 'treatment' at Dr Apolant's sanatorium, the secret arrangements for the wedding had been going on undisturbed in Vienna. And as the Okhrana would discover to their chagrin, the selected church was not Russian Orthodox, the priest was not a Russian and neither were the two witnesses. Michael and Natasha had been married by the Serbs.

The Okhrana agents throughout Europe had been alerted to watch for Michael and Natasha and for any other member of his party who might have slipped away from Berlin or Bad Kissingen, but not anyone else. The man they did not spot was undoubtedly Aleksei Matveev, Natasha's brother-in-law.

In planning their runaway marriage Michael and Natasha needed help and looking about them, there was only one man they could trust absolutely. It is not difficult to identify Matveev as that man, not only because he was family, but because he had the necessary professional skills to handle the details, as his efforts in handling George's birth certificate had amply demonstrated. He left no calling-cards in Vienna, but neither did anyone else.

The steady Matveev was not the sort of man who would have gone to Vienna on the off-chance of finding a suitable church, a pliable priest and an accommodation address which would involve more questions than answers. The plan had to be in place before Michael and Natasha left Russia, not made up as they went along.

The choice of Vienna was deliberate. Michael and Natasha needed to marry in an Orthodox church; they also knew that a Russian church abroad would almost certainly mean prior discovery. So what was the alternative? The obvious and most convenient answer was to be found in Vienna, whose population contained a large number of Serbs, then subjects of the Austro-Hungarian empire. As Michael and Matveev remembered, but the Okhrana seemingly forgot, a Serbian Orthodox wedding was as legal in Russia as one conducted by a co-religionist Russian Orthodox priest.

Twenty-two years earlier, in 1890, the Serbs living in Vienna had established their own church, on the ground floor of a modest three-storey building at Veithgasse 3 and it was there in 1912 that the bearded and worldly Father Misitsch served as priest-in-charge of the Church of St Savva, taking care of the spiritual needs of those Serbs living in the capital.[15]

Without any pretensions and hardly known outside the closed world of the *émigré* Serbs in Vienna, the church looked the very last place that one would expect a Russian Grand Duke and brother of the Tsar to be married; therein lay its greatest appeal. Nevertheless, a cautious Matveev would not have disclosed the identity of 'his clients' on making his preliminary enquiries and Father Misitsch is therefore unlikely to have known about Michael and Natasha until Matveev turned up again, towards the end of September 1912, when Senior Agent Bint and his team were plodding into Bad Kissingen, 350 miles away.

Astonished though Father Misitsch must have been to discover the truth, and since Matveev had to hand over to him copies of birth certificates for both Michael and Natasha the truth was hardly avoidable, the priest proved a ready accomplice, no doubt hugely enjoying the extraordinary role cast for him. He could also be trusted to keep quiet, for the fee was exceptionally generous.

Father Misitsch was bound by the Habsburg writ and not by that of the Romanovs and in consequence he neither cared nor knew anything about the Tsar's secret agents. His usual congregation was of humble means and on average he conducted only one wedding per week, though none at anything like the price which Matveev had been prepared to suggest for an hour of his time on a quiet Tuesday afternoon. The French ambassador Paléologue, years later, would repeat informed gossip that the priest was given 1000 Austrian crowns,[16] more than he could ordinarily hope to see in two months or so.* In view of that, it is hardly surprising that a shrewd Father Misitsch not only co-operated to the full, but that the two formal witnesses he provided were members of his own family, one of them his wife Vrikosova.[17] It made for better security; it also made for better business.

Matveev's next task was to secure a discreet accommodation address which would satisfy the residential qualifications required of Michael, but which would not lead to embarrassing and premature disclosure. Fashionable Vienna had to be ruled out, for Austrian society gossiped as eagerly as did its counterpart in St Petersburg. Michael would not be long in Vienna

* It was then the equivalent of £42; as a measure of what that was then worth, Father Misitsch could have spent a night at the Ritz Hotel in London, with dinner and wine included, for about £1.

but his name would be registered as living in the city for a month beforehand and there could be no risk in that time of it being discovered, talked about and the Okhrana alerted. The Archduke Franz-Ferdinand, the Austrian heir by whose side Michael had ridden in procession at the funeral of Queen Victoria and with whom he had dined and chatted on all three of the state occasions they had both attended in London, was only one of the many people who would have been more than curious at learning that Grand Duke Michael Aleksandrovich was 'living in Vienna'.

Grand hotels and grand addresses with grand neighbours were therefore ruled out. Instead, Matveev entered into a discreet arrangement with an obliging manager at the quiet Tegetthof, a five-storey hotel at Johannesgasse 23 in the centre of Vienna[18] but conveniently placed for the Veithgasse.

A hotel room is not usually sufficient for residential qualifications, so it may be that Matveev 'borrowed' the manager's private flat in the same building; as he would have explained, Michael was not actually going to be living there, so vacant possession was not one of the requirements. Since Father Misitsch entered only the address, Johannesgasse 23, in the marriage registry and not the name of the hotel,[19] it is quite possible and perhaps more than probable, that the priest was privy to the arrangement at the Tegetthof and indeed that Matveev went there on his recommendation. If so, one reason might have been that the manager was a Serb and a member of the priest's flock. Father Misitsch, it may be remembered, was the kind of man who liked to keep business among his own; Matveev's cash reinforced by the priest's parochial authority was a powerful inducement to remain silent.

Having finalised matters in Vienna, there would have been no reason for Matveev to remain to excite possible attention from the local men of the Okhrana and it is therefore most probable that he slipped back into Russia as quietly as he had left, confirming his arrangements in a coded telegram to Bad Kissingen. Certainly, the banns proceeded without any interruption or attracting any notice, being read out on September 30 and again on the two following Sundays, October 7 and 14.[20] As Matveev would have insisted, the name mumbled by Father Misitsch would have been stripped of rank and reduced to its barest and virtually unrecognisable essentials. Since no one in his Serb congregation knew a Michael Romanov, the watching eyes remained glazed, the listening ears deaf. Whoever Romanov was, he was obviously a man of no substance. No one who had any social ambition married at St Savva.

The three-week period in which the banns were being read coincided almost exactly with the period in which Michael and Natasha were in Dr Apolant's sanatorium in Bad Kissingen. It was an effective diversion. They went in just before the first banns were being read in Vienna; they came out just before the last banns and in the interval the Okhrana went to sleep.

When Michael and Natasha left Bad Kissingen on Monday, October 15, their Opel tourer took them only to Würzburg, some thirty miles away.[21] There they took the overnight train via Munich and Salzburg to Vienna, while their chauffeur loaded their car on to another train for the long journey south to Cannes. Next morning, on reaching Vienna, they went directly to the Tegetthof Hotel. Michael, who needed a room in which he and Natasha could bath and change before their wedding, presumably now signed the hotel register for the first and last time, for the Okhrana report rightly records Michael as having gone to the hotel on arriving in Vienna,[22] though for their own self-preserving reasons the authors remain silent about the Tegetthof and Johannesgasse 23 being one and the same place, since that would be to admit more from the marriage register than was good for them.

At 4 p.m. that same day[23] Michael and Natasha arrived at the church, to be met by Father Misitsch and his two witnesses. There was no one else present; Father Misitsch had kept his word and the marriage was conducted in absolute secrecy.

The marriage register at St Savva for October 16, 1912, shows that the wedding of Michael and Natasha was the thirty-fifth that year and the third that month. The bride was identified as 'Noblewoman Nathalie Sergeyevna Brasova, daughter of the hereditary nobleman Sergei Aleksandrovich Sheremetevsky and of Julia Vladislavovna'. Michael was entered simply as Michael Aleksandrovich, Grand Duke of Russia, born on November 22, 1878; both were said to be 'living at Johannesgasse 23, Vienna (I)',[24] the hotel in which they had spent only a few hours and in which they would never stay, even for a night.

The ceremony could not have been simpler and at the end of it Grand Duke Michael Aleksandrovich and Madame Brasova were duly pronounced man and wife. The question now was what the Tsar would do by way of reprisal.

It was Michael, not the still blissfully ignorant Okhrana, who broke the news of his marriage to Nicholas. He and Natasha had the briefest of honeymoons; immediately after their wedding they went by train to Venice, where next morning they were to be found taking snapshots of each other feeding the pigeons in St Mark's Square[25]; three days later they were in Milan and on October 22 they were established at the lavish Hotel du Parc at Cannes.[26] Within the week Tata and George were there with them,[27] hustled out of Gatchina and escorted out of Russia by Natasha's sister Olga and her husband Matveev. The house on Nikolaevskaya Street was then securely locked up, with no one to know when, if ever, Michael and Natasha would see it again.

Michael knew that he could not long delay in confessing what he had done to his brother and mother, yet he had reason for pausing before doing so. He had no worries about the validity of the marriage itself, for the careful Matveev had made sure that the ceremony had complied with the law in every detail, from residency to the calling of the banns. The Tsar could not, therefore, declare the marriage null and void; there was less certainty, however, about what actions he might take with respect to the children.

Before telling Nicholas it seems that Michael and Natasha therefore decided to ensure that Tata and little George were safely out of the country, worried perhaps that otherwise the expected wrath of the Tsar might be such that the children's exit would be impeded once news of the marriage came out. However remote that risk might be, there was a troubling precedent: ten years earlier, when Michael's widowed uncle, Grand Duke Paul, followed his divorcée mistress Madame Pistolkors out of Russia, Paul's two children – Dimitri and his sister Marie – had been placed by Nicholas in the guardianship of Grand Duke Serge and his childless wife Ella, sister of Empress Alexandra. Paul did not see his children for several years.[28]

Indeed, it was almost certainly because of their fears about retribution being visited on the children, or at least on George, that Natasha, eleven days before leaving Russia, had collected a certified copy of her son's birth and baptism certificate, for what Nicholas had given with one imperial decree he might take away with another and what had been 'doctored' once might be 'doctored' again; Michael had no intention of allowing George Mikhailovich Brasov to vanish as mysteriously from the archives as had George Vladimirovich Wulfert and the certified birth certificate was its own insurance policy against that, though he knew there was nothing the Tsar could do about the validity of the marriage itself.

Even so, Michael still hesitated, though now because of the difficulty in deciding quite what he was to say. It was not until October 31, two weeks after his marriage, that Michael sat down to compose the first of the two letters which would admit what had happened. His mother was on holiday at Hvidore and he wrote to her there:

My Dear Mama, If only you knew how painful and distressing it is for me to upset you, yet I know my letter will bring you great sorrow and I ask you in advance to hear me out and forgive me. I so much want you to believe me, when I say it's more than painful for me to distress you, dear Mama, but I am obliged to inform you that on the 16/29 October, that is two weeks ago, I was married to Nathalie Sergeyevna Brasova. I have suffered greatly over this last period, but was unable through force of circumstances to talk to you of that, which has been the main focus of my life for all these years, moreover you yourself evidently never wished it.

It is now five years since I met Nathalie S. and I love and respect her more each year. But, morally it was always very hard on me and in particular the last year in St Petersburg convinced me that the only way out of this painful and false situation was marriage. But I never wanted to distress you and might never have had decided on this step, were it not for little Alexis's illness and the thought that as Heir I could be separated from Nathalie, but now that can no longer happen.

Let me say again, that more than anything I am tortured by the fact of distressing you and Nicky so terribly, but to go on living as before was simply not bearable. And so I beg you, my dear Mama, to forgive and understand me as a mother, whom I love deeply with all my heart. Your Misha.[29]

The following day he wrote in similar vein to his brother, then readying himself to leave his Polish hunting lodge at Spala. It was not, in the circumstances, the most tactful of letters, for it came just after the most serious crisis yet in the life of eight-year-old Alexis, whose haemophilia had a month earlier brought him to the brink of death. While at Spala, Alexis had caught himself in a rowlock while jumping into a boat;[30] the bruise later brought on extensive haemorrhaging in his thigh and groin and the bleeding could not be stopped.

Michael knew about the crisis, for on his postcard telling Nicholas that he was going to Cannes, he also said that he was 'greatly upset to learn about Alexis being unwell'.[31] Daily bulletins on the state of Alexis's health were then being published in Russia and special prayers were being said for him in church; at the height of the agony, the doctors had prepared their evening bulletin 'in such a manner as to be able to follow it by an announcement of the child's death'.[32] Had that happened Michael would at once have been Heir Presumptive again and in all likelihood, being ten years younger than Nicholas, the next Emperor.

Michael unwisely chose to use that as one of the factors in his decision to wed, claiming that if Alexis had died, he would then have had to have given up Natasha entirely. Seemingly unwilling to admit that he had planned his wedding as carefully as he had, he preferred instead to suggest that it had been prompted by the grave news about Alexis. It did not help his cause that he should say so:

Dear Nicky, I know that my letter will cause you a lot of sorrow and I ask you in advance, as your brother, to listen and understand me. I am even more sorry to distress you, when you are already so preoccupied by Alexis's illness, but it was precisely this circumstance and the thought that I could be separated from Nathalie Sergeyevna Brasova, that prompted me to marry her. I have already loved her for five years and can no longer say that on my side it was only a distraction. On the contrary, with each year I have become more deeply attracted to her and the thought that I could be deprived of her and our child was simply unbearable.

He then set out what were, in fact, his true reasons for his marriage, even if in Cannes these did not, on their own, appear sufficient explanation to give his brother:

At first I did not consider the possibility of marrying her, but the last five years and particularly the past one in St Petersburg, changed my intentions. You should know that, even during the two difficult years living apart (when I was in Orel), we were always a family and I always looked on Nathalie Sergeyevna as my wife and always honoured her, which is why the humiliations and insults which she inevitably had to bear in St Petersburg because of her position, were so terribly painful for me.

I give you my word that I did not act under pressure from anyone. Nathalie S. never talked to me about it or demanded it. I myself came to the conclusion that to live in this way was dishonourable and that I had to escape from a false position. All this prompted me to take the decision and get married to Nathalie Sergeyevna. Our wedding took place at the Serbian church of St Savva in Vienna on October 16/29 October. I know that punishment awaits me for this act and I am ready to bear it.[33]

After receiving her letter from Michael the Dowager Empress had written at once to Nicholas and her horror at the news she had so long feared could not have been greater. She viewed the marriage as an imperial disaster, for at a stroke it ruined her hopes that one day her beloved Michael would take a 'proper' wife and perhaps eventually succeed Nicholas. Anna Vyrubova, an intimate friend and companion of the Empress Alexandra, privately believed that the Dowager Empress continued to harbour her own ambitions for Michael and that 'possibly she felt in her secret heart that it should have been her own strong Michael who was the acknowledged successor of Nicholas'.[34] Michael's mother was therefore distraught on receiving his letter, as her own to Nicholas, heavily underlined, amply demonstrates:

My dear sweet Nicky! I must tell you of a terrible cruel new blow! I have just received a letter from Misha, in which he informs me of his marriage! I simply can't believe it and can hardly understand what I am writing, it's so unspeakably awful in every way and has completely killed me! I only ask that it should remain a secret, so there shouldn't be another scandal, there have been other marriages in secret, which everyone pretended not to know about.

I think it's really the only thing that can be done now, otherwise I won't be able to show myself any more, it's such a shame and disgrace! May God forgive him, I can only pity him. But my God! What a sorrow and how hard it is to bear such blows! Thank God, dear Xenia is with me, she is supporting me, it's a great comfort to talk to her. But now I must end, I'm not in a state to write about it any more, it's too painful.[35]

Nicholas, who had received Michael's letter while *en route* from Spala to his home at Tsarskoe Selo, replied at once, his shock having turned to anger that Michael should not only have 'broken his word' but that his excuse was that little Alexis might die. Anna Vyrubova was called into the Tsar's study and found him still clutching Michael's letter and in a state of great agitation, repeating again and again, 'He broke his word – his word of honour'.[36]

My dear sweet Mama . . . I was also going to write to you about this new sorrow, which has befallen our family, but you had already the appalling news. I enclose the letter I received in the train on the way here. Read it and see for yourself, can he really, after everything he has written, remain in the service and in command of your cavalry? . . . Alas, everything is over between him and me now, because he has broken his word. How many times did he tell me, without my asking, he himself gave his word that he would not marry her. And I believed him implicitly![37]

In an age when a 'word of honour' was thought sacrosanct, this was a grave indictment of Michael; repeated by Nicholas it would win him additional sympathy and increase the sense of outrage within the family. Nicholas, by his own account, was a trusting brother who had been grievously deceived and he did not spoil the effect by mentioning that for the past years the Okhrana on his orders had been spying on Michael and trailing him abroad. Some trust, some honour.

Nicholas, with better cause, now condemned Michael for his unwise excuse that it had been news of Alexis which had pushed him into marrying Natasha. He told his mother:

What upsets me particularly – is that he refers to Alexis's illness as having forced him into this rash step! He doesn't seem concerned about your distress, or our distress, or the scandal this event will cause in Russia . . . It's shameful and awful! My first thought was also to keep the news quiet, but on reading his letter two or three times I realised that it's impossible for him to return to Russia now. Sooner or later everyone here will find out and will be surprised if nothing has happened to him, as the others were dealt with very severely.[38]

Despite his reference to Alexis, Nicholas knew perfectly well that his son's illness was irrelevant to the issue, for he ended his letter by revealing that

Frederiks had learned that some two months earlier Michael had ordered the transfer abroad of a large sum of money 'and apparently he even bought an estate in France'. That was evidence enough that Michael had planned his marriage well in advance and not simply because of the crisis over Alexis. In reporting that to his mother, Nicholas ended by declaring, 'Now all is clear'.[39]

Michael had indeed transferred very substantial sums abroad before departing from Russia in early September, but the 'estate in France' was merely his excuse for doing so. The money, transferred to an account at the Crédit Lyonnais on the Boulevard des Italiens in Paris[40] was not for the purchase of an estate but simply to ensure that he had sufficient money to maintain himself abroad for some months ahead.

Any idea of keeping the marriage secret swiftly faded. 'By now everybody knows of the marriage', Nicholas told his mother in his next letter. 'In Moscow it is the same; probably the news came from her relations!'[41]

Within the imperial court the view was that Michael had been hypnotised by a 'malicious vamp'. Baron Frederiks now submitted to the Tsar a memorandum setting out the proposed response to Michael; its harshness must suggest Alexandra's hand in its drafting and her approval of it before it went to Nicholas. For one of the proposals – that Grand Duchess Olga, Alexandra's eldest daughter, should replace Michael as co-Regent with her mother – goes far beyond anything that Frederiks himself would have felt able to put forward; indeed, it is impossible to think of anyone other than Alexandra who would have thought of it. There were ten points in all, some more vindictive than others.

1. *For the present – no letters, nothing at all, complete silence, complete 'non-recognition' of the marriage; to regard his letters announcing his marriage as written by somebody who is utterly unconscious of what he is doing under the hypnotic influence of a malicious vamp – in short, to regard these letters as written exclusively by her and not by him, which in fact is the case; and her letters are not to be answered and the marriage performed without the Sovereign's consent is not to be recognized as a lawful one;*
2. *To announce that he is to return to Russia immediately and alone . . . and that his estate is to be put under trusteeship;*
3. *To ban her from Russia forever . . . as somebody who has demonstrated criminal disregard for the Head of State and publicly injured the dignity and status of a member of the Imperial House;*
4. *All associates are to be exiled or, at least, deprived of their official status;*
5. *If he refuses to come without her, to give him, privately, a leave of absence for another 11 months with a warning that . . . if there is no voluntary*

divorce within those 11 months, very severe and irrevocable measures will be taken;

6. *If he comes alone and promises to divorce her, even if not immediately, to promote him to a General, giving him individual assignments or a brigade – there is no question of his remaining in the regiment;*
7. *Until he promises a divorce, he is not to be received by the Sovereign, who will thus show him his disfavour – not as his brother, but as his Emperor – and who will be thus spared unpleasant conversations;*
8. *Should the divorce take place, the son is to be given a title as somebody who is entirely innocent and in whom there is his blood. She is certainly not to be given a title, for she has already been given a surname. He is to be forgiven everything on account of his unconscious state and due to the fact that no steps were taken in time;*
9. *As the marriage, due to her and her associates, has taken place and, on her insistence, has become common knowledge – for the purpose of sowing discord and discrediting him in the eyes of loyal people and elevating him in the eyes of ill-intentioned ones – and in case he does not agree to a prompt and voluntary divorce and bearing in mind the time in which we are living, there should be prepared a manifesto naming Grand Duchess Olga Nikolaevna Regent, with Empress Alexandra Fedorovna named as guardian.*

   However this manifesto should not be made public for at least a year, although made known to all members of the Imperial Family, who are to be asked to leave on it their signatures as tokens of their being notified of the Emperor's will; the idea of an 11-month leave of absence is also appealing because this period will cover the jubilee celebrations, on which she pins her hopes, believing that they will be forgiven;*
10. *The guardianship, particularly over the estates, should be established as soon as possible . . . for she, as I foresee, will try or is trying already to turn everything upside down . . . There have recently been so many categoric orders coming from him – through her and over my head – conducive to nothing but total disorganisation . . .*[42]

With this on the table, Nicholas drew up a document containing the text of Michael's renunciation of his rights to the throne and despatched 'the good Mordvinov'[43] to Cannes, with instructions that he was to present the paper to Michael with an ultimatum: 'he must either sign it, or divorce her'.[44]

Hating Natasha as he did, Mordvinov had been as condemning as anyone else at Tsarskoe Selo. But when he arrived at the Hotel du Parc, Michael found him 'difficult to understand, for he was nervous'. Nevertheless, the

* 1913 was the tercentenary of the Romanovs as Tsars of Russia.

essential message was clear enough: get rid of Natasha, or else. Given that, there was little point in further discussion. 'I can certainly not agree to a divorce and a return to Russia without my family,' Michael responded in a letter to his brother. He apologised 'if certain phrases in my letter caused you distress' – a reference to Alexis – but at the same time he refused to sign the paper renouncing his rights for 'I must first clarify certain conditions about my future life'.[45] He also insisted in his sealed letter that Mordvinov should not be sent to him again; he was 'no longer on good terms' with his former aide. Mordvinov left the Hotel du Parc with the letter and a paper listing Michael's terms but with nothing else.

The terms were four in number. First, that he should be allowed to return to Russia with his family, to live in the country and promising 'to play no political part whatsoever'. Second, that he should retain control over his 'personal fortune and property, which I have never squandered and never will'. Third, that Natasha should be given the title of countess and little George that of count. Fourth, that he retained his title, 'which belongs to me by right of birth' – Mordvinov having told him that Baron Frederiks had threatened 'to divest me of my title'. Finally, he asked what was to happen to the *Zarnitsa*, his imperial yacht.[46]

Tsarskoe Selo was not in a bargaining mood. Encouraged by a loose-tongued Mordvinov, whose hatred of Natasha now knew no bounds, Michael's letter was ignored. Ready to believe anything that the embittered Mordvinov chose to invent, Nicholas told his mother:

> *Poor Misha is evidently not responsible for his own actions at the moment, he thinks and reasons as she tells him and it's utterly useless to argue with him. Mordvinov has very much asked us* NOT TO WRITE *to him* AT ALL, *as she not only reads any telegrams, letters and notes, but takes copies which she shows to her people and then keeps them in the bank together with the money.* She's such a cunning, wicked beast that it's disgusting even to talk about her.*[47]

Nevertheless he did talk about her, as did everyone else. All Europe was agog and at Sandringham Michael's cousin George, now George V of England, was as distressed as anyone else, writing to Nicholas to say so. Expressing his sorrow at the problems of little Alexis, the king added that 'I have also felt for you so much on account of dear Misha. I am so fond of him that I am in despair that he should have done this foolish thing & I know how miserable you must be about it. What a lot of worries & anxieties there are in this world.'[48]

* There is, in fact, no evidence supporting Mordvinov's claims in any of Natasha's files in Moscow or in her family papers in England.

In the midst of it all, Michael seemed more concerned about his mother's reaction than his brother's. Nearly a month after breaking the news of his marriage and while still waiting to hear about what Nicholas intended to do, Michael wrote again to the Dowager Empress:

> *My dear Mama, I await stern punishment for my act, which was dictated to me solely by my conscience. I am ready to bear all the punishments and deprivations. I do not fear them, the only thing which is very painful is the distress, which I have unintentionally caused you. Dear Mama, surely I have only acted as befits any honourable man – in that my conscience is clear. With all my heart I beg you not to judge me harshly, but to give me your blessing, as a mother whom I love deeply. May the Lord keep you, my dear Mama. I embrace you warmly. I love you with all my heart, Misha.*[49]

Michael would not have to wait long to find out what Nicholas had decided to do about him. With the memorandum on his desk and Alexandra at his elbow, he would go further than even Michael feared, not only banishing him but freezing all his assets remaining in Russia and most astonishingly making him personally subject to guardianship, a measure normally reserved for minors or madmen. On December 15 the Tsar issued at Tsarskoe Selo an imperial ukase to the Ruling Senate. It read:

> *Deeming it expedient to establish a guardianship over the person, estate and affairs of the Grand Duke Michael Aleksandrovich, we have considered it advisable to take upon ourselves the chief control of the guardianship and to entrust to the Central Administration of the Imperial Domains the direct control of all estate, personal and real and also funds possessed by the Grand Duke Michael Aleksandrovich.*[50]

Two weeks later, on December 30, he issued an imperial manifesto removing Michael from the regency:

> *By our Manifesto given on the first day of August 1904, we, in the event of our decease before the attainment of his majority by our beloved son, his Imperial Highness and Heir, the Tsarevich and Grand Duke Alexis Nikolaevich, appointed our brother the Grand Duke Michael Aleksandrovich, to be Regent of the State until our son should come of age. Now, we have deemed it advisable to divest his Imperial Highness, the Grand Duke Michael Aleksandrovich of the obligations laid upon him by our Manifesto of August 1, 1904.*[51]

Both the ukase and the manifesto were published for the world to see in the *Official Messenger* No. 2 of January 3, 1913. Two days earlier the same official gazette had announced that 'the Grand Duke Michael Aleksandrovich, Colonel and Commandant of the Chevalier Gardes Regiment of the Empress Marie Fedorovna has been granted eleven months' leave and is relieved of his command'.[52] This series of official statements caused a considerable stir, among the diplomatic world as well as society at large. Sir George Buchanan, the British ambassador, telegraphed the news at once to the British foreign minister Sir Edward Grey, adding that 'in the event of no one being specially appointed to act as Regent in place of the Grand Duke Michael the Regency would, as I am informed, devolve by law on the Empress'.[53]

Even hardened members of St Petersburg society were astonished at the severity of the punishment which, as one observer put it, was 'as unfortunate as it was unwarrantable'.[54] And because Alexandra was judged to be behind this humiliation, sympathy in some quarters swung to Michael rather than to Nicholas. Given the choice between condemning Michael and condemning Alexandra, society was tempted to forgive him in order to denigrate her. At the same time, few could think of anything which would be to the credit of Natasha. He was foolish; she was unspeakable. Yet there was also one point which the ultra-cynical held in her favour: no one who was hated by Alexandra could be all bad.

ELEVEN

Exile in Europe

Troubled as he was by his rift with his family, Michael was not so disturbed that he regretted what he had done. Nevertheless, he did try to explain himself to Nicholas, while accepting that he had broken his word not to marry. 'I really did promise not to do it,' he admitted to his brother in a later letter from Cannes. 'I said it sincerely and in good faith . . . but our last year in St Petersburg convinced me of the contrary.' Marriage was the only solution 'to the painful position we were in'. There was no going back. Whatever his brother might hope, Michael insisted that 'it must remain a lawful marriage before God and people. To be married in church and then divorce immediately would be an act of blasphemy.'[1]

As he saw it, he had been put in a position in which he had no choice but to act as he did. As Natasha would say later, she did not expect to be received by the imperial family; she simply wanted to be allowed to live in peace and dignity. That never happened and so there was never hope of a compromise which would have cost both sides something, but perhaps Russia nothing. Kings and princes have had mistresses throughout history; not all have been unhappy arrangements.

'Uncle Bertie' provided a good example of that. His mistresses, first Lillie Langtry, then Mrs Alice Keppel* were accepted by society and enjoyed considerable status because of, not despite, the fact that they were royal mistresses. To be sure, neither were divorcées and that was an extra difficulty in the case of Natasha; even so, a generation later, British society did not turn on the American Mrs Wallis Simpson because she was a divorcée, but because King Edward VIII was resolved to marry her and make her Queen.

Michael was never that naïve. He did not make it a condition that Natasha should take his rank, but only that he should not be required to give her up and that she would be treated with that respect, at least in private, which he would expect to be accorded to her, as the woman he loved and the mother of the son he acknowledged. That respect was denied to her and therefore to him. St Petersburg society took its lead from the imperial

* Mrs Keppel was the great-grandmother of Camilla Parker Bowles, a close friend of Charles, Prince of Wales.

family; had they been more sympathetic, society would have understood and the gossip would have lost its edge.

In Michael's letters on his marriage he emphasised that Natasha had not attempted to influence him and asked for nothing, willing to remain no more than his 'unmarried wife'. Cynics remarked that in asking for nothing she merely demonstrated how clever she was. One biting comment was that 'she played her cards exceedingly well and not only refrained from mentioning that alarming and obnoxious word "marriage" to the Grand Duke, but made him feel, on the contrary, that for love of him she was sacrificing all that a woman holds dear, without asking anything of him in return ... she never complained, never suggested to him what he ought to do, but played on his affections and on his feeling of chivalry'.[2]

It was a superficial judgement, but it was how society and the imperial family saw matters. The truth was that had society tolerated Natasha, there would have been no marriage. Michael knew his duty, though never to the extent of taking a wife for form's sake and he had indeed given his word that he would not break the law. It can be argued therefore that in forcing him into an action he would have avoided, given the chance, other members of his immediate family bore some blame.

Yet Michael was never a reluctant husband. Married or not, he had thought of Natasha as his wife. Now that he was no longer living a lie and obliged to hide her away, he appeared in a relaxed mood. Banishment was a punishment but it was also liberty. And not everyone shared the view that he was a pariah. The Hotel du Parc attracted a steady stream of friends. There were picnics, dinners, parties and a holiday atmosphere. An unashamed practical joker, and to the delight of nine-year-old Tata, he 'filled various unfortunate people's beds with hair brushes and damp sponges, sewed up pyjama legs and filled them with confetti, filled certain domestic utensils with fizzy powders, set alarm clocks to ring at some ungodly hour of the morning and generally produced turmoil'.[3]

Among Michael's victims was Chaliapin, then singing in Monte Carlo. Tata's English governess Miss Rata, convalescing after typhoid, returned to the fold wearing a wig to conceal a head shaved in hospital. During coffee one morning, while Chaliapin was holding forth at some length, Michael signalled to Miss Rata to take off her wig, which she did, hiding it under a cushion. When the expansive basso turned and saw the bald governess, he was so startled that he froze to the spot, unable to speak. The rest of the room burst into roars of laughter.[4]

Baldness was not usually a joking matter for Michael. He hated the fact that his own hair was thinning. At Brasovo he had shaved his head in the hope of stimulating growth and at Cannes he was always on the lookout for fresh remedies and willing to try out every new 'miracle cure'.[5]

He had complained about his receding hairline in one of his first letters to Natasha, three years earlier, when he had reminded her about her first serious admirer, Dimitri Abrikosov, the good-looking but shy law student who had once dreamed of marrying her. She had mentioned him while telling Michael about her early life in Moscow, but it was enough to worry him. 'Here is a foolish question for you!' he wrote. 'Are you sorry that I am not as handsome as Dimitri Abrikosov? Probably so . . . it's stupid for a man to talk about such things, but honestly I am really bothered by the fact that I am losing my hair. I've always hated baldness and I also think my face is looking older. When I am with you my face seems younger and my eyes look brighter somehow and now they seem half-alive, dull – disgusting to look at!'[6]

Natasha did not care a fig about his receding hairline, but Michael never ceased to worry about it. He also mocked himself, posing one day for a photograph in which he wore a black wig while holding up a bottle of the magic elixir which had supposedly brought about the extraordinary transformation.[7]

His obsession with his hairline was obvious to everyone around him and to Tata's annoyance it would provide advantage in later years to her then sworn enemy, a new English governess, Miss Neame, Tata claimed 'got into the good graces of Uncle Misha by professing to know a cure for incipient baldness . . . he had always said he would give a fortune to anybody who made his hair grow again. So Miss Neame suddenly developed a knowledge of scalp massage and succeeded in rubbing off the remaining hair that Uncle Misha had. This she explained away by saying that the old had to make way for the new. The whole of the household was in fits of laughter over these massage sessions; it seems a shame to laugh over Uncle Misha's hair, but all men have their weaknesses and this was the one vanity of an otherwise remarkably modest man.'[8]

Michael was also modest in many of his habits, but as Tata observed, 'one cannot say that he would have been happy without money, for he had been born to riches and not to consider his income,' but that said, 'his personal tastes were far less extravagant than my mother's'.[9] In the management of her household Natasha was as prudent as her bourgeois upbringing had taught her to be; but in the dress shops of Cannes, as in those of Paris, Vienna, Berlin and later London, Natasha was treated as a grand duchess and she ran up bills to match. Few beautiful women in her position would, perhaps, have done otherwise.

Natasha possessed exceptional taste, reflected in the way she decorated and furnished her homes and her own fashion sense. She favoured white or cream in the summer months, as indeed did most women of a period which many would come to regard as the last age of elegance, so shortly to be swept away for ever. She particularly loved broderie anglaise, the finest Swiss lawn and slim-fitting gowns which showed off her slender figure.

Of all the cities she visited, Paris provided the best opportunity for a spending spree. Michael and Natasha stayed in a suite at the fashionable Hotel Mirabeau at 8 rue de la Paix, a short stroll from the Opéra and at the very heart of haute-couture, high-temptation Paris. Michael made no complaint; on the contrary, he encouraged her, taking pleasure from her pleasure. Money was not his immediate problem.

His presents to Natasha usually took the form of jewellery, of magnificent diamonds and precious stones, of perfect ropes of pearls and superb sables and over time her collection would be worth a fortune. For her first birthday after their marriage, he added one surprise which in itself said much about his attitude towards his bank account. He bought her a Rolls-Royce.[10]

In any case, set against his other expenses, Natasha's dress account was relatively inconsequential when compared with the costs of the floor rented at the Hotel du Parc and the wages paid to his entourage. There were personal maids to house and feed, as well as a governess, nanny, valet, chauffeur and a new private secretary in substitute for the defector Mordvinov.

The new secretary, hired in December 1912, was Nicholas Johnson, who despite his name was a Russian. Johnson was a shortish, round-faced young man who spoke three languages, though his heavily-accented English[11] would never be as good as Michael's, who spoke it as well as any Englishman. He was also a more than competent pianist, his mother having been a court music teacher, and his keyboard talent was one reason why Michael and Johnson got on so well. Michael shared his musical interests, taking lessons and playing the guitar, the balalaika and the flute, as well as the piano. In the evenings he would often sit down with Johnson and play duets, including one piece, a plaintive air, which Michael composed himself.[12]

For someone who could afford to buy whatever he wanted his interests were not judged extravagant. Apart from motor cars and photography, his hobby was collecting watches, though his attempts to take them apart and then reassemble them were often disastrous.[13]

He was not a gambler and had never been a womaniser; he smoked the occasional cigar and sometimes a pipe; he preferred barley water to alcohol but would drink champagne on social occasions. His tastes in food were simple: fish, chicken, porridge and beetroot, but included a passion for strawberries. He never ate cheese, lobster or mushrooms and would not touch red meat.[14] Forgetting that he had a gastric ulcer, Tata thought his likes and dislikes in food were dictated by his great belief in physical fitness. 'He always insisted that I rode and took exercise ... for himself he had physical training instructors always in attendance and was constantly going out for long walks or sharp sprints.'[15]

Natasha was much the more sociable of the two and more inclined to accept invitations to parties and to entertain in style. Because of the inevitable notoriety which attended their runaway marriage and the attention which they attracted when they went out in public, Michael preferred to go to private homes rather than to public places. He had, in any event, what Tata would call 'a retiring nature',[16] but there was one incident which shortly served to remind both him and Natasha that marriage had not removed them as subjects for either gossip or irritating scrutiny.

In February 1913, dining in an exclusive restaurant in Monte Carlo, they found themselves being stared at continually by an aristocratic Englishwoman seated at a nearby table; as one course followed another, the same woman sat there gazing at them through her lorgnette, until an irate Natasha raised a spoon to her eye in imitation and stared back. Only then did the woman turn away.[17] It was an annoying reminder that they had not left behind the clucking tongues and biting gossip which had made life such a misery in St Petersburg.

Because of such public attention, Michael preferred the company of old friends and discouraged the acquaintanceship of others. There were, of course, many in rich and flamboyant Cannes who were only too eager to be on social terms with Grand Duke Michael Aleksandrovich and who cared nothing for the supposed disgrace of his marriage, but they were largely disappointed. Michael and Natasha preferred to live their own lives.

To Michael his family was all important and in that family he treated Tata as if she was as much his child as George. When a group of Russians, 'in the hope of favours to come', turned up at the Hotel du Parc and presented little George with an array of beautiful presents, but gave Tata only a small box of chocolates, Michael on their departure went out and bought her a fountain pen 'which I had long desired'.[18]

Whenever it was George's birthday 'there was always a less important present for me from Uncle Misha, so that I should not feel out of it'. When it was Tata's birthday and she was made to feel 'queen of the party', Michael ensured that George, likewise, was not forgotten, with a small present of his own in consolation.[19] He was, as she would say, 'truly a good man'.[20]

The photographs which Michael and Natasha took over that winter in Cannes could be of any family on a seaside holiday, paddling in the water, making sandcastles for the children on the beach, or with Natasha posing prettily on a fisherman's boat, or picking up her skirt at the water's edge to expose her long, shapely legs. There are dozens of such pictures of Michael and Natasha and the two children, neatly pasted into his photo albums, as a memento of a time which was precious. The album for Cannes also shows Michael and Natasha playing tennis, out riding in the country, watching a polo match and of Michael dressed up as a clown at a Christmas party.[21]

The real-life picture was not, of course, as tranquil as the camera would make it seem. In January 1913, after reading in the newspapers the reports of Nicholas's action against him, Michael was so outraged that he could not bring himself to write to his brother even in protest. When he did do so, a month later, he explained that 'it took me some time to get over the guardianship decision, which you had announced for all the world to know. I will never believe that it was your own idea and it is painful to know that you listened to those people who wished to discredit me in public opinion.' Knowing what was being said, he added: 'It has already done a lot of harm.'

His main point in writing, however, was to protest about his uncle Grand Duke Paul. 'I have received a very harsh letter from him, in which he orders me to present myself to him in Paris. Not having had any message from you, I refused to go, for I consider such tone and manner on his part insulting.'[22] It was also inappropriate, given that Paul himself had been banished to Paris years earlier for running off and marrying a divorcée. Paul had nothing to teach Michael.

However, his rift with his estranged family could not be shrugged off and despite the cheerful face which he presented, he remained privately distressed. His once devoted sister Olga would not speak to him and she would never see or speak to Natasha again, or even admit that they had once been friends. The loss of Olga's love and friendship was for Michael perhaps the bitterest price of all.

Yet Michael was not entirely ostracised by his imperial relatives. The first to visit him in Cannes was his cousin Grand Duke Andrew,[23] whose ready sympathy owed much to the fact of his own long-standing relationship with Kschessinska. Andrew had no intention of marrying his mistress, but he understood perfectly why Michael had felt he must. Society had never ostracised and insulted Kschessinska as it had Natasha. Andrew had everything to lose and nothing to gain by marrying Kschessinska; Michael lost everything by marrying Natasha, but reckoned that he had gained more.

In the spring of 1913 there were also some attempts within Michael's immediate family to heal wounds. Unlike Olga, Michael's other sister Xenia wanted a reconciliation. Now thirty-seven and the mother of seven children, Xenia had suffered heartbreak in her own marriage to Sandro: he had secretly taken a pretty American girl as his mistress and two years earlier, at Biarritz, had planned to elope with her to Australia, giving up his position and buying a farm near Sydney.[24]

It came to nothing, but Sandro compounded his folly by confessing it all to Xenia; she retaliated by taking her own lover, a married man whom she identified in her private diaries only as 'Prince F'.[25] One consequence was that Xenia's own sad experiences made her less condemning of Michael than she might have been otherwise.

The day after saying goodbye in Cannes to his cousin Andrew, Michael and Natasha were in Paris, staying again at the Hotel Mirabeau. From there, on March 4, Michael telegraphed to Xenia in St Petersburg telling her that she should come to Paris next week 'if you want to see me'.[26] Xenia could not travel that quickly but she arranged to be in Paris two weeks later, going to see Nicholas before her departure to hear what he might want her to say. 'We talked a lot about Misha,' she noted in her diary. 'Nicky has said and repeated to me, that he can come to Russia whenever he wants – but she is forbidden.'[27]

Perhaps Xenia in Paris could rescue Michael. Determined to try, she met her brother there on March 19 and afterwards recorded what happened in her diary:

> *Now that I have told him everything and got it all off my chest after three months, I feel somewhat better. He sat with me for two hours and we talked the whole time. As I told him about Mama, the terrible winter and her health and state of mind, I was unable to hold back my tears – nor was he. We cried on each other's shoulders. Poor Mishkin, he is suffering so much . . . I told him about Alexis's illness and about Nicky; here he was more attentive and occasionally made a remark or asked a question. He says that he was unable to do otherwise, that he suffers for Mama and regrets having to break his word to Nicky, but that he was obliged to act in this way. Of course, there were many things I didn't touch on, there was no time . . .*[28]

Xenia stayed in Paris for a further three days, seeing Michael again just before she left to go on to England, to join 'Prince F'. As she wrote afterwards: 'It was so sad saying goodbye to Misha, when will we meet again? He was so sweet and touching and kept thanking me the whole time for coming, my poor little boy! It's hurtful and sad that he has slipped away from us again.'[29]

There would, however, be more attempts over the next few months to arrive at some reconciliation. And in the course of that, Natasha for the first time would come face to face with the formidable Dowager Empress.

At the beginning of the summer of 1913 Michael and Natasha packed up their winter quarters at Cannes and set off with their entourage for Chexbres, where four years earlier Natasha had spent the summer and from where she had successfully travelled in secret to Copenhagen. This time they moved into the secluded Hotel du Signal, a popular family hotel which enjoyed a spectacular setting, in fifty acres of private hilltop grounds overlooking the glistening sunlit waters of Lake Geneva.* Tata would say of her return to Chexbres that 'I have never enjoyed myself so much. The hotel was very simple and not full of smart people and there were at least thirty children of different nationalities . . . the official language was French . . . we had a grand time.' When not playing Cowboys and Indians, games in which the boys were always cowboys and the girls were always Indians, Tata sometimes went off for drives with her mother and Uncle Misha: 'the great treat was to go to Montreux to the roller-skating rink'.[30]

The arrival of Grand Duke Michael and Natasha at the Hotel du Signal would be long remembered in the village itself, for even some eighty years later there would still be people there who could recall hearing 'that the Grand Duke used to book two floors and had amongst the first cars anyone had ever seen'.[31] One other reason why they were remembered was that while most hotel guests could only afford one or two weeks, Michael and Natasha settled down for two months. They arrived on May 22 and the hotel was their base until the end of July.[32]

On Natasha's birthday, June 27, Michael sent her a greetings telegram from the village post office: 'My dearest Natashechka, From all my heart I congratulate you and from the depth of my soul wish you the best of health and happiness for a thousand years. I regret that there are very few suitable articles as presents here, but to them is added a Rolls Royce which will be awaiting its mistress in Paris. Kissing you very tenderly. Your Misha.'[33]

Michael had bought a six-seater Rolls-Royce Silver Ghost in August 1911, registered by the makers as No. 1682, which had been delivered to him in Bad Kissingen. There is no record of how much it cost, but the next Rolls to go out was to the Maharajah of Mysore, who paid £1367 for his.[34] Now Michael ordered a five-seater Colonial type, registered as No. 2429, with a four-speed gearbox, which was despatched on July 9 to a garage on the rue Mesnil to await collection by Natasha in September, by which time they planned to be in Paris.[35]

When he gave his instructions to Rolls-Royce, Michael had not expected to be in London, but circumstances changed just as the car was being despatched to Paris. On June 10, Sandro's eldest brother Nicholas had arrived at Xenia's Paris hotel 'bringing a confidential letter from Misha complaining about us all, that we don't write, that we don't care about him, don't do anything that he asks etc.; I was completely destroyed for the whole day, the whole thing is untrue!'[36] A week later Xenia noted the receipt of another long letter from Michael: 'he's still complaining about everyone'. She also noted that the Dowager Empress, then in London, had telegraphed 'hoping that he might come to England. But how to arrange

* A samovar, left behind by Michael, is still preserved at the hotel.

it? I wrote and telegraphed him about it.'[37] A week later, Xenia, now in England with her mother, was recording that 'I sat with Mama talking about Misha, she was crying. She so wants to see him! Sandro sent him a telegram saying that he must come.'[38]

Michael did come, but with Natasha. On July 11, Xenia travelled up to London with the Dowager Empress from Sandringham; she was met at Liverpool Street Station by 'Prince F', who 'said that he had seen Misha – with her – and that he looked rather embarrassed for her!'[39]

Michael and Natasha were staying at the Ritz Hotel in Piccadilly and the Dowager Empress was at Marlborough House, then the London residence of her sister, now the Dowager Queen Alexandra. Marlborough House is only a few minutes' walking distance from the Ritz. Michael walked there for the first meeting, leaving Natasha behind. As Xenia recorded it, the Dowager Empress had been 'very agitated at the prospect of seeing him' and was 'completely unable to sleep – she was so excited and upset'. At last he arrived 'and they disappeared into the next room for a minute, but returned looking quite calm! Thank God it went all right. I was so anxious for Mama . . .'[40]

That evening Michael came back again, this time with Natasha, and he and his mother 'had a good quiet talk, thank God and he was happy to be able to speak'.[41] Then it was Natasha's turn to face the Dowager Empress Marie Fedorovna and let her speak her mind. Natasha was a proud-spirited woman, but it was not the occasion for answering back. There could be no hope of a 'good quiet talk' now and there was nothing that a nervous Natasha could do but to keep her head up and allow the anger to wash over her. As Xenia reported the meeting to her diary, the Dowager Empress 'saw his wife and told her a few home truths in front of Misha, which she also repeated to me in front of him. She is so sad and upset. In general it's terribly *penible* [unpleasant] on all sides.'[42]

The Dowager Empress gave her account of the meeting with Michael in a letter to Nicholas, written when she returned to Sandringham:

> *Although our first meeting was rather disturbing and we both were rather shy at first, which, after all, was only too natural, I was happy to see that he has remained the same; just as nice and good and even kinder than ever. We talked everything over quite frankly and all was said so nicely and quietly without a bitter word, that for the first time after all those dreadful worries my heart felt relieved and so, I think, did his . . .*[43]

She made no mention at all of her confrontation with Natasha, for it had served little purpose other than to allow her the satisfaction of tongue-lashing the woman who had caused her such heartbreak.

TWELVE

Mistress of Knebworth

The unexpected trip to London to meet the Dowager Empress had one positive consequence for Michael and Natasha: it made up their minds about where they should live in the immediate future. They could have chosen almost anywhere in Europe, in particular the places which they so enjoyed on holiday and to which they returned again and again. Instead they chose England, a decision which was made more by Michael than by Natasha.

Michael knew Britain well enough and felt at home there. His first cousin was its king, his aunt its Dowager Queen. London was familiar and he spoke English perfectly. And there was good reason for seeing it as a place where he and Natasha might live more easily than elsewhere, for his namesake cousin Grand Duke Michael Mikhailovich – known to his friends as Miche-Miche – and his morganatic wife Countess Torby appeared to have settled down well since their banishment from Russia many years earlier. Totally accepted by British society, Grand Duke Michael Mikhailovich and Countess Torby were living proof that there was life after St Petersburg.

Miche-Miche, now fifty-two years of age, was the grandson of Tsar Nicholas I and as an elder brother of Sandro he was a brother-in-law of Michael's sister Xenia. Thus, while seventeen years older than Michael, there was a close family connection. The two Michaels also had in their wives another point in common, for the marriage of the elder Grand Duke had caused almost as much uproar as had Michael's.

Miche-Miche had been involved in a number of romantic affairs in Russia, but since they always involved commoners, he was barred from marrying any of them. In 1888 he had been sent abroad by Michael's father, after asking Alexander III for permission to marry Countess Ekaterina Ignateva. So when he next fell in love, with Sophia, the granddaughter of the famous Russian poet Aleksandr Pushkin, he decided to marry her without troubling to ask permission, which he knew from experience would have been denied anyway. He and Sophia married at San Remo in 1891, with somewhat tragic results: when his mother, Grand Duchess Olga, received his telegram announcing his marriage she collapsed with a heart attack and died.[1]

Alexander III promptly banished Miche-Miche and stripped him of his military rank. Like Michael and Natasha, Miche-Miche and Sophia started off their married life at Cannes and then moved to London. Sophia was given the title of Countess Torby by a relative, the Grand Duke of Luxembourg,[2] and the couple settled down happily in British society, eventually in 1909 taking a long lease on Kenwood, a magnificent house owned by the Earl of Mansfield, overlooking London's Hampstead Heath.[3] Miche-Miche, pushed by his wife, was eager to acquire for her a more solid title than Countess, particularly since it was granted by Luxembourg, a country which few people could, with confidence, have found on a map. A few years earlier, King Edward VII had complained about her sitting on the duchesses' bench at a palace ball and Countess Torby had smarted about that ever since.

In 1912, just before Michael's runaway marriage, Miche-Miche's ambitions for his wife had prompted a sour letter from King George V to Nicholas about 'that good fool of a Michel, who I am sure bores you with many grievances as he does me'. Nicholas had written to George to tell him that Miche-Miche had asked his permission for his wife to accept a British title and that he had given his consent, subject of course to George's agreement. In his reply George pointed out, 'I have not the power to grant a title in England to a foreign subject and still more impossible in the case of a Russian Grand Duke'. Gloomily accepting that Miche-Miche would be turning up to make a formal request for his wife's title, George added that 'I do not look forward to our interview with any pleasure, as I fear I have no alternative but to refuse his request'.[4]

It was a bitter blow for Countess Torby. However, there was nothing to be done about the decision by George V, save to go on behaving as if she were a grand duchess anyway and by ensuring that her name appeared as often as possible in the Court Circular, published daily in *The Times* and the *Morning Post*. In doing so, with conspicuous success, Countess Torby did not welcome the news that another and more senior Grand Duke Michael was arriving in England, with a wife who provided an uncomfortable reminder of the scandal which had once attached to her own name.

Countess Torby was not going to open any doors for Natasha.

Because they wanted to be back in Chexbres before George's third birthday on July 24, Michael and Natasha had little time to find a suitable house in England, but they made initial enquiries, decided on their requirements and Nicholas Johnson stayed behind to handle the details. In August they left Chexbres for a nostalgic holiday in Bad Kissingen and in September they moved on to Paris, staying on this occasion not at the Mirabeau but at the luxurious Hotel Astoria, which stood then on the Champs-Elysées, just below the Arc de Triomphe on the corner of the rue de Presbourg.[5]

Natasha's new birthday Rolls-Royce was waiting for her and they set off for a celebration drive, with Michael at the wheel. Delighted though she was at having her own Rolls-Royce, like almost all women of her time, Natasha did not know how to drive, nor had any great ambition to do so. Sitting in the passenger seat, her greater pleasure came when Michael drove the Rolls into the rue de la Paix and she could get out and go shopping.

Sometimes she shopped on her own, for the prospect of facing yet another dress designer can weary even the most devoted husband and it was on one of those mornings that Michael went off and like any tourist climbed to the top of the Eiffel Tower. From there he sent a souvenir postcard to Natasha at the Astoria, scribbling on it the message: '*Gatchina is almost visible from this height. Kissing you tenderly, Your Misha*'.[6]

Those few words said much about Michael. Cheerful by nature and passionately in love, he was, deep down, homesick for the place which would always mean more to him than anywhere else and which he knew he might never see again.

Home now was Knebworth House, some twenty miles north of London, near Stevenage in Hertfordshire. Owned by the Earl of Lytton, a former Viceroy of India, it was available on a one-year lease, for an annual rental of £3000; for the purposes of the lease, signed on his behalf by Johnson, Michael was described as 'at present residing at Palace Anichkov in St Petersburg'.[7] The drafting lawyers of Robinson, Williams and Burnands in Belgravia knew that His Imperial Highness Grand Duke Michael Aleksandrovich of Russia, 'hereinafter called the tenant of the other part', ought properly to be described as being 'of no fixed abode'. However that would have appeared unseemly. The palace sounded more respectable.

Built in 1531 but extensively remodelled in Victorian times, Knebworth House was and is a stately home of considerable historical and architectural stature and as Tata said when she got there: 'I was very impressed . . . It was far grander than anywhere we had lived before and I was very much in awe of the butler and the footmen, who at night wore knee-breeches and powdered hair.'[8]

The staff, including a small army of gardeners, came with the house and taken together with the splendour of the building itself Knebworth House was indeed very grand, if never as grand as the massive palace at Gatchina. However, neither Natasha nor Tata had ever lived at the palace and thus Tata was right: compared with the 'darling little house' in Moscow, the villa in Gatchina, or even the wood-built country mansion at Brasovo, Knebworth House, with its impressive oak banqueting hall, picture gallery, state drawing room, library and four-poster bedrooms, was quite magnificent.

The house was theirs from September 1, 1913* – and it would mark the beginning of what Natasha would afterwards describe as the happiest year of her life.[9] It was certainly the most tranquil.

It was at Knebworth that Natasha could, for the first and last time, play the role of mistress of a stately home and she filled the house with Russian friends, all suitably impressed by the fourteen footmen who waited upon them. Even Tata had her own footman, called James, as well as a new governess, Miss Dyer – little George inheriting Miss Rata as his nanny; she also had her own maid, Lillian, smartly attired in a green-and-white uniform.[10]

All wealthy travellers going on extended holidays in the years before 1914 took with them vast amounts of luggage. In September 1912, knowing they were leaving Russia for the foreseeable future, Michael and Natasha had taken with them even more than they would have normally and this great mound of baggage had trailed them across Europe, much of it unopened until they had somewhere to settle. At Knebworth the first days were spent unpacking possessions they had not seen since leaving Gatchina a year earlier.

They also had their dogs – Natasha's beloved mongrel Jack and Tata's pet terrier Tom. British quarantine laws were strict and could not be avoided. However, Michael's cousin King George V arranged one concession for him: the two dogs could be quarantined at Knebworth in kennels specially constructed for them, rather than being confined for six months in one of the official kennels.[11] Jack and Tom, who could not understand why they were 'behind bars', whined continually and there were constant pleas to let them out, since no one else would have known anyway. However, Michael was on his honour to keep them there and he did so, despite the pleading look in Jack's eyes and the equally desperate looks from Natasha and Tata.

Having settled in, life at Knebworth took on the routine which was to be found in any grand country house in England at that period. Michael hired a head groom, Mr S. Bennett, to look after his horses and Tata was bought a pony, conventionally named 'Beauty' which Mr Bennett taught her to ride, with Michael providing supervision.[12] It was not long before Miss Rata and Mr Bennett began walking out together, the 'downstairs' romance being indulgently encouraged by Michael and Natasha and providing amused comment at the dinner table. Ordinary things had become important again and that in itself was a kind of happiness.

There were also disappointments to be shrugged off. The Court Circular

* Dates outside Russia are hereafter given according to the Western calendar.

in *The Times*, read by everyone of consequence, had announced that Grand Duke Michael Aleksandrovich was taking possession of Knebworth and normally this would have been enough for crested invitations to fall thick and fast on their doormat. Society, however, turned a polite back on Michael and Natasha, taking its lead not only from Buckingham Palace and Marlborough House, but from Countess Torby.

Michael and Natasha could have assumed that the connections made by Miche-Miche and his wife would provide them with a ready-made social circle to which they could easily be introduced and easily adopt. They were to be disappointed. Anxious to protect her own status as morganatic wife, Countess Torby saw Natasha not only as a rival but a threat; she and Miche-Miche had worked hard to establish themselves in English society and she had no intention of compromising their position by being seen to endorse a woman twice-divorced. Countess Torby was also not best pleased by the prospect of finding that there would now be two Grand Duke Michaels in the Court Circular, for whenever their names appeared on the same day she knew from past experience that the name of Michael Aleksandrovich, as the son of a Tsar, would always be printed several paragraphs above that of Miche-Miche, the grandson of a Tsar.

Accordingly, Countess Torby did not welcome the arrival of Michael and Natasha, she hated it. The two women never met and the doors of Kenwood, Miche-Miche's mansion home in Hampstead, remained shut in Natasha's face.

That in itself sent a signal to English society, so that Natasha found herself not so much ostracised as cold-shouldered. She was not insulted, as she had been in St Petersburg and Gatchina, for that was not the English way. She was politely ignored and simply excluded from guest lists, though one reason for that was the peculiar British fear of making a mistake in addressing her. Was she 'Madame De Brassow', or 'Countess de Brassow'? No one was sure, particularly since her writing paper carried her initials NB displayed under a coronet.[13]

Even Buckingham Palace officials were confused about her name and on their three attempts in the Court Circular they changed it each time. She was the 'Comtesse de Brassow' when she stayed at the Ritz Hotel towards the end of December, 1913, 'Mme De Brasov' when she went to a luncheon some two weeks afterwards and 'Countess' in May when she came back from Cannes.[14] The maxim 'when in doubt, leave out', may explain why the Court Circular listed her so infrequently and perhaps also why there were so few invitations on the Knebworth mantelpiece.

At Christmas that year they celebrated both the English and the Russian festivals, decorating a huge Christmas tree in the hall at Knebworth[15] and inviting in the children on the estate, with presents for all; thirteen days later they had Christmas all over again, for themselves. On New Year's Day, as the English reckoned it, they organised a grand dinner for the servants, with Natasha supervising the setting of the long trestle tables at which would be seated housemaids, footmen, gardeners and stable lads.

For their own 'above stairs' staff, including Mr Bennett and Miss Rata, Michael and Natasha hosted a private party in the panelled dining room. Natasha had special menus printed for this, with the imperial arms at the top.[16]

After the dinner, all the guests – her sister Olga among them – signed the back of the menu as a souvenir. Olga was first to do so, followed by Miss Rata and Mr Bennett, with Michael adding his full name and then Natasha scrawling a Napoleonic 'N' for Nathalie followed by 'de Brassow',[17] the name which served as reminder that no one, including Buckingham Palace, really knew who she actually was.

The luncheon at which in January, 1914, the Court Circular recorded her as 'Mme De Brassow' was at the home of Sir Frederick Pollock and the guests included Walter Hines Page, the American ambassador and his wife and the Russian actress Princess Baryatinskaya, whose stage name was Lydia Yavorska.[18] The actress was playing, at the Ambassadors Theatre, the title role in an English adaptation of Tolstoy's *Anna Karenina*, a love story with some uncomfortable reminders of Natasha's own life and Michael and Natasha had gone to the opening night with the Russian chargé d'affaires and the consul-general.[19] Their Russian connections apart, Michael's other interest was a business one: he had joined with Sir Frederick Pollock in a theatrical enterprise, the New International Theatre, which had backed the play. Michael took a five per cent stake in the company,[20] though after some 'unlucky' investments it was to prove ultimately a total loss.[21]

Never the less, there were odd victories in the social battle, unmarked but none the less gratifying. Michael's cousin Grand Duke Andrew came to Britain and stayed at Knebworth,[22] as he had stayed at Cannes. And in early 1914 Michael and Natasha went off to St Moritz to join Andrew and his long-time mistress Kschessinska, though it was only Michael and Andrew who liked skiing. Natasha was content to remain looking elegant, going for sleigh rides with Kschessinska, but never actually tempting fate on the slopes, though she did ice-skate.[23] They made an interesting foursome: two Grand Dukes and two of the best-known women in Europe – both the mothers of illegitimate sons, with Kschessinska admired as the celebrated prima ballerina *assoluta*, Natasha as the most notorious woman in high society. In their own ways, each was outrageous and what made them more so was that each was clearly adored by the two proud Grand Dukes hovering around them. Society, pretending to turn away in disapproval, could only stare in wonderment.

Because of the guardianship order and the freezing of his fortune and property in Russia, Michael was now financially stretched. The cash he had transferred to Paris in 1912 was exhausted and he was dependent on the monthly allowance which his brother permitted to be sent to him – in effect, his normal allowance from the imperial fund paid to all Grand Dukes. It was 20,000 roubles, or some £2000 a month, but even so it was not enough to balance the books. Rental and the upkeep of the estate, including gardeners, maids, cooks, footmen and a butler, plus the wages of his own staff and his personal living expenses consumed more than that. He had many millions of roubles in the bank and an income from his own estate of an additional one million a year; in the two years since he had left Russia the income generated by his estates had therefore been more than £200,000.[24] Not a penny had come to him.

In March 1914 he wrote to Nicholas about it. 'Life in England is very expensive ... this month I had to pay a six-month rent for the estate in which I am living, which is why I have been left without any money.' Six-month rental in advance was the equivalent of some 14,000 roubles (£1500) and paying it in a lump sum stretched his resources. He therefore asked Nicholas to increase his monthly allowance to 30,000 roubles.[25]

His guardianship caused him difficulties in other respects. 'I have become sadly aware', he told Nicholas in another letter, 'of the unfair and discourteous treatment on the part of the staff involved and of the department in question.' It was hardly surprising, for Mordvinov – rewarded for his efforts by being made an ADC to Nicholas – had been put in charge of Michael's estates and monies, despite Michael's continued protests that he did not want 'this man anywhere near me or my affairs'.[26] He wanted him removed and he would still be insisting on that in July 1914. He was also outraged that the guardianship order itself remained in force. As he put it to Nicholas:

> *The combination of trusteeship over my estate with the guardianship over my person, without doing anything to protect my fortune, has put me in the position of an imbecile or a madman and made my situation totally unbearable. As things are, even a short visit to Russia is impossible for me, for I shall be seen as a man who has been subjected to a humiliating punishment . . .*[27]

Outwardly, however, he gave no sign of his private distress. He and Natasha went on holiday to Cannes, to the Hotel du Parc as before, and returned in time to offer 'open house' at Knebworth to the stars of the Ballets Russes, then taking London by storm.

The Ballets Russes by 1914 had conquered Paris, Berlin, Rome, Vienna and Budapest, as well as London, and in 1912 Michael and Natasha had seen the wonderful Diaghilev company in both Paris and Monte Carlo. It was in 1910 that the Paris Opéra had presented the great choreographer Michael Fokine's production of Rimsky-Korsakov's *Scheherazade* – Fokine also arranged the dances for *Firebird* which Diaghilev commissioned from Stravinsky. Paris had never seen anything like it. Fokine created *Le Spectre de la rose* for Tamara Karsavina and Nijinsky, which was premièred in Monte Carlo in 1911, the same year Karsavina premièred *Petrouchka* in Paris.[28]

The Ballets Russes had their first season at Covent Garden in 1911 and achieved the same sensation as in Paris. The following year Diaghilev returned with Nijinsky, his lover.[29] In St Petersburg, Nijinsky had been with the Imperial Ballet Company at the Maryinski until, legend had it, he offended the Dowager Empress by appearing on stage in too-tight tights instead of more modest knickerbockers. Following a message of imperial disapproval Nijinsky was dismissed.[30]

In the summer of 1914 the Ballets Russes were back in London and Natasha invited the dancers *en bloc* to Knebworth, together with the stars of the Russian opera who were also appearing as part of Sir Joseph Beecham's 'Russian season' at Drury Lane.* Natasha's old friend Chaliapin, who had been their guest in Cannes, was among them.[31] Another guest was the celebrated Russian sculptor and stage designer Sudeikin, who 'paid for his supper' by creating a bust of Michael, George and Tata. Tata remembered 'fidgeting badly' when sitting for Sudeikin, 'though I must say he was a sport and did not complain'. She was 'very much struck by Karsavina and I thought her remarkably pretty'.[32]

Natasha was in her element during those days at Knebworth, when the house rang with laughter and music and no one went to bed until the early hours. 'On the mornings after the parties, the gardeners were not allowed to start work near the house, so as to leave undisturbed the slumber of guests who would eventually arise, yawning, just in time for lunch.'[33]

The noisiest man at Knebworth was Michael. In addition to a new two-seater Detroit-built Hupmobile he had bought a three-wheeled car, a 'Bedelia' to which he became devoted. 'He used to go off early in the morning. One could always hear him coming back, with a series of frightful explosions roaring away at the other end of town. Then I knew it was time to get ready for lunch,' Tata recalled. The car was a tremendous joke, not only to Natasha and the servants, but to the inhabitants of the surrounding villages. 'I think he eventually crashed it when a wasp tried to sting him.'[34] He was unhurt but that was the end of the Bedelia.

* Sir Joseph was the father of the conductor Sir Thomas Beecham.

The 'Russian season' in London that summer included more than the stars, dancers and singers brought over to Drury Lane. The Dowager Empress had arrived for an extended visit to her sister Alexandra at Marlborough House. Michael's sister Xenia and her husband Sandro also came from Paris to stay at the Piccadilly Hotel and they were followed to London by Xenia's daughter Irina and her new young husband Prince Felix Yusupov, who owned an apartment at 15 Parkside, Belgravia.[35] As summer wore on the Russian imperial contingent increased when Grand Duchess George Mikhailovich, Sandro's sister-in-law, arrived at Claridge's with her two daughters,[36] bringing to nine the number of Romanovs in England in addition to Michael and his cousin Miche-Miche.

Royal Ascot was another fixed feature of the London season and Countess Torby was there, of course; because she was divorced, Natasha was not. The ban on divorced people entering the Royal Enclosure at Ascot would still be in force for another half-century, so that even in the 1950s a British prime minister* would not be allowed through the gates.

The principal guests invited to Windsor Castle for Ascot week were the ambassadors of Russia and Austria and each day, as part of the traditional royal procession, they would drive together down the racecourse in an open landau drawn by four bays.[37] On Gold Cup Day, June 18, they stood beside the king and watched Aleppo, owned by a Mr Fairlie, romp home at 6–1.[38] Afterwards they could look down on the cream of British and indeed European society strolling around immaculate lawns, sipping champagne. The sky was cloudless and all was in its place.

The scene at Ascot was much the same as many had known it for all their lives and no one, including the two top-hatted ambassadors in the Royal box, had reason to suppose that it would be any different next year. They still thought that when on June 29 their newspapers reported the assassination in Sarajevo of the heir to the Austrian throne, Archduke Franz-Ferdinand.

It was a sensation, but the Balkans had always been a troublesome place. Ireland was of more immediate political concern in Britain and the Irish question, like the Balkan question, was something which many pondered but few pretended to understand.

The season was not concerned about either issue. There was Wimbledon to think about and at Buckingham Palace the main attention was being focused on the State Ball fixed for July 16, when the grandest members of society, including Miche-Miche and Countess Torby, would be present,[39] and predictably Michael and Natasha would not. This would be followed by racing at Goodwood and by the regatta at Cowes, which the Kaiser's

* Sir Anthony Eden (prime minister 1955–7); his second wife was Clarissa, niece of Sir Winston Churchill.

brother, Prince Henry of Prussia, brother-in-law of the Russian Empress Alexandra, was to attend in his steam yacht *Carmen*.[40]

German royals were as prominent as the Russians in London in the last summer of old Europe. At the State Ball in Buckingham Palace the most distinguished guests included the Tecks, Battenbergs, Saxe-Coburg-Gothas and Schleswig-Holsteins,[41] all of them closely related to the British royal family.

That ball in Buckingham Palace would be the last time old Europe danced the quadrille. Three weeks later the world exploded.

PART II

WAR AND REVOLUTION

THIRTEEN

Going to War

On the evening of Saturday, August 1, 1914, Germany declared war on Russia.* As the news came to Knebworth 'everyone looked grim and endless telegrams were delivered and the telephone never stopped ringing'.[1] Michael, determined to return to the army, cabled Nicholas immediately to ask permission, more for Natasha than himself for he was not prepared to leave her behind.[2] Ordinarily she would never have been allowed to return, 'as somebody who has demonstrated criminal disregard for the Head of State'.[3] But with Russia at war, private wars could be put aside. As promptly, Nicholas cabled back his agreement: Michael and Natasha could both return.

There was much to do in the next frantic days. The Schlieffer family, who had spent the summer at Knebworth, had been stranded in Paris on their journey home and were returning to Knebworth,[4] so that, with family, friends, secretaries, governesses, valets and servants, there would be twenty people seeking passage back to Russia in the Grand Duke's party.[5] The best route was across the North Sea to Norway, thence through Sweden and Finland to St Petersburg. A ship was found, the s.s. *Venus*, which could accommodate the whole party and it would be leaving from Newcastle, 200 miles away on the River Tyne.[6] Miss Rata was among those going back to Russia, but first she wanted to marry Mr Bennett, who was staying behind to look after the horses. A marriage had therefore to be fitted in at St Mary's, the twelfth-century church which stood in the park, a short distance from the main house.

The lease at Knebworth was to end in September and Michael had already settled on a move to Paddockhurst, a much larger estate in Sussex owned by Lord Cowdray,[7] which he had agreed to rent for two years at £3460 a year,[8] a little more than for Knebworth. Although he would not now be moving there himself, he still needed a property in England. Most of the family possessions taken to or acquired at Knebworth would have to stay behind and therefore furniture, books, pictures and linen, as well as cars and horses, would have to be housed somewhere; besides, the war –

* The date on the Russian calendar was July 19, 1914. Until Michael has returned to Russia the dates continue according to the Western calendar.

which Britain joined on August 4 – would not last for long. As eleven-year-old Tata understood it, 'everybody thought that we should be back in England by the following spring at the latest'.[9] Certainly Miss Rata prayed that it would be so; with luck, she hoped she might be back at Christmas, for the war would surely be over by then. Everyone said so.

Since Paddockhurst, its farms, extensive outbuildings and its 3000 acres would be of no immediate value to Michael other than as storage, he wrote to the British War Office and offered to place the estate at their disposal, for billeting or training. He also offered them his Opel touring car. The War Office accepted the use of some of the outhouses and stabling, but on examination of the head-lease it was clear that full use of the property was impractical; the damage clauses for which Michael was responsible did not envisage the kind of damage the heavy-handed British Tommy could inflict, even by Christmas. However, they gratefully took his German car.[10]

Like Michael, Nicholas Johnson also wanted to get back to Russia to take part in the war, but his widowed mother, now part of the household, was staying behind in England. She had been so terrified on the Channel crossing from France that she declared that she would never go on a ship again.[11] It was agreed that she would go to Paddockhurst with Mr Bennett.

On the morning of Thursday, August 13, Michael went up to London to say farewell to his cousin King George V.[12] Just over two weeks earlier the king had met another cousin at Buckingham Palace, Prince Henry of Prussia, the Kaiser's brother and the brother-in-law of Empress Alexandra. Henry had arrived at Cowes, little expecting that the crisis in the Balkans was about to plunge all Europe into war; hurrying home on July 26, Henry stopped off at the palace, where George had told him grimly that war appeared likely and if so it was almost certain that Britain would be 'dragged in' against Germany.[13] Gloomily the two men had shaken hands. Now it was the turn of Michael and a more cheerful handshake, for at least they were on the same side. But as with Henry, the farewell would also prove to be goodbye. King George would never see either cousin again.

At Knebworth all was ready for departure. That afternoon there was a champagne wedding breakfast for Miss Rata and Mr Bennett, married by special licence, and Tata went off with the Schlieffer children to make 'hurried farewells to our favourite nooks' and to place a last bunch of flowers on the cairn erected in memory of Tom, her mourned terrier who had died a few weeks earlier.[14] As his parting gift to Knebworth, Michael left behind a Meissen figure modelled on Catherine the Great's favourite lapdog.* Next day all the servants at Knebworth, together with local

* It is still on display at Knebworth House.

villagers, gathered at the local railway station to say farewell as Michael and Natasha set off on the first leg of their journey home.[15]

That Friday night they boarded the s.s. *Venus* at Newcastle and when they woke up in the morning they were well out to sea. Natasha and Miss Rata stayed in their cabins, feeling seasick, but the news that British destroyers had closed in as escort roused the governess to go on deck, joining Michael in giving them a cheer.[16]

Arriving in Norway, the party crossed over to Sweden, then travelled on to Finland. A week after leaving Knebworth, they were back in St Petersburg, now renamed Petrograd, patriotic sentiment having deemed that Petersburg sounded too German. They booked into the Hotel de l'Europe,[17] where at least now they could use the front door as they had not done before.

The Dowager Empress had also returned to Russia but after a more eventful journey. She had left London hurriedly,[18] travelling with Xenia through Germany; by the time her train reached Berlin the war had already started; hostile crowds broke the windows of her carriage and tore down the blinds. She was lucky, however: her train was allowed to go on to neutral Denmark and from there she got back to Russia via Sweden and Finland.[19]

She was naturally anxious to see Michael on his return but after their meeting in London the Dowager Empress had no intention of seeing Natasha a second time. Michael still had his rooms at the Anichkov Palace, but he would never live in them again; nor would he return to his apartments at the Gatchina palace. Where Natasha could not stay, he would not stay.

Michael and Natasha remained at the Hotel de l'Europe for several days before moving on finally to Gatchina, to the house in Nikolaevskaya Street. Securely locked up when the children left to join them in Cannes in 1912, it had to be reopened and made a home again. Michael also bought the property next door, to house guests as well as some of his staff.[20]

When Michael arrived back he had no idea what role he would be asked to play. He was nearly thirty six, with some sixteen years of soldiering behind him; he had been colonel of two cavalry regiments, the Chernigov Hussars and the élite Chevalier Gardes; and he had proved his leadership. It was remembered, after the 1911 manoeuvres, that 'he displayed such excellent qualities as a regimental commander that the Chernigov Hussars were unanimously found to be the smartest cavalry regiment reviewed by the Tsar'.[21] That was not evidence of competence on the battlefield, but at the outset of war it went to Michael's military credit, when as with other peacetime commanders there was nothing else to go on.

Michael's actual appointment came therefore as a surprise to the army itself. He was given command of a new division to be made up of Muslim horsemen from the Caucasus, tribesmen who had never been in the army before. Michael was promoted to the rank of major-general but none the less his new command was seen by many as a snub intended to remind him that he was not forgiven; having walked out on the Guards cavalry, he was not to think he could walk back in, or be given a regular division.

There were two main fronts: the northern, in East Prussia, facing the Germans; and the southern, in Galicia, facing the Austro-Hungarians. On the outbreak of war, the German plan was to defeat France first, leaving their eastern border manned only by a defensive 'holding army' until the German armies in the west could turn and attack Russia, a plan neatly summarised by the Kaiser as 'lunch in Paris, dinner in St Petersburg'. The counter to this, as the French were pressed back to Paris, was that the Russians should draw off the German army by launching an offensive on the eastern front, even before they were fully ready for it. The Russians gallantly obliged, but a month after the war began they were heavily defeated at Tannenberg in East Prussia and then suffered humiliation at the Masurian Lakes. In the first thirty days they lost some quarter-of-a-million men in East Prussia alone. One of the dead was the beaten commander of the Russian Second Army, General Aleksandr Samsonov, who walked into a wood and shot himself.[22] Berlin, only 150 miles away, was not going to be the cavalry canter some had boasted it would be.

Tannenberg could be explained away as a necessary sacrifice made for France and a month later there was better news elsewhere. In Galicia, the advancing Russians won important successes. Their losses were no less appalling, but they had more to show for them, advancing 100 miles across the frontier, capturing 100,000 prisoners and inflicting battle casualties of some 300,000 on the Austrians.[23]

Michael's division, assigned to the Galician front, was called the Caucasian Native Cavalry; it comprised six regiments, each known by the name of the tribe or place from which it was recruited: Daghestan, Kabardin, Chechen, Tartar, Circassian and Ingush.[24] It would prove itself to be among the very best of the fighting units in Russia and quickly earned such a reputation that it would be known simply as the 'Savage Division'.[25]

Each horseman – or rider as they were known within the division[26] – was a volunteer because Russian conscription laws did not apply to the Caucasus, under the terms agreed when it became part of the empire.[27] The regimental officers were, however, mostly professional Russian cavalrymen, many of them from the Guards; the divisional staff was also drawn from Russian regulars.

Michael's Muslim tribesmen, natural brigands, were difficult to discipline, for they would fight each other as readily as they would Russia's enemies, but they were superb horsemen, fearless in a charge and terrifying to face in battle. On a training exercise, one regiment ordered to carry out a sham attack, switched to real cartridges when they ran out of blanks. As bullets whizzed past Michael's head, their urbane colonel murmured, 'I can only congratulate you on being for the first time under real fire.' The brigade commander, standing beside them, was furious, but 'the Grand Duke laughed'.[28]

Michael's uniform was the picturesque *cherkeska*, the long Circassian coat which fits tightly at the waist and folds gracefully down below the knees and over the top of soft high boots in polished leather. His fur cap was of grey astrakhan from a new-born lamb and he carried a sword and a razor-sharp dagger.[29] In the Savage Division it passed for *chic*, but it was a far cry from the dress of the Chevalier Gardes or the Blue Cuirassiers. Natasha hated it.

In September Michael went down to Tiflis, the capital of the Caucasus, to oversee the final formation of his division and to select his own personal staff, though one of his aides-de-camp, the young Prince Vyazemsky, was recommended to him by Natasha who had met and become friendly with his wife, whom she liked 'very much'. Princess Vyazemskaya had been married twice before and her new husband 'is half her age' but 'she is madly in love with him . . . really smitten'.[30]

Prince Vyazemsky never regretted joining the Savage Division. 'You cannot imagine', he wrote to a nephew, 'how colourful the whole outfit is: the customs, the whole spirit of the thing. The officers are mostly adventurous souls with a devil-may-care attitude. Some of them have had a "tumultuous" past, but they are far from dull . . .' As for the men, the riders, 'they seem to think that the war is a great holiday and their Muslim fatalism precludes all fear of death. They adore the Grand Duke . . .'[31]

Michael's personal appointments also included the chaplain who would serve the needs of the minority Christians in the division. The job went to Father Peter Pospelov,[32] the priest who had baptised little George in Moscow and who had then signed the 'corrected' certificate, a favour not forgotten. But his most unusual recruit was an American boxing coach. Boxing was one of Michael's enthusiasms and he saw no reason why the war should interrupt it. The commander of his Tartar regiment, Colonel Peter Polovtsov, remembered Michael as 'tall, very slim, a perfect sportsman, an excellent horseman, a very good shot and his American boxing teacher always told me that it was a pity that he was a Grand Duke, because he would have done very well as a prizefighter in the ring'.[33]

Michael was well pleased with his division in its first weeks and at the end of October he went north to the supreme headquarters, called Stavka, to meet his brother, who had arrived there from Tsarskoe Selo in his long, magnificently-equipped blue-and-gold train, its carriages including a mahogany dining car which could seat twenty people at its table and a study furnished with a desk and leather chairs. The headquarters were set in a clearing inside a forest of pines and birches, just outside Baranovichi, 'a miserable little country town'[34] which before the war had been base for three railway battalions. The site had been chosen because it was an important railway junction and because it was roughly at the centre of the 500-mile Russian line. Stavka staff worked, ate and slept in a dozen trains standing fan-wise among the trees, but some wooden barracks had been put up for the Cossacks guarding the site. It was a closed world, for there was nowhere else to go and no amusement save conversation at dinner or walks in the surrounding woods. Sir Alfred Knox, then a British liaison officer, was surprised at the peace and quiet of it all, 'in fact, anything less warlike ... would be difficult to imagine'.[35]

Nicholas found Michael enthusiastic about his new command. Three days later, on October 27, Nicholas wrote to Alexandra: 'I had the pleasure of spending the whole of Saturday with Misha who has become quite his old self and is again charming.' A little wooden church had been built beside the railway tracks and Michael and Nicholas went there for evening service, 'and parted after dinner'.[36]

Michael went on to Gatchina briefly to finalise his affairs there and before returning to the front and the risks of the battlefield he wrote to his brother on a matter of vital importance to him: that his four-year-old son George was still illegitimate.

While a divisional commander's life expectancy was considerably better than that of a junior officer, rank was no protection against artillery shells, snipers, or a random bullet. Michael was also not a man to hang back in the rear; as one of his commanders would say of him later, 'the only trouble he gave us was through his constant wish to be in the fighting-line; we sometimes had great difficulty in keeping him out of danger'.[37]

Were he to be killed in the war, as might happen, Natasha would not inherit anything. The 1912 manifesto by which Michael's assets had been placed in administration remained in force; he was still legally in the same position as 'a minor or a lunatic'[38] and technically without rights to the management of his estates or monies. But to leave innocent little George as a bastard was surely to take punishment beyond anything which was reasonable. He said as much to Nicholas:

As I am leaving for the war, from which I may not return, I want to ask you for one favour, which I hope you will not refuse me and which depends entirely on you. It is very hard for me to go away, leaving my family in such an ambiguous position. I wish for my only beloved son to be accepted by society as my son and not as the son of an unknown father, as he is registered on his birth certificate.

It hurts me to think about it, I am possessed by this thought at a time when my soul is full of longing and readiness to serve our beloved country. Remove from me the burden of the worry that, should something happen to me, that my son would have to grow up with the stigma of illegitimacy . . . You alone can do this, as it is your right.

I beg you . . . give the order for my son Georgy, born to Nathalie before our marriage, to be recognised as our legitimate son. Spare him in this way from the difficult position I have outlined . . . At the moment he is not aware of the situation, but in the future he will feel it very much. And after all, he is not to blame! Take pity on him and on me as a father . . .[39]

Michael then set off to rejoin the Savage Division; now judged ready for action, it had moved by train to the Austrian border where the wide-gauge Russian railway ended. The Russian frontline was far forward into the Carpathian Mountains and the division rode the rest of the way to the positions selected for it as part of the Second Cavalry Corps.[40]

The Austrians would have good reason to fear Michael's Muslims in the future, but the first to do so were the unfortunate inhabitants they met as they advanced over the border. Finding themselves on conquered territory, the men of one regiment, quartered in an Austrian village, decided to take the spoils of war and that night there was chaos as excited Tartars raced around the village, chasing dishevelled girls. It was only at dawn that order was restored and the most serious offenders lined up to be flogged, twenty-five lashes being considered the usual punishment, though rapists convicted at court martial could be shot.[41]

Later, two men in that regiment would be and when they were condemned the staff at Michael's headquarters offered to provide a firing squad from another regiment. However, the Tartars insisted on carrying out the execution themselves, the two men preferring, it was said, to die facing friendly faces.[42]

The Savage Division was difficult to handle behind the lines, but when it reached the enemy it behaved with the courage expected of men who relished battle, whether on foot or on horseback. Michael, of course, kept well away from the actual fighting and was never for a moment in any danger. Or so he told Natasha.

With Michael away at the front Natasha had toyed with the idea of moving back to Moscow. Gatchina held bitter memories for her and to live there alone was something she dreaded. After he had left she went to stay with her family in Moscow, but finally realised that she had no choice but to go back to Gatchina: 'there is no hope of settling in Moscow, for everything I have looked at is totally unsuitable and it's so dirty here, that I don't know how people can live here at all'.[43]

Since Gatchina had to be her home, she did her best to make it so. On her return she put her energies into redecoration and into buying new furniture for the two-storey house on Nikolaevskaya Street. She could not know how long she would be there, but any idea that the war would be over by Christmas had long gone. Every day there were railway trains passing through Gatchina carrying wounded men. No one was cheering now, as they had when war began.

In 1908 Michael had inherited a mansion house in St Petersburg, formerly owned by his bachelor uncle Grand Duke Alexis, but he had never considered it as a marital home with Natasha. With the war, he decided to turn the house into a hospital and Natasha took over the organisation, busily finding the equipment, beds and the doctors and nurses who would staff it, putting her friends the Schlieffers in charge of the day-to-day administration.[44] The hospital could accommodate 100 soldiers and twenty-five officers[45] and from the moment it was opened no bed would be empty. In Gatchina, Natasha had also organised a small infirmary on Baggout Street, which took another thirty wounded.[46] Founding hospitals and equipping hospital trains was expected of the grander members of society and in this regard Michael and Natasha did as much as anyone else.

Busy though she was, Natasha had the opportunity to socialise as she had not been able to do in the half-world in which she had lived before her marriage. People still stared at her in Gatchina and some still showed their open disapproval, but at least she was now Michael's wife, not his mistress. When she went to Petrograd, as she did frequently, her favourite luncheon spot was the busy glass-roofed palm-filled Winter Garden restaurant of the Astoria Hotel, opposite St Isaac's Cathedral. The hotel, rivalling in luxury the Europe on Nevsky Prospekt, had opened two years earlier in 1912 and was now so crowded with officers coming from and going to the front that it was popularly known as the 'Hotel Militaire'.[47] Natasha adopted it as a meeting place; one of the new friends she would entertain there regularly was Princess Olga Putyatina.

Princess Putyatina had first met Michael in the spring of 1912 at a tournament held at the Chevalier Gardes riding school; her husband Pavel, an officer in the regiment, was recovering in hospital after a bad fall from his horse while out hunting; Michael came up to her and asked 'with characteristic kindness' about her husband's progress.[48] The princess was fulsome in her praises of 'the tall, slim, well-proportioned, youthful-looking' Michael, for he was not only 'the personification of a sporting horseman, brave and strong; but from the first words he spoke I felt in him kindness, tenderness, reliability. Perfectly straightforward, he won me over at once, as much by the natural charm which infused his whole personality as by the melting and caressing look in his beautiful eyes.'[49]

Olga Putyatina, on meeting Natasha in the autumn of 1914, was astonished to find that she was nothing like the woman so scorned in society gossip. She thought Natasha 'an enchantress ... she was really endowed with all the attractions bestowed by beauty, grace and elegance – a fine mind added to all this captivated those who were struck by her stunning beauty'. As she became a regular guest at Gatchina, Princess Putyatina would say later that 'our long conversations in the evening, peacefully by the fire, convinced me of the great love she felt for her husband'.[50]

Princess Putyatina had one child, a daughter of the same age and with the same name as Tata and the two eleven-year-old girls also struck up a close friendship, though in comparing notes Natasha's daughter would think that the other was the luckier: 'She was allowed to stay up an hour later in the evening, was allowed to have coffee after lunch' and was encouraged to air her views at the table whereas 'if I dared open my mouth, apart from asking for the cruet, I would get half-murdered.'[51]

As she would do often over the next months, Natasha made time at the beginning of December to travel southward to Lvov to see Michael for the few days' leave that he could snatch from his frontline division. Lvov, captured by the Russians in September, was a Polish city fifty miles inside Austro-Hungary and known there as Lemberg; Michael's headquarters were in a village some 100 miles to the south-west of it.[52] He could be in Lvov by car in a few hours; it took her two laborious days, but to Natasha it was worth it.

Apart from her natural fears for Michael's life, what troubled Natasha particularly was her belief that he had been posted to the Savage Division in retribution for his marriage. On her return to Gatchina she wrote to say: 'You are naturally talked about more than the division and what pains me most of all, is that they say that you did not go to war of your own accord, but were sent to atone for your guilt towards Russia – so your heroism, with which you wished to surprise the world, has been totally wasted ...'[53] What she was trying to tell him was that there was no point in being killed. He was not in the frontline to be a hero, he was there to be punished by his brother.

Michael spent Christmas at the front, his day and those of his officers, greatly improved by a vast hamper of provisions sent to him by Natasha. From Yeliseev's in Petrograd she sent him 'a whole ham, two tongues, five pounds of butter and five boxes of fresh Siberian hazel-grouse', together with 'a whole case of chicken, turkeys, butter and so on'. She also sent him, in a special wooden case, 'a little Christmas tree which we decorated ourselves ... only with those things that cannot break or be damaged. I am sending the candles, candlesticks and four little lanterns separately.'[54]

She also remembered the wounded soldiers in their hospitals in Gatchina and Petrograd, buying each 'a silver watch with your monogram engraved', as well as tobacco pouches. Christmas was to be made as happy as possible, but she could not bear to think of New Year in Gatchina. 'I am going with the children to Moscow to stay with the Matveevs, so as not to be on my own ... it would feel so sad to be alone ...'[55]

Over Christmas, however, Natasha's house was filled with friends old and new. One unexpected new friend was Grand Duke Dimitri, twenty-three and a handsome Horse Guards officer with the admired Cross of St George on his chest. In the early weeks of the war, at the battle of Kaushin, he was returning from a cavalry charge when he saw a corporal lying wounded; under heavy enemy fire he dismounted, put the man on his back and carried him to safety, before returning for his horse.[56] Two years earlier Dimitri had been a member of Russia's Olympic equestrian team at Stockholm and had been something of a popular hero for that, also.

Like many other young men born to considerable wealth and high position, Dimitri was something of a rake in his private life. He was a familiar figure in Petrograd nightclubs and after a noisy evening he and his riotous companions would roar off drunkenly in their fast cars to the gypsy restaurants on the islands.[57] For many years his closest friend was the older Prince Felix Yusupov, whose own reputation for wildness verged on the legendary. The friendship between the two temporarily ended when a worried Tsar, alarmed by the gossip about them, ordered Dimitri to stop seeing the notorious Yusupov.*

Dimitri's mother, Princess Alexandra of Greece, died giving birth to him; he was eleven when his father Grand Duke Paul was banished for marrying the divorcée Olga Pistolkors and he was put in the care of his uncle Grand Duke Serge and his wife, Alexandra's sister Ella. He was fourteen when Serge was assassinated in 1905, after which Ella retreated into a convent, forming her own order of nuns. Thereafter it was Nicholas and Alexandra who took responsibility for Dimitri and his sister Marie, treating them almost as their own. For a time Alexandra thought that Dimitri might marry her eldest daughter Olga.[58]

Until December 1914 Natasha knew little about Dimitri; thirteen years

* It amused Yusupov to dress up in women's clothes; on one occasion at a theatre in Paris, Britain's King Edward VII was so struck by the 'lovely young woman' sitting in the stalls that he asked for an introduction which, as Yusupov would boast later, 'greatly flattered my vanity'. *Youssoupoff, p. 90.*

younger than Michael, Dimitri had played no part in their lives before they left Russia. Natasha saw him for the first time on her way back from Lvov, when the train stopped at Baranovichi, Stavka headquarters. Like most passengers, she took the opportunity to go to the station restaurant for a meal; as always the beautiful and ever elegant Natasha attracted admiring glances.

Dimitri was also at the station. A staff officer, he was returning on leave to the capital by the same train. They did not meet, but afterwards Johnson, who was escorting Natasha home, told her that he had overheard Dimitri asking his companions, 'Who is that tall lady in brown?'[59] It was virtually the same question Michael had posed almost to the day seven years earlier in the riding school at Gatchina. In the first instance, of course, the answer was that she was the wife of a lieutenant; now it was that she was the wife 'of your cousin, Grand Duke Michael'. Dimitri's eyes widened in astonishment, but he made no attempt then to meet her.

Next day, Friday, December 5, Natasha was having lunch in the Astoria. Dimitri turned up at the hotel and asked Johnson to introduce him. 'He sat with us for a very long time, after which he drove us in his open automobile around various shops,' Natasha told Michael. On the following Monday Natasha went back to Petrograd, having invited him to lunch, and they sat together until 4 p.m. 'I found him a remarkably intelligent and interesting conversation partner and he made the best possible impression on me,' she wrote to Michael afterwards. 'I haven't found in him what you said to me about him . . . It's simply bad company and loneliness that have left their mark on him, but his soul is pure and craving for kindness and endearment and it is capable of all the good that is here on earth.'[60]

That Christmas Dimitri became a regular at Gatchina. Tata, aged eleven, thought him 'extraordinarily good looking; very tall, very slender'.[61] She and her two bosom friends, the Schlieffer daughters Tania and Marina, promptly fell in love with him, forming 'a secret Dimitri Club'. Tata kept a diary all about him, hiding it under her bed and breathlessly recording such red-letter days as the occasion when 'I was in the *same sleigh* as Dimitri and Mamma'.[62]

Inevitably the little diary was discovered, read and laughingly revealed to the household. The next time Dimitri came to the house, a blushing Tata was to hear her mother announce to him, 'You know, Dimitri, this child is madly in love with you'. Tata was not, however, to be discouraged: continuing to dream about him, she started a book, in which Dimitri played the hero, called Dennis, and Tata disguised herself as the heroine, Nina. Tata, of course, ensured that handsome 'Dennis' fell madly in love with the adorable 'Nina'.[63]

In fact, the young and gallant Dimitri had already fallen madly in love – with her mother.

FOURTEEN

Lily-of-the-Valley

At the end of 1914 Michael's division was in a sector of the frontline which was quiet enough to allow him to take two weeks' leave. He could not get home for New Year's Eve, but he would be there early on January 2. Thrilled at the news, Natasha cancelled her trip to her sister's home in Moscow, her own New Year's Eve made joyous merely by knowing that Michael was already on his way.

'Arrived in our beloved Gatchina at 8.30 a.m.,' Michael wrote in the new blue-and-gold embossed diary, a Christmas present from Natasha. 'Our Baby was so touchingly glad to see me and became quite affectionate ... What a joy to be back in my family in lovely Gatchina.'[1]

Next day, January 3, he went 'to the detestable Petrograd', inspected his new hospital, called on his mother, spent the afternoon shopping with Natasha and then took the train to Tsarskoe Selo to see Nicholas.[2] Michael was still concerned about his son's status; nothing had been done about it despite his letter two months earlier. He hoped to speak privately to his brother about it.

Nicholas avoided the subject, however, for Michael's son was a sore point at Tsarskoe Selo. Alexandra opposed any concessions suggesting acceptance of Michael's marriage, and legalising little George would have gone some way towards that. Michael returned without the assurances he had hoped to get and without any chance to press for them.

Over the next days Michael went to the Gatchina palace on a nostalgic trip around his childhood home and collected crystal ornaments and other personal items from his old rooms in the Arsenal. He also took Natasha on sleigh rides around the snow-covered park, mildly irritated perhaps at her enthusiastic reminders about Dimitri's fast Swedish sleigh. 'Such a pity you've never had anything of this kind,' she had told him after an outing with Dimitri at Christmas.[3] Natasha could be disconcertingly honest, saying what she thought without regard for its consequences.

It was so in her letters to Michael about Dimitri. He had been surprised to hear about the friendship. Telling her that he 'couldn't help smiling' at the news, he was taken aback by her reply. 'Of course it was hard to imagine that we could become friends or, in fact, even become acquainted in the first place. However, it has happened ... I feel quite clearly that he has taken a certain place in my heart and in my life and that we shall always have a deep and tender affection for each other.'[4]

That was not quite the kind of letter a man wants to receive in the frontline, a thousand miles from home, when necessarily imagination has to substitute for knowledge. But once home his concern vanished. Natasha adored Michael; nothing had changed.

With Michael's arrival from the front the house was full of people, with a core of regulars – the Viazemskys, Olga Putyatina, Koka and Maggie Abakanovich, the Schlieffers and some British friends, Major and Mrs Simpson. He and Natasha shopped in Petrograd and in Gatchina he went hunting in the Game Reserve, armed with a hunting rifle and bagging a wolf.[5]

All too soon the leave was over and he set off back to his divisional headquarters at Lomna, sixty miles south-west of Lvov. 'It is so sad to leave,' he wrote in his diary for January 11, 1915, though Natasha insisted on accompanying him as far as Lvov, giving them another day-and-a-half together. On arrival they parted hurriedly, for the Austrians had launched an offensive and the Russian line was being pushed back. 'The fighting is unceasing,' he told Natasha in his first letter home.[6] One of his colonels had been killed the day before and three staff officers seriously wounded, one of whom, the adjutant of his Tartar regiment, would die two days later. Sixty of his horsemen were casualties.[7]

Natasha had watched him go off. 'My darling Mishechka, I am awfully worried for you, my darling and I beg you to be careful . . . believe me, darling Misha, that whatever you do and no matter how daringly you put yourself at risk, there'll be no gratitude and no appreciation. Do what you will, you still won't prove anything to anyone.'[8] Five days later, back home, she was still fearful. 'You can't imagine how worried I am about you, it makes me really sick.'[9]

Michael's headquarters had been pulled back in the fighting and in the confusion of the move all his belongings were mislaid, 'so until last night I did not have even a bar of soap'.[10] But by January 20 he was able to report that 'the crisis is over and the enemy is in retreat along our entire frontline. We are now dealing mainly with the Hungarian troops, who fight with great persistence. Yesterday, our infantry (on our right flank) lost about 1000 men, but in my division the losses were quite small.'[11]

The Carpathians are a thick belt of mountains, with one rising above another, often with a slope of one in six and covered in trees. These heights dominate the passes, which were deep in snow and each had to be fought for at the point of a bayonet. It was a savage business and no one who was there could think that war was glory. Temperatures fell to minus 17 degrees and 'the poor soldiers, especially at night, freeze terribly and many have frostbitten feet and hands. The losses in the infantry attached to us have been very great,' Michael wrote home.[12] The enemy suffered as greatly and sometimes more. One Austrian regiment of some 1800 men froze to death as it lay waiting to advance the following morning. In the Austrian Second Army 40,000 men were casualties to frostbite. Rifles locked solid by ice had to be heated over fires before infantrymen could be sent into battle.[13] Trenches were so difficult to dig that men could often do no more than bury themselves in the snow.

The casualty figures in all armies were horrific and beyond anything known to history before. After six months of fighting the Russians had lost a million men, dead, wounded, or captured.[14] 'Corps have become divisions, brigades have shrunk into regiments,' Nicholas confessed to Alexandra.[15] The slaughter appalled Michael; the war itself he saw as a catastrophe, entered into blindly by men who little knew what they were doing. As he told Natasha:

> *The war and all the great horror it involves cannot help inspiring sadness in every sensible person; for example, I feel greatly embittered towards people in general and most of all towards those who are at the top, who hold power and allow all that horror to happen. If the question of war were decided by the people at large, I would not be so passionately averse to that great calamity; but . . . nobody ever asks the nation, the country at large, what course of action they would choose.*
>
> *I even sometimes feel ashamed to face the people, i.e. the soldiers and officers, particularly when visiting field hospitals, where so much suffering is to be seen, for they might think that one is also responsible, for one is placed so high and yet has failed to prevent all that from happening and to protect one's country from this disaster . . . I know that you'll understand . . .*[16]

Natasha understood completely. 'I agree with all you write about the war,' she replied, 'and your opinion does you credit.' But she did not elaborate, for her letters went through the private office which dealt with Michael's affairs – the 'Department', as she called it – and 'the gentlemen there are capable of anything'.[17] Past experience had taught her to be cautious in her letters, though she would sometimes write things she wished would be noted by curious eyes and passed on. She was never hesitant, for example, in complaining about the way Michael was treated; she also held nothing back when she wrote about her love for him, for she did not care who knew it and nor did he.

All that he wanted, he wrote, was that this 'disgusting and dreadful war finish soon in our favour, so that I can return to you and never part from you again . . . I miss your love and caresses so dreadfully'.[18] And then again, 'if you could only know how I yearn for you, my tender, darling wife . . .

my heart always frets for you, yet I would not think I had the right, at a time which is so hard for Russia, to live somewhere quietly ... That would be too selfish – in other words, I do not really complain about anything but our separation, which is killing me.'[19] Michael also fretted about his separation from his son, while reminding Natasha about her hope years before of having a girl. 'Baby is so touching in that he's remembered me and asked why I didn't come. Will we ever have a girl with blue eyes – I think we never will!'[20]

Yet he also confessed that in the past days he had been haunted by the memory of her new affection for young Dimitri. At Gatchina he had put it out of his mind, but back in the frontline he found himself brooding over what she had said and written. 'I keep thinking of the impression he has produced on you and I can't say that I find the thought pleasant – until recently there was no one apart from me and now there is someone else and he has taken a certain place in your heart and I can't allow that, for I love you too much. I always said to you that I wasn't jealous, but that was only because there was no reason to be jealous.'[21]

He would have been even more jealous if he had known that Dimitri had declared his love to Natasha, in a hotel room in Moscow. It was to be one of the rare instances in Natasha's life when she decided, wisely, that there were some things it might be best that Michael did not know.

Natasha had gone to Moscow on January 21, 1915, for the saddest of reasons. The day before she had received the tragic news that her beloved sister Olga had died of pneumonia. 'I can't get used to the idea that she, poor love, has died,' she told Michael. 'It turned out that she had a very weak heart and did not survive her very first serious illness.'[22] Michael had already heard about Olga's death from her grieving husband Aleksei Matveev. 'I just can't believe it ... do ask him to come and stay with you in Gatchina for a while,' he suggested to Natasha.[23] Michael had been exceptionally fond of his sharp-witted and clever sister-in-law Olga, but hers was one death in a world in which, on some days, he was counting his own dead by the hundreds.

After Olga's funeral Natasha decided to stay on in Moscow for a week or so. She had taken a suite at the National Hotel and apart from her daily visits to her parents at their apartment on the Vozdvizhenka, 'I am seeing many friends here, they are all so kind to me and I am not feeling as lonely as I did in Gatchina'.[24]

Dimitri was also in Moscow and one evening he came round to the hotel to see her. In the sitting room of her suite, he suddenly blurted out his love for her. She was seated at her writing desk in the corner next to the bedroom door, 'with a kind, tender and somewhat sad expression on your face,' as Dimitri would later remind her.[25] 'I can't describe to you, "dearest friend", the feelings that possessed me when I was talking to you about my thoughts and feelings when looking at you then in your hotel room ... maybe I should not have told you all that, but I felt better afterwards. Of course, it had something to do with your own agitation at the time, but you were agitated because you understood what was being said and thought ...'[26]

Natasha, facing a second Grand Duke who had fallen in love with her on sight, had good reason to be 'agitated'. Here was the young, handsome and charming Dimitri declaring to a woman eleven years older than himself that he was madly in love with her; it was frightening and yet enormously flattering. Because she had become so fond of him, he could not be cruelly spurned; at the same time he could not be encouraged. Somehow she managed gently to extricate both of them from a situation in which Dimitri might well have been humiliated, or Michael betrayed.

That she did so successfully is evidenced by the fact that afterwards they went together to the apartment of Natasha's eldest sister Vera and that Dimitri would later recall 'that wonderful evening at your sister's ... and continued the evening which began so strangely and remarkably ...'[27]

Yet Natasha felt that she could not allow Dimitri to go on seeing her, now that his love was openly declared; in the event, it was Dimitri who made that decision for them both, telling her that he was going back to the front. Michael heard that he had been offered a squadron in a Cossack regiment in the Caucasus,[28] although Natasha was doubtful that Dimitri, suffering from tuberculosis, was at all well enough for such a post. 'I personally think he will not go to any front for he is very ill, much more seriously than he supposes. How could he fight at 10,000 feet when he coughs up blood. I have seen a red stain on his handkerchief with my own eyes, but he just laughs it off.'[29]

After Dimitri and Natasha said goodbye in Moscow she then wrote and told Michael as much as she thought he should know, but without mentioning the scene in the hotel room. Dimitri had seen her twice in Moscow and once at Vera's, she said. 'We kept teasing each other all the time, then we called a one-day truce to say goodbye, for he told me that we would not see each other for a very long time and said that he loved me very much, believed me to be very good and honest and because of all that he had decided to run away from me'. She added:

> *Yet if I happened to suffer grief again, I was to write to him and then he would be by my side and do everything to help me. Isn't it touching to hear it from such a person as he is? I am genuinely grateful to him for such an attitude and I feel less lonely for it. Even if we never ever see each other again, it is still*

easier to live knowing that you are loved and respected. I feel deeply sorry for him and I fear he will die pointlessly and far too early. The better I know him the more I see that I was right in my opinion of him.[30]

However, Natasha did not allay Michael's fears and he continued to brood – a characteristic of his. 'I find it strange that even more people are not in love with you than there are. On the other hand, I feel you have enough admirers already – not even counting Dimitri . . .'[31] His mood did not improve on reading her latest references to his cousin.

So you have seen each other again and teased each other and professed moving feelings. And you have reproached me for falling for somebody all the time, whereas it has never happened and I have never said moving things to anyone! When I think about it, my heart sinks and there's a nagging pain in my chest. Since we started living together, I have experienced this feeling for the first time – it is a complicated feeling, there is frustration, jealousy and deep sadness and all that is made worse by our present separation.[32]

It would not be the end of his torment over Dimitri, whom Natasha likened innocently to a 'lily of the valley'. Michael never let her forget that delicate description, referring thereafter to his young cousin Grand Duke Dimitri Pavlovich as simply Mr Lily-of-the-Valley. Sometimes he would do so through gritted teeth.

Natasha had intended to go directly from Moscow to Lvov, hoping to meet Michael for a few days, but she postponed her trip when he wrote to her to tell her on February 3 that 'the situation is such that it is difficult to say when we might have a few free days.'[33] The fighting had not stopped since his return to the division three weeks earlier. It was a brutal business and on going forward to one captured position 'we saw such horrors as I am not going to describe'.[34] But Michael also tried to reassure Natasha that he was in no great personal danger: 'most of the time I sit at home and feel miserably bored. To be at war and not even take advantage of the fresh air seems so stupid!'[35]

That was far removed from reality. The day before, as his diary noted, he had been climbing on foot through freezing snow up a mountain identified on his map as Height 673 inspecting positions which within hours would be under heavy enemy assault, 'with intense shooting from the front and both flanks, causing great losses'. One regiment 'lost 300 soldiers'.[36]

Natasha was not convinced by the assurances he gave her in his 'soothing letters'. She had heard from the courier who brought his letters, 'and from others' that he was 'under fire'.[37] Michael replied that 'it was not quite so . . . besides, if our positions had been under fire we would certainly have moved to a safer place, but I repeat, it has never happened'.[38]

The impression he gave her of his being merely bored was, however, reinforced by two requests to Natasha: to send him some 'piquant books' and a photograph of her 'in an evening dress with the lowest neckline possible'.[39] He suggested that she should go to Boissonnas & Eggler, a Petrograd studio and have the picture taken specially. In reply to the first request Natasha pointed out, with a touch of disapproval, that 'I honestly didn't know what "piquant books" I could send you . . . I have hardly read any such books and know nothing apart from the *Journal d'une femme de chambre*, but you read it in England.'[40] She ignored the second request.

Michael continued to press her about the photograph, however. Two weeks after first mentioning it he wrote that 'I am looking forward with impatience to a photograph in a low-cut (as low as possible) dress'.[41] He would go on asking again and again for that picture. 'I would so much like to have a portrait of you with a low décolletage as I asked you before and without any fur, for the furs conceal everything – please do it for me when you are in Petrograd next!' he would remind her in June.[42] Almost a year later – in May, 1916 – he would still be pleading for the same picture. Natasha's reluctance to comply was hardly surprising: she was a loving wife, but it was asking a great deal of her that she should go to Boissonnas and pose in quite the way Michael wanted. 'Piquant books' were one thing,* piquant photographs another.

What she would do without question was to travel to the front to see him. To do so, in the midst of winter, across a thousand miles of track in trains which were often sidelined to make way for military transport, was a daunting prospect but on February 10, 1915, a week after returning to Moscow, she set off on her postponed trip for Lvov for the third time in three months.

On this occasion she was lucky to see him at all. The Austrians had just regained two towns, Chernovitsy and Stanislavov, and the Eighth Army Commander General Aleksandr Brusilov had ordered the Savage Division 'to straighten out the situation'.[43] It involved a long cross-country move and the establishment of new headquarters in the town of Stryj, forty miles from Lvov. It gave him little time to see her, but none the less he was waiting for her as she stepped off the train.[44] It was a brief reunion. After thirty-six hours together he returned to Stryj, leaving a tearful Natasha behind in the Governor's house on Yagellonovskaya Street in Lvov. 'It was awfully hard and sad to part with you,' she would write later, 'and to watch

* Michael did read serious works, however, as many of his letters to Natasha demonstrate. In one he listed the books he was then currently reading: they included Dostoevsky's *Crime and Punishment*, *A History of the French Revolution* and a biography of Robespierre, as well as a couple of literary novels.

you leave from the balcony. My heart was breaking with grief.'[45]

Back at his headquarters he sent a note to say that 'fighting is on and it is impossible to say how long it will last, maybe five maybe more than ten days. Therefore I cannot ask you to stay on in Lvov and I suggest you leave at once . . . Yesterday there were heavy losses in the 2nd Brigade.' He added, however, that 'there is no need to worry about my safety for I am far from the battle area'.[46]

That was not true. He was with the frontline troops, moving from village to village, finding lodgings where he could and 'walking with the main forces' as they came up to the Austrians, led by their famous and rightly respected Tyrolese riflemen. Outnumbered two to one, Michael's Tartars and Chechens, fighting on foot, met the Austrians in a forest. There was a bloody hand-to-hand battle, but the bayonets of the 'stalwart Tyrolese' wavered in the face of the swords and daggers of 'the active little Tartars', their commander proudly reported.[47]

Half his men lay dead among the trees and when Michael rode up 'he was very much impressed' by the fight the regiment had put up, but also clearly saddened as he rode through the woods full of corpses. 'A battlefield after a fight is not a beautiful picture,' noted the Tartar colonel, 'and I think that the kind heart of the Grand Duke suffered from the sight.'[48]

During their brief reunion in Lvov, Michael had seemed less sure of Natasha's love for him, perhaps in part because of what she had told him about Dimitri. When she got back to Gatchina, she wrote to reassure him:

> *I keep thinking of how tender and loving you were to me . . . and my heart overflows with love and gratitude to you. You have unjustly reproached me . . . for loving you less than before – I think, the change is not in me, but in you – I love you just as I did before, whereas you, either because of our separation or for some other reason, now love me more and really appreciate what you used to take for granted or even failed to notice altogether. You must admit, that my love for you has gone through severe trials and it might have ended very sadly, yet I have retained the same ardour for you, Misha and you know it perfectly well, my darling boy – so there's no need for you to worry or get upset.*[49]

Just over a week later, she set off on the long 2000-mile round trip to Lvov yet again. Michael's division had been pulled back from the front for a rest after its successes against the Austrians and Michael told her that they could meet for a week or so.

She arrived in Lvov on March 1, 1915. 'What a joy to be with Natasha again,' Michael penned in his diary next day. 'We got up very late . . .'[50] When they did arise it was to hear that Michael was being honoured with Russia's highest gallantry award, the Order of St George Fourth Class, on the recommendation of the tough-minded Eighth Army commander Brusilov. Appointments to the Order were made rarely and only after approval and scrutiny by the Council of St George in Petrograd; to prevent favouritism any commander making a recommendation to the Council which misrepresented the facts was liable to court martial. No one could receive a higher class in the Order until they had been awarded the Fourth. The names of Knights were engraved in the St George Room at the Kremlin and a plaque installed at the military school from which they graduated.[51]

Michael's citation said that he was awarded the Order in recognition of 'his conduct . . . at the time of the fighting for command of the Carpathian passes in January, during which he exposed his life to great danger, inspiring and encouraging the troops under constant enemy fire by the example of his personal bravery and courage and, when resisting attacks by superior enemy forces . . . and later, when moving onto the offensive, he contributed to the successful development of our manoeuvres by his energetic actions . . .'[52]

This was not quite the picture that Michael had given Natasha – of him sitting far away from the battlefield, bored and reading naughty French novels to pass the time – but she was immensely proud none the less. News of the award, published in the newspapers, impressed even cynical, backbiting Petrograd. A Russian war correspondent, Nikolai Breshko-Breshkovsky, wrote glowingly that Michael 'always wanted to be wherever there was danger, or where deadly fire had been unleashed by the enemy. The personal courage of a physically strong sportsman and cavalry officer . . . drove Grand Duke Michael into this fire . . . seeing the Grand Duke at their forward positions the ranks were ready to follow him to a loyal death . . .'[53]

Such blushful comments were echoed by others, sometimes in terms so extravagant as to be embarrassing. One society commentator would later write that 'the idol of his men . . . he shared the dangers of his soldiers'; the truth of that, however, was not helped by adding that Michael 'never allowed himself any luxury which they did not have, sleeping in the open with them and living the same life as they did, without the least indulgence as regards meals or anything else . . .'[54] That might occasionally be the case, but generals, Grand Dukes or not, did not live like ordinary soldiers in any army and it would never occur to them or their soldiers that they should. A more realistic comment was that of his brother-in-law Sandro, who said that Michael was 'a particular favourite at the front', his division, 'led by him through innumerable battles, being recognised by GHQ as our best fighting unit'.[55]

With the Council of St George's approval of the award, Nicholas's reaction was a curious mixture of pleasure, pride and almost begrudging condescension. Writing to Alexandra on March 3, he told her about 'the splendid behaviour of Misha's division in the February fighting, when they were attacked in the Carpathians by two Austrian divisions. The Caucasians not only repelled the enemy, but actually attacked him and were the first to enter Stanislavov, while Misha was the whole time in the line of fire. Everybody is asking me to give him the Order of St George, which I shall do.' He then added: 'I am very glad for his sake, as I think this time that he has really earned this military distinction and it will show him that he is, after all, treated exactly as all the others and that by doing his duty well he also gets his reward.'[56]

In her own comments about Michael's gallantry award Alexandra could also not resist a moralising tone. She replied to Nicholas: 'About Misha, I am so happy, do write it to Motherdear, it will do her good to know it. I am sure this war will make more of a man of him – could one but get her out of his reach, her dictating influence is so bad for him.'[57] It was a patronising letter blindly unaware of its own irony. For what was truly the problem, as Russia was beginning to realise as never before, was 'the dictating influence' of Alexandra. Natasha was certainly formidable and she would not have survived the past years if she had been otherwise. But at least she was entirely sane. Some people wondered if the same could be said about Alexandra.

In the apartment at Lvov which they had rented for their nine days together, Natasha sat at the table and wrote a letter which she wanted Michael to read as soon as he arrived back at his headquarters. 'My dear Mishechka, I am so terribly sad to part with you. When you return from the station read these lines and know that my thoughts will always be with you, that I love you dearly and will miss you terribly. Embracing you tenderly, may God bless and guard you.'[58]

Natasha went home via Moscow. Her eldest sister Vera was seriously ill after an operation for appendicitis and with Olga having died only eight weeks earlier Natasha was concerned. When she saw Vera in hospital on the afternoon of Thursday, March 12, she appeared to be in no 'great immediate danger', so she called on her old friends Sergei Rachmaninov and his wife Natalya and then went with them to a performance of his *Vespers* in the Great Hall of the Assembly of the Nobles. The Rachmaninovs are both 'so incredibly nice', she wrote afterwards.[59]

Next afternoon, before returning to Gatchina, she visited Vera again. 'She was in a terrible state of mind and said that she felt that she was about to die and that she wanted to be discharged from hospital so that she could die at home.'[60] The doctors, however, did not seem overly concerned, for she had almost recovered from the surgery. Worried, but assured that Vera was not in any real danger, Natasha travelled back to Petrograd.

At the station she was met by the Abakanovichs and after doing some shopping they went to the Astoria for lunch. Dimitri was there, lunching at another table, but later he came over to join Natasha. 'He was very amiable and in high spirits,' she reported later to Michael. 'Tomorrow we are lunching together again.'[61]

Michael had written to say that he could not get back for Easter, 'for we are in contact with the enemy and I as commander have no right to leave my unit at such a moment'.[62] He added: 'In my thoughts I'll be with you every second and inseparably in the Gatchina palace church which I love so tenderly . . .'[63]

Natasha very much wanted to go to the palace church, but she had not yet done so on her own, feeling still that she was not welcome there. Instead, in Michael's absence, she went to the nearby town church, though it was so crowded that 'it is impossible to pray'. Accordingly she asked the palace administrator Krestyanov for permission to attend the palace church at Easter, telling Michael defiantly that 'if someone resents my presence then let them not come'.[64]

As it happened, she would not need permission. For when she met Dimitri for their luncheon date on Tuesday, March 17, she invited him to spend Easter at Gatchina the following weekend. He accepted eagerly.[65] With her arm on his, there was no question of her going anywhere but the palace church, resented or not. The sight of her arriving with another Grand Duke gave smart Gatchina reason to gossip, but that was something Natasha had long stopped worrying about.

With her marriage there were some who had come cap-in-hand, hoping that by ingratiation their past comments would be forgotten. But there remained those of the 'old guard' who could not bear Natasha, married or unmarried. One of the most offensive was Baron Girard, who 'has always sniffed openly', she complained to Michael. On one occasion he 'spat after my motor when I was driving away from the Warsaw station. Everyone saw that.' And one evening, when she went to the cinema with Johnson, 'he snorted loudly' when he saw her come in.[66]

Michael was infuriated by such stories. In January he had written to Natasha to say, 'I now look at people with different eyes, not the way I looked at them before, when, with a few exceptions, everyone seemed to me nice and kind – when, in actual fact, such truly nice and honest people with integrity are few and far between'.[67]

As for the spiteful Baron the response of Michael was to have it made known to him 'that I ask him never to telegraph me again and that if I ever encounter him I will not give him my hand and will treat him in the way that he treated you'.[68]

Michael and Natasha had endured insults for so long, however, that a few more hardly mattered. What mattered more was to learn on March 26, 1915, four days after Easter Sunday, that Vera had died. Within two months Natasha had lost both her sisters.

FIFTEEN

Love and Duty

With the news of Vera's death following so swiftly upon Olga's, Michael decided to leave the front for a few days and go to Moscow, though he could not, in fact, get there in time for the funeral itself. He met Natasha at Matveev's apartment before going to the cemetery where 'they gave a *panikhida* at the graves of Olga and Vera' before a large crowd.[1]

Having given himself a few days' leave he went on home, anxious to see his son. George had been ill with abscesses in both ears and Natasha had been deeply worried about him. 'Poor Baby', she had written to Michael ten days earlier, 'he is terribly thin and pale, his little arms have become like threads and the bones are sticking out in all directions. And yet he is so meek and never complains about anything, always content, quiet and obedient and I keep thinking he won't stay long in this world.'[2]

That came as a shock and Michael was therefore anxious to see how he was faring. 'Baby has, thank God, completely recovered, although he is very thin and sluggish,' he wrote that night in relief. 'Before dinner, I played with him and Tata. We had a sad evening.'[3]

Having come home from the frontline, albeit briefly, Michael decided to invite 'Mr Lily-of-the-Valley' to Gatchina. His intent was sociable; Dimitri was at home in Petrograd and Michael thought it would be a good opportunity to show that he bore him no ill will over his attentions to Natasha. A guilty Dimitri clearly assumed, however, that Michael was not so generously inclined. After he picked up the telephone Dimitri's line unaccountably went dead and when Michael called back he refused to come to the telephone. So 'it's his own fault that he never came to see us', Michael told Natasha.[4]

One relief on that leave was that George had at last been legitimised, six months after Michael's request. However, it had taken another letter to make that certain. From the frontline on March 14 Michael had written to Nicholas again about his son. 'Something that upsets me very much is that neither when we saw each other in January, nor in your letter afterwards, have you said anything in response to my personal request which means so much to me ... please remember about it during Easter.'[5] This time Nicholas did as asked, legitimising George – as Count Brasov – on March 26;[6] but he still kept Michael's estate in administration: if Michael was killed there might be some discretionary bequest to his son; his widow would have nothing.

When he returned to the front Natasha went with him only as far as Brasovo. She was back in Gatchina on April 7, to continue with her task of making 24 Nikolaevskaya Street as comfortable as it could be, though she made no secret of her dislike for Gatchina itself. 'It is like a graveyard,' she told him. 'Johnson is right when he says that Gatchina should be renamed "Pompeii" . . . it is just as dead a place and the weather is impossible.'[7]

Nor was their home easy to get right. 'Everything has been neglected. It seems to me that one day our house and all that's around it will just collapse and fall to pieces, so old is everything.'[8] Natasha felt caught between spending too much on a house which might prove only a temporary home and living in a place which was so shabby that she was ashamed of it.

Michael, dependent still on the allowances which the Department of Estates paid him monthly, could not afford major improvements. He had enough to live on, but no more. When he needed extra monies he was obliged to ask his brother directly, as he did in February, in the midst of the fighting in the Carpathians. The half-yearly rent, plus a bill for running costs, was due on Paddockhurst, the estate he had left behind in England and Michael did not have the money. He wrote to Nicholas from his village headquarters asking him to order the 'Department' to forward the necessary £2530. 'I can't pay,' he explained, 'for most of my money . . . is spent on maintenance of our three hospitals for the wounded.'[9] With millions tied up in the 'Department' it was humiliating to be in the position of begging for small amounts, but Michael had no choice. A war hero he might be, but legally he remained in the role of madman.

Yet the house in Nikolaevskaya Street needed money, as Natasha was only too aware. 'I realise that it is impossible to leave everything as it is, for it all looks "beggarly" and it's not appropriate for you to live in such a tumbledown,' she told him. 'In six years we haven't yet made ourselves a real home, because you don't care how you live and I couldn't do anything single-handed. Now, little by little, the circle of my acquaintances is growing larger, for I can't behave like a hermit and refuse all invitations – at the same time these invitations embarrass me, because I feel and see that my house is inferior to those of other people and so I can't receive them in the same style as they receive me and as I would like to receive them. And I happen to be very popular – the Putyatins keep inviting me all the time and now all their acquaintances are beginning to follow suit.'[10]

It had taken a very long time for Natasha to become accepted by any section of Petrograd society, much of it still hostile to her, but slowly she was indeed widening her circle, social and political. Among her newest friends was Countess Kapnist, whose husband Dimitri was one of the twenty-two members of the Octobrist party in the Duma.* Count Kapnist was much taken by Natasha; as she recounted to Michael, he 'told Johnson that for the sake of a woman like me a man could forget and give up anything'.[11] Natasha could be accused of many things; excessive modesty was not one of them.

For the sake of Natasha, one person Michael gave up was his sister Olga, who was nursing in a hospital she had set up in Lvov. He had not forgiven her for opposing his marriage and they had not spoken since. Having given her unwavering loyalty in her affair with Kulikovsky, he expected the same from her in return.

Michael was exceptionally easygoing, but it was a characteristic which could mislead people into thinking that he would protest at nothing. He did allow himself to be imposed upon, but when he believed that someone had betrayed his trust, he would cut them off completely. It was so with his former ADC Mordvinov, as it was with anyone else in his entourage who had spoken out against Natasha. He would not fly into a rage, or have a heated row; instead, it would be as if a shutter had come down. Before that stage was reached his apparent willingness to suffer in silence could infuriate Natasha, who was always ready and eager to do battle. His 'character' was sometimes her despair.

After one protesting letter from her, Michael replied: 'You say that someone has only to write a tearful letter to me for me to forgive that person. Well, if that is so, it only applies to people whose fault is not really great; but this forgiveness of mine will never be granted to such people as Mordvinov ...'[12] He might have added, 'or even Olga'.

Olga wanted a reconciliation but there was none to be had as yet, though she was well aware that Michael's headquarters were only a few hours away and that he had been in Lvov several times with Natasha, including those nine days at the beginning of March. As Alexandra reported to Nicholas, Olga 'feels sad Misha is with his wife there and she has never seen him for four years'.[13]

One chance for a possible reconciliation came a month later, when Natasha was at home at Gatchina. Nicholas arrived in Lvov on a 'victory tour' of the Galician front and to see the newly-captured fortress of Przemysl, seventy miles east of Lvov. He might have been expected to meet Michael, so recently decorated for heroism, and to have arranged a family reunion, for Xenia had travelled to Lvov to see her sister. But Michael was not

* Octobrists, led by Aleksandr Guchkov, were so called because they supported the 1905 October manifesto and were conservatives who generally favoured a 'constitutional monarchy'.

invited; the first he knew that Nicholas had been in Lvov was when he read about it in a local newspaper.[14] One reason for that may have been Alexandra.

People might have thought he had been forgiven.

Built upon tribesmen unused to conventional military discipline, the Savage Division had been forged into an exceptional fighting force and much of the credit for that lay with Michael. 'We were all devoted to him,' said a colonel.[15] Ordinary soldiers called him simply 'Dzhigit Misha' – meaning 'our Caucasian horseman Michael', a compliment they gave to no other Russian officer – and because they did not distinguish rank as carefully as they should have done they often called him 'Your Majesty' rather than 'Your Highness'.[16] The men trusted him implicitly, believing that whatever their grievances they could go to him for justice.

One such dispute involved an Ingush Cossack rider who had captured two officers. Taking an officer prisoner earned a medal and the simple Ingush reasoned therefore that he was entitled to two medals. Stubbornly refusing to accept what he was told by his own officers he argued his way into divisional headquarters and was brought before Michael. Having heard him, Michael burst out laughing. 'Lord, what am I to do with him?'

His staff had no doubt. 'You must tell him that he is wrong, Your Highness.'

'I know perfectly well he is wrong, but he is offended. He places his hopes on me and it is not within my power to help him.'

With that, the Ingush bowed. 'Do not help me,' he said. 'I thought that they were lying, but if you say it, that means it is true. Do not be angry.' Michael gave him the single medal he was entitled to and settled the matter of the second officer by handing the grateful rider twenty roubles.[17]

Some matters ended badly. On April 17 three of his men, condemned to death by a court martial for looting, were taken out for execution. In the process they broke free and were shot dead, with one guard killed and another wounded in the confusion. Michael was horrified, noting, 'it all turned out to be very horrible and tragic and such a shame, as a telegram with their pardon had been received and was to be read to them at the place of execution for greater effect – and it all failed!'[18]

There was for the moment relatively little action on his front, as his diary noted. Other divisions in other sectors would be fighting desperate battles, with worse to come, but it was not so in the map references which were the world of the Savage Division. On April 19 a German plane dropped five bombs on his headquarters 'without causing any damage', there was sporadic firing from the enemy outposts and 'we buried a soldier, Veris, killed the day before yesterday'.[19] One dead soldier in two days; that was almost peace. Five days later Michael was home, his division, after six months in the line, being withdrawn for rest and refitting.

His month's leave passed so quickly that afterwards it seemed the briefest of interludes. Michael saw his brother twice at Tsarskoe Selo and had tea with his mother at the Anichkov Palace. Otherwise he spent his whole time with Natasha. They went to Peterhof with a party of friends, drove off on picnics in his American Packard, rode in the Gatchina park, had tea in the private garden at the palace and went to the theatre to see a play based on Dickens's *Cricket on the Hearth*.[20]

His memories would become photographs kept in his frontline quarters and when he first looked at the pictures he told Natasha how well she looked in them. She was 'charming ... touching ... not without a touch of coquetry ... demure ...' but of all the pictures his favourite was the one in which she was standing by a cherry tree in the palace garden at Peterhof. 'I have no words to tell you how much I like you in that picture: *tu est si belle et désirable* – that turn of the head, those feet, those hands, that charming bosom – you look such a beauty.'

Then he added: 'How magnificently stupid on my part to show all my love and all my admiration in such a way, for it's the best way to lose your love for me. No, it's not I who am confident of your constant love, as you always told me, but you of mine!'[21]

When Michael returned to the front on May 23, Natasha travelled with him this time only as far as Brest-Litovsk, a large town and railway junction 132 miles from Warsaw and some 200 miles north of Lvov. Parting yet again on a railway platform, she wrote to him immediately afterwards. 'My darling Misha, I wish to write you a few words to tell you how sad it was to part with you. My dearest, don't forget your promise to be careful and you must always remember this promise. You know that I have no one but you and my entire life is you alone.'[22]

Natasha had not seen Dimitri since Easter, but he had sent her a postcard on April 28, to say that 'one shouldn't, oh, one shouldn't ruin what has been built' and signed it 'Deeply devoted to you, Dimitri'.[23] He had not, as he had hoped, gone to the front; instead, he was at Baranovichi, serving as an orderly officer at Stavka. On her way home to Gatchina on May 24 Natasha's train stopped for almost a full day at Baranovichi; there Dimitri came to see her four times in the space of ten hours.

'Lily-of-the-Valley came flying in about 11.30 a.m. I was not ready yet, so I talked to him through the door; he left around noon, for they have lunch at noon and returned at one. He was awfully nice and moving and was terribly happy to see me. He said he hadn't expected himself that he would be so happy to see me.' He left again at three; then returned at 6.30 p.m., then left to get permission to dine with Natasha, returning shortly afterwards and to stay with her until her train was ready to leave at 9.40 p.m.[24]

Afterwards she wrote to him, reminding him of his comments in his earlier postcard and adding that 'it is for the sake of that, that I have been avoiding you lately. I felt so sad and I did not want to "ruin what has been built". Let us go into the past, but go as thoughts and touching memories like the fragrance of lilies of the valley in Spring. Darling, darling, Lily-of-the-Valley, what else can I say to you? There is a lot I would wish to, but I can't . . .'[25]

Dimitri clearly took that to heart for a few days later, in Petrograd, Natasha was 'amazed to see Lily-of-the-Valley in a car on Morskaya Street . . . and he hasn't even telephoned me or given any indication of his being here. I feel quite hurt,' she told Michael.[26]

He was almost gleeful in his reply. 'It seems to me that one day you two will have a furious quarrel and all your friendship will be over.'[27]

Michael returned to a war which had started to go badly for Russia. Ground won on the south-western front was now ground lost. The Tsar's victory tour of early April proved premature, for shortly afterwards the Germans masterminded a new offensive, launched with an overwhelming artillery barrage which reduced Russian divisions to a fraction of their normal strength. Trenches collapsed and reinforcements brought up melted away under the barrage of metal. Many soldiers hastily marched into the battle zone were unarmed and dependent on picking up the weapons of soldiers who had fallen. A month after the offensive began, Przemysl was recaptured and three weeks later, on June 9, the Russians lost Lvov.

'I feel so distressed because of Lvov,' wrote Michael, but adding that 'to lose heart and think that we won't win is just sinful. The morale of the army at the front is good, what I am concerned about is the attitude of the Russian public at large . . . One should look at the English for a good example – they have more steadfastness than we do, they do everything in a more systematic way and if they set themselves an objective, they will never give it up halfway.'[28]

Natasha voiced her own concerns. There was a desperate shortage of shells, rifles, bullets and 'those joining the volunteer corps lately were given old rifles left over from the Turkish campaign,* which can only shoot at thirty paces. So the soldiers are aware that they are sent to their deaths unarmed – it is appalling! All Russia's faults and blunders are coming to the surface, yet many prefer to be blind to them. You must admit that everything

* The Russo-Turkish war of 1877–8.

is done as I have always said . . . our retreat will not stop at the frontier, but will go as far as the Germans wish.'[29]

The retreat did not stop at the frontier. Caught up in it, Michael's division withdrew behind the River Dniester, but held its ground thereafter. 'Oh, how I wish this atrocious slaughter could be over soon!' he wrote to Natasha. In two days there were 1000 wounded.[30]

His letters home were not always full of gloomy passages about the war. There were also moments of light relief, as when the Ninth Army commander General Lechitsky visited an artillery position with a large entourage of braided staff officers; it was a target too good to miss and in consequence the general and his staff 'had to spend two hours crouching in an empty trench'. It was their own fault, said Michael, for he often went to the same position 'without all that pomp and retinue' and nothing ever happened.[31]

Michael sent Natasha photographs of the half-dozen pilots attached to his division and of their new Voisin, a French reconnaissance plane, with a 130-horsepower engine and a speed of sixty miles per hour. Natasha was immediately suspicious, taking the photographs to mean that 'you are dying to fly, particularly since it would be so easy to keep it from me'.[32]

He promptly denied that he had any such idea and then enthused about an air battle in which his Voisin had helped in chasing off two German planes, even though in the rush to get into the fight the pilot had forgotten to take a machine-gun.[33] A few days later his divisional Voisin shot down a German plane just above his position. 'The pilot was killed and the navigator could not crawl over and get behind the controls. Our pilots had a machine gun and they had only rifles. The plane fell right before our eyes' and crashed in flames. Michael raced across to the Voisin as it landed and welcomed 'our wonderful pilots', as he noted that night in his diary.[34] Since the story would only have confirmed to Natasha that he was indeed hoping to fly, he did not tell her about it, or mention his planes again in his letters.

In the midst of this fighting, with Michael's division being driven back, then counterattacking to regain ground lost, Grand Duke Konstantin Konstantinovich died at the age of fifty-seven at his home in Pavlovsk; on Saturday, June 6, 1915, he was buried with great pomp in the fortress of St Peter and St Paul.[35] The only member of the imperial family absent was Michael.

There was comment about that which upset Natasha. She wrote to him in bewilderment: 'Darling Misha, why do you always harm yourself and why didn't you come for K.K.'s funeral? Literally all your relatives came *en masse*, only you didn't appear . . . your absence was conspicuous. Even assuming that you did not feel like showing your face at a family gathering, you could have still taken that opportunity just to come home! Boris had only just left and he came back again till June 20.'[36]

Michael explained what seemed to him needed no explanation: that he was in the middle of a war.

> *I did not come to the funeral of Konstantin K. because I had only returned from a long leave a short while before that and did not think I had a right to leave here again: there is a war on, not children's games with soldiers . . . while I am in command of a division, it is impossible for me to leave it so often; and if any of my relations do just that, they are wrong and they are not an example for me to follow. I am not having fun here, I am quite miserable and you know perfectly well that if only I manage to return home I will be the happiest of men.*[37]

There was another reason why he could not go back, and he tried to explain that, too. 'Our division is not a regular army unit, and it's not so easy to command it; there are a lot of different things to sort out – jealousy and rivalry between the regiments, their mutual complaints, etc. When I am here, everything gets into a more peaceful vein, but without me . . . it is more than difficult to control.'[38]

Natasha, having complained about his absence from the state funeral, was plainly in a bad mood that day, for she added more personal criticism in the same letter. At Stavka as well as in Petrograd the officers she saw were all smartly dressed, in crisp uniforms, polished boots and with an elegant style that looked well in the Astoria. In contrast, Michael, a fighting general, looked shabby, ill-dressed and muddy in almost all the photographs he sent her. 'You want me to like your looks so badly, yet you do very little to ensure it – look how awfully you now dress,' she chided him. 'Your boots are horrible, you've done away with your aiguillettes and instead of the St George you wear a piece of some narrow ribbon . . . You used to be so elegant and I regret to see you so changed.'[39]

Natasha had sent Michael a St George, made up for her at Fabergé,[40] not understanding that the only person likely to admire the gleam of a Fabergé St George was an enemy sniper. Personal appearance was not the uppermost consideration in the frontline. None the less, her parade of complaints 'to be honest, deeply upset me'. He added that he could well understand 'why Lily-of-the-Valley can be much more attractive and interesting than I'.[41]

One reason for Michael's despondent mood was that he had been feeling dreadful. 'Since yesterday I have had a bandaged head because I have abscesses in both my ears . . . very painful . . . I can't seem to get well . . . I feel terribly sluggish,' he confided to his diary. 'I've been feeling awful since the end of May, I have had no strength . . .'[42]

Both became upset at the letters each was writing to the other. 'Misha, it's awfully sad for me to read your letter, it is so unloving,' Natasha complained.[43] He replied: 'It's so unkind and unfair on your part to write to me in such a way.'[44] Nevertheless, their tiffs went on.

'I know you were upset by what I said about your appearance,' Natasha replied in her letter, 'but Mishechka, it is true . . . I like elegant people and that is exactly why I pay attention to the way you're dressed. If I hadn't cared, I wouldn't have noticed.'[45]

Michael lamely defended himself. 'You know how difficult it is to get any sense out of tailors and shoemakers when you don't see them or hardly ever see them and can't explain to them what you want.' However, he took note of her point. A shell hole remained a shell hole, but in future he would dive into them looking better dressed. 'At present I wear linen jackets and breeches with yellow boots – I think you would approve.'[46]

Someone who did approve was an American war correspondent, Stanley Washburn, who visited his headquarters shortly afterwards. He was impressed to find the brother of the Tsar in a 'simple uniform with nothing to indicate his rank but shoulder straps of the same material as his uniform and, barring the St George (won by personal valour on the battlefield), without a decoration . . .' He rated Michael highly. 'He evinced the same stubborn optimism that one finds everywhere in the Russian army,' he commented, while appearing 'as unaffected and democratic a person as one can well imagine'.[47]

But what surprised Washburn was that he should find Grand Duke Michael 'living so simply in a dirty village in this far fringe of the Russian front . . .'[48] He thought it praiseworthy. Natasha thought it only a humiliation imposed upon Michael by a family determined to punish him for his marriage. She could not understand why he put up with it and many of her criticisms were merely symptoms of her frustration over his apparent acceptance of his lot.

'All your "saintly" deeds have achieved nothing except cause you pain,' she told Michael with her usual frankness.[49] Her theme was that Michael was fooling himself if he believed that he would eventually earn recognition for his marriage. All he achieved was the sacrifice of 'our happiness'.[50]

Michael did not see it that way. 'You are not always fair towards me and you criticise me too much for everything – though I am not saying that I am always right,' he answered.

> *As for my conscience, it is torn into two parts: I feel that at such a difficult time I must serve Russia and serve here at the front, no matter how hard it might be for me (that's one half). And the other half of my conscience, knowing how much you suffer because of my service, gives me no peace day or night . . . I am a patient person, maybe even too patient and because of my patience the*

people who are dearest to me might even suffer some injustices. But the present time is so hard for Russia that my conscience could not allow me not *to join the frontline service – and I am convinced that having done that, I also brought you some good in terms of public opinion, which, unfortunately, we can't totally ignore.*[51]

Sometimes Natasha could hit below the belt, as when she claimed that Michael would have left her behind in England, if she had been refused permission to return with him when war was declared.[52] 'Natashechka, you know perfectly well that, if it hadn't been for this dreadful war, we would have lived quietly abroad and I would never have dreamt of going to Russia – even for a day – without you. And you had no reason whatever to hurt me by writing that . . . I would never have returned on my own. No, I wouldn't have done that and it's as certain as my writing to you now.'[53]

Yet he never failed to declare his love for her, whatever she said to him. 'The longer I live with you, the more I love you, cherish you and respect you.'[54] And having heard that Natasha had torn a ligament in her foot he was full of concern: 'My tender, darling girl . . . my poor little darling, I feel so sorry for you that I can't say and I'm so annoyed I can't be with you now! I could have massaged your poor injured foot and would have sat by your side all the time . . .'[55]

Natasha had intended to go to Moscow at the beginning of June, but had postponed her trip because of serious rioting which had broken out there. The defeats suffered by the Russians since the spring resulted in revenge attacks on Germans living in Moscow. Many had been there for generations, owning important businesses and thinking themselves German only in name.

'It was really appalling,' wrote Natasha. 'Enormous mobs were looting all shops with foreign signboards and then proceeded to do the same with the Russian shops and especially the wine cellars . . .' All the windows in the Nikolaevskaya Palace had been smashed, because 'a drunken mob' believed that Grand Duchess Ella was hiding her German brother, Grand Duke Ernst of Hesse.[56] He was rumoured to have come secretly to Russia to negotiate a peace settlement.

There was particular ill-feeling against Ella, Natasha reported, 'because everyone knows how she cares about the German prisoners of war. In short, there has happened the same thing as in London, but their crowds are certainly more cultured and they only went against the Germans, while here they immediately got drunk and all hell broke loose . . .'[57]

Three weeks later Natasha went to Moscow and saw some of the damage for herself. 'All that's left of the shops and houses with German names are just bare walls, with the insides looted and burnt ... It was real pillage, well organised and made possible by the indifference and inaction of the authorities and police ...' One business friend whose home was ransacked 'told me that members of the intelligentsia were among the rioters – obvious connoisseurs came to his house and chose the best pictures to destroy. So many wonderful paintings are lost, such a shame!'[58]

Michael felt 'very sorry for the unfortunate victims' and wrote that the pogrom 'clearly demonstrates the hatred that the Russian people have long felt for foreigners living in Russia ...'

> *The government ought to be ashamed that it can't prevent such things, with many victims as a consequence. How I wish for a 'wise government' for my dear Russia, so that we could boast of it to all European states, but who knows if that will ever come and if it does, I am afraid it won't be soon! I know you will understand what I mean and will read between the lines ...*

He added that 'many people now feel that I was right to have married a Russian and not a German ...'[59] It was not difficult for Natasha to 'read between the lines'. His barbs were aimed at Alexandra and her circle.

On Natasha's return home from Moscow she celebrated her thirty-fifth birthday. Michael had missed Christmas, New Year, Easter and now her birthday also. 'It is so sad for me not to be with you, my darling Natasha,' he wrote. 'I am wishing you a happy birthday from the very bottom of my heart ... and I am asking God to bring us together again soon.'[60]

He was rather put out, however, to find that Dimitri had specially telephoned her and that they had 'chattered about all sorts of silly nonsense for 35 minutes or so ... He wished me a happy birthday in the most charming way and said he would come the next day to lunch, which he did. I was delighted to see dear Lily-of-the-Valley. I love him tenderly, I really do. You know, I have nothing to amuse him with here and therefore if he comes it is only to see me, which means he is fond of me ... He later said to Johnson that he'd been delighted with his visit to Gatchina and that I always received him so well and that he greatly appreciated my friendship.'[61]

The letter shocked Michael.

> *What you are writing to me about Lily-of-the-Valley, i.e., how tenderly, tenderly you love him and also that he comes to see you because he likes you and has totally succumbed to your charm and besides, you say that conquering such a heart means much to you – I believe that if you just stop to consider the meaning of these several sentences you have written, you will realise what pain you have given me by writing them; alas, I am now getting more and more convinced that I was right when I said that your feelings towards me and*

your love have changed and that intense, undiluted feeling that used to be is no longer there and will never be again.

But my feelings for you are the same as ever. Yes, it is sad, so sad – I used to believe your absolute love for me, I almost believed it more than my own and I never thought it could ever change. You will probably say that's all nonsense and it's not true – no, Natasha, it is not nonsense and it is true![62]

Natasha had not meant to give that impression and she was quick to reassure Michael that in saying one thing she had not intended to suggest another. She started well:

My dearest Mishechka, it makes me very sad to know that you are so upset because of Lily-of-the-Valley. Believe me, my affection for him does not in the least interfere with my love for you. It is true that I am very fond of him, he is very precious to me and so is his regard for me, but none of this can affect my attitude to you – and especially now that I have succeeded in directing my relations with Lily-of-the-Valley into the channel of my choice, which is the only channel I can ever allow for the relations between myself and anyone else – i.e., just very warm and affectionate terms, with a touch of flirtation if you like, witty and amusing and with mutual teasing, but certainly nothing beyond that.

That was almost what Michael wanted to hear and reading it he felt relief. Natasha would have done better to have left it at that, but she pressed on, to explain more than was necessary about Dimitri.

He no longer talks to me about his love, as though it has never happened, but I can feel that he admires me and that imparts a certain piquant interest to our meetings. Besides, we seem to be very like each other in character and I could even say that we are kindred souls . . . No one who knows him well can help loving him . . . and even those who start off being prejudiced against him, change their opinion once they get to know him. So I, knowing him better than others, also know what to love him for.[63]

The French ambassador Paléologue, attempting to understand the nature of Russian women, would later repeat one judgement which impressed him – that 'one of their serious defects is that they cannot lie . . . and this it is which often makes them seem cruel'.[64] Natasha, having explained Dimitri, now explained herself.

You have been so used to having my entire self in your possession and my entire life too, that I can easily imagine how sad it must be for you now to think that there's somebody else in my life besides you – yet in our first years, in the years when the love between us was so intense, you had a life completely separate from mine, where there was no part for me and which had nothing to do with me – friends, pleasures, service, balls, picnics with the ladies – and I had to put up with it all.[65]

In writing that, she had been prompted by re-reading her old letters from Bad Kissingen, written in 1911.

What a terribly unhappy time it was and what a nightmare my entire life was then! I now feel almost as if I have risen from the dead and, despite the war and the difficult times we are all living through, I now see things in an entirely different light and I am gradually becoming my old joyful and merry self again . . . I am so happy that those days are gone for ever and nothing can induce me now to live them again and suffer as I suffered then. When you come home, I'll let you reread these letters and you will see from what burden I have been released.[66]

Fortunately for Michael's peace of mind he was coming home and shortly. And then the problems and misunderstandings that often arose when they were apart could, as always before, be forgotten. He left the front on July 15, going first to Stavka;[67] there he met Dimitri. In the circumstances it was a meeting which could have been greatly embarrassing. To Dimitri's relief, Michael could not have been more charming and agreeable and afterwards Dimitri wrote in relief to Natasha: 'I was very pleased. He touched me deeply with his kindness and understanding . . . I could have written so much, dearest, but sometimes it is best not to express one's thoughts . . .'[68]

By the time that Natasha got that letter Michael was already at home. It was as well that he was, for reasons other than the strains in his marriage. Michael had diphtheria, dreaded as one of the great killers of the age.

SIXTEEN

Alexandra the Great

Natasha had long worried about Michael's health, often with good reason. Michael, a potential 'prize-fighter' as his American boxing coach had described him, a superb horseman and a man who prided himself on keeping fit, hid from the world the fact that he suffered from gastric ulcers.

For years only Natasha and his doctors knew about it. However, as Natasha told Princess Putyatina when Michael went off to war in 1914, 'whenever he strayed, no matter how slightly, from the diet ordered by the doctors he suffered painfully'.[1] The frontline did not have special diets; a soldier ate what he got. That was why men with stomach ulcers were invariably graded as physically unfit for military service, or at best given desk jobs at home depots.

As Tata put it, 'Uncle Misha would have been the first to protest at such an insult to his endurance'; his advantage was that 'in his exalted position he could ignore the authorities of the medical world and carry on'.[2]

Diphtheria he could not ignore, for more died than survived it. There were no antibiotics and many sufferers died from asphyxiation as their throats closed up. Those who survived took a long time to recover. Michael caught diphtheria, a highly-contagious disease, while he was still at the front and he was fortunate to have arrived home on leave just as the first symptoms appeared. On July 22 'I stayed in bed because I had a high temperature and a sore throat', he noted.[3] Three days later his Gatchina doctor, Dr Koton, arrived to tell him that he had found diphtheria bacilli. By next day his condition had worsened, 'although out of stubbornness I continued to sit on the couch and not lie in bed'.[4] Fearing a spread of the infection, a desperately worried Natasha sent the two children to friends nearby. When Michael did go to bed that night he would stay there for the next ten days. To cheer him, Count Pavel Tolstoy, an old friend and son of an equerry to Nicholas, came in one afternoon and played the piano in the 'schoolroom' next to his bedroom and he and Natasha 'sang Russian songs at half-voice, that was very nice to listen to'.[5]

A week after the first symptoms he began to feel better and was well enough to have 'played the guitar a little'.[6] A few days later a specialist confirmed that he had 'anaemia and high blood sugar' but by August 5 he could write that 'I got up and went downstairs for breakfast for the first time'.[7]

The beginning of his recovery was good news, but there was little else to cheer him. On August 7 he grimly noted only that 'the war is so bad that I don't want to write about it'.[8] Next day he tersely recorded, 'Kovno and Novo-Georgievsk have been captured!' Six days later he took up his diary and wrote that 'Brest-Litovsk has surrendered! We've been in a bad mood for the past few days'.[9]

Michael had long thought that Russian strategy was wrong, as events would prove it to be. The war was not about holding or taking territory, he told Natasha, but about destroying the enemy's army.

> *What's happening is that they are trying to achieve the opposite. All high commanders panic over every inch of land captured by the enemy instead of taking a huge fist and punching the enemy where it hurts. This simple and, one would think, reasonable tactic has not so far been used. They want to be strong everywhere, along the entire frontline, which, of course, is impossible and as a result, we are everywhere equally weak.*[10]

Over the past three weeks the advancing Germans had captured Warsaw, then the string of Russian fortresses which in theory should have barred an enemy advance into Russia proper. Millions of shells had been locked up in them, along with hundreds of guns and tens of thousands of men. Now they had all gone, without anything to show for them.

In the first year of the war the Russian army had lost one and a half million men, the equivalent of the whole of its peacetime army; whereas it had been fighting until the spring beyond its own frontiers, now for the first time since Napoleon an enemy was advancing deep inside Russia's homeland, driving back not only the army but hundreds of thousands of refugees flooding east in desperate flight from homes and crops burned behind them.

Something had to be done and that something was firstly the dismissal of the disastrous war minister Sukhomlinov; he was not only incompetent but corrupt, supporting his high-spending and pretty young wife – at thirty, half his age – with bribes taken from army contracts.

For very different reasons the Supreme Commander, Grand Duke Nicholas Nikolaevich – 'Uncle Nikolasha' – was also to be brought down. The Grand Duke was well regarded by both the French and British, and by the Germans no less, and his great height and soldierly bearing had impressed foreign correspondents. He was not the best general in the Russian army, but he looked the part. He was also more victim than villain in the scandal of an army without enough shells, rifles and boots. Neither the public nor the army sought him as scapegoat. Nevertheless, he was removed.

But what shocked Russia was the name of his successor. The new Supreme Commander was to be a man who had never been on the battlefield and whose last military command had been almost a quarter of a century earlier and then only as an officer in a squadron of the Hussar Life Guards. The Tsar appointed himself.

Few approved. Michael's cousin Grand Duke Andrew observed that 'thoughtful people believe that this step will cause general ill-feeling and discontent and have serious consequences'.[11] The British military observer Sir Alfred Knox, who saw the army's reaction at first hand, concluded that misgivings 'were almost universal ...'[12] The French ambassador wrote gloomily that 'the news has produced a deplorable impression ...'[13] General Brusilov would say that Nicholas 'struck the last blow against himself'.[14]

But if Nicholas was to be at Stavka, then who would represent him in the capital and handle the day-to-day affairs of state? The man who knew nothing about war answered that by appointing someone who knew nothing about politics. He gave the job to his wife.

The move was made almost casually within days of his arrival at headquarters and after a letter in which Alexandra wrote: 'Do not fear for what remains behind ... don't laugh at silly old Wify, but she has "trousers" on unseen ...'[15] His reply was as she had hoped. 'Think my Wify, will you not come to the assistance of your hubby now that he is absent? What a pity that you have not been fulfilling this duty for a long time, or at least during the war!'[16]

The invitation was eagerly accepted. 'Oh, Sweetheart, I am so touched you want my help. I am always ready to do anything for you, only never liked mixing up without being asked ...'[17]

Since there was no formal announcement that Alexandra was now effectively Regent on the home front, it took some time before the public realised that henceforth Russia was to be ruled by a domineering, neurotic and hysterical Empress and behind her, hiding in her shadow, by the scandalous and hated figure of her hypnotic 'holy man', Grigory Rasputin.

The power of Rasputin had grown massively over the past ten years as again and again he appeared to demonstrate that only he could save Alexandra's son from the 'bleeding disease'. When Alexis lay at the point of death at Spala in 1912 an anguished Alexandra sent Rasputin a telegram begging his help and received back a cable to say that 'the Little One will not die. Do not allow the doctors to bother him too much.'[18] Shortly afterwards the crisis passed. A man who could save her son even by telegram was surely a man sent by God and she would ever after be utterly dependent on him.

Rasputin was not the first mystical figure to influence affairs at Tsarskoe Selo. His most notorious predecessor was a hypnotic French quack, a former butcher's assistant from Lyons and a man well known to the French police. Calling himself Dr Philippe – his real name was Philippe Nizier-Vachod – he appeared on the scene in 1901, long before the birth of Alexis. Like Rasputin he was known as 'our Friend' by both Nicholas and Alexandra; indeed, Alexandra's references to Dr Philippe could easily be confused with her later references to Rasputin: 'how rich life is since we know him and everything seems easier to bear', she would write that year.[19] Grand Duke Konstantin would note disturbingly that after sessions with Dr Philippe, the Tsar and Alexandra would return 'in an exalted state, as if in an ecstasy, with radiant faces and shining eyes'.[20]

It was Dr Philippe who persuaded Alexandra that she was going to give birth to her long-awaited son; in August 1902, as St Petersburg eagerly waited for the bells to ring and the cannon to roar, there was unexpected disappointment. It was a phantom pregnancy,[21] although Russia could not, of course, be told that. Even so, 'our Friend' survived that embarrassing setback; it was another eighteen months before Nicholas, with regret, felt it would be wiser to dismiss him.* Someone was bound to step into his shoes and in the event his successor was Grigory Rasputin.

Face to face, what struck many people about Rasputin was his eyes. Even down-to-earth Paléologue remarked on them: 'The whole expression of the face was concentrated in the eyes – light-blue eyes with a curious sparkle, depth and fascination . . . When he was excited, it seemed as if his pupils became magnetic.'[22] By 1915 Paléologue concluded that Alexandra 'lives in a kind of hypnosis'. Whatever Rasputin's opinion or desire 'she acquiesces and obeys at once. The ideas he suggests to her are implanted in her brain without provoking the slightest opposition.'[23]

Because few people outside court circles knew about the carefully guarded secret of Alexis's haemophilia, wider society did not understand why Rasputin was tolerated at all at Tsarskoe Selo, or how it was that he had come to hold such power over the Empress – though the same might have been said about Philippe. Meetings between Alexandra and Rasputin usually took place outside the Alexander Palace and in the nearby villa of her long-time companion Anna Vyrubova, who was devoted to 'our Friend'. Rasputin lived in an apartment in Petrograd, but would regularly be summoned to Tsarskoe Selo whenever the Empress wanted his advice, encouragement, or blessing in relation to some particular matter, now increasingly political in nature. He and the Empress, with Vyrubova in attendance, might be closeted together for hours, with police keeping guard around the little villa at 2 Sredniaia, just 300 yards from the palace. 'As the Emperor never ventured to decide anything without his wife's opinion, or

* He died in France in August 1905.

rather approval, the net result is that it is the Empress and Madame Vyrubova who really govern Russia!' commented Paléologue.[24] No mention of these meetings appeared in the newspapers, but they were known about none the less. Rasputin himself boasted about them.

Had Rasputin been a discreet man and modest in his private life, his association with the Empress would have attracted comment but perhaps no more than that. As it was, his outrageous public behaviour appalled Petrograd and Moscow and as scandal followed scandal the reputation of the Empress followed Rasputin's into the gutter.

Thus it was in the spring of 1915, when Rasputin was embroiled in a disgraceful scene in the exclusive Yar restaurant, in Moscow's Petrovsky Park. One witness was the British diplomat Robert Bruce Lockhart. From one of the 'cabinets' there came wild shrieks, a man's curses, the sound of broken glass and the banging of doors. 'The cause of the disturbance was Rasputin – drunk and lecherous and neither police nor management dared evict him.' It was not until a direct order came from the assistant minister of the interior, General Dzhunkovsky, that Rasputin was arrested and taken away, 'snarling and vowing vengeance'. Rasputin was released next day on 'instructions from the highest quarter'.[25] In Petrograd the story quickly spread and it was said that one cause of the uproar was that Rasputin had started talking about the Empress, calling her 'the old girl'. Showing an embroidered waistcoat he was wearing under his caftan he said: 'The old girl made me this waistcoat ... I can do anything I like with her ...'[26]

When she got her hands on a copy of the official report Alexandra was enraged, denouncing the honest Dzhunkovsky for 'a vile, filthy paper'. Her fury increased when she learned that Dzhunkovsky had shown his report to Dimitri, 'who repeated all'.[27] There was never any chance that the story might be hushed-up anyway; such was the public clamour that Nicholas ordered Rasputin to return to his home village in Siberia, in the futile hope that it might dampen the outrage certain to be voiced in the new session of the Duma.

On his departure Rasputin warned a tearful Alexandra: 'Remember that I need neither the Emperor nor yourself ... But neither the Emperor nor you can do without me. If I am not there to protect you, your son will come to harm.'[28] Two weeks later Alexandra prevailed over her husband and Rasputin was back as if nothing had happened. And three weeks after that, the man who had arrested him was sacked.

Dzhunkovsky's downfall was inevitable once Alexandra had set her mind to it, for, as many learned, they crossed her at their peril. Grand Duke Nicholas, the army's Supreme Commander, had failed to realise that and had duly paid the price. His dismissal served as a warning and as an example to all who thought themselves a power in the land.

Over the past months the Tsar had been bombarded by Alexandra with complaints about Grand Duke Nicholas. She had protested about Nicholas taking him on his victory tour in April, thinking that Nikolasha would steal his thunder. 'Show that you are master ... be more decided and sure of yourself ... They must remember who you are and that first they must turn to you,' she urged.[29] Fearing that Nikolasha was usurping the Tsar's authority, she came to believe that he was intent on usurping his crown. Rasputin was also deeply hostile to the Grand Duke, for when he had cabled him, offering to come and bless the troops, the ramrod commander-in-chief had sent the reply: 'Yes, do come. I'll hang you'.[30] One jealous, the other vengeful, Alexandra and Rasputin worked together to bring down Grand Duke Nicholas.

When the Tsar went off in April on his battlefield tour of the south, rumours that the visit had been less than a triumph quickly seeped back to the capital. 'Everyone has been struck by the indifference, or rather coldness, with which the Emperor was received by the army,' noted the French ambassador. 'The legend which has grown up around the Empress and Rasputin has been a serious blow to the prestige of the Emperor both with the men and their officers.'[31] Later he commented that Rasputin 'is always railing' against Grand Duke Nicholas, whom he accuses of 'blank ignorance of the military art and of having no other ambition than to gain an illegitimate popularity with the troops with the ulterior object of supplanting the Emperor'.[32]

In the Moscow pogroms at the end of May the mobs had chanted insults against the German-born Alexandra, shouting that she should be locked up in a convent, Rasputin hanged, the Emperor deposed and the crown transferred to Grand Duke Nicholas.[33] Reports such as that were seized upon at Tsarskoe Selo as evidence that their true enemy was in Stavka, where 'Uncle Nikolasha' and not the Tsar seemed to reign supreme. Alexandra regarded as intolerable a headquarters with Nikolasha in command. When Nicholas went there for two weeks in June Alexandra wrote to him sometimes twice a day, her letters dripping with spite against the man she saw as a potential usurper. Invariably her criticisms of Nikolasha – 'N' in her letters – were supported by references to Rasputin.

Our Friend dreads yr. being at the Headquarters as . . . involuntarily you give in to them, when your own feeling has been the right one, but did not suit theirs. Remember you have reigned long, have far more experience than they – N. has only the army to think of . . . after the war he is nobody. No, hearken unto our Friend, believe Him, He has your interest & Russia's at heart – it is not for nothing God sent Him to us – only we must pay more attention to what He says – His words are not lightly spoken – & the gravity of having not only His prayers but His advice – is great.[34]

Then again, 'Nobody knows who is the Emperor now – you have to run to the Headquarters and assemble yr. ministers there, as tho' you could not have them alone here ... It is as tho' N. settles all, makes the choices & changes – it makes me utterly wretched ...'[35] A week later she was still persisting that 'all are shocked that the ministers go with reports to him, as tho' he were now the Sovereign'.[36]

A few days later Nicholas was safely at home and she could preach the same message to his face. The result was inevitable. Nikolasha was sent away to be commander of the distant Caucasus and a nervous Nicholas took his place. A jubilant Alexandra dismissed all criticism now levelled at her husband, writing to him: 'Those who fear & cannot understand your actions, will be brought by events to realise your great wisdom. It is the beginning of the glory of yr. reign, He said so & I absolutely believe it.'[37]

Nicholas was nothing like so sure, thinking that he went to Stavka more as sacrificial lamb than warrior leader. Nevertheless, having completed the awkward business of facing Nikolasha and despatching him to the sidelines, Nicholas could write to her, 'Thank God it is all over ... I feel so calm – a sort of feeling after Holy Communion!'[38]

Others were anything but calm. Grand Duke Andrew, visiting a 'terribly worried' Dowager Empress, reported that she feared that the removal of Nikolasha 'will be the ruin' of the Tsar and 'laid all the blame' on Alexandra. 'It is all her work ... she alone is responsible for all that is happening now. It is too awful.' Her son was 'lovable, honest, good' but with Alexandra behind him the Dowager Empress could only wring her hands and cry, 'What are we coming to, what are we coming to?'[39] Duke Alexander of Oldenburg, known in the family as Uncle Alex, was in equal despair when he saw the Dowager Empress. As she would tell Andrew afterwards, 'he rolled on the floor'.[40]

Alexandra was quite frank, and startlingly so, in showing her dominance over her husband. When the British ambassador, Sir George Buchanan, met her at Tsarskoe Selo and told her of his worries about Nicholas assuming the Supreme Command, she told him: 'The situation requires firmness. The Emperor, unfortunately, is weak; but I am not and I intend to be firm.'[41] However true, to say that to the ambassador of an allied country was unforgivable.

None the less the Tsar ended his first day as Supreme Commander on a confident note. 'We had only just finished playing dominoes,' he wrote to Alexandra, when news came that the southern army had captured 'over

150 officers, over 7,000 men, thirty guns and many machine-guns. And this happened immediately after our troops learnt that I have taken upon myself the Supreme Command. This is truly God's blessing . . .'[42] To underline his delight, he sent the same news by telegram next day, so that she could read all over again about 'our glorious success' and that 'this happened immediately after the declaration of my appointment'.[43]

Nicholas needed a sign from heaven. He had done what Alexandra had insisted he should do but, as he was to confess nine months later, in March 1916, taking command of the armies had been 'a terrible moment for me. I thought God had deserted me and a victim was necessary to save Russia.'[44]

Michael was soon to find out for himself what life was like at Stavka with his brother as Supreme Commander, for two weeks after Nicholas took over the armies he summoned Michael to join him. With the Russian armies in retreat, general headquarters had been forced some weeks earlier to withdraw from Baranovichi and find somewhere safer. The place chosen was the provincial capital of Mogilev, 180 miles further east, and it was there, on his way back from the front eight weeks earlier, that Michael had met Dimitri and breakfasted with Nikolasha in the tent set up beside the commander-in-chief's train, never thinking that the next time he saw Stavka it would be with his brother in charge.

The first and most obvious change he would find at headquarters was that the Supreme Commander no longer lived in a train. 'In view of the dampness of the wood, where the train was standing', Nicholas took comfortable quarters in the Governor's mansion.[45]

The picture of life at Stavka, as presented by Nicholas in his letters home, was not that of a crisis-ridden headquarters, desperately struggling to rescue a reeling Russian army from a powerful enemy and now led by a warrior-Tsar. It was almost as if it was an escape from the daily turmoil at Tsarskoe Selo and a retreat to an ordered life of respectful officers, in a pleasant provincial town. The war was coloured flags on a wall-map and the real work could be done by staff officers, the chief of whom was the highly competent General Mikhail Alekseev, former commander of the north-western front.

Alekseev was the son of a former non-commissioned officer and he had risen through the army by dint of hard work and dedication. Uninterested in small talk and in evenings at the imperial dinner-table,[46] the industrious Alekseev was the real commander-in-chief and it could hardly be otherwise, given that Nicholas's military expertise was confined to saluting troops, reviewing parades and handing out medals.

The suggestion that Michael should be called to Mogilev came from Alexandra. While at the front he had been ignored, but now ill and back at

Gatchina, with 'that wife' of his to tell him what was being said in Petrograd, there was no knowing what might happen. Alexandra wished for no more rival courts and to make sure of that she wanted Michael with his brother, not with his wife.

Thus, as Nicholas arrived at Mogilev, Alexandra wrote to him: 'Won't you send for Misha to stay a bit with you . . . would be so nice and homely for you, & good to get him away from her & yr. brother is the one to be with you'.[47] Six days later she was anxiously enquiring: 'Have you news from Misha? I have no idea where he is. Do get him to stop a bit with you – get him quite to yourself.'[48]

Four days later, on Thursday, September 10, a still groggy Michael set off on the 500-mile journey southwards to Mogilev. He got there next day and Nicholas immediately cabled Alexandra to say so, adding surprisingly that 'he looks well'.[49] Two days later Nicholas wrote home again: 'The weather continues to be lovely. I go out every day in a car with Misha and we spend a great part of my leisure together, as in former years. He is so calm and charming . . .'[50] It was encouraging news for Alexandra, who replied by continuing to impress on Nicholas the importance of having Michael at his side – 'your very own brother, it's just his place and the longer he stops with you, away from her bad influence the better it is and you will get him to see things with your eyes'.[51] She meant her eyes.

With Michael in her camp Alexandra hoped to tighten her grip elsewhere. The Dowager Empress, fiercely critical of Rasputin, had to be muzzled. As Alexandra said to Nicholas: 'When you see poor Motherdear, you must rather sharply tell her how pained you are, that she listens to slander and does not stop it, as it makes mischief and others wld. be delighted, I'm sure, to put her against me – people are so mean.' Her pen raced on. 'How I wish Misha could be a help in that.'[52]

But to be a help Michael had first to be won back and to be won back he had to be wooed away from Natasha. Alexandra saw hope of this in two allies: Michael's sister Olga and his former aide Mordvinov, now at Mogilev as Nicholas's ADC. She therefore urged Nicholas to 'speak often about Olga when you are out together, don't let him think badly of her'; spinning her web around Michael, she added: 'I hope he is at last nice with good Mordvinov and does not cut that devoted, loving soul who tenderly loves him'.[53]

Mordvinov continued to denigrate Natasha even now. While waiting for Michael's arrival he had written to Alexandra's eldest daughter Olga and that letter had prompted a warning back from Alexandra to Nicholas: 'I fear Misha will ask for his wife to get a title – she can't – she left two husbands already & he is your only Brother.'[54]

Although Michael had not raised the subject again since his letter to

Nicholas in November, 1912 – when he asked that Natasha should be made a countess – there was good reason for Alexandra to fear that he might. Only a few weeks earlier, on August 15, Grand Duke Paul's morganatic wife, the former Olga Pistolkors, had been given the title of 'Her Serene Highness Princess Paley';[55] that being so, there was less reason to deny a similar title for Natasha. Both women were divorcées, both were commoners, both had sons who were illegitimate at birth. True, Natasha was twice-divorced rather than once, but in every other respect the cases were identical. If Princess Paley, why not Princess Brasova?

That was a question which Alexandra had already considered – 'what reason to Misha later', she had asked Nicholas in April,[56] when Paul was pressing his case. His wife had acquired a Bavarian title after their marriage in 1902, becoming Countess Hohenfelsen, but 'Uncle Paul' wanted more. Alexandra had thought the request 'vulgar'[57] but had given way none the less.

She would not concede the same to Natasha. She had decided that the answer to the question of why one wife should get a title and the other not was that 'Paul was of no consequence'[58] whereas Michael was the Tsar's brother. There were also other reasons, which she did not admit to herself. Ever since being allowed to return to Russia Paul's wife – Dimitri's stepmother – had set out to ingratiate herself with Alexandra, flattering her at every turn, and persuading Paul to build a palace in 1913 at Tsarskoe Selo so that she could live on the Imperial doorstep.

Natasha, in contrast, scorned Alexandra and made no secret of it. That served to increase Alexandra's hatred for her, as did reports that Paul's son Dimitri had become a regular guest at Gatchina and seemed to think more of Natasha than was good for him. Alexandra was therefore immovable on the question of any title for Natasha, hoping instead that if Michael could be kept within the embrace of his *only brother*, then perhaps the baleful influence of 'that woman' could be removed for ever.

Nicholas's letters did not encourage Alexandra in her hopes of a repentant brother-in-law eager to admit the errors of his ways and ready to dump Natasha. Nor was there anything to show him a stalwart champion of Nicholas against the dark forces of the Duma. Despite their long hours together, nothing that was said between the two brothers went back to Tsarskoe Selo. The best she could learn was that 'Misha often sits with me'.[59]

But alone together, there was plenty to say that week and Michael did his best to say it, though, as he would reveal later, it was sadly to no avail.

Michael's week at Mogilev gave him, as nothing else would do, a clear insight into how his brother was conducting affairs in the midst of the greatest military, parliamentary and governmental crisis since 1905. The enemy was within the gates. The Duma had been in such uproar that Nicholas had ordered that it be adjourned. Ministers were openly quarrelling among themselves. And every day he saw Nicholas sit down, cigarette in hand, and read what Alexandra believed he should be doing.

A letter might be fifteen pages long, Alexandra's pen leaping from one thought to another and from one demand to another. She always wrote in English and at such speed that she often seemed to be rambling incoherently, with words frequently misspelt. She spent long hours writing to 'my own sweet darling ... my very own beloved ... my angel ... my sweet precious one'. In that week she wrote six letters to Nicholas at Mogilev, each containing an average of 2000 words. 'I long to put my nose into everything – to wake up people, put order into all & unite all forces,' she had written just before Michael's arrival.[60]

Alexandra had always interfered, in almost everything. Once, when Nicholas was having his portrait painted by an eminent artist, Alexandra had interrupted the work so often with critical advice to the artist that eventually, exasperated, the man pushed the palate into her hand and said, 'You do it.'[61] Her meddling began even before her marriage to Nicholas. In 1894, when Alexander III was dying, she was horrified on her arrival from Hesse-Darmstadt to find Nicholas being ignored by doctors, court officials, government ministers and members of the imperial family itself and that her husband-to-be was anything but master of the drama around him. So she crept into his room, took up a pen and hurriedly scribbled into his diary a message, written in English, which was to become the first of many such messages in the years to come:

> *Darling boysy, me loves you, oh so very tenderly and deep. Be firm ... Don't let others be put first and you left out. You are Father's dear son and must be told all and be asked about everything. Show your own mind and don't let others forget who you are. Forgive, my love.*[62]

What she said here was, in all its essentials, what she would be saying almost a quarter of a century afterwards, for nothing had changed except the subject matter. Over the next days she hurled advice, pleas and vitriol. In one letter she lashed out right and left at the most senior men in government. Why was foreign minister Sazonov 'such a pancake?' Interior minister Prince Shcherbatov was 'a coward & rag'. The recently-appointed Procurator of the Holy Synod was a 'stupid, insolent fellow'. Agriculture minister Krivoshein 'is an underhand enemy'.[63]

Pausing only to stub out one cigarette and light another, Nicholas read through letters like these impassively. He would read that the little silver bell which Rasputin's charlatan predecessor Dr Philippe had given her and which hung on an icon, 'has indeed helped me to "feel" people – at first I did not pay enough attention, did not trust to my opinion, but now I see the Image & our Friend have helped me grasp people quickly. And the bell would ring if they came with bad intentions & would keep them from approaching me . . .'[64]

And always, as at the very beginning, there would be fevered urgings 'to be firm . . . you are the master, the Autocrat'. Ministers and the Duma had to be taught that they could not interfere with the will of the Tsar.

The Duma, which had not met since January, was largely composed of conservative and liberal members – landowners, industrialists, lawyers, academics and well-off businessmen. What they wanted was a greater voice in government, a share in policy-making and ministers who were more accountable to them. The current Duma was the fourth since the 'October Manifesto' of 1905. The first two Dumas had lasted for only a few weeks, but the third had run its full course of five years. The fourth Duma had been elected in 1912 and still had two years to run.

The session which opened on July 19 had seen the emergence of a new 'Progressive Bloc', a liberal–conservative alliance which represented 250 of the 402 Duma deputies. Because of the military disasters at the front, this majority group demanded the creation of a government 'of public confidence'. Alexandra had vehemently opposed the Duma being called at all – 'it's not their business . . . they speak too much . . . Russia, thank God, is not a constitutional country'[65] – and by the end of August she was urging Nicholas 'only quickly shut the Duma'.[66] He did, four days later.

The closure was marked immediately by strikes at the giant Putilov munitions works in Petrograd and did nothing to solve a growing crisis in the government itself. Most ministers favoured working more closely with the Duma and believed that what was needed was co-operation not confrontation, but their efforts were frustrated by the aged prime minister Ivan Goremykin, whose sole policy seemed to be that 'for me, an imperial command is law'.[67]

The man who had briefly succeeded Witte in 1906, but had proved too ineffective to last for more than a few weeks, he had been the surprise appointment as prime minister in 1914. Seventy-six in June 1915, he was exhausted and broken; 'the candles have already been lit round my coffin,' he said, 'and the only thing required to complete the ceremony is myself'.[68] By mid-September the majority of his ministers were in open revolt, demanding his removal, and six of them signed a letter to the Tsar to say so. The response was a curt summons to the ministers to present themselves at Mogilev.

Alexandra was in no doubt about the right response to the ministerial rebellion. 'Clean out all, give Goremykin new ministers & God will bless you ... Show your fist, chastisen [*sic*], be the master & lord, you are the Autocrat, & they dare not forget it, when they do, as now, woe unto them.'[69] Competence was no longer the determining factor in government. 'The ministers are rotten', she had written before the crisis meeting at Stavka, 'be decided, repremand [*sic*] them very severely for their behaviour.'[70] She offered Nicholas mystical support in his forthcoming confrontation, with a comb blessed by Rasputin. Having told him that it 'would bring its little help' if he used it 'before all difficult talks & decisions',[71] she now urged him 'to comb your hair with His comb before the sitting of the ministers'.[72] Divinely groomed, Nicholas dealt briskly with them and proudly cabled Alexandra afterwards to say 'the conference passed off well. I told them my opinion sternly to their faces ...'[73]

At Mogilev Michael witnessed the political drama which took place that week. It did little to encourage him in his hopes that his brother would make the kind of changes which he believed were now essential. He would say later that he had 'no influence' over his brother.[74]

The political battle and not the war dominated Michael's time at Stavka and inevitably it was politics and not military matters which he also discussed with his cousin Dimitri in that week. Dimitri was still serving at headquarters as an orderly officer and he and Michael had ample opportunity to talk between themselves about the crisis around them and in particular their worries about the influence of Alexandra. She continued to fuss about Dimitri and he still on occasion went to have tea with her, but it was from duty not affection.

In mid-August, on learning that the Tsar was to dismiss Nikolasha, a shocked Dimitri had travelled home to Tsarskoe Selo, hoping to persuade Nicholas that Grand Duke Nicholas should, at least, be retained at Stavka as Quartermaster-General. While waiting for an invitation to the Alexander Palace he talked to Paléologue, who was dining with Dimitri's father and stepmother. If his compromise was not accepted, he said, 'the consequences may be incalculable, as disastrous to the dynasty as to Russia'. When the French ambassador replied that he doubted that the Tsar would change his mind, Dimitri angrily threw away his cigarette and cried: 'Then we're lost. Henceforth it will be the Empress and her *camarilla* who command at Stavka! It's maddening.'[75]

Later that evening, after repeated requests from Dimitri, Nicholas invited him to his palace. They played billiards and while doing so Dimitri pressed his arguments; Nicholas seemed persuaded, thanking him for 'his devotion and frankness'.[76] Two days later, reading the newspapers in Petrograd, Dimitri discovered that Nicholas had taken no notice of him whatsoever. As would be often said about Nicholas, 'to avoid opposition he invariably acquiesces in everything which is said to him and always complies with one's requests. The moment his back is turned he orders the opposite . . .'[77]

At Mogilev it was Michael's turn to tackle Nicholas. It was not easy to warn his brother about 'the dangerous influence' of his wife;[78] nevertheless, in this week at Mogilev, he tried his best to do so. Predictably, it had no effect.

Michael's response to the political crisis in Russia could never have been the same as that of his brother. Nicholas firmly believed in autocracy, and was married to a determined woman who held views even more reactionary than his own; Michael was attracted to the principles of constitutional monarchy, and was married to a determined woman of liberal sentiments, whose background and sympathies were shared by many in the Duma. Nicholas strove unsuccessfully to be like his father Alexander III; Michael thought it more sensible if they remembered that they were not living in their father's world. Michael would have been even less effective as an autocrat than his brother and as one friend observed, had he attempted to act as one, his reign 'would have been a real tragedy'.[79] The relevant point, however, was that Michael had no desire to be another Alexander III; though the crown was never his ambition, his leaning was to constitutional monarchy, a role in which he would have been at ease. In that respect he was more suited to the changing political circumstances than was the intransigent Nicholas.

The differences between the two brothers made any chance of mutual understanding impossible. Nevertheless, in his week at Mogilev, Michael tried to convince Nicholas that without concessions the situation could only get worse, not better, while acutely aware that his own position had been deeply compromised by his marriage and that to an extent he had forfeited his right to speak at all. Even so, he made the attempt, pointless though it was.

The day after the ministers departed from Mogilev, Michael left also, knowing that there was nothing more he could say that would be of any use. Afterwards, Alexandra, blind to anything but her own conviction, wrote to Nicholas to say that 'you must miss Misha now – how nice that you had him staying with you – I am sure that it must have done him good in every sense.'[80]

She was to be disappointed. Seeing things through his brother's eyes had done Michael no good whatsoever.

SEVENTEEN

Rival Courts

As he slowly recovered from his illness Michael settled down happily in Gatchina, the place he loved best. Even Natasha was beginning to enjoy it more than she had thought possible. 'The house is becoming better and better every day,' she had written at the end of May.[1] She had supervised a team of workmen who had covered the courtyard with fine gravel. She had planted large numbers of flowers, had the summerhouse painted white and bought white Finnish furniture for the garden. There was a new tennis court and a little summerhouse for the children.[2]

The house at the end of Nikolaevskaya Street could never be grand, but she was no longer ashamed of it as she had been. Her excellent taste and her good eye for colour, had been used to the best effect. It was, at last, a family home, though gloomily Natasha wondered for how long. 'I have been thrown from place to place all my life,' she told Michael, 'especially since I started living with you, so probability theory tells me that as soon as I have settled here and made it my home I'll have to give it up and run away.'[3]

Nevertheless, she was rightly proud of what she had achieved in transforming the 'tumbledown' into a proper house. Michael loved it and wanted nothing more. He had, by imperial standards, only a handful of servants, some of whom had quarters in his house and others in the guest house next door. They included his valet and chauffeur, Natasha's personal maid Ayuna, a cook, the maids who cleaned and helped in the kitchen and a washerwoman living above the washhouse in the back courtyard. For Tata and George there was now a new English governess, the redoubtable Brighton-born Margaret Neame, a friend of Miss Rata who had departed to have a baby.[4]

Michael also had two ADCs and an adjutant, though they all lived elsewhere in their own quarters, as did the faithful Nicholas Johnson, who had an apartment on Baggout Street near the Warsaw railway station.[5] But his household had no butler to wait at table, or liveried servants in attendance at formal dinner parties and in that respect he did not live as grandly as at Knebworth, or could have done at the Gatchina palace, where an army of retainers continued to preserve state rooms which in the main only they walked through. Michael made full use of the park and he took advantage of the gymnasium sited in one of the quadrangles adjoining the main palace, but otherwise he was not seen there at all.

He took no precautions for his personal safety. There were no guards and apart from the low wooden picket-fence, 24 Nikolaevskaya Street lay open to the front. Beyond the house was a field which led to the barracks of the 23rd Artillery Brigade.[6] When Michael returned home he simply parked his car on the short drive to the side of his house, walked through his front door and stepped into the living room.

He was a familiar figure in the streets and shops; he took his family to the palace church on Sundays. He spoke to the townspeople as freely as they would speak to each other and regularly attended social gatherings and other like activities of a small community. Evening after evening was spent in committee work on various charities and when he was convalescing Tata would 'often remember him coming in dead tired' after an exhausting round of lengthy meetings.[7]

He liked children and could often be seen 'involved in an earnest discussion with some chubby little boy who barely reached his knees'.[8] He was an indulgent father and less strict with the two children than Natasha, who made rules and expected them to be obeyed. 'Time and time again he would come between me and my mother who was not of so gentle a nature,' said Tata.[9]

Michael always treated Tata as his own: 'though I was his stepdaughter, child of another man by my mother whom he adored . . . he never made any differentiation between me and George, his own son'.[10] When she was ill he sat at her bedside for hours, reading to her and cheering her up by drawing 'all sorts of pictures, chiefly boats, or modelling figures in plasticine'.[11]

He was a keen handyman and when he got up in the morning he would often go first into the garden, to his workshop, and there 'with his sleeves rolled up to the elbow he would plane, chisel and saw. He loved working on a lathe'.[12] In the evenings his favourite pastime was music and often he noted in his diary that he had 'played the guitar', sometimes with his aide and fellow guitar-enthusiast Prince Vyazemsky, or with Johnson as accompanist on the piano. He also loved the balalaika.

One official posted to the garrison was 'astonished by the Grand Duke's approachability and simplicity'. He first encountered him when he went to the local cinema one evening, before he knew what Grand Duke Michael looked like. The cinema, crowded with ordinary soldiers and townspeople, was 'a filthy hovel . . . a stuffy shed'; in the semi-darkness the officer looked for a seat and asked a young-looking man in the audience if the place in front of him was free. The man said it was and the officer settled down, realising as he did so that the man he had just spoken to seemed to be in the uniform of a general. Surprised at that, the officer later whispered to his neighbour, enquiring the general's name. The neighbour glanced round. 'What, behind us?' was the reply. 'Why that's Grand Duke Michael Aleksandrovich.'[13]

Usually good-natured, he surprised everyone when he lost his temper. On one occasion in Gatchina his neighbours were startled to hear him yelling from his windows and then to see him leaping into the roadway, half shaved and still in his nightshirt, wielding a whip and bellowing as he broke up a dog fight in front of his house. 'There were blows and curses . . . in his temper he was quite oblivious to his appearance or dignity.'[14]

In the best sense of the term, Michael was a simple man; sometimes he was too trusting of others. When beggars approached him in the street, he would give them money; when asked to provide job references, 'he never refused'. Inevitably his open trust was abused, as when he recommended a man who had been sacked three times for bad conduct.[15]

But those were trivial instances. More seriously in the weeks ahead he would be blamed for one of the notable frauds that bedevilled the Russian war machine. Cheating and corruption were endemic and there were constant scandals about misdeeds among government officials, manufacturers and politicians. In Michael's case it would not be alleged that he was dishonest or corrupt in any way, but that he had been embarrassingly gullible.

An 'invention' was brought forward by an engineer officer called Bratolyubov who claimed that he had developed a devastating new war machine, a monster flame-thrower. The officer, recommended by Rasputin, had gone first to Stavka and from there the Tsar instructed his brother to authorise the funds required. On Michael's signature, Bratolyubov received huge sums; it was not, however, until he presented a demand for 14 million gold roubles that suspicious officials discovered that the 'invention' was merely a money-making swindle. Bratolyubov was arrested, although subsequently released on the intervention of Rasputin.[16] Nevertheless, since Michael had signed the engineer's invoices, albeit on his brother's orders, he was made to look naïve.

Another version of the story claimed that Natasha first introduced the 'inventor' and persuaded Michael to authorise the payments.[17] That was not so; on the contrary, Natasha was livid on discovering that Michael had been duped. In a noisy scene at Nikolaevskaya Street a furious Natasha stormed at Michael: 'But you promised me not to sign anything without consulting me.' An abashed Michael replied that 'it was impossible to live if one could not trust anybody'.[18]

Other than on official business – the 'invention' being an unfortunate example – Michael went to 'detestable' Petrograd primarily for the theatre, ballet, or a concert. In the last three months of 1915, when still on home leave after diphtheria, he visited the capital six times,[19] but never to parties there, or to mingle socially with the bankers, diplomats, politicians and businessmen who thronged the capital; he kept himself within a small circle of friends and was never happier than to be back in Gatchina. Natasha would go to Petrograd to shop and lunch, but usually without Michael.

When Nicholas came back from Stavka, Michael would occasionally drive over to Tsarskoe Selo to see him for breakfast or tea and in November they met at the Anichkov Palace for tea with the Dowager Empress.[20] Natasha, of course, was never present.

Neither Nicholas nor Alexandra came to see him at Gatchina, for Gatchina was where Natasha lived. Alexandra, in particular, thought of Gatchina as an enemy camp, with 24 Nikolaevskaya Street as the headquarters. Alexandra divided the world into good and bad and while often those on her bad list were people who had once been on her good list, Natasha enjoyed the special status of simply being so bad that Alexandra could not bear even to mention her by name.

She was certainly right to classify Natasha as an enemy. The two women hated each other and their own circles reflected that. No one at Tsarskoe Selo had a good word to say about Natasha; at 24 Nikolaevskaya Street, Alexandra was condemned by all, including the three Grand Dukes who were often to be found there – Boris, his brother Andrew and of course Dimitri.

Boris was a recent addition to Natasha's guest list at Gatchina; he met her for the first time when he came to lunch one Sunday in August, 1915. His impression of Natasha, Michael was pleased to note, 'was most favourable. He liked her very much and found her "charmante"'.[21] With Dimitri's sister Grand Duchess Marie also happy to be seen at Gatchina, it could not but enrage the jealous-natured Alexandra.

Another addition to Natasha's circle was Dimitri Abrikosov. They had not seen each other since the days when, as a very young man, he had 'held her hand' while listening to Tchaikovsky and had thought himself in love with her. Still a bachelor, he was now in the diplomatic service, working in the foreign ministry in Petrograd, and although he knew that Natasha was in Gatchina 'she had risen to such high position that I did not dare to renew our acquaintance'.[22]

One day, walking down the street, he saw 'a very elegant lady' about to climb into a car bearing the imperial crest. 'Suddenly she rushed towards me and accused me of having forgotten her. I replied that our paths had separated so that I did not want to annoy her, but she called this nonsense. She insisted that I come to Gatchina the first Sunday.'[23]

Abrikosov duly arrived at Nikolaevskaya Street and became a regular visitor over the next months. Admiring though he was of Natasha and possibly still a little in love with her, Abrikosov came to think more of Michael. 'I found him to be far superior to her. When you were as clever and ambitious as she, you could not remain a thoroughly good woman; such a pure character as that of the Grand Duke, on the other hand, could not be spoiled.'[24] Michael's tastes were simpler, 'but he bowed to the wishes of his wife, who liked crowds and flattery,' judged Abrikosov.[25]

Of Michael he said: 'I have never met another man so uncorrupted and noble in nature ... He did not want to admit that there was wickedness and falsehood in this world and trusted everybody.' But that, he admitted, was a questionable virtue. 'Had his wife not watched over him constantly, he would have been deceived at every step.'[26]

Abrikosov remained fascinated by Natasha, noting that she had 'acquired a certain amount of regal manners – a vacant look, an artificial smile, elegance ...'[27] Natasha may indeed have adopted some royal manners, but she was still only the title-less Nathalie Sergeyevna Brasova. On letters home Michael addressed the envelopes to 'Her Excellency',[28] which was a couple of notches higher than the French 'Madame', but it was only a politeness not a rank.

Nevertheless 'Countess Brasova' became the name by which Natasha was generally known, a courtesy title accepted by society at large, by her friends and ultimately by herself, for as at Knebworth she had stationery printed with her initials NB displayed below a coronet.[29]

There were occasions, however, when her real position was painfully obvious, as on October 18, 1915, when Michael and she went to the Maryinski, one of the three imperial theatres in the capital – the others being the Michael and the Alexandra. It was the first time Petrograd society would see them together since their marriage.[30]

The chandelier-lit Maryinski was packed with uniformed officers, men in white-tie-and-tails and women who had taken the greatest trouble to appear at their bejewelled best. For Natasha the Maryinski held bitter memories. It was here, three years earlier, that she had been humiliated by a drunken Blue Cuirassier officer and that another officer who had dared to appear in her box had been disgraced and thrown out of the regiment. Snubbed, scorned and treated with contempt as she had been, it was a testing moment for her as she made her entrance.

All eyes were on the imperial family box situated to the side of the Tsar's ornate gala box which, with its huge turquoise blue-and-gold drapes and adorned with the imperial arms, dominated the rear of the theatre. Boris had joined Michael and Natasha for the evening and they had dined together before the ballet. Just before the curtain rose, the two Grand Dukes walked into the box reserved for members of the imperial family.[31] As they did so,

Natasha swept into sight, not into the imperial box but into one nearby. The opera glasses raised to stare at the Grand Dukes swivelled to gaze at her, eyes fascinated by the sight of this woman deemed unfit to sit beside her husband in public. Natasha was now wife not mistress, but in an imperial theatre like the Maryinski, where rigorous social convention applied, it gave her no more position than had been hers before.

However, Natasha turned the situation to her advantage: in the interval, the imperial box emptied and moments later the two Grand Dukes appeared in her box on the first tier,[32] sipping champagne and making clear to all those staring up at them that wherever Natasha sat was where they would prefer to be.

She and Michael stayed that night at the Astoria and next evening they went with Boris in a party to the Maly Theatre on the Fontanka. Because the Maly was not an imperial theatre they were all seated in the same box.[33] Three days later they went back to Petrograd, to the Michael Theatre, and this time Michael and Boris sat in the imperial box and Natasha and the Schlieffers were in one adjacent.[34] A month later, when they went to the Maryinski to see Kschessinska dance in *Swan Lake* they again sat apart, with Michael, Boris and Kschessinska's lover Andrew joining Natasha in the interval in row 11 of her first-tier box.[35]

Abrikosov, who was present on one evening at the Maryinski, noted the sensation Natasha caused as she swept into her box. Glittering with jewels, she was the focus for all eyes, and Abrikosov was in no doubt that 'she enjoyed attracting the attention of the whole theatre as she appeared . . .'[36] These scenes seemed to make her more rather than less important and in consequence the ban on Natasha rebounded in her favour.

Natasha, at thirty-five years of age, was more beautiful than ever. She turned heads wherever she went, as the French ambassador would confirm for himself when he chanced upon her for the first time in January 1916, at Soloviev's, a bookshop in the Liteiny. Paléologue was already in the shop and glanced up as she walked in. Though he did not know who she was he could not take his eyes off her. That night, he devoted his diary to her.

> *As I was examining several fine 18th-century French editions in the back of his empty shop, I saw a slender young woman of about thirty come in and take a seat at a table on which an album of prints was laid out. She was a delight to watch. Her whole style revealed a quiet, personal and refined taste . . . Her pure and aristocratic face is charmingly modelled and she has light velvety eyes. Round her neck a string of superb pearls sparkled in the light . . . There was a dignified, sinuous and soft gracefulness about her every movement.*[37]

Leaving the bookshop he saw a 'very smart car' parked behind his and his chauffeur, noticing his interest, asked him: 'Didn't your Excellency recognise the lady?'

'No, who is she?'

'The Countess Brasova, wife of His Imperial Highness the Grand Duke Michael Aleksandrovich,' replied the chauffeur.[38]

Paléologue recognised the name at once. The woman he had seen in the shop was not only extraordinarily beautiful, but from what he had heard, dangerous.

Unknown in political circles on her return to Russia in August 1914, Natasha was being widely talked about a year later. She would regularly meet friends in Petrograd, holding court at her lunch table in the Astoria's Winter Garden. Often seated beside her would be a member of the Duma, intrigued, fascinated and flattered by the attentions of the beautiful, elegant wife of the Tsar's brother.

She liked to entertain and be entertained, but she preferred intelligent society and serious conversation. She had strong opinions and voiced them frankly, careless of what might be repeated afterwards. And so it was that the French ambassador recognised at once the name of a woman regarded as a mortal enemy at court. That night, in his rooms at the French embassy, he penned an ode to her beauty, but also drew a portrait of a woman who was 'ambitious, clever and utterly unscrupulous'.[39]

Paléologue had heard enough in his round of the salons and at his own dinner table to know that 'she has been parading very strong liberal opinions for some time. Her circle, quite small though it is, is frequently open to deputies of the Left. In court quarters she has already been accused of betraying Tsarism – a fact which pleases her enormously, as it makes her views notorious and lays the foundations of her popularity. She becomes more independent every day and says the most audacious things – things which in the mouth of any other would mean twenty years in Siberia!'[40]

Natasha could not have wished for a greater tribute and would have agreed with almost every word of it, except his description of her as 'utterly unscrupulous', for that would mean that she was without principles, whereas it was the very strength of her principles that offended her critics. Abrikosov, who knew her as Paléologue did not and who was critical as well as admiring, did not think that she was merely driven by ambition but that 'her mentality remained that of an independent girl who could not hide her feelings'.[41]

At Gatchina he had seen and heard Natasha often enough to know that she said what she thought without regard for the company she was in. He remembered one Sunday luncheon at which the guests included two Grand Dukes, Boris and Andrew. They were discussing with Michael the defeats suffered by the Russian armies and the scandal over the shortage of munitions. Natasha suddenly exploded: 'It was you Romanovs who brought Russia to such a state!' There was a general hush in the room, 'and the Grand Dukes looked down at their plates'. Afterwards, Abrikosov took Natasha aside and told her 'that it was no wonder she was regarded at court as a revolutionist'.[42]

Paléologue's views of Natasha were based, however, on the prejudices of the dinner tables at which she was discussed and were chiefly influenced by Princess Paley, one of his regular sources of information. The French ambassador never met Natasha or Michael. While admitting that 'he fought bravely' he otherwise dismissed Michael as 'the feeblest of men',[43] a description probably borrowed from Princess Paley, for she would so describe Michael herself.[44] Paléologue was a magnificent observer of the Petrograd scene, but he was only as good as his sources. In the case of Natasha, those sources told him that, ambitious for her husband, she 'is working to secure him his revenge in another field'.[45]

Natasha had indeed developed links with many members of the Duma, though they were by no means 'deputies of the left'; her first Duma friend, Count Kapnist, was hardly a left-winger, though his party leader Aleksandr Guchkov was so regarded by Alexandra and had been since 1912, when Guchkov had spoken out in the Duma against Rasputin. 'Oh, could not one hang Guchkov?' Alexandra demanded of Nicholas.[46] 'The personal enemy of Their Majesties,' was how Paléologue would describe Guchkov.[47]

Natasha shared that distinction with him, as well as his political views generally. That in itself would have been enough to put her on a collision course with an imperial court now so stridently dominated by an increasingly mad Alexandra.

Whereas Alexandra wanted the Duma to be shut down, Natasha promoted its cause and the ideal of a ministry responsible to it. And she said so openly at her lunch-table in the crowded Astoria. As in her letters to Michael, she could sometimes have said less than she did, but that was not in her character. Had she been acknowledged by the imperial court as wife of the Tsar's brother she might have learned to keep a check on her tongue; as it was she spoke as she pleased. Unfortunately, comments overheard were repeated and no doubt embellished for dramatic effect. Petrograd thrived on such gossip.

It was not always gossip. One of the most remarkable statements with which the names of Michael and Natasha were linked politically came at a conference of the majority Progressive Bloc on October 25, 1915, when relations between crown and Duma were at rock bottom. The conference, with the Duma suspended, was in effect the Duma by another name.

The first speaker, a non-party liberal, M. M. Fedorov, was quoted as saying: 'Grand Duke Michael has been told about the situation through a person close to his wife. He has spoken to the Tsar and says the Tsarina, Goremykin and Rasputin are even prepared to go as far as closing the Duma.' That was true: Alexandra wanted it shut down permanently, never to be heard of again.

Fedorov then went on to say: 'To the question of whether or not he would be prepared to succeed to the throne the Grand Duke replied: "May this cup pass me by. Of course, if this were, unfortunately to come about, I sympathise with the British system. I can't understand why the Tsar won't take it calmly." '[48]

Aleksandr Kerensky, a leading socialist destined to play a decisive role in Russian affairs, was also to recount an incident so astonishing and so unlike Michael, that at face value it cannot seem true. 'In the autumn of 1915,' he recalled in his memoirs, 'I was visited by an old friend, Count Pavel Tolstoy, the son of one of the Tsar's equerries. He was a close friend of the Tsar's brother, Grand Duke Michael, whom he had known since childhood. He told me that he had come at the request of the Grand Duke, who knew that I had connections with the working class and left-wing parties and who wanted to know how the workers would react if he took over from his brother, the Tsar.'[49]

Since Michael would never have stooped to any approach on the lines which Kerensky claimed, the question arises as to whether the young Tolstoy was prompted by Natasha, with whom he was also on friendly terms. It is hardly likely; Natasha knew that if Nicholas was forced to abdicate it was his son Alexis who would succeed. Michael's role could only be as Regent, though that itself would have been triumph indeed. Natasha could never be Empress, but could she be wife of the Regent? Many believed that to be her ambition. It would be wonderful revenge.

More probably, in circumstances less formal than Kerensky described, Tolstoy posed hypothetical questions of his own and Kerensky interpreted them to mean more than they did. Nevertheless, Natasha was not entirely innocent: she handed out the ammunition and to that extent she had some liability for the shots fired by others, even when they were blanks.

Although Michael never sought or desired his brother's downfall, he feared for his future if Nicholas did not bring about change, curb the power of Alexandra and dismiss Rasputin. On one Sunday, in the early evening, Abrikosov was in the Gatchina house with Michael. Everyone else had gone for a drive. It was shortly after Michael's return from Mogilev and his discussions with Nicholas.

'He told me that he often thought how difficult it was for his brother, who sincerely wanted to do only what was good for the people, but who was hindered by his wife. Several times he had tried to convey to his brother what people were saying about him and about the dangerous influence of the Empress; Nicholas would listen with great tenderness but would say nothing until Michael felt so upset that it was his brother who consoled him.'

Michael thought that 'Nicholas seemed indifferent to his fate, leaving everything in the hands of God, but under the influence of Rasputin, God had assumed a strange shape'. Abrikosov recorded that 'tears choked his voice'. Dusk had fallen as they sat on the verandah and when Abrikosov turned on the light 'I was shocked by the utter despair on the pale face before me . . .'[50]

In public Michael refrained from saying anything critical of his brother, confining comments to technical matters. He was particularly interested in transport and the state of roads and railways, knowing that their efficiency was vital to the supply of the front. When the British consul Bruce Lockhart met Michael in Moscow he observed that Michael 'talked quite freely about the war,' but made only one comment which could be said to have political overtones. 'Thank God,' he said, 'the atmosphere at the front is so much better than the atmosphere of St Petersburg.' The diplomat left Michael, thinking that here was 'a prince who would have made an excellent constitutional monarch'.[51]

This was also the image which Natasha indirectly projected among her contacts in the Duma by her own support of the reforms the 'constitutionalists' sought. If Michael were Regent, all would be accomplished. Much was inferred, but what could not be ignored was the stark contrast between the wife of the Tsar and the wife of the Tsar's brother. Both were strong-minded; one hated the Duma and wanted unrestricted autocratic power, the other believed in parliamentary government and a constitutional monarchy; both were thought of as having a decisive influence over their husbands. Inevitably Natasha was seen as an ally by those who viewed Alexandra as an enemy.

In February 1916 Abrikosov went with Natasha to the reopening of the Duma at the Tauride Palace. They were in the box for distinguished visitors, but several members of the Duma were also seated there. Abrikosov noted that 'from the respect they showed her it was obvious she was becoming known in Duma circles'.[52]

That day was an historic occasion for the Tsar had elected to be present. On the rare occasions when he had addressed the Duma over the past ten years he had done so at the Winter Palace. Now for the first time he was going to them. It was not, however, the signal of a new relationship between crown and Duma, but a ploy to smooth over the introduction of his newly appointed and controversial choice for prime minister, Boris Stürmer.

The old prime minister, Goremykin, had finally been retired in January.

Stürmer, at sixty-eight, was only ten years younger, but Alexandra had pressed his appointment on Nicholas because Stürmer 'very much values Grigory wh. is a great thing'.[53] In the real world he was damningly seen as 'worse than a mediocrity', with a 'third-rate intellect, mean spirit, low character, doubtful honesty, no experience and no idea of State business,'[54] but at Tsarskoe Selo he had the blessing of Rasputin and therefore of God.

To give himself moral support at the Duma, Nicholas took along Michael; it was their first state appearance together in Petrograd since Michael's marriage and banishment. Michael, pushed to the sidelines since his return to Russia, was now being brought centre-stage, for the convenience of the moment. In the eight years in which she had known Michael, this was the first time that Natasha, sitting in her box, had ever seen the two brothers together. It would be the only day she would do so.

That morning Michael and Natasha had breakfasted with Duma deputy Count Kapnist,[55] who had then escorted Natasha to the Duma while Michael went off to the Pavilion at the Tauride Palace to join his brother for the ceremonial entrance into the adjacent Catherine Hall. Nicholas was 'deadly pale and his hands were trembling with agitation'.[56] He was not looking forward to the ceremony.

The Catherine Hall was packed, with diplomats as well as Duma members, for the Tsar's visit was taken as an important sign of change for the better, an expectation which Michael's presence could only encourage. As the Kadet party leader Pavel Milyukov put it to Paléologue, what Nicholas had never understood about the members of the Duma was that they 'were not the opposition *against* His Majesty but His Majesty's Opposition'.[57] Perhaps today he would alter that view. Most hoped so.

After a *Te Deum*, throughout which Nicholas stood pale, his mouth tightened and his discomfort obvious, he made a short welcoming speech, 'stopping and stumbling over every word'. To Paléologue it was 'painful to watch'.[58] It was also disappointing for those members who hoped that he was going to announce some important reform. His visit proved a gesture and no more.

After Nicholas left, Michael sat in the semi-circular assembly hall for the whole of the three-hour session, which closed with the Progressive Bloc calling for a government of 'public confidence'. Michael thought that Serge Shidlovsky, the Progressives' leader, 'spoke well', but he was unimpressed by the new prime minister Stürmer, 'who could hardly be heard'.[59] Mikhail Rodzyanko, President of the State Duma, was also less than impressed by Stürmer, who left the speaker's tribune 'amid dead silence ... from the very outset Stürmer revealed himself as an utter nonentity'.[60]

That evening, Michael and Natasha were also at the opening session of the 192-strong Council of State, of which half the members were appointed by the Tsar and the others by an amalgam of institutions, including the Church, universities, landowners and the nobility. Once again, Nicholas made a brief appearance, gave a speech and left, having been received 'in an atmosphere of cold officialdom'.[61] Having said goodbye to Nicholas, Michael returned to the assembly room and joined Natasha's box where she was sitting with their friend Count Kapnist. Once again he stayed for the full session.[62]

Merely by being there, in the company of a Duma deputy, Michael and Natasha were making their own political statement and endorsing as clearly as could be their support for a new start in Russian government. But at Tsarskoe Selo that would be thought of only as confirmation that it was time that Michael got back to the war. As Alexandra had already told Nicholas, 'I assure you that it is far better that he should be in his place there, than here with her bad set'.[63]

In Alexandra's mind, Natasha's 'bad set' was some sort of rival court. It was a view which would harden over the next year, with even the experienced and worldly Madame Naryshkina, Grand Mistress of the Court and a senior member of the imperial circle, convinced that Natasha was an arch-conspirator. To her diary, she confided that 'I think the danger will come from a direction from which it is not expected, from Michael. His wife is very "educated", from an intelligentsia background of limited means. She has already gained sway over [Grand Duchess] Marie Pavlovna. At the theatre her box is full of Grand Dukes. She and Marie Pavlovna are making arrangements . . . I have a feeling that they are hatching a conspiracy. Poor Misha will be drawn into it in spite of himself, first he will be Regent, then Emperor. They will achieve everything . . .'[64]

EIGHTEEN

War on Two Fronts

Michael went back to the war immediately after the reopening of the Duma in February, 1916. The 2nd Cavalry Corps, his new command, comprised the six regiments of his old Savage Division, as well as a Cossack division and a Don Cossack brigade. The corps was part of the Seventh Army under General Shcherbachev and its front was on the far left of the Russian line, south of Tarnopol and therefore in the same general area where Michael had been in 1915.[1]

Michael had spent Christmas with his family at Brasovo, their first time there since the spring of 1912;[2] Nicholas had at last given up his control of Michael's assets, his manifesto in October 1915 removing the 'madman' order imposed after his marriage. In the three years in which Brasovo had been subject to the guardianship order it had been sadly neglected, as Michael and Natasha discovered. The administrator appointed by the Tsar had been a bad manager and he was dilatory in rendering his accounts and in handing over estate papers, jeopardising urgent repair work.[3]

There were other concerns. After Michael departed for the front, an arrested moneylender in Petrograd was rumoured to have a large number of promissory notes signed by Michael, the implication being that Michael had been borrowing heavily during his guardianship and had been dealing with a crook. Natasha was furious and demanded a formal denial from the authorities. A search of the moneylender's papers confirmed that there were no promissory notes, but the malicious gossip persisted anyway.[4]

Michael was disgusted. 'It seems to me that there's no point in even trying to deny these rumours, for they are really beneath contempt.' Remembering the uproar over the fraudulent engineer, he added: 'Natasha, please remember one thing: I have never in my entire life been involved in any sordid affairs and it was only at the end of last year that, it is true, I could have ended up having trouble due to my trustfulness – but, fortunately, the matter has been completely resolved and forgotten. And this episode does not mean that I will go on making mistakes. On the contrary, this unpleasant experience will be a hard but a useful lesson for me and nothing of the kind will ever happen again. But of course I will always remember this mistake with shame and vexation.'[5]

He would stick rigidly to that position thereafter, though with the release of his monies and assets there were constant attempts to lure him into speculative ventures of one kind or another.[6] As Michael wrote, 'I refuse once and for all to be involved in any such ventures. I never used to have anything to do with commercial activities of any kind and now one should be more careful and keep away from all that sort of thing.'[7]

Now that he was master of his assets again, Natasha complained endlessly about inefficiencies in his personal office in Petrograd – based in rooms set aside at his embankment hospital – and about the way in which, in his absence, his various retainers, servants and appointees were either incompetent, greedy, or sometimes light-fingered. Every month Michael had money transferred to England to pay the rent and bills on his Paddockhurst estate, but 'they never send it on time, there is always a delay of about two weeks'.[8] When their hospital in Gatchina was temporarily closed for repairs, Natasha reported that the supply manager continued ordering provisions for it, selling them to local shopkeepers and pocketing the difference. He succeeded in stealing a whole 'railway car full of meat, cereals and flour'.[9]

Petitions to his office from wounded soldiers were also causing difficulties. A month after Michael returned to the frontline they were running at some sixty per day and rising. Michael was generous but, as Natasha warned, the word had got around, so that every soldier satisfied brought in other soldiers equally anxious to claim the same. 'You can't support the entire wounded army on your own money,' Natasha pointed out. There had to be a budget, 'otherwise there will never be enough'.[10]

Michael had arranged that Natasha had her own money, so that she was financially independent, with enough funds to do charitable works of her own choosing. One of her interests was a hospital in Kiev, funded from her account but bearing Michael's name. When she founded the hospital she was asked to provide a large portrait of herself for the entrance hall. But in June 1916, arriving there unannounced, she found that it had been taken down and hidden in a back room. The hospital was expecting a visit by the Dowager Empress and the management had decided that the sight of Natasha's picture was likely to cause offence to her mother-in-law.

Natasha was incensed. Not only was it her hospital, but she had bought beds, pillows and sheets for it, as well as sending presents to staff and wounded soldiers there. 'All the walls are hung with portraits of people who have done nothing for that hospital, while mine is as good as chucked out like an offensive object. You must admit it's insulting, whatever I do is an utterly wasted effort and I lose all incentive to do anything else.'[11]

The incident continued to rankle and she wrote again to Michael about it. 'I have no ambition but I have pride,' she said. The portrait had not been her idea and she had refused at first, for 'I am not in the habit of presenting my portraits to hospitals' and there was none even in her own Gatchina hospital. 'It was extremely disrespectful . . . for my own part I will completely detach myself from this hospital and if they want more money they can ask the people whose pictures do cover their walls.'[12]

Two weeks later she would complain bitterly to Michael that even his own hospital in Petrograd was the subject of official slights, with attempts to remove his name from it. 'It's absolutely disgraceful. It can only be done by people who know that there is somebody very powerful behind their backs.'[13] Natasha did not excuse her mother-in-law, but mostly she blamed Alexandra. 'She hates you and does all she can to prevent your name from even being mentioned. Petrograd is full of hospitals bearing the names of the Heir, of Nikolasha, of Olga and others – and in your name there is only one, which they are trying to get rid of. And that's a hospital where the officers' ward exists entirely on your money, so it is in fact virtually your hospital. I do hope you will assert your rights and will not allow them to treat you in this manner . . .'[14]

But that was precisely what Tsarskoe Selo continued to do, as one particularly unpleasant incident amply demonstrated, only a few days later.

Just before Michael had gone back to the front, he and Natasha had gone to the studios of Boissonnas & Eggler and had a series of pictures taken together, as well as separately. One photograph was of Natasha in a low-cut dress, the picture he had been demanding for the past year. He got the proofs after he returned to the front and was delighted. 'I love those shoulder-length photographs of you – they are very piquant,' he commented. But he wanted more. 'Could the shoulders be made a little clearer, and the bottom cut off a bit, so that the dress would not be seen in the picture at all . . .'[15] Once again she ignored his request.

A leading Petrograd society magazine opted to feature one of her photographs on its front page, together with a glowing description of her hospital work. There was more to come: Boissonnas & Eggler decided to mount a window exhibition devoted to Michael and Natasha, using the photographs taken at the February session. It was flattering publicity for the woman Tsarskoe Selo had tried so hard to keep in the shadows and it greatly enhanced Natasha's standing in society.

It was all too much for Alexandra. When news of the exhibition reached Tsarskoe Selo, she ordered Prince Obolensky, governor of the imperial palace, to have it removed. On Friday morning, July 15, he arrived with the police, who then stood by to ensure that the photographers cleared the window. The affair was another public slap in the face for Michael and Natasha.

'I cannot tell you how incensed I am at such disgraceful treatment,' Natasha wrote. It was humiliation, with 'the public driving past to witness how the shop was cleared of our pictures with police being present and all the stir it created . . .[16] Knowing Alexandra's vengefulness, Natasha was not surprised by the order to remove the pictures; what troubled her was the way in which the order was contemptuously carried out, in full public view, at a busy time of day, instead of discreetly, 'in a decent manner'.[17]

It was two weeks before that letter reached Michael, probably because in the interval Natasha dashed off to Brasovo to oversee some refurbishing work. He slept badly after reading it on August 4 and had another bout of stomach pains,[18] which he revealed to his diary, but not to Natasha.* Alexandra's order outraged him, but he was also furious with Obolensky, who had served under him in the Chevalier Gardes. 'I was greatly appalled,' he wrote. 'That's such impudence, such disgraceful breach of tact . . . It's not for nothing that I have always despised Petrograd high society . . . there are no people more devious than they are; with a few exceptions, they are all scum.'[19]

Even before the latest series of petty humiliations, Michael had wearily recognised that there was little chance of a new start back in Russia. Four years earlier he had left Russia to marry Natasha, entirely because of the treatment meted out to her by the same 'scum'. He had hoped for better things on his return, but by early 1916 he accepted that he would be driven out of Gatchina again. 'It is sad that we can't live quietly and normally in that dear place, but in the circumstances we'll have to leave it . . . I would so much want to see you completely happy at last, calm and content. Yes! That is what I want more than anything else in the world.'[20]

Natasha also saw little alternative but to return to England after the war. 'Actually, in my position, it would be better not to live in Russia at all . . . you can't protect me and to live in the position of an innocent culprit and a criminal is too hard . . .'[21]

At the same time, it seemed to Natasha that some of their problems were self-inflicted, because Michael was unwilling to bang his fist on the Tsarskoe Selo table. Silent dignity was all very well and doing his duty in the war was praiseworthy, but more was needed. There was a limit to penance.

> *I believe that while living here you must also assert yourself in such a way as to make people reckon with you and respect you. It is your own fault that by your kindness you have spoilt everyone to such an extent that your relatives regard you as a nonentity, while all the rest – as a turkey stuffed with truffles and they are crowding around you, each trying to get hold of a bigger truffle.*[22]

His appointment to command the 2nd Cavalry Corps seemed further proof of the intention at Tsarskoe Selo to keep Michael and Natasha as far

* He never mentioned in any of his frontline letters to Natasha that his stomach ulcer gave him problems; unable to follow a strict diet, there was nothing that could be done about it.

apart as possible. 'None of the other Grand Dukes sits in such a hole as you do, so why should you be worse off than the others?'[23]

To add insult to it all, she pointed out that there had been no announcement of his new command. 'Even some army people don't know you have a corps.'[24] To Natasha it could mean only one thing: Tsarskoe Selo had deliberately suppressed it. 'They shove you into the worst possible place, taking advantage of your meek temper' and they do so, she said, because 'they want to get rid of you'.[25]

Michael objected to the idea that he was only at the front because of court machinations. 'It is a matter of my conscience, too. I would be ashamed to be somewhere on the home front, when the Russian people are shedding their blood for their country and for future peace.' If the war had any purpose now, he said, it was as 'a war for the sake of peace'.[26]

But even he could not close his eyes to some snubs, as when he was promoted to lieutenant-general. As a Grand Duke it was the convention that on promotion to that rank he would simultaneously be made an ADC to the Tsar – an adjutant-general. In itself it meant little, but he would have worn different epaulettes, and aiguillettes in gold rather than in silver. Upon hearing of his promotion, Michael had cabled Matveev* to get him the gold insignia, 'assuming naturally that, as is always the case with members of the imperial family, I was promoted to the next rank with a formal position in the Retinue'.[27] It was only then that he discovered that he was to be an exception.

It was another public slap, but coming as it did at the same time as the police were removing their photographs at Boissonnas, Natasha was not surprised. 'The Tsar is deliberately set against you,' she said.[28]

'All I will say,' Michael replied, 'is that it is not a misunderstanding, but was deliberately done that way. Therefore I believe that no one should remind or ask the Sovereign about it, not even in ten years' time.'[29]

The private war between Tsarskoe Selo and Gatchina did not isolate them from all the members of the family. Boris, Andrew and Dimitri stood firmly 'in our camp',[30] as Michael would put it. In particular, the lovelorn Dimitri remained devoted to Natasha.

They still met occasionally and after one lunch at the Astoria a few months earlier Dimitri had sent her a thank-you letter, telling her that her kindness had left him 'elated'.[31] In January she had sent him a present of two crosses and he wrote to express his delight:

They proved you were thinking of me and I knew that. My thoughts went to

* After the death of Olga in 1915, Michael appointed the widowed Matveev to be his 'executive secretary'; Matveev moved to Petrograd, taking an apartment on the Fontanka.

> *the hotel at Moscow, oh, I would like so much to be there again but this time, alas, is gone. It is gone and I, yes I, must see that it does not repeat . . . Please know, dearest, that when I am writing that I am possessed by the same feelings as then and it seems to me that my thoughts are inadequate and that my thoughts are running faster than my pen. I can't write down everything that is in my head and in . . . but this is exactly what must be finished.*[32]

A month later, Natasha met Dimitri in Petrograd, just after Michael had gone back to the front. She and Johnson had gone to Kschessinska's jubilee performance, where they shared a box with Countess Kapnist and Olga Putyatina. 'In the interval, the curtains of the box moved slightly apart and dear Lily-of-the-Valley looked in and then Boris and Andrew,' she told Michael.

> *Lily-of-the-Valley was exceedingly charming and docile . . . Next day he dined with me at the Astoria and one of these days also came to tea. Both times he was awfully nice but quite different from what he was like before and did not say anything in the 'touching' vein at all. I am very pleased that our relations have taken such a shape and I cherish the delightful, friendly conversations that we have. I can now see that the infatuation is gone, yet something more solid and thoroughly good has remained in the heart.*[33]

Michael was relieved to hear it. 'Your friendship last year – well, I can't say it left me unperturbed,' he replied. At the same time he was again worrying about whether she loved him now as she once had, dreading the thought that their marriage might end up in a rut. 'How did you sleep last night, Nathalie Sergeyevna? Thank you, Michael Aleksandrovich, a little better and the pain in my stomach was less.' Even as he penned that illustration of domestic boredom, he realised that it was hardly a situation ever likely in his life with the volatile Natasha. Perhaps smiling to himself, he added: 'What a silly thing I've just written.'[34]

The persistent problem between Michael and Natasha, apart from their separation, was his refusal to ask Nicholas for a command more suited to his rank. To Natasha, that meant an élite Guards Corps, one added advantage being that she would see more of him – 'the entire Guards are within twelve hours of Petrograd,' she pointed out. She had little hope that Michael would pay any attention to her. 'I am used to everything being worse with us than with other people and living with you one should always be prepared for the worst,' she wrote.[35]

In his own mind Michael had decided that he would continue with the 2nd Cavalry Corps, at least for several more months, but to pacify Natasha he finally agreed that he would seek a headquarters posting thereafter. At the end of March, he tackled his brother about it when Nicholas arrived at

Kamenets-Podolsky on the south-western front for a brief inspection of units. Michael saw his brother twice,[36] but got nowhere. They parted on strained terms.

Nicholas's version of their conversation came in a letter to his wife. 'He asked to be recalled in June and to be appointed to Stavka. Then I began to preach to him about our father, about the sense of duty, example to others and so on. When I had finished and we had said goodbye to each other, he again asked me coldly and quite calmly not to forget his request, as if I had not spoken at all. I was furious!'[37]

So was Michael. He had no need of any lecture, for he had accepted without complaint his punishment for having failed in his duty by marrying Natasha. Yet he had seen more frontline service than any other Grand Duke, had commanded a battlefront division, 'with personal bravery and courage' as his gallantry award testified and he now commanded a front-line cavalry corps. That was his example to others. Both brothers wore the insignia of the Order of St George, but Michael had won his, with 'Swords', having 'exposed his life to great danger, inspiring and encouraging the troops under constant enemy fire', whereas Nicholas got his for being Tsar and without having been in any battle ever.[38] Small wonder, then, that Michael spoke to him coldly.

Michael, who normally recorded every meeting with Nicholas, made no mention in his diary of seeing him at Kamenets-Podolsky. He would not speak to him for another five months and when next in Tsarskoe Selo, during a short home leave in May, he would not trouble to call at the Alexander Palace. He did, however, bump into Alexandra. There was no enthusiasm on either side. He stopped for a moment, politely, then hurried on. Alexandra simply reported to Nicholas that 'going to church, met Misha, stopped, talked a minute and then he went back to Gatchina'.[39] The days of 'darling Misha' and 'give the sweet boy a kiss from me' were over.

Natasha was not surprised by the outcome of the meeting with Nicholas. As she would say later, Nicholas was only 'interested in keeping you as far away as possible and in having as little public attention to you as possible. Besides, he is also awfully afraid of your popularity and takes it out on you in every way. If I were you I'd never go to Stavka and would never ask for anything, for he will simply do the opposite of what you want.'[40]

As one family breach widened, another seemed to close. In May, Michael had met Olga in Kiev, where she had set up her hospital after the retreat from Lvov. The Dowager Empress had recently moved to Kiev to be near her youngest daughter; Michael, passing through the city, saw his mother on occasion and in so doing could not avoid Olga. There had been four years of bitterness between them, but Olga's grip on the high moral ground had slipped. Michael had broken the imperial law by marrying a divorcée and a commoner; the disapproving Olga was now to put herself in a like position: ending her marriage in order to marry a commoner, her long-time lover Kulikovsky.

This time it was she who was facing heavy criticism from Tsarskoe Selo. Alexandra was furious. 'I cannot tell you the bitter pain it causes me for you,' she wrote to Nicholas. 'She an Emperor's daughter & sister! Before the country at such a time when the dynasty is going through heavy trials & many countercurrants [*sic*] are at work – is sad. The society's morals are falling to pieces & our family, Paul, Misha & Olga show the example, not speaking of the yet worse behaviour of Boris, Andrew and Serge . . . We have been far to [*sic*] weak and kind to the family . . .'[41]

Nevertheless, for once her objections were ignored. Olga's marriage had always been a farce and even the Dowager Empress was in favour of it ending, accepting the marriage to Kulikovsky though she would never think of him as family.

Michael could only wish Olga well. They kissed and Olga wept.[42] A week later his mother was writing with relief to Nicholas: 'Misha spent a day here. At last he has made it up with poor Olga. I am so happy and have shed tears of joy! Thank God all that is now settled and I can die in peace.'[43] However, Michael had not 'made it up'. He would not see Olga again, nor would he go to her wedding.

The Dowager Empress had left Petrograd in the spring of 1916 because she could no longer bear Alexandra and the insidious influence of Rasputin. In February, Grand Duchess Marie Pavlovna – mother of the three 'Vladimir' Grand Dukes, Kirill, Boris and Andrew – told Paléologue at a dinner party that 'I spent two hours with Marie Feodorovna the other day; all we could do was to grieve together'. The Dowager Empress had tried to make Nicholas see the damage being done by his wife and her association with Rasputin, 'but the moment she begins to lecture her son, her feelings run away with her . . . Then he stands on his dignity and reminds his mother that he is the Emperor. They leave each other in a rage.'[44]

Since the Dowager Empress had moved to Kiev, Natasha urged Michael to speak to his mother about his treatment not only by the Tsarskoe Selo court but by the Dowager Empress herself. She believed that Michael's mother was so ashamed of his marriage that by her example she had encouraged the conduct of Nicholas and Alexandra towards them. It was a recurring theme in her letters in the summer of 1916:

'I believe you ought to have it all out with your mother and stop pretending that everything is fine and you're on good terms with her. I believe her to be chiefly responsible for the attitudes towards me and until you talk it all over with her, everything will be the same. Do understand that I don't need to be received by them at all, but it is their duty to respect my position in Russia. And you must do all you can for that, or sever your relationship with them. Otherwise our life together will be a failure.'[45]

Then again she would write: 'Go to see your mother just to tell her how you have been treated and ask her to write to the Tsar about it. If she declines, you'll have an excuse to have a quarrel with her, for it is really appalling what they are doing to you and it should not be allowed to go unpunished[46] . . . Any open conversation, even a quarrel, will be better than the silence which you've been keeping.'[47]

She could also mock her mother-in-law. When their favourite dog Jack died and some weeks later another died as suddenly, she wondered if 'somebody is deliberately poisoning our dogs'. Maybe, she teased him, 'they might just be practising on them before poisoning us' – Michael's mother having 'decided to get rid of me by simpler means, having despaired of the possibility of divorce'.[48]

At the time, the death of Jack, the mongrel dog which had been part of their lives ever since they had met, was not something either could joke about. It was as if a child had died. 'In fact, after you and the children Jack was all I loved in the world,' a grieving Natasha wrote. 'I spent more time with him than I spent with you, he was constantly by my side . . . I always used to talk to him and he understood me better than any person . . .'[49]

Michael had been no less shocked. 'This news has stunned me and I can't believe we have lost our dearly loved and devoted Jack. I won't keep it from you that I am crying bitterly even as I am writing this letter and I can't express the grief that I feel . . .'[50] He suggested that Jack be buried in the garden in a lead case, which would could then be taken with them whenever they moved from Gatchina.

Natasha did as he asked. Jack was that special to them. But the manner of his burial was its own evidence of their lack of faith in any future together in Russia.

Michael's corps was involved in heavy fighting all that summer. The Brusilov Offensive, so called because it was his south-western armies which launched it, promised heady rewards, with the prospect of a breakthrough across the Carpathians to Vienna – a repeat of the hopes of a year earlier. By the end of June Michael noted that 'the approximate count of prisoners in the whole offensive was 5620 officers and 266,000 men, 312 guns, 833 machine-guns.'[51] The Austrians had been mauled, but then so had the Russians. On both the western and the eastern fronts in the First World War, casualties were horrific and indeed when Michael was recording his statistics the British had suffered 58,000 casualties, half the men involved and 20,000 of them dead, on just the *first day* of their offensive on the Somme. In the previous year, the total casualties on the western front – French, British and German – had been some two million. In the past few months, the battle at Verdun had turned into a bloodbath.

Michael hated the slaughter, on both sides. The sight of a dying Czech prisoner in a field dressing station could sadden him, enemy or not. 'There are so many such unfortunate heroes who are dying away from their country and worse still – away from their nearest and dearest and in strangers' hands. I was sorry for that poor Czech as much as for anyone else,' he told Natasha.[52]

As the summer wore on the casualties on the Russian front continued to mount but the prize slipped away. Elation was followed by disappointment. Although the Russian line had been pushed forward, overall there would be little to show for the sacrifice. The Guards Army, the best troops of all, were wasted by clumsy generalship – one corps ruined by incompetence on the part of its newly-appointed commander Grand Duke Paul, 'whose only failing was that he knew absolutely nothing about military affairs'.[53] Paul had been seriously ill for months, stricken with gallstones, and he was in no condition to go to war. After the mishandling of his corps he was quietly removed from his post.

In contrast Michael would earn his second high gallantry award – the red enamel cross of the Order of St Vladimir with Swords 'for distinction in action against the enemy'.[54] As a corps commander he was, of course, less exposed to personal danger than before, but occasionally there were brushes on the frontline, albeit inadvertent. On August 23, returning from a military conference at Savage Division headquarters, his driver took the wrong turning and headed straight for the Austrian lines. After half a mile 'we were bombarded by an Austrian outpost . . . several bullets whizzed by'. To get them out of it, 'I took the wheel, because I knew how to drive better'.[55] He did not tell Natasha about that, though he admitted that 'there has been very severe and very bloody fighting all this time'.[56]

There was then a lull in his sector. He took the opportunity to go to Mogilev, arriving there on August 31.[57] It was his first meeting with Nicholas since their near-quarrel in April and Michael was determined to raise again his request for a Stavka appointment. Natasha was opposed, but Michael persisted, saying that it was 'essential for a favourable result. I certainly feel very reluctant to go there . . . but I promise that it is going to be the last time and if on this visit I achieve nothing then I will never go to Stavka again and in general I will change my attitude . . .'[58]

He and Nicholas met privately in the Tsar's salon before tea. This time there were no lectures and it was Nicholas who now offered his brother the headquarters appointment he had refused earlier. It 'suits me well'

Michael briskly noted.[59] He was also belatedly promoted to Adjutant-General.[60]

These concessions signalled no change in the family war conducted from Tsarskoe Selo. What Michael did not tell his brother was that Natasha, whom he had not seen for three months, had also come to Mogilev and was staying in his carriage. In the four days she was there she kept well away from the headquarters proper, going for walks in the town and having lunch in the restaurant of the Bristol Hotel. She also went to the cinema, while Michael was dining with his brother.

It was after Michael had left that Nicholas found out about Natasha. His source was a furious Alexandra. 'You know Misha's wife was at Mogilev!!' she exploded in a letter to him. 'Georgi [Grand Duke George Mikhailovich] told Paul he sat near her at the cynema [*sic*]. Find out where she lived (perhaps wagon) & how long, & forbid strictly it happening again.'[61]

It would not happen again. Michael never took up an appointment at headquarters and the next time he saw Nicholas it would be in circumstances so desperate that both had more important matters to worry about.

By September 1916 the war Michael had been fighting on two fronts had taken its toll on his health, always suspect at the best of times. Natasha was also worn out with the battles against his family, their courtiers and officials. The strain had affected both considerably and it showed in many of their letters to each other. Natasha, feeling herself a hostage in an enemy camp, blamed Michael for allowing it to happen, as if he regarded it all as part of his 'punishment', to be endured without protest; Michael, torn between his duty to his service and to his wife, felt guilty about both, knowing that to satisfy one was to neglect the other.

Their letters reflected this torment; Natasha could not hide her depression at her position, made worse by her belief that Michael was deliberately kept as far away as possible from home and that 'the family' was intent on destroying their marriage and if not that, her. When her second sister Vera died, her grief had been coupled with a sense of doom. It would be her turn next: 'it will be better and easier for you if it happens and then nobody will stand between you and your service and your duty,' she had told him then in her despair.[62]

Gatchina added to her misery. 'You know very well, under what circumstances we made our home here ... everyone tried to kick me, to forget to bow to me in the street or to insult me in some other way. You also know that you never used to help me in anything and never do ... I am living here against my wishes and without any joy, feeling utterly depressed by this life.'[63] Without Michael Natasha felt abandoned and isolated. Wherever she went she was reminded of the people who had made her life a misery. In the palace church she saw her enemy Mordvinov. 'God, how assiduously he prayed ... he almost beat his head on the floor,' she told Michael. 'He must have been asking God to punish me, just as the Germans ask God to punish England. *Gott straffe England*.'[64]

She also became alarmed when she heard rumours that the Dowager Empress intended to replace the amiable palace commandant Krestyanov. If that happens, said Natasha, 'they will eat us alive'. One day 'you'll get a surprise from them – they'll put Mordvinov in charge'.[65]

In blaming Michael for failing to stand up for her against people like Mordvinov, Natasha could be brutally frank: 'Honestly, you have a most unfortunate character which is totally useless in life ... fate seems to have deliberately muddled everything up for you and you are caught between the devil and the deep blue sea and don't know how to get out of it all ... for eight years I have been a loyal wife and have never so much as looked at anybody but you, yet in all these eight years I have seen nothing but trouble and I am so worn out that I can't bear it any longer or live the way I have lived all this time ... and while it is so, our relationship can't improve, for what I see in it is a lacking in your love for me and your unwillingness to take my side.'[66]

That was so unfair as to be outrageous; in taking her side he had given up his own position and left Russia, though he would never for a moment complain about that; nevertheless, it was distressing to read her letters; she was vulnerable and what she wanted was what he could not do; he could not come home.

She knew that too, but it did not help as the months went by. 'It is very sad to know nothing about each other for weeks and it can't help drawing us apart emotionally as well. You complain about our relationship, but I am convinced it all comes from constant separation. Just think that out of seven years together we spent five apart from each other.'[67]

She could also be perverse, as when she told him that 'you shouldn't go to the trenches so often. You might get killed by a stray bullet. Perhaps this is what you are looking for ... and I regard it as another proof that you have stopped loving me.'[68]

In these exchanges, Michael sounded just as depressed. 'Strange that you should accuse me of what I am accusing you – of lack of love. If I am feeling so low and desolate, it is mainly for two reasons: 1) because I notice that you are ceasing to love me and 2) because of the thought that I am now good for nothing!!!'[69] Two days later he was in no better mood. 'It is so hard and painful to think of your unjust attitude to me all this time. This heavy thought does not leave me for an instant and I am feeling extremely depressed, humiliated, dejected and utterly without hope for the future.

The worst thing is that you no longer love me the way you did – I know that it is so.'[70]

Natasha denied that.

> *I haven't stopped loving you, but our eternal separation has brought us apart and I am now used to having a life of my own which is quite separate from yours and to having my own interests that are different from yours.*
>
> *But it was not I who always went away from you, but you from me, therefore none of it is my fault,* je ne demande pas mieux que d'etre toujours et toujours avec toi, *[I have never wanted more than to be always and always with you] – yet I had to be on my own for years.* Partir c'est mourir un peu *[To part is to die a little] and indeed, this endless separation does kill the soul.*
>
> *However, I see no reason why you should go into such deep depression and as a result upset me. I don't even understand what the phrase about your being good for nothing is supposed to mean. Pull yourself together, my darling Misha and stop cherishing your spleen.*[71]

The ceaseless fight was also draining her strength. 'I feel so frightfully exhausted and listless of heart as though life was gradually leaving.'[72] Michael chided her for refusing to get treatment and advised her to have injections of arsenic, used in those days as a tonic.[73] Nothing cheered her. 'If I go on feeling worse and worse I'll summon you to me Misha and I beg you to come to me, for I don't want to die without seeing you for the last time.'[74] When ill, Natasha inclined to the dramatic.

Yet their letters were also full of the very love which each claimed the other lacked. 'You must know and believe that I am always lonely for you,' wrote Natasha, 'and in my thoughts I am always with you. You know that I now have no one but you and my entire life is you alone.'[75]

Some two weeks later she would write: 'My dearest, I am always with you in my thoughts and I love you with all my heart. Let God keep you, please be well and don't forget me, my dear boy. I am kissing you tenderly. Don't forget your Natasha . . . You must know that without your love I'll be done, for it is the only thing that gives me strength to live. The rest is all too sad and frightening.'[76]

Michael was no less ardent, as his letters over the next three weeks made repeatedly clear. On July 24 he wrote:

> *I do want to believe you when you say that <u>you have not stopped loving me,</u> for there is only one kind of happiness in my life, only one joy – and that is your love for me; and if you ever stop loving me, the meaning of my life will collapse – that's why I often feel so desolate when I notice that you are changing towards me: it just kills me, it does!*[77]

Again, nine days later: 'In my thoughts I am with you all the time and without you I am only tortured by separation – you don't know how uneasy I am in my heart and how sad and dark it feels! I don't any longer know any joy or any hope; everything seems to have collapsed and there is a feeling that it has got lost irretrievably ...'[78] Then again, 'My entire tortured being and all my thoughts are always and only with you – it is awful how I suffer because of my separation from you and I repeat that the only thing that sustains me is the hope that it is the last time that we are parted for so long ... If you only knew how homesick I am and how tired I am to live like this ...'[79]

Having written those last lines, on Saturday, August 13, at his quarters in the little village of Ustse-Zelena, he came back to add more to his letter:

> *I've just returned from vespers, the church was empty, lit with the rays of the evening sun and I was trying to imagine myself in Gatchina, in the palace church (my favourite), where we had prayed together so many times . . . I will never forget how in 1908, in Gatchina, we were together, although not alone, at vespers . . . and we stood next to each other and our souls were full of joy . . .*
>
> *What is sad is how fast time is flying: how many years have passed since our first meeting – it will be nine in December, just think, Natasha! My heart sinks at this thought – why is time flying so fast, when I want us both to be always young together, as we have been so far! My Natasha, my tender one, my darling angel, my only comfort is my love for you, which still fills my entire being and besides my love I have a desperate wish never to be apart from you – if you only knew how I suffer, yearn and melt away without you!*[80]

However, the prospect of at last being together cheered them both. 'On September 4 I hope to be in Brasovo and in your tender arms – you can imagine my joy! I can't find words to express it ...'[81]

Natasha could not wait that long, hence her decision to travel discreetly to Stavka. Leaving Mogilev together, they were in Brasovo on September 4 as planned. Natasha had worked wonders in the house, decorating it and refurnishing it. Brasovo was a haven and it became the one place in Russia where both Michael and Natasha felt entirely at ease; the home into which the world outside could never intrude. If, to live in peace, they had to go abroad, then it would be 'to delightful Brasovo' they would want to return whenever they came back to Russia.[82] That was the dream which would sustain them both when all else seemed impossible.

Michael went fishing on the mill pond, catching 150 fish in one morning in a big sweep-net; with Vyazemsky he chopped down thirty-six trees near the house; he went riding with Tata; and one Friday evening he climbed the tower of the house to watch the sun set. 'The sky was magnificently beautiful, black-red clouds moved with great speed.'[83]

Leaving Brasovo they all went to Moscow, staying for thirteen days at the National Hotel.[84] On October 17 they were back in Gatchina and going for a drive in their new 12-cyclinder Packard, which had just unexpectedly arrived from America.[85] Ordered in peacetime Paris, and intended for England, the car had been half-forgotten; given that its delivery was hardly an essential on Russia's strained supply lines, it seemed astonishing that almost three years later it should turn up at all. But since it had, Michael could not wait to get behind the wheel.

His pleasure was short-lived. Next day he succumbed to a fever and no sooner had he recovered than he went down again with a new attack of his 'damned stomach pains'; a week later he was still ill. After being examined by a team of specialists in Petrograd, he was advised to go to the warm Crimea and rest. A month of sitting doing nothing and he would feel a different man; if he ignored their advice and returned to the army, the problem would only get worse.

But before departing there was one thing he had to do: to write to Nicholas. He had warned him face to face about the political risks he was facing; now for the first time he did so in writing:

> *A year ago . . . you invited me to share my thoughts with you candidly whenever I felt it called for. The time has come . . . I am deeply concerned and worried by what is happening around us. There has been a shocking alteration in the mood of the most loyal people; on all sides I observe a way of thinking which fills me with the most serious apprehension not only for you and for the fate of our family, but even for the integrity of the state order.*
>
> *The public hatred for certain people who allegedly are close to you and who are forming part of the present government has, to my amazement, brought together the right, the left and the moderate; and this hatred, along with the demands for changes are already openly expressed at every opportunity. Please don't think that I am writing this under someone's influence: these impressions I have tried to verify in conversations with people of various circles – level-headed people whose loyalty and devotion are beyond any doubt and, alas, my apprehensions have been confirmed.*

Having underlined the fact that he was speaking from his own experience, not merely repeating what Natasha and her 'bad set' had told him, he did not mince his words thereafter:

> *I have come to the conviction that we are standing on a volcano and that the least spark, the least incorrect step could provoke a catastrophe for you, for us all and for Russia . . . it seems to me that, by removing the most hated persons and replacing them with unblemished people, towards whom there is no evident mistrust on the part of society (which now means Russia as a whole), you will*

find a good way out of the situation in which we now are; and for such a decision you will certainly find support both in the Council of State and the Duma . . . It seems to me that the people who are urging you to follow an opposite course are concerned far more with keeping their own posts than with protecting you and Russia. Half-measures in this case are only prolonging the crisis and thus making it more acute.

I am deeply confident that everything that is said in this letter will be confirmed by all those among our relatives who are at least slightly familiar with the moods pervading the country and society. I am afraid, these moods are not so strongly felt and perceived at Stavka . . . the majority of those who come with reports will never tell you the unpleasant truth, for they are protecting their own interests . . . I cannot help feeling that if anything happens inside Russia, it will be echoed with a catastrophe as regards the war. That is why, painful as it is for me to do it, my love for you has urged me to share all my worries with you without keeping anything back.[86]

He could hardly be clearer; and it was not necessary to mention Alexandra. He had done that often enough before. Would Nicholas pay any heed? He had never done so, but the letter had to be written anyway, though there was no reply.

Six days later, on November 17, Michael and Natasha, accompanied by her brother-in-law Alexei Matveev, set off to stay at Xenia's beautiful wisteria-covered house at Ai-Todor, on the shores of the Black Sea, twelve miles from Yalta.[87] For the next three weeks no one would be able to get through to them, and the blame for that would be pinned firmly on Natasha. That, anyway, was what Nicholas told Alexandra – that two of Michael's aides had written to Frederiks complaining 'bitterly about Misha's wife, who does not allow them to speak to him, even if it is only about his health'. He added that 'judging from what they write, the doctors who attend him insist on serious treatment and a rest in a warm climate . . . but he, or perhaps she, wishes to return to Gatchina, of which the doctors do not approve and nobody can penetrate to Misha to explain it to him . . .'[88]

In fact it was not Gatchina but Brasovo to which Michael and Natasha were bent on returning. They had always intended to spend Christmas there and had arranged that a party of friends, as well as the children, were to join them. They set off from Ai-Todor on December 18 and were in Brasovo two days later,[89] shortly before the children, staff and their house party arrived from Petrograd.

Of their guests, only one – Grand Duke Dimitri – failed to turn up. As they would discover, Dimitri had been arrested.

NINETEEN

Murder Most Fair

The crisis facing Russia in the autumn of 1916 was the beginning of the end for Nicholas and Alexandra. On the battlefield the summer offensive had ended in stalemate, with horrific casualty lists. Industrial and politically motivated strikes had been almost unknown in the first months of the war, but by the end of 1916 the number of strikers would reach a million, double the figure for the previous year. Facing their third winter of war, Russians now looked inwards and not outwards. Talk of betrayal was commonplace, with many convinced that the source of that treachery lay in the boudoir of the German-born Empress Alexandra Fedorovna and in the government she had largely created.

Alexandra was never a traitor; a more telling complaint was that she and Rasputin now dictated political affairs almost without hinder from the Tsar at Stavka. Two of the best ministers who had survived her original purge were now dismissed. The first to go was the effective war minister Polivanov. Alexandra, who had pestered Nicholas for his removal, thought him 'simply a revolutionist';[1] Knox judged him the 'ablest military organiser in Russia' and thought his dismissal 'a disaster'.[2] In July the long-serving and respected foreign minister Sazonov was also removed, again on Alexandra's insistence, after he warned the Tsar about 'the dangerous part that the Empress had begun to play since Rasputin gained possession of her will and intellect'.[3]

Stürmer now became both prime minister and foreign minister. The government had fallen into the hands of men who in the majority were appointed merely because they had been approved by 'our Friend'. Among them, shortly, would be the new fifty-year-old interior minister, Aleksandr Protopopov. An Octobrist recruited from the Duma, where he had been a vice-president, he became an overnight convert to Alexandra's brand of mystical autocracy; increasingly deranged, he was destined to become as hated as his mentor Rasputin.

The dismissal of Sazonov was bad enough in itself. 'We have all been shocked ... it's really something incredible,' Natasha wrote to Michael.[4] He agreed. 'We were all greatly surprised here ... I did not know Sazonov well but it was apparent that he was trusted and now with Stürmer, I am afraid we are in for some rotten business ... such unsuitable people are chosen for such responsible posts, it's too awful for words!'[5]

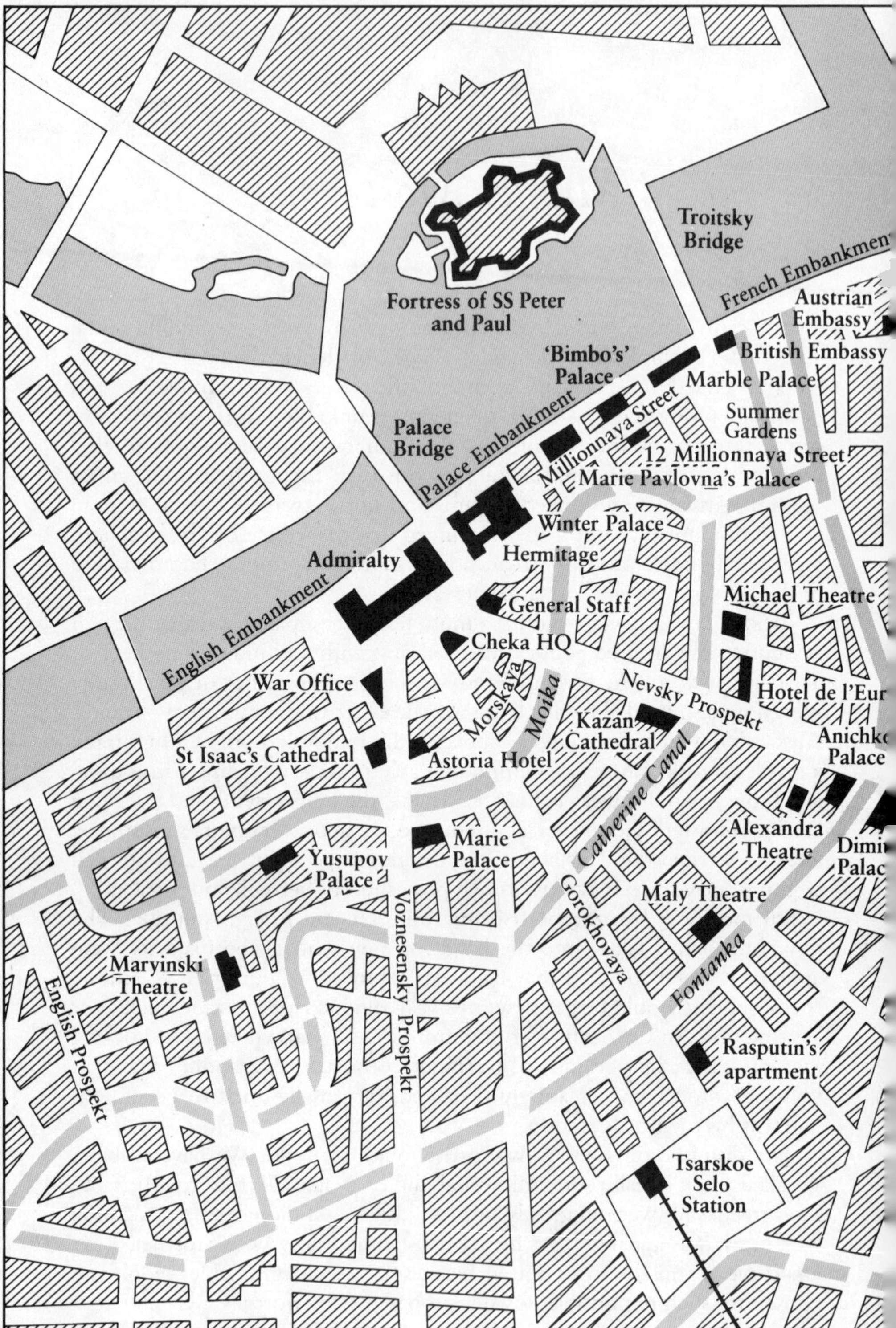

Troitsky Bridge
French Embankment
Fortress of SS Peter and Paul
Austrian Embassy
'Bimbo's' Palace
British Embassy
Marble Palace
Summer Gardens
Palace Bridge
Palace Embankment
Millionnaya Street
12 Millionnaya Street
Marie Pavlovna's Palace
Winter Palace
Hermitage
Admiralty
English Embankment
General Staff
Michael Theatre
Cheka HQ
War Office
Morskaya
Moika
Nevsky Prospekt
Hotel de l'Eur
Kazan Cathedral
St Isaac's Cathedral
Astoria Hotel
Catherine Canal
Anichk
Palace
Alexandra Theatre
Dimi
Palac
Marie Palace
Yusupov Palace
Voznesensky Prospekt
Gorokhovaya
Maly Theatre
Maryinski Theatre
English Prospekt
Fontanka
Rasputin's apartment
Tsarskoe Selo Station

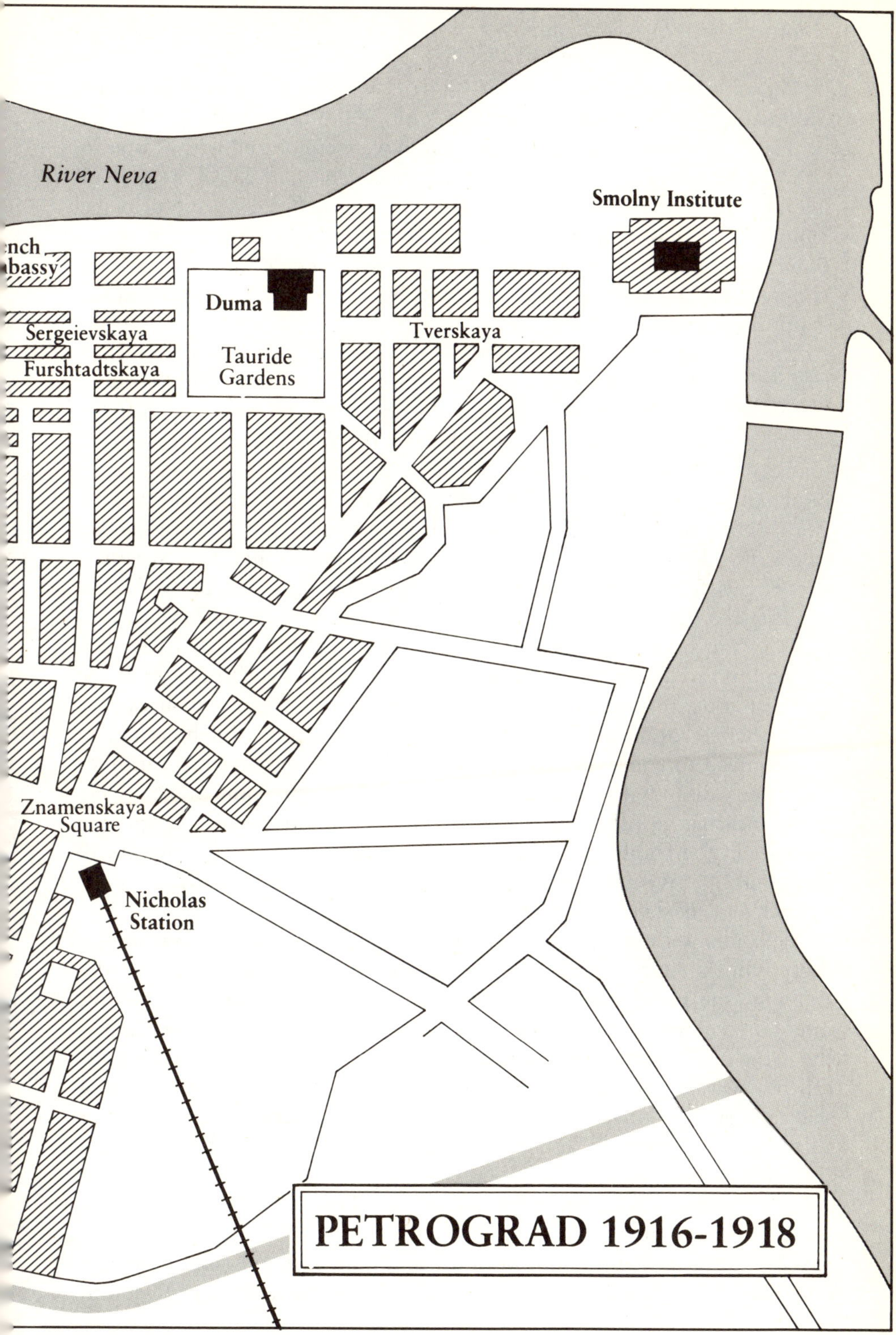
River Neva
Smolny Institute
nch
bassy
Duma
Tauride
Gardens
Sergeievskaya
Furshtadtskaya
Tverskaya
Znamenskaya
Square
Nicholas
Station
PETROGRAD 1916-1918

The only encouraging sign for Michael was the arrest of Prince Andronnikov, a shady political intriguer, and of the notorious pro-German banker D. L. Rubinstein and his wife. Both were connected with Rasputin. 'It's almost too good to be true!' wrote Michael 'Why, if it goes on like this, they might finally get to Rasputin himself, i.e. to the principal scoundrel.'[6] Natasha was more realistic. 'Rasputin has gone to Pskov, where Rubinstein is imprisoned and will do all he can to help him ... Mark my words, he will soon be released.'[7] He was, by imperial order. Alexandra and Rasputin saw to that.

Michael had warned Nicholas about the need to step clear of his wife's fatal influence. So had his brother-in-law Sandro and cousin Dimitri, to no better effect. In November, Sandro's brother George, reporting that the 'hatred for Stürmer is extraordinary', begged the Tsar to form 'a responsible ministry', for only that 'can avert a general catastrophe'.[8] His other brother Nicholas – 'Bimbo' to the family – also made the attempt a few days earlier, at a meeting in which he reinforced his points in a letter he then handed to the Tsar. 'You trust her,' he wrote, 'that is quite natural. But what she tells you is not the truth; she is only repeating what has been cleverly suggested to her ... You are on the eve of new troubles ... Believe me, if I insist so much on your freeing yourself from the chains that have been forged, I do so ... only in the hope of saving you and saving the throne of our dear country from the most serious and irreparable consequences.'[9]

By chance and not realising what the letter contained, Nicholas passed it on unread to Alexandra. Her response was a furious attack on Bimbo: 'am utterly disgusted ... He has always hated & spoken badly of me ... He is the incarnation of all that's evil ... He and Nikolasha are my greatest enemies in the family ... Sweety mine, you must back me up for your & Baby's sake ... We must show that we have no fear & are firm. Wify is your staunch One & stands as a rock behind you.'[10]

Alexandra was not a rock but a millstone. Her elder sister Ella was among those who knew it. Alarmed by the mounting public outcry against the Empress, she had gone to Tsarskoe Selo from her convent in Moscow, intent on making Alexandra see reason. However, as soon as she mentioned the name of Rasputin, Alexandra coldly cut her short. Rising, the Empress called a servant and ordered her sister to leave. On reaching Petrograd a shaken Ella went to see the Yusupovs, who were waiting eagerly at their palace on the Moika to hear how her meeting had gone. She came into their private drawing room trembling and in tears. 'She drove me away like a dog!' she cried. 'Poor Nicky, poor Russia!'[11] The two sisters would never see each other again.

Reason was proving futile, for both the imperial family and desperate politicians alike. The Tsar would never consent to the removal of Rasputin

Colonel-in-exile.
Michael as colonel of the Chernigov Hussars at Orel, September 1909.

A pregnant Natasha, July 1910.
A photograph taken by Michael at Udinka in early July, 1910, just three weeks before she was to give birth to their illegitimate son, George. Although she looks tranquil, she was under great strain, and with reason. The birth certificate would describe her as the 'divorced' wife of Lieutenant Wulfert; she was not.

Moments of domestic bliss

Above left: Natasha with Tata, then aged seven.

Left: At Brasovo a 1911 birthday portrait of Natasha, aged 31, on the garlanded chair which became a family tradition.

Above and inset: Michael with a toddling little George, 1912.

A wife in all but name. Scorned in public, but happy in their private world.
Below: With Koka and Maggie Abakanovich at Brasovo, before moving back to St Petersburg to take command of the Chevalier Gardes.
Above right: The summer of 1912: a storm ahead.

The Getaway Car. Michael and Natasha at Bad Kissingen, in his grey Opel tourer. On October 16, 1912, he and Natasha would drive off in his car ostensibly for Cannes, watched by the Okhrana. Later that day they would be married in Vienna.

The Getaway Man. Michael just before his secret marriage, with the Okhrana having gone off in another direction, believing that he had left for Cannes.

The Honeymooners. St Mark's Square, Venice, October 17, 1912.

Life at Cannes 1912-13

Above: A picnic with Nicholas Johnson and Grand Duke Andrew (right).

Right: Michael flexing his muscles on the beach.

Left: Michael and Natasha on the balcony of the Hotel du Parc.

Below: Lunch at the hotel, with Andrew, Johnson, Tata, and Tata's governess, Miss Rata.

1914 and the last summer.

Above: Skating in Switzerland.

Above right: Driving in Provence.

Right: Putting Jack through his paces.

Below: Summer in the garden of Knebworth with guest Madame Schlieffer and her two children – and a contented Jack, freed from quarantine.

Mistress of Knebworth. Michael and Natasha off to see the Russian ballet in London, July, 1914. She would think her time at Knebworth the most tranquil in her life.

and seemed helpless against the tirades of his wife. Dimitri told Prince Felix Yusupov, son-in-law of Michael's sister Xenia, that at Stavka he had become convinced that 'the drugs administered to the Tsar were paralysing his will power and were given with this intention'.[12] Rasputin seemed to confirm this, telling Yusupov that 'the Emperor is given a tea which causes Divine grace to descend on him. His heart was filled with peace, everything looks good and cheerful to him.' The 'tea' was provided by a quack doctor called Badmaev, using 'herbs provided by nature herself ... God makes them grow, that's why they have Divine properties.'[13]

Paléologue also knew about Badmaev, 'an ingenious disciple of the Mongol sorcerers', and observed that 'judging by its effects, the elixir must be a mixture of henbane and hashish,' for 'every time that the Tsar has used this drug ... he has not only recovered sleep and appetite, but experienced a general feeling of wellbeing, a delightful sense of increased vigour and a curious euphoria'.[14]

Yusupov and Dimitri concluded that something would have to be done.

For most of Russia's élite, the death of Rasputin was the best news of the year. He was murdered in the early hours of Saturday, December 17, at the Yusupovs' magnificent palace on the Moika. Apart from Yusupov and Dimitri, three others were involved: Vladimir Purishkevich, a right-wing member of the Duma, Dr Lazovert, an army doctor and Captain Serge Sukhotin, a friend of Yusupov.

As a preliminary to the murder, Yusupov cultivated Rasputin's friendship. At one meeting Rasputin was boastfully frank. Alexandra 'has a wise, strong mind and I can get anything and everything from her'. Nicholas was 'a simple soul ... he is made for family life, to admire nature and flowers, but not to reign'. As for the ministers, 'all owe their positions to me ... they know very well that if they don't obey me, they'll come to a bad end ... All I have to do to enforce my will is to bang my hand on the table.'[15]

He also told Yusupov about the future: 'We'll make Alexandra regent during her son's minority. As for *him*, we'll send him to Livadia for a rest. He'll be glad to go, he's worn out and needs a rest ... The Tsarina is a very wise woman, a second Catherine the Great. Anyway, she's been running everything lately and, you'll see, the more she does, the better things will be. She's promised to begin by sending away all those chatterboxes at the Duma.'[16]

Rasputin condemned himself. The plan was to poison him, lacing cakes and drink with cyanide potassium provided by Dr Lazovert. The bait they offered Rasputin was Yusupov's wife Irina – she wanted to meet him, he was told; in fact, she was in the Crimea. A basement was hurriedly converted into a dining room. Yusupov collected Rasputin from his apartment on

Gorokhovaya Street on the evening of Friday, December 16, and drove him back to the Moika. He told Rasputin that Irina would join him as soon as she could get rid of the last of her guests upstairs; to keep up the pretence of a party the other plotters were talking noisily in the room above and playing 'Yankee Doodle' on a gramophone.[17]

Yusupov handed out cakes and watched in horror as Rasputin took one after another without the poison having any apparent effect. He also drank glass after glass of wine, firstly Crimean then Madeira. None of that had any effect either. Two hours after his arrival Rasputin was seemingly no worse than he had been before. Frantic, Yusupov went upstairs to report that the poison had failed entirely. Aghast, the plotters decided to shoot him. Dimitri offered to do it, but when Yusupov insisted that it should be his task, he handed Yusupov his revolver.[18]

Yusupov went back, gave Rasputin another glass of Madeira and, after suggesting that he look closely at a crucifix on the cabinet, shot him through the chest. Rasputin gave 'a wild scream' and crumpled on to the bearskin.[19] When the others rushed down at the sound of the shot they found Rasputin lying on his back, his blouse blood-stained and his face twitching. In a moment he was motionless; the doctor, examining him, pronounced him dead.

The plotters went upstairs, leaving the body in the basement. Dimitri, the doctor and the captain then drove off to Gorokhovaya Street, the captain in Rasputin's overcoat and cap, so as to pretend that Rasputin had returned home safely. Dimitri then went to collect his closed car in which the body was to be taken away to be dumped in the frozen Neva. It was reasoned that the corpse, weighted with chains, would remain hidden under the ice until the spring thaw.

While Yusupov and Purishkevich were waiting for Dimitri to return Yusupov went back to the basement to check the body. As he bent over Rasputin he was horrified to see an eye open, then with a violent effort the 'dead man' leapt to his feet and rushed at Yusupov, his hands reaching out to strangle him. Yusupov struggled and freed himself, then rushed upstairs to Purishkevich. The two men came back just in time to see Rasputin, 'gasping and roaring like a wounded animal',[20] stumbling out through a side door in the basement to the courtyard outside. Suddenly there were two shots as Purishkevich fired at the fleeing Rasputin, then two more. Rasputin collapsed into the snow.

This time he really seemed to be dead. However, the firing had been heard and a curious policeman arrived. Yusupov stood so that he could not see the body in the courtyard and told him that there had just been some 'horseplay' in which a dog had been shot. The man went away, but returned, his superiors also having heard the gunfire. This time Purishkevich confronted him and boldly told him what had happened, adding 'that if you love your country and your Tsar you'll keep your mouth shut'.[21]

By now Dimitri and the others had returned. They took Rasputin's body and, bundling it into Dimitri's car, drove off through the dark, early-morning streets to Petrovsky Island, where they threw it from a bridge into the icy Neva below. In their haste, however, they had forgotten the chains intended to weigh down the body;[22] two days later, on Monday, searching police found Rasputin's corpse, visible just below the ice, with one arm outstretched. At the post mortem examination it was found that there was water in his lungs, suggesting that he was still alive when he was thrown into the river.[23]

Poisoned, shot, or drowned, it came to the same thing: Rasputin was dead.

There was never any chance that the identity of those involved in the murder would remain unknown. The policeman made a report: two men-servants had seen the body in the snow-covered courtyard, Purishkevich had admitted the shooting and at Tsarskoe Selo they knew that Rasputin was going to the Yusupov palace on Friday evening, for he had told Anna Vyrubova earlier in the day when she came to visit him at his apartment.[24]

By Saturday evening the city was alive with rumours. Paléologue had the bare details by seven o'clock,[25] though by then most people seemed to know about the murder and the names of those involved. That same night, at the Michael Theatre, Dimitri had to leave 'before the end of the performance so as to escape an ovation of the audience'; outside his palace on Nevsky Prospekt* 'people knelt to pray'[26] and in churches across Russia candles were being lit before icons of St Dimitri.[27]

Yusupov, who had intended to set off that Saturday for the Crimea – for the house just vacated by Michael and Natasha – was ordered by the police to remain in the capital.[28] Next day, at lunchtime, Dimitri was told by telephone at his palace that he was under 'house arrest'. In both instances the order came from Alexandra. Yusupov, who had just arrived at Dimitri's palace, saw him go to the telephone. 'He returned looking upset: "I'm under arrest by order of the Empress," he said. "She has no right to issue such an order. Only the Emperor can have me arrested." '[29] Yusupov later claimed that Alexandra's first instinct was not to have Dimitri arrested but shot.[30] There was also the danger of a revenge attack by Rasputin supporters; the interior minister Protopopov was suspected of planning that police guarding Dimitri would, in fact, murder him; as a counter-move the

* Inherited from his assassinated uncle Serge, it became the Anglo-Russian hospital, Dimitri retaining only an apartment.

Petrograd governor ordered troops to Dimitri's palace to protect him.[31]

On Sunday, the day after the murder, Dimitri's father Grand Duke Paul came to see him. 'Can you swear to me', he asked, 'that there is no blood on your hands?' Dimitri crossed himself in front of the icon hanging in the corner of the room and replied: 'I swear by the name of my mother.'[32] It was true that he had not himself shot Rasputin and in that sense there was 'no blood' on his hands, but no court would have excused him on that score. If it had been an ordinary murder he would have hanged.

Two days later Dimitri gave his father a letter for the Emperor. In it he said that at any enquiry or court martial he would refuse to answer questions or give any explanation, for he had taken an oath on that. Afterwards he proposed to shoot himself, 'and by such an act he would justify himself in the eyes of the Emperor.'[33] In the event there was to be no enquiry and no legal proceedings of any kind.

Rasputin was buried in near-secrecy at Tsarskoe Selo on December 23, on a plot of land owned by Anna Vyrubova, with a grief-stricken Alexandra pinning a farewell note to his body.[34] Afterwards, the punishment Nicholas decreed for Dimitri was his immediate exile to Kasvin, on the Persian front; Yusupov was banished to his estate in Kursk. However, Purishkevich was deemed too powerful; he escaped punishment entirely.[35]

Some friends had urged Dimitri to challenge any order against him; there had also been hotheaded talk by Kirill, Boris and Andrew of a night march by four Guards regiments on Tsarskoe Selo. This excited plot, aimed at the seizure of Nicholas and Alexandra – he to abdicate, she to be placed in a nunnery – envisaged the newly popular Dimitri leading a *coup d'état*, but he had refused to 'lay hands on the Emperor' because of his oath of allegiance.[36] 'All that he sought in joining the plot against Rasputin was to uphold the throne and he did not now intend to reverse that attitude,' said his sister Marie.[37] Resigned to his exile, he went to his room to pack and to look through the papers in his desk. Dimitri had been permitted to take no more than a suitcase with him. Marie watched as he drew out and 'thoughtfully examined several large photographs of a very pretty woman, hesitating as to which he would take with him; but they were all much too large and, with a sigh, he thrust them back into the drawer'.[38]

Natasha's portraits had to be left behind.

On Monday, December 19, the day that Rasputin's body was found under the ice, Michael wrote in his diary to say that 'we read in the papers that Grigory Rasputin was assassinated in Petrograd',[39] though there was only a short paragraph – thereafter newspapers were prohibited from giving details of the murder. However, when Princess Putyatina, the children, the Viazemskys, Johnson and the governesses and staff from Gatchina arrived they brought with them all the rumours from the capital.

The still infatuated Tata was 'thrilled to the core' by learning that 'my darling Dimitri' figured among the plotters[40] and she was downcast only when she heard the news of his arrest and that he would not be joining them for Christmas.[41] Tata was even more upset when she heard around the table at Brasovo that his punishment was inevitable and that he was bound to be banished 'to some remote outpost of the imperial domain'.[42] So, of course, was a worried Natasha. There is no evidence that Natasha had any prior knowledge of Dimitri's involvement in the murder plot, but she had made no secret of her views about Rasputin. Had she influenced him to act? She would never know, but she could hardly do other than wonder.

Alexandra certainly believed that Natasha and her 'bad set' bore some responsibility. Five months earlier she had written to Nicholas about Dimitri: 'Don't let him go to that lady so often – such society is his ruin – nothing but flattery and he likes it . . . and don't let him be too free with his tongue either.'[43] The death of Rasputin was to Alexandra evidence enough that Dimitri had been ruined by the people around him.*

At Brasovo, Rasputin's murder dominated minds no less than at Tsarskoe Selo, but 700 miles from events and tucked away on an estate, 'covered in dazzling snow and looking like a fairy kingdom',[44] the rituals of Christmas and the demands of children briefly shut out the dramas in the capital. Setting aside her schoolgirl sorrow at the absence of Dimitri, 'we proceeded to have a wonderful time', Tata wrote.[45]

Early on Christmas Eve Michael and Vyazemsky cut down a tree on the estate, carried it into the house and set it up in the children's room and after breakfast everyone set about decorating the branches. In the evening a local priest conducted a service and later, 'to liven things up' as Michael put it, he played the guitar and 'in the living room we hung mistletoe, which we brought from the Crimea, on the chandelier'.[46] Presents were distributed before they sat down to 'a long and elaborate dinner, to be followed by more games'.[47] On Christmas Day, Michael and the children tobogganed 'down the hill, to the great pleasure of Tata and Baby,' he noted happily.[48] That evening the Christmas tree was lit up again and the workers on the estate were invited into the house to join the guests for drinks.

Princess Putyatina was impressed by her first sight of Brasovo. 'Nathalie, thanks to her artistic taste, had succeeded in making it an elegant dwelling as well as a comfortable home, thereby creating for the Grand Duke a place

* Dimitri's passion for Natasha was 'common knowledge' says his son, Paul Ilyinsky; Alexandra was in no doubt therefore about 'that lady's' influence over Dimitri, and resentful of it.

where he found comfort, peace and happiness.' But what she remembered most was its magnificent setting amidst fields and pines. 'A great deal of snow fell that year . . . Brasovo estate, surrounded by the huge forests for which Orel is famous, presented a truly magical sight in winter. A marvellous view unrolled before our eyes from the windows of the house; a blanket of snow sparkling white and glinting in the sun like myriads of diamonds stretched as far as the eye could see. "What splendour!" I thought looking out at this scene.'[49]

Unhappily, that Christmas at Brasovo was to end abruptly. One of the guests was an old school friend of Natasha, Maria Lebedeva, who had arrived from Moscow with her two daughters. The elder, Irina aged thirteen, complained just after Christmas of a sore throat and was sent to bed. The next day her condition worsened and Dr Koton, who was among the house guests, diagnosed diphtheria. Two days later Irina was dead.[50]

With the other children – Tata and George, Princess Putyatina's only daughter and Marie Lebedeva's younger child – all at risk of infection, there was no option but to leave immediately. Looking back at the house as the sleighs took them to the station, Princess Putyatina remembered that 'it was with hearts filled with unhappiness and dark forebodings that we all left together the place where we had spent such happy days'.[51]

None of them would ever see Brasovo again.

TWENTY

Palace Plotters

Michael and Natasha returned to a world where the death of Rasputin had done nothing to ease tension, for it had provided drama but no other tangible improvement in political conditions. The government had not fallen, the hated Protopopov was still interior minister, claiming that he was now guided by Rasputin's ghost[1] and Alexandra was still effectively Regent, grieving but otherwise unchanged in her purpose. The only desperate action came from an officer who attempted to assassinate Alexandra on December 28, *en route* between the palace and her hospital. Caught, he was hanged next morning, although his arrest and execution were kept 'absolutely secret'.[2]

Nevertheless, there was still talk of a palace coup, as there had been before Christmas. At one champagne supper party, Boris was reported to have been openly discussing the timing and the regiments which could be used, seemingly indifferent to the fact that the whole conversation could be overheard by servants, gypsy singers and with 'harlots looking on and listening'.[3]

Nicholas seemed prepared to face any family challenge head on. After Dimitri's departure, his sister and stepmother, worried that he would not survive the rigours of frontier life in Persia, sent a letter, signed by several members of the family, asking Nicholas to revoke his order. The letter came back to Grand Duke Paul with a scribbled note in the margin: 'No one has the right to kill . . .'[4] Bimbo, one of the instigators of the letter, was banished to his remote estate on New Year's Day and it was enough to stop the family rebellion in its tracks. Paléologue judged that Nicholas 'obviously intended to frighten the imperial family. He has succeeded. They are terror-stricken.'[5]

A week later, the Tsar told Grand Duchess Marie Pavlovna that 'in their own interests' it would be best if her sons Kirill and Andrew should leave the capital for a few weeks.[6] They went quietly, leaving their mother to scurry around in search of other allies. Mikhail Rodzyanko, president of the State Duma, recorded a 'peculiar interview' with Marie Pavlovna in her palace on Millionnaya Street. It was common knowledge that the Grand Duchess hated Alexandra and that she cherished ambitions to see one of her three sons on the throne. The Third Lady in Russia, with only Alexandra and the Dowager Empress ranked above her, she began to talk about the government, Protopopov and the Empress. 'On mentioning the latter's name she became more and more excited . . . that things must be changed, something done, removed, destroyed . . .'

'What do you mean by "removed"?'

'Well, I don't know . . . The Duma must do something . . . She must be annihilated . . .'

'Who?'

'The Empress.'

'Your Highness,' said Rodzyanko, 'allow me to treat this conversation as if it had never taken place, because if you address me as the President of the Duma, my oath of allegiance compels me to wait on His Imperial Majesty and report to him that the Grand Duchess Marie Pavlovna has declared to me that the Empress must be annihilated.'[7]

Rodzyanko was not, at this stage, one of those willing to act against the Tsar, hoping still that he could be persuaded to change course. Among those Duma deputies who thought otherwise, the view was that nothing could now be expected of the Grand Dukes. The right-wing Kadet deputy Maklakov, who had been privy to, but had declined to take part in, the plot to kill Rasputin, concluded that 'they want the Duma to put the match to the powder. In other words, they are expecting of us what we are expecting of them.'[8]

At Tsarskoe Selo, an unhappy Grand Duke Paul was telling the French ambassador that 'the Emperor is more under the Empress's thumb than ever. She has persuaded him that the hostile movement against her . . . is nothing but a conspiracy of the Grand Dukes and a drawing room revolt.'[9]

She was deluding herself. There were more serious plots afoot. All were intended to bring about the abdication of the Tsar and thereby Alexandra's removal from the political scene and the substitution of twelve-year-old Alexis as Emperor under the Regency of Grand Duke Michael Aleksandrovich. The question in January 1917 was no longer whether this might be done, but when and by whom.

Because Michael returned from Brasovo only on December 30 he did not sign the family petition on behalf of Dimitri, pointless though it was; however, at Gatchina there was never any doubt as to where sympathy lay. Indeed, Natasha would be one of the first to hear from the exiled Dimitri. Soon after his arrival he wrote to her: 'Natasha, dearest, how often I remember now our charming conversations, how much I miss them, be happy and do not forget me . . .'[10] A month later came a second letter. 'My dearest Natasha, you remember Moscow, that beloved city. You remember our meeting there . . .' It was just over two years since his confession of love at the National Hotel. 'Oh, Natasha, Natasha, where is that magic time, where is that Moscow, where is that wonderful time now? . . . We are so far apart, 2500 miles separate us, my lot is a very miserable one . . . yet I love life even more than before . . . please don't forget your sincerely devoted and truly loving friend.'[11]

Though there was constant discussion at Gatchina about the political crisis looming in both court and government, Michael strove otherwise to make his family life as normal as possible on the return from Brasovo. On December 31 he had a dinner party at home, 'and Tata brought in the New Year for the first time. The tree was lit and all was joyful'.[12] On January 5 he was delighted when a group of sailors arrived from his imperial yacht *Zarnitsa* and presented six-year-old George with a model ship the boatswain Kuzmenko and four of the crew had built for him. 'It was ideally made, the length of the model was seven feet. You can raise the 14 sails.'[13]

Nevertheless, these domestic interludes were small pleasures in an increasingly grim world. The telephone brought news of developments in the capital, including the family intrigues against Tsarskoe Selo. Although Michael had no part in any palace coup directed against his brother, he was convinced that Alexandra had to be removed from any further influence on affairs. To that end he conducted his own diplomacy.

Early in the New Year he saw Nicholas at Tsarskoe Selo and heard his side of the story, including his account of an uncomfortable meeting a few days earlier, on December 30, with British ambassador Sir George Buchanan.

The ambassador, alarmed by the open talk in the capital of an impending palace coup, had been given permission by London to deliver his own warnings, but not to speak on behalf of the British government or of King George V. It is rare for an ambassador to ask for an audience at which he is speaking personally and not officially and Buchanan was in consequence nervous, but nevertheless determined to have his say. Normally he would sit in the Tsar's study and chat over a friendly cigarette, but on this occasion, as if Nicholas had been forewarned that he was there on his own responsibility, he was shown into the audience chamber, with the Tsar standing formally in the middle of the huge room.[14]

'My heart, I confess, sank within me,' said Buchanan afterwards; none the less he decided to say what he had come to say: that interior minister Protopopov 'is bringing Russia to the verge of ruin', that in the event of revolution 'only a small part of the army can be counted on to defend the dynasty' and that the only safe course now was for the Tsar to 'break down the barrier that separates you from your people and to regain their confidence'. Drawing himself up and looking hard at the ambassador, Nicholas replied: 'You tell me that *I* must regain the confidence of the people. Isn't it rather for my people to regain *my* confidence?'[15]

The meeting clearly shook Nicholas, however much he concealed his reactions from the British ambassador. A government minister who had an audience with the Tsar immediately afterwards found him 'trembling and distrait'.[16] Buchanan's strictures appear to have stung Nicholas, for when Michael arrived he recounted the conversation to him.

Shortly afterwards Michael called at Rodzyanko's apartment at 20 Furshtadtskaya, near the Tauride Palace. Rodzyanko was surprised to see him. When they had sat down, Michael asked him abruptly: 'I should like to talk to you about what is going on and to consult you as to what should be done. We understand the situation perfectly.'

Rodzyanko's response was as frank as the question invited him to be. 'The entire policy of the government must undergo a radical change. Ministers must be appointed whom the country trusts, not men whose very presence in the government is an insult to public feeling. I am sorry to tell you that this can only be done on condition that the Empress is removed. She exercises a deplorable influence on all appointments, even those in the army ... Alexandra Fedorovna is fiercely and universally hated and all circles are clamouring for her removal. While she remains in power, we shall continue on the road to ruin.'

'Buchanan said the same thing to my brother,' Michael replied. 'The whole family is aware of her evil influence. She and my brother are surrounded by traitors. All decent people have gone. But things being so, what is to be done?'

'Your Highness, you, as his only brother, must tell him the whole truth; point out the pernicious results of the Empress's influence ...'

'Do you think that there must be a responsible ministry?'

'The general demand is only for a strong government ... the country's desire is to see at the head of the Cabinet a man enjoying the confidence of the nation. Such a man would form a ministry responsible to the Tsar ... for God's sake, Your Highness, use your influence to get the Duma summoned and Alexandra Fedorovna and her set put out of the way.'

According to Rodzyanko this interview lasted more than an hour. 'The Grand Duke agreed with everything and promised to help ...'[17]

Rodzyanko's wife thought Michael was there 'on some mysterious mission, I think he was sent secretly by his brother'. But she reported to a relative that 'he knows and understands everything and listened attentively to all that was said and promised to prevail upon the Emperor to see [my husband]'. When Nicholas then did agree to meet Rodzyanko, she wrote that 'it is more than likely that the audience was granted after Michael Aleksandrovich's expostulations'.[18]

On Saturday, January 7, Tsar and Duma president met at Tsarskoe Selo.

The Duma president was frank about the disastrous influence of the Empress and blunt about the mistakes which now threatened to plunge Russia into anarchy. 'Your Majesty, do not compel the people to choose between you and the good of the country. So far, the ideas of Tsar and Motherland have been indissoluble, but lately they have begun to divide.'

It was much the same litany that Nicholas had heard from the British ambassador and from Michael; unless he agreed to grant concessions and removed Alexandra from political influence, he faced disaster.

The Tsar pressed his head with his hands and said, 'Is it possible that for twenty-two years I tried to act for the best and that for twenty-two years it was all a mistake?'

It was a trying moment. 'Yes, Your Majesty, for twenty-two years you have followed the wrong course.'[19]

Like everyone else, however, Rodzyanko achieved nothing in the end. Once he had bowed and departed for the capital, Nicholas went on as before. Nothing changed. At Tsarskoe Selo the last word lay with Alexandra.

If the last word at Gatchina had rested with Natasha, Michael might have been found talking to people other than his brother and Rodzyanko, but Michael would not undermine Nicholas by allowing a breach between them to surface in public. Like Dimitri, he wanted to save the throne, not usurp it. In all the gossip in the capital, his name was never mentioned among those members of the imperial family willing to see Nicholas abdicate in order to remove Alexandra, though the same cannot be said about Natasha. Michael's loyalty was perhaps ill-judged, but if his brother was forced to abdicate, he would not have it said that he was party to it. 'May this cup pass me by' was not cynical hypocrisy, but his hope that Nicholas would yet save himself.

Michael's involvement in the unfolding drama was necessarily interrupted when on January 19 he left Gatchina to return to the front. Three days later he was in Kiev and on his way to the south-western front and the headquarters of his 2nd Cavalry Corps.[20] His new appointment, effective as of January 29, was that of Inspector General of Cavalry, but before taking up the post he needed to hand over his Corps formally and to make his farewells to the divisions, brigades and regiments. Over the next days he travelled the frontline by sleigh, inspecting trenches and outposts.

After the atmosphere in Petrograd it was almost a relief to him to be at the frontline and he enjoyed his tour. He 'thanked the riflemen for their service, tasted the food, inspected the wooden barracks of the lower-ranking men and then went to a hut and had a bite to eat'.[21] Fortunately he did not have to make any formal speeches to gathered regiments as had happened when he left the Savage Division some ten months earlier. Doing so 'must have taken at least three years of my life', he lamented. 'I am always so frightfully nervous, but I pulled myself together and spoke loudly, slowly and clearly.'[22]

On his farewell tour he found nothing in his Corps to suggest that morale was low, or that the ferment in the capital had affected his troops. As before, they cheered him, played trumpet farewells, sang songs, gave him tea and looked sorry to see him go.[23]

Yet politics could not be kept at bay. Before returning to Gatchina he went to say goodbye to his commander-in-chief Brusilov at his headquarters in Kamenets-Podolsky, arriving there on Wednesday, February 1. 'I was very fond of him,' Brusilov recalled, 'for he was an absolutely honourable and upright man, taking no sides and lending himself to no intrigues . . . he shunned every kind of gossip, whether connected with the services or with family matters. As a soldier he was an excellent leader and an unassuming and conscientious worker.'[24]

At their meeting Brusilov thought the situation too serious for merely polite talk. 'I expounded most earnestly . . . the need for immediate and drastic reforms . . . begging him to explain all this to the Tsar and to lend my views his personal support.'

Michael agreed to do so, but added: 'I have no influence and I am of no consequence. My brother has time and time again had warnings and entreaties of this kind from every quarter, but he is the slave of influence and pressure that no one is in a position to overcome.'[25]

The two men shook hands and Michael set off for home next day. It was a slow journey. 'We are moving with a delay of 3 hours, probably because of snowdrifts. I say "probably", as you can never know the real cause of happenings. But the truth is that everything is in complete disorder everywhere . . .'[26]

It was going to get worse.

The serious plotters were now well advanced in their plans for a palace coup. Discounting the near-hysterical 'champagne plot' at the Vladimir palace, which served only to extinguish any hopes that the Romanovs could put their own house in order, there were a number of conspiracies, none knowing much, if anything, of the others. All necessarily were shadowy and perhaps only two were credible.

By the end of December the Progressive Bloç of conservatives and liberals had prepared a list of ministers who would form the government after a coup, with Michael as Regent, though they were still vague as to how this was to be accomplished.

Demands that something should be done could be heard on all sides. Vladimir Stankevich, a henchman of the left-wing Duma deputy Aleksandr Kerensky, saw 'a general determination to have done with the outrages perpetrated by court circles and to overthrow Nicholas. Several names were suggested as candidates for the throne, but there was unanimous agreement that Michael Aleksandrovich was the only one who could guarantee the constitutional legitimacy of government.'[27]

Talk was not action. Among those determined to act were Aleksandr Guchkov, the fifty-five-year-old leader of the Octobrists and sometime president of the Third Duma, the liberal Nikolai Nekrasov and industrialist Mikhail Tereshchenko.[28] Nekrasov and Tereshchenko were both young men, the former thirty-six, the latter only twenty-nine.

Guchkov's reasoning was that without change a revolution was inevitable and that if it was left to extremists and the street mob then it would be they who would rule afterwards: 'I fear that those who make the revolution will be at the head of that revolution'. The alternative was a bloodless palace coup; they did not want Alexis as the new Emperor and Michael as Regent to 'take their oath surrounded by lakes of blood'.[29] From the beginning of October 1916 the three men worked on their plans; in the end they decided 'to capture the Tsar's train while it was travelling between St Petersburg and Headquarters', presenting the country next morning with a *fait accompli*. To make this possible they needed the help of 'like-minded' army officers; the man recruited to find them was 'a valued collaborator ... Prince Viazemsky'.[30]★

But would Michael agree to be Regent? Encouraged perhaps by direct or indirect contact with Natasha, the plotters assumed Michael's willingness to accept the Regency, even though his well-known loyalty made it impossible to ensure this in advance, or even to sound him out. Certainly, Guchkov seemed confident. Besides, 'it would be His Majesty's decree', he argued. 'The only illegality would be the moral pressure exerted. After that the law would come into effect.'[31]

A second and unrelated plot involved Prince Lvov, the popular leader of the civic and volunteer organisations across Russia, who had secured the support of General Alekseev, the chief of staff at Stavka. Their intention was to arrest Alexandra on one of her regular visits to Stavka and to compel the Tsar to remove her to Livadia; if he refused, then abdication would be forced upon him.[32] Since he would have refused, the aim of this plot matched the other. The plan had not been developed because Alekseev had been ill for several weeks, but it remained in being.

A third plot, or perhaps the inspiration for the action plan devised by the 'Guchkov conspiracy', was the arrival in the capital in January of General Aleksandr Krymov, a forty-six-year-old cavalryman serving on the south-western front. Michael knew Krymov and it appears that Natasha knew at

★ Prince Dimitri Vyazemsky, a relative of Michael's aide-de-camp, Prince Vladimir Vyazemsky.

some point about Krymov's involvement in the Guchkov plot, for she later spoke about it.[33]

Krymov approached Rodzyanko and asked for his agreement for an unofficial meeting with members of the Duma, to acquaint them with the critical situation at the front. Rodzyanko called the meeting at his apartment, inviting Duma deputies and members of the State Council.

Krymov spoke bluntly. 'The feeling in the army is such that news of a *coup d'état* would be welcomed with joy. A revolution is imminent and we at the front feel it is to be so. If you decide on such an extreme step, we will support you. Clearly, there is no other way . . . the Emperor attaches more weight to his wife's nefarious influence than to all honest words of warning. There is no time to lose.'

The meeting lasted far into the night. As he would do the following day, in his 'peculiar interview' with Grand Duchess Marie Pavlovna, Rodzyanko stood firm against a *coup d'état*. 'I shall never countenance a revolution . . . I have taken the oath of allegiance.' But others were less squeamish, one man quoting Brusilov's remark, 'If it comes to a choice between the Tsar and Russia, I will take Russia.'[34]

Yet the question remained: 'Who will have the courage to undertake it?'[35] The only realistic answer seemed to be the men around Guchkov, more so when now in Krymov they had a general who was willing to lead the troops they needed to capture the train.

Their plan would be to strike in the middle of March.[36]

TWENTY-ONE

'Make Yourself Regent'

Michael arrived back home in Gatchina on Saturday, February 4, knowing that the situation was serious but still hoping that his brother would see reason and yield the concessions. Meeting his brother-in-law Sandro in Petrograd, he proposed that they should go together to see Nicholas and press the need for a responsible ministry and the removal of Alexandra from any further role in political affairs.[1] Sandro agreed, but insisted that firstly he saw Alexandra on his own and spoke his mind to her. Although unwell, Alexandra agreed to see him.

Nicholas led Sandro into her mauve bedroom. 'Alix lay in bed, dressed in a white negligée embroidered with lace . . . I kissed her hand and her lips just skimmed my cheek, the coldest greeting given me by her since the first day we met in 1893. I took a chair and moved it close to her bed, facing a wall covered with innumerable icons lit by two blue-and-pink church lamps.'

With Nicholas standing silently, puffing away on his cigarettes, Sandro told her bluntly that she had to remove herself from politics. Their exchange became heated, until all pretence at politeness vanished. 'Remember, Alix, I remained silent for thirty months!' he shouted at her in a wild rage. 'For thirty months I never said as much as a word to you about the disgraceful goings-on in our government, better to say in *your* government! I realise that you are willing to perish and that your husband feels the same way, but what about us? Must we all suffer for your blind stubbornness? No, Alix, you have no right to drag your relatives with you into a precipice! You are incredibly selfish!'

'I refuse to continue this dispute,' she said coldly. 'You are exaggerating the danger. Some day, when you are less excited, you will admit that I knew better.'

He got up, kissed her hand, received no kiss in reply and left. 'I never saw Alix again.'

Passing through the mauve salon he went straight to the library, ordered a pen and paper and sat down to write a letter to Michael. As he did so he looked up and saw the Tsar's ADC watching him, as if on guard. The aide refused to leave and 'in a fury' Sandro got up and stormed out of the palace.[2]

The next day he returned to Tsarskoe Selo with Michael. Meeting them in his study, Nicholas smoked, listened, but seemed unimpressed by anything that Michael said. Sandro judged that they were 'wasting his time and ours'. When it became Sandro's turn to argue he found by the end that 'I was hardly able to speak, nerves and emotion choking me'.[3]

On February 10 Michael went again to Tsarskoe Selo,[4] for another meeting as pointless as the first. He was there when Rodzyanko turned up, with another fateful warning that without change they all faced disaster. Rodzyanko recounted that 'I was received very coldly ... I began to read my report. The Emperor listened not only with indifference, but with a kind of ill-will ... and he finally interrupted me with the request that I hurry a bit, as Grand Duke Michael Aleksandrovich was waiting for him to have a cup of tea ...'[5]

Four days later, on February 14, Sandro wrote to his brother Nicholas, told him about his depressing meetings at Tsarskoe Selo and added, 'Misha can also see no way out, except sending her to Livadia'.[6]

Over the next days the pressure on Nicholas to yield to the demands for a responsible ministry seemed to have produced results for at one point he told his prime minister, Prince Golitsin, that he was prepared to go to the Duma next day and concede that constitutional reform. But suddenly he changed his mind. There would be no appearance at the Duma and no concessions. Instead he went to Stavka.

Next day, hardly back at headquarters, Nicholas received a letter from Alexandra. It was like all the others, written in English, with the same urging that she had scribbled into his diary twenty-three years earlier, at the deathbed of his father: 'Be firm ...'[7]

This time Nicholas's reply showed a touch of irritation. 'What you write about being firm – the master – is perfectly true. I do not forget it – be sure of that, but I need not bellow at the people right & left every moment. A quiet sharp remark or answer is enough very often to put the one or the other into his place ...'[8]

It was not going to be enough ever again.

The revolution intended to come from above came instead from below and without any real warning. It was a spontaneous rising, with no master-plan, or even a decisive leader who could be identified afterwards. Unrest became disturbance, disturbance grew into rebellion and rebellion turned into revolution. And yet all this was in large part confined to the capital, with the rest of the country unaffected, at least in the beginning, and with some regions unaware of events until they were all over.

There were many factors. The ostensible cause was fear of a bread shortage: although supplies were adequate, the fear was self-fulfilling in that housewives hoarded, creating the shortage. There had been large-scale strikes, following a lock-out of workers at the giant Putilov factories and by February 24 the Okhrana calculated that there were 158,000 men idle[9]; many thousands of these were gathering at demonstrations or taking part in protest marches through the streets.

Petrograd was a vast military camp, with 170,000 armed troops in barracks,[10] many of them susceptible to agitators. The government was hated. For months the talk had been of revolution. German agents were actively fomenting resentment, it being German policy to bring about revolution and thus remove Russia from the war.

On Saturday, February 25, 1917, Michael noted that 'there were disorders on Nevsky Prospekt today. Workmen were going about with red flags and were throwing grenades and bottles at the police, so that troops had to open fire. The main cause of disorders – is lack of flour in the shops.'[11] Three demonstrators and three policemen were killed, with some 100 other people injured.

But what had greater significance that day was an incident in Znamenskaya Square, which stood at the far end of Nevsky Prospekt, beside the Nicholas station, the main terminus for Moscow. A grey-coated police inspector called Krylov had ridden forward into a crowd of demonstrators gathered around the statue of Alexander III, intending to seize a red flag and was killed by a Cossack trooper.[12] The Cossacks were the most feared of Tsarist troops and the traditional scourge of rioters and demonstrators. If they were no longer reliable, no one was.

That afternoon the Tsar, in his headquarters at Mogilev, sent a telegram to the military governor Khabalov: 'I command you to put an end to all disturbances in the streets of the capital, which are inadmissible at this difficult time when we are at war with Germany and Austria.'[13]

Next day, Sunday, there were placards all over the city, forbidding meetings or gatherings, with notices that troops were authorised to fire to maintain order. The crowds took no notice of these warnings and that evening Michael would note in his diary: 'The disorders in Petrograd have gathered momentum. On the Suvorov Prospekt and Znamenskaya Street there were 200 killed.'[14] He did not know that there had been an even more ominous development: a company of the Pavlovsk Guards regiment mutinied in their barracks and when their colonel came in to confront them, he was attacked and his hand cut off.[15]

Rodzyanko now sent a desperate telegram to the Tsar at Stavka. 'The situation is serious. The capital is in a state of anarchy. The government is paralysed. Transport service and the supply of food and fuel have become completely disrupted. General discontent is growing. There is wild shooting in the streets. In places troops are firing at each other. It is necessary that some person who enjoys the confidence of the country be entrusted at once with the formation of a new government. There must be no delay. Any procrastination is tantamount to death . . .'[16]

Nicholas, reading that telegram, dismissed it as panic. 'Some more rubbish from that fat Rodzyanko,' he said.[17] However, he did decide to put together a loyal force to march on the capital and to return to Tsarskoe Selo himself.

He was not the only one still taking matters more lightly than circumstances warranted, for in some parts of the capital fashionable life continued almost as before. While Paléologue noted on the previous evening that the Maryinski had been half full for a symphony concert – an indication of the nervousness felt by many about braving the streets – on Sunday night, returning from a dinner party, he passed a house blazing with lights on the Fontanka, with a line of cars and carriages outside. 'Princess Leon Radziwill's party was in full swing; I caught a glimpse of the car of Grand Duke Boris as we passed.'[18]

It would be the last party in the capital of imperial Russia. Next morning, Monday, February 27, a column of marchers crossing the Neva were met by a regiment of troops ordered to bar them from the city centre. Looking out from his window, Paléologue expected a violent collision; instead, soldiers and marchers merged into one. 'The army was fraternising with revolt.'[19] A few hours earlier the Volynsky Guards regiment mutinied and an NCO shot dead a company commander, Captain Lashkevich; this was followed by a mutiny in the Litovsky regiment, its soldiers plundering the arsenal and disappearing into the suburbs with rifles. The Preobrazhensky Guards also mutinied, killing their commander, Colonel Bogdanovich, before scattering through the city, taking their arms with them.[20]

The rebels were not frontline soldiers but depot reservists, many of them raw recruits, the scrapings of the military barrel. Their officers were men convalescing after being wounded at the front, or young inexperienced subalterns fresh from the military academies. It was certain, observed General Knox, that 'if the men went wrong, the officers were without the influence to control them'.[21] Military discipline was a thin veneer which was easily stripped away, turning such troops into a uniformed mob. Nevertheless, they had guns and were no worse trained than those soldiers who would be facing them. By noon 25,000 troops had gone over to the side of the demonstrators, but among the rest, the great majority of soldiers, there were relatively few still willing to march out either with or against them. The bulk of the available forces simply stayed in their barracks as the armed rebels and the mob took command of the streets.

The Arsenal on the Liteiny was captured, putting into the hands of the rebels thousands of rifles and pistols, and hundreds of machine-guns. The headquarters of the Okhrana, across the Neva and opposite the Winter Palace, as well as a score of police stations, were overrun and set on fire.

The prisons were opened and their inmates freed, criminals as well as political detainees. By the evening, only the very centre of the city, around the Winter Palace, could be said still to be in government control.[22]

Michael would begin his diary entry for Monday, February 27, by writing that it was 'the beginning of anarchy'.[23]

On Monday, February 27, sitting in his quarters at Stavka, Nicholas puffed on a cigarette and read Alexandra's latest letter, written the day before from Tsarskoe Selo. She was dealing with her own crisis at home, for three of the children – Alexis, Olga and Tatiana – had gone down with measles, as had her devoted companion Anna Vyrubova and she expected that the other two children 'may still catch it'. Alexandra, wearing her Red Cross uniform, was nursing the patients herself and she was following *only* intermittently the reports from the capital. Nevertheless she was cheerful and confident 'for they say it's not like 1905, because all adore you & only want bread ... it seems to me it will be alright – the sun shines so brightly'. There was also the consolation of her prayers at the grave of Rasputin, who had been buried in the palace grounds. 'I felt such peace & calm on His dear grave – He died to save us.'[24]

Nicholas was also striving to be calm. The day before, in church, he had felt 'an excruciating pain in the middle of my chest, which lasted for quarter of an hour. I could hardly stand & my forehead was covered with beads of sweat. I cannot understand what it was, as I had no heart beating, but it came & left me at once, when I knelt before the Virgin's image.'[25] Now on Monday he told Alexandra 'how happy I am at the thought of meeting you in two days', then reported that 'after the news of yesterday from town – I saw many faces here with frightened expressions. Luckily Alekseev is calm ...'[26]

Calm was the watchword. Early that afternoon the war minister General Mikhail Belyaev cabled Mogilev to reassure Nicholas that while 'it has not yet been possible to crush the rebellion ... I am firmly convinced that calm will soon arrive. Ruthless measures are being adopted to achieve this. The authorities remain totally calm.'[27] If he had written 'totally panic-stricken' it would have been nearer the mark, but Belyaev, fifty-four and appointed only seven weeks earlier, could not bring himself to admit to Mogilev that he had already lost control of the army in Petrograd.

At the Tauride Palace the Duma was in uproar. Just thirteen days after its new session had begun, deputies arrived to find that the Duma had been shut down again. Prince Golitsin, the third prime minister in a year and a reluctant appointee, used a 'blank' decree left with him by the Tsar to prorogue the Duma,[28] thinking it would defuse tension by silencing the more radical elements. However, the deputies refused to disperse, adjourned to another chamber in the building and set up a 'temporary committee' under the chairmanship of the Duma president Rodzyanko. Within twenty-four hours this would claim to be the *de facto* government.

Rodzyanko cabled Nicholas to protest strongly at the suspension of the Duma and to demand that the decree be rescinded. 'The last bulwark of order has been eliminated,' he told him. 'The government is absolutely powerless to suppress disorders . . . regiments are in rebellion. Officers are being killed . . . civil war has started . . . Sire, do not delay . . . tomorrow it may already be too late.'[29]

As excited deputies crowded into their unofficial session, it was still far from clear what role they should take. The dilemma of the Duma members was captured by Rodzyanko: 'I have no desire to revolt. I am not a rebel . . . on the other hand there is no government . . . everyone wishes to know what to do. What shall I do? What shall I do?'[30] Another Duma member remembered that 'we did not have an idea of what was happening and certainly no plan or idea of how to deal with it'.[31]

While the debate continued, Rodzyanko slipped out to telephone Michael at his home in Gatchina, to tell him what had happened and to urge him to come to the capital immediately. The call would appear to have been some time after 3 p.m. for immediately afterwards Michael called Matveev at his embankment office in Petrograd only to find that Natasha's brother-in-law had left at 3.30 p.m. and was on his way home to the Fontanka. Instead Michael spoke to his chauffeur Kozlovsky, ordering him to be with a car at the Warsaw railway station just after 6 p.m. When Matveev found out what was happening and spoke to Natasha at Gatchina an hour or so later, she told him of Rodzyanko's call and that Michael and Johnson were already on their way to the capital.[32] Their special train left Gatchina at 5 p.m.[33]

Arriving at the Warsaw station in Petrograd just over an hour later Michael was relieved to find that 'things were comparatively quiet'.[34] This may have been so on the streets, but at the crowded Tauride Palace there was feverish excitement and in the government ministries noisy confusion and deepening despair. At 8 p.m. Johnson telephoned Matveev to tell him that Michael was in the Marie Palace on St Isaac's Square and was in conference with Rodzyanko and other leading members of the Duma, as well as with the prime minister Prince Golitsin and the war minister Belyaev.[35]

The atmosphere was one of immense crisis, for it was clear that the capital was in the grip of a revolution and there was neither government nor parliament in place to deal with it. At the Tauride Palace, the Duma members had finally agreed to set up a 'temporary executive committee' intended to provide some means of controlling events, but the committee itself had no legal status and was still unsure about what to do.

In the government, there was only defeatism. A few hours earlier the hated interior minister Protopopov had been persuaded to resign and as he shuffled off into the night he muttered that there was nothing now left to him 'but to shoot himself'.[36] No one really cared what he did and no one bothered even to say goodbye to the man so trusted by the Empress, so distrusted by the nation. Yet his departure left the government little better off. Golitsin accepted that his ministry was finished, but did not know how to write out the death certificate. He hoped Michael would do it for him.

There was not a moment to lose. As Michael would note afterwards: 'By 9 p.m. shooting in the streets began and almost all the armed forces became revolutionary and the old rule ceased to exist.'[37] What was to be the new rule? In the conference which followed Rodzyanko would later claim that he urged Michael to 'assume on his own initiative the dictatorship of the city . . . compel the personnel of the government to tender their resignations and demand by telegram, by direct wire from His Majesty, a manifesto regarding the formation of a responsible cabinet.'[38]

These were dramatic proposals; the Duma president was urging Michael to break his oath of allegiance – something which Rodzyanko himself had consistently refused to do – seize power in the capital, effectively proclaim himself Regent and present his brother with a *fait accompli*.

Rodzyanko purported to be disappointed that Michael declined to take such bold measures, complaining that this 'irresoluteness of Grand Duke Michael Aleksandrovich contributed to a favourable moment being lost. Instead of taking active measures and gathering around himself the units of the Petrograd garrison whose discipline was not yet shattered, the Grand Duke started to negotiate by direct wire with Emperor Nicholas II . . .'[39]

What Rodzyanko did not consider were the consequences, had Michael in fact 'seized power'. Nicholas would have repudiated any such action, in which case the result would have been a collision between the Tsar and the self-appointed and unlawful Regent. If Michael had sacked the Tsar's government, Nicholas would have simply reinstated it. As Rodzyanko knew, the Tsar would refuse a demand for a responsible ministry, so what then? Was Michael to form one of his own, in which case there would then be two governments, one legal and the other illegal? To whom would any troops rallied by Michael have been loyal – to the Tsar and the old regime or to the Tsar's brother and Russia's new 'popular government'? Would Michael have been defending the crown or usurping it? If this had ended one revolution would it merely be replaced by another?

However, this picture of an 'irresolute' Michael and a decisive, ruthless and clear-headed Duma president depends on Rodzyanko's own self-serving account, written long afterwards and published in 1922, when many of his contemporaries were revising their roles in the revolution of 1917 and its aftermath. Rodzyanko was then anxious to rebut criticism that he himself had been irresolute and it is that which more easily explains his improbable scenario of February 27; since its impracticality was never demonstrated by being put to the test, it helped to excuse all that followed.

Nevertheless, discounting his references to a 'dictatorship', the two-hour conference in the Marie Palace adopted in a broad sense the measures described by Rodzyanko. Michael was to present to his brother the proposals which all agreed were necessary to halt the revolution. Michael would offer to act as Regent in the capital, with the power to appoint a new prime minister, but one competent to choose his own Cabinet, rather than have ministers foisted upon him by the Tsar or approved by Alexandra.

This was a constitutional change Nicholas had absolutely refused to consider, resisting the clamour in the Duma for just such a 'responsible ministry'. Now Michael, who had argued for the reform privately, was prepared to speak openly. He would wrap it all up in the politest of language, but the message to Mogilev was clear: the Tsar's brother was telling the Tsar that autocracy was over.

Michael was, however, to disappoint Rodzyanko in one important respect that evening. When it came to the choice of the new prime minister, Michael nominated someone else for the post the Duma president assumed would be his by right. At Gatchina Michael had clearly been more in touch with political opinion than Rodzyanko might have expected and knew that the majority Progressive Bloc in the Duma had already opted for Prince Georgy Lvov.

Lvov was not at the conference and was not a member of the Duma, but he was more popular and more trusted among the radical elements than the authoritarian bull-voiced Rodzyanko; he was also the best-known civic leader in Russia, as long-time chairman of the powerful union of local authorities, the Zemstvos. Pavel Milyukov, the Kadet leader, would believe that the choice of Lvov rather than of Rodzyanko 'was rendered easier by the reputation of Prince Lvov everywhere in Russia; at that time he was irreplaceable. I cannot say, however, that Rodzyanko was reconciled to this decision.'[40]

The real question, of course, was whether the Tsar would accept anyone at all on the terms to be put to him. The next four hours would be decisive: if Nicholas agreed to Michael's proposals and empowered him to act, there could be a new government by early next morning, with the popular prestige necessary to assert its authority. Numerous though they were, the rebel troops were still a minority and the great mass of soldiers sitting tight in their barracks had refused to join them. Michael, as lawful Regent acting on behalf of his absent brother and with a name respected in the army, was better placed than almost anyone else to rally such troops in support of a new government. But every hour counted: the longer the revolution went unchecked, the harder it would be to win back control.

Leaving the Marie Palace, Michael crossed the square to the residence of the war minister on the Moika and there, at 10.30 p.m., he began his despatch to his brother.[41] He was using the Hughes apparatus, a kind of primitive telex, with a keyboard, in which one party typed out a tape and waited for a reply tape. It was slow, but it was the best they had over such a long distance. At the receiving end in Mogilev was chief-of-staff General Alekseev and Michael 'talked' to his brother through him.

Grand Duke Michael Aleksandrovich on the apparatus. I beg you to report the following to His Majesty the Emperor on my behalf: I am firmly convinced that in order to pacify this movement, which has assumed huge proportions, it is essential to dismiss the whole Council of Ministers, a course urged on me by Prince Golitsin.

If the Cabinet is dismissed, it will be essential to appoint replacements at the same time. All I can suggest in current conditions is to settle your choice on someone who has earned Your Imperial Majesty's trust and enjoys respect among wide sections of the population, entrusting him with the duties of the Chairman of the Council of Ministers and making him solely accountable to Your Imperial Majesty.

It is essential that he be empowered to appoint a Cabinet at his own discretion. In view of the extraordinarily serious situation, Your Imperial Majesty may wish to authorise me to announce this on behalf of Your Imperial Majesty as a matter of urgency. For my part, I would suggest that the only possible candidate at this moment is Prince Lvov. ADC General Michael.

Alekseev's reply came back on the tape. 'I will report Your Imperial Highness's telegram to his Imperial Majesty immediately. His Majesty the Emperor is leaving for Tsarskoe Selo tomorrow. *ADC General Alekseev.*' Then there was another tape: 'I will take the liberty of informing you that if His Majesty the Emperor gives any orders now I will telegraph them to Your Imperial Highness immediately.'

Michael replied: 'I shall be waiting for your answer in the house of the War Minister. Please send it by direct wire. I would also like to ask you to tell His Imperial Majesty that I am convinced it may be advisable to delay His Majesty the Emperor's journey to Tsarskoe Selo for several days.'[42]

While he waited, the chauffeur Kozlovsky telephoned Matveev to tell him where Michael was, though he did so by hints, 'apparently fearing to speak openly of the Grand Duke's whereabouts on the telephone'. He also told Matveev that the car was hidden in the courtyard of the war minister's house. It was then midnight.[43]

At Mogilev Nicholas did not choose to answer his brother in person and his reply, when it came, was uncompromising, almost contemptuous. Forty minutes after Michael's message had gone through to Mogilev, the Hughes machine in the Moika began to stutter out its reply, sent through Alekseev.

> *Is His Imperial Highness Grand Duke Michael Aleksandrovich at the apparatus? His Majesty the Emperor has instructed me to thank Your Imperial Highness on his behalf and to inform you of the following.*
>
> *Firstly. In view of the extraordinary circumstances His Majesty the Emperor does not consider it possible to delay his departure and will leave tomorrow at half past two p.m. Secondly. His Imperial Majesty will not deal with any measures touching on changes to his personal staff until his arrival in Tsarskoe Selo. Thirdly. ADC General Ivanov is leaving for Petrograd tomorrow as Commander-in-Chief of the Petrograd Area and has a reliable battalion with him. Fourthly. As of tomorrow four infantry regiments and four cavalry regiments from amongst our most reliable units will begin moving from the Northern and Western Fronts to Petrograd.*

Reading that, Michael knew that his brother had ignored everything he had said and that his wire had been a waste of time, as had the discussions at the conference in the Marie Palace. Michael had been told to mind his own business. Alekseev was clearly unhappy, for he added a message of his own, essentially supporting Michael's original proposals. 'Allow me to conclude with a personal request that, when making personal reports to His Imperial Majesty, Your Imperial Highness will be so kind as to give firm support to the ideas which you expressed in your preceding message, both as regards to the replacement of the present members of the Council of Ministers and as regards the method by which a new Council is to be selected and may the Lord God aid Your Imperial Highness in this important matter.'

Michael made a last attempt to keep his brother at Mogilev, where at least he could be in immediate contact with events. 'For my part I wish to tell you personally that I am afraid that time may be wasted before His Majesty's return since under the present conditions literally every hour counts. Thank you, Mikhail Vasilevich, for the work you have taken upon yourself. I wish you every success. *ADC General Michael.*'

Alekseev then came back on the line to promise that he would raise the matter again at the morning conference, because 'I realise perfectly well . . . that time lost cannot be compensated for'.[44]

It was a dispiriting end to a long night, in which Michael had achieved precisely nothing. He summarised his efforts in his diary, concluding with one word: '*Alas*.'[45]

Alas indeed, for by refusing to empower Michael, his brother now had no government at all. When the lights failed at around midnight in the Marie Palace, the last of the ministers there simply drifted away into the night and they never met together again. At 11.25 p.m. in Mogilev the Tsar sent his prime minister a telegram to say that 'I personally bestow upon you all the necessary powers for civil rule,'[46] but when it arrived there was no prime minister, no power and no rule. Prince Golitzin had gone home; over the next twenty-four hours, he and most of Nicholas's other ministers would be arrested by the revolutionary mob and for some their ultimate fate would be a firing squad.

After this 'unsuccessful attempt to help matters' Michael decided to return to Gatchina, but this was impossible 'because of heavy machine-gun fire and grenade explosions'. Michael lingered on at the Moika but by 3 a.m. 'things had quietened down somewhat' and he decided to make an attempt to reach the station, still hoping to get back home. However, as his car and a military escort drove through the streets they encountered revolutionary patrols 'and in one spot we were nearly stopped, but accelerating managed successfully to escape, but our escorting car was arrested. We could not proceed any further and decided to make for the Winter Palace.'[47]

When Michael got there he found the war minister Belyaev with the dejected garrison commander Khabalov, 'and a force of 1000 troops'.[48] With only a few machine-guns and little artillery, the troops had been in the Admiralty building until a few hours earlier, but although that made for a better strongpoint they had been marched out when their commander, General Zankevich, decided it would be more symbolic to 'die in defence of the palace'.[49]

Michael recognised a different kind of symbolism – that it had been from the Winter Palace that troops had fired on the crowds in the first revolution of 1905. When that massacre took place he had been with his brother at Tsarskoe Selo and twelve years later the memory of that day, and the lesson, remained with him. Despite Nicholas's offhand dismissal of his proposals, events might swiftly force the Tsar to change his mind and authorise Michael to act as his Regent in the capital. Given that, Michael could not risk another 'Bloody Sunday' if he was to have any hope of winning public support.

Khabalov, highly agitated, proposed that the troops should fire on any crowd advancing on the palace, but Michael would not hear of it. It would be said that not 'wishing to spill a drop of Russian blood'[50] he was not going to permit troops for a second time 'to fire on Russians from the

House of the Romanovs'[51] and there was truth in that, for that would be to hand a propaganda victory to the revolutionaries. He was also too experienced a battlefield commander to be impressed by heroic gestures. To make the scarcely defensible Winter Palace the centre of resistance would mean 'the inevitable destruction of the palace by the revolutionary troops',[52] backed as they were by the guns of the rebel-held fortress of St Peter and St Paul, facing the palace across the river.

The troops were therefore withdrawn back to the Admiralty, 'the poor General Khabalov' being 'very grateful'[53] to avoid a battle he could only lose. At 5 a.m. that Tuesday morning Michael and Johnson left the palace themselves, deciding to make for the nearby apartment of Princess Putyatina, 500 yards away at 12 Millionnaya Street.[54]

The 'street of millionaires', so called because it had been built as the residence of wealthy foreigners in the late eighteenth century, runs from Palace Square to the Summer Gardens; on the left in 1917 were the barracks of the Preobrazhensky Guards and a number of Grand Ducal palaces; on the right stood a line of five-storey houses, painted yellow ochre, with carriage gates leading to inner courtyards. The double-fronted door of number 12 was opposite the palace of Grand Duke Nicholas Mikhailovich – 'Bimbo'.

To avoid patrols of revolutionaries Michael and a weary Johnson made their way on foot, going firstly through the Winter Palace itself into the courtyard of the Hermitage, then through the courtyard of Bimbo's palace, before crossing the snow-covered road and knocking on the door of number 12.[55] The concierge heard their banging and, recognising the voice of Grand Duke Michael, let them in and led them up two flights of stairs to the apartment of Princess Putyatina, opening the door with her passkey.

Princess Putyatina, whose husband Pavel was away on duty at the front, was alone with her young daughter. 'I woke with a start hearing violent knocking on my bedroom door. At this noise, seized with fright, I could only imagine that armed soldiers had burst into my apartment.' She was reassured when she recognised the voice of Johnson. Dressing hurriedly she went into the study where Michael was waiting. He was 'very tired and seemed very upset', but apologised with his 'usual good grace' for having disturbed her, adding: 'Are you not afraid, Princess, of putting yourself at such risk by having such a dangerous guest?'[56]

Her maid produced coffee and they were sitting in the dining room when they suddenly heard shouting from the apartment above, occupied by the Tsar's Chamberlain, Nikolai Stolypin, a brother of the former prime minister, assassinated in a Kiev theatre six years earlier. A squad of armed soldiers, coming through the service entrance at the rear of the building on a pre-dawn raid, had forced their way into his apartment. As Princess

Putyatina would discover later, they behaved 'so brutally towards Madame Stolypin that she had a nervous breakdown'.[57] Her protesting husband was dragged away under arrest.

Such break-ins would go on over the next two days, as mutineers went around the town looking for officials and ministers who, like the unfortunate Stolypin, were identified with the old regime. Princess Putyatina had so far been lucky, 'thanks to the intelligence of the concierge' who told the rampaging mobs that in her apartment there was only a soldier's wife and their daughter.[58] She was not likely to remain so, however, if the mutineers discovered that the Tsar's brother was there, in an unguarded building they could enter with one blow of a rifle butt.

For the moment that was a problem for the morrow. Michael and Johnson, exhausted, collapsed on settees and went to sleep.

TWENTY-TWO

Address Unknown

As Michael was slipping out of the Winter Palace and making his way to Millionnaya Street in the pre-dawn of Tuesday, February 28, the train carrying his brother back to Tsarskoe Selo was leaving Mogilev, its windows darkened, its passengers asleep. Another train, carrying members of his suite, had set off an hour earlier, at 4 a.m.[1] To leave the direct line north clear for the relief force ordered to the capital, the imperial trains took a roundabout route, heading east to join the main Petrograd–Moscow line, adding nine hours and 200 miles to the normal 450-mile journey. With luck he would arrive at around eight o'clock on Wednesday morning.

'Every hour is precious,' Michael had told his brother on the wire from the war ministry and he had urged him not to leave Mogilev at all, so that he could be in direct communication throughout the crisis. On his train Nicholas would be virtually *incommunicado* all day and all night. Russia no longer had a government and over the next crucial twenty-seven hours or more it would, for all practical purposes, be without an emperor.

Nicholas had gone to bed in the train at 3.15 a.m. having talked late with General Nikolai Ivanov,[2] the former commander on the south-western front and the man now charged with restoring order. What Nicholas hoped was that when he reached Tsarskoe Selo next morning he would hear that Ivanov had crushed the rebellion. Ivanov had been given a battalion comprising 800 men who had each won the Cross of St George[3] and from Mogilev General Alekseev had commanded the despatch of reliable battle-hardened formations to be sent on the direct rail route to the capital, giving Ivanov another four infantry and four cavalry regiments, plus artillery.[4] Late that Tuesday afternoon, at Tsarskoe Selo, Alexandra received a confident telegram: 'Left this morning at 5. Thoughts always together. Glorious weather. Hope are feeling well and quiet. Many troops sent from front. Fondest love. Nicky.' The telegram, sent from Vyazma at 3 p.m., arrived at Tsarskoe Selo nearly two hours later, at 4.49 p.m.[5]

It was reassuring news. Vyazma was 420 miles away, but if the trains kept to schedule Nicholas would arrive at Tsarskoe Selo in another sixteen hours, certainly by 9 a.m. Darkness had fallen, but Alexandra knew that all around the palace there were well-armed and reliable troops who would

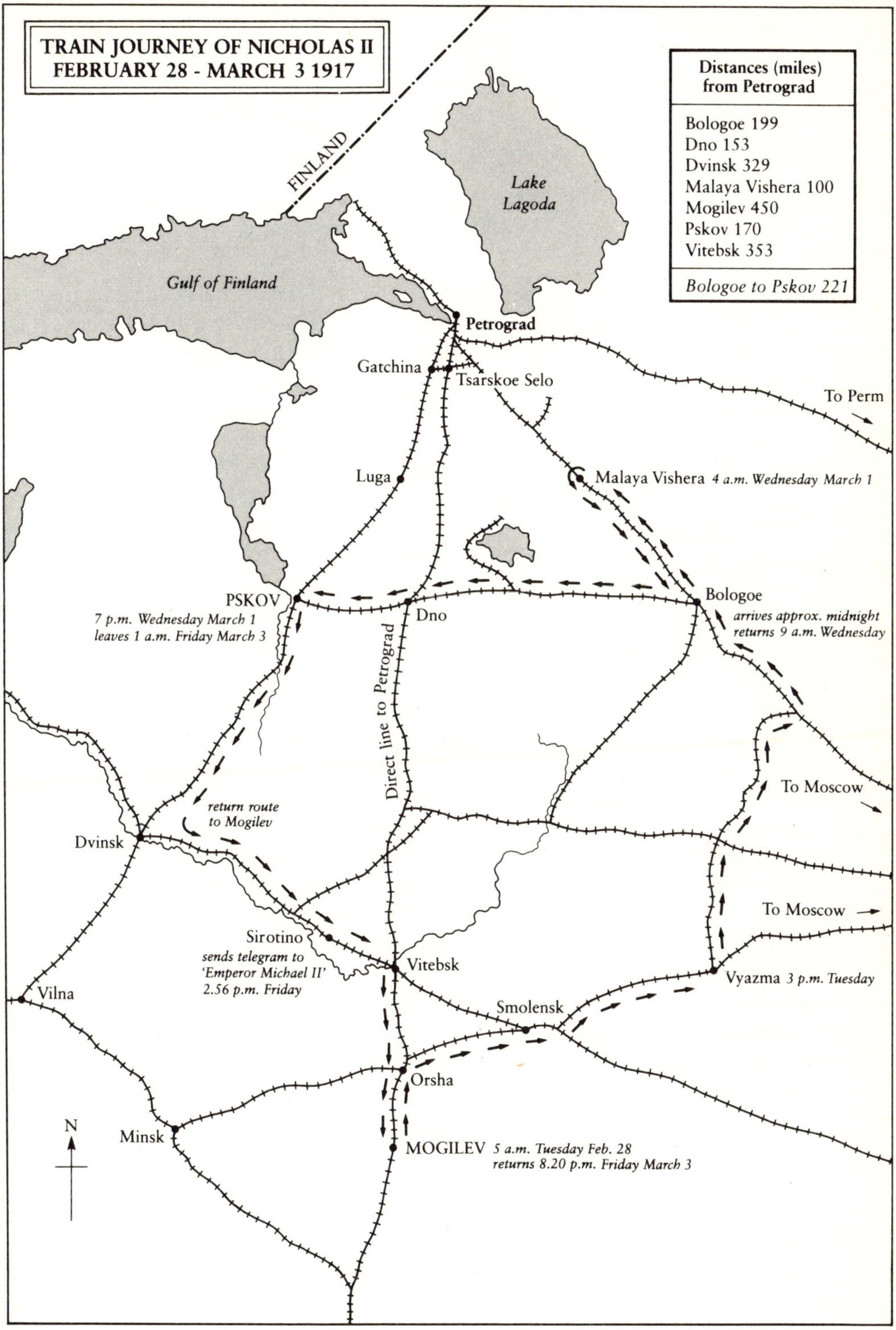

TRAIN JOURNEY OF NICHOLAS II
FEBRUARY 28 - MARCH 3 1917
Distances (miles) from Petrograd
Bologoe 199
Dno 153
Dvinsk 329
Malaya Vishera 100
Mogilev 450
Pskov 170
Vitebsk 353
Bologoe to Pskov 221
FINLAND
Lake Lagoda
Gulf of Finland
Petrograd
Gatchina
Tsarskoe Selo
To Perm
Luga
Malaya Vishera 4 a.m. Wednesday March 1
PSKOV
7 p.m. Wednesday March 1
leaves 1 a.m. Friday March 3
Dno
Bologoe
arrives approx. midnight
returns 9 a.m. Wednesday
Direct line to Petrograd
To Moscow
return route to Mogilev
Dvinsk
To Moscow
Sirotino
sends telegram to
'Emperor Michael II'
2.56 p.m. Friday
Vitebsk
Vyazma 3 p.m. Tuesday
Vilna
Smolensk
Orsha
Minsk
N
MOGILEV 5 a.m. Tuesday Feb. 28
returns 8.20 p.m. Friday March 3

stand guard throughout the night. The men protecting the imperial family were hand picked and their personal loyalty to the Tsar was beyond question. There were Guardsmen, Cossacks of the Emperor's Escort, artillerymen, riflemen and the tall marines of the *Garde Equipage*, whose proud commander was Grand Duke Kirill.[6] They were not just crack troops: as Alexandra said to her long-standing confidante, Lili Dehn, they were 'our personal friends'.[7]

Rodzyanko, alarmed at the dangers posed to Tsarskoe Selo, had sent court officials a message urging them to evacuate the palace and remove the Empress and children to safety by train,[8] but the illness of the children made that seem impossible. The ring of troops around the palace also seemed to make it unnecessary. Besides, the Tsar was due back in the morning and Ivanov and his battalion of heroes were hastening towards them, followed by eight regiments of frontline troops.

Alexandra was concerned, but not alarmed. Truckloads of mutineers had arrived in the town itself, but their revolutionary fervour had been diverted into looting the wine shops.[9] There was the sound of shooting beyond the palace gates, but as darkness fell, the palace itself seemed entirely secure. In the late evening, with a black fur coat thrown over her nurse's uniform, she and her seventeen-year-old daughter Marie walked among the troops, praising them for their loyalty.[10]

When she came back, Alexandra seemed 'possessed by some inward exaltation. She was radiant ... "They are all our friends ... so devoted to us," she told Lili Dehn.[11] Tomorrow, Ivanov would march into town, Nicholas would be back and all would be well again.

Nicholas also expected to arrive on schedule. At around 4 a.m. on Wednesday morning he was less than 100 miles away, having covered 540 miles. It was then that the train stopped, at the town of Malaya Vishera and the Tsar was told that revolutionary troops were blocking the line ahead.[12] It was a bitter moment for Nicholas; no more than five hours from home, he was told that he would have to turn back.

After discussion it was decided that the two trains should go back down the line to Bologoe, halfway between Moscow and Petrograd, and then head west for Pskov, headquarters of General Nikolai Ruzsky's Northern Army. It was the nearest safe haven, but it would still leave Nicholas 170 miles from home and worse off than if he had stayed at his general headquarters, where he could command the whole of his armies. His journey had been entirely wasted. 'To Pskov, then,' he said curtly and retired back to his sleeping car.[13] But once there, he put his real feelings into his diary. 'Shame and dishonour!' he wrote despairingly.[14]

The return to Bologoe would take around five hours and from there it was 221 miles on the branch line to the ancient town of Pskov. For the next and decisive fifteen hours the Emperor of All the Russias would once again vanish into the empty snow-covered countryside.

At Tsarskoe Selo, an ever more worried Alexandra would wait for a man who was not coming and when she dashed off a desperate telegram to ask Nicholas for news, ordering it to be sent immediately to 'His Imperial Majesty', it was returned, with the stark message scrawled across it in blue pencil: '*Address of person mentioned unknown*'.[15]

With no government and a nomadic Tsar lost in a railway train, power in Petrograd passed on Tuesday, February 28, to the revolution, with competing bodies in the Tauride Palace trying to establish their own agendas in the reshaping of Russia. The home of the Duma, the parliamentary building, now also housed a noisy mass of workers, soldiers and students, joined together in a new organisation, a Soviet on the lines which had emerged in the revolution of 1905. The few hundred respectable deputies who formed or backed the Temporary Committee of the Duma now jostled for places in rooms and hallways packed with a thousand excited street orators, mutineers and strike leaders. It was chaos and it would remain so for days to come.

When Vladimir Nabokov, a lawyer destined to play a leading part in the events of that week, arrived at the smoke-filled Tauride Palace it looked to him like an improvised camp: 'rubbish, straw; the air was thick like some kind of a dense fog; there was a smell of soldiers' boots, cloth, sweat; from somewhere we could hear the hysterical voices of orators addressing a meeting . . . everywhere crowding and bustling confusion . . .'[16]

In that crush of people, the man who was beginning to stand out as the dominant figure of the revolution was Aleksandr Kerensky, a lawyer, socialist deputy and, at thirty-six, a man who bestrode both camps – as a member of the Temporary Committee and as a vice-chairman of the newly formed 'Petrograd Soviet of Workers' and Soldiers' Deputies'.

'He spoke decisively, authoritatively, as one who had not lost his head,' said Vasili Shulgin, a right-wing member of the Duma committee. 'His words and his gestures were sharp and clear-cut and his eyes shone . . .'[17] He was also the finger of justice. When the mutineers dragged in their first important prisoner, Ivan Shcheglovitov, the chairman of the State Council and a former minister, Kerensky strode up to him and shouted dramatically: 'Your life is not in danger. The Imperial Duma does not shed blood.'[18]

The arrested man was led off to the Government Pavilion, a separate building with some anterooms previously reserved for ministers who had come to address the Duma. It was connected to the main hall by a glass-roofed passage and technically was not part of the parliamentary building, so that deputies avoided the stigma of 'turning the Duma into a prison'.[19]

Over the next hours and days the numbers of prisoners would run into hundreds, so that the Government Pavilion became crammed to the doors with downcast and often frightened men, so recently powerful figures in the Tsar's government machine and now fearing to be shot. It was not difficult for the hunting squads of troops to find most of them, for their home addresses were all openly listed in the 1916 Petrograd telephone directory.

Prince Golitsin, Belyaev, Stürmer – one by one they were rounded up and taken into the Tauride Palace. It was to Kerensky's credit that he protected them from violence, even when the hated Protopopov, who had been hiding in a tailor's shop, crept in to surrender himself. The former interior minister, 'trembling with terror',[20] was almost unrecognisable: a shrunken, frightened figure, all posturing gone. This was the man who so recently had fallen on his knees before Alexandra, crying out: 'Oh, Majesty, I see Christ behind you.'[21] If any minister was likely to be torn to bits it was Protopopov, but Kerensky stood over him and with his stretched-out arm he cried: 'Don't touch that man.' The crowd fell back silent as Kerensky pushed on, one arm raised, the other dropped, pointing at the cringing Protopopov following in his wake. 'It looked as if he were leading him to execution, to something dreadful ... Kerensky dashed past like the flaming torch of revolutionary justice and behind him they dragged that miserable little figure in the rumpled greatcoat, surrounded by bayonets.'[22]

Goremykin, prime minister until a year ago, was another prisoner brought to the Tauride Palace, though at first he was treated with special consideration on the insistence of the 'old school' Duma deputies. It would be a brief respite. Kerensky found him in Rodzyanko's room. 'In a corner sat a very old gentleman, with exceedingly long whiskers. He wore a fur coat and looked like a gnome.' Kerensky, noting that he had taken the trouble to hang round his neck the Order of St Andrew, refused to be impressed. 'In the name of the revolutionary people I declare you under arrest,' he shouted.[23] Rodzyanko, faced with this challenge to his own authority, backed down helplessly. Two soldiers led away the confused and crestfallen old Goremykin to join the others.

Kerensky was everywhere. 'I was summoned and sent for from all sides. As in a trance, regardless of day or night ... I rushed about the Duma. Sometimes I almost lost consciousness for fifteen or twenty minutes until a glass of brandy was forced down my throat and I was made to drink a cup of black coffee.'[24]

Kerensky would become more and more excitable as the hours and days passed. Nabokov, seeing him for the first time, was struck by his 'loss of emotional balance'. He was also astonished when Kerensky, coming out of one meeting 'excited, agitated, hysterical', put up his hands, grabbed the corners of his wing collar and ripped them off, 'achieving a deliberately proletarian look, instead of that of a dandy'.[25]

His power, nevertheless, was enormous for there was no doubting among the Duma deputies that the new Soviet, with a thousand members milling around the Tauride Palace, was master if it chose to be. Kerensky was the bridge between two rivals in an uneasy coalition and for the Duma members, he was a bridge they could not afford to cross. The Temporary Committee of the Duma had the better claim to government, but the other members knew already that they could only lead where Kerensky was willing to follow.

On Tuesday, February 28, Princess Putyatina had kept her apartment doors locked all day in constant dread of boots ringing on the stairs and armed men breaking in to hunt down the Tsar's brother. Across the city, armoured cars with machine-guns and flying red flags were roaring up and down the main streets, past buildings sometimes in flames, while squads of armed mutineers searched for officials and government ministers. There was fierce firing around the Admiralty building until the last of the loyal troops, holed up there since the evacuation of the Winter Palace at 5 a.m., surrendered after warnings that the guns of the St Peter and St Paul Fortress would be turned on them.[26] Thereafter the streets belonged to the revolution and the head-hunting gangs seeking out policemen, officials and anyone judged a 'traitor' to the revolution.

At the Astoria Hotel, a mob stormed in, after claiming that shots had been fired from there, and wrecked it. A number of guests, women as well as men, were hauled off to the Tauride Palace under arrest.[27] It was a terrifying experience for all such 'prisoners of the revolution', not knowing when and if they would be freed, or whether they would live or die.

There were also individual acts of plunder and revenge. At the height of winter, when the fuel depots were empty and people were freezing in their homes, four military lorries, laden with sacks of coal, had arrived at Kschessinska's mansion on Kammenny-Ostrov Prospekt.[28] To the mob she was not an admired ballet dancer but the pampered recipient of blatant imperial favours and a profiteer in arms deals; a vengeful crowd therefore descended on her house and sacked it from top to bottom. Kschessinska, forewarned that she was to be a target, fled with a shawl over her head, but not before remembering to pack a small suitcase with the most valuable of her jewels.[29]

After a few restless hours on a settee, Michael was awakened by 'the noise of heavy traffic and movement of cars and lorries filled with soldiers, who were shooting mainly in the air and there were also explosions of hand grenades. The soldiers shouted and cheered, waved red flags and had red ribbons and bows on their breasts and buttonholes.'[30]

Peering cautiously out from the apartment windows, Michael guessed from the jubilation of the troops driving by that there was no longer any resistance in the capital. Trapped where he was, he could only sit tight and wait until the morning, when there would be news of Nicholas and of the troops ordered to the city. He was trying to contact Natasha to tell her where he was, but the telephones and telegraphs had stopped working. He ended by scribbling a note, delivered by a courier who managed to reach Gatchina safely. He had left the Winter Palace (he coded it as 'Rastrelli's) 'because a further stay would have been in many respects inconvenient'. He added that 'our brains are wide-awake and the order of the day is to find a way of contacting representatives of the area where we are renting an estate' – a reference to his English property, and thus code for the British ambassador Buchanan.[31]

Keeping in contact with the outside world, while keeping their presence secret, carried risk but fortunately, their luck held. 'The day passed peacefully and no one bothered us.'[32] Next morning, March 1, there were fresh alarms. Still unaware that the Tsar's brother was on the second floor, a squad of uniformed men ransacked the top-floor apartment, the home of the Procurator of the Holy Synod, and dragged him away shouting that he was 'under arrest'. In the house next door, an old general, Baron Staekelberg, and one of his servants, defended their apartment for hours against a mob of soldiers and sailors and when the attackers finally broke in they lynched the servant and killed the general, dragging his body to the Neva and throwing it into the river.[33]

Michael could not spend another day hostage to a mob which could arrive at any time. Besides, he expected Nicholas to be home later that day and, not knowing that his brother had already turned back, Michael was determined to see him at Tsarskoe Selo. To do so, he had to be free to move. With local telephone lines working again, Johnson called Rodzyanko and asked what could be done.[34] Rodzyanko organised an armed guard of five officers and twenty cadet officers to be sent to Millionnaya Street. By lunch-time the apartment was secured.[35]

The presence of guards, 'acting on the orders of the Temporary Committee of the Duma', sufficed to prevent further attacks; after that, 12 Millionnaya Street was left untouched. The officers and cadets were housed in the study and in the empty flat below, with sentries placed at the street door as well as the apartment door and at the service entrance in the rear courtyard.

After the guards were in position, visitors started arriving. Matveev turned up at lunch-time,[36] as did Michael's ADC Wrangel, whose wife trudged into Millionnaya Street with a scarf around her head to make her look like a peasant woman.[37] There was also a lawyer, Nikolai Ivanov, an aide of Rodzyanko, who brought with him an imperial manifesto which he wanted Michael to sign, as Grand Duke Paul and Grand Duke Kirill had done before him.

The intention was that the manifesto should be delivered to Nicholas for endorsement and published under his name. It proposed the creation of a constitutional monarchy as soon as the war was ended. In the meantime it promised the recall of the Duma and of the upper house, the State Council and the formation of a government 'that enjoys the trust of the country'.[38] The manifesto had been drafted by Paul, Rodzyanko and Ivanov, and Paul had already shown it to Alexandra, who had treated it with her usual scorn. 'Paul has worked out some idiotical manifesto about a constitution after the war,' she would write to Nicholas in a letter that would reach him when it no longer mattered.[39] Nevertheless, to Rodzyanko it seemed increasingly to be the Tsar's last chance. 'To strengthen Rodzyanko's hands' Michael added his signature.[40] 'With this manifesto Russia's new existence will begin,' Michael scribbled in another note to Natasha, adding that 'things are happening with terrifying speed'.[41]

In the afternoon the British ambassador Buchanan arrived at the apartment and discussed the manifesto, agreeing that such a reform might just save Nicholas's throne. Michael told him that he 'had repeatedly urged the Emperor to grant reforms, but in vain' and that he greatly regretted that Nicholas 'had not done spontaneously what he would now have to do by force'.[42] Buchanan, knowing that Michael was planning to see Nicholas that night – but equally unaware that the Tsar was now heading for Pskov – asked him 'to beseech the Emperor, in the name of King George, to sign the manifesto, to show himself to his people and to effect a complete reconciliation with them'.[43] As both men would shortly realise, such pious hopes were already being overtaken by events.

One man who seems already to have recognised this was Grand Duke Kirill, who had signed the manifesto the day before.[44] However, at the very moment when Michael was being asked to add his name, Kirill was marching into the Tauride at the head of a battalion of his marines, to 'declare his loyalty' to the Duma Committee. His marines guarding Tsarskoe Selo would also be withdrawn on his orders. Attached to his naval captain's uniform, he was wearing a big red bow.[45] Like Michael and every other Grand Duke, he had sworn an oath to 'serve His Imperial Majesty, not sparing my life and limb, until the very last drop of my blood'; now, on March 1, he joined the revolution, while Nicholas was still Tsar. Paléologue, driving later past Kirill's palace on Glinka Street, would see a red flag flying on the roof.[46]

One of those who saw Kirill's arrival at the Tauride Palace was General Polovtsov, formerly commander of the Tartar regiment in Michael's Savage Division. In Petrograd by chance, he had been recruited by Guchkov to serve on the Duma's 'military committee'. Polovtsov noted that the appearance 'of a Grand Duke under a red flag made a great impression and was understood by the crowd as a sign that the imperial family refused to fight for its rights and recognised the revolution as an accomplished fact'. He added: 'The monarchists in the Duma did not like it'.[47]

Kirill's explanation would be that the Duma Committee was the only effective authority in the capital and because it had ordered all units to march to the Duma 'to show their allegiance to the government' he had no choice, as commander of one of those units, but to obey. 'They were the only loyal and reliable troops left in the capital . . . to have deprived them of leadership would simply have added to the disaster.' His main concern, he protested, 'was to do my utmost to re-establish order in the capital . . . so that the Emperor could safely return'.[48]

Not many people believed this, either then or on reading his subsequent *apologia*, which he boldly entitled *My Life in Russia's Service*. Kirill's hostility to Tsarskoe Selo was well known, as were his own ambitions. However much he attempted to excuse himself afterwards, he was bound to be suspected of having gone to the Duma in the hope of ingratiating himself with the Duma Committee, hoping that if Nicholas abdicated it would be the 'loyal' Kirill who would be asked to be Regent, or even Emperor. However, as Nicholas's abdication came to be seen by the Duma Committee as the last hope of saving the monarchy – and as the price of a deal with the Soviet – the only man being talked about as Regent was Michael.

Kirill was outraged, as was Grand Duke Paul, who suspected it to be the work of Natasha. Paul wrote hurriedly to Kirill: 'The new intention to make Misha Regent displeases me greatly. It is inadmissible and it is possible that it may be merely the intrigues of Brasova . . . If Nicky signs the manifesto which we have sanctioned about a constitution, the demands of the people will have been satisfied . . .'[49] Kirill replied at once. 'I completely agree,' he wrote back furiously, 'but despite my entreaty to work together and in conformity with the family, Misha sneaks away and communicates secretly with Rodzyanko. I have been left completely alone during these days to bear responsibility towards Nicky and to save the situation while recognising the new government.'[50]

Kirill's petulant response was understandable: his march into the Tauride Palace, which broke his oath of allegiance to the Emperor, had gained him nothing but odium. As for Paul, his manifesto was already dead even as he was advancing its merits. It had been vetoed by the Soviet and as that became clear, Michael wrote to Rodzyanko telling him to remove his name.[51] With that, the Grand Dukes' manifesto ceased to matter and was put in a drawer.[52] It was simply too little, too late.

Ironically, Nicholas still believed it was too much, too soon. At about seven o'clock that evening, after travelling 860 miles, his train crawled into the station at Pskov and he was at last back in touch with the world, if not as yet the same world emerging around him. He was disappointed not to find Rodzyanko waiting for him; indeed he had hoped that the Duma president would have met him earlier, at one of the stations on his cross-country journey. However, Rodzyanko was struggling to keep his own position in the Duma Committee and had no time for train rides into the countryside,[53] or even to Millionnaya Street for a planned meeting with Michael.[54] So at Pskov Nicholas had to be content with talking to the sixty-three-year-old army commander, General Nikolai Ruzsky; shortly after the train arrived, he turned up at the station, 'bent, grey and old, wearing galoshes', his eyes behind his spectacles 'unfriendly'.[55]

Sitting in the Tsar's study aboard the train, Ruzsky was uncomfortable about discussing constitutional issues, but he was convinced of the need for concessions and he pressed on doggedly to say so. There was a gloomy dinner, then the talks resumed. Nicholas thought Ruzsky rude and the general would later admit that 'we had a storm brewing'.[56] As stubborn as ever and still blind to his own peril, Nicholas refused to give up his autocratic rights, though he was willing to appoint Rodzyanko prime minister, but with a Cabinet responsible to the Tsar. Ruzsky was getting nowhere, until a telegram arrived from General Alekseev at Mogilev, urging the same concessions.[57]

Yet even now Nicholas did not give up entirely, insisting that the war, navy and foreign ministers should continue to be responsible to him. Ruzsky proved just as stubborn as Nicholas and persisted in arguing for a ministry wholly responsible to the Duma. Nicholas could not finally ignore his own generals. At 2 a.m. he called Ruzsky to his carriage and told him that he had 'decided to compromise'; the manifesto granting a responsible ministry, already signed, was on the table.[58] Ruzsky was authorised to notify Rodzyanko that he could now be prime minister of a parliamentary government. Michael, better informed, had rightly told Nicholas that Lvov was the only man capable of playing that role; either Nicholas forgot that, or he chose to ignore it.

His concession was no longer enough in any case. When, at 3.30 a.m., Ruzsky got through to Petrograd on the direct line, Rodzyanko's reply was shatteringly frank: 'It is obvious that neither His Majesty nor you realise what is going on here ... Unfortunately the manifesto has come too late ... and there is no return to the past ... everywhere troops are siding with the Duma and the people and the threatening demands for an abdication in favour of the son, with Mikhail Aleksandrovich as Regent, are becoming quite definite.'[59]

When Ruzsky finished his long and painfully slow discussion on the direct wire, with the machines stuttering out the words fed in by ready-made tapes at a speed of only twenty words a minute, the time was 7.30 a.m., on Thursday, March 2.[60] Before the day was out Nicholas would abdicate not once, but twice.

TWENTY-THREE

A Father's Feelings

His discussion on the wire with Rodzyanko was the first time that Ruzsky knew that the crisis in Petrograd had moved beyond demands for a constitutional monarchy to that of the abdication of Nicholas. He therefore ordered that the taped record of his discussions be sent to General Alekseev in Mogilev. At 9 a.m. that Thursday morning, after reading the print-out, Alekseev cabled back to Pskov headquarters 'my deep conviction that there is no choice and that the abdication should take place ... It is very painful for me to say so, but there is no other solution'.[1]

Having made his own views clear, at least to Ruzsky and without waiting for a reply, Alekseev then sent out his own telegrams to his other army commanders and to the admirals commanding the Baltic and Black Sea fleets. Russia had a war to fight and Alekseev was determined that the revolution in Petrograd should not undermine the frontline armies waiting to begin their spring offensive.

He summarised Ruzsky's discussions and Rodzyanko's comments, putting the case in black and white and more bluntly than the Duma president had done himself. 'The dynastic question has been put point-blank,' he told his commanders. 'The war may be continued until its victorious end only provided the demands regarding the abdication from the throne in favour of the son and under the regency of Grand Duke Michael Aleksandrovich are satisfied. Apparently the situation does not permit another solution ... It is necessary to save the active army from disintegration; to continue the fight against the external enemy until the end; to save the independence and the fate of the dynasty.'[2] Alekseev favoured abdication. Did his commanders agree?

His cables went out at 10.15 a.m. Less than four hours later, at 2.15 p.m., he wired the Emperor at Pskov, giving him the first replies. They would prove decisive.

Nicholas had been given a transcript of the early-morning tapes when he arose in the late morning and he also read the cable from Alekseev, recommending abdication. There was 'a terrible moment of silence', Ruzsky remembered, as Nicholas absorbed the shock,[3] but he gave no sign of his inner turmoil when he went for a walk along the station platform with Ruzsky at lunch-time. A few hours earlier he had assumed that in granting a responsible ministry he had given more than enough; now he was being asked to contemplate the unthinkable: that he should give up the throne. Later it would be said that Ruzsky bullied him into this, shouting at him and thumping the table with his fist, saying 'Will you make up your mind to go!'[4]

Nicholas, however, was waiting to hear what his other army commanders had to say. But there was no comfort there. Alekseev's cable incorporated all three responses. The first was from 'Uncle Nikolasha', the former Supreme Commander, now commander on the Caucasus front:

> *As a loyal subject I feel it my necessary duty of allegiance and in the spirit of my oath, to beg Your Imperial Majesty on my knees to save Russia and your heir, being aware of your sacred feelings of love for Russia and for him. Make the Sign of the Cross and hand over to him your heritage. There is no other way . . .*

The next was from Brusilov, the most successful fighting general in the army and commander on the south-western front:

> *. . . At the present time the only solution that could save the situation . . . is the abdication of the throne in favour of the heir Tsarevich under the Regency of Grand Duke Michael Aleksandrovich. There is no other way out; speed is necessary, so that the popular conflagration which has grown to large proportions can be rapidly extinguished otherwise it will result in incalculable catastrophic consequences. By these acts the dynasty itself would be saved in the person of the lawful heir.*

The third was from General Aleksei Evert, the commander on the western front:

> *. . . Under the conditions which have been created and not seeing any other answer, I . . . implore Your Majesty . . . to make a decision which would be in agreement with the declaration of the President of the State Duma . . . as the only measure which apparently can stop the revolution and thus save Russia from the horrors of anarchy.*[5]

Early that afternoon, with Alekseev's cable in his hand, Ruzsky went back to the Emperor in his railway carriage. He handed it over, letting it speak for itself. Nicholas, smoking one cigarette and then lighting another, read through the paper and put it down on the table. Ruzsky and the two generals he had brought with him as moral support, stood silently as Nicholas got up and went to the window, staring out unseeingly. He had little regard for politicians, but the views of his army commanders mattered. They had just passed a vote of no confidence in their Tsar and their Supreme Commander. He could not sack them, as he could sack politicians, nor could he argue with them. Suddenly he turned and said calmly: 'I have decided. I shall renounce the throne.' He made the sign of the Cross and the three generals, suddenly realising the enormity of what had just been said, followed suit.[6]

Two short telegrams were drafted. The first was to Rodzyanko: 'There is no sacrifice which I would not bear for the sake of the real welfare and for the salvation of our own dear Mother Russia. Therefore I am ready to abdicate the throne in favour of my son provided that he can remain with me until he comes of age, with the Regency of my brother the Grand Duke Michael Aleksandrovich.' To Alekseev, he wrote in similar terms.[7]

Just as Ruzsky was about to have these despatched, a cable arrived from Petrograd to announce that two members of the Temporary Committee, Guchkov and Shulgin, were on their way to Pskov to see the Tsar and were leaving at 3.35 p.m. Not knowing the significance of this, Ruzsky held up despatch of the abdication cables and went back to Nicholas with the unexpected news from the capital.[8] Perhaps the two delegates were coming with some offer that would make abdication unnecessary. Perhaps, after all, there was to be a last-minute reprieve for the reign of Nicholas II.[9]

However, fifteen minutes later, reality returned to the imperial carriage. The frontline commanders had spoken and Nicholas knew now there could be no hope. Ruzsky had returned to him his telegram to Rodzyanko and now Nicholas handed it back to him, telling him to send it and release the other to Alekseev. It was 3.45 p.m.[10]

Michael was keeping closely in touch with developments at the Tauride Palace and on that Thursday, March 2, there were constant comings and goings at Millionnaya Street as Duma emissaries arrived with news. Michael had known the night before that while 'all the power is now in the hands of the Temporary Committee' the Duma men 'are in difficulties because of the strong pressure by the Committee of Deputies of Workers and Soldiers'.[11] By morning he knew also that his brother had offered a responsible ministry, under a government headed by Rodzyanko, but that it looked as if this would no longer be enough. Nevertheless, anxious to do whatever might help swing the arguments in his brother's favour, he wrote to Rodzyanko offering to come to the Tauride Palace himself, 'if his presence could do any good'.[12]

The prospect of Grand Duke Michael Aleksandrovich arriving at the Tauride Palace was one which Rodzyanko properly viewed with dismay. Its dramatic effect apart, the result could have been only to arouse alarm in the ranks of a Soviet already suspicious of the 'gentlemen of the Duma'. Kirill's appearance at the head of his marines had created astonishment, rather than uproar, and if anything it had seemed to increase the authority of a Duma who could now command even a Grand Duke. That was also the case, if less surprisingly so, when later that day another Grand Duke, – 'Bimbo' – presented himself to the Duma Committee and also offered them his support.[13] Bimbo had just arrived back at his Millionnaya Street palace, having taken the revolution as signal that he could end the exile imposed on him on New Year's Day by the Tsar. Tall, bald, fat and still a bachelor at fifty-eight, Bimbo was a notorious gossip who had never concealed his contempt for Nicholas and Alexandra; as a young man in the Chevalier Gardes he had been known as 'Philippe Egalité' because he insisted on addressing his soldiers as 'my friends'.[14] At the Tauride Palace his support was welcomed, but it was not judged politically significant. Even the Soviet hardly noticed that he was there.

But Michael was not the discredited Kirill or the somewhat eccentric Bimbo: he was the Tsar's brother, the man the Duma Committee was promoting as the Regent and the means by which they hoped to bring about a constitutional monarchy and thus forestall the Soviet's ambitions for a 'democratic republic'. The last thing Rodzyanko wanted was to see Michael walking into the Tauride Palace as advocate for his brother, or even as apparent ally of the Duma Committee. It would have enraged the mob, risked his life and compromised, possibly fatally, the authority of the new government then being formed. The best thing that Michael could do that Thursday was to keep well out of sight and say nothing.

As it happened, by the time Rodzyanko replied to Michael, events had moved beyond the point of anything that Michael could have done for his brother anyway. As Rodzyanko's letter to him reported that evening, Nicholas had abdicated and named Michael as Regent. Indeed, this news had by now reached even London, for that night Michael's cousin King George V wrote in his diary: 'Heard from Buchanan that the Duma had forced Nicky to sign his abdication and Misha had been appointed Regent . . .' The British king was in no doubt about the reasons behind the abdication: 'I fear Alicky [*the Empress*] is the cause of it all and Nicky has been weak'. King George ended his diary note by writing, 'I am in despair'.[15] Yet there was also reason for optimism, for tomorrow, with a new government and a new monarchy, hopefully Russia could turn the page and start again.

Unfortunately, what the world did not yet know was that Nicholas had already changed his mind.

Sharing the Tauride Palace, the Duma Committee and the Soviet shared little else. Both were the product of revolution, both needed the other to ensure their own survival, but both hoped for different outcomes. The Duma was intent upon a constitutional monarchy, the Soviet upon a democratic republic. On Monday night, February 27, it might still have been possible for Nicholas to save his throne by conceding a responsible ministry and appointing his brother Regent in the capital, but when he failed to do so the revolution became an accomplished fact. After that, the question was whether the monarchy itself could survive.

The struggle for the future of Russia began just after midnight on Wednesday, March 1, in the meeting room of the Duma Committee. The Soviet executive, led by their chairman Nikolai Chkheidze, a fifty-three-year-old Georgian schoolmaster and socialist deputy, included many radical members of the intelligentsia, with a sprinkling of men just freed from the Kresty prison across the Neva. With the exception of Kerensky, none of the Soviet members saw themselves as competent, or wished to be part of a new government. Nevertheless, they were determined to fashion its agenda.

Political convictions apart, the great difference between the Duma and the Soviet was that the members of the latter had their necks at stake. If the revolution ended in failure, the gallows beckoned for the men who led the Soviet, as it did for many of the soldiers who thronged the Catherine Hall. Kerensky would escape, for he could claim to have saved the lives of his prisoners by taking them into 'protective custody'. The 'gentlemen of the Duma' could also be sure of emerging unscathed, for in any counter-revolution their act of rebellion against the crown could be excused as a necessary defence against anarchy and besides, they would be needed if order was to be restored. Win or lose, the Duma deputies had nothing to fear.

What, though, would the position be if the revolution resulted in a 'half-way house', with Nicholas gone, but with Russia still a monarchy? Among the mutinous troops, those who had killed or participated in killing their officers or policemen had most to fear. Officers who had broken their oath of allegiance by siding with the revolution were also likely candidates for the gallows. In August, 1916, when mutineers in the 2nd Brigade murdered their colonel, twenty men were shot; in Petrograd in October 1916, when two regiments called to a strike at the Renault factory fired on police, 150 men were executed.[16] But those were relatively minor incidents; for a revolution on the scale of 1917 the number of those who faced execution was likely to run into many hundreds, including men from every regiment which had taken part.

Although the rebellious regiments had sworn allegiance to the Duma, their true loyalty was to the Soviet, for soldiers and Soviet both knew that if they did not hang together now, they would be hanged together later. The Soviet did not pretend it could form a government which could rule Russia – it had neither the men nor the experience; however, as one of its terms for supporting a new Duma-created government the Soviet executive demanded a complete amnesty for all revolutionaries, including mutinous soldiers and anyone accused of terrorism or murder. It also, significantly, wanted guarantees that the garrison in Petrograd would not be dispersed into the army as a whole, or disarmed. With these and other measures, the Soviet would continue to hold a loaded pistol at the head of a new government, should it afterwards seek revenge.

When the Soviet delegates filed into the Duma Committee with their agenda they found Rodzyanko at a far table, drinking soda water. Facing him, at another table, was the white-haired Milyukov, sitting behind a pile of papers, notes and telegrams. In the centre of the room the Committee members, including Prince Lvov, occupied a line of chairs and armchairs, with otherdeputies standing around them.[17] After desultory conversation, the Soviet deputation read out its conditions. The real issue over the next forty hours would be their 'Point Three': in effect, the future of the monarchy.

The man who would have nothing to do with the Soviet's demands for a republic was Pavel Milyukov, though he was willing to yield on every other issue. 'He spoke for the entire Duma Committee; everyone considered this a matter of course,' one of the Soviet members noted. 'It was clear that Milyukov here was not only a leader but the boss of the right wing.' He insisted that Russia remain a monarchy and on this the 'bourgeois leader was irreconcilable'. He made no attempt to defend Nicholas, for he agreed that he was 'unacceptable' and 'must be removed'. But Alexis had to be Tsar and Michael the Regent.[18]

Milyukov attempted to make a reformed monarchy appear harmless, a mere principle which could not possibly affect the kind of government which Russia would enjoy, or the safety of those who had actively participated in the revolution. There could be nothing the Soviet need fear, for Alexis 'was a sick child' and the Regent Michael was 'a thoroughly stupid man'.[19] This ploy, judged 'naïve' by one,[20] failed to impress the three men staring back at him across the table. By eight o'clock on Thursday evening, March 2, with Nicholas's abdication in favour of his son then known to all, the status of the monarchy was still not settled.

It was then that Milyukov clinched matters, by telling the Soviet that if there was no Tsar then he would not be in the government. 'Now, if I am not here, there is no government at all. And if there is no government, then . . . you yourselves can understand . . .'[21] Was this an ultimatum, or was it a bluff? Either way, the Soviet grudgingly decided to give way, agreeing that the status of Russia should be settled by an elected Constituent Assembly, rather than now by the Soviet. The revolution was to end with Russia still a monarchy, although the Soviet made clear it would 'engage without delay in a broad struggle for a democratic republic'.[22] The monarchy had been reprieved, but only just.

By Thursday afternoon, Russia had a new government, composed largely of the same men who, a year earlier, would have been part of a 'ministry of public confidence'. Milyukov, perched on a table, jotted their names on a sheet of paper and distributed the portfolios with little discussion.[23] The prime minister was Prince Lvov, the man Michael had put forward to his brother on Monday evening as the 'only possible candidate'. Rodzyanko, the man Nicholas had assumed would be prime minister, was not even in the twelve-man Cabinet. Milyukov was foreign secretary, Guchkov – then on his way to Pskov – was named as war minister. The minister of justice was Kerensky, the only member of the Soviet to be included.

The name of this self-appointed government was chosen casually. Milyukov suggested 'The Provisional Committee of the Duma'. The Soviet member, Nikolai Sukhanov, suggested 'The Provisional Government'; Milyukov nodded and scratched that name down.[24]

By 10 p.m. on Thursday, March 2, 1917, the Provisional Government had been born. All that remained was to acquire at Pskov the formal signed abdication of Tsar Nicholas II. At that very moment, however, Nicholas was bungling even that.

Aleksandr Guchkov and Vasily Shulgin arrived at Pskov on their special train not knowing that Nicholas had already abdicated in favour of his son. They were expecting, therefore, to have a struggle on their hands.

Earlier that day, as the talks with the Soviet dragged on, Guchkov had resolved to take decisive action, regardless of any agreement with the revolutionaries about the status of Russia.

> *In this chaos, in everything that goes on, the first thought should be to save the monarchy. Without the monarchy Russia cannot live. But apparently the present Emperor can no longer reign. An imperial order by him is no longer an order: it would not be executed. And if that is so, then how can we calmly and indifferently await the moment when all the revolutionary riffraff starts to look for an issue itself? They would destroy the monarchy . . . We should act secretly and swiftly without asking anyone. If we act following an agreement with 'them' it will surely turn out to be least favourable for us. They should be faced with an accomplished fact. Russia must have another Emperor. Under this banner must be gathered what can be gathered in order to organise resistance. For this purpose we must act swiftly and resolutely.*[25]

With that, he and Shulgin had set off for Pskov at around 3 p.m. The 170-mile journey took them seven hours, some two hours longer than normal. On arrival they were led across the tracks to the brightly-lit imperial carriages and shown into a large saloon car. Hors d'oeuvres had been set out on a table along one side of the carriage. Waiting for them was the bent figure of old Baron Frederiks. Shulgin suddenly felt uncomfortable, conscious that he was 'unshaved, with a crumpled collar, in a business coat'.[26] Then Nicholas came in, wearing a grey Circassian coat, his face calm. He gestured and the two delegates sat down. For Guchkov it was an extraordinary moment: for months he had been planning a coup in which Nicholas would be arrested on his train and made to abdicate. In Guchkov's mind he had pictured a scene not unlike the very one of which he was now part. It would have been two weeks later and there would have been no revolution, but otherwise there were uncanny resemblances between fact and forecast.

Yet Guchkov found himself curiously disconcerted as he faced Nicholas. He shook hands with Nicholas and sat facing him across the polished tabletop. 'The Emperor sat, leaning slightly against the silken wall and looked straight ahead. His face was absolutely calm and impenetrable.' Guchkov, recovering his own composure, put his hand on his forehead as was his habit when speaking and began talking, looking down rather than at the Emperor.[27]

As Guchkov made out the case for abdication, Ruzsky came in, bowed to the Emperor and whispered to Shulgin, to tell him that 'the matter has been decided'. However, Guchkov would not know that until he had finished and Nicholas replied: 'I have made the decision to abdicate the throne.'[28] What was even more startling was that he went on to say that he had decided to name Michael and not his son, as his successor. No one had expected that, or thought it a possibility, for the law was clear: an emperor could not deprive the next in line to the throne of his right to succeed; it had been so since the days of Paul I. The law was silent on abdication because that had never been foreseen, but it did not affect the principle.

Nevertheless, after signalling his willingness to abdicate and while waiting for the arrival of the two delegates from Petrograd, Nicholas had talked to Professor Sergei Fedorov, the court physician, about his son's health. Fedorov had always told him that Alexis's haemophilia was incurable and now he ventured that as Emperor he would most certainly be removed from the care of his parents.[29] It was the last prospect which Nicholas could not face: separation from his beloved child. Accordingly, he looked across the table at Guchkov and told him: 'I have come to the conclusion that, in the light of his illness, I should abdicate in my name and his name simultaneously, as I cannot be separated from him'. He paused, as if seeking understanding. 'I hope you will understand the feelings of a father,' he said quietly.[30]

Guchkov was bewildered and protested: 'But we had counted on the figure of the little Alexis Nikolaevich as having a softening effect on the transfer of power.'[31] An innocent boy Emperor would have attracted sympathy, rallied loyalists, signalled continuity and disarmed those who paraded the crimes of the Romanovs as justification for bringing down the monarchist state.

No one had a copy of the *Fundamental Laws* at Pskov and there was no time for lengthy discussions. Every hour counted and there could be no question of Guchkov and Shulgin returning to Petrograd without Nicholas's abdication in their hands, or lamely going back to the Duma to discuss whether a double abdication was acceptable. They left the carriage to confer with Ruzsky and his generals.

For some moments they also wondered about a further complication: Michael's marriage to Natasha. Could he be Emperor with a morganatic wife? Someone mentioned Alexander II's marriage to his mistress Catherine Dolgorukaya, a commoner and mother of his illegitimate children. Was that a precedent? No one was sure, for Alexander had been Emperor when he married his mistress.[32] Besides, Alexis was problem enough and if they were to start raising doubts about the next in line the monarchy was finished. No one there wanted that. Irregularities would have to be accepted and if necessary they could be sorted out later. After all, Nicholas was still an autocrat and what one Tsar ordained perhaps another could set aside, a view which it would seem that Nicholas himself adopted.

Guchkov, Shulgin and Ruzsky returned to the salon and told Nicholas that they would accept the abdication in the form stipulated. A manifesto had been drafted earlier at Stavka and sent down to Pskov for signature, and it was this which Nicholas took with him into his study for amendment and signature. It was then 11.40 p.m. but by agreement it was settled that the manifesto should be timed as of three o'clock that afternoon, when Nicholas had decided to abdicate.[33] It was also agreed that Nicholas should issue two other edicts, one naming Prince Lvov as prime minister of the new government, the other reappointing Grand Duke Nicholas Nikolaevich as Supreme Commander. To give them legality, these were antedated to 2 p.m., one hour before the time shown on the abdication manifesto.[34] It would have been better law if Nicholas had also antedated Alexis's removal from the succession on the grounds of his ill-health, citing independent medical evidence in support and separating it from his own abdication. That said, it would have been better politics not to have done it at all.

A sealed copy of the abdication was handed over to Guchkov and another given to Ruzsky for transmission to the army commanders, and to Petrograd and other key centres, including the garrison headquarters at Tsarskoe Selo. The original text had been elegantly written at Stavka and the changes made by Nicholas in no way diminished the style. Beginning with a declaration about the need to continue the war 'to a victorious end' and 'the duty to draw Our people into a close union', the manifesto concluded:

> *We have judged it right to abdicate the Throne of the Russian State and to lay down the Supreme Power. Not wishing to be parted from Our Beloved Son, We hand over Our Succession to Our Brother the Grand Duke Michael Aleksandrovich and Bless Him on his accession to the Throne of the Russian State . . . In the name of Our Dearly beloved native land, We call upon all true sons of the Fatherland to fulfil their sacred duty to It by their obedience to the Tsar at this difficult time of national ordeal and to help Him, together with the people's representatives, to lead the Russian State onto the path of victory, prosperity and glory . . .'*[35]

Throughout the formalities Nicholas had given no sign of distress. Guchkov was so astonished by the 'simple, matter-of-fact way' in which the business was concluded that 'I even wondered whether we were dealing with a normal person'. Even with a person of 'the most iron character, of well-nigh unequalled self-control, one might have expected some show of emotion ... but nothing of the sort.'[36] Others would also remark on Nicholas's composure: 'He renounced the throne as simply as if he were turning over command of a cavalry squadron', one of his aides remarked.[37]

Within himself, however, he was anything but calm. When he went later to his diary and confided his innermost thoughts his private agony was revealed: 'At one o'clock this morning, I left Pskov with a heart that is heavy over what has just happened,' he wrote. 'All around me there is nothing but treason cowardice and deceit!'[38]

Nicholas was then on his way back to Mogilev, the headquarters he had left in that same train forty-four hours earlier. No one had yet told Michael that he was Emperor, nor had it yet occurred to Nicholas that he should contact his brother to explain what had happened and why he had not been given any warning.

At Millionnaya Street Michael was asleep on a makeshift bed, aware only that he would be Regent when he woke up on Friday morning. However, by virtue of his brother's manifesto he had been, as from 3 p.m. on Thursday afternoon, His Majesty Michael II, Emperor of All the Russias, Polish King and Grand Duke of Finland . . .

At the Tauride Palace they still believed that Michael was to be Regent – 'the majority of the Provisional Committee of the Duma still took it for granted,' said Kerensky[39] – and the news of that had been enough in itself to have caused consternation among some of the soldiers. On Thursday afternoon, with Guchkov and Shulgin on their way to Pskov, Milyukov had gone to the colonnaded Catherine Hall and had made a speech to the crowd gathered there about the programme of the new government, then just formed. He then, without the issue having finally been settled with the

Soviet, announced that 'the old despot who has led Russia to the brink of ruin will either voluntarily abdicate, or be set aside. The power will go to the Regent, Grand Duke Michael Aleksandrovich . . .' There were some cheers as well as indignant protests, but when he added that the Tsarevich would be Emperor there were shouts: 'But that's the old dynasty'.

Milyukov replied firmly: 'Yes, gentlemen, that's the old dynasty, which you may not like and which I may not like, but . . . we cannot leave unanswered the question of the form of government. We have in mind a constitutional monarchy . . . but if we stop to quarrel about it now, we will come to no decision, Russia will drift into civil war and we shall have a ruined country.'[40]

That evening, as word spread that Michael was to be Regent, a frightened Rodzyanko, 'accompanied by a handful of officers who reeked of alcohol', came running up to Milyukov. 'In a quavering voice', recalled Milyukov, a shaken Rodzyanko 'repeated their assertions that after what I had said about the dynasty they could not go back to their units. They demanded that I retract what I had said. This I could not do; but on seeing the behaviour of Rodzyanko, who knew that I had spoken not only in my own name but in the name of the Progressive Bloc as a whole, I decided to issue a statement saying that I had expressed only my personal view.'[41]

The officers went in fear of retribution, but fear worked two ways and Rodzyanko was certainly one of those who was as scared of the revolution as the revolution was scared of the monarchy. Later, Milyukov would describe him as being in a 'blue funk' and this would become a significant factor in the next hours, for Rodzyanko would be the first to crumble[42] when the news came, early in the morning, that Nicholas had changed his abdication manifesto and had named Michael as Emperor.

The Duma Committee had been willing to back Milyukov when they believed that the abdication would be in favour of Alexis, with Michael as Regent for his nephew, for that transfer of power was lawful and more importantly it faced the Soviet with the difficult task of waging war on a child. Little Alexis could not be compelled to abdicate, because he was too young to sign anything and they could be sure that Michael would never sign such a manifesto on his behalf. Alexis was also likely to attract the sympathy of the sentimental, God-fearing peasant soldiery, wavering between loyalty and rebellion, who so far had stayed in their barracks.

As written, the manifesto removed that advantage; furthermore it created confusion in the ranks of those who had been prepared to defend the expected, but were thrown off balance by the unexpected. The authority of the Duma men had been based in great degree on the continuity of the legal order and that order had been jeopardised by Nicholas. It weakened resolve; it diluted courage.

Now it was the Duma men who saw their necks at stake. Fear is infectious and it was fear that Rodzyanko spread through the Duma deputies and into the new government. No one was anxious to admit that, of course, and instead they advanced whatever reason could excuse a change of mind.

One objection was Michael's morganatic marriage 'to a woman well known for her political intrigues'; another, that 'he had never been interested in affairs of state'.[43] Even Kerensky, a republican, recognised them as 'irrelevant arguments'; the real issue for the new government was whether it stood by the monarchy, or caved in to the Soviet. The test was courage.

In those early hours of Friday morning there was not much courage about. Milyukov was one of the few who did not lose his head, arguing that 'what mattered was not *who* should be Tsar but that there should be a Tsar'.[44] However, their nerves rattled by Rodzyanko, the abdication manifesto was seized on as excuse for abandoning the very case which the Duma Committee had argued so strenuously with the Soviet. Kerensky, hearing his own case being made for him, thought that 'the decision of Nicholas II had really cut the Gordian knot. Everyone felt with great relief that once the lawful and rightful succession had been broken, the immediate question of the dynasty was settled.'[45]

But Michael was already Emperor and his succession was being telegraphed across the country. Within hours the army would be taking an oath of allegiance to him. Somehow, that would have to be stopped while the new government decided what best to do. Rodzyanko immediately drove to the war ministry to wire Pskov and to ask General Ruzsky to hold up the manifesto.

It was 5 a.m. when Rodzyanko's tape stuttered over the direct wire.

> *It is extremely important that the manifesto . . . should not be published until I advise you of it . . . It is with great difficulty that we managed to restrain the revolutionary movement within more or less bearable limits, but the situation is as yet far from settled and civil war is quite possible. Perhaps they would reconcile themselves to the Regency of the Grand Duke . . . but his accession as Emperor would be completely unacceptable . . . A mutiny of soldiers has flared up, the like of which I have not seen . . . little by little the troops were brought to order during the night, but the proclamation of Grand Duke Michael Aleksandrovich would pour oil into the fire and a merciless extermination of everything that can be exterminated would start . . .*[46]

At 6 a.m. he was sending the same message to General Alekseev at Mogilev.[47] Alekseev, who had already sent out the abdication manifesto, was disturbed by his wire conversation with Rodzyanko and his concern increased when he received a print-out of Rodzyanko's previous conversation with Ruzsky. At 7 a.m. he wired his views to his other army commanders that 'there is no frankness or sincerity in the communications of Rodzyanko' and that 'there is no unity within the State Duma and the Temporary Committee'.[48] Alekseev now suspected that it was the Soviet which was dictating affairs in Petrograd. His response was to propose that the army should demand that the manifesto as written be implemented and that there should be a meeting of all army commanders to 'establish unanimity in all circumstances and in any eventuality'.[49]

At the Tauride Palace, the new government knew that it could not delay much longer its meeting with Michael. Everyone knew where he was. As they waited for Rodzyanko to return from his wire talks with the army, Kerensky picked up a copy of the Petrograd telephone directory, flicked through the pages and ran his finger down the column to the name of Princess Putyatina.[50] Her number was 1–58–48. A few moments later, at 5.55 a.m., the telephone rang in 12 Millionnaya Street.[51]

PART III

THE LAST EMPEROR

TWENTY-FOUR

Emperor Michael

There was never any real hope of keeping secret the succession of Michael as Emperor. In the four hours which had elapsed between the first telegraphed despatches from Pskov and the desperate call from Rodzyanko the news had spread not only to the army but to cities across Russia. At first light, thousands of troops in frontline units were swearing an oath of allegiance to Emperor Michael II, and in the Fourth Cavalry Division General Krasnov announced the succession to 'an enormous cheer'; over the next two days he decorated soldiers with the Cross of St George in the name of the new Emperor.[1]

At Pskov itself, with Nicholas departed for Mogilev, a *Te Deum* was ordered for the new Emperor in the cathedral. Dimitri's sister Marie went to the morning service, as did General Ruzsky. The square beside the church was crowded with soldiers, many of them wearing a red rosette, 'their faces agitated'; inside, a packed congregation heard the manifesto of Nicholas read out, and then prayed 'for the prolongation of the days of the new Tsar'.[2]

As the morning wore on, even in far-off Crimea, and around the ex-Tsar's favourite home at Livadia, people celebrated Michael's succession. The American-born Princess Cantacuzène, granddaughter of US President Grant, and one of Petrograd's leading hostesses, was on holiday at Yalta in March, 1917. She remembered that Nicholas's portrait disappeared 'from shop windows and walls within an hour after the reading of the proclamation; and in its place I saw by afternoon pictures of Michael Aleksandrovich. Flags were hung out, and all faces wore smiles of quiet satisfaction. "It was very bad; now it will be better", was the general, calm verdict. The supposition of a constitutional monarch was the accepted idea.'[3]

In Moscow, where the garrison had also gone over to the revolution, although without any of the excesses which had occurred in Petrograd, the succession of Michael was greeted with 'wooden indifference' on the part of those who were sympathetic to the revolution,[4] but there were no marching protests or riots and no sign of resistance of the kind so feared by Rodzyanko. When Alexandra's sister, Grand Duchess Ella, heard the news at the Chudov Abbey, of which she was abbess, her objection was largely purist: that Michael was married to Natasha; told by a monk that in the next service the liturgy would be changed to 'our Right Orthodox and Sovereign Lord and Emperor Michael Aleksandrovich', she protested: 'But the Grand Duke cannot possibly reign! What about . . .'

The monk broke in hurriedly, 'Ah, Matushka, there will be no mention of the lady.'[5]

There would be no prayers for Natasha, but elsewhere the faithful crossed themselves and prayed for Michael. Even in Petrograd, the storm centre of the revolution, the news of his succession was greeted with cheers, at least in some quarters.

At the Warsaw station, when the train arrived bringing Guchkov and Shulgin from Pskov, the two delegates decided to make the first proclamation about the succession. 'Long live Emperor Michael,' they cried as they hurried from their train. The excited crowd cheered. When Shulgin walked into the station's huge entrance hall, a battalion of troops was drawn up there, surrounded by a curious crowd. Shulgin read out the manifesto and, lifting his eyes from the paper, called for three cheers for 'His Majesty the Emperor Michael II'. The regiment and crowd responded with cheers that 'rang out, passionate, genuine, emotional'.[6]

Shulgin strode back into the station, the crowd making way for him as he went forward looking for Guchkov. Suddenly he was aware of an urgent voice telling him that he was wanted on the telephone in the station-master's office. When he walked in and picked up the receiver he heard the croaking voice of Pavel Milyukov. 'Don't make known the manifesto,' said Milyukov. 'There have been serious changes.'

A startled Shulgin could only stammer a reply. 'But how? . . . I have already announced it.'

'To whom?'

'Why, to all here. Some regiment or other. The people. I have proclaimed Michael Emperor.'

'You should not have done that,' Milyukov barked into the telephone. 'Feelings have become much worse since you left . . . Don't take any further steps. There may be great misfortune.'[7]

Shulgin put down the phone in bewilderment. Guchkov, he was told, had gone off to a meeting of 2000 men in some nearby railway workshops, intent on spreading the glad tidings of Michael's succession. Shulgin decided to go after him, then remembered that he still had the abdication manifesto in his pocket. The railway shopmen had been staunch supporters of the Soviet; if he went in, would he get out? At that moment the telephone rang again. This time it was Bublikov, the man whom the Duma Committee had appointed as Railway Commissioner. He was sending his own man to the station. 'You can trust him with anything . . . Understand?'

Shulgin understood. A few minutes later, Bublikov's messenger thrust himself through the crowd and Shulgin slipped him the envelope bearing the manifesto. The man took it, and disappeared back to the transport ministry offices, where the document was hidden under a pile of old magazines. Shulgin then headed for the workshops, where Guchkov was standing on a platform above a dense mass of workers. The meeting was being harangued by its chairman, sneering protests about a new government led by a prince, and full of landowners and wealthy industrialists. 'Is this what we had the revolution for, comrades? Prince Lvov?' It was clearly not the moment to cry out 'Long Live Emperor Michael'.

As Shulgin joined Guchkov on the platform, the seething railwaymen began to move forward menacingly towards them. Here were two representatives of this bourgeois government, sent secretly to confer with the Tsar at Pskov. Whom did they represent? 'Shut the doors, comrades,' cried the leaders.

The situation looked nasty, but then the workers began to argue among themselves, with some shouting that the shopmen on the platform were behaving 'like the old regime'. Pushing, shoving, the crowd began to turn on its own, with voices demanding that Guchkov be allowed to speak. He did so, defending the government, but prudently deciding to make no mention of Michael. As tempers cooled, the doors were opened again, and a shaken Guchkov and Shulgin were allowed to leave.[8]

By then the news of the proclamations read out at the Warsaw station earlier had raced across the city. Vladimir Nabokov, unaware that he would soon be playing a critical role in the future of the monarchy, heard about Michael's succession twice over as he was walking to work from his apartment on the Morskaya, and when he reached his office he found 'great excitement, with crowds on the stairs and in the big conference hall'.[9]

Curiously, one of the last to discover the name of the new Emperor of All the Russias was Michael himself. When Kerensky telephoned the Millionnaya Street apartment at 5.55 a.m. he did not disclose that Nicholas had abdicated in favour of Michael. It was merely arranged that a delegation would come to see him at the apartment.

Millionnaya Street was half awake when Kerensky made his call. The apartment was spacious; even so, it was exceptionally crowded this Friday morning. Officers of the guard were sleeping in the study, and Michael, Johnson and Matveev were also camping out, on settees and makeshift beds. Johnson took the call from Kerensky and learned that the 'Council of Ministers' would be arriving for a meeting in about an hour. They were not surprised, for they were expecting news of Nicholas's abdication; but, as Matveev would firmly record, 'in the light of the letter from the President of the State Duma' delivered the previous evening, the assumption was that the delegation was coming 'to report on the Regency'. While they waited, Michael was 'therefore thinking over the appropriate reply expressing his consent'.[10]

At Tsarskoe Selo there was no such ignorance. Some time around 3 a.m. the text of the manifesto from Pskov was received at the garrison headquarters, and given to the town's new commandant. Deciding that it would be best if the news was first disclosed to the Alexander Palace by Grand Duke Paul, the commandant tried to telephone him repeatedly but failed to get through. An officer was sent to Paul's palace at 4.15 a.m. Paul came down in his dressing gown to find a pale-faced and tearful officer with a message that the Commandant wished to speak to him urgently. 'We realised at once that all was finished,' said Paul's wife Princess Paley.[11]

Five minutes later an artillery colonel, wearing a large red bow on his chest, was shown in to them. The colonel apologised for the early hour, then read them the abdication manifesto. Paul and his wife were 'thunderstruck' and Princess Paley sat mute, shivering, her teeth chattering.[12]

Paul could not bring himself to go to the Alexander Palace until eleven o'clock that morning. There he found Alexandra in her room, dressed in her hospital uniform. As yet no one had dared tell her of the abdication, and it fell to Paul to break the news to her. Tears rolled down her cheeks, and she bent her head as if praying. 'If Nicky has done that, it is because he had to do so ... God will not abandon us ... I am no longer Empress ... As it is Misha who is Emperor, I shall look after my children and my hospital. We shall go to the Crimea.'[13]

That Alexandra would not know of the abdication until 11 a.m. was understandable; that the new Emperor was not formally told as soon as the news reached Petrograd was astonishing. The silence was deliberate.

Although the Duma Committee had taken control of the war ministry after the arrest of the war minister Belyaev on Tuesday, February 28, authority there had not quite passed to the new government, for the new war minister was Guchkov, who as yet did not know of his appointment, and who was still travelling back to Petrograd throughout the early hours of Friday, March 3. At the war ministry the man they knew best was Rodzyanko, and it was he who still appeared to be in control when he arrived there at 5 a.m. to begin his long discussions with Pskov.

In asking that the abdication manifesto be suppressed, Rodzyanko also wanted it kept from the new Emperor, though he said nothing about this in his discussions with Pskov. Kerensky would later gloss over the details of his own call to Millionnaya Street, but some of his comments are revealing. He would say of Michael that 'we did not know how much he knew,' while adding that it was important 'to prevent whatever steps he was planning to take until we had come to a decision'.[14] Michael could not be allowed to 'take steps' while the new government was arguing over what its position should be; it would have been awkward to find the new Emperor telephoning them at 3 a.m. and demanding that his new government attend on him immediately. It would have been particularly awkward if Michael had also insisted on going to the war ministry to communicate directly with the army headquarters at Pskov and Mogilev. In the circumstances it was best that Michael did not find out until the ministers were ready to tell him.

At 6 a.m. it was thought that the Duma men could be at Millionnaya Street about an hour later. The streets would still be dark, the capital hardly awake and the chances that Michael had been informed independently about the manifesto relatively small. Kerensky, though he does not say so in his later accounts, would have reported back after his telephone call that Michael did not know about the manifesto, for that was an important factor in the discussions at the Tauride Palace. 'How much does he know?' was a question he himself admits to asking and after his telephone call he had the answer, from the reaction of Johnson on the telephone. Michael, as Matveev recorded, believed he had become Regent.

He found out otherwise because the meeting was delayed, partly because of the time taken in working out the new government's response, and partly because of the delay in the arrival of Guchkov and Shulgin, held up by their adventures in the railway workshops. In consequence it was not until 9.15 a.m. that the delegation began to assemble at Millionnaya Street. By then, Michael knew what the government had not thought fit to tell him.

Natasha certainly heard about Michael's succession, and her first instinct would have been to contact him. On Friday, March 3, Tata remembered that 'the telephones never stopped ringing',[15] suggesting that at least locally – there were 250 telephones in Gatchina[16] – the service was working and that there were a large number of calls to and from Nikolaevskaya Street, as might be expected. However, the telephone service between Gatchina and the capital was disrupted; no matter how much she persevered, she could not get through to Michael.

One immediate source of intelligence, nevertheless, was 'Bimbo', Grand Duke Nicholas Mikhailovich, who lived in his palace across the road, and whose younger brother George was at Gatchina, staying with Natasha.[17] On Wednesday, his first day back in Petrograd since his exile by Nicholas on January 1, Bimbo had spent the evening with Michael, discussing the situation;[18] he also, it seems, came back early on Friday morning.

Princess Putyatina recalled a conversation between Michael and Bimbo which could only have taken place on Friday morning, at some time around or before 9 a.m. Grand Duke Nicholas Mikhailovich 'was up-to-date with everything, and he knew that the Emperor had abdicated,' she wrote.[19] The meeting was 'very moving' as Bimbo 'embraced his nephew tenderly'.* Her version of what was said, given by her several years later, plainly cannot be verbatim, but what matters is not the precise words used but their meaning.

'I am very happy to recognise you as Sovereign,' said Bimbo, 'since in fact you are already the Tsar! Be brave and strong: in this way, you will not only save the dynasty but also the future of Russia!' He then asked: 'When are you going to appear as Tsar?'

Michael replied: 'I shall leave as Tsar from the same house where I was received as Grand Duke.'[20]

While that is hardly Michael's conversational style, nevertheless it would seem from Princess Putyatina's account that it was Bimbo who brought news, or confirmed the news, of Michael's succession. And that Michael, in whatever words, had decided to accept the crown before the first knock on the door announced the arrival of Rodzyanko and Prince Lvov.

Two miles separate the Tauride Palace and Millionnaya Street. On snow-covered streets a car could make the journey in around ten minutes, driving down the street towards the Winter Palace, then turning into the archway leading to the large inner courtyard behind the Putyatin apartment. Once inside the courtyard the several cars arriving from the Duma building would be concealed from view as the cadet guards closed the heavy black metal courtyard doors behind them. The delegation had not told the Soviet executive about the meeting and they did not want the 'true revolutionaries' to know about it until afterwards.

Matveev, wearing his uniform as a reserve lieutenant in the Zemstvos Hussars,[21] was given the role of meeting the delegates arriving at Millionnaya Street. The well of the staircase was crowded with armed cadet officers, and the Duma men threw off their fur coats there and climbed the shallow-stepped granite staircase, with its elaborate wrought-iron bannister, to the apartment landing where Matveev was waiting to show them into the drawing room,[22] warmed by a roaring fire.

The room had been prepared to provide an informal setting. The settees and armchairs were arranged so that Michael, when he took the meeting, would be sitting in a tall-backed easy chair, facing a semicircle of delegates. He remained outside the drawing room while the others assembled, and after Rodzyanko asked that the meeting should not begin until the arrival of Guchkov and Shulgin, who were bringing 'important news'.[23]

* He was not a nephew, but first cousin once removed; Bimbo was the brother of Michael's brother-in-law Sandro.

Within fifteen minutes or so there were a dozen men in the drawing room. Seven of them were ministers in the newly named Provisional Government and five were Duma deputies, led by Rodzyanko. Before the meeting it had been agreed at the Tauride Palace that Lvov and Rodzyanko, now supported by the majority of the government and by the rump of the Duma Committee, would press Michael to abdicate the throne to which he had just succeeded, and that Milyukov would argue the minority view, that he should exercise the supreme powers.

It had also been agreed that, whichever side prevailed, those advancing the losing argument would then withdraw from the government.[24] Put another way, if Michael refused to abdicate, he would be left with only a foreign minister and, assuming the absent Guchkov's support, a war minister. The prime minister, and the other seven ministers, would all resign. The president of the State Duma, Rodzyanko, would not take office in any replacement Cabinet.

Michael would be Emperor with no government and surrounded by mutinous troops who had every reason to want him dead. However, as Rodzyanko would blandly comment, the decision none the less would be one for Michael alone.

At 9.45 a.m., with the delegates deciding that they could no longer wait for Guchkov and Shulgin, Matveev was told that they were ready to begin the meeting.[25] The drawing-room door opened, ministers and deputies all stood up, and in walked the man being hailed across the country as His Majesty Emperor Michael II. He moved around the room to greet each one individually. 'We shook hands and exchanged courtesies', Kerensky would remember.[26]

Then Michael sat down, looked around the men facing him and the meeting began.

TWENTY-FIVE

Playing for Time

Michael had expected a meeting at which he would be sitting in his chair as Regent, not as Emperor, for taking the crown was a possibility he had never considered. The removal of Alexis from the succession was so contrary to every ambition hitherto held for him that it hardly seemed credible. Alexandra had been obsessed with 'Baby's rights', had fought like a tigress to protect them and had brought Russia to the brink of ruin in consequence. Now, in a moment, Alexis had been swept aside.

But could Nicholas do that? The fact was that he had, and that same fact faced everyone at Millionnaya Street that morning. Nothing could change that. Nicholas was on his train, trundling back to Mogilev. He had left Pskov some eight hours before, at 1 a.m., and he would not arrive at Stavka until 8.20 that Friday evening.[1] For the second time in a week, Nicholas had vanished at the height of a crisis leaving chaos in his wake. Four days earlier, when it might have made a difference, he had refused to name Michael as Regent in Petrograd; now, without discussion, he had handed him the crown.

Whatever Michael's suspicions about the mood of the new government which came to him, he would quickly learn that the majority had already decided that their own survival required that he give up the throne. They would pretend that it was his decision, but they would make sure that it was the one they had already made for him. Nekrasov, the transport minister, had drafted an abdication manifesto at the Tauride Palace, ready to be produced when Michael formally gave them what they had come to get.

Just before the meeting began, it seems that Michael had been alerted to the political manoeuvring within the Tauride Palace, for apparently Bimbo knew something of it and had warned Michael, if only in general terms, when he saw him that morning.[2] Thus, on walking into the drawing room, Michael had good reason to look, as Kerensky put it, 'much perturbed'.[3]

Although everyone stood up as he entered, it seems that there was a collective decision not to address Michael as 'Your Majesty' but as 'Your Highness', a distinction which underlined the point of the meeting: that the purpose of the majority was to convince Michael that he could not reign.

Looking around the room Michael saw a group of men who were

exhausted, unshaven, bedraggled and, as Prince Lvov would put it, unable even to think straight any more.[4] Kerensky would admit that he himself had been 'near collapse'. At dawn the previous day he had walked back to his apartment at 29 Tverskaya, and had fallen into bed, lying there for two or three hours in 'a semi-delirious state',[5] but that was the only rest he had managed since Monday morning. Milyukov was so exhausted that he 'was falling asleep where he sat . . . He would start, open his eyes, then begin to fall asleep again'.[6]

In some cases it was not exhaustion but terror that marked the faces of the men from the Duma. Dread of the Soviet would be the recurring theme of the morning's discussions, and that fear would be heightened by Kerensky, the only man in the new government who could claim to speak for the mob. Kerensky, a master of the theatrical posture, would convince some there that he also was 'terrified' and that at any moment a gang of armed men might break in and murder the Grand Duke, if not the rest of them.[7]

Fear was a weapon, and it was the principal weapon which Rodzyanko himself would use that morning. As he had done in his wire conversations with the army commanders, he drew a black picture of the world outside the windows, where civil war loomed, and a bloodbath threatened. He himself was terrified, though there was no sign of this in Rodzyanko's own account, written as it was from the safety of his memoirs. The only man fearing for his life at Millionnaya Street, as he preferred to remember it, was Michael:

> *It was quite clear to us that the Grand Duke would have reigned only a few hours, and that this would have led to colossal bloodshed in the precincts of the capital, which would have degenerated into general civil war. It was clear to us that the Grand Duke would have been killed immediately, together with all his adherents, for he had no reliable troops at his disposal then, and could not sustain himself by armed support. The Grand Duke asked me outright whether I could guarantee his life if he acceded to the throne, and I had to answer in the negative.*[8]

Quite why Michael, with the Order of St George and the Order of St Vladimir pinned to his chest, should look to a fearful Rodzyanko to guarantee his life is not easy to answer, nor is it immediately apparent why Michael was willing to risk being killed as Regent but not as Emperor, since he had no more troops at breakfast than were available to him in mid-morning. However, Rodzyanko survived to write his memoirs, and Michael did not.

Milyukov, with Guchkov not yet arrived, was the sole spokesman for those who believed that Rodzyanko and Lvov were leading the government to ruin. Rousing himself, he argued that it would be immeasurably more difficult in the long term if the established order was simply abandoned, for in his reasoning the 'frail craft' of the Provisional Government alone, without a monarch, would soon be sunk 'in the ocean of national disorder'.[9]

As he advanced his case the combative Milyukov progressively found himself fighting against a babble of angry voices; all idea of a measured debate had been swept away in a torrent of noisy argument. To latecomer Shulgin, now arrived with Guchkov, 'Milyukov seemed unwilling, or unable, or afraid to stop talking ... This man, usually so polite and self-controlled, did not let anybody else speak, and interrupted those who tried to answer him.'[10]

Milyukov said afterwards: 'I was amazed that my opponents, instead of producing arguments of principle, had started intimidating the Grand Duke. I saw that Rodzyanko was still in a blue funk. The others were also frightened by what was happening ... I admitted that my opponents may have been right. Perhaps indeed those present and the Grand Duke himself were in danger. But we were playing for high stakes – for the whole of Russia – and we had to take a risk, however great it was.'[11]

Part of that risk might have been avoided if, as Milyukov saw it, the succession of Michael had been presented as a *fait accompli*, with the Soviet having to confront the fact, rather than the prospect, but that aim had been frustrated at the Warsaw station by Guchkov and Shulgin, giving the extremists time to gather strength in opposition, and indeed to call for Michael's arrest as they were to do later that day.

Guchkov and Shulgin had not helped their own cause by their premature disclosure of the manifesto, though in fairness they could not have known beforehand that the Provisional Government had shifted its ground in the hours in which they had been away. But after the incident at the railway station the odds had shifted even further in favour of the 'defeatist' and frightened majority.

Tereshchenko, twenty-nine, and now the new government's finance minister, was one of those whose views were apparently swayed by threats that morning. Late in the meeting he motioned Shulgin to leave the room for a moment. 'I can't go on anymore ... I will shoot myself ... what's to be done?' he moaned.

Shulgin, still bewildered by the change in the mood of the government, asked him: 'Tell me, are there any units we can rely on?'

'No, not one.'

'But I saw some sentries downstairs ...'

'That's only a few people. Kerensky is terrified ... he is afraid ... any moment someone could break in ... there are gangs on the prowl. Oh, Lord!'[12]

In the latter stages it was the republican Kerensky, more than Rodzyanko or Prince Lvov, who dominated the proceedings. In effect the Soviet spokesman, his references to the risks of 'an internal civil war', appeared more menace than warning. There was also an oblique personal threat to Michael, when he ended dramatically: 'I cannot answer for Your Highness's life.'[13] When Guchkov attempted to support Milyukov, his intervention 'made Kerensky almost beside himself with passion, and provoked him to a torrent of invective and threats which terrified everyone there,' Paléologue would record next day, after hearing accounts of the drama at Millionnaya Street.[14]

During the whole of the meeting, Michael had sat sprawled in his armchair, saying little himself. To Kerensky he seemed 'embarrassed' by what was going on, and then 'to grow more weary and impatient'.[15] That would hardly be surprising; there was little prospect of winning sustained support from these quarrelling and frightened men, and this divided and helpless government.

After more than two hours of wrangling, there was little more that could usefully be said, and Michael calmly rose and announced that he would like to consider the whole matter privately with just two of the men in the room, and that he would then make his decision.

Kerensky stirred uneasily, thinking that this meant that Michael would retire with Milyukov and Guchkov, his natural supporters; to his surprise the choice fell on Prince Lvov and Rodzyanko, and 'a weight fell off my mind, as I thought to myself that if he wants to speak with those two, it means that he has already decided to abdicate'.[16] Because the gathered delegates had agreed in advance that they would not permit private discussions, Rodzyanko at first demurred, glancing at Kerensky as he did so. In fact, since it seemed now to his advantage, Kerensky immediately supported the idea. 'I felt that since the Tsar's brother was about to make such a momentous decision, we should not refuse him this request, and I said so,'[17] though it is unlikely that he would have been so gallant if the choice had been Milyukov and Guchkov, as he had first feared.

Kerensky's restrained portrait of his own part that morning was, however, not quite that reported to the French ambassador Paléologue by one of those present, probably Milyukov. Paléologue's diary entry recounts that, as Michael was making for the next room, Kerensky leaped in front of him and shouted: 'Promise us not to consult your wife!' Michael, reported Paléologue, replied with a smile: 'Don't worry, Aleksandr Fedorovich, my wife isn't here at the moment, she stayed behind at Gatchina.'[18]

The choice of Lvov and Rodzyanko, both committed to the idea that Michael's accession would make matters worse rather than better, may seem, as Kerensky believed, its own evidence of Michael's mind by this stage; but there were more obvious reasons for the decision. Lvov was the prime minister and the man Michael himself had recommended for the post, and Rodzyanko was president of the Duma and a man he had long trusted.

There could never be a question of Michael, who believed completely in constitutional government, seeking a private meeting with anyone other than the two most senior figures present. In any case, there were other reasons why he should want to talk privately to Lvov and Rodzyanko.

First, given the atmosphere in the drawing room, it was clear that any discussion initiated by him would lead only to further noisy dispute and he had heard quite enough of that already; second, it was only natural that he should want reassurances from Lvov and Rodzyanko that the Provisional Government could indeed restore order and secure the conditions necessary for elections to a constituent assembly, for if that were not so, then all that had taken place was no more than hot air.

In his conversations with the two army commanders that morning, Rodzyanko had stressed that the commitment to a constituent assembly 'does not exclude the possibility of the dynasty returning to power',[19] and this is certainly a point he would have made strongly to Michael, encouraging him to believe that his abdication would not necessarily be fatal to the crown. Presented as a short-term expediency, it was a plausible argument.

Michael had little real choice in the matter. From the outset he had been in the position of a man damned if he did and damned if he didn't. However powerfully Milyukov argued his case, there was never any real possibility of Michael dismissing the views of Lvov and Rodzyanko since without their support there was no chance of any alternative government coming into being.

Michael stayed behind for a few moments after Lvov and Rodzyanko returned to the smoke-filled drawing room, then conferred briefly with Matveev, who throughout that morning had been lingering outside the meeting room, listening as best he could to what was being said. The choice put to Michael was stark: if he abdicated, the Provisional Government would be able to restore order and pursue the war against Germany to a victorious conclusion; if he ruled, the majority of the new government would immediately resign and there would be a civil war, with the risk that Russia would be compelled to seek peace with Germany.

Political reality demanded that he had to abdicate immediately, as the majority expected. He had been given command of a ship in which the crew had mutinied and the officers had taken to the lifeboats. It was hardly a surprise, therefore, when Michael walked back into the drawing room and announced that, in the circumstances, he had to follow the advice of the two senior men present.

Or words to that effect. Nothing was written down, and afterwards no one could remember precisely what he said.[20] However, those present in the drawing room understood that he had decided to abdicate, for in the black-and-white world of Petrograd the issue was a straight choice between taking or giving up the throne. Shulgin would add dramatic effect to his later account by saying that Michael wept,[21] though no one else remembered that; on the contrary, what was remarked upon at the time was Michael's composure.

Already Nekrasov was fingering the abdication manifesto in his pocket: '*We by God's Mercy, Michael II, Emperor and Autocrat of all the Russias* . . .'[22] After that preamble the rest could be filled simply enough. It would need a few flourishes, perhaps, to give the required sense of occasion, but essentially 'abdicate' was the word that mattered. Allowing five minutes or so for regretful comments, and funereal courtesies, Michael's manifesto could be signed by lunch-time, and posted around the city by late afternoon.

In fact, it would turn out to be rather more complicated than that.

With Michael's statement, and the apparent resolution of the issues debated all morning, the meeting adjourned, but without getting his signature on anything. Michael showed no signs of hurry, however, intimating that he would deal with these matters after lunch. Princess Putyatina now emerged on to the scene as hostess, inviting those who wished to do so to join her in the dining room.[23] It was an unexpected development, but in their surprise no one seemed able to voice an objection.

Some half-dozen of the fourteen men in the drawing room accepted the invitation and shuffled in to sit at the lunch table. These included Prince Lvov, Kerensky, Shulgin, Nekrasov and the finance minister Tereshchenko. Princess Putyatina sat at the head of the table, with Michael at her right hand, and Prince Lvov beside him. Matveev and Johnson were also present.[24] Rodzyanko, the other ministers, and the remaining Duma deputies left, their victory delayed.

Michael now had an opportunity to find out what had happened at Pskov. He spoke across the table to Shulgin. 'Tell me, how did my brother conduct himself?'

'His Majesty was very pale but at the same time very calm and resigned . . . Amazingly calm.'[25]

Shulgin then told him the full story, including Nicholas's reasons for bypassing his son. Michael made no comment. The references to Alexis's health he understood without need of explanation, and he made no open criticism of his brother. In front of Michael, no one else did either.

Nothing further was said about the meeting that morning, until lunch was finished, and Princess Putyatina withdrew. The members of the delegation present were all waiting for the moment when Michael would turn to the question of his manifesto and Nekrasov fingered again the abdication document in his pocket.

Matveev, sitting quietly at the table, now asserted himself. Nekrasov's version of the proposed manifesto was produced, glanced at, and politely returned to him.[26] The delegation members shuffled uneasily as they began to realise that Matveev was not quite the nonentity they had assumed, and that the manifesto was not yet the cut-and-dried document that they expected to take away with them after lunch. Michael suggested that Matveev should help 'to set down in proper form what had taken place'.[27]

Matveev was advising Michael, and his first piece of advice was to point out 'that in preparing the Act it was necessary to have before us the original abdication of the Tsar and the *Fundamental Laws*'.[28] This was lawyer talk, and it was also awkward.

An embarrassed Prince Lvov knew from Shulgin that he had handed over the original manifesto for safe-keeping to someone from the transport ministry. It was still hidden under a pile of dusty magazines in the office of the transport commissioner Bublikov,[29] but no one in the government knew that. And where could they get hold of a Code of Laws?

Since Michael had Matveev, they would now need their own legal expert. The man they settled on was Vladimir Nabokov – at forty-seven the lawyer who would that night find himself appointed Head of Chancellery – and Prince Lvov volunteered to call him. He was an acceptable choice; Michael knew of him, for Nabokov's sister Nadine was one of Natasha's closest friends and her daughter Sophie was a playmate of little George.[30] Lvov tried Nabokov's office first in the General Staff building, then his home number. He was at neither, but his wife offered to find him. She traced her husband promptly to the home of General Manikin, Nabokov's chief, and Nabokov promised to leave immediately.[31]

At almost that very moment a telegram was sent to Michael from Sirotino, a station some 275 miles from Pskov. Nicholas, having 'awoken far beyond Dvinsk',[32] had suddenly remembered that he had neglected to mention to his brother that he was the new Emperor. He hastily scribbled out a telegram to Michael; despatched at 2.56 p.m. and addressed to 'Imperial Majesty, Petrograd', it read:

> *To His Majesty the Emperor Michael: Recent events have forced me to decide irrevocably to take this extreme step. Forgive me if it grieves you and also for no warning – there was no time. Shall always remain a faithful and devoted brother. Now returning to HQ where hope to come back shortly to Tsarskoe Selo. Fervently pray God to help you and our country. Your Nicky.*[33]

As so often during the past days, Nicholas had acted when it was too late to matter.

There were no cabs or cars available to Vladimir Nabokov, but hurrying along the crowded Nevsky Prospekt, past crowds burning the imperial emblems torn down from the Anichkov Palace on the corner of the Fontanka, he reached Millionnaya Street just before 3 p.m. After briefing him for a few moments on the events of that morning, Prince Lvov explained that 'the draft of the Act had been outlined by Nekrasov, but the effort was incomplete and not entirely satisfactory, and since everyone was dreadfully tired and in no condition to think straight, not having slept all night, they requested that I undertake the task'.[34]

But as Matveev had already made clear, they could not begin without the Code of Laws and the abdication manifesto. Nabokov had neither with him, and knew nothing of the manifesto, but he agreed with Matveev that the *Fundamental Laws* were essential. After discussion it was decided that he should call the distinguished constitutional jurist Baron Nolde – 'that astute and exacting specialist in state law'[35] – at his office in Palace Square and ask him to come at once to Millionnaya Street, bringing the first volume of the Code of Laws, so that they could all start work. Baron Nolde hurried from his office, and reached the apartment ten minutes later.

He, Nabokov and Shulgin now retreated into the bedroom of Princess Putyatina's young daughter, with only a small school desk at which to write. The problems which immediately confronted the two lawyers were precisely those which had exercised Michael that day. There was nothing to justify Nicholas abdicating on behalf of his son; at the same time he had done just that, and circumstances made its undoing impossible. It was the same problem all over again: political expediency in conflict with constitutional law.

This conflict clearly exercised Nabokov and Nolde no less than it had Michael and Matveev, for as Nabokov recognised, Nicholas's abdication manifesto as published contained 'an incurable, intrinsic flaw'. Thus, as Nabokov sat down at the school desk, he knew that the whole business made doubtful law, and that 'from the beginning Michael must necessarily have felt this'. Rightly, he judged that 'it significantly weakened the position of the supporters of the monarchy. No doubt it also influenced Michael's reasoning.'[36]

That said, Nabokov and Nolde were left in the same position as Michael: the fact was that Alexis *had* been bypassed and he could not now be restored in any practical sense. Besides, if Nicholas's abdication had to be overturned in that respect, might it not be overturned in its entirety? That was unthinkable.

It being swiftly clear that legal considerations were not the issue, Nabokov and Nolde concentrated on the task they had been brought in to complete: the drafting of a political manifesto which would appear lawful. The result after several hours was a document which even they would later casually describe as 'an abdication manifesto'.[37] Curiously, for those who bothered to read it, of the 122 Russian words meticulously written out at the school desk by Nabokov 'in his beautiful handwriting'[38] the one word which did not appear was 'abdicate'.

When Nabokov and Nolde began their task, handing out drafts of the manifesto to Matveev for perusal and approval by Michael, they began with the same formula used by Nekrasov: '*We, by God's mercy, Michael II, Emperor and Autocrat of all the Russias* . . .'[39] They started off therefore on the premise that Michael was Emperor, and that in abdicating he 'commanded' the people to obey the authority of the Provisional Government, in which he was vesting his powers until a constituent assembly determined the form of government. This formula gave legitimacy to the new government, which otherwise was simply there by licence of the Soviet. No one had elected the Provisional Government; its ministers had simply appointed themselves and in that respect it had no more authority, and arguably less, than the Soviet Executive, which could at least claim to have been endorsed by elected soldier and worker delegates.

Michael could make the new government official and legal, as no one else could, and therefore it was important that his manifesto be issued by him as Emperor. If he was not Emperor, he had no power to vest, and no authority to 'command' anyone. This political necessity therefore overrode the flaws in his succession. The new government needed Michael to give up the throne, but first they needed him to take it.

It was not that simple. Michael discussed the draft manifesto with Matveev, then came back into the room to say that he would not agree to it in the style presented. 'He did not wish the manifesto to mention him as a monarch who had accepted the throne';[40] since he was accepting the throne conditionally, it could not be said that he had accepted it yet, and therefore in the meantime he was not prepared to call himself Emperor. But whatever the form of words applied to his succession – whether conditional acceptance or temporary refusal – they amounted to the same thing: he was not abdicating. In the course of the afternoon, Michael went to the school desk several times to remind Nabokov of that.[41] Nothing was final. Rodzyanko had said so, and Michael was putting that on paper.

It was an extraordinary answer to an extraordinary problem. There was no precedent. If Michael was Emperor he could only reign or abdicate; he could not suspend the crown; 'the Russian laws of succession . . . do not permit the Imperial Throne to remain vacant',[42] but Michael said it was, temporarily. He could not do that. Like death, abdication or renunciation of the throne was permanent. At the same time, since Nicholas lawfully could abdicate only for himself, then Michael equally could abdicate only for himself, not for the other Grand Dukes in line of succession. In that case, the next in line – Kirill, on the face of it – would immediately become Emperor in his stead. No one ever suggested that, for it would have been to defeat the entire purpose of the meeting.

Thus 'temporary' was the only answer, and that was the position Michael insisted upon, helped perhaps by the fact that the law was being heavily bent all around him, and so an added twist was not likely to make much difference. The result was a manifesto which would make him Emperor and non-Emperor, past Emperor but potential future Emperor, all at the same time.

It is a measure of the confusion then obtaining and of the impossibility of reconciling law and political necessity that Nabokov and Nolde finally presented a manifesto which, if it ever came to it, would survive the scrutiny of a constitutional court for no longer than the time it took to read, which is to say about ten minutes, if taken very slowly.

> *A heavy burden has been thrust upon me by the will of my brother, who has given over to me the Imperial Throne of Russia at a time of unprecedented warfare and popular disturbances.*
>
> *Inspired like the entire people by the idea that what is most important is the welfare of the country, I have taken a firm decision to assume the Supreme Power only if such be the will of our great people, whose right it is to establish the form of government and the new basic laws of the Russian state by universal suffrage through its representatives in the Constituent Assembly.*
>
> *Therefore, invoking the blessing of God, I beseech all the citizens of Russia to obey the Provisional Government, which has come into being on the initiative of the Duma and is vested with all the plenitude of power until the Constituent Assembly, to be convoked with the least possible delay by universal suffrage, direct, equal and secret voting, shall express the will of the people by its decision on the form of government. Signed: MICHAEL.*[43]

By this manifesto Michael was accepting the throne 'thrust upon him' but only if his acceptance was confirmed by a future Constituent Assembly. At the same time he was vesting powers in the Provisional Government which were not his to give, if he was not yet Emperor. He had changed the imperious word 'command' which appeared in the first version into merely 'beseech' and he had removed all use of the imperial 'We', as well as the original preamble describing him as 'Emperor and Autocrat',[44] but he had signed it with an imperial *Michael*, rather than a grand ducal *Michael Aleksandrovich*.

Politically it was brilliant, for it could mean whatever it was required to mean. The Provisional Government had its powers and was now legitimised by the new Emperor even though he said he was not yet the Emperor but might be; the Soviet could be told that Michael had been the Emperor but had abdicated though he had not; Michael had conditionally accepted the crown while temporarily refusing it; and Russia had become a republic while remaining a monarchy.

Legally it was nonsense but as Nabokov was to explain later, 'we were not concerned with the juridical force of the formula, but only its moral and political meaning'.[45] In saying so, Nabokov clearly did not remember the afternoon at Millionnaya Street with any great pride.*

Rodzyanko and Kerensky had returned to Millionnaya Street by the time the all-things-to-all-men manifesto had been finalised, and they were present when Michael sat down at the school desk and put his signature on the document, which, as Nolde would recall, 'was in essence the only constitution during the period of existence of the Provisional Government';[46] Nabokov also recognised it as 'the only act which defined the limits of the Provisional Government's authority'.[47] When Milyukov was asked where the government derived its authority, he replied, 'We have received it, by inheritance, from the Grand Duke Michael.'[48]

To Nabokov, standing beside the school desk, Michael 'appeared rather embarrassed and somewhat disconcerted' as he came into the room, sat down, and took up the pen. 'I have no doubt that he was under a heavy strain, but he retained complete self-composure.'[49] Nolde was also impressed, describing Michael as having 'acted with irreproachable tact and nobility'.[50] Shulgin, watching him in the room, thought to himself 'what a good constitutional monarch he would make'.[51] Even Paléologue, hitherto unimpressed by Michael, would praise him next day, writing in his diary that his composure and dignity never once deserted him' and that Michael's 'patriotism, nobility and self-sacrifice were very touching'.[52]

The theatrical outburst, predictably, was left to Kerensky. 'Believe me', he cried out, 'that we will carry the precious vessel of your authority to the Constituent Assembly without spilling a single drop.'[53] In fact, he would spill it all, but that no one could then foresee.

When the delegation returned to the Tauride Palace the arguments over the manifesto continued. Professor Lomonosov had arrived from the

* Nabokov's account was published in 1921; he was murdered in Berlin in 1922 by a Russian reactionary. His son, also called Vladimir Nabokov, was destined to become a world-famous writer, and author of *Lolita*.

transport ministry with Nicholas's original abdication, which was to be printed jointly with Michael's manifesto. Should these be presented as the Acts of two Emperors? How was Michael's to be described? Because it was a political rather than a legal document, at midnight there was still no clear answer to the question of whether Michael had refused the crown, or whether he had abdicated, though curiously no attention seems to have been paid to the obvious point that he had done neither. 'Foaming at the mouth, Milyukov and Nabokov tried to prove that the abdication of Michael could only have legal meaning if it was recognised that he had been Emperor.'[54] It was not until 2 a.m. that agreement was reached, and Nabokov set about the final form in which the manifesto would appear, in the form judged best to appease the Soviet. At 3.50 a.m. it was taken away to the printers.[55]

The final confusion in the Duma rooms at the Tauride Palace was understandable. Michael's manifesto was an extraordinary document produced in extraordinary circumstances; its aim was to buy time, but its meaning was ambiguous. But would that matter? The next few days, even the next hours, would be decisive in determining what happened thereafter. The Provisional Government hoped, as did Michael, that it would restore order and create the conditions in which a constituent assembly could be elected, composed largely of men like themselves. Six months is a long time, and if Russia won great victories in the summer, the mood of the country might be very different. Old loyalties might reassert themselves, and a constitutional monarchy might well have the overwhelming support of the people.

Given that scenario, Michael's manifesto could be seen not as the surrender of the throne to the mob, but as a shrewd holding operation which kept the monarchy in being until the election, hopefully, of a moderate constituent assembly, and better days. The sovereign powers passed over to the Provisional Government were not abandoned but delegated for a specified and limited period of time, and in the interim the manifesto preserved Russia as a monarchy.

Besides, as Michael might wryly have reflected, the idea of having his succession confirmed by being 'elected' Tsar was not without precedent. The first Romanov, his namesake Michael I, had been elected by a national assembly in 1613. After 300 years, a second 'election' would change the Romanovs from autocrats into constitutional monarchs, but it would also strengthen their position as the ruling house. No one on March 3 could know that an assembly would vote to retain the monarchy, but equally no one could know that it would not.

Following these events in the Crimea, Princess Cantacuzène was optimistic, saying, 'we looked forward to the probability of the Constituent

Assembly being in favour of a constitutional monarchy'.[56] In *The Times* of London the judgement of Robert Wilton, that newspaper's respected correspondent in Petrograd, was that 'perhaps in the end it will be all for the best'. Accepting that while 'at present we must be content to go on with the new Provisional Government until quieter days supervene', he concluded that were it possible to bring about the Constituent Assembly 'there could be little doubt as to the election of Grand Duke Michael to the Throne by an overwhelming majority'.[57]

A less generous view came from Michael's brother. Just after 9.30 that evening he was settling back into his house at Mogilev when Alekseev arrived with Rodzyanko's version of the events at Millionnaya Street. Nicholas wrote in his diary for March 3: 'Misha, it appears, has abdicated. His manifesto ends by kowtowing to the Constituent Assembly, whose elections will take place in six months. God knows who gave him the idea of signing such rubbish.'[58]

Given the chaos which he himself had created, and the impossible position in which he had placed his brother, his effrontery had an epic quality about it. Certainly, when he said much the same to his brother-in-law Sandro a few days later, Sandro confessed himself to be 'speechless'.[59]

But what, finally, did Michael wearily say himself of that day? His diary entry for Friday, March 3, 1917, was breathtaking in its brevity.

> *At 6 a.m. we were woken up by the telephone. It was a message from the new Minister of Justice Kerensky. It stated that the complete Council of Ministers would come to see me in an hour's time. But actually they arrived only at half-past nine a.m.*[60]

And that was all, from the man who woke up that morning thinking he was about to become Regent, and went to bed having been Emperor.

TWENTY-SIX

Retreat to Gatchina

Michael left Millionnaya Street next morning, Saturday, March 4, at eleven o'clock, the first time he had set foot outside the apartment in four days. The previous afternoon, while waiting for the final draft of his manifesto, he had sent off a courier with a hastily pencilled note to Natasha to tell her that he expected to return next morning. 'Awfully busy and extremely exhausted,' he had scribbled. 'Will tell you many interesting things. I kiss you tenderly. All yours, Misha.'[1]

There was certainly no point in remaining in Petrograd. He had no further role to play, and was not likely to have one until and if a constituent assembly decided to support a constitutional monarchy, and that could not be for several months hence. The new government had its mandate, and needed no more.

As Michael left the apartment and stepped out on to the landing, the first sight to greet him was as surprising as it was agreeable. Lining the staircase leading down to the street was a guard of honour made up of the officers and cadets stationed in the building. There was an order to present arms and as Michael, saluting, walked down the stairs and outside into his waiting car, a cry of 'Long Live Russia'.[2]

But what might follow? Would there be hostile demonstrations at the station, agitators demanding his arrest, as the Soviet executive had done only yesterday? The Soviet leaders had resolved 'to arrest the Romanov family'; in Michael's case this was not to be house arrest but 'an actual arrest', though having taken him away the Soviet intended 'to announce officially that he is subjected only to the surveillance of the revolutionary army'.[3]

Michael's manifesto, or more probably the 'abdication' gloss put on it by the new government, was sufficient to strike out the Soviet demands directed against Michael, though not against his brother; passions were calmed and instead, Michael found himself going home in something akin to triumph. Followed by another car filled with armed cadets, he and Johnson were driven off to board a special train arranged for them at the Baltic station. Joined by General Yuzefovich, his old chief of staff, he stepped out of his car and into a station 'overcrowded with soldiers ... everywhere were machine-guns and boxes of ammunition'. Flanked by his armed escort he walked to his waiting train, and to another reception of the kind which he had not expected. 'A military detachment was lined up by my carriage and I greeted them, and a gathered crowd cheered me.'[4]

The scene at the Baltic station, with saluting mutineers and applauding bystanders, was not without its irony. Here was evidence that the decision taken at Millionnaya Street, difficult though it had been, was the right one, at least in the short term. Now Michael was being hailed, not hunted, and if Lvov, Rodzyanko, Kerensky and their other supporters at Millionnaya Street had been present at Michael's departure for Gatchina it would have given them immense satisfaction. 'It seems that order in general is being established,' Michael would note that night in his diary.[5]

The restoration of order, with all its consequences for the conduct of the war, had been the deciding factor for Michael in the meeting at Millionnaya Street. That evening, in explanation of his manifesto, he had told Princess Putyatina that it would 'calm the passions of the populace, make the soldiers and workers who had mutinied see reason, and re-establish the shattered discipline of the army'.[6] He said much the same on his return to Gatchina on Saturday afternoon. Bimbo's brother George, still taking refuge in Nikolaevskaya Street, wrote afterwards that Michael 'fears that if he is proclaimed Emperor at once, without knowing the wish of the country, matters will never calm down . . .'[7]

Natasha later told Colonel Boris Nikitin, a staff officer with the Savage Division, and one of Michael's old friends, that a decisive factor in Michael's judgement at Millionnaya Street was the bypassing of Alexis; Nikitin himself felt that Michael had been in 'a deadly grip' and thought that 'a government which was inclined against him would never give him the chance to work'.[8] There was truth in that.

For the moment, however, Michael was simply glad to be away from the madness that was Petrograd. 'I sighed with relief,' he wrote in his diary, 'when at last I was home.'[9] Next day he went with his family to the palace church for Sunday service, and they all took a walk in the gardens before lunch. Afterwards he and Natasha spent the afternoon on a sleigh ride in the Game Reserve. 'When we met soldiers, many of them did not salute me,' he noted with disapproval. 'After tea we read the papers which were printed today after a week's interruption.'[10]

Off the streets that week because of strikes, the Petrograd newspapers returned with their first reports of what had been happening in the past dramatic days. Almost without exception they presented Michael's manifesto in the way that the government intended. Nicholas's abdication manifesto was followed immediately by Michael's 'conditional' manifesto, though they were treated as if both were the same, their intentional juxtaposition helping that effect. What counted was satisfying the appetite of the Soviet; it was a case therefore of telling them what they wanted to hear.

In four newspapers – *Birzhevye Vedomosti, Den, Petrogradsky Listok*, and *Petrogradskaya Gazeta* – the headline was identical: 'Abdication of Grand Duke Michael Aleksandrovich'.[11] There was nothing in the text to support that, but the accompanying statement issued by the Provisional Government had used the word 'abdication' and that was enough to justify the headlines.*

From 'abdication' grew the assumption, fed by triumphant Soviet propaganda, that the monarchy was finished. Even the British and French ambassadors seemed to think in consequence that Russia was now a republic. Both were to be corrected by Milyukov, the new foreign minister: 'the Constituent Assembly alone will be qualified to change the political status of Russia,' he explained to Paléologue;[12] and when he overheard Buchanan referring to the new government as republican, 'he caught me up, saying that it was only a Provisional Government pending the decision of the future Constituent Assembly'.[13]

Correcting the impressions gathered by two experienced and senior ambassadors was one thing; it was quite another with the country at large. Michael had been wasting his time at the school desk at Millionnaya Street. What he had signed was not his conditional acceptance of the throne, but his abdication. Everyone knew that, because it said so in the newspapers. Some people, reading the manifesto, would say that he had 'refused the throne' rather than 'abdicated', but the effect was the same. What was intended as temporary was taken as permanent.

Some people would never forgive Michael for being Emperor but not being Emperor. Grand Duke George wrote to his wife that while 'Misha's manifesto seems to have calmed the republicans, the others are angry with him . . .'[14] The right-wing Duma member Vasily Maklakov, who was not at Millionnaya Street, called the manifesto 'strange and criminal . . . an act of lunacy or treason, had not the authors been qualified and patriotic lawyers'.[15] Princess Paley was another scornful of Michael, a 'feeble creature' and a 'weakling'.[16] In short, in some circles it would be Michael who would be blamed for the fall of the House of Romanov. 'Not us', was the cry, 'it was him.'

Not all thought so. Mossolov, former head of the Court Chancellery, observed that when Michael 'became Emperor, those Grand Dukes who were in Petrograd failed to rally around him'.[17] Bimbo cannot be counted among them, but certainly Paul, Kirill and Boris did nothing to help – none of them made contact with Michael on March 3.

But in casting blame, in the final analysis the ultimate responsibility lay with

* Only *Rech*, the newspaper supporting the Kadet party of which Milyukov was leader, avoided the word 'abdication'. Its headline called the manifesto a 'Declaration'.

Nicholas and, above all, Alexandra. Dimitri, brooding over events in faraway Persia, was in no doubt about that. 'The final catastrophe,' he judged, 'has been brought about by the wilful and short-sighted obstinacy of a woman. It has, naturally, swept away Tsarskoe Selo, and all of us at one stroke.'[18]

At Millionnaya Street the meeting had been conducted on the basis that Michael was working in concert with the Provisional Government; the ministers and Duma men were there as delegates seeking his help and co-operation in the difficult task of restoring order and lawful government. Michael's manifesto bound him, but it also bound the Provisional Government; the powers they inherited from the crown were temporary, until a constituent assembly determined the status of Russia. The assembly might opt for a republic; on the other hand it might confirm Michael as Emperor, or even elect to offer the crown to Alexis or to any other Grand Duke. Michael could end up as Emperor, Regent, or citizen – but until then the Provisional Government could not pre-empt a decision for which it had no mandate.

So it seemed on March 3. The reality was very different. Michael did not surrender the Romanovs; the new government would do that for him, yielding to the clamouring pressures of the Soviet. There would be no place in the new order for Grand Dukes; their rank, privilege, wealth, land, and even liberty were now at the disposal of a government in hock to the Soviet. The meeting at Millionnaya Street had not intended it, but long before any constituent assembly could come into being, the Romanovs would be out of business. Indeed, that seemed to be the case almost immediately, such was the weakness of the new government.

On his return to Gatchina Michael had assumed that he would continue with some role in the army, or at least do so when conditions allowed it. Technically he was still Inspector-General of Cavalry with the rank of colonel-general, but he was willing to serve in any capacity. He was to be immediately disappointed; there would be no job for him or any other Grand Duke. 'They do not allow us to go to the front fearing that we might start a counter-revolution,' wrote Grand Duke George from Gatchina, though no such idea has 'even crossed our minds.'[19] Perhaps so, but in Petrograd the government knew that the Soviet would never believe that. On April 5, one month after he signed his manifesto, Michael noted with scarcely concealed bitterness: 'Today I received my discharge from military service,' adding caustically 'with uniform'.[20] It was another pointer to the way reality had overtaken the meeting at Millionnaya Street.

Next day Michael and Natasha, together with his cousin George, went by train to Petrograd, Michael's first visit to the capital since the meeting in Millionnaya Street. They were intent on organising the removal of his furniture from the unoccupied Anichkov Palace before it was stolen by 'the workers'.[21] It would be the first and only time that Natasha would ever set foot in the palace in which Michael had been born.

As Michael settled into his carriage at Gatchina, 'a soldier came running to the compartment in which Misha sat by the window, and taking off his military fur cap, made a deep bow'. At the same station a group of soldiers stood to attention as Grand Duke George came up to them. 'They seemed delighted to talk to me,' he wrote. 'I could do anything with these soldiers who now want a republic with a Tsar!'[22]

For a Grand Duke to think it worth mentioning that soldiers had stood to attention when he approached them, or that one had bowed to Michael was a measure of just how greatly discipline had deteriorated in the army over the past month. The cause of the collapse in ordinary standards was not the revolution itself but the notorious Order No. 1 which had been issued on March 1 by the Petrograd Soviet. Formally addressed only to the garrison in the capital, the 'order' was widely interpreted as applying to all troops including those facing the Germans.

Guchkov, the new war minister,* found out about Order No. 1 only after it was published, and he failed to get it rescinded. On March 9, just a week after the Provisional Government came into being, he cabled General Alekseev: 'The Provisional Government has no real power of any kind and its orders are carried out only to the extent that this is permitted by the Soviet ... in the military department it is possible at present to issue only such orders as basically do not contradict the decisions of the above-mentioned Soviet.'[23]

The effect was disastrous, for it essentially made officers subservient to the dictates of 'soldier committees' established in every military formation, which took away the control of arms from officers, and in some instances dictated what military action might, or might not, be taken against the enemy. Off-duty soldiers were to be treated as civilians, with no requirement to salute or stand to attention; officers were 'prohibited' from speaking to soldiers rudely. In some units soldier committees insisted on electing their officers, and expelling those thought too strict or who were simply suspected of wanting to get on with the war.[24] It was small wonder that there was no place in the new 'democratic people's army' for Grand Dukes, including 'Uncle Nikolasha', whose reappointment by Nicholas as Supreme Commander had immediately been revoked by the new government.[25]

Paléologue estimated that there were well over a million deserters roaming Russia.[26] 'Units have been turned into political debating societies,' reported

* After the Millionnaya Street meeting, both Milyukov and Guchkov were persuaded to serve in the new government despite the original understanding that the 'losers' would not do so; neither remained long.

the British military observer Knox after a tour of the northern front. The infantry refused to allow the artillery to shoot at the enemy, and fraternised daily with the German soldiers facing them. In Petrograd 'the tens of thousands of able-bodied men in uniform who saunter about the streets without a thought of going to the front ... will be a disgrace for all time to the Russian people and its government'.[27]

Michael said much the same in a letter to his British friend Major Simpson: 'I want you to know that I am very much ashamed of my countrymen, who are showing too little patriotism ever since the revolution, and who are forgetting their agreement with the Allies, who have done so much to help them. But nonetheless I hope that the return of their good feelings will prevent them becoming traitors.'[28]

One consolation for Michael was that his own Savage Division had remained immune to the breakdown in discipline. Officers and men were as rock-steady after the February revolution as they had been before. He would also have been proud to know that when an officer returned from Petrograd to his Muslim regiment, he found that 'one question seemed to interest the men most – the fate of Grand Duke Michael'. When he replied that he was in Gatchina, and that he was 'safe for the present', the men would shake their heads and mumble, 'Allah preserve him – he is a real *dzhigit*. Why didn't he come to us when it all happened: we would never have given him up.'[29]

Almost from the first days of the new government the fifty-four-year-old Grand Duke George had been determined to get out of Russia at the first opportunity. He had accepted the emergence of the Provisional Government, because 'there is no doubt that the old regime could not work any more'. But what he had seen after that 'is enough to make your hair stand on end. I would like to leave the country at once,' he wrote to his wife.[30] He was also becoming anxious to leave Gatchina; 'Misha is so nice but his wife is so vengeful about the Romanovs ...'[31] George was not sure how much more he could take of her outbursts.

He wanted to go to England, where his wife, the daughter of the late King George I of Greece, had been stranded since the outbreak of war. Accordingly George was delighted when Michael agreed that he also would like to go to England. They had been walking together in the palace park at Gatchina, and afterwards George reported that 'Misha and I have decided to leave our poor country, never to return'.[32]

It was George who approached the British ambassador about going to England. In so doing he told Buchanan that he was also acting on Michael's behalf. He believed it would help his case. While his wife was closely related to the British royals,* as was Michael, George had no such connection in his own right. By joining Michael to his application he believed it would increase the chance of a favourable reply. George saw no hope for Russia. 'Everything was being confiscated ... and to think that these brutes will probably govern the country ... it will become a country of savages ... every decent person will leave.'[33]

Yet Michael was more sanguine about events. In many respects his own day-to-day life changed little as the days went by. He was free to move about within the Petrograd area, though not beyond without a permit. He could drive into the country in his Rolls-Royce or his new Packard, have friends to stay, and afford servants. Many townspeople still bowed to him in the street.[34] There were now guards posted in Nikolaevskaya Street but they were there only to keep away hooligans and looters. As even George admitted in one letter to his wife, 'the government is trying to be as polite as possible with us, I must own that they have been quite correct towards us'.[35]

Although Michael's annual income from the imperial purse had been stopped, as it had for all Romanovs, and his imperial train carriage requisitioned, he still had ample cash in the bank. He also received some income from his retained private holdings – including a sugar factory in the Ukraine as well as his Brasovo estate.

His real concern about Brasovo was that he could not go there. Just after the Millionnaya Street meeting the new government, in deference to the Soviet, had refused to grant him a travel permit.[36] The man a future constituent assembly might confirm as Emperor was thus immediately a prisoner in his own country. That alone made a mockery of the promises given by the Duma men on March 3.

None the less, while a disillusioned Grand Duke George schemed to get away to England, Michael and Natasha looked set to stay. Michael had bought a third house, on Baggout Street in Gatchina, and wanted to rent another in Kseniinsky Street, by the Priorate. 'The house has two floors, we're thinking of it for our servants,' he noted in his diary.[37]

It was true that on May 5 he would write to Major Simpson in England to say that 'as I had to resign and am forbidden to go to the Front, we are quietly staying here in Gatchina waiting patiently for permission to leave the country'.[38] But that same day he was at Baggout Street inspecting his new property, planning to enlarge the garden, and discussing with Natasha

* Grand Duchess Marie Georgieevna was niece of Dowager Queen Alexandra, whose brother George, elected to the Greek throne in 1863, was assassinated in Salonika in 1913. Marie's marriage was not, for her, a happy one; according to her grandson, Prince David Chavchavadze, she may have gone to England for a trial separation.

the final furnishings, due for delivery nine days later.[39] He wanted to go abroad, but only for a short time.

One reason why Michael was keen to go to England was his 'damned stomach'. There had been past discussions about having treatment in Britain but because of his military duties 'it was impossible for him to get to the great specialists who could have dealt with it radically'. His enforced idleness after March 1917 provided the opportunity to seek treatment and raised for Natasha 'the idea of sending him out for this purpose'.[40]

However, the impression George gave to the British ambassador in late March – as, indeed, he did to his wife – was that he and Michael were leaving Russia permanently. That served only to diminish their chances. That was not George's fault. It was just that Buckingham Palace was set against providing sanctuary for the Romanovs. King George V had his own problems.

The Romanov who posed the greatest difficulty for Britain was the ex-Tsar Nicholas, notwithstanding ties of family and friendship, and the loyalty he had shown as an ally. His downfall had been generally welcomed by liberals worldwide – by President Woodrow Wilson as well by British prime minister Lloyd George – but liberal sentiment was not the problem. Nicholas was a hated figure among British socialists, holding as they did an idealised view of the Russian revolution; what enraged them was the prospect that Nicholas might be offered refuge in England.

On March 9 Nicholas, escorted by Duma deputies, returned to Tsarskoe Selo on his imperial train.[41] One week after abdicating he began what was in effect a prison existence. He and his family were confined to their apartments in the palace, and restricted to a small area of the park outside. They were guarded day and night, and while the bayonets were protection from possible attacks by Soviet extremists they were also a bar to the outside world. The family were captives, under threat that they faced worse than house arrest. The Soviet continued to clamour for their confinement in the fortress of St Peter and St Paul.[42]

There were endless petty humiliations. Soldiers enjoyed taunting them; spectators at the outer railings would peer in, hissing and booing. It was an ordeal borne with dignity, and in the confidence that it was only temporary, and that they would shortly be sent abroad into exile. Pierre Gilliard, the Swiss tutor employed at Tsarskoe Selo, would remember that 'there was talk about our imminent transfer to England'.[43] The Provisional Government, worried by Soviet threats, was anxious to remove Nicholas from reach of the extremists; the British government appearing willing to take the whole family.[44]

Buckingham Palace thought otherwise. King George was increasingly worried about having Nicholas in England. It was not just that left-wing opinion was violently opposed to the ex-Tsar – 'bloody Nicholas' as they branded him – but that British royals were themselves facing increasing hostility over the fact that they were all of German descent. When even a dachshund could not venture into the street without risk of violence, the British king was understandably sensitive about being ranked as a German, with a German wife, and German relatives all around him. British republicanism was not deep-seated, but it was noisy.

It was very awkward, and by midsummer anti-German sentiment would mean a general name-change for the British royals. The Battenbergs – Alexandra's eldest sister Victoria was one of them* – and the Tecks would vanish to re-emerge as Mountbatten, Carisbrooke, Milford Haven, and Athlone; the British royal house re-christened itself the House of Windsor, by Order-in-Council, July 17, 1917.

With all this looming before him, King George was not pleased to find himself caught up in the problems of a Russian autocrat for whom there was little British sympathy. His objections were at first set aside by the British government, on the grounds that they could not go back on their offer. It was at this point that the names of Michael and Grand Duke George were added to the list of those seeking to come to England.

The British ambassador's cable to London about them on March 23 reopened Buckingham Palace's case against any Romanov coming to Britain.[45] 'I do trust that the whole question . . . will be reconsidered,' wrote the king's private secretary, Lord Stamfordham, to the British foreign secretary Balfour. 'It will be very hard on the King, and arouse much public comment if not resentment.'[46]

More shots came in from Buckingham Palace. 'The residence in this country of the ex-Emperor and Empress . . . would undoubtedly compromise the position of the King and Queen . . . we must be allowed to withdraw from the consent previously given.'[47] Yet George V was aware of the dangers facing his cousin: 'I fear that if poor Nicky goes into the Fortress of St Peter and St Paul he will not come out alive,' he wrote in his diary.[48]

Could the problem be solved by persuading Nicholas to go instead to France? Buchanan asked the question, and the British ambassador in Paris provided the reply. 'The Empress is not only a Boche by birth but in sentiment . . . She is regarded as a criminal or a criminal lunatic, and the ex-Emperor as a criminal from his weakness and submission to her promptings.'[49]

As the British agonised, the Provisional Government itself stepped away from the idea of sending Nicholas abroad. When word of the proposal to

* Princess Victoria Battenberg re-emerged as the Marchioness of Milford Haven.

London reached the Soviet, the new government was obliged to backtrack and to pledge that it would not give permission for any member of the imperial family to leave Russia without the agreement of the Soviet.[50] That conveniently allowed the British to let their invitation wither on the vine.

Unaware of the changed British attitude, Michael blamed the delays over his own application on the Provisional Government's unwillingness to do anything which would offend the Soviet. As the weeks slipped by, the Soviet seemed ever more demanding, as did the Bolsheviks, spurred on by Lenin and Trotsky, both now back from exile. If Michael could not get an exit permit to England, could he get one for Finland? In the circumstances it might be a useful 'insurance policy', though he remained adamant that he had no intention of leaving Russia permanently.

General Polovtsov, his old friend from the Savage Division, had recently been appointed commander of the Petrograd garrison and, on an official trip to Gatchina in June, Polovtsov had been contacted about a meeting by Michael's ADC Prince Vyazemsky.

'It was completely out of the question that I should openly visit the Grand Duke, whom I liked so much,' said Polovtsov. 'A plot would have at once been suspected, and that would have led to serious trouble both for him and for me but I was delighted to think that a secret meeting with his ADC could be arranged.' It took place in the Gatchina palace. In the course of this meeting Vyazemsky asked if Michael could be given a permit to cross into Finland with two cars.

Back in Petrograd, Polovtsov casually approached Kerensky. 'By the way, I have had a request from the Grand Duke Michael to deliver him a permit for crossing the frontier into Finland with his family in two cars. You always say that you admire him so much for his correctness and straightforwardness, so I expect you will have no objection . . .'

Kerensky looked at him through half-closed eyes. 'If I was not in Petrograd at the moment, what would you do?'

'I would deliver it on my own responsibility.'

'Then deliver it on your own responsibility,' Kerensky replied.[51]

There were, however, no such discreet concessions for Nicholas. After three months' imprisonment at Tsarskoe Selo no solution had been found to the question of what to do with the ex-Tsar and his family. In July an attempted coup by the Bolsheviks in Petrograd was to force a decision. The uprising, crushed by loyal government troops after two days of serious disorders, was a serious setback for the Bolsheviks and a humiliation for its leadership, with Lenin fleeing to Finland; but it also settled the immediate future of Nicholas. Believing that the Bolshevik failure might encourage a monarchist counter-revolution Kerensky decided to remove the ex-Tsar from the political chess board while there was opportunity to do so. He chose Tobolsk, in the Urals; his reason, he would say, was 'because it was an out-and-out backwater'.[52] The move was fixed for the early hours of Thursday August 1.

Michael heard about it 'only by accident' in the afternoon of the previous day. He drove at once to Petrograd with Natasha and Johnson, going directly to the Winter Palace, now home and office to Kerensky. Johnson was sent to persuade him to allow Michael to see his brother that night.[53]

Kerensky had taken to working at Alexander III's desk and sleeping in his bed; the red flag flying over the Winter Palace was also lowered whenever he was out of town, as had happened with the imperial standard in the old days.[54] It was as if Kerensky had become Tsar. The Provisional Government which had met Michael at Millionnaya Street was largely dissolved. Only three of the original ministers remained in office – Kerensky as prime minister, and minister of war and the navy; Tereshchenko, now foreign minister; and Nekrasov, who remained as transport minister. Milyukov and Guchkov had resigned in disgust within the first two months; Prince Lvov, utterly out of his depth, had quit as prime minister after the abortive Bolshevik uprising in July. The others had vanished. In their place came men from the Soviet, though no Bolsheviks, who refused to 'collaborate'.

It was around 7.30 in the evening when Johnson was led in to see Kerensky. A meeting between Michael and his brother was quickly agreed for midnight at Tsarskoe Selo, when Kerensky would also be there. After Johnson re-emerged into the palace square, Michael drove to Matveev's Fontanka apartment, where they all had dinner. At 10 p.m. Michael and Natasha drove to Tsarskoe Selo, stopping at Boris's English-style villa on Town Street; from there at midnight Michael was taken to the Alexander Palace by the Guard Commandant, Colonel Eugen Kobylinsky.[55] Entering through the kitchen, they went through the basement to the stairs leading to Nicholas's study. In the anteroom they were met by Kerensky.

It was five months since the brothers had seen each other, the last occasion being in February when Michael had gone to Tsarskoe Selo to beg Nicholas to make the concessions necessary to save the throne. Kerensky accompanied Michael into Nicholas's study; as the door closed behind them, little Alexis came into the anteroom and asked Kobylinsky: 'Is that Uncle Misha who has just come in?' Told that it was, he hid himself behind the door. 'I want to see him when he goes out,' said Alexis, peering through a crack in the door at the study beyond.[56]

In the study Kerensky retreated to a table and pretended to be absorbed in a book.[57] Privacy was impossible. However low their voices, he could hear everything they were saying. There was an awkward silence, then ten minutes of polite conversation in which they both contrived not to say anything of substance.

'How is Alix? How is mother?' asked Michael. The answers hardly mattered. 'They stood fidgeting all the while, and sometimes one would take hold of the other's hand or the buttons of his uniform.' After ten minutes Kerensky motioned that the meeting was over. 'May I see the children?' asked Michael, not knowing that Alexis was outside the door looking in.

'No,' answered Kerensky, 'I cannot prolong the interview.'[58]

Michael and Nicholas clasped hands, and murmured their goodbyes. Then Michael, his eyes filled with tears,[59] turned and left as he had come. 'I found that Nicky looked rather well,' was all that he said to his diary.[60]

He would never see his brother again.

TWENTY-SEVEN

Citizen Michael

Michael stayed at home on Monday, August 21, while Natasha and Johnson went by train to Petrograd. At 7 p.m. a column of trucks roared into Nikolaevskaya Street. Armed troops, some sixty in number, jumped down and were ordered into position around the house. As they lined up, Captain Andrei Kosmin, deputy chief of the Petrograd District accompanied by the local Gatchina commandant, walked to the front door, to be met by a startled Michael. They told him that on the orders of Kerensky he was now under arrest and confined to his house under guard.[1]

Half an hour later Natasha and Johnson returned from the capital, to be told that they, too, were under arrest. Kosmin handed them an order, nodded and left, leaving the guard to the local commandant. The order, signed by Boris Savinkov, a former revolutionary terrorist who was now 'Director of the War Ministry', read:

> *To the Commander-in-Chief of all Forces of the Petrograd District. Based on the resolution of the Provisional Government an order is given to arrest the former Grand Duke Michael Aleksandrovich as a person whose activities are a threat to the defence of the country . . . and to the freedoms won by the revolution. This person must be kept under the strictest house arrest . . . This order must be declared to the former Grand Duke, who should be kept under arrest until a further special order.*[2]

The arrest of Michael, now identified as a 'former' Grand Duke though there had been no decree to that effect, was a panic measure by a government fearful of a 'counter-revolution' in favour of the monarchists. A week earlier General Lavr Kornilov, the recently-appointed Supreme Commander, had been given a hero's reception by the rightist delegates at the State Conference held in Moscow and in consequence Kerensky had become convinced that 'the next attempt at a blow would come from the right, and not from the left'.[3] His suspicions were fuelled by reports that Mogilev was a hotbed of monarchist conspirators, a view encouraged by the fact that 'in the evenings, in order to tease the local democrats',[4] the officers opened the windows and played on the piano the old national anthem, 'God Save The Tsar' and not the 'Marseillaise', which the revolutionaries had adopted – though their version sounded more like a 'lugubrious chant' than a rousing march.[5]

Michael was arrested in this climate of an imagined monarchist counter-revolution, though the immediate cause was a farcical 'plot' to rescue Nicholas and his family from Tobolsk. The central figure appeared to be Margarita Khitrovo, a former maid-of-honour at the imperial court. The blindly devoted Margarita journeyed to Tobolsk taking to Nicholas and Alexandra a large number of letters concealed in a pillow; within hours of her arrival on August 18 her hotel room was searched and the letters discovered. Arrested, she was sent back to Petrograd the following day.[6]

Although the letters turned out to be merely innocent correspondence, in the frantic atmosphere of Petrograd the news of her detention at Tobolsk was taken as evidence of a major counter-revolutionary plot. 'Highly exaggerated tales of this conspiracy reached the government', but when the excitement died down it was found to be no more than a romantic adventure and the matter was quietly dropped.[7]

Bemused rather than alarmed, Michael and Natasha were not greatly bothered by their arrest. He wrote a letter of protest to Kerensky, but was told in reply only that 'the present position of democracy and the State is such that it was found necessary to keep me in isolation'. They had been caught up, as he put it four days later, 'in a plot which never existed'.[8] As it happened, they were now to be embroiled in another plot which never existed, the so-called 'Kornilov Affair', an event which was to prove more tragedy than farce.

At 3 a.m. on Tuesday, August 29, a week after their first arrest, Michael and Natasha were awakened by an excited Gatchina commandant and told that they had to be ready to leave for Petrograd in an hour's time. Because the military drivers could not get Michael's cars started – 'they had to call out our chauffeur Vedikhov as we had suggested in the first place' – it was not until 5.10 a.m. that the convoy set out for Petrograd.[9]

From the viewpoint of their guards, their departure was just in time. Later that morning Michael's old Savage Division rode into the woods around Gatchina. General Kornilov had been provoked into rebellion.

General Kornilov had intended to strengthen the government, not rebel against it. He had replaced Brusilov as Supreme Commander in mid-July after the failure of the so-called 'Kerensky Offensive' launched on June 18. He was determined to restore discipline in the army and to reimpose the death penalty. No army could wage war when regiments refused to advance, or simply deserted to the rear whenever the enemy counter-attacked. The 'Kerensky Offensive' had shown that the 'world's first democratic army' would, when tested, vote with its feet.

Kornilov, the son of a Cossack peasant, did not think of himself as a counter-revolutionary – 'I despise the old regime', he said[10] – but he wanted a strong government which could free itself of its dependency on the dictating policies of the Soviet and Bolsheviks. On August 7, he ordered General Aleksandr Krymov's Third Cavalry Corps on the Romanian front to move northwards so that it could deal with any attempted coup by the Bolsheviks in either Petrograd or Moscow. He was prepared, he told his chief-of-staff, to disperse the Soviet, hang its leaders, and finish off the Bolsheviks.[11]

In mid-August there came intelligence reports that the Bolsheviks were indeed planning an all-out bid for power in mid-September. On August 22 Kerensky asked Kornilov to provide a cavalry corps to defend the government, intending that this should come under the government's direct control. It would therefore be available to deter any Bolshevik uprising, but it would also be on hand to deter any counter-revolutionary threat from the right. Kerensky was now more concerned about the ambitions of Kornilov than the threat from the Bolsheviks.

His ploy backfired. Kornilov ordered forward Krymov's Third Cavalry Corps, which included the Savage Division and two Cossack divisions, as well as artillery. This was a force which seemed deliberately chosen for its immunity from Soviet and Bolshevik agitation, which was staffed by monarchist officers, and commanded by a 'political' general remembered as one of the key figures in the Guchkov conspiracy, which only six months earlier had been intent on replacing Nicholas with a Regency under Michael. Kornilov, it seemed, was sending a Trojan horse. Sensing trouble, Boris Savinkov, Kerensky's emissary at Mogilev, urged that Krymov be replaced; he also sought to have the Savage Division, widely thought of as 'Grand Duke Michael's private army'[12] and now commanded by his old friend Prince Bagration, removed from the corps.[13]

Kornilov ignored him. There would be no point in sending a cavalry corps 'acceptable' to the Soviet and the Bolsheviks. If Krymov and the Savage Division scared Petrograd, then that was precisely what was required. As he told his chief-of-staff, the government might not like it, but they would thank him for it afterwards.[14]

Kerensky was now caught between a determined Kornilov and a clamouring Soviet, and unable any longer to claim the middle ground. Persuading himself that Kornilov was intent on arresting him, and becoming dictator in his place, Kerensky was determined to brand Kornilov as a conspirator and traitor, and to present the advancing columns as a counter-revolution, conveniently forgetting that it was he himself who had ordered them to Petrograd.

In the early hours of August 27, after a Cabinet meeting called to deal with 'the emergency', Kerensky demanded and got dictatorial powers and the Provisional Government ceased, for all practical purposes, to exist. After sending Kornilov a cable sacking him as Supreme Commander, Kerensky asked the Soviet to help in defending the revolution; they promptly agreed to set up a military committee, which passed at once into the control of the Bolsheviks. On Kerensky's authority some 40,000 weapons were issued to the workers,[15] so that in defence of 'democracy' he armed the very people determined to overthrow it and himself.

In response an enraged Kornilov defiantly declared his intention to 'lead the people through victory over the enemy to a constituent assembly, where it will decide its own destiny and choose its own political system'.[16]

Unfortunately his last-minute rebellion made it look as if he had intended to rebel from the outset; Kerensky had wrongly accused him of treason, but his response made the charge seem justified. Other generals sympathised, but they were in no position to support him. Neither, as it turned out, was the Third Cavalry Corps.

At his own headquarters in Luga, seventy miles from the capital, Krymov hesitated. Railway workers had blocked the line to Petrograd and his communications with Mogilev had also been cut so that he could not contact Kornilov. On August 29, as his forward columns reached Gatchina and Tsarskoe Selo, he received a cable from Kerensky claiming that Petrograd was calm, no disorders were expected, and 'there is no need for your corps'. He was 'commanded' to stop the advance 'ordered by the removed Commander-in-Chief'.[17] Bolshevik agitators, swarming out of Petrograd, also came out to the corps to insist that all was peace, all was quiet.

The Third Cavalry Corps was stopped in its tracks. Two days later Krymov went to Petrograd at Kerensky's invitation and met him at the Winter Palace. He denied a rebellion and pointed out that he was advancing in support of the government and not against it, as ordered by Kornilov and at the request of Kerensky himself. He then went to a friend's apartment, wrote a letter to Kornilov, then another to his wife. That done, he picked up a revolver and shot himself dead.[18]

Next day, September 1, Kerensky declared Russia to be a democratic republic. He also appointed himself the new Supreme Commander, but that was of necessity. No one else wanted the job. Michael was still under arrest. On arrival in Petrograd on August 29 he and Natasha, their two children, their British governess Miss Neame, and the faithful Johnson, were taken first to military headquarters, and then told that they were to be housed under guard in a small apartment on the Morskaya. Escorted by sixty-five soldiers they were taken by car and led into their new 'prison'. Michael immediately protested. 'The premises were absolutely unfit for our stay, without any elementary conveniences and with only three beds,' he complained.[19]

Faced with a furious Natasha and a stubborn Michael, the officer in charge seemed incapable of simply locking the door and leaving them to make the best of it. Eventually Johnson discovered that Matveev was at home and that they could all stay at his apartment on the Fontanka. It won them their point. The orders were changed, and they were given permission to go there, provided the apartment was kept under close guard.

Michael and Natasha had left Gatchina at dawn that Tuesday morning; it was now early evening. Tired – and with two exhausted and fretful children to worry about – they all trooped back into the street and were driven off again in their armed convoy to the Fontanka.[20]

A week later they were still there, with sentries on the doors. 'That is how dangerous criminals are guarded!' Michael fumed. 'We can't find out anything about ourselves and we are frustrated and melancholic.'[21] His stomach problem had also worsened and Natasha, always frantic about his health, insisted on specialists being allowed to see him. Eventually on Monday, September 4, three of them were permitted to examine him at the apartment. They recommended a strict diet, hot-water bottles, and complete rest, 'but where can one find this under present circumstances?' he asked.[22] That same night, at 9 p.m., Kerensky's ADC Grigorev arrived to tell Michael that he would be released shortly.

These concessions appear to have been due to the intervention of the British ambassador Buchanan, to whom Johnson had gone to seek help. Buchanan in turn saw Tereshchenko, who remained foreign minister in the new five-man 'republican government'. Buchanan also reported matters to London, in a cable to Lord Stamfordham, the king's private secretary: 'The poor Grand Duke Michael has, I am afraid, had rather a bad time of it lately ... I protested strongly to Tereshchenko against the treatment to which HIH had been subjected and Tereshchenko in turn complained to Kerensky. From what his secretary has since told me I hope that the Grand Duke will be released at once.'[23]

He was not, in fact, released, but Tereshchenko did agree that Michael should be transferred back to his home at Gatchina, and kept under arrest there. Indeed, he had already left Petrograd by the time Buchanan sent his telegram. They were back in Gatchina by midnight on September 6.

'Our cortege consisted of five cars, two of them ours,' Michael recorded. 'Natasha, children, Kosmin and I were in the Packard, in the front were two cars with our belongings and servants, and at the back were Miss Neame, Johnson and the Commandant, and at the rear – the Rolls-Royce with the guard. As soon as we arrived, I went to bed. It was so nice to be back at home at last.'[24]

Buchanan had proved a useful ally, but he was unable to help in another direction: the British government was not prepared to admit Michael – or Nicholas, or any other Grand Duke for that matter – and the British foreign secretary Balfour had reconfirmed that to Buchanan with a 'private and secret' telegram dated September 5, 1917 (August 23 in Russia).[25]

Three days after that telegram, Tereshchenko approached Buchanan to tell him that at 'a secret sitting of Cabinet' held that day it had been decided that certain members of the imperial family 'were to be allowed to go abroad'. The Dowager Empress was to be the first to be free to go whenever she pleased, 'whether to England, Denmark, or Finland' and 'Grand Duke Michael would be next'. Tereshchenko 'begged that what he had told me might be kept secret'.[26]

That was the day before the 'Kornilov Affair' turned into open rebellion and the Savage Division reached Gatchina. However, given Kerensky's fevered belief in a coming 'counter-revolution', it may well be that the decision to allow Michael to go abroad was intended to remove him as a rallying point for the monarchists. The alternative, that it was an act of kindness, is not consistent with the political situation. Kindness was not on the agenda in August 1917. It may also be that Buchanan's telegram to Stamfordham, twelve days after he reported the secret decision to allow Michael to go abroad, was a diplomatic attempt to change minds in London. It failed. The door remained shut.

Not until Wednesday, September 13, three weeks after his first arrest, was Michael told that he was free again. 'But why we were under arrest is unknown, and of course, no accusations were made, there couldn't be. Where is the guarantee that this won't be repeated?' Two days later, 'quite unexpectedly', Captain Kosmin returned to Gatchina and 'brought me a written permit to go to the Crimea whenever we wished'.[27]

Michael now had two permits: the first given by Polovtsov, which allowed him to go to Finland, and this new one for the Crimea. Nevertheless, Michael seemed unwilling to go anywhere in a hurry. Since he had been unable to take a trip to England, as he had originally hoped, he appeared content to stay where he was, and see how matters developed. Michael's support for the Kerensky government, while falling far short of enthusiasm, was based on his belief that it would yet bring about the Constituent Assembly, and that a freely-elected government would end the struggle for power in Russia.

On September 1 a desperate Kerensky declared Russia to be a 'republic' – in breach of the undertaking that only a constituent assembly could change the status of the country; Michael shrugged that away. Republic or monarchy, what did it matter, he wrote, 'if only there is order and justice in the land'.[28] That is what he wished of the new Assembly; elections had been fixed for November 12 and it was due to convene on November 28. He saw, therefore, no urgent reason to leave; after the elections, perhaps, they would go to the Crimea for the winter. He had the permit to do so.

Anxious friends urged him to leave at once while he could, but he took no notice. Could he have got away, even abroad? Princess Putyatina thought so, recording a curious incident which seems at odds with the official British position on giving refuge to Grand Dukes. 'I remember perfectly', she said, a visit from two representatives of the British embassy; they had brought two passports, and suggested to Michael 'that he should move to a secret address, from where, some days later, he could leave for England'; Michael refused, saying that 'he believed in the Russian people.'[29]

About that time Natasha sent off a telegram to Persia, addressed to Dimitri, who had sensibly opted to move into the British Legation in Teheran. Taken under the wing of the British ambassador, Sir Charles Marling, Dimitri became an honorary officer in the British army.[30]

In his diary Dimitri wrote that he was 'surprised that she suddenly decided to make contact and wrote favourably and touchingly – this may mean that things have taken a little turn for the better in Gatchina'.[31] When Natasha sent her cable, that might momentarily have been true; when Dimitri received it, some time in early October, things were getting worse, not better.

Kerensky's arming of the Bolsheviks in the face of Kornilov's advancing columns proved as disastrous as it was desperate. He had humbled Kornilov, now under arrest, but in the process he had lost the trust of the other generals. He had made his bed in the extremist camp and he now had to lie on it. The Bolshevik coup, rumoured for mid-September, became fact in October and there was now no Savage Division, no Krymov, and no Kornilov, to crush it. Kerensky was on his own, as he discovered when the three Cossacks divisions he ordered to the defence of the capital refused 'to saddle up'.[32] In the capital itself, the bulk of the Petrograd garrison refused to rally to him, and for the defence of the Winter Palace Kerensky had to rely on officer cadets and a 'Women's Battalion'.[33]

At Gatchina the Bolshevik threat dominated discussion from October 19, when Michael noted that 'an action ... is expected daily'. Five days later he wrote that 'all bridges in Petrograd are swung apart because of the action expected every moment by the Bolsheviks'. On October 25, Petrograd fell. 'The Winter Palace is occupied by the Bolsheviks ... The Council of the Republic is dismissed by the Bolsheviks and the military staff of the District is in their hands. There is shooting in some streets. The whole garrison went over to the Bolsheviks ... Kerensky has gone to Dno to summon help.'[34]

Next day he recorded that 'all power is in the hands of the Military Revolutionary Committee. All the banks, ministries, are seized. The Winter Palace, which was heavily bombarded was defended by cadets and the Women's Battalion and many lives were lost. All Cabinet ministers were arrested and are in the Kresty prison. In short, the Bolsheviks have won a complete victory . . . but for how long?'[35]

Gatchina was still in the hands of loyal government troops. Cossacks with artillery came into town and a desperate Kerensky arrived at the palace, having fled the capital in the hope of rallying troops to his support. Michael and Natasha drove around the Game Reserve and also walked about the town to see what was happening, and to hear the latest rumours. Troops were said to be rallying to the government; the Bolsheviks in the town had fled. Michael was briefly encouraged. 'It appears that the Bolsheviks are not feeling so well,' he noted optimistically.[36]

In the midst of this excitement and drama, and after an early dinner on October 27, they went out that Friday evening, driving in their Rolls-Royce to the local cinema to see the film *She Put Him to Sleep Forever*, starring the seventeen-year-old Italian actress Franchese Bertini.[37] At the onset of the Bolshevik Revolution it was a curious place to find the last man to be proclaimed Emperor of All the Russias; as a gesture of contempt for the Bolsheviks, it was not, perhaps, without style.

In any case, Bolshevik success was by no means certain. General Peter Krasnov, commander of the Third Cavalry Corps, was confident. The corps was not what it had been under Krymov, but he and the few hundred Cossacks available to him in Gatchina, were marching to Tsarskoe Selo, and expected next day to reach Petrograd, where an armed uprising was claimed to be awaiting their arrival. However, in the only battle between loyal troops and Bolshevik forces, an outnumbered Krasnov* was forced to retire to Gatchina.[38] It was the end for Kerensky.

By October 30 Michael accepted at last that it was time to leave. His only hope was the Finnish permit; if he was to use it, he would have to do so now. The plan for departure involved one of Natasha's closest friends, Nabokov's sister Nadine Vonlyarlarskaya. Johnson, sent to the palace for the latest news, returned at 11.30 that Tuesday night to report that 'the position of Gatchina was critical'.[39] It was now or never. With that the household began packing valuables, working until 4 a.m., with the ever-practical Natasha 'sitting down and prising out the precious stones from various Oriental orders' which had been awarded to Michael over the years. 'I can only congratulate her on her foresight,' Tata would say.[40] After a few

* General Krasnov would fight Bolshevism until the end; he served in the German Army during the Second World War. In 1947 he was hanged in Russia as a traitor.

hours' sleep they continued packing during the rest of the day. Michael went out, and returned to report that a truce had been declared 'until midday tomorrow'.[41] There was no time to lose.

As specified in the permit, they would use two cars. The children would leave first, and go to Batovo, an estate owned by Nabokov, some fifteen miles to the south of Gatchina. They would wait there until Michael and Natasha arrived in the second car.

Early next morning the Packard set off with George, Tata, Miss Neame, Nadine, and her little daughter Sophie. Arriving safely, the car started back to Gatchina to collect possessions and provisions while the children, governess, and Nadine sat down to breakfast. 'Suddenly the manageress of the estate came hurriedly in to say that Bolshevik centres were being formed in all surrounding villages; that our car had been seen coming to the house; and that the Commissars intended to arrest the occupants, thinking that they were members of the Provisional Government trying to escape.'[42] Telephone lines to the house had already been cut.

Realising that Michael had to be warned if he was not to fall into the same trap, Nadine decided to go on horseback to the local hospital and use their telephone. When she arrived she found one line working, and called Nikolaevskaya Street. Speaking in English to confuse eavesdroppers, she told Michael what had happened, and he replied that he would send the car back with a message. The little party waited all day and it was not until 8 p.m. that the Packard returned, but with an armed Bolshevik seated next to the chauffeur.[43] They had been too late. Gatchina was now in the hands of the Bolsheviks, and sailors had arrived at Michael's house to confiscate his cars.[44] Their only concession was to allow the Packard a final run to Batovo to pick up the children, Michael having persuaded the new local Bolshevik commandant that they had gone only on a day trip.

It was Wednesday, November 1. Kerensky was a refugee hiding in a peasant cottage. The Provisional Government born on March 3 was no more.

Three days later the Bolshevik commandant in Gatchina, Semen Roshal, came to Nikolaevskaya Street. Roshal was one of the prominent figures in the Petrograd party, and a leader of the Kronstadt sailors whose revolutionary fervour had made them the 'shock troops' of the Bolshevik coup. Roshal produced an order of the Military Revolutionary Committee that Michael was to be taken to the Bolshevik headquarters in Petrograd. Michael protested, and after a long argument Roshal compromised: Michael could select his own accommodation in the capital and he would be free to go out provided he stayed in the city.[45] Once more Michael was under arrest, but on rather more generous terms than had been the case under Kerensky.

Michael telephoned Princess Putyatina's apartment on Millionnaya Street and then Matveev. The princess was away in Odessa, but her sister who was staying at Millionnaya Street with her husband and brother immediately offered to provide rooms. The children and Miss Neame were to stay with Matveev.[46] Next day, Sunday, Michael's cars were returned to him for the journey and at 5.30 p.m. the household departed in convoy, accompanied by Roshal and a guard of sailors.[47]

At Millionnaya Street Princess Putyatina's brother-in-law came out to welcome them. Michael put a finger to his lips to warn him to be careful in what he said, and it was then that he noticed that behind Michael stood two armed sailors and 'a tall man with dark, piercing eyes', dressed in a soldier's tunic and wearing a fur cap. Roshal motioned them inside, and after a few minutes of final instructions to Michael on the conditions of his 'arrest' he departed, leaving the two sailors on guard.[48]

Although officially 'under surveillance', Michael was not troubled by the Bolsheviks in the next days. He walked about the city, going first to the square in front of the Winter Palace, where he 'admired its appearance', as he caustically put it. 'All the walls were spotted with bullet holes, and also the windows.' On his return to Millionnaya Street, he and Natasha entertained friends. The conversation, having turned to politics, became so heated, with Natasha and the others becoming so 'worked up and shouting' that 'we had to take drastic measures' – Michael suggesting that he should be given 'a chairman's bell to restore order' and that if that did not work, 'a revolver'.[49]

Ten days after his removal to Petrograd Michael was told that he could return to Gatchina 'under house arrest'.[50] Natasha stayed behind, however, for she was determined to rescue her valuables held at the State Bank in a strong-box. The bank was closed because of a strike, but was to reopen in two days' time. Natasha would therefore return on Saturday.[51]

Michael wrote to her as soon as he was back home with the children, Miss Neame, and Johnson, laconically addressing in the envelope to 'Comrade Nathalie Sergeyevna Brasova from Comrade MAR'.

I have found the toothpaste and thread in a suitcase and am sending them to you . . . Come soon. Without you here I feel sad and forlorn and very lonely at night. Two of our people kept watch in the house during the night because our guard had been removed, but, as of tomorrow, we are supposed to have a guard again. Everything is quiet and comfortable here, it was a great pleasure to return home and breathe the wonderful fresh air.

Johnnie is going to town tomorrow and will call at Millionnaya for a minute, and will come back with you on Saturday. It is now 9.30 p.m. and he and I are going for a little sledge ride in the wonderful moonlight, maybe we will

The Fighting General with the Order of St. George on his chest. Michael with members of the staff of his Savage Division, and one of his pilots, in May 1915. Two months earlier he had been awarded Russia's highest gallantry award, the Order of St. George. A year later he would be awarded a second high gallantry medal. The Savage Division proved itself to be among the best, perhaps the best, in the Russian army. Natasha believed he was given the division as a punishment.

Postcard general, real-life general. The official 'souvenir postcard' of Grand Duke Michael Aleksandrovich (top left) bought by thousands of Russsians, and the real-life front-line general, dete mined on victory but horrified by the slaughter.

And the man who astonished an American. This is how American war correspondent Stanley Washburn saw Michael at his headquarters in 191 (left) ... in a 'simple uniform with nothing to indicate his rank but shoulder straps of the same material as his uniform ...'

The house on Nikolaevskaya Street. 'A tumbledown', Natasha called it, telling Michael that the police had complained about the dangerous state of the picket fence at the front. The man at the window loved it. So, when she had managed to make it comfortable, did Natasha.

Michael and his beloved Jack. When Jack died in March, 1916, Michael was stunned. 'I won't keep it from you that I am crying bitterly even as I am writing this letter and I can't express the grief that I feel ...'

Dimitri Abrikosov, September 1915. Natasha's one-time boyfriend, with Michael in the garden at Gatchina. 'I have never met another man so uncorrupted and noble in nature.'

One of the photographs removed by the police. Michael and Natasha in a studio portrait at Boissonnas & Eggler in February, 1916. Natasha hated Michael's Savage Division uniform. A few months later the photograph was one of those removed by the police from a window display, on the orders of Alexandra.

Natasha and the besotted Grand Duke Dimitri, October, 1916. Dimitri and Natasha at 24 Nikolaevskaya Street, two months before Dimitri was arrested for his part in the murder of Rasputin. From his exile he would write: 'I can't describe to you, "dearest friend", the feeling that possessed me when I was talking to you about my thoughts and feelings when looking at you.'

Emperor Michael II at Millionnaya Street. The meeting place on March 3, 1917, in the drawing-room with the pedimented window. Cars came in through the courtyard gate; sentries were on the front door.

Exile in the Korolev Room. The hotel in Perm where Michael was exiled. His room was directly above the main door to the right. It was from there that he was abducted on June 12, 1918. The sign on the contemporary postcard reads 'Hotel No.1'.

Prisoners of Perm, April, 1918. The last known picture of Michael, with Nicholas Johnson, taken by a street photographer in Perm in April 1918, just after their release from prison. Michael wrote on the back of the photograph, 'Prisoner of Perm', and also vowed that he would not shave off his beard until he was free again.

The Executioners. The five men who plotted the murder of Michael. (Left to right) A.V. Markov, Ivan Kolpashchikov, the leader, Gavriil Myasnikov, V.A. Ivanchenko and N.V. Zhuzhgov. They posed together after the murder.

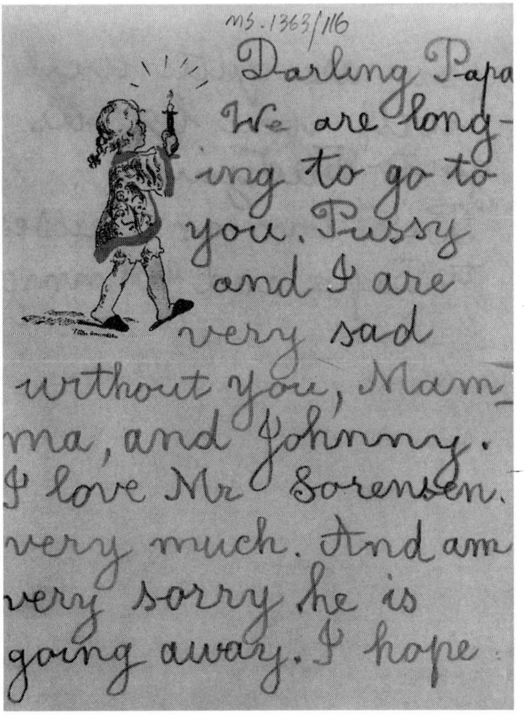
MS.1363/116

Darling Papa
We are long-
ing to go to
you. Pussy
and I are
very sad
without you, Mam-
ma, and Johnny.
I love Mr Sorensen.
very much. And am
very sorry he is
going away. I hope

George's last letter to his father, July 1918. Written from Denmark in July, 1918 to 'Darling Papa ... Pussy and I are very sad without you...'

The last photograph of George, 1931. He 'looked so like Michael, the same walk, the same way of talking ...'

Reunion with Dimitri, 1919. Grand Duke Dimitri, in British uniform, at Snape.

Natasha, a woman alone. 'Oh, Misha! Oh, George!'

sleep better afterwards. Until we meet again, my dear Natasha, I embrace you and kiss you strongly and tenderly. May God protect you. Yours ever, Misha.[52]

Natasha got what she wanted at the bank. Telling officials that she needed access to her strong-box in order to examine papers, she was escorted into the vault and the box given to her. Somehow, as she sorted through the papers, she managed to divert attention from her real purpose; when she left the bank her muff was 'stuffed full of some of her more valuable and portable jewellery'.[53] She would need it all in the days to come.

Although Michael was released from 'house arrest' shortly after his return to Gatchina, he would not be free from minor harassment. On November 23 a party of soldiers arrived at the house with an order authorising them to confiscate wine and provisions. They took '80 bottles of our wine and a quantity of sugar . . . some bottles were drunk and smashed on the spot'.[54]

Determined to put an end to petty looting and to obtain some form of guarantee that the Bolsheviks would 'leave me in peace', Michael went back to Petrograd next day, and walked into the party headquarters to confront one of Lenin's henchmen, Vladimir Bonch-Bruevich. Michael asked for assurances that he would no longer be subject to arrest. Bonch-Bruevich, Secretary of the Soviet of the People's Commissars, promised that he would not be, and drew up a permit on official paper declaring Michael to have 'free residence' as an ordinary citizen.[55]

For the next three months the Bolsheviks left Michael Romanov in peace. He walked around town without anyone molesting him, though unaware for some time that volunteers among the local people had organised a discreet watch over him in case of trouble, and were also guarding his house against hooliganism. When he did find out about this 'private watch' he made it known that 'nobody needs me and nobody will touch me here. I do not have any right to give orders, but I want the guard to be removed'.[56]

One change for the better at Gatchina was the appointment of the young Vladimir Gushchik as palace commissar. Gushchik regarded Michael almost with awe. 'The Grand Duke,' he would say 'has three rare qualities: kindness, simplicity, and honesty . . . None of the parties were hostile towards him. Even socialists of all colours treated him with respect . . .'[57] Gushchik became a close friend of Johnson and so trusted that he even became guardian of confidential papers which Michael did not feel it was safe to keep in his house. Gushchik proved a valuable friend and ally, and did what he could to make life as tolerable as the situation allowed. He would later burn the confidential papers in his charge;[58] what they would have revealed about Michael and Natasha's political activities and contacts is unknown.

Everyday life at Nikolaevskaya Street settled down into an ordinary and unremarkable routine. At Christmas 'we lit the tree, danced around it, and played cat-and-mouse. The children made masks and danced around the room in a comical way ...' On New Year's Eve 'we sat down to eat at 12, not so much to greet the New Year as to say goodbye to damned 1917, which brought so much evil and misfortune to everyone'.[59]

The New Year brought no improvement. In the elections for the Constituent Assembly the Bolsheviks had captured less than twenty-five per cent of the vote, winning some 170 of the 700-plus seats;[60] when the Assembly met for its opening session on January 5, 1918, the Bolsheviks closed it down the same day by sending in armed and drunken troops, and that was the end of that.* Two prominent liberal members – Aleksandr Shingarev and F. F. Kokoshkin, both former ministers in the Provisional Government – were murdered directly afterwards. Russia was no longer a monarchy, a republic, or a democracy; henceforth it was to be ruled by Bolshevik diktat, with opponents shot or arrested. Murder and robbery became commonplace. For most ordinary people – including Michael's staff, though not Michael himself – the war had ceased to matter. The very British governess Miss Neame was as patriotic as anyone, but 'it had come to such a pitch of terror', she said later, 'that we were all praying and waiting anxiously for the arrival of the Germans, as we then knew we would be safe'.[61]

The Bolsheviks could not afford to continue fighting Germany. Over the next two months Michael's diary was dominated by the negotiations with the Germans for a separate peace. 'What a disgrace to Russia!' he wrote when he first heard of the talks.[62] They would stop and start and in the end the peace terms agreed would be worse than the ones first on offer. The Treaty of Brest-Litovsk, signed on March 3,† ended the war between Russia and Germany, and cleared the way for a civil war. Russians would now concentrate on killing each other.

For the nervous servants at Nikolaevskaya Street the regret was that the advancing Germans had stopped short of Gatchina. 'Everyone was in despair,' wrote Miss Neame.[63] Four days later, at 11 a.m. on Tuesday, March 7, Michael was on his bedroom balcony, overlooking the snow-covered road. It was a beautiful morning, with bright, hot sunshine. Troubled by stomach pains he was lying on his couch, but had just begun his diary for the previous day, noting that he had been playing the guitar in the afternoon. As he started to write: 'In the evening ...'[64] he was interrupted by the sight

* Socialist Revolutionaries emerged as the largest group, with around 375 seats. On one analysis the total votes cast were 36.2 million; on another, 41.7 million. Of the 815 or so seats in a full Assembly, more than a hundred had not been awarded at the opening. Whatever its final complexion, it would not have produced a Bolshevik government.

† From February 1, 1918, the Bolsheviks adopted the Western calendar, February 1 becoming February 14. All dates therefore follow the new-style calendar from February onwards.

of a group of armed men running up the street towards the house. Minutes later they burst in and raced up to his balcony.[65] Brusquely he was told that he and Johnson were under arrest.

The order was signed by Moisei Uritsky, the head of the feared Petrograd Cheka. The Cheka – formally the Extraordinary Commission on the Struggle Against the Counter-Revolution, Speculation and Sabotage – was designed as an instrument of terror, with powers which in effect made it a law unto itself.

Miss Neame would never forget Michael's arrest. He shook her hand, and said, 'we must hope for the best ... Promise me you won't fret too much.' Watching him go, she was struck by the 'sad look in his eyes – so tired and ill, he was so hurt at all the injustice'.[66] Taken to the capital, Michael was imprisoned in the Smolny, once an exclusive girls' school, now Bolshevik headquarters.[67] This time there were no polite discussions about private accommodation, or time given for packing possessions.

Natasha followed Michael to the capital, and spent the night at the home of her friend Maggie Abakanovich on the Moika. Next morning, Wednesday, March 8, she met Princess Putyatina, and together they walked to the grey-painted Smolny. Passing through the colonnaded entrance, past machine-guns and guards with fixed bayonets, they were given permission to see Michael and found him in a large room, furnished now with eight beds and a few chairs. Armed Red Guards were sitting around smoking, talking loudly, and laughing. Michael was standing in the window recess, talking to Johnson. When Natasha walked in, Michael came over 'and kissed her hand without speaking'.[68]

As they settled down to talk, the door opened and Uritsky came in, dressed in a leather jacket, high boots and a grey fur hat. Princess Putyatina remembered 'a man of under-average height, with a prominent, fleshy nose, large lop-ears, small ferrety eyes with an expression of cold cruelty'. He gave a short nod, sat down, and lit a cigarette. After a few vague promises about improving conditions, he got up and left.

Next day, Natasha and Princess Putyatina returned and were allowed to see Michael for only thirty minutes. Desperate to do something, Natasha decided to go directly to Lenin, who was somewhere in the same building. 'Noticing that there was a sentry in front of one of the doors, we presumed that must be his office. Natasha brusquely opened the door, without giving the sentry time to bar the way', though he was able to stop the princess.

Lenin was sitting at his desk when Natasha marched in. He might have called for the guard and had her thrown out, had Natasha given him a chance to recover from his surprise.

Outside, the princess collapsed on a bench. 'I do not know how long I waited, but I do know that I got up several times and paced the corridor nervously.' At last the door opened and Natasha peeped out and beckoned her in. The sentry, now utterly confused, stood there blankly as the princess swept by him.

Natasha was standing in the office on her own. Lenin had disappeared through another door, promising to look into the matter, but 'saying that it did not only depend on him'. After a long wait, the inner door opened and instead of Lenin his friend Bonch-Bruevich walked in to tell Natasha that the question would be reviewed later in the day.[69]

That evening, twenty-four Commissars met at the Smolny; among them Lenin and the man who would one day succeed him, Joseph Stalin.[70] The Bolshevik leadership, fearing that the capital was too close to the German lines, and too near the counter-revolutionary movement in Finland, was about to move to the greater safety of Moscow. One of their last decisions in Petrograd was to decide the fate of 'the former Grand Duke M.A. Romanov'; he was to be exiled 'until further notice' to the Urals. Johnson was also to be exiled, but 'shall not be accommodated in the same city'. The arrangements were 'entrusted to Comrade Uritsky'.[71]

Next morning a protesting Natasha was refused permission to see Michael. Afterwards she and the princess went to the Cheka offices on Gorokhovaya Street, formerly the headquarters of the City Governor. Natasha waited by the steps, and the princess went inside to find Uritsky. He was in his office, and motioned her in, telling her that she had come 'just at the right time'. He gave her the news that Michael was to be exiled to the town of Perm. Shocked, the princess went out to a waiting Natasha. 'It was a terrible blow, but she bore it with courage and resignation.'[72]

Late that night Michael sat down in his prison room at the Smolny and wrote to Natasha. 'Uritsky has just read to us the resolution of the Soviet of People's Commissars ordering our immediate move to Perm. They gave us half an hour to be ready ... everything has happened so unexpectedly ... Don't be disheartened, my dearest – God will help us to go through this dreadful ordeal. I kiss and most tenderly embrace you. Your Misha.'[73]

At one o'clock on the morning of Saturday, March 11, Michael and Johnson were taken by car through the freezing, snow-covered streets to the darkened Nicholas station. After three hours' wait[74] they were marched to the train which would take them into exile.

TWENTY-EIGHT

Prisoner of Perm

In peacetime two ordinary trains left daily from the Nicholas station in St Petersburg to Perm, covering the 1000 miles south-eastwards in two days; there was also a twice-weekly Siberian express which could do the trip in thirty-seven hours. The train on which Michael and Johnson left at 4 a.m. on Saturday, March 11, took more than eight days for the same journey. By Tuesday, and after some 80 hours, they had got only as far as Vologda,[1] 371 miles from the capital, crawling along at an average of less than five miles an hour; it would be like that all the way. The weather was bitter and they were housed in a battered carriage attached to a freight train, sitting in a grubby, unheated compartment, grandly marked 'First Class', but which had all its windows broken or missing.[2]

The armed six-man escort – Latvians commanded by a Russian[3] – treated them with indifference for the first day but by Sunday evening, impressed by finding that their imperial prisoner made no complaint, their attitude towards him changed. 'As we were getting ready to settle down to sleep,' Johnson later reported, 'two of the escort even took off their coats and hung them over the windows to keep out the draughts.' They began to address Michael as 'Michael Aleksandrovich' and after that 'they did their best to take care of us.'[4]

Two days later, as the freight train reached Vologda, the guards made no objection when Michael asked for permission to send a telegram. He drafted it out, in terms as reassuring as possible, and Johnson took it for despatch to a frantic Natasha. 'Everybody well. Fellow-travellers are nice. Moving extremely slowly by freight train.' In his farewell letter, Michael had told her, 'Uritsky assured me that you and the family will have no difficulty in following me whenever you like'.[5] In his cable, he added: 'It will be quite impossible to travel with children . . . but taking a direct passenger train will be considerably quicker. Must take food for entire journey . . .'[6] That said much about what might be expected at restaurants at the stopping stations *en route*; so far Michael and Johnson had been given barely enough to sustain them.

The order that Michael and Johnson should be separated on arrival and obliged to live in separate areas continued to vex Michael, and on the next evening, when the train stopped at the small station of Sharya, he fired off a protest telegram to Lenin, but sent it under Johnson's name. Using Michael's 'poor health' as justification, the telegram asked Lenin to revoke the order.[7] It was.

Finally, on Sunday, March 19, Michael and Johnson – unshaven, filthy, exhausted, and ravenous – arrived in Perm, almost grateful to find themselves being taken to a small room in the Hermitage Hotel where they could at least wash and look forward to sleeping in a bed.[8]

Perm, with a population then of 62,000, was the capital of a government of the same name, which also included Ekaterinburg, 235 miles to the south-east. The gateway to Siberia, and situated above the broad River Kama, it was normally a thriving and even attractive town with nineteen churches, a new university and, fittingly as the birthplace of Diaghilev, boasted the largest theatre outside St Petersburg and Moscow, with the third-largest ballet company in Russia. There were worse places to be in exile; Michael was resolved to make the best of it.

Their first shock, two days after their arrival, was to find that they were not to be left in peace, as promised. The local authorities, having no instructions about Michael, decided to put him in prison. In Petrograd, a Bolshevik newspaper explained that away by saying that he 'has become insane'. The story was republished worldwide, and even *The Times* in London reported the claim.[9]

Upon his arrest, Michael was allowed to send a telegram to Natasha telling her that he was 'to be kept until further notice in solitary confinement.'[10] He also sent telegrams to three of the Petrograd Commissars, Bonch-Bruevich, Lunacharsky and Uritsky, demanding that the local Soviet be instructed to release him at once. 'Urgently request issue of directives immediately,' he wrote.[11]

Five days later Michael's valet, Vasily Chelyshev, who with the chauffeur Borunov had arrived in Perm just as Michael was being arrested on March 21, reported to Natasha that there had been 'no reply to the telegrams of our "boss" ... very important that the local authorities receive directions ...' Uritsky was being 'evasive', Chelyshev also told her.[12] He and Borunov had brought clothes, books, and a variety of toilet and medical supplies packed by Natasha, but they were not allowed to see Michael.[13]

Natasha was busy banging on doors, demanding Michael's release. It was frustrating work, but her persistence eventually paid off; early in April, some two weeks after Michael was imprisoned, she heard that orders had been given for his release. Robert Wilton, *The Times* man, lobbied perhaps by Natasha, helpfully filed the story of his release, making it difficult for the Commissars to retract their decision.[14] Even so, Michael was still in prison while the outside world was reading on Saturday, April 6, that he was at liberty. The local Perm Soviet stubbornly dragged its heels over the next four days, as if determined to show its independence. Michael's valet Chelyshev badgered the Perm Bolsheviks until they eventually gave way. In the late evening of Monday, April 9, the prison doors opened and Michael walked out.[15]

Chelyshev had arranged accommodation for him in the Korolev Rooms at 3 Siberia Street,* not far from the embankment of the Kama river. The handsome three-storey hotel had opened eleven years earlier in 1907, and prided itself on providing the most luxurious accommodation in town. Though it was now administered by the local Soviet – and renamed Hotel No. 1 – a guest was entitled to a three-course dinner every day, with tea or milk.[16] The hotel was a long, flat-fronted building painted yellow ochre, with tall arched windows; inside there were elegant columns and stucco mouldings.[17] Michael was given a large room, number 21, with a wrought-iron balcony on the first floor, immediately above the main entrance, and overlooking the busy street outside.[18] It was the very best on offer and, after what had gone before, a joy to behold. Johnson, Chelyshev, and Borunov also found rooms in the same hotel.[19] Michael wrote at once to Natasha.

My very own, dearest Natasha, At last I can write to you openly, as up to now, i.e. up to last night, we were under arrest and all my correspondence was being checked by the local Soviet. I did not want to write letters, knowing that they would be read by all and sundry . . . Yesterday morning we were told that we would be released and we have spent a wearisome day awaiting the results. Thanks to the insistence of Vasily, we were at last released at 11 p.m. and went straight away to the rooms we have rented in the Korolev Rooms . . . My head is going round and round – so much I want to tell you, as I have lived through so much in the last five weeks of my arrest.

My dearest Natashechka, I thank you from all my heart for the lovely letters and also for all the trouble you have taken to help me. Thank God, the first step was successful, and we are free. This is already a great relief. The second step would be to get away from here and go home, but I am afraid that this won't be soon. I am terribly lonely without you, my darling, come here as soon as possible. As from today, I will start looking for some lodgings for us and as soon as I find something suitable, will send you a wire . . .

You can be quite sure and certain that you continue taking the greatest part of my heart . . . I still want your caresses . . . I think constantly about you, my angel, and it hurts me to think that you have to go through these dreadful times. There is nothing to do about it but to be patient and rely on God.

How vexing it is not to be in our dear Gatchina at this lovely time of the year. I was always used to spending the spring there, and where I have so many perfect and delightful memories of my childhood and also of the

* Now 5 Karl Marx Street.

later years. It always seems to me that only there is there a real spring. And if you think of Pushkino, which you love so much, you will then understand me better.

May God keep you and bless you. I embrace and kiss you tenderly with all my love. Adoring you, all yours. Misha.[20]

After the tumult of the past five weeks it was a letter that made the best of the position he now faced. There was hope that somehow the worst was really over.

The arrest of Michael was alarming enough for Natasha, but it was also a reminder that the Bolsheviks could not be trusted to leave any Romanov alone, including the children. Nicholas's family had been taken, and it could be assumed therefore that little George was also at risk. He was only seven years of age, but would that matter to the ruthless men who now wielded such arbitrary power? Natasha was not prepared to wonder. Somehow, George had to be sent to safety.

She was also worried about Tata, now approaching her fifteenth birthday. The risk in her case was not as great, since she was still legally a Mamontov by name, and without any title or Romanov connection other than the fact that she was Michael's stepdaughter. It would be best if both could be sent out of the country, but if that jeopardised the chances for George then Tata would have to stay behind.

But how could George escape? Natasha could not go too, not only because that in itself would greatly increase the odds against him, but because she would not leave Michael behind, and no less could she leave Tata. Princess Putyatina's husband suggested an approach to the Danes. After all, Michael was a cousin and friend of King Christian; George was 'family'. The Danish embassy was next door to the Putyatin apartment in Millionnaya Street. The senior diplomat there, George Scavenius, agreed to seek permission from Copenhagen to help; he also put Prince Putyatin in touch with Colonel Cramer, the Danish official in charge of prisoner-of-war exchange, who was living in the former Austrian embassy on Sergeyevskaya Street. Colonel Cramer volunteered to take George into his care until there was news from Denmark.[21]

On March 16 Miss Neame and George moved to Sergeyevskaya Street, and were hidden there for the next forty days. On April 25 they were ready to move, though the only route was through Germany, with no assurance that they would get any further. They would travel on a train taking prisoners of war back home. For Miss Neame it was a daunting prospect; she was to pose as the wife of a repatriated Austrian officer, with a false passport made out in the name of Silldorff. Although she would be accompanied all the way by a Danish officer, Captain Sorensen, neither she nor George spoke German; if she was stopped in Germany she could be arrested as an enemy alien, even as a spy. There was no knowing what would then happen to the boy.

Nervously, she and George boarded the packed Red Cross train which would take them first to Pskov, where she would pass into German-controlled territory. To her immense relief, the Bolsheviks took no special notice of her as they stamped her passport and that of 'her son'. A few days later they were in Berlin, and went at once to the Danish embassy, where the American-born wife of the ambassador Count Carl Moltke took them into her care. They were there for a week, as Count Moltke carefully broached with the German foreign ministry the question of getting them across the border into Denmark. Their identities were disclosed – a delicate decision given that Miss Neame was British and properly faced internment.

Happily, the Kaiser was told about the situation. 'He not only kindly allowed us to go on, but we had a reserved first-class carriage,' said Miss Neame. 'Orders were sent ahead that on the frontier we were to be passed and neither we nor our luggage were to be searched.'[22] They left Berlin in style. Arriving in Copenhagen they were met at the station by a court official, taken to the palace and invited to stay with the king and queen. 'You and the boy must settle down and be happy with us,' King Christian told Miss Neame. 'I admire you for undertaking such a dangerous journey.'[23]

Danish help did not stop there. In Petrograd the embassy also took steps to secure the house at Gatchina from the attentions of the mob. The embassy 'rented' part of 24 Nikolaevskaya Street and every day, to keep up the pretence, two Danish officials would arrive there to make it appear that they were actually in residence. To add further protection, a Danish flag fluttered above the house.[24]

Once in the Korolev Rooms Michael's position began to look tolerable. The latest orders to Perm from Petrograd, signed by both Uritsky and Bonch-Bruevich, were that 'Michael Romanov and Johnson are entitled to live in freedom under the surveillance of the local Soviet authorities'.[25] The surveillance amounted only to a requirement that Michael report every day to the militia headquarters next to the hotel; otherwise he was at liberty. He tagged himself as the 'Prisoner of Perm' on a photograph of him and Johnson, taken in a muddy street just after his release from prison. He had grown a beard which he vowed not to remove until he was freed,[26] but he was more cheerful than he had been for weeks. Michael's obvious popularity, among the townspeople at large did not endear him to the more fervent members of the Perm Soviet, but for the moment they did no more than grumble about it.

There would always be some people who avoided Michael for fear of offending the Soviet, and on one occasion, when Michael went to a bootmaker's, the door 'was shut in our faces'.[27] One 'refugee' from nearby Ekaterinburg who also booked into the Korolev Rooms remembered that 'at first I was afraid of staying there' because the presence of Michael would 'attract the attention of the Soviet authorities' but he quickly discovered that Michael was 'at complete liberty and walked around the town without anyone following him'. Even the Soviet commissar who ran the hotel as if he owned it was careful to treat Michael 'quite correctly'.[28]

Sometimes in a shabby raincoat, tweed cap and boots, and on fine days in a grey suit, soft hat and carrying a stick,[29] Michael became a familiar figure as he strolled around the town. Princess Putyatina in Petrograd would hear that people meeting him in the street 'treated him with great respect' and that they 'brought him all sorts of delicacies'. Robert Wilton, who was in Perm some months later, would report that 'his rooms were always full of provisions'. Wilton also learned that Michael, when out walking, 'found himself running the gauntlet of popular ovations'.[30]

Michael, reviewing his position in those first days of relative freedom, could afford a degree of optimism. Apart from Johnson he had his valet Chelyshev and his chauffeur Borunov with him – though ex-chauffeur was possibly a more apt description since the last of Michael's cars had been seized at Gatchina – and despite the loss of his income, he still had enough cash to meet his immediate needs.

With Natasha pressing for a permit to join him,[31] Michael's main problem in the last two weeks of April was of finding an apartment where they could live out their exile. It proved more difficult than he expected, and indeed he cabled her to say that 'it is not practical to rent a flat. We can live in our hotel. Waiting impatiently.'[32]

The waiting was to last three weeks, for it was not until the beginning of May that Natasha received her travel permit. With Good Friday falling on May 10, Michael was particularly delighted that Natasha would be in Perm by then: 'My darling, beloved, and very dearest Natasha, thank God that we, nevertheless, are able to celebrate Easter together, if not at home. Shall we hope that we will return to our beloved Gatchina very soon. Wishing you all that you wish yourself most, and kissing you three times and very tenderly embracing you. Misha.'[33]

With Tata being looked after at home by Princess Vyazemskaya, Natasha arrived with her friend Maggie Abakanovich and Prince Putyatin after a two-day journey aboard the Siberian express. There was never greater joy than at the moment when Michael saw Natasha stepping down on to the platform at Perm. Everything else was forgotten as they fell into each other's arms, and only the present mattered.

Natasha intended to stay in Perm indefinitely and accordingly she and Michael started to look for a home. It was not easy. However, shortly after Michael's arrest, Colonel Peter Znamerovsky – former commandant of the Gatchina railway gendarmerie – had also been exiled to Perm; his wife had joined him, and they were living together in an apartment at 8 Kungurskaya Street.[34] Natasha was encouraged by that example.

On Michael's and Natasha's first weekend together in Perm they looked at an apartment and 'a nice house' on Siberia Street. On Saturday evening they went to the Perm 1500-seat opera house where the French actress Beauregard was playing in *Dream of Love*. Michael's party included two of Perm's best-known society figures, Sergei and Olga Tupitsin, neither of whom had any love for the Bolsheviks; afterwards Beauregard joined them in their crimson-and-gold box,[35] with the ever-elegant Natasha holding court, as oblivious to the sullen stares of the new Bolshevik 'aristocracy' as previously she had been to the disapproving eyes of imperial society.

Michael and Natasha returned to the theatre twice in the following week, to a piano recital, and to a concert given by a group of artists from the Maryinski in Petrograd. The bottom left-side box became Michael's regular place at the theatre. On other evenings they gave small dinner parties, for the Tupitsins and the Znamerovskys, and during the day they went for walks along the river bank, or strolled into the marketplace on the Monastyrskaya and to the shops still open for business.[36]

Michael's diary for the period was so full of ordinary events that it might have been written at Gatchina in happier times. Theirs was a simple enough routine, remarkable in the circumstances, and it might have gone on like that had not the Bolsheviks suddenly found themselves threatened by an unexpected new enemy: a large armed force of Czechs who had taken control of Chelyabinsk, a town 390 miles to the south.

Chelyabinsk was the junction for the Trans-Siberian railway from Moscow to Vladivostok; the Czechs were former prisoners of war who had opted to change sides and fight their old masters, the Austro-Hungarians. Under the terms of the peace treaty between Russia and Germany they had been released from their camps and were travelling to Vladivostok, with the intention that they would then be shipped out to join the Allied armies. Under the same treaty, Austrian prisoners of war were being transferred westwards to rejoin their army. At Chelyabinsk, when a Czech and an Austrian train met at the station, an Austrian ex-prisoner threw a slab of concrete at the jeering Czechs, injuring one of them. The Czechs lynched the offender, and when the local Bolsheviks intervened the Czechs took over the town. Shortly, the entire Czech Legion, strung out along the railway line to Vladivostok, would turn and decide to fight the Bolsheviks, adding a new and dangerous dimension to the civil war being waged elsewhere in Russia.

The news alarmed Perm, located as it was within a day's journey from Chelyabinsk and an armed force whose future moves were unpredictable. Michael, warned by Colonel Znamerovsky that the nervous local Bolsheviks might react harshly, decided that it would be best if Natasha left and returned to Petrograd immediately. Natasha would leave on the first available train, expected in Perm on Saturday morning, May 18. No one knew when there would be another.

On their last full day together, Friday May 17, they took an afternoon walk, and then had a quiet dinner in the hotel, after which Natasha spent the rest of the evening packing. 'It is very sad to be left alone again,' Michael wrote in his diary that night.[37]

Next morning, miserable at parting, they left the hotel at 9.30 and took a cab to the station. 'We waited a long time for the train on the platform there because the Siberian Express was late by approximately 36 hours . . . Natasha found a seat in a small compartment of the international carriage, sharing with another lady. The train left at 12.10.' As he had done on their first parting nine years earlier at the railway station in Copenhagen, he stood and watched the train pull away, until it was out of sight. Then he took a cab back to the hotel and that night he wrote in his diary that 'it has become so sad and so empty now that Natasha has gone, everything seems different and even the rooms have changed . . .'[38]

In Perm Natasha had made it clear that she would go to Moscow and once again confront Lenin, demanding Michael's release and, she hoped, secure permission for him to leave the country.

After his move to Moscow on March 10, Lenin made the Kremlin the seat of his government, choosing for himself one of the buildings of the old Court of Chancellery, opposite the Arsenal, taking a five-roomed apartment on the second floor, with offices on the same floor.[39]

The Kremlin bells now played the 'Internationale' instead of 'God Save the Tsar' and the double-headed Romanov eagles mounted on the gates had been stripped of their crowns, but otherwise it was the same Kremlin Natasha knew well from her childhood. She stayed at her parents' apartment at 6 Vozdvizhenka, only a few hundred yards from the Troitsky Gate and the Kremlin beyond.

With guards at the Troitsky Gate and on every building within the Kremlin, entry without authority or permit was near impossible. 'Near impossible' was not a term which Natasha recognised, however, and somehow she talked her way in and – as she had done in Petrograd – yet again into Lenin's office.[40]

Finding Natasha at his desk once more was not the most welcome sight for Lenin, though as before she changed nothing. Yet Natasha did not take 'No' for an answer, going on to badger other members of the Bolshevik regime as she had done earlier. Among them was Trotsky – who had been 'ill-tempered and answered rudely' when tackled by Natasha in Petrograd;[41] another was Yacob Sverdlov, styled the Red Tsar. 'She imagined that personal intercession with the Red chieftains would move them to let him go,' the *Times* man Wilton would comment. 'Of course, it was an illusion excusable only in a distracted wife.'[42]

At 11 a.m. on Tuesday, May 21, at almost the same time that Natasha arrived in Moscow, Michael and Johnson appeared by order at 33 Petropavlovskaya-Okhanskaya, the Perm offices of the sinister Cheka. Until then they had reported only to the local militia. However, in view of the growing Czech threat, the Perm Soviet decided that it could no longer be responsible for Michael's 'safety'; responsibility was transferred to the provincial Cheka.[43]

The change seems to have coincided with a resolution by the workers in nearby Motovilikha that if the Perm Soviet did not arrest Michael, they would 'settle with him themselves'.[44] The Bolsheviks at Motovilikha, some two and a half miles away, were largely employed in the huge government munitions factory, and were noticeably more militant than those in Perm. In his diary afterwards, Michael wrote that at the Cheka offices 'I was given a piece of paper ordering me to go there every day at 11 o'clock (good people, tell me what this means)'.[45]

The switch to the Cheka seemed at first merely an irritation. They took a more officious approach, demanding that he appeared promptly at a fixed time, instead of at his convenience as had been the case at the militia. Telegrams from Natasha in Moscow were now delivered to the Cheka, and read there before being handed to him.[46] It was an unpleasant reminder of his real position.

Nevertheless, Michael continued to go about the town without restriction. He listened to a string orchestra in the City Garden, saw 'a dreadful farce' at the opera house, spent an evening at the Triumph Cinema, visited a waxworks exhibition and went in search of walking boots, buying a pair of 'simple soldiers' lace-up boots'.[47] At one of the shops in Siberia Street the manager asked him why it was, in view of his comparative freedom, that he did not escape. Michael only laughed. 'Where would someone as tall as I am go. They would find me immediately.'[48]

The Cheka was not quite so sure. Perm was now more crowded, as thousands of people trying to make their way eastwards found themselves stranded there, with the railway line to Chelyabinsk cut. Among these unexpected newcomers were two Americans, who called on Michael after dinner on Saturday, May 25. 'Mr O'Brien and Mr Hess'[49] were the kind of people the Cheka looked upon warily, as possible messengers for plotters intent on rescuing Michael; at the very least they were a reminder that Michael could meet anyone coming from anywhere, including members of monarchist organisations bent on saving him.

Colonel Znamerovsky certainly had plans for escape, and given the worsening position in Perm, it would be odd if he had not; he feared that 'the Motovilikha workmen might be goaded into violence'.[50] Curious messages also arrived at the Korolev Rooms, of which two survive, though their meaning is not known. '*The mignonette is not a flower of brilliant beauty, but its fragrance is divine*', says one, and '*Turkeys are yours*' is another.[51]

A week after Michael's first visit to the Cheka the town of Perm was declared to be 'in a state of war'. Next day he noted in his diary that 'it is difficult to work out what is going on, but something major is brewing'.[52] On Monday, June 3 he wrote to Natasha, telling her what he knew about the situation. 'My dearest sweetheart, my own darling Natasha . . . It is now 16 days since you went away. I can't describe how I feel – depressed and desperate from all the surroundings here, from this dreadful town, where I am in absolute uncertainty and living an aimless life. Why do I write all this when you know it so well yourself!'

He went on to tell her of his efforts to find an apartment, for he was finding the Korolev Rooms increasingly expensive, and a drain on his reserves of cash. 'The price for the rooms is going up all the time and the cook serves us with enormous bills,' he wrote. He had his eye on an apartment with 'a nice view from the balcony over the river'.[53] The apartment at 212 Ekaterinskaya Street was owned by the Tupitsins, and it would be free in the middle of the month.[54]

The military situation made it impossible to know when they might meet again. 'It seems to me that everything is again delayed and we will not be able to see each other for another two months, which would be dreadful, but I will hope that you would be able to come here sooner, provided that there isn't any military coup.'

He ended by writing: 'My dear soul, Natashechka, I will hope that God will allow us to be together again or that we would be able to return home soon! I embrace you and kiss you very tenderly. God bless you I am all yours. Your Boy.'

Then he added a postscript, jokily 'headlining' it as *The Recent Political Review*, and signing off as *Correspondent-on-Tour*:

Everything here is outwardly calm, but the authorities admit that things are rather acute and serious. We have to continue to give our signatures daily in the Committee of 'charms'. In the town squares the railwaymen and party-

workers are receiving military training, drill and similar body exercises . . . The town is full of rumours and disturbed by news that in the east – not very far away, in 'Katia's Burg' there are activities of either 'Czecho-slovaks' or 'Slovako-czechs'. It is rumoured that they have besieged 'Katia' from three sides and even taken Chelyabinsk, thus cutting off Siberia. What their further plans are, nobody knows, but our town is now declared under military law . . .*[55]

Shortly after sending this letter Michael suffered a bout of his 'infamous stomach pains', the first for some time. Next day he went as usual to report to the Cheka and 'had a bit of a run in with one of the "comrades" there, who was very rude to me'.[56] The 'comrade' was Gavriil Myasnikov, the former chairman of the nearby Motovilikha Soviet, who had been appointed just ten days earlier to the Perm Cheka, taking over the department dealing with counter-revolutionaries.[57]

On Myasnikov's arrival the local Cheka changed from being officious to being menacing. Before the February revolution in 1917 Myasnikov had spent four years in a labour camp for terrorist acts. Aged nineteen when first arrested and imprisoned for crimes and violence, for the next five years his life had been an unending series of escapes, periods in hiding, and prison, until in 1913 he went to a labour camp.[58] Myasnikov, now twenty-nine, hated what Michael represented and bitterly resented the freedom he was allowed in Perm.

Among the workers at Motovilikha there had been fierce criticism of the relatively benign treatment afforded Michael in Perm. 'The people of Perm did not realise that their attentions to the exile might arouse suspicion among his Red enemies,' Wilton would comment. 'Znamerovsky warned that the Reds at the suburban Motovilikha arsenal were beginning to grow restive and openly agitating against the liberty allowed to the exiles.'[59]

At Easter the sight of Michael and Natasha going to Perm's SS Peter and Paul Cathedral had been one trumpeted cause for Bolshevik fury. 'The blatantly monarchist ceremonies of the bourgeoisie and the new Tsar-Saviour's almost daily processions to the cathedral along roads covered with carpets and fresh flowers angered the working class,' claimed Cheka agent A. A. Shamarin.[60] Bolshevik agitators at Motovilikha loved spouting this sort of story, and Myasnikov thought it incredible that nothing had been done to curb popular support for 'His Imperial Majesty', as he sneeringly called Michael.[61]

A fellow Bolshevik, the secretary of the Perm Party Committee, thought Myasnikov to be 'a bloodthirsty and embittered man, and not altogether

* Ekaterinburg where Nicholas and Alexandra were now imprisoned. Michael carefully followed news of his brother and family, at one point cabling the 'moderate' Bolshevik commissar Anatoli Lunacharsky in the hope of improving the conditions in which they were being held.

sane . . .'[62] Local Bolsheviks were also frightened of him, believing him capable of utter ruthlessness. Myasnikov suspected that some members of the Perm Soviet might try to protect Michael, and also that 'there is an organisation of officers attempting to liberate him'.[63]

There appears to have been some effort by the 'moderates' to remove Myasnikov from the local Cheka, for a week after his appointment it was proposed that he be 'promoted' to the Ural Regional Cheka. Myasnikov refused to go and the appointment went instead to F. N. Lukoyanov, the local Cheka chairman,[64] whose removal from Perm left Myasnikov in an even more powerful position. Lukoyanov was no saint; Myasnikov was a cold-blooded killer.

An unknowing Michael went on as before. After his first 'run in' at what he called the 'Committee of Charms' he shrugged off the row and went off on the Kama in a motor boat. In the afternoon he had 'wonderful coffee and cake' with the landlady at the Korolev Rooms, and in the evening he walked to the City Garden to listen to the string orchestra.[65]

Over the next three days he would spend much of his time in bed, suffering from stomach pains. On Saturday, June 8, 'I ate nothing after midday because I was in pain all the time'. On Sunday he 'spent the whole day in bed by the window' and in the evening Znamerovsky arrived 'and told me much of interest about rumours circulating in the city'.[66]

On Monday he was on his feet all day 'but felt very poorly'; he also noted that he had received a telegram from Natasha in Gatchina. 'She arrived there last Wednesday.' Next day, Tuesday, he felt much better, and the pains were 'not as intense and did not last long'. Znamerovsky, with Michael's godson Nagorsky, came to tea; at 10 p.m. Nagorsky came back again to say goodbye, for as Michael wrote in his diary next morning, 'he is going to Petrograd today.'[67]

It was Wednesday, June 12.

TWENTY-NINE

Death in the Woods

At the beginning of June, 1918, the leaders of the Bolshevik regime in Moscow had still to make a final decision about the fate of those Romanovs held in custody in one form or another. The ex-Tsar had been moved at the end of April from Tobolsk to Ekaterinburg and he and his family were kept there in virtual prison conditions in a large house commandeered from a merchant called Nikolai Ipatev. Six other members of the imperial family – Kschessinska's ex-lover Grand Duke Serge Mikhailovich, Alexandra's sister Ella, three of the sons of Grand Duke Konstantin, and Dimitri's half-brother Vladimir Paley – were being held in the Napolnaya school on the outskirts of Alapaevsk, an industrial town some 180 miles north-east of Ekaterinburg, from which they had been transferred towards the end of May.*

The Napolnaya school had no more than five or six small rooms. The furniture was simple, with two or three plain tables, some chairs and stools, and iron cots. The Alapaevsk exiles, guarded by Latvians and members of the local Soviet, were allowed to walk in the town and to talk to local residents, mainly the young who came to the school to play football and skittles with the young Konstantin princes and Prince Vladimir Paley. Their principal occupation was working in the garden, planting vegetables, and in the evenings they sat around and read books supplied to them by the local library. At first their meals were cooked and brought in to them, but later the system changed and they were given food to cook for themselves.[1]

Conditions at Alapaevsk were not as strict as at Ekaterinburg, where Nicholas and his family were confined to the Ipatev house and its small courtyard, with their windows whitewashed to prevent them seeing out, and with restricted opportunity for exercise.[2] But if it was a more tolerable existence at the Napolnaya school, it could not compare to the relatively pleasant conditions Michael enjoyed in Perm.

* Nicholas, Alexandra and their daughter Marie arrived in Ekaterinburg on April 30, 1918; the other four children joined them three weeks later. Alexandra's sister, Ella, and the other Romanovs, originally imprisoned in Viatka, were confined in an Ekaterinburg hotel from May 3 to May 20 when they were transferred to Alapaevsk. There was no contact between the two groups.

The last Emperor would be the first of the Romanovs to die.* The order to 'execute' him appears to have been given by the Perm Cheka, though responsibility is clouded by the conflicting statements of the men involved. The Ural Regional Soviet at Ekaterinburg and the Bolshevik leadership in Moscow would not admit having any hand in the murder, but each had good reason for pleading ignorance; each endorsed it afterwards and both conspired in the cover-up.

The actual execution was entrusted to Myasnikov. He later claimed to have acted on his own initiative, without the authority of the Perm Cheka; this view is contradicted by other leading Cheka members actually involved in the conspiracy and murder. The Perm City Soviet also knew, approved and took part.

Perm's Bolsheviks were excited by the fear that the Czechs could reach Perm; martial law was in force in the town. Myasnikov claimed the discovery of a plot by an organisation of officers to rescue Michael. These factors, he said, determined the decision: Michael had to be killed because 'he was the only figure around whom all the counter-revolutionary forces could unite' and the 'danger to Soviet power if Michael escaped and became the head of the counter-revolutionary forces would be immense'.[3]

The testimony of another Cheka department head, Pavel Malkov, is consistent with this: Michael was killed because of the advance of counter-revolutionary forces, and also because of his 'suspicious behaviour';[4] another leading Bolshevik, A. A. Mikov, describes a meeting attended by Malkov, Myasnikov and others in a *dacha*. Malkov told the assembled men that 'it was dangerous to "keep" Michael any longer; he might escape even though he was being watched closely'. Mikov suggested killing him. 'I was sure they were all in favour.'[5]

Mikov dates that meeting as 'in the middle of June . . . I remember it well, it was a Sunday evening'.[6] If so, it was June 9, 1918. At dawn the following morning, in Ekaterinburg, a group of 'Whites' raided the town in a bid to rescue Nicholas and his family; however, the Cheka had sufficient warning of the attempt and Red reinforcements rushed into Ekaterinburg. The name 'Whites' was used to describe those actively fighting the Bolsheviks; some were monarchists, some were not; these Whites were ex-Tsarist officers. The fighting lasted all day, and it was not until late evening that the Whites were finally overcome. Their leader was captured and shot.[7]

That raid on Ekaterinburg increased fears in Perm. The president of the Ural Soviet at Ekaterinburg was Aleksandr Beloborodov, who had worked as a clerk in Perm. He had close connections with the town, where his own

* Grand Duke Nicholas Konstantinovich, aged sixty-one, died in February, 1918, in Tashkent; contrary to rumours that he was murdered, he died of pneumonia, as Grand Duchess Tatiana told her aunt Xenia in a letter from Tobolsk on February 28, 1918. (*source: Prince Nicholas Romanov*)

family still lived; one of his close friends there was Gavriil Myasnikov.[8] On the afternoon of Wednesday, June 12, some thirty-six hours after the abortive White attack on Ekaterinburg, Myasnikov took the first steps in the plan to abduct and execute Michael, as approved by the Cheka. The involvement of the Ural Regional Soviet cannot be established but equally cannot be excluded. The murder was set for that night.

Once the decision had been made, Myasnikov acted with considerable speed. His first task was to recruit an execution squad. 'I needed hard men who had suffered from the autocracy . . . men who were ready to bite through someone's throat with their teeth. I needed men who could hold their tongues, who trusted me more than they did themselves, and were ready to do anything if I told them it was necessary in the interests of the revolution.'[9] The four men who met his criteria were all from the Motovilikha arsenal:

Nikolai Zhuzhgov, aged thirty-nine, was a member of the Perm Cheka and assistant chief of the Motovilikha militia. A small man, with sunken eyes, he had spent seven years in labour camps and had been a friend of Myasnikov since 1905.

Vasily Ivanchenko, aged forty-four, was another veteran Bolshevik, and since April he had been head of the Perm militia and a deputy in the local Soviet. In 1906 he had been arrested for the murder of two Cossacks and sentenced to fifteen years' hard labour. Like Myasnikov, he had been released after the 1917 February revolution.

Andrei Markov, aged thirty-six, was the Perm 'commissar for nationalisation', who worked as a foreman in one of the Motovilikha workshops. A thickset man, he had been for some time in prison with Myasnikov, who regarded him as someone who could be relied upon to do whatever he was told.

Ivan Kolpashchikov was a powerfully built man with a curiously squeaky high-pitched voice and, like all the others, was a veteran of the prison camps. When not working at the arsenal he served as a Red Guard.[10]

Myasnikov called the four men to a meeting that Wednesday evening in the projection room of the cinema in Motovilikha. There, he set out the reasons why Michael had to be killed. He said that if 'His Imperial Majesty' was not dealt with, then 'tomorrow he may not be here, tomorrow he may be standing at the head of the massed forces of the counter-revolution'. However, the execution would have to be presented officially as an escape, for Lenin and Sverdlov would then be able to avoid complications with the 'bourgeois governments' and 'we will not compromise them.'[11]

The four men having vowed silence, Myasnikov then revealed the details. To ensure secrecy the killing would be done that very night. Michael was to be abducted from the hotel room, taken to a wood and shot. As cover for the abduction the execution squad would present him with a forged order, pretending that he was being evacuated for security reasons and because of the threat to Perm from advancing White forces. On the morrow it would be announced that he had escaped, and his entourage would be arrested for complicity and shot.

The time was now 9.30 p.m. The abduction was set for midnight. The place of execution was to be a small wood near a place called Malaya Yazovaya, not far from Motovilikha. If all went as planned by Myasnikov, 'His Imperial Majesty' had four hours to live.

At the beginning of June, in accordance with an order from Moscow, the clocks in Bolshevik Russia had been advanced by two hours.[12] It was a fuel-saving device, and in consequence it did not become dark in Perm on June 12 until after eleven o'clock. On that date darkness lasts for six hours and thirteen minutes,[13] so that with sunset at 10.52 p.m. sunrise would be at 5.05 a.m. The distance between the hotel and the proposed execution scene was six and a half miles,[14] and by horse-drawn carriage, travelling slowly over bad roads in darkness, that journey would take about an hour. There would be no difficulty in finding the wood beyond Malaya Yazovaya for it had been a favoured meeting spot for Bolsheviks in the days when they held illegal gatherings and secret meetings.[15] Allowing an hour or so for grave-digging, the execution squad would be back in Motovilikha before dawn.

There was a great deal to do. Myasnikov telephoned the works and arranged horses for the two phaetons to be used in the abduction. At ten o'clock the horses were ready and the party set off for Perm.[16]

On their arrival the five men went into the Cheka offices to prepare the forged order. The wording drafted by Myasnikov read: 'In view of the approach of the front, Comrade Nikolai Zhuzhgov is hereby instructed to evacuate Citizen Michael Romanov to Central Russia'. The order was to be triple-signed, ostensibly by the Cheka chairman, the head of the counter-revolutionary department, and the secretary. When it was finished, Myasnikov, Markov, and Kolpashchikov provided the three signatures.[17]

During Markov's typing of the document Myasnikov claimed that they were interrupted by the unexpected arrival of Malkov and of Sorokin, the chairman of the Provincial Executive Committee. They saw what was being written, guessed its purpose and appeared 'confused and frightened'; he had to swear them to silence.[18] That was nonsense. Malkov and Sorokin and the other local leaders had already decided 'to shoot Michael Romanov immediately in complete secrecy'; Myasnikov was their agent.

Myasnikov's motives in describing that scene in that way may owe much to his desire to make himself a hero. When he told his story, in 1935, he was a political renegade in Paris;[19] the statement he gave to the Soviet embassy there was intended to win him a pardon in Moscow and permission to return.* To exaggerate his own role, he diminished that of Malkov.[20]

What may be true, however, is that Malkov feigned surprise when he walked into the Cheka offices, for officially he did not know anything about the plot. His role was to pretend afterwards that Michael had escaped. In the meantime, he stayed where he was. He would do nothing more until he received a telephone call from the hotel, to tell him that Michael had been abducted.

It was now 11.45 p.m.[21] Their task completed, Myasnikov and his men marched out, Zhuzhgov folding the typewritten order and thrusting it into his pocket.

Shortly before midnight, the two phaetons bearing the executioners clattered into Siberia Street and stopped outside the Korolev Rooms. While Ivanchenko and Kolpashchikov turned the carriages round so that they were facing towards the town, Zhuzhgov went to the hotel's entrance and banged hard on the door. A Red Guard opened it and peered at the group. Zhuzhgov flourished the order, told the guard that they were there to evacuate Michael and pushed his way inside.

There is no complete record of how Michael spent Wednesday, June 12, although it was probably as any other day, with a stroll in the town and perhaps along the river embankment. He may have gone to Ekaterinskaya Street to look at his new apartment, for Johnson made an appointment that day to conclude negotiations for the rental with the Tupitsins.[22] Certainly Michael was back in the hotel by 6 p.m. for Colonel Znamerovsky joined him then, leaving at 9 p.m.[23] Michael may well then have returned to his letter to Natasha, which he had started the previous day. The first pages, beginning as always with 'My darling, beloved Natasha' would be on his writing desk. At midnight he was in a dressing gown, talking to Johnson in his room; Chelyshev had just interrupted them to tell Michael that his bath was waiting for him.[24]

What happened then in the Korolev Rooms chiefly depends on the evidence of four men. There are the accounts subsequently given by Myasnikov and Markov and the statements of Michael's valet Chelyshev, who was present throughout the scene, and of a witness called Krumnis, a guest in the hotel. On the main points they broadly agree.

Krumnis was playing cards in the hotel when he heard raised voices in the hallway. He went out to find three armed men standing in the office of Ilya Sapozhnikov, the hotel commissar. Myasnikov, Zhuzhgov and Kol-

* He was successful, though he would later regret being so; he was executed by the Soviets in 1945.

pashchikov were telling the commissar that they had orders to evacuate Michael. The commissar said he would telephone the Cheka for confirmation, but the armed men refused to allow it.[25] Leaving the others in the hallway, Zhuzhgov approached a kitchen maid and asked her to take him to Michael's room; the girl led him upstairs to room 18, occupied by Borunov.[26] Chelyshev was then in Michael's room and when he came out, followed by Johnson, they found Borunov 'talking to a man in a soldier's greatcoat'. The man was flourishing a piece of paper and demanding to know where 'Michael Romanov lived'. Told it was room 21, he stepped forward, pulling out a revolver when Chelyshev attempted to bar his way.[27]

Michael stood up, read the order but refused to comply, insisting that he would do nothing before he had spoken to Pavel Malkov, the chairman of the Cheka.[28] Zhuzhgov, staring up at a man eight inches taller than himself, appears to have become uncertain as Michael demanded the telephone. Zhuzhgov had a gun, and a piece of paper, but neither seemed to impress Michael.

Zhuzhgov left the room and called to Kolpashchikov to join him. The argument continued for so long that Markov, waiting outside, hurried into the hotel to find out what was happening.[29] With his arrival there were now three armed men in the room; Michael still stubbornly refused to leave, citing illness, demanding a doctor, and insisting that he spoke to Malkov – unaware, of course, that he was privy to the plot.

With time slipping by one of the men – probably the burly Kolpashchikov – grabbed Michael roughly by the shoulder and snarled: 'Oh, these Romanovs. We're fed up with you all.'[30] Realising that it was futile to resist any longer, Michael began to get dressed. Johnson insisted that he, too, go with them, and after some discussion between the three men he was told to get ready also. Michael was informed that his other effects would be sent on after him. Zhuzhgov then reached up and grabbed Michael by the collar, ordering him to go outside, motioning Johnson to follow.

As they were leaving the room, Chelyshev remembered about Michael's medicine and ran forward holding out the bottle. 'Please, Your Highness, take it with you,' he called out.[31] The men roughly shoved Chelyshev aside, pushing Michael outside into the stairway.

Downstairs, Krumnis watched as the three armed men came down with Michael and Johnson. He remembered Michael and Johnson 'were dressed in the everyday suits that they usually wore when they went out walking. They did not have coats with them, but carried sticks in their hands.' Michael and Johnson both seemed calm and composed: Krumnis 'did not notice any particular agitation on their faces'.[32]

Myasnikov, who had remained at the commissar's office in the hotel lobby,[33] led the way out into the street. Chelyshev, watching from the hotel balcony, saw Michael 'violently pushed' into the first phaeton. Zhuzhgov clambered in behind him, with Ivanchenko on the reins. Johnson climbed into the other phaeton, with Malkov and Kolpashchikov.[34]

The presence of Johnson had not been allowed for in the original plan, so there was no room in either of the three-seat phaetons for Myasnikov and 'contrary to plan, I found myself left behind'. Nevertheless, he told them to move off – 'I will catch you up. If I don't, then wait for me at Motovilikha.'[35]

As the two carriages clipped away towards the Siberian Highway, Malkov and Sorokin came running up from the Cheka offices. They and Myasnikov now went to the militia office next to the hotel, where Malkov and Sorokin confirmed that they would arrest Michael's servants and associates and would also circulate the story of an escape.[36] Myasnikov's 'personal initiative' was now openly a plot involving the Cheka executive.

At the militia headquarters Myasnikov ordered the officer in charge, Vasily Drokin, to drive him to Motovilikha in a militia carriage. Going at a fast trot they caught up with the two phaetons just as they reached the militia offices in Motovilikha. Zhuzhgov climbed down and came over to Myasnikov, who quickly checked the details for the final stage of the journey. Yes, they had spades. No, there was no point in Myasnikov going with them, they could manage without him.[37]

Myasnikov stood in the roadway and watched as the two phaetons set off and disappeared into the darkness. Then he went into the militia offices and telephoned the Perm Cheka. Malkov was there, and confirmed that the escape story was now being circulated, search parties organised and telegrams sent out announcing that Michael Romanov had been abducted by counter-revolutionaries.[38]

By this time the phaetons had reached the paraffin stores some three miles beyond Motovilikha. Michael had sat silently on the journey to Motovilikha but when they moved off again he began questioning Zhuzhgov about their destination. Zhuzhgov told him that it was Mogilev, the first name that came into his head. It was not a reassuring answer, since Mogilev was 1400 miles to the west, and the carriages were heading east. Zhuzhgov hurriedly covered up his invention by telling him that they were heading for a railway crossing and that arrangements had been made that they would be put on a train there, so as to avoid the attention which they would have attracted at 'a busy station'.[39] It was not a convincing story but Michael 'didn't seem frightened', said Zhuzhgov afterwards.

Six hundred yards past the paraffin stores[40] the two phaetons slowed as they reached the wood selected for the executions. According to Markov's account the carriages turned right and drove into the wood for 250 yards before stopping; according to Myasnikov, quoting Zhuzhgov, the carriages remained on the road and the men all walked into the wood, Michael having been told that it was a short cut to the railway crossing.

Whether they drove in or walked, the result was the same when they reached and stopped at the spot selected for the execution. There was no ceremony, no explanation, no macabre ritual of a cigarette and blindfold, just cold-blooded murder. Zhuzhgov lifted his Browning and aimed at Michael, standing a few feet away, and simultaneously Markov shot Johnson, wounding him. Zhuzhgov's gun either misfired or he also succeeded only in wounding Michael, for knowing that he was about to die Michael ran forward with his arms out wide, 'begging to say goodbye to his secretary'.[41] As he did so Zhuzhgov fired again, but because he was using home-made bullets his gun jammed, as did Kolpashchikov's gun as he attempted to fire a second bullet at Johnson. With Michael still moving forward with his arms outstretched he was shot in the head at close range. Markov boasted that he did so, though in Myasnikov's account, Zhuzhgov claimed to fire the fatal shot; as Michael fell he 'pulled Johnson, who had been shot by Ivanchenko, down with him. I went up to them. They were still moving. I put my Browning to Michael's temple and shot him. Ivanchenko did the same to Johnson . . .'[42]

The time was approximately 2 a.m. on Thursday, June 13.

Markov would claim later, in his statement about the killings, that because 'it was quickly getting light' it was decided to leave the bodies covered with twigs and to return that night to bury them.[43] However, that cannot be right, for there were some three hours of darkness ahead of them, which was ample time in which four men armed with axes and spades could dig the single grave into which both bodies were thrown. In Myasnikov's more credible version on this point, Zhuzhgov told him that digging the grave 'didn't take very long'.[44]

Before burying Michael and Johnson their bodies were stripped of all their clothes and possessions, which were put into the phaetons and taken back to Motovilikha, apparently in order 'to prove' to Myasnikov that the executions had been carried out as planned. They had been told not to touch personal effects, but the temptation of trophies proved too much for them. From Michael's pockets they took a watch, a cigar case, a penknife and a tobacco tin.[45] Johnson's pockets yielded, among other things, a handsome silver watch which Markov appropriated for himself, and which he would go on wearing for the rest of his life.*

* He would still be wearing it in 1965, when his statement about Michael's murder was lodged in Perm archives.

At Motovilikha, having reported to Myasnikov, the killers took the bloodied clothes, poured kerosene over them, set them on fire, and scattered the ashes. No one as yet has found the grave in the wood beyond Malaya Yazovaya.

Myasnikov, lighting a cigarette, looked at his watch. It was 4 a.m.[46]

The first telegrams from the Perm Cheka announcing the 'escape' of Michael Romanov had already been despatched. Malkov telephoned Myasnikov at 2.20 a.m. to confirm that he had cabled the Soviet of People's Commissars at Moscow, marked for the attention of Trotsky and Feliks Dzerzhinsky, the Cheka supremo. A copy was also sent to Petrograd and to the Ekaterinburg Soviet and Cheka. The message read: '*Last night Michael Romanov and Johnson were abducted by persons unknown in military uniform. Search as yet unsuccessful, most energetic measures taken*'.[47]

The 'energetic measures' involved ordering out token search parties, which were sent everywhere except on the road to Motovilikha and beyond. They also involved the immediate arrest of Chelyshev and the chauffeur Borunov as 'accomplices'.[48] Chelyshev would subsequently recount what had happened in the hotel room to his then fellow prisoner Aleksandr Volkov, a valet in the imperial household.[49] Chelyshev was in no doubt that Michael had not been rescued by friends but abducted by enemies.

Nevertheless, the story of the 'escape' was spread so convincingly that most ordinary people accepted it as fact. In the local Soviet newspaper, the Perm *Izvestiya*, Michael was said to have been abducted 'soon after midnight' by three 'unidentified armed men in military uniform ... Orders were immediately given for Romanov's arrest and mounted militia units were despatched along all highways, but no traces were found...'[50]

Many of Perm's townspeople saw 'the hand of God' in Michael's disappearance. Prayers were said for him in the cathedral, 'for the health of God's servant Michael'; rumour had it that he would reappear at the head of an army and restore order.[51]

One of the few who wondered if all was as it seemed was Krumnis, the hotel guest who had watched Michael being led out of the hotel. He noted that 'everything about the escape seemed strange, all the more because there were no house searches'.[52] The sister of the senior Cheka man, Lukoyanov, admitted that the news 'had been received rather strangely at the Cheka; they weren't particularly worried'.[53] What was also odd was the relaxed reaction of the Moscow leadership, given the threat which Michael's escape would have posed for them. No vengeful tribunal descended on Perm to exact punishment on those charged with Michael's security. No one demanded an accounting by the local leadership, or the arrest of those whose negligence had permitted the rescue. There was no enquiry, no scapegoat, no consequence. At the Perm Cheka, Malkov kept quiet and he did so easily because he was never asked to speak out.

Moscow knew, in fact, about the murder of Michael very soon after it occurred. According to Myasnikov, a local Bolshevik leader, M. P. Turkin, was sent to Moscow immediately after the murder to report it. Turkin's message was to be that Michael had been killed in order to foil an escape organised by officers intent on liberating him, and to prevent the emergence of Michael as the leader of a counter-revolution. The story was to be told firstly to Sverdlov, with the proviso that he 'isn't to tell everyone about this, just Lenin and anyone else who needs to know . . .'[54]

Myasnikov claimed that Turkin returned from Moscow having done as he had been asked, and that Sverdlov 'had been very, very pleased. There and then he spoke to Lenin on the phone and immediately organised a meeting . . . Lenin was also very pleased . . . they decided to say that he had escaped.'[55] Since Myasnikov was eager to say so in his account submitted to the Soviet embassy in Paris, it can be assumed that firstly it was true, for otherwise the claim would do him no good, and secondly that by 1935 he believed that it was not official policy to deny approval of Michael's murder, but only prior knowledge of it.

Andrei Markov, in his account given in 1965, also claimed to have gone to Moscow, 'and with the help of Sverdlov he was received by Lenin, whom he told about the event'.[56] There is no evidence of Markov's visit, but there is a record of Turkin having been there at about that time, for he is listed as a delegate to the All-Russian Congress which took place at the beginning of July 1918.[57] Markov's claim was probably therefore only an old man's boast, in which he adopted the role actually given to Turkin.

Moscow's approval for the murder appears therefore certain. There is also evidence that Myasnikov obtained from the Ural Soviet formal retrospective authority for the murder already committed.

Some time after Michael's death Myasnikov went to Ekaterinburg, to a meeting of the Ural Regional Soviet at the Hotel Amerika on Pokrovsky Prospekt. Those present were the leaders of the Ural Soviet, headed by its president Beloborodov. The purpose of the meeting was to draw up a resolution for the execution of the leading Romanovs. Although he was already dead, Michael's name was included as one of those the Regional Soviet 'considers it indispensable to execute . . .' The Regional Soviet recognised, however, that 'for reasons of foreign policy', it might be necessary to keep the executions 'absolutely secret'.[58]

The meeting unanimously endorsed the resolution, and also agreed that the Ural Soviet should send immediately two envoys to Moscow to obtain the endorsement of the Bolshevik leadership for their decision. The first envoy was the Ural secretary and war commissar Filipp Goloshchekin; the second was Myasnikov, who it was said was also carrying a 'personal report' for Lenin; he would travel separately, as escort for Beloborodov's wife and family who were also going to Moscow.* The two envoys were instructed to return 'not later than July 15'.[59]

The man who had been Michael II was dead. Now, five weeks later, they were going to kill Nicholas II and every other Romanov in reach of the Ural Soviet.

* On the journey, Beloborodov's family drowned in a cross-river ferry accident; Myasnikov survived, but the accident would explain why he did not return to Ekaterinburg with Goloshchekin or play any further role in immediate events.

THIRTY

Long Live Michael

The first that Natasha knew about events at Perm was a terse telegram sent to her on the morning of June 13 by Colonel Znamerovsky: 'Our friend and Johnny have vanished without trace'.[1] It was the last contact Natasha would have with the colonel. That very day he and his wife were arrested and thrown into prison to join Chelyshev and Borunov. The Archbishop Andronik of Perm, whose crime was to have prayed for Michael, was also arrested; none of them would survive. Comrade Zhuzhgov subsequently boasted of having killed the archbishop as well as Michael.[2]

Natasha was also immediately arrested. She had been in Petrograd staying at the house of Maggie Abakanovich on the Moika. After receiving Znamerovsky's telegram, she and Maggie went at once to the offices of Uritsky to demand an explanation. It was a stormy meeting, which ended with Uritsky ordering Natasha to be detained in the women's prison on the fourth floor of Cheka headquarters at 2 Gorokhovaya Street, beside the Alexander Gardens and opposite the Admiralty. Like Znamerovsky and the others in Perm, she was charged with being an accomplice in Michael's escape. Maggie Abakanovich was also arrested.[3]

More worried about Michael than herself, Natasha continued to insist on an explanation for his disappearance, though it was futile in face of Uritsky counter-demanding explanations for his 'escape'. More satisfactorily, Natasha made 'a thorough nuisance of herself . . . continually complaining about everything and demanding all sorts of impossible things'. Unawed by her gaolers, she refused from the outset to accept the prison conditions, insisting that she be allowed to bring in her own furnishings as well as her own food. The Cheka guards, whom she 'treated as a collection of half-witted menials',[4] shrugged and gave in.

Next day a procession of workmen arrived bearing 'an enormous pile of luggage . . . beds, bedding, linen, crockery, books, candles, cushions, towels, and all spare available food'. Natasha and Maggie pinned sheets to the dirty walls and having reorganised it to make the room look more like a parlour than a prison, they 'retired to their separate beds and stayed there'.[5]

At 2 Gorokhovaya the women's prison was a set of two intercommunicating rooms, the smaller one of which, reserved for political prisoners, housed Natasha and her friend Maggie. In normal circumstances prisoners were kept at Gorokhovaya for only a short period before being moved to a prison proper. However, Natasha would be there for the next ten weeks, facing the threat of a transfer to prison in Moscow to stand trial for conspiracy.

Natasha was refused contact with the outside world for the first four weeks. It was only then that Tata was allowed to see her. Escorted from Gatchina by Princess Vyazemskaya, Tata took flowers, some eggs and butter to Gorokhovaya Street. A condition of the meeting was that it took place with Uritsky present, and a nervous Tata was led into his office. He was sitting beside his desk, 'a fattish man, with protruding ears, very pale, with reddish hair and agate eyes'. He nodded, but said nothing to her.[6]

'Eventually Mamma came down, escorted by a guard with bayonet fixed. She and Uritsky glared at each other like a couple of angry cats,' Tata remembered. Natasha had got 'a lot thinner and was very pale'. They hugged, and were allowed to sit together for thirty minutes, before Natasha was led away to her prison floor upstairs. Princess Vyazemskaya then whispered to Tata to thank Uritsky for allowing her to see her mother; Tata went up to his desk and, like any well-brought-up girl, mouthed her party piece and curtseyed.[7] But good manners counted for little at Gorokhovaya Street; next time Tata would be a prisoner there herself.

Over the past weeks Natasha had been interrogated by Uritsky on a number of occasions, and although she learned no more from him than he did from her, of one thing she became certain: Michael was alive and well and in safe hands. It was not just that Uritsky insisted that Michael had escaped, but that the whispers reaching the prison said the same thing. The rumour was that Michael might yet return to Petrograd as Emperor.

Under the terms of the Brest-Litovsk peace treaty the Germans had re-established a diplomatic presence in Russia; their embassy, staffed with Russian experts, was in the Bolshevik capital of Moscow, but they had an important consulate in Petrograd. The ambassador, Count Joachim von Mirbach, had been Counsellor in the pre-war embassy in St Petersburg; he took up his new post on April 26, 1918; his chief assistant, Riezler, was equally experienced.[8] The Germans were still the dominant military force in the region; they were in easy striking distance of Petrograd and were also effectively masters in supposedly independent Ukraine. The Bolshevik regime depended for its existence on German tolerance of it.

Like the French, the British had withdrawn their embassy personnel in February, leaving a skeleton staff behind. Among them was the British naval attaché, Captain Francis Cromie, now a key source for intelligence. Based on reports from a spy in the German general staff, he reported by telegram on June 29, 1918, that the Germans believed that they would follow up their seemingly successful offensive in the West by a new effort in Russia. Their intention was 'to break the Brest peace, and declare a monarchy . . . Considerations will be more favourable than Brest Peace Conference, return of all territory to Russia, even Ukraine . . . Economic conditions will be onerous but less so than at present. Candidate for throne is Grand Duke Michael and a high German Agent has already been sent to Perm to open negotiations, but Grand Duke has temporarily disappeared.'

The despatch to London, which fitted the facts as Cromie understood them, urged that, since the Germans appeared bent on restoring the monarchy, albeit for their own interests, the best course for the British was to forestall them and back the monarchists first. 'In Ukraine there are 200,000 officers of whom 150,000 will at once join up, but only in support of monarchy,' Captain Cromie reported, adding that 'Grand Duke Michael is the most popular candidate.'[9]

The Germans in Petrograd were sending similar messages to Berlin and to the Kaiser's brother, Prince Henry, who was primarily responsible for questions relating to the Romanov dynasty, and whose concern about their fate was both political and personal, since the ex-Empress Alexandra and the Grand Duchess Ella were his sisters-in-law and his wife Princess Irene was aunt to the five children of Nicholas.

A report sent to Prince Henry in early July made many of the points already raised in London by Captain Cromie in Petrograd. Of all the candidates for a restored monarchy the leader was undoubtedly Michael – believed now to be in Siberia, and the author of a manifesto published in his name – and on that both the German and British viewpoints tallied. For the Germans their evidence, in part, was the reaction of the people in Petrograd to two news reports, the first being of the 'death' of Nicholas II and the second the 'rescue' of Michael.

When Michael was reported as having escaped, the Ekaterinburg Soviet simultaneously spread the rumour that Nicholas had been killed by a Red Guard while being evacuated aboard a special train taking him and his family from Ekaterinburg to Perm. The story was that in the evacuation, necessary because of the threat from advancing Czecho-Slovak troops, the ex-Tsar and the soldier had been involved in a furious row, and it was then that the Red Guard had killed him with a bayonet thrust.[10]

This wholly false story was intended to test both public and foreign reaction to the death of Nicholas. From the Bolshevik standpoint the result was encouraging, as the German despatch to Prince Henry confirmed. The report, passed on by Henry to the Kaiser, stated that although the 'murder' of Nicholas on the train was widely believed, *the effect of this news on the masses was scarcely perceptible. Even the Russian church, whose interests can only be bound up with the imperial family, did not react in any way. Although the rumour was not retracted for almost two weeks, a requiem mass did not take place anyway. This notoriously proved that the ex-Tsar has lost all sympathy from the people . . .*

Grand Duke Michael is a different matter. The newspapers which carried the news of his flight and his alleged manifesto in Siberia were read feverishly and he is seen as the only possible source of deliverance from the unbearable circumstances. The famous Russian writers Kuprin and Amfiteatrov even attempted to publish a newspaper article about the Grand Duke, in which His Imperial Highness was characterised as the only Romanov not to have been discredited in any way. Both were, of course, immediately arrested.

The report, largely confirming Cromie's assessment of German intentions, concluded: 'only the restoration of the monarchy in Russia with German assistance . . . will guarantee Germany an alliance with Russia and the maintenance and support of German interests in East Europe'. What was needed was that 'a general Church Congress, presided over by the Patriarch, offers the Grand Duke the crown'.[11]

In Moscow, Ambassador von Mirbach also advised Berlin that of all the Romanovs who might be considered as Emperor in a restored monarchy the most popular in Russia was Michael, although given his known support for the Allies he was not Mirbach's preferred choice. However, Mirbach concluded, there was no support for Nicholas and he judged the ex-Tsar's cause to be hopeless.[12]

Of more immediate concern to von Mirbach was the news that Michael was at the head of an army in Siberia, that he was supporting the British and French – the Entente – and not Germany, and that his 'manifesto' called on all officers to support him. On July 3 von Mirbach* sent off a gloomy cable to Berlin: 'Effect of Michael Aleksandrovich's support for Entente on generals and officers, including those of the groups who lean towards us, considerable according to impressions here. Groups here have shown themselves noticeably more restrained towards us during the last week.'[13]

No one involved in these assessments was in any doubt that Michael was alive. In London on June 27, 1918, *The Times* reported rumours that Michael 'is at the head of an anti-revolutionary movement in Turkestan' and that 'he had issued a manifesto to the Russian people . . . leaving the decision as to the form of government to be adopted by the Duma which

* Von Mirbach was murdered in his embassy three days later by two Socialist Revolutionary (SR) members of the Cheka as part of a power struggle between the SRs and the Bolsheviks. The SRs were hoping to provoke a resumption of the war with Germany, and thereby prevent a German-led counter-revolution.

was to be convoked'. On July 3 the newspaper reported other rumours of him being at Omsk 'at the head of the Siberian revolt'.[14] Five days later this appeared to be confirmed when the military attaché in Tokyo cabled London that 'a counter revolutionary movement headed by Grand Duke Michael has started in Omsk'.[15] Nine days later, the German military attaché in Moscow cabled Berlin to the same effect, but worrying that it would damage German efforts to rally support from ex-Tsarist officers; if Michael was leading a pro-Allied force, then 'this would place Russian officers of a monarchist tendency in a difficult position'.[16]

Four days later even a Moscow newspaper was reporting Michael's reappearance. 'Rumour has spread here,' said a despatch from Vyatka, 'that the former Grand Duke Michael Romanov is in Omsk and has taken command of the Siberian insurgents. There are claims that he has issued a manifesto to the people calling for the overthrow of Soviet power and promising to convene Assemblies of the Land to resolve the question of what regime there should be in Russia.'[17]

The news of Michael reached even Persia, where Dimitri recorded in his diary the rumours that 'Misha is advancing on Moscow with Cossacks and has been proclaimed Emperor'.[18]

The belief that Michael still lived was widespread and accepted as fact in Denmark, where little George was being cared for by King Christian. Just after his eighth birthday on July 24, 1918, George wrote to his father, in English, a pencilled letter on lined notepaper: 'Darling Papa, We are longing to go to you. Pussy and I are very sad without you . . . I hope you are quite well . . . Best love and kisses'.[19] To Natasha he wrote: 'Dear Mama, how are you. Here is very, very, very bad . . . I want you so much . . . We are very lonely here . . . I have not forgotten Papa.' At the end of July he wrote again to his mother: 'Pity that you were not here for my Birthday. It was a nice day. I write my letters by myself now' and ended by asking, 'Where is Papa?'[20]

It was a difficult question. The first official 'sighting' of Michael was not until August 26 when a British agent identified as ST12 reported from Stockholm that 'a Swede arrived from Omsk reports that Grand Duke Michael Aleksandrovich is living in the Governor's House in Omsk with the Imperial Russian flag flying, with guards and procedures as in old regime days'.[21]

For the Germans, long convinced that Michael was not only alive but leading a monarchist army in Siberia, the question which commanded most attention, at least in Berlin, was whether he could be wooed away from his support for the Entente and persuaded to back Germany. The Moscow embassy on July 17 reported that 'General Brusilov, formerly supreme commander,* has therefore sent a lieutenant-commander to the Grand

* He would later join the Red Army.

Duke to prevent him aligning himself with the Entente . . .'[22]

This was good news for Berlin. There had already been encouragement on July 22 in a report that 'attention should be paid to news which has repeatedly come in recently that certain differences of opinion exist between Grand Duke Michael and the Omsk government about the Entente, as the Omsk government is pursuing solely Russian objectives and in any case wishes to avoid a war with Germany'.[23] By August 23 a despatch from the German Ukraine Delegation in Kiev to Berlin suggested that Michael 'is by no means as pro-Entente as he is said to be'.[24]

German interest in Michael would persist until the very end of the war, and their eagerness to win him to their cause was to have one significant and practical result: it would save Natasha from the Bolsheviks.

The news that Michael was leading armies in Siberia suited the Bolsheviks. So long as Michael was 'alive' then, as 'the most popular of all the Romanovs', it would be difficult, even impossible, for any other candidate for the throne to emerge. The indifferent public reaction to the 'death' of Nicholas effectively sealed his fate, but the outstanding question was what should be done about the other Romanovs. The only factor which stood in the way of their execution was fear of the German response.

It had been in German interests to bring down the Romanov dynasty, and then to support the Bolsheviks, so as to force Russia out of the war. But the Germans were no friends of the Reds for in Germany there were plenty of home-grown Reds eager to emulate their comrades in Russia. Imperial Germany would not countenance the wholesale murder of Russian royals and in particular of those Romanovs who were both Germans and relatives. Apart from family considerations the Kaiser, when a young man, had been deeply in love with Grand Duchess Ella; he had made an earlier attempt to bring her out of Russia into Germany but she so loathed him that she had refused.

There were special reasons, therefore, why the Kremlin should tread carefully in its dealings with the Romanovs. Moscow could not afford to provoke Berlin; at the same time, it did not intend to leave the Romanovs as a 'live banner', as Lenin would put it, for the monarchists. The answer was clear enough in Moscow: the Romanovs in their hands would be killed, but with the sole exception of Nicholas, the deaths of the others would be concealed. Michael's 'escape' had proved how successful deception could be.

In the early hours of Thursday, July 18, Nicholas and his family were awakened in their rooms at the Ipatev house in Ekaterinburg and told, as Michael had been told, that because of the threat posed by advancing

Whites it was necessary to evacuate them. They went quietly downstairs, were placed in a basement room, and shortly afterwards massacred there by a squad of gunmen. It was an horrific killing which would revolt the world.[25]

At Alapaevsk the next day, the horror of the Ekaterinburg massacre was repeated with equal ferocity by, and to the equal shame of, the regime which ordered, permitted, and then concealed it. The Romanov prisoners there were told that they were being evacuated; on peasant carts, they were taken out into the night to a disused mineshaft into which they were thrown alive. A shot fired into the shaft killed Grand Duke Serge, the bullet striking him in the forehead and passing out through his jaw; the others, including Ella, were still alive at the bottom when their killers shovelled earth and rubble on top of them. When White troops captured Alapaevsk, Red Guard prisoners who had been at the murder site admitted to interrogators that they had heard hymn singing coming from the shaft for some time afterwards.[26] As in Michael's case the Alapaevsk Romanovs were said to have been abducted by Whites and to have escaped.

Moscow announced on July 19 that Nicholas had been shot dead. However the Bolsheviks assured the world that the ex-Empress and her five children were all alive and well, although of necessity they had been evacuated from Ekaterinburg to keep them out of the hands of advancing Whites. They also cynically continued in negotiations with the Germans for the release of Alexandra and the children as part of a wider settlement of issues between them.[27]

Official confirmation of Nicholas's execution on July 19 had no greater effect on public opinion than had the false report five weeks earlier. In Moscow the British diplomat Bruce Lockhart noted that 'I am bound to admit that the population of Moscow received the news with amazing indifference,'[28] though it might not have been so if they had known the truth about the killing of the entire family and the savage slaughter at Alapaevsk.

With her mother in prison, and her stepfather missing, Tata was left at Gatchina in the care of Princess Vyazemskaya and a new English governess, Miss Trevelyan, though shortly afterwards the latter was repatriated by the rearguard British embassy. Because of money and food shortages, the domestic staff had been reduced to four: an aged housekeeper, a porter who lived above the washhouse, his mother who came in daily to clean, and the gardener, whose interest in the vegetable patch seemed increasingly proprietorial. There were no cars and the family transport was reduced to a dog-cart and a pony. The standard meal became a fish pie, with potato on top, and a few vegetables when the gardener could be prevailed upon to release them. Sugar, butter, and eggs came through the back-door, usually late at night, from the local black market.[29]

The Danish embassy continued to 'rent' part of the house, flying their flag and sending their daily caretakers to help protect the house against looters, but it was the local Cheka which presented the great nuisance. The Gatchina chief, Serov, took particular pleasure in his regular appearances, flanked by guards, and in baiting Tata, who proved no more tactful than her mother.

Fortunately for Tata and the household, there was continuing help from Vladimir Gushchik, their friendly Bolshevik commissar at the Gatchina palace. He became a regular visitor to Nikolaevskaya Street, often bringing with him a chicken, eggs, or fish,[30] and he also gave the household warnings when Serov planned a nuisance raid, ostensibly looking for illegal supplies of food, valuables, or hidden stacks of arms. The warnings allowed the food to be hidden; jewellery and other valuables were already carefully concealed – the silver was buried in the garden – or had been smuggled out to friends in Petrograd. Searches for arms were, of course, ludicrous but they gave an excuse for turning the house upside down.

In early September Serov found himself with a better reason for raiding Nikolaevskaya Street. Almost three months after being arrested and imprisoned at Gorokhovaya Street, Natasha had escaped. There was swift reaction. On Saturday, September 7, Serov arrived at 24 Nikolaevskaya Street and arrested Tata.[31]

Kept overnight in the local Cheka office, she was bundled next day on to a train and taken under escort to the same prison room where her mother had been, though it was now so crowded that Tata spent the night sleeping on a table. One of the women there remembered Natasha, 'and was full of admiration for Mamma and said . . . that it was marvellous the way she had them all rushing around executing her orders and pandering to her whims'.[32]

Tata would say afterwards that nothing the Cheka ever did could compare with having been in the hands of an English governess like Miss Neame, but that was schoolgirl bravado. Told by Serov that she would be sent to a correction camp for young criminals, 'I burst into a flood of tears'.[33]

The threat turned out to be a bluff. After interrogation to find out what she knew about her mother's whereabouts, she spent another night sleeping on a tabletop, but next day, Tuesday, September 10, she was suddenly told that she was being released.

It was pouring with rain when she got outside. She had no money and had not eaten for two days. Knowing that she could not go back to Gatchina, she took her suitcase and struggled with it to the Fontanka, hoping to find refuge at the apartment of her 'Uncle Alyosha', Natasha's brother-in-law Matveev. Climbing the stairs she reached the apartment door, only to find that Matveev was no longer there. He had disappeared. The housekeeper refused to allow her in, complaining that she had not been paid and that she was tired of having the Cheka turning up every day to look for Natasha. With that the door was slammed in Tata's face.

She sat down on her suitcase on the landing and started to cry. Suddenly she heard a door open on the floor above and footsteps on the stairs. A voice called her name, and when she looked up, startled, she saw 'a completely strange woman with flaming red hair'. It was Princess Vyazemskaya, disguised by a wig. Moments later Tata was running upstairs and into the arms of her mother. Since her escape Natasha had been hiding out in the apartment immediately above the one which the Cheka searched every day.[34]

Natasha had escaped from Cheka custody just in time to save her own life. She had been in the women's prison for ten weeks, until the end of August 1918. Helped by a co-operative doctor, who confirmed that she was 'suffering from tuberculosis', she was transferred under guard to a nursing home.[35] Once there, she simply got up one night and walked out.

The timing of her escape increased the Cheka's determination to find her, for it came just after the murder in Petrograd of her old enemy Uritsky, gunned down on August 30 by a Jewish student, apparently revenging himself for the execution of a friend. Uritsky's death was followed, coincidentally, by the shooting and wounding of Lenin in Moscow. In revenge the Bolsheviks brought in two decrees which inaugurated what would be known as the Red Terror. The first instituted the execution of hostages as reprisal for further attacks on Bolsheviks; the second commanded the execution of anyone 'with links to the White Guard organisations, conspiracies, and seditious actions'.[36] No one was to be spared, even those with diplomatic immunity, as was shown when a band of Cheka agents forced their way into the British embassy and killed the resisting naval attaché Captain Cromie, shot down at the top of the staircase. His body was hung out of the window and left there for days.[37]

Natasha, in custody, would have had little chance of avoiding the firing squad; cheating the executioners by escaping made her re-arrest a priority for the Cheka. Her disappearance was followed not only by the arrest of her daughter, but by an announcement in Perm that Michael and Johnson had been recaptured. Coincidence or consequence, the news of their 're-arrest' suggests that at some level in the Bolshevik leadership there was disquiet about the encouragement which Michael's 'escape' had given to the monarchists. The disappearance of Natasha may have contributed to the decision to announce his 'recapture', in the sense of it being the 'last straw', but what is certain is that by September 18 the Perm Soviet was resolved to remove Michael from the scene officially. To do that they passed off Michael's valet Chelyshev as being Michael, and the chauffeur Borunov as Johnson.

A statement issued on that date by the Perm Cheka, signed by the chairman Malkov, announced that six days earlier a local Cheka agent had arrested two men who, walking along a road, were 'behaving in a suspicious manner'. One of these suspects, 'a tall man with a light-brown beard, particularly drew attention to himself'. Taken to Cheka headquarters for interrogation, it was noted that the men were 'wearing make-up'. When this was removed, 'they were identified as the former Grand Duke Michael Romanov and his secretary, Johnson' and were immediately 'detained under close guard'.[38]

Two days later the Russian Telegraph Agency reported that 'Michael Romanov and his secretary have been detained by agents of Perm Provincial Cheka. They were taken to Perm.'[39]

On the following day, under Warrant No. 3694, Chelyshev and Borunov were taken from prison and shot dead.[40] A month earlier, Sverdlov had cabled Perm that 'as to the Romanov servants I give you permission to act as you see fit in accordance with the circumstances',[41] which was effectively their death warrant. There can be little doubt that their killing was intended to provide bodies for Michael and Johnson, but that this purpose was frustrated because for some reason the decision to 'kill off' Michael was rescinded, at a level higher than the Perm Cheka, possibly by Moscow.

Evidence of confusion and of countermanding can be seen in the fact that the text of Malkov's announcement of Michael's 'recapture' appeared in only one newspaper and that was then blacked-out by being covered in printer's ink; in the regional newspapers the announcement was removed at the last moment from the presses.[42]

The reversal in policy was not enough, however, to save Chelyshev and Borunov, who were doomed anyway in the wave of Bolshevik killings which followed the inauguration of the 'Red Terror'. Madame Znamerovsky, arrested with her husband immediately after Michael's murder, was among the victims, taken out with a group of other prisoners to a sewage farm outside Perm and there shot dead.[43] Had Natasha remained in Perm, instead of returning in May, or had she not escaped from custody in Petrograd, it was a fate she would certainly have shared.

No further attempt was made to promote the story of Michael's 'recapture' and in consequence no real attention was paid to the agency story from Perm. The German report to Berlin mentioned a newspaper reference to it, but dismissed it cynically as 'same as always'.[44] Michael was back in play, and the Germans returned to the business of finding a way in which he could be brought over to their side.

A cable to Berlin on September 30 reported that Petrograd monarchists were planning a dictatorship under General Lechitsky, 'who is supposed to prepare the accession to the throne of Grand Duke Michael'.[45] Lechitsky, former commander of the Ninth Army, under whom Michael had served in 1915, was a competent general but he was not the stuff of which dictators were made, nor was he ever likely to attract the kind of support from other White generals which would be necessary, but in Petrograd the monarchists were so desperate that any general was better than none, and any hope better than none.

Three weeks later, in a telegram from Kiev, Berlin received apparently authoritative confirmation that 'Grand Duke Michael is in Siberia in the safe hands of the "Siberian government"'.[46] That report, passed on to Natasha, must have given her enormous joy; it was also sufficient to spur the Germans on to the next stage of their plans for Michael. Natasha was to be their bait.

From early summer the Germans had been taking the keenest interest in Natasha. As soon as news of Michael's 'escape' was announced, Armin von Reyer, a key figure in the negotiations between the German legation and the monarchist organisations in Petrograd, went to see Natasha. They met just before her arrest and he reported their conversation back to Prince Henry in Berlin, emphasising Michael's popularity and recounting her story of the scenes at Easter when the townspeople of Perm had overwhelmed him with gifts.[47]

Von Reyer was never in any doubt that Michael was alive, though his first information 'from a trustworthy source' was that Michael had been 'brought by ship to Rybinsk',[48] a river port on the Upper Volga, 200 miles north-east of Moscow, and about 1000 miles westwards by river from Perm. That was in flat contradiction of later and more credible reports placing him some 1600 miles to the east in Omsk, which at least was behind friendly lines. Nevertheless, it served to confirm that reports of an escape were genuine enough, whatever the confusion about Michael's whereabouts.

Michael's pro-Allied stance was the greatest hurdle for the Germans and in Berlin it raised questions about backing another candidate whose loyalty might be more certain. But these alternatives were never of any substance and the issue became one of winning over Michael, not backing someone better disposed to the Germans.

But how to win him over? The answer seemed to be Natasha. If the Germans smuggled her safely out of Russia and into the German-controlled Ukraine, then Michael would surely hasten from wherever he was and join her. He would be in German territory and in German debt.

The Germans therefore provided her with a false passport and the necessary permits for entry into the Ukraine. The passport – issued in the name of Frau Tania Klenow, dated October 1, 1918, and numbered 4594 – was prepared by the Ukrainian consulate-general in Petrograd, effectively German-controlled. The affixed photograph showed Natasha wearing the white head-dress of a nursing nun.[49] Since Natasha did not dare venture outside into the streets, the nun's outfit must have been smuggled into her hide-out apartment and the photograph taken there.

The Germans equally appear to have been involved in helping to get Tata out of Russia and into the Ukraine. In her case she travelled on a false passport made out under her real name of Nathalie Mamontov,[50] thought safe enough since it was unlikely to be connected with Brasova in routine checks at railway stations or at the border crossing into the Ukraine.

After their reunion, Natasha had decided that it would be best if Tata went back to Gatchina, as if she had no notion whatsoever about her mother's whereabouts. She was to stay there until given the signal to leave. Shortly afterwards a 'strange man arrived ... who he was I have never discovered, he vanished as silently as he had appeared, leaving my passport; the tickets he would hand to me at the station the next day'.[51] It had been arranged that Tata would travel in the company of one of her mother's friends, a Madame Yakhontova, who had property in the Ukraine and was travelling on a genuine passport.

Next morning Tata set off for the station. On reaching Petrograd the stranger, either a German or German agent, was waiting for her with her tickets. He had arranged reserved seats in the train, packed with people trying to get out of Russia, and her suitcase, taken by him the day before, was already on the rack, along with other cases belonging to her mother, including a kitbag filled with dirty clothes, under which were Natasha's sables as well as other valuables. The stranger thrust money into Tata's hands and waved goodbye.[52]

The route southwards out of Bolshevik-controlled Russia was through Vitebsk to the border crossing at Orsha on the Dnieper; a distance of only some 420 miles. At Orsha the following morning, there was a long wait for examination of exit permits and luggage. It was a worrying prospect, given the valuables – including Natasha's pearl ear-rings, 'the size of hazel nuts', secreted inside a bar of soap[53] – hidden in their suitcases. Mme Yakhontova found a man who assured her that the Bolshevik guards checking the luggage could be bribed; fortunately the man proved a genuine 'fixer', and to their relief the guards passed their luggage with only casual scrutiny.

Across the border Tata 'was struck by the look of order and tidiness that pervaded the territory occupied by the Germans ... It was in such marked contrast to Bolshevik Russia ...' There was also ample food to buy, and they purchased bread, butter, cold meat, cream cheese and bottles of *kvas*, a kind of beer. Across the border they boarded a new train which took them through the old Stavka town of Mogilev, then to Gomel and on to Kiev, a journey of 300 miles. At stations *en route*, the locals on the platforms would offer for sale apples, pears, plums and watermelons. After Bolshevik Russia 'it seemed a land of plenty'.[54]

On arrival in Kiev, Tata was met by Princess Vyazemskaya, who had left Petrograd days earlier and had travelled much as Tata had done. Accommodation had been prepared in an apartment owned by a friend of Princess Vyazemskaya and Tata settled down to await her mother. There had been no news of her and no one knew when or if she would arrive. At last, in early October, about a month after Tata's departure from Petrograd, there was a telegram from the station at Gomel,[55] the halfway point from the border crossing. Natasha, wearing her white uniform of a nursing nun, had successfully escaped and would be in Kiev within hours, no doubt having changed into something more attractive.

The Bolsheviks still hunting her in Petrograd learned of her escape when, on October 21, the Russian Telegraph Agency reported her crossing the border. 'Brasova was greeted with great honour by the German local authorities . . . She was presented with an officer's carriage for her journey to Kiev.'[56]

By the time that story appeared in the Bolshevik press the Germans in the Ukraine were already involved in the next stage of their plans for Natasha, which were intended to make her – and thus Michael – even more obliged to them for their help. King Christian X of Denmark had cabled an invitation to her to go to neutral Copenhagen to join her son. The Germans saw benefit to themselves in helping her get there.

As Berlin was told: 'As we are losing considerable ground with the monarchists . . . permitting the journey might be a suitable way to place the monarchic circles under an obligation to us. The precondition, though, would be that a political influencing of the Copenhagen court by the countess to our disadvantage is not to be feared'.[57]

In short, Natasha was not to say anything detrimental about the Germans.

A few days later, on October 24, there was another request to Berlin to approve Natasha's journey, along with her daughter, Princess Vyazemskaya, and two other companions. The telegram to Berlin described Natasha as 'extremely agitated as a result of the strain she has endured and worrying about the fate of her husband'.[58] Two days later Berlin received yet another formal request from Kiev.

Having received confirmation from Copenhagen that the king approved – though later 'he did comment to the minister that he had invited the countess alone, and did not expect that she would appear with so many companions'[59] – the Berlin foreign ministry finally agreed to the trip and signalled permission to Kiev on October 30.[60] The assumption, of course, was that Natasha would bring little George back with her to the Ukraine, for they knew how desperate she was to be reunited with Michael. In turn, Natasha and George would be irresistible bait for Michael; and with a grateful Michael in the Ukraine, the monarchists everywhere would surely rally to the Germans.

Natasha, or Gräfin von Brassoff as the Germans now called her, posed once more for a passport photograph, wearing a hat and an elegant dress, and completed the details for the exit visa. The young clerk typing out the necessary details looked up and asked her for her date of birth. Natasha did not hesitate, telling him it was June 27, 1888. The clerk inserted that without blinking, and at the end of the line typed in her age as thirty.[61] No matter what the circumstances, she was damned if she was going to admit to being thirty-eight.

With the papers in her hand, bags packed, farewells made, and money organised, Natasha was ready to leave. Unfortunately the date was Monday, November 11, 1918. And that morning, at eleven o'clock, the war ended. Natasha was holding a passport to nowhere.

Now it was the turn of the British to rescue Natasha. With German authority at an end it could only be a question of time before the Bolsheviks seized power in Kiev, and Natasha was once more at risk. Knowing that, she and Tata, along with Princess Vyazemskaya, fled to Odessa, hoping to discover some way of escaping by sea. On arrival they found a room which they all shared at the Hotel de Londres; Natasha's brother-in-law Matveev had also arrived there after his escape from Russia.[62]

Nerves were tense. There were no ships in the harbour, there was widespread looting and the only exit route to safety seemed to be through Romania, though the rumours were that the border had been closed. Then came hope: the arrival of a French battleship. Its sailors came into the town and swiftly restored order, though there was no sign of any willingness to evacuate any civilians in Odessa.[63]

Some days later, Natasha, Tata, and Princess Vyazemskaya went for an afternoon walk down to the quay, and to their delight saw a new ship moored there. Running forward, they found it was the destroyer HMS *Nereide*. The destroyer, just 772 tons, was an old ship with a crew of seventy-two, including six officers.[64] Nevertheless, 'our hearts stood still', Tata recalled. 'The British had arrived.'[65]

Tata ran up the gangway and asked permission to go aboard. A few minutes later all three of them were being invited into the wardroom for tea with the captain, Lieutenant-Commander Herbert Wyld. 'After that the officers of the *Nereide* took us under their wing. They commandeered a car from somewhere, and that car was put at our disposal; they came up *en masse* for tea at our hotel, and we in return were invited to meals on board.' Tata would recall.[66]

By now Odessa was entirely blocked landward, and there was the sound of shelling as the Bolsheviks started to approach. One of the British officers gave Natasha a small pistol for self-protection, but she 'was so frightened by it that she promptly locked it away in a suitcase'.[67]

Another British warship, the 2800-ton light cruiser HMS *Skirmisher*, with a crew of 268, had also arrived in the harbour.[68] With the situation in Odessa deteriorating almost by the hour the British now decided to take Natasha, Tata, and Princess Vyazemskaya aboard the *Skirmisher* for greater safety. They stayed there for a few nights and then, as the two warships prepared to leave, all three were transferred back to the *Nereide* and told that they were being evacuated.[69]

Shortly afterwards the ship moved away from its berth and headed out to sea. Standing on the deck, looking back at Odessa, Natasha knew not whether she would ever see Russia again, but she still believed that somewhere out there was Michael, and that he was alive and well, for everyone had said so.

Aboard the *Nereide* Natasha carried with her the very last letter received from Michael. His final words then were now the very same prayer in her own heart as she stared across the sea at the fading coastline. '*My dear soul . . . I will hope that God will allow us to be together again . . .*'

PART IV

THE FINAL TRAGEDY

THIRTY-ONE

The Death of Hope

It took many weeks for Natasha to travel from Russia to England. The *Nereide* took her to Constantinople, where later she was given passage in a British battleship, *Agamemnon*, to Malta; from there a merchant ship took her to Marseilles, where she continued on by rail to Paris and then to London.[1] It was not until March 1919 that she finally arrived at the house which Mme Johnson had leased on Michael's behalf. It was a comfortable Tudor house, 'Snape', at Wadhurst in Sussex; all the possessions stored at Paddockhurst had been transferred there, although of the horses only Tata's pony, 'Beauty', still remained, as did Natasha's 1913 birthday Rolls-Royce.[2]

Natasha's first concern was to bring back George from Copenhagen and he arrived with Miss Neame just after Easter.[3] Natasha was also thrilled to hear that Dimitri had arrived safely in England from Teheran and was living in London, though now, as an honorary captain, in British uniform rather than Russian.[4] The British ambassador, Sir Charles Marling, and his wife brought Dimitri back with them, in defiance of the ruling that barred the admission of Romanov Grand Dukes. Sir Charles would be rapped over the knuckles for that, but he and his wife had become fond of Dimitri.[5]

Dimitri's sister Marie was also in London; her first marriage, to Prince William of Sweden, had been dissolved and in September 1917 she had married Prince Sergei Putyatin, a kinsman of Princess Putyatina's husband Pavel.[6] Marie and her husband escaped to England through the Ukraine and Romania, leaving behind their baby son, Roman, with Sergei's parents; unhappily, the baby died shortly afterwards of influenza. The Putyatins and Dimitri set up home in a small rented house in an 'unfashionable' part of London; Marie began to eke out a living knitting and selling sweaters, while Dimitri started a private course in economics and social science.[7]*

Dimitri's fellow conspirator in the Rasputin murder, Felix Yusupov, was also in London but the two scarcely met. Felix had his Belgravia apartment, and ample cash – he escaped from Russia with, among other things, two Rembrandts;[8] but he had also disclosed the details of the planning and killing of Rasputin, disregarding his vow to Dimitri that neither would ever

* His tutor was the Socialist Dr Hugh Dalton, later to be Chancellor of Exchequer in the 1945 British Labour government.

speak of it. Dimitri kept his word, but was deeply offended that Felix did not.[9]

Dimitri went to Snape as soon he discovered that Natasha was there.[10] They had not seen each other since October 1916; and in those thirty months much had happened. Together again, their reunion was clouded by the news of the execution of Dimitri's father, Grand Duke Paul,* and by Natasha's desperate worries about Michael. Where was he? Dimitri had heard that he was alive and so, repeatedly, had Natasha.

For the first weeks Dimitri became a constant visitor; Tata was eager to see him when she returned from Paris where, *en route* for England, Natasha had enrolled her in a French convent. 'I had quite got over my passion for him, but would nevertheless have loved to see what he looked like.'[11] The real question was whether Dimitri had got over his passion for Natasha. The bond was still there, and they teased each other as before, but Natasha was tormented by her fears about Michael and could hardly think of anything else. By the time that Tata arrived for the summer holidays, Dimitri had drifted away, trying to pick up the pieces of his own life.[12]

Natasha had other worries. She had brought from Russia a small fortune in jewellery, but she needed more money than had remained in the Paris account. It was more of a cash-flow problem than a crisis for she still expected to return home reasonably soon, believing, as did most exiles, that the White Armies would ultimately crush the Bolsheviks with the aid of the foreign troops now landed in their support. There were British, French, Japanese and American forces helping the Whites, albeit half-heartedly, but as Tata remembered, 'at most we expected ... to live abroad for perhaps three years'.[13]

In September 1919 Natasha sent George, then nine years old, to St Leonards-on-Sea College, a boarding school on the English south coast.[14] With this and Tata's school fees, Natasha required funds from somewhere. On Christmas Eve she was relieved to receive a much-needed cash payment of £1500 from Copenhagen. The money, in a Danish account of Michael's, was transferred on the authority of General Biryukov, who had been on Michael's personal staff in Russia,[15] and had escaped to Denmark. A second £1500 would be paid to her shortly afterwards.[16] These sums gave the illusion of financial security, though they were the last she would receive from this source. There was nothing more to get.

With both George and Tata away at school, Natasha was left with little else to do but worry about Michael. She still believed she would see him again. In February 1919 there had been excitement when her brother-in-

* Grand Dukes Paul, Dimitri Konstantinovich, George and his brother Nicholas Mikhailovich (Bimbo) were executed by firing squad in the fortress of SS Peter and Paul on January 19, 1919.

law Matveev, living in Paris, contacted her to tell her that the French Colonial Office had received a 'Top Secret' report that Michael was in French Indo-China. A man claiming to be Grand Duke Michael Aleksandrovich was asking for a visa; the French authorities wanted photographs for identification. Natasha sent these to Matveev, who gave them to the French. They all waited on tenterhooks for news. There was bitter disappointment: the man was a fraud.[17]

There were other false alarms. Michael was in Japan. Michael was in Siam.[18] Each time there was joy, to be followed by despair. At the same time, there was nothing to say that he was dead. It was torture.

Natasha now faced another ordeal. The Dowager Empress, who had been evacuated by the British with her daughter Xenia, was staying at Marlborough House with her sister the Dowager Queen Alexandra. Natasha was summoned to see her, the first meeting with her mother-in-law since the dressing-down at Marlborough House six years earlier. On July 25, 1919, Natasha wrote to a friend, Captain Shirley Litchfield-Speer* to tell him that 'I have to go to London with Georgie tomorrow morning as the Empress wants to see us. It will be a very *penible* interview, so I am quite upset and even getting ill at the thought of the meeting.'[19]

In 1913 she had faced the Dowager Empress with Michael to give her support. This time she took Mme Johnson. To her delighted surprise the meeting turned out to be a happy occasion. The Dowager Empress made a fuss of her grandson, and even seemed pleased to see Natasha. 'She was rather nice to me,' Natasha reported to Litchfield-Speer, 'but I feel she does not like me and will never forgive me that I married her son. She told me that I had changed so much she would never have recognised me. I could not ask if it was for the better or the worse.'[20]

The Dowager Empress was, in fact, impressed by Natasha. The day afterwards she met Mme Johnson again, and said of Natasha: 'What a beautiful woman, she is so pretty, I had quite forgotten'. Repeating that to Litchfield-Speer, Natasha added: 'I can tell you that, because you know me enough to know that I am very modest and not at all of that opinion.'[21]

The Dowager Empress refused to believe that Michael was dead, as she refused to believe the reports that Nicholas and his family had been murdered at Ekaterinburg. She would never accept the fact of their deaths, and would go on thinking that all were alive until her own death nine years later, in Copenhagen. At their meeting, Natasha tried to sound confident about Michael's safety, but in her heart she feared the worst.

'I am feeling quite rotten,' she told Litchfield-Speer, 'because although

* Captain Litchfield-Speer, of the *Agamemnon*, which took Natasha to Malta; after Natasha arrived in England, Litchfield-Speer and his wife became her close friends.

I had two good reports of my husband from Russia, I had one very bad one from Colonel Davidson. He wrote to Mme Johnson that there is no more hope that my husband and her son are alive. It has become for me a real open wound, as I am thinking of this night and day, and begin to lose the last hope. Alas! It is so hard to live without any hope!'[22]

Yet the hope went on, even after the blackest of news. In September 1919 Admiral Kolchak, signing himself as Supreme Commander of the White Army, sent a telegram to Omsk from Sukin. 'In reply to the letter of Countess Brasova, please inform her that all information I possess does not give any indication that the Grand Duke Michael Aleksandrovich is at present in Siberia or the Far East. His destiny is quite unknown after he was taken away ... and all attempts to find out where he is have not produced any results.'[23]

The only good news was for Princess Vyazemskaya. She had left Snape at the beginning of the year for Japan, hoping to find her husband who was reported there. Kolchak confirmed that he was alive, and 'at present in the general forces on the Eastern front and was seen recently in Omsk safe and well'.[24]

Kolchak* did not say that Michael was dead, only that his fate was unknown. It was the cruellest news; to know the worst would have allowed her to mourn; to be left with hope when there was none was ceaseless torture. Even in October 1919 Natasha was clinging desperately to the idea that Princess Vyazemskaya might yet tell her something about Michael.[25]

In truth, Princess Vyazemskaya knew more than she told Natasha. As early as March 1919, Tata had written secretly to Litchfield-Speer: 'The fact is we have received very bad news about my stepfather; they say he has been caught somewhere in the Ural mountains and murdered on the spot. Ghastly details we have also been given. Mother knows nothing about this. The princess is trying to find out all about it, she is sending letters to anybody she can think of that might know something.'[26]

Yet rumours continued to torment Natasha. After Michael was reported to be in Shanghai, Natasha wrote that 'I have to hope, otherwise it is too hard to live! ... I sometimes feel so depressed and tired of life and think it would be better to die, than to live such a miserable and aimless life. But I try not to complain, and I always have a smiling face.'[27]

Her comfort was her son. She wrote to George several times a week and apologised whenever she missed a regular letter. 'I have not written to you for three days, but that doesn't mean that I have not been thinking of you

* Admiral Kolchak was captured and shot by the Bolsheviks in 1920.

my darling . . .'[28] She also went to see him, hiring a driver to chauffeur her to the school in her Rolls-Royce.[29]

By 1920 Natasha had decided to remove Tata from her French school and to enrol her at Cheltenham Ladies College in Gloucestershire. Tata was now seventeen, and a touch too precocious for Natasha's liking; a year or so of strict discipline would do her no harm. There had been growing concern about her at home in Gatchina and just before his exile to Perm, Michael had written in his diary: 'Before dinner, Natasha, Miss Neame and I had a serious talk with Tata. She has a very difficult personality'.[30]

Money was becoming a worry again. Litchfield-Speer's son John would remember being in London with Natasha in her Rolls-Royce and stopping at a Bond Street jewellers, where she sold an enormous pearl.[31] She would sell more and more of her jewellery over time, though as yet she still thought of her financial problems as temporary. Even the news, passed on to her by friends, that 24 Nikolaevskaya Street had been destroyed in fighting in Gatchina, did not cause her great distress. The house, she told Litchfield-Speer, is 'quite destroyed', but she said no more about it.[32] What would have incensed her was to have discovered that the Bolsheviks later changed the name of the road to Uritskaya Street, in memory of her hated enemy at the Cheka, and the man who had exiled Michael to Perm.*

The lease on Snape came to an end in 1920; Natasha moved to Percy Lodge near Richmond, Surrey, which had the advantage of being nearer London. She was still able to think of living in style; she was also sufficiently confident of her financial position to enrol George at Harrow, one of Britain's most famous and expensive public schools. The headmaster, Lionel Ford, booked him into his own House, which he would join from his preparatory school in January, 1924, when he was thirteen.[33]

At Percy Lodge Natasha entertained lavishly, wining and dining a new circle of friends. She needed people around her, for she could not bear to be alone. 'Gradually the full realisation must have borne in on her that she could no longer hope to see Uncle Misha again,' said Tata. 'Since he was the one person above all others that she loved, the private emotions must have been terrible.'[34] People helped her forget, and to cope, and it mattered not that sometimes they were people more interested in her connections than in her friendship.

One added problem with which she had to cope was as unexpected as it was distressing. Tata, barely turned eighteen, and still at school, had secretly married.

*

* It is still Uritskaya Street; No 24 is now a small apartment block. Gatchina was badly damaged during an abortive White advance on Petrograd in October 1919; Gatchina was, for a time, renamed Trotsk in honour of Trotsky, who had commanded the successful defence of Petrograd; on Stalin's orders he was murdered in 1941 in Mexico.

Tata's husband was Val Gielgud, then an undergraduate at Oxford, later head of BBC radio drama.* In 1921 what mattered was that Tata was a schoolgirl, he a student, and both were far too young for marriage. Natasha, when she found out about it, was at first disbelieving and then enraged.

Natasha had met Val Gielgud earlier, when Tata introduced him to her at Percy Lodge. Natasha had not been impressed. 'She paralysed him by asking his intentions. When he told her that he wished to marry me, and she found out that he had no money, he was more or less shown the door,' said Tata.[35] Natasha ordered Tata not to see him again, threatening to cut off her pocket-money.

Determined to marry none the less, Tata wrote to her father Sergei Mamontov then working for an opera company in Tallin, Estonia; Mamontov had not seen Tata for some years, but he gave permission willingly, enclosing £10 as a wedding present.[36]†

The wedding took place on August 12, 1921, during the school holidays. Afterwards they celebrated with a lunch and an afternoon at the cinema. Tata then returned to Percy Lodge in time for dinner, her wedding ring strung around her neck on a chain.[37]

Natasha found out about the marriage just before Tata was due to return to Cheltenham Ladies College. She was so furious that she ordered Tata out of the house. Tata, with her husband away in the country, ended up on the doorstep of a house in London's Primrose Hill, the home of her old governess Miss Rata.[38]

With Tata gone, Natasha moved again, this time to a fashionable apartment at 26 Bolton Gardens, in South Kensington. By now, all hope had faded for Michael. There was no trace of him anywhere, and all that was reliably known was that on the night of June 12/13 he had been abducted from his hotel in Perm. The inescapable presumption was that he was dead, even if the circumstances of his death were as yet a mystery.

By 1924, six years after his disappearance, Natasha accepted the fact that Michael had been shot dead by the Bolsheviks in June, 1918, though she did not know the full details and never would. She was alone, and she needed to find a means to survive. She began the battle to recover Michael's funds; to do so she would need a court order effectively declaring Michael to be legally dead.

On July 5, 1924, the High Court in London gave such an order in granting Natasha 'letters of administration of the English estates of the late Grand Duke Michael Aleksandrovich of Russia, Michael, in the words of the grant, 'died on or since the 12th day of June 1918, at a place unknown,

* The elder brother of the actor Sir John Gielgud.

† Mamontov died in December, 1939.

intestate'.[39] The value of Michael's assets in Britain was given as only £95, but it was the order not the money which was of significance.

It was also to have immediate significance for Grand Duke Kirill. Since Michael was legally dead, Kirill would now declare himself Emperor.

There had been an unwritten agreement among the Romanovs that, while the Dowager Empress was alive and still unable to accept the deaths of her sons, no member of the family would claim the throne.[40] Kirill ignored this, waiting only for the moment when Michael's death was sufficiently established to allow him to succeed him.

In June 1917 Kirill had been given permission by Kerensky to go to Finland; he remained there with his family until 1920, when they all left for Germany. Later, he and his wife Ducky and their three children made their home in St Briac, a fishing village on the Brittany coast.[41] From there, on August 8, 1924 – a month after the High Court order in London – Kirill issued his first manifesto, declaring himself 'Guardian of the Throne'.[42] That was a meaningless title, which confused everyone, but it emboldened him to move on a month later to a second manifesto in which he proclaimed himself 'Emperor of All the Russias'.[43]

In this manifesto he stated that 'the Russian laws of succession . . . do not permit the Imperial Throne to remain vacant after the death of the previous Emperor and His nearest Heir have been established'.[44] That neatly covered Nicholas, Alexis, and Michael. Kirill based his claim on being 'the senior member of the Tsarist House, and sole legal heir'.[45]

His action divided the Romanovs, as well as the many thousands of monarchists now living in exile, in France, Britain, Germany, the Balkans, and the United States. Of the seven surviving Grand Dukes, his brothers Boris and Andrew acknowledged him as Tsar, as did Michael's brother-in-law Sandro. The four others – the former Supreme Commander 'Nikolasha', his brother Peter, Miche-Miche and Dimitri – did not; neither did the Dowager Empress, who was scathing in her condemnation. She wrote in protest to Nikolasha from Hvidore:

> *I was most terribly pained when I read Grand Duke Kirill Vladimirovich's manifesto proclaiming himself* EMPEROR OF ALL THE RUSSIAS.
>
> *To date there has been no precise information concerning the fate of My beloved Sons or My Grandson and, for this reason, I consider the proclamation of a new* EMPEROR *to be premature. There is still no one who could ever extinguish in me the last ray of hope.*
>
> *I fear that this manifesto will create division. This will not improve the situation, but, quite the opposite, will worsen it, while Russia is tormented enough without such a thing.*

> *If it has pleased THE LORD GOD, as he acts in HIS mysterious ways, to summon My beloved sons and grandson to HIMSELF, then, without wishing to look ahead and with firm hope in the Mercy of GOD, I believe that HIS MAJESTY THE EMPEROR will be elected in accordance with Our Basic Laws by the Orthodox Church in concert with the Russian People . . . I am sure that, as the senior member of the HOUSE OF THE ROMANOVS, You are of the same opinion as Myself. Maria.*[46]

Kirill expected bitter opposition. He told Michael's sister Xenia, 'I know full well that I can expect no mercy from all the malicious attacks and accusations of vanity'.[47] The attacks on him were, however, founded on more than malice and charges of self-aggrandisement.

The greatest practical objection to Kirill's action was that the 'White Russians' were united only in their opposition to the Bolsheviks; even among those who favoured a return of the crown, many wanted the decision on the form of government to be settled by a constituent assembly – in short, the same terms as those set out in Michael's manifesto of March 1917. A constitutional monarchy might follow the downfall of the Bolshevik regime, and monarchists naturally hoped that it would, but the critical need was to overthrow the Bolsheviks, not divide the opposition.

Nikolasha, still widely respected by White Russians, summarised their views when he issued his own manifesto, in the wake of Kirill's. The aim, he said, was to re-establish the rule of law in Russia without stipulating the form of government[48] – in effect, a restatement of Michael's manifesto. And if Russia were to restore the monarchy, it was not necessarily Kirill who enjoyed greatest support as Emperor. The so-called Supreme Monarchist Council, which claimed to represent majority monarchist opinion, favoured Dimitri.[49] This high-minded organisation, clinging to the small print of the imperial laws, held that the three Vladimir brothers – Kirill, Boris, and Andrew – were excluded from the succession because their German-born mother had not adopted the Orthodox faith at the time of her marriage.[50] It did not help that Kirill had married a divorcée and, more importantly, his first cousin.

One other objection was the abiding memory of the red flag on the tower of his palace in Petrograd and his arrival at the Duma wearing a red bow as he marched his marines to pledge their support to the revolution, breaking his oath of allegiance while Nicholas was still Tsar.

Kirill damaged the imperial cause then; by proclaiming himself Emperor in 1924 – dividing monarchists and dismaying the White movement at large – he damaged it again. He would never admit that, nor would his son, Prince Vladimir, elevated to 'Grand Duke' and 'Tsarevich' in his father's manifesto.[51] Under the rules introduced by Alexander III, only the sons and grandsons of Tsars could be Grand Dukes; Vladimir was the great-grandson of Alexander II and was thus entitled to be styled only as a prince. But since Kirill called himself Emperor, it followed that Vladimir should be called Grand Duke.*

They were all empty titles. But Kirill handed them out anyway.

Natasha was given the title of princess in 1928, to be formalised seven years later as 'Her Serene Highness Princess Romanovskaya-Brasova'; George found himself Prince Brasov.[52] In the case of Natasha, being a princess was worth about as much as being called countess. What was still worth something was having been Michael's wife.

Michael's assets outside the reach of Bolshevik Russia were still considerable; so were his brother's. Natasha and George had some claim to both; George also could expect some legacy on the death of his grandmother the Dowager Empress. No one was sure how much was involved, but clearly it would take a long time before any substantial monies would be released.

The most identifiable and substantial claims Natasha could make on her own behalf, or through George, were in Finland and Poland, both now independent countries. In Finland, there was a small estate at the village of Halida, which Michael's father had purchased privately in 1892 for 100,000 roubles; that produced some money, for the Finnish government agreed a settlement.[53] Natasha also knew of 100,000 roubles in the Ukraine, from a sugar refinery which had once belonged to Michael,[54] but that proved impossible to get. In Poland, Michael had owned land estimated by the 1930s to be worth £600,000[55] – a sum which would have made Natasha a very rich lady indeed, if she could get her hands on it.

As for Nicholas's assets, their value would be the subject of immense dispute but the assumption was that they would amount to many millions of roubles, in bank accounts in London and Berlin. The Berlin court dealing with the German-based assets would be told – by Prince Lvov and Kerensky in evidence they provided on behalf of the former Provisional Government – that the estimated figures in foreign funds were between seven and fourteen million roubles.[56] Not all of that was in Germany;[57] but whatever the sum involved, Natasha and George could establish a right to some part of it, along with the other identifiable heirs with equal claim.

However reassuring the future prospects, the reality for Natasha during the 1920s was that while lawyers haggled, the actual cash in her pocket was

* After his father's death in 1938, Vladimir did not claim to succeed him as Emperor, but became 'Head of the House of Romanov'; he would style his only child, Maria, a 'Grand Duchess', and her son by a Hohenzollern prince would become 'Grand Duke Georgy', though at birth he was Prince George of Prussia – a German, not a Russian.

ever dwindling. She had survived so far, partly by selling jewellery, as well as her birthday Rolls-Royce.

Since 'life in London is three times more expensive than in France', Natasha moved to Paris in 1927.[58] It made more sense anyway: she had family connections there, including her brother-in-law Matveev and many of the Mamontovs, her former in-laws. Her old friends the Putyatins were in Paris, and the Vyazemskys had a restaurant in Nice. Dimitri had also moved to Paris, and was working for a champagne company; in 1926 he had married in Biarritz an American heiress, Audrey Emery of Cincinnati.*

Leaving George to complete his last year at Harrow, Natasha moved into an apartment at 9 rue Berlioz.[59] George joined her in July 1927. He had done moderately well in his three years at Harrow, where he was registered as 'Count Brassow'. He was naturally good at languages, but the school would later say that 'his academic progress may have reflected a certain lack of tuition earlier in his life'. His first reports showed him 'next to last' but thereafter he rose to 'middling' and stayed there.[60] In Paris, Natasha enrolled him in the exclusive, and equally expensive, École des Roches at Verneuil, fifty miles to the west of Paris; he would go on from there to the Sorbonne.[61]

George brought with him to France his prized and beloved Norton motor cycle, which he insisted on driving at high speed, much to the terror of Natasha.[62] He was now growing to be as tall as his father had been, with the same slim figure. 'He was uncannily like Uncle Misha,' thought Tata. He had the same look about him; his voice was similar; he even walked in much the same way.[63]

Some *émigrés* among the divided Russian colony in Paris mentioned his name as the 'true successor' to the imperial throne in preference to the disliked and discredited Kirill, but George 'treated the claims made on his behalf with indifference, tinged with amusement'.[64]

It was in Paris that George, though not his mother, became the first beneficiary of the various interests which, on paper, sustained Natasha's hopes of financial security in the future. In 1928 the Dowager Empress died, three years after the death of her sister the Dowager Queen Alexandra. Hvidore, their joint property in Denmark, was sold. King George V and his sisters waived their claims; the proceeds were therefore divided equally between Michael's two sisters, Xenia and Olga, and George.[65]

It was a handsome legacy. The full amount was £11,704. George's one-third share was a very welcome windfall. He put some of it immediately into the purchase of a new Sports Chrysler motor car.[66]

* Their son, Paul, would be born in London in 1928. The marriage failed, however, and in 1937 Audrey went back to the United States, taking Paul with her. He would become a colonel in the U.S. Marines, and later Mayor of Palm Beach, Florida. Dimitri died of tuberculosis in Switzerland in 1942, at the age of fifty-one.

In July, 1931, having finished his final examinations at the Sorbonne, he decided to celebrate with a holiday in the south of France. He and a Dutch friend, Edgar Moneanaar, planned to drive to Cannes, George promising Natasha that he would be back in two weeks in time for his twenty-first birthday.[67]

Before leaving, George and his friend had a meal in Natasha's apartment; she then walked downstairs with them to watch them go off. That afternoon, as Natasha was playing bezique with friends in the sitting room, the telephone rang in the hallway at 5 rue Copernic, the apartment she had taken off the Place Victor Hugo.[68] The Chrysler had skidded on the road near Sens, and crashed into a tree. The nineteen-year-old Dutch boy, who had been at the wheel, was killed. George was in hospital; both thighs were broken and he had severe internal injuries.[69]

Natasha, distraught, took the first train southwards, arriving at the hospital in Sens just before midnight. She sat by his bed all night, but there was no hope for him. George died without recovering consciousness at 11.30 a.m. on Tuesday, July 21, 1931.[70]

His body was brought back to Paris and he was buried in the cemetery at Passy. The funeral was attended by hundreds; Dimitri, who so many years earlier had vowed that, should Natasha ever suffer grief, he would be at her side, walked alone behind the coffin; Natasha, her stricken face hidden behind a black veil, followed behind.[71] In public she refused to weep. 'I must pay tribute to my mother,' Tata would write. 'George was her favourite child and her last link with the man she had loved; yet in spite of the crushing blow she refused to show her deep sorrow in public. She met the situation with amazing courage; that is a virtue she never lacked.'[72]

Natasha bought two plots lying side by side at Passy, the fashionable cemetery near the Trocadero in Paris.* George was laid in one. The other she kept for herself.

Life meant very little to Natasha after the death of George. At fifty-one she was still beautiful but her hair was snow-white. In private she gave way to her grief. At the apartment of her close friend Princess Tamira Eristova, whose husband had served with Michael, she would collapse sobbing, 'What is left for me now? Why should I go on living? My son! My son! My son! I can't bear it. Oh, Misha! Oh, Georgie![73]

Natasha could not be consoled. 'She would weep and weep ... eventually she would cease her terrible crying, drink a glass of tea, and leave – eyes dry, back held straight, head held high, to return to her empty apartment.'[74]

* Natasha was not over-impressed by the title which Kirill gave her. She used it, but the cemetery receipt shows that she bought the plots in the name of Mme de Brassow.

Tata was an added cause for her distress. Her first marriage to Val Gielgud ended in 1923; her next husband was a distinguished writer and music critic, Cecil Gray, by whom she had a daughter, Pauline, in 1929; her third husband, Michael Majolier, had been a midshipman on the *Agamemnon* which had taken Natasha and Tata to Malta.[75] As in Natasha's case, Tata's third marriage to her Michael – by whom she would have another daughter, Alexandra – would last for the rest of her life, though Natasha would not know that.* Thinking about Tata, Natasha had little reason for cheer; she rarely saw her, and because of 'that absurd gypsy life you lead'[76] she often did not even know where she was living.

In Paris, Natasha never gave any outward sign of her sorrow or her personal anxieties. In 1933, just after moving to a new apartment at 22 rue Washington, she obtained an identity card, made out in her new name of 'Princess Brassow'; she had dyed her hair to remove any trace of white; and on the official form she completed she gave her birth year as 1886, reducing her real age from fifty-three to forty-seven.[77] As always, Natasha believed in being no older than she looked.

Despite her continuing cash problems there still seemed reason for optimism. The lawyers representing her claim on the Polish estates had been sufficiently confident to advance her a subsidy against her prospects, in return for a percentage of the proceeds;[78] the case would drag on for several years more, but at the end of it she could expect that her financial position would be secure. Nothing could fill the void in her life, but at least she would not be poor.

Under the 1921 Treaty of Riga, by which Bolshevik Russia recognised the independence of Poland, the Polish government was entitled to sequester any imperial property within its borders; Natasha argued that at the time of that treaty Michael was already dead – a fact which would be established in 1934 by disclosures in the Soviet Union, albeit without admission of any responsibility – and that his estates belonged to his heirs, who were commoners; therefore the land was not imperial and not subject to the treaty provisions. In 1937, after a three-day hearing, the Polish judges found against her. Natasha got nothing.[79]

She did a little better, however, in respect of the assets of Nicholas and Alexandra. She began the action in December, 1933, joined by Michael's two sisters, Alexandra's two surviving sisters – Victoria, the Marchioness of Milford Haven, and Princess Irene of Prussia – and Alexandra's brother Grand Duke Ernst of Hesse. In January, 1934, a Berlin court recognised all six claimants as heirs.[80]

The value of German currency had been virtually destroyed by hyper-

* Tata died in England, at Wanstead, Essex, in 1969.

inflation, and it was estimated that the real value of Nicholas's assets had shrunk to the equivalent of £25,000 at best – though that was not a small amount in those days. It was not until 1938, however, that a certificate of inheritance was issued to the heirs.[81] It was the first time Natasha had ever been treated as an equal of the Romanovs.

That was not the end of it, however. Shortly afterwards there was a petition to have the certificate revoked. The plaintiff claimed that her name was Anastasia, the daughter of Nicholas;[82] her story, which she would maintain with extraordinary success for forty years,* was that she had escaped the massacre of her family; if she was Nicholas's daughter, the money was hers. That claim would fail ultimately, but not until 1961.[83]

Natasha's expenses over twenty years had been far greater than any money she had managed to acquire, or borrow. To meet her costs she had continued to sell her jewellery, piece by piece. Some bills remained unpaid. When Natasha left England she had put a large number of possessions into storage but had never paid the fees, now amounting to £200. Tata, living in England, learned through a newspaper notice that the goods 'deposited by Countess Brasova' were to be sold unless payment was made. Neither Natasha nor Tata had the money.[84]

Desperate to find something to sell, Tata rummaged through the cases in the storehouse, and discovered a mass of elaborate orders and decorations, in gleaming gold and silver. Apart from Michael's Russian orders he had been given others by Britain, Germany, Denmark, Norway, Italy, Portugal, Japan, and Siam. Tata persuaded her reluctant mother to sell them, and then took them to Sotheby's, the London auction house. There was much excitement. It was the best and most important collection of chivalric orders ever available on the market. The auction was fixed for December 15, 1938.[85]

The Sotheby's brochure described the collection in mouthwatering terms. The Most Noble Order of the Garter, presented to Michael by 'Uncle Bertie' in 1902, was 'magnificently complete' and it was 'probably the first time that the complete regalia has been in an auction room'.[86] Then there was the Order of the Bath, the Russian Order of St Andrew, the Badge of the Danish Order of the Elephant, the Collar and Star of the Norwegian Order of St Olaf, the Badge and Silver Collar of the House of Hohenzollern, the Order of Merit of Oldenburg, the Habsburg Order of the Golden Fleece, the Italian Annunziati, the Portuguese Order of Christ and St Benedict, the Japanese Order of the Chrysanthemum, the Siamese Order of Maha Chakrakri – worth perhaps together £10,000.[87] Indeed, it might be very much more.

* DNA testing eventually demonstrated that she was not Anastasia.

Tata was elated. 'For a week or so we wined and dined out daily.'[88] The celebrations proved premature. Firstly the Danish court wrote to Sotheby's to complain. Their decorations were not for sale. The Order of the Elephant was thus withdrawn. Then Buckingham Palace demanded return of the two British orders.[89] There was some surprise about that. As *The Times* explained, 'it is a rule when a member of either Order dies for his heir to return the insignia to the authorities. There has, however, been a general impression that the rule did not apply to royalty, British or foreign.'[90]

Palace officials in London were 'kind but firm', said Tata. When she said that she had borrowed against the sale, their reply was that she should have been better advised. However, they did murmur that an ex-gratia payment might be made to Natasha; in fact, Natasha got nothing.[91]

With the British blocking the sale, the other countries followed suit. The sale was cancelled. Only one country, Japan, took back its decoration but courteously made an ex-gratia payment in exchange.[92] At the end of this fiasco, Natasha was even worse off. Money had been borrowed against the expectations of wealth; experts who verified the insignia had to be paid fees. In consequence more had to be sold. Michael's beloved golden flute went for £100.[93] Other items in storage were taken out and sold off. Natasha made no complaint, but Tata was desperately sorry for her. 'I could cry when I think of my mother,' she wrote, 'of the hopes I raised and the sore disillusionment which followed. She is without means.'[94]

Natasha's only consolation was to refuse ex-King Alfonso of Spain his curious claim to have title to the Austrian Order of the Golden Fleece, as an heir of the Habsburgs. Natasha would have none of it. 'Why should I,' she wrote to Tata, 'he's only another refugee like me.'[95]

Tata, living in England, would not see her mother for many years after that dispiriting experience. War broke out in September 1939, and in June 1940 Paris was occupied. Tata would know no more about her mother until 1946 when her young daughter Pauline went to Paris to find her grandmother. 'I was shocked by her plight,' Pauline would remember. 'She did not complain at all, but I could see that she was starving, and her clothes, though clean and well-pressed, were very shabby. Her poor little gloves were more darns than material.'[96]

There was no trace of any money now. Home was a boxroom in the roof space of an apartment block at 11 rue Monsieur, on the Left Bank.[97] The tiny room had been offered to her by a Russian *émigré*, Mlle Annenkova, who seemed to find satisfaction in their change of fortunes. Mlle Annenkova took no rent, but 'she took pleasure in treating Natasha like dirt and being as rude as she possibly could,' noted Pauline.[98] Natasha never made any protest. She had nowhere else to go.

The Mamontov family in Paris did what they could for her; despite her long-ago divorce they 'welcomed her cordially' and gave her 'tea and drink and things to eat, as she looked so pale and thin'.[99] Natasha had come almost to the end. Sometimes friends – Prince Felix Yusupov among them – would give her a little money, and from England Pauline sent her a regular sum, saved from her own small salary,[100] though it could never be enough. Five years after Pauline first met her, Natasha discovered she had cancer. On learning that, her landlady threw her out.[101]

Natasha, the 'uncrowned Empress' as Sandro once described her,[102] was taken to the Laënnec, the charity hospital around the corner. She died at 3.50 p.m. on January 23, 1952.[103] Afterwards they buried her beside her beloved George. Their grave is marked by a Russian cross of stone, above a chest-tomb of green-and-black marble, with the simple, gold-lettered inscription: *Fils et Epouse de S.A.I Grand Duc Michel de Russie.*[104]

In far-away Perm there is no known grave for Michael. However, in 1996 a local group privately erected in his memory a simple wooden cross in the wood where his remains are presumed to lie. If one day Michael should have a permanent memorial, the epitaph might be that written by Vladimir Gushchik, the Bolshevik commissar at Gatchina palace who so admired Michael: '*And now, remembering this man, I wonder how You, Russia, will wash away his innocent blood? Will you ultimately be able to redeem the death of Michael the Last?*'[105]

ACKNOWLEDGEMENTS

It would not have been possible to write this book without the help of a large number of people and a variety of institutions and organisations, in several countries. We are grateful to all. We should begin at the beginning by thanking Pauline Gray for her many memories of her grandmother Natasha and, not least, for the invaluable collection of Michael's and Natasha's letters, telegrams, papers, and photographs which she generously deposited with the Leeds Russian Archive at the University of Leeds; we also thank Alexandra Majolier Smith for her recollections of her grandmother.

No one attempting a study of Michael and Natasha can do so without the Leeds Russian Archive; in our case we were especially fortunate in that the archivist there is Richard Davies, for without him we might not have had a book at all. His enthusiasm, guidance, and friendship has been a constant support and encouragement; his contacts among academics in Russia have opened doors we might otherwise never have known about; his knack of discovering new material in the most obscure places never ceased to astonish us.

Richard Davies was our gateway into the Moscow archives and our introduction to a number of people who have also made the book possible. Dr Aschen Mikoyan, whose grandfather was chairman of the Supreme Soviet, gave up several months of her life, and much of her nights' sleep, to the editing of some 3000 pages of Michael's and Natasha's letters in the State Archive of the Russian Federation; as befits one of the outstanding lecturers in Moscow University's English Department, she did so brilliantly; without her the book would have been the poorer, for she added substantially to the amount of research possible, some of which might well otherwise have eluded us. In assembling the files, she and we had the advantage of the unfailing 'detective work' of Dr Aleksandr Ushakov. The State Archive of the Russian Federation itself could not have been more helpful: we are immensely grateful to the director, Sergei Mironenko, the deputy director Alya Barkovets, and the historian Vladimir Khrustalev, as well as to the tireless research staff in the depository and reading rooms – Lyubov Tyutyunnik, Vera Khitrova, Nina Semenova, and Nina Abdullaeva; all made it a pleasure to work there. We are also greatly indebted to the efforts of Dr Sergei Romanyuk, who spent days in several other Moscow

Archives, uncovering turn-of-the-century files which many thought had vanished.

In St Petersburg, we owe much to Alina Adazhiy's persistent research at the Russian State Historical Archive, and to the kindness of Tatyana Kozlova and the knowledgeable staff at Gatchina Palace, who gave us access to documents and opened up apartments, not yet fully restored, in which Michael and his family lived during his childhood. At Gatchina they still remember with affection 'our Grand Duke', or Emperor Michael II as the palace rightly records him in their roll of Romanov Tsars. In Perm, we must thank Madame T. G. Rozhnova, director of the Diaghilev House Museum, and Elena Soldatkina; Nesta Macdonald's efforts at Perm on our behalf are also greatly appreciated.

Archive research also took us to the United States. Michael's original diaries for 1915–18 are in the Malcolm Forbes Collection in New York, and we were able to have them fully translated for the first time. For that we owe our thanks to Margaret Kelly and Mary Ellen Sinko, as well as to the excellent translation work of Janel Plank of Columbia University. The Hoover Institution at Stanford University is another major research centre for Russian documents, and we received there every help and consideration; our greatest thanks therefore to Carol Leadenham, Molly Molloy, and to Viktoria Kats for her translation work. The Hon. Paul Ilyinsky, Mayor of Palm Beach, Florida, and the son of Grand Duke Dimitri, generously gave us permission to quote from his father's diaries, and we are also grateful to Leslie Morris at the Houghton Library, Harvard University, where the diaries are deposited, as well as to William Lee who shared with us his research work on them. Prince David Chavchavadze in Washington DC is another to whom we are greatly indebted.

There are many others who helped as we 'followed' Michael and Natasha across Europe. In Vienna, Professor Dr Ferdinand Opll and the staff at the *Stadt-und Landesarchiv*; in Copenhagen, Hans Berggreen, of the Royal Danish Archives, Ann-Mett Skovsgaard, of the Hotel d'Angleterre, and the library staff of the *Politiken* newspaper; in Switzerland, M. R. de Gunten, of the Hotel du Signal at Chexbres – all deserve our particular thanks. In Paris, our evening in Martine Rumeau's apartment at 11 rue Monsieur was made the more memorable by a chance meeting there with fellow guest Danielle de Manneville, who was as astonished to discover that Natasha had spent her last years in the upstairs boxroom (now a bathroom) as we were to discover that Danielle was a great-niece of Natasha's first husband, Sergei Mamontov.

In Britain, where Michael and Natasha lived in 1913–14, and Natasha from 1919 to 1927, we received endless help. We are particularly indebted to Lady Cobbold and the staff at Knebworth House, to the archivists at

Paddockhurst, and to East Sussex Council for their documentation on Snape.

Jill Kelsey, Anne Dimond and Pamela Clark, of the Royal Archives, Windsor, and Dr J. E. O. Screen and Kate Hallett at the School of Slavonic and East European Studies, University of London, have provided invaluable material, and have always been ready to help; Richard Thornton's genealogical expertise has provided vital clues to documentation we might otherwise have missed; Val B. Insley gave us the fascinating letter which Miss Neame wrote to his family from Copenhagen; George Behrend provided us with much detail about train travel in the 1900s; Dr Angus Macleod told us everything we needed to know about medicine; we also thank Harrow School for records of Michael's son George, and Cheltenham Ladies College for those on Tata.

There are many institutions to which we owe our thanks, including the Danish Foreign Ministry, the Admiralty library at the Ministry of Defence, London, the Imperial War Museum, the Bank of England public affairs office, the British Meteorological Office, the Royal Geographical Society, the Rolls-Royce Enthusiasts Club, the Royal Opera House archives, Sotheby's, the British and French Jockey Clubs, Lloyd's Register, and John Entwhistle, Reuters' librarian.

We must also offer our greatest thanks to Martin Pearce for his immense contribution in dealing with Russian-language material which has appeared from a variety of sources; Hilary McLellan not only assembled, edited and dealt with all French material, but tramped with us across St Petersburg and Gatchina; she also spent countless hours in reading and discussing early drafts of the book. Finally, our special thanks to Prince Nicholas Romanov for his help and guidance on a variety of matters relating to the Romanovs, for providing access to documents in his possession, and for his patience in dealing with our many questions.

Any errors in the book are, of course, entirely our responsibility.

CHAPTER NOTES

CHAPTER NOTES

MA = Michael
NS = Natasha
MA's diary = Michael's diary 1915–1918
N = Nicholas II (letters), or in 'N's Diary'
AF = Empress Alexandra
DE = Dowager Empress Marie Fedorovna
BK = Browder/Kerensky: *The Russian Provisional Government 1917*
GAPO = State Archive of the Perm District
GARF = State Archive of the Russian Federation, Moscow
LRA = Leeds Russian Archive, University of Leeds
MM = Maylunas/Mironenko: *A Lifelong Passion*
PRO = Public Record Office, London
RA = Royal Archives, Windsor
RGIA/BF = Russian State Historical Archive, St Petersburg (Baron Frederiks' file)
SK = Steinberg/Khrustalev: *The Fall of the Romanovs*
SSEES = School of Slavonic and East European Studies, London
Vienna SLA = Wiener Stadt -und Landesarchiv
Dates are according to Russian calendar, unless shown in *italics*

PART I

ONE 'That Sinner'

1. Letter, N to AF, September 28, 1898, cited MM, p. 176
2. Princesse Olga Poutiatine, 'Les Derniers Jours du Grand-Duc Michel Alexandrovitch', *Revue des Deux Mondes*, Paris, November 1 & 15, 1923 (hereafter: Poutiatine)
3. General P. A. Polovtsov, *Glory and Downfall*, Bell, London, 1935 (hereafter: Polovtsov), pp. 126–7
4. Grand Duke Alexander (Mikhailovich), *Once a Grand Duke*, Cassell, London, 1932 (hereafter: Alexander), p. 161
5. Prince Nicholas of Greece, *My Fifty Years*, Hutchinson, London, 1926 (Nicholas of Greece), p. 181
6. S. P. Melgunov, *Martovskie dni 1917 goda*, Editeurs réunis, Paris, 1961 (hereafter: Melgunov), p. 229
7. Ian Vorres, *The Last Grand Duchess*, Scribner, N.Y., 1965 (hereafter: Vorres), p. 64
8. Queen Victoria's Journal, *October 8, 1899*, RA
9. MA to NS, November 1, 1909, GARF 622/12
10. MA to Baby-Bee, October 1, 1902, GARF 668/36
11. *Ibid*, October 24, 1902
12. Xenia's Diary, December 9, 1903, cited MM, p. 232
13. *Ibid*, December 21, 1903, pp. 232–3
14. *Ibid*, January 14, 1904, p. 239
15. *Ibid*
16. MA to Baby-Bee, January 1, 1904, GARF 668/44
17. *Ibid*, April 10, 1905, GARF 668/51
18. Princess Catherine Radziwill, *Secrets of Dethroned Royalty*, Cassell, London, 1920 (hereafter: Radziwill, *Secrets*), pp. 87–8
19. Hoover Institution, 'Angel Sapon'ko', f. 61014-A
20. *The Times*, London, *January 13, 1913*
21. Radziwill, *Secrets*, p. 88
22. Princess Romanovsky-Krassinsky, *Dancing in Petersburg: The Memoirs*

of Kschessinska, Victor Gollancz, London, 1961 (hereafter: Kschessinska), p. 44
23. *Ibid*, p. 51
24. *Ibid*, p. 43
25. Radziwill, *Secrets*, p. 88
26. MA to N, July 20, 1906, GARF 601/1301
27. N to DE, July 25, 1906, *The Letters of the Last Tsar: The Confidential Correspondence between Nicholas II and His Mother, Dowager Empress Marie Feodorovna*, (ed.) Edward J. Bing, Nicholson & Watson, London, 1937 (hereafter *Letters*), pp. 213–14
28. N to MA, undated, but circa July 25, 1906, GARF 601/1301 ff.166–7
29. DE to N, August 5, 1906, *Letters*, pp. 214–15
30. *Ibid*, p. 231
31. *The Times*, London, obituary, *January 14*, 1974
32. Sunday, *October 7*, 1906, in Britain. *Inter alia*, the story was headlined in *The Sunday Times*, *Observer* and *Reynolds News* of that date.
33. Donald Read, *The Power of News: The History of Reuters, 1849–1989*, Oxford University Press, Oxford, 1992, pp. 143–5
34. *Observer*, London, *October 7*, 1906
35. *The Times*, *Morning Post*, London, *October 8*, 1906
36. Xenia's Diary, May 3, 1907, cited MM, p. 301
37. *Ibid*, July 30, 1907, p. 306
38. *Ibid*
39. Grand Duke Konstantin's Diary, July 27, 1907, cited MM, p. 305; Xenia's Diary, July 30, 1906, *ibid*, p. 306
40. N to DE, September 22, 1907, *Letters*, p. 230
41. Vorres, p. 89
42. N to DE, September 22, 1907, *Letters*, p. 230
43. *Ibid*
44. RA W58/133, 114
45. Letter from Fisher to King Edward VII, *September 14*, 1907, RA W58/113
46. Admiralty Library, Ministry of Defence, London
47. *The Times*, London, *September 14*, 1907
48. Logbook, HMS Minerva, Friday, *September 13*, 1907, PRO/ADM 23718
49. DE to N, October 23, 1907, *Letters*, p. 231
50. *Ibid*
51. *Ibid*
52. Xenia's Diary, October 27, 1907, cited MM, p. 306
53. MA to NS, November 3, 1909, GARF 622/12
54. *Ibid*

TWO Darling Floppy

1 *Baedeker's Russia*, 1914
2. A. A. Mossolov, *At the Court of the Last Tsar*, Methuen, London, 1935 (hereafter: Mossolov), p. 65
3 Count Paul Vassili, *Behind the Veil at the Russian Court*, Cassell, London, 1913 (hereafter: Vassili), p. 156
4. Mossolov, p. 121; Vorres, p. 58
5. Vorres, p. 59
6. *Ibid*, p. 72
7. Vassili, p. 105
8. *Ibid*, p. 114
9. Alexander, p. 72
10. *Ibid*, p. 73
11. *Ibid*, p. 74
12. *Ibid*, p. 78
13. Count Sergei Witte, *Memoirs*, Doubleday, Page, Garden City, N.Y., 1921 (hereafter: Witte), p. 39
14. Alexander, p. 80
15. *The Times*, London, *November 3*, 1894
16. Vorres, p. 33
17. *Ibid*
18. *Ibid*, p. 23
19. *Ibid*, p. 27
20. *Ibid*, p. 23
21. *Ibid*, p. 45
22. *Ibid*, p. 40
23. *Ibid*, p. 32
24. Blue Cuirassiers regimental roll, 1902, Prince Nicholas Romanov to authors
25. Alexander, p. 52

26. *Ibid*, p. 194
27. *Ibid*, p. 102
28. *Ibid*, p. 103
29. Anon., *Russian Court Memoirs*, Herbert Jenkins, London, 1917 (hereafter: *Court Memoirs*), p. 19
30. Baroness Sophie Buxhoeveden, *The Life and Tragedy of Alexandra Feodorovna, Empress of Russia*, Longmans, London, 1928 (hereafter: Buxhoeveden), p. 92
31. Mossolov, p. 33
32. Witte, p. 194
33. *Ibid*
34. *Ibid*, p. 194
35. Mossolov, p. 95
36. *Ibid*
37. Grand Duke Konstantin's Diary, February 26, 1904, cited MM, p. 240
38. E. J. Dillon, *Eclipse of Russia*, Dent, London, 1918 (hereafter: Dillon), pp. 310–11
39. *Ibid*
40. Witte, pp. 40–41
41. Dillon, p. 44
42. Prince David Chavchavadze, *The Grand Dukes*, Atlantic International Publications, N.Y., 1990 (hereafter: Chavchavadze), p. 128
43. August 13, 1906, Princess Catherine Radziwill, *Nicholas II: The Last of the Tsars*, Cassell, London, 1931 (hereafter: Radziwill, *Nicholas II*), p. 173
44. August 12, 1906, *ibid*, pp. 172–73
45. N to DE, August 30, 1906, *Letters*, p. 217
46. Imperial manifesto of August 1, 1904, *The Times*, London, *January 17*, 1913
47. MA to N, July 20, 1906, GARF 601/1301
48. Chavchavadze, p. 107; Radziwill, *Secrets*, pp. 44–6
49. Chavchavadze, p. 104
50. Mossolov, p. 76
51. Chavchavadze, p. 235
52. *Ibid*, p. 242
53. Radziwill, *Secrets*, p. 60
54. *Ibid*, pp. 69–70; Chavchavadze, p. 128
55. December 1916, see 'Murder Most Fair', Chapter 19
56. Kleinmichel, Countess, *Memoirs of a Shipwrecked World*, Brentano's, London, 1923, pp. 66–8; Chavchavadze, p. 138
57. N to DE, October 20, 1902, *Letters*, p. 170
58. Vorres, p. 115

THREE The Lieutenant's Bride

1. On her French identity card issued in 1933, Natasha gave her height as 1m. 67c., LRA MS 1363/88
2. Natalie Majolier, *Stepdaughter to Imperial Russia*, Stanley Paul, London, 1940 (hereafter: Majolier), pp. 29, 39
3. Richard Stites, *The Women's Liberation Movement in Russia*, Princeton University Press, Princeton, N.J., 1978, p. 182
4. *Court Memoirs*, p. 197
5. Chavchavadze, p. 108
6. V. Trubetskoi, 'Zapiski kirasira', *Nashe nasledie*, Moscow, 2–4, 1991 (hereafter: Trubetskoi), p. 60
7. Sergei Sheremetevsky qualified as a lawyer in 1879, *Spiski prisiazhnykh poverennykh Moskovskogo sudebnogo okruga*, Moscow, 1916, p. 27
8. Savva Mamontov founded his Private Opera Company in 1885; it was housed in the massive Solodovnikov Theatre on Bolshaya Dmitrovka.
9. After 1899 the Mamontov company was known as the Association of Russian Opera; Nikolay Rimsky-Korsakov, *My Musical Life*, Knopf, N.Y., 1923, p. 385
10. Majolier, p. 59
11. *Ibid*
12. Kyril Fitzlyon and Tatiana Browning, *Before the Revolution*, Allen Lane, London, 1977 (hereafter: Fitzlyon/Browning), pp. 25–6
13. Natasha's rank appears on her birth certificate, Moscow Historical Archive, f. 203–777–41–12
14. Fitzlyon/Browning, pp. 25–6
15. State Archive of the Moscow Region, f. 2170–8–1–64
16. *Vsya Moskva*; Moscow Historical Archive, f. 179–24–237–15

17. Moscow Historical Archive, f. 203–777–41–12
18. Aleksei Khludov is named as godfather on Natasha's baptism certificate, *ibid*
19. Moscow Archive of Scientific and Technical Documentation, Prechistenskaya chast, d. 38; *Vsya Moskva*
20. G. T. Lowth, *Around the Kremlin*, 1868, p. 14
21. Majolier: p. 15, on Natasha's birth certificate Yuliya Sheremetevskaya's patronymic is given as Vyacheslavovna, whereas on Natasha's 1912 Vienna marriage certificate it is given as Vladislowowna; her maiden name was Sventitskaya, or Swentizki as it is given on Natasha's 1952 Paris death certificate.
22. Pauline Gray, *The Grand Duke's Woman*, Macdonald, London, 1976 (hereafter: Gray), p. 5
23. *Ibid*, p. 7
24. Dimitri I. Abrikossow, *Revelations of a Russian Diplomat*, University of Washington, Seattle, 1964 (hereafter: Abrikossow), p. 42
25. *Ibid*, p. 231
26. Sergei Mamontov was born in Moscow on October 1, 1877; he died in Tallin on December 30, 1939. Biographical notes on him appear in S. G. Isakov, *Russkie v Estonii, 1918–1940*, Kompu, Tartu, Estonia, 1996.
27. The actual date of Natasha's first marriage in 1902 is not known, but Tata's birth on June 2, 1903, suggests the summer of 1902 and around her twenty-second birthday.
28. Majolier, p. 14; Gray, p. 8
29. Tallin newspaper obituary 1940, LRA MS 1363/138
30. *Vsya Moskva*, 1905, the apartment building opened in 1902
31. Gray, p. 9, she quotes June 15, 1903; in Russia the date then would be June 2.
32. Sergei Bertensson and Jay Leyda, *Sergei Rachmaninov*, Allen & Unwin, London, 1965, p. 100
33. Gray, p. 10
34. *Ibid*
35. *Ibid*
36. Sidney Harcave, *Years of the Golden Cockerel*, Hale, London, 1970, p. 361; Alan Moorehead, *The Russian Revolution*, Collins, London, 1958, p. 72
37. Majolier, p. 14
38. Ibid, p. 15
39. Gray, p. 11
40. *Ibid*
41. Trubetskoi, 4, p. 108
42. Maurice Paléologue, *An Ambassador's Memoirs*, Doran, N.Y., 1925 (hereafter: Paléologue), *February 10*, 1916, Vol. II, p. 172
43. Trubetskoi, 4, p. 112
44. *Ibid*
45. *Ibid*, 3, p. 145
46. *Ibid*
47. Address on MA's letters to NS, 1908, GARF 668/71
48. Majolier, p. 16
49. Aleksandra Tyutcheva, *Pri dvore dvukh imperatorov*, Moscow, 1990, p. 111
50. *Baedeker's Russia*, 1914
51. Alexander, p. 271
52. *Ibid*
53. Prince Felix Youssoupoff, *Lost Splendour*, Jonathan Cape, London, 1953 (hereafter: Youssoupoff), p. 66
54. Trubetskoi, 4, p. 109
55. Gray, p. 15
56. *Ibid*
57. *Ibid*

FOUR An Innocent Abroad

1. Mossolov, p. 182; Majolier, p. 126; *Kratkii ocherk Brasovskogo imeniya ego Imperatorskogo Vysochestva . . . Georgiya Aleksandrovicha*, Orlovsky vestnik, Orel, 1895 (hereafter: *Kratkii ocherk Brasovskogo imeniya*); Majolier, p. 231
2. MA's stable of cars included Rolls-Royces, an Opel, Hupmobile, Renault, Bugatti and later Packards: references to them include MA's Diaries, Majolier, Vorres, SSEES
3. Nicholas of Greece, pp. 181–2

4. MA to NS, April 15, 1908, GARF 622/08
5. Majolier, pp. 16–17
6. *Ibid*, p. 17
7. *Ibid*
8. Vorres, p. 93
9. Majolier, pp. 19–20
10. Vorres, p. 86
11. *Ibid*
12. *Ibid*, p. 87
13. *Ibid*, p. 105
14. Trubetskoi, 4, p. 110
15. Vorres, p. 105
16. *Ibid*, p. 89
17. MA to NS, September 19, 1908, GARF 622/08
18. *Ibid*, September 24, 1908
19. *Ibid*, September 28, 1908
20. *Ibid*, October 8, 1908
21. *Ibid*, October 13, 1908
22. *Ibid*, October 8, 1908
23. Majolier, p. 250; letters from Olga, GARF 668/81
24. MA to NS, October 21–3, 1908, GARF 622/08
25. N to DE, October 9, 1908, *Letters*, p. 236
26. DE to N, October 26, 1908, *Letters*, p. 237
27. *The Times*, London, *November* 5, 1908
28. MA to NS, October 21–3, 1908, GARF 622/08
29. *The Times*, London, *November* 5, 1908
30. *Ibid*
31. *Ibid*
32. *Ibid*, *November 10*, 1908

FIVE Scandal in Gatchina

1. NS to MA, December 1,1909, GARF 668/71
2. Gray, p. 20
3. Trubetskoi, 4, p. 110
4. *Ibid*, 2, p. 61
5. Yousoupoff, p. 51
6. Trubetskoi, 4, p. 109
7. *Ibid*, p. 108
8. Gray, p. 20
9. Majolier, p. 19
10. *Ibid*
11. *Ibid*, p. 20
12. Natasha's parents moved to Flat 52, at 6 Vozdvizhenka in 1906 and her father remained there until 1924; *Vsya Moskva*
13. MA to NS, December 23, 1908, GARF 622/08
14. *Ibid*, December 28, 1909
15. MA's photo albums, SSEES, Vol. III, 1909
16. Letter to Pauline Gray, September 7, 1973, LRA 1363/133
17. MA to NS, March 26, 1909, GARF 622/9
18. *Ibid*, but filed as GARF 622/22, ff. 93–4
19. *Ibid*, March 27, 1909, *ibid*, f. 95
20. *Ibid*, March 31, 1909, *ibid*, f. 97–9
21. *Ibid*
22. *Ibid*, April 1, 1909, GARF 622/9
23. *Ibid*, April 3, 1909
24. Majolier, p. 17
25. *Ibid*, p. 18
26. *Ibid*
27. *Ibid*, p. 20
28. MA's photo albums, SSEES, Vol. I ('Gatchina' 1909)
29. Paléologue, *January 22*, 1916, Vol. II, pp. 152–3
30. Majolier, p. 22
31. NS to Wulfert, July 17, 1909, GARF 622/23
32. *Ibid*, Natasha uses the word 'rape'
33. Majolier, p. 22
34. MA to NS, June 17, 1909, GARF 622/9
35. *Ibid*

SIX Pistols at Dawn

1. MA to NS, June 17, 1909, GARF 622/09
2. *Ibid*
3. *Ibid*, June 18 & 20, 1909
4. NS to Wulfert, June 21, 1909, from Berlin, GARF 622/23
5. MA to NS, June 23, 1909, GARF 622/09

6. *Ibid*, June 26, 1909, addressed to 'Hotel d'Angleterre'
7. *Ibid*, June 26, 1909
8. *Ibid*, postcard, July 1, 1909
9. *Ibid*, June 30, 1909
10. *Ibid*, July 2, 1909
11. *Ibid*, July 5, 1909
12. *Ibid*
13. NS to Wulfert, July 16, 1909, GARF 622/23
14. MA to NS, July 12, 1909, GARF 622/09
15. *Ibid*
16. NS to Wulfert, June 21, 1909, from Berlin, GARF 622/23
17. *Ibid*, July 17, 1909
18. MA to NS, July 19, 1909, GARF 622/09
19. *Ibid*
20. *Ibid*, July 22, 1909
21. *Ibid*, July 5, 1909, addressed to 'Grand Hotel'
22. *Ibid*, September 13, 1909, GARF 622/10
23. NS to Wulfert, July 28, 1909, GARF 622/23
24. MA to NS, July 28, 1909, GARF 622/09
25. *Ibid*
26. *Ibid*
27. Vladimir Gushchik, *Taina Gatchinskogo dvortsa*, Literatura, Riga, 1927 (hereafter: Gushchik)
28. MA to NS, August 2, 1909, GARF 622/09
29. *Ibid*, July 8, 1909
30. *Ibid*, July 25, 1909
31. MA to NS, July 22, 1909, GARF 622/09
32. *Ibid*, August 2, 1909
33. *The Times*, London, Tuesday, *August 18*, 1909 (August 5, Russia)
34. *Baedeker's Berlin*, 1912
35. Gray, p. 26
36. *Baedeker's Berlin*, 1912
37. Gray, p. 26
38. MA to NS, November 25, 1909, GARF 622/12
39. Hotel d'Angleterre, Copenhagen
40. *Ibid*
41. *Politiken*, Copenhagen, *August 18*, 1909 (August 5, Russia)
42. *Ibid*, *August 21–6*, 1909 (August 8–13, Russia)
43. Gray, p. 27
44. *Politiken*, Copenhagen, *August 26*, 1909 (August 13, Russia)
45. MA to NS, aboard *Zarnitsa*, August 14, 1909, GARF 622/09

SEVEN Mistress in Moscow

1. MA to NS, August 19, 1909, GARF 622/09
2. Trubetskoi, 4, p. 107
3. MA to NS, August 29, 1909, GARF 622/09
4. Baron Frederiks to MA, January 19, 1910, RGIA/BF
5. War Minister to Baron Frederiks, December 14, 1909, *ibid*
6. MA to NS, August 17, 1909, GARF 622/09
7. Gray, p. 27 (LRA 1363/53)
8. Gray, p. 28
9. MA to Baron Frederiks and reply, September 8, 1909, RGIA/BF
10. *Ibid*
11. Gray, p. 28
12. *Ibid*
13. MA to NS, August 27, 1909, GARF 622/09
14. MA to N, September 22, 1909, GARF 622/10
15. N to DE, September 27, 1909, *Letters*, pp. 249–50
16. MA to NS, November 10, 1909, GARF 622/12
17. *Ibid*, October 29, 1909
18. *Ibid*, October 8, 1909
19. *Ibid*, October 12, 1909
20. *Ibid*, October 8, 1909
21. *Ibid*, October 12, 1909
22. NS to MA, November 22, 1909, GARF 622/11
23. *Ibid*, December 2, 1909
24. *Ibid*, October 8, 1910, GARF 668/75

25. MA to NS, October 7, 1909, GARF 622/12
26. *Ibid*, October 12, 1909
27. *Ibid*
28. Interior Ministry report to Baron Frederiks, November 5, 1909, Report no. 138438, RGIA/BF
29. MA to NS, October 29, 1909, GARF 622/12
30. *Ibid*, October 10, 1909
31. *Ibid*, November 31, 1909
32. Majolier, p. 23
33. MA to NS, November 5, 1909, GARF 622/12
34. *Ibid*, November 13, 1909
35. NS to MA, November 22, 1909, GARF 668/71
36. MA to Baron Frederiks, November 28,1909, RGIA/BF
37. Baron Frederiks to MA, December 4, 1909, *ibid*
38. War Minister to Baron Frederiks, December 14, 1909, *ibid*
39. MA to N, December 3, 1909, GARF 601/1301
40. *Ibid*
41. Baron Budberg to NS, January 8, 1910, GARF 622/02
42. Natasha's petition, December 31, 1909, RGIA/BF
43. Baron Frederiks to MA, January 19, 1910, *ibid*
44. Prince Odoevsky-Maslov to Mordvinov, January 21, 1910, *ibid*
45. NS to MA, January 11, 1910, GARF 668/72
46. *Ibid*
47. Mordvinov to Grand Duchess Olga Aleksandrovna, September 17, 1909, GARF 643/98
48. NS to MA, January 11, 1910, GARF 668/72
49. *Ibid*
50. *Ibid*
51. MA to NS, January 13, 1910, GARF 622/13
52. MA to Baron Frederiks, January 13, 1910, *ibid*
53. Baron Frederiks to MA, January 19, 1910, RGIA/BF
54. NS to MA, November 22, 1909, GARF 668/71
55. *Ibid*, November 25, 1909
56. MA to NS, November 11, 1909, GARF 622/12
57. NS to MA, November 22, 1909, GARF 668/71
58. *Ibid*
59. MA to NS, October 12, 1909, GARF 622/12
60. NS to MA, November 22, 1909, GARF 668/71
61. *Ibid*, November 21, 1909
62. *Ibid*, November 24, 1909
63. *Ibid*, January 4, 1910, GARF 678/72
64. *Ibid*
65. *Ibid*, January 13, 1910
66. *Ibid*, January 14, 1910
67. *Ibid*, January 31, 1910
68. *Ibid*, February 10 1910
69. *Ibid*, February 11, 1910
70. Chief Procurator, Holy Synod, to Baron Frederiks, February 22, 1910, RGIA/BF
71. *Ibid*
72. MA to Baron Frederiks, March 22, 1910, RGIA/BF
73. MA to N, March 29, 1910, GARF 601/1301
74. MA to NS, April 27, 1910, GARF 622/14
75. *The Times*, London, *May 12*, 1910
76. MA to NS, May 1, 1910, GARF 622/14
77. MA to Baron Frederiks, May 8, 1910, RGIA/BF
78. *The Times*, London, *May 21*, 1910
79. MA to NS, May 5, 1910, GARF 622/14

EIGHT A Son is Born

1. MA to NS, May 26, 1910, GARF 622/15
2. Majolier, p. 29; NS to MA, November 22, 1909, GARF 668/71
3. Robert Walker, *Rachmaninov: His Life and Times*, Pitman Press, London, 1980, p. 52

4. NS to MA, February 19, 1910, GARF 668/73
5. Abrikossow, p. 232
6. MA to NS, May 20, 1910, GARF 622/15
7. NS to MA, February 11, 1910, GARF 668/73
8. *Ibid*, September 29, 1910, GARF 668/75
9. Grand Duchess Olga to MA, March 27, 1910, GARF 668/81
10. MA to NS, October 29, 1909, GARF 622/12
11. NS to MA, January 4, 1910, GARF 668/72
12. MA to NS, June 1, 1910, GARF 622/15
13. NS to MA, June 2, 1910, GARF 668/75
14. *Ibid*, June 10, 1910
15. *Ibid*, June 15, 1910
16. Baron Frederiks to MA, June 19, 25, 1910, RGIA/BF
17. NS to MA, June 22, 1910, GARF 668/75
18. Majolier, p. 25
19. *Ibid*, p. 26
20. *Ibid*, p. 28
21. *Ibid*
22. *Ibid*, p. 24
23. *Ibid*, p. 25
24. *Ibid*
25. *Ibid*, p. 26
26. MA to NS, July 24, 1916, GARF 622/21
27. Birth/baptism certificate, LRA MS 1363/111
28. Majolier, p. 29
29. MA to NS, August 4, 1910, GARF 622/15
30. *Ibid*, August 5, 1910
31. NS to MA, August 5, 1910, GARF 668/75
32. *Ibid*, August 28, 1910
33. *Ibid*, September 28, 1910
34. *Ibid*, October 14, 1910
35. *Ibid*, October 15, 1910
36. MA to NS, October 27, 1910, GARF 622/16
37. Birth/baptism certificate, LRA MS 1363/111
38. *Ibid*
39. Letter to Pauline Gray, December 17, 1973, LRA MS 1363/136
40. Gray, p. 35
41. Birth/baptism certificate, LRA MS 1363/111
42. *Ibid*
43. *Ibid*
44. *Ibid*
45. Gray, p. 35

NINE A Woman Scorned

1. N to DE, October 4, 1910, *Letters*, pp. 257–8
2. MA to N, October 14, 1910, GARF 601/1301
3. NS to MA, August 24, 1911, GARF 668/76
4. *Ibid*, August 18, 1911
5. *Ibid*, August 24, 1909
6. MA's photo album, SSEES, Vol. VI, 1910
7. NS to MA, January 21, 1911, GARF 668/76
8. *Ibid*
9. NS to MA, January 24, 1911, GARF 668/76
10. *Ibid*, February 25, 1911
11. *Ibid*
12. MA to N, May 25, 1911, GARF 601/1301
13. Majolier, pp. 32–3
14. *Kratkii ocherk Brasovskogo imeniya*
15. Memorandum to the Tsar, November 1912, GARF 601/1301
16. Majolier, p. 32
17. NS to MA, May 12, 1911, GARF 668/76
18. *The Times*, London, *June 15*, 1911
19. Majolier, p. 32
20. *Ibid*, p. 33
21. *Ibid*
22. MA to NS, July 31, 1911, GARF 622/17
23. NS to MA, August 4, 1911, GARF 668/76
24. *Ibid*, August 7, 1911
25. *Ibid*
26. Seals used in GARF files 622/17 and 668/76

27. NS to MA, August 20, 1911, GARF 668/76
28. MA to NS, August 25, 1911, GARF 622/17
29. NS to MA, August 18, 1911, GARF 668/76
30. *Ibid*, August 20, 1911
31. *Ibid*, August 18, 1911
32. Okhrana order, September 6, 1911, cited MM, p. 345
33. MA's photo album, SSEES, Vol. VI, 1910
34. *Ibid*
35. MA to N, March 3, 1911, GARF 601/1301
36. *Ibid*, March 30, 1911
37. Trubetskoi, 4, p. 110
38. Letters from MA to NS, GARF 622/18
39. NS to MA, August 8, 1911, GARF 668/76
40. Radziwill, *Secrets*, p. 92
41. Trubetskoi, 4, p. 110
42. *Ibid*
43. MA to NS, February 11, 1912, GARF 622/18
44. MA to N, May 2, 1912, GARF 601/1301
45. Majolier, p. 35
46. Trubetskoi, 4, p. 117
47. *Ibid*
48. Abrikossow, p. 232
49. Rodzyanko (Paul), pp. 138–9
50. MA to NS, July 20, 1912, GARF 622/18

TEN A Runaway Marriage

1–3. Okhrana report from Paris, December 17, 1912, cited MM, pp. 364–5 (hereafter: Paris Okhrana report)
4. *Baedeker's Berlin*, 1912
5. Paris Okhrana report
6. MA to N, October 6, 1912, GARF 601/1301
7–8. Paris Okhrana report
9. MA to N, October 14, 1912, GARF 601/1301
10–14. Paris Okhrana report
15. Vienna SLA
16. Paléologue, *February 10,* 1916, Vol. II, p. 172
17. Extract from St Savva marriage register, No. 35, 1912, Vienna SLA
18. Paris Okhrana report; Vienna SLA
19. Marriage register, Vienna SLA
20. *Ibid*
21–3. Paris Okhrana report
24. Marriage register, Vienna SLA
25. MA's photo album, October 17, 1912, SSEES, Vol. XVI
26. *Ibid*, October 22, 1912; Paris Okhrana report dates the arrival as October 21
27. *Ibid*, the first picture is dated October 28, 1912
28. Chavchavadze, p. 128
29. MA to DE, October 31, 1912, cited MM, p. 360
30. N to DE, October 20, 1912, *Letters*, p. 276
31. MA to N, October 14, 1912, GARF 601/1301
32. Buxhoeveden, p. 133
33. MA to N, November 1, 1912, GARF 601/1301
34. Anna Vyrubova, *Memoirs of the Russian Court*, Macmillan, London, 1923 (hereafter: Vyrubova), p. 87
35. DE to N, November 4, 1912, cited MM, p. 362
36. Vyrubova, p. 95
37. N to DE, November 7, 1912, *Letters*, pp. 283–4, also MM, pp. 362–3
38. *Ibid*
39. *Ibid*
40. The only surviving records of accounts with the Crédit Lyonnais are in Natasha's documents, LRA 1363/72; in 1912 the bank also had a branch at 48 Nevsky Prospekt, St Petersburg
41. N to DE, November 21, 1912, *Letters*, p. 285
42. The ten-point memorandum about Michael is undated and unsigned, but was clearly written in early November 1912; Frederiks was the court minister responsible for matters relating to the Grand Dukes, GARF 601/1301 f. 175–6

43. N to DE, November 21, 1912, *Letters*, p. 285
44. *Ibid*
45. MA to N, November 16, 1912, GARF 601/1301
46. MA's 'terms' were attached to his letter to N, November 16, 1912, *ibid*
47. N to DE, November 21, 1912, cited MM, p. 363
48. George V to N, *December 16*, 1912, cited MM, p. 363
49 MA to DE, December 7, 1912, *ibid*
50. British ambassador to Sir Edward Grey, *January 16*, 1913, PRO/FO 371/1743
51. *Ibid*
52. *Ibid, January 4*, 1913
53. *Ibid, January 16*, 1913
54. Radziwill, *Secrets*, p. 94

ELEVEN Exile in Europe

1. MA to N, December 7, 1912, GARF 601/1301
2. Radziwill, *Secrets*, pp. 92–3
3. Majolier, p. 40
4. *Ibid*, p. 39
5. *Ibid*, p. 40
6. MA to NS, July 5, 1909, GARF 622/09
7. MA's photo album, November 2, 1912, SSEES, Vol. XVI
8. Majolier, p. 89
9. *Ibid*, p. 79
10. LRA 1363/06
11. Majolier, p. 46
12. *Ibid*, p. 80
13. *Ibid*, p. 79
14. *Ibid*, p. 81
15. *Ibid*
16. *Ibid*, p. 78
17. *Ibid*
18. *Ibid*, p. 82
19. *Ibid*
20. *Ibid*, p. 84
21. MA's photo album, December 14, 1912, SSEES, Vol. XVI
22. MA to N, February 14, 1913, GARF 601/1301
23. MA's photo album, March 3, 1913, SSEES, Vol. XVI
24. Alexander, p. 267
25. Prince F is first mentioned by Xenia in her diary entry for June 15, 1908, cited MM, p. 312
26. Xenia's Diary, March 4, 1913, *ibid*, p. 375
27. *Ibid*, March 15, 1913
28. *Ibid*, March 19, 1913
29. *Ibid*, March 22, 1913, p. 376
30. Majolier, p. 41
31. Letter to authors from Hotel du Signal
32. MA's photo album, May–July 1913, SSEES, Vol. XVII
33. MA to NS, June 27, 1913, LRA 1363/06
34. Archives, Rolls-Royce Enthusiasts Club
35. *Ibid*
36. Xenia's Diary, June 4, 1913, cited MM, p. 379
37. *Ibid*, June 17, 1913
38. *Ibid*, June 23, 1913
39. *Ibid*, July 11, 1913
40. *Ibid*
41. *Ibid*, July 12, 1913
42. *Ibid*
43. DE to N, July 27, 1913, *Letters*, pp. 287–8

TWELVE Mistress of Knebworth

1. Chavchavadze, p. 178
2. *Ibid*
3. *The Times*, London, *September 17*, 1909
4. George V to N, *October 6*, 1912, GARF 601
5. *Baedeker's Paris*, 1913
6. LRA 1363/08
7. Knebworth House archive
8. Majolier, p. 43
9. Pauline Gray to authors
10. Majolier, p. 43
11. *Ibid*, p. 42
12. *Ibid*, p. 44
13. Natasha continued to use her Knebworth notepaper on her return to Russia, GARF 668/77–8

14. *The Times*, London, *December 30*, 1913, *January 10*, 1914, *May 13*, 1914
15. Photo, LRA 1363/327
16. Knebworth House archive
17. *Ibid*; when abroad, Natasha rendered the Cyrillic Brasov as 'de Brassow', using the German 'w' to represent the Russian 'v'; for the same reason, the Russian 'Vulfert' translates into the German 'Wulfert'
18. *The Times*, London, *January 10*, 1914
19. *Ibid*, *December 2*, 1913
20. On *May 9*, 1914, LRA 1363/38
21. May 19, 1920, *ibid*, 1363/39
22. Photo, *ibid*, 1363/333
23. *Ibid*, 1363/386
24. The memorandum to the Tsar, November, 1912, included an estimate of income from Michael's estates at one million roubles a year.
25. MA to N, March 8, 1914, from Knebworth, GARF 601/1301
26. *Ibid*, April 23, 1914, from Cannes
27. *Ibid*, July 7, 1914, from Knebworth
28. Gillian Freeman and Edward Thorpe, *Ballet Genius*, Thorsons, Wellingborough, England, 1988 (hereafter Freeman/Thorpe), pp. 12–14
29. Freeman/Thorpe, p. 11
30. *Ibid*, p. 13
31. *The Times*, London, *July 4*, 1914
32. Majolier, p. 47
33. Gray, p. 38
34. Majolier, p. 46
35. *The Times*, London, *June 17*, *July 1*, 1914
36. *Ibid*, *July 20*, 1914
37. *Ibid*, *June 17*, 1914
38. British Jockey Club
39. *The Times*, London, *July 17*, 1914
40. *Ibid*, *July 15*, 1914
41. *Ibid*, *July 17*, 1914

PART II

THIRTEEN Going to War

1. Majolier, p. 49
2. MA to NS, June 20, 1915, GARF 622/20
3. Point 3 in the memorandum to Nicholas, November 1912, GARF 601/1301
4. Majolier, p. 49
5. *The Times*, London, *August 20*, 1914
6. Majolier, p. 49
7. *The Times*, London, *August 1*, 1914
8. MA accounts, 1914–16, Paddockhurst Estate Office
9. Majolier, p. 49
10. William Clarke, *The Lost Fortune of the Tsars*, Weidenfeld & Nicolson, London, 1994 (hereafter: Clarke), p. 32
11. Majolier, p. 46
12. George V's Diary, *August 13*, 1914, RA
13. Harold Nicolson, *King George the Fifth*, Constable, London, 1952, pp. 245–6; *The Times*, London, *July 27*, 1914
14. Majolier, p. 49
15. George V's Diary, RA, although for security reasons the departure was not reported in the Court Circular until *August 20*, 1914 (*The Times*, London)
16. Majolier, p. 52
17. Poutiatine
18. *The Times*, London, *August 3*, 1914
19. Yousoupoff, p. 180
20. Majolier, p. 53
21. *The Times*, London, *January 17*, 1913
22. W. Bruce Lincoln, *Passage Through Armageddon*, Simon & Schuster, N.Y., 1986 (hereafter: Lincoln), p. 76
23. *Ibid*, p. 83
24. Sergei Kournakoff, *Savage Squadrons*, Harrap, London, 1936 (hereafter: Kournakoff), p. 55
25. *Ibid*; Richard Pipes, *The Russian Revolution, 1899–1919*, Collins Harvill, London, 1990 (hereafter: Pipes), p. 318; Lincoln, p. 419
26. Kournakoff, p. 80
27. Polovtsov, p. 115
28. *Ibid*, p. 127
29. *Ibid*, p. 116–17

30. NS to MA, September 27, 1914, GARF 668/77
31. Kournakoff, p. 55
32. *Ibid*, p. 358
33. Polovtsov, pp. 126–7
34. Paléologue, *March 16*, 1915, Vol. I, p. 302
35. Major-General Sir Alfred Knox, *With the Russian Army*, Hutchinson, London, 1921 (hereafter: Knox), p. 46
36. N to AF, October 27, 1914, *Letters of the Tsar to the Tsaritsa, 1914–1917*, Bodley Head, London, 1929 (henceforth: N to AF), p. 10
37. Polovtsov, p. 138
38. Paléologue, *February 10*, 1916, Vol. II, p. 172
39. MA to N, November 15, 1914, GARF 601/1301
40. Polovtsov, p. 134
41. *Ibid*, p. 128
42. *Ibid*, p. 132
43. NS to MA, September 27, 1914, GARF 668/77
44. MA's Diary, January 3, 1915
45. *Ibid*
46. *Ibid*, January 2, 1915
47. *V. D. Nabokov and the Russian Provisional Government, 1917*, Yale University Press, New Haven, 1976 (hereafter: *Nabokov*), p. 40
48. Poutiatine
49. *Ibid*
50. *Ibid*
51. Majolier, pp. 93–4
52. MA to NS, November 11, 1914, GARF 622/19
53. NS to MA, December 10, 1914, GARF 668/77
54. *Ibid*
55. *Ibid*
56. Grand Duchess Marie (Pavlovna Jnr.), *Education of a Princess*, Viking, N.Y., 1931 (hereafter: Marie), pp. 180–81
57. Yousoupoff, p. 95
58. Christopher Dobson, *Prince Felix Yusupov*, Harrap, London, 1989, p. 11
59. NS to MA, December 10, 1914, GARF 668/77
60. *Ibid*
61. Majolier, p. 57
62. *Ibid*
63. *Ibid*, p. 58

FOURTEEN Lily-of-the-Valley

1. MA's Diary, January 2, 1915
2. *Ibid*, January 3, 1915
3. NS to MA, December 20, 1914, GARF 668/77
4. *Ibid*
5. MA's Diary, January 6, 1915
6. MA to NS, January 16, 1915, GARF 622/20
7. MA's Diary, January 17, 1915
8. NS to MA, January 14, 1915, GARF 668/78
9. *Ibid*, January 19, 1915
10. MA to NS, January 15, 1915, GARF 622/20
11. *Ibid*, January 20, 1915
12. *Ibid*, January 22, 1915
13. Lincoln, p. 121
14. *Ibid*, p. 89
15. N to AF, November 19, 1914, p. 14
16. MA to NS, January 22, 1915, GARF 622/20
17. NS to MA, January 30, 1915, GARF 668/78
18. MA to NS, January 22, 1915, GARF 622/20
19. *Ibid*, January 26, 1915
20. *Ibid*
21. *Ibid*, January 22, 1915
22. NS to MA, January 30, 1915, GARF 668/78
23. MA to NS, January 22, 1915, GARF 622/20
24. NS to MA, January 30, 1915, GARF 668/78
25. Dimitri to NS, February 6, 1917, GARF 622/28
26. *Ibid*, January 20, 1916
27. *Ibid*
28. MA to NS, January 22, 1915, GARF 622/20
29. NS to MA, January 30, 1915, GARF 668/78

30. *Ibid*
31. MA to NS, February 4, 1915, GARF 622/20
32. *Ibid*, February 5, 1915
33. *Ibid*, February 16, 1915
34. *Ibid*, February 4, 1915
35. *Ibid*, January 22, 1915
36. MA's Diary, January 21–2, 1915
37. NS to MA, January 30, 1915, GARF 668/78
38. MA to NS, February 5, 1915, GARF 622/20
39. *Ibid*, January 22, 1915
40. NS to MA, January 30, 1915, GARF 668/78
41. MA to NS, February 5, 1915, GARF 622/20
42. *Ibid*, June 20, 1915
43. MA's Diary, February 9, 1915
44. *Ibid*, February 12, 1915
45. NS to MA, February 19, 1915, GARF 668/78
46. MA to NS, February 16, 1915, GARF 622/20
47. Polovtsov, p. 135
48. *Ibid*, p. 138
49. NS to MA, February 19, 1915, GARF 668/78
50. MA's Diary, March 2, 1915
51. Robert Werlich, *Russian Orders, Decorations, and Medals*, Quaker Press, Washington, D.C., 1981, pp. 9–12
52. *Fund of the Imperial Russian Cavalry*, Hoover Institution archives
53. A. Krylov, 'Istoricheskie miniatyury', *Moskva*, Moscow, 3, 1990
54. Radziwill, *Secrets*, p. 96
55. Alexander, p. 303
56. N to AF, March 3, 1915, p. 32
57. AF to N, March 4, 1915, *Letters of the Tsaritsa to the Tsar, 1914–1916*, Duckworth, London, 1923 (hereafter: AF to N), p. 54
58. MA copied the letter into his diary, March 10, 1915.
59. NS to MA, March 16, 1915, GARF 668/78
60. *Ibid*
61. *Ibid*
62. MA to NS, March 20, 1915, GARF 622/20
63. *Ibid*, March 21, 1915
64. NS to MA, March 16, 1915, GARF 668/78
65. Dimitri to NS, March 22, 1915, GARF 622/28
66. NS to MA, April 20, 1915, GARF 668/78
67. MA to NS, January 22, 1915, GARF 622/20
68. *Ibid*, April 12, 1915

FIFTEEN Love and Duty

1. MA's Diary, March 29, 1915
2. NS to MA, March 16, 1915, GARF 668/78
3. MA's Diary, March 30, 1915
4. MA to NS, April 12, 1916, GARF 622/20
5. MA to N, March 14, 1915, GARF 601/1301
6. Imperial ukase of March 26, 1915, cited Jacques Ferrand, *Il est toujours des Romanov!*, Ferrand, Paris, 1995, p. 25
7. NS to MA, April 20, 1915, GARF 668/78
8. *Ibid*
9. MA to N, February 22, 1915, GARF 601/1301
10. NS to MA, April 20, 1915, GARF 668/78
11. *Ibid*
12. MA to NS, April 12, 1916, GARF 622/20
13. AF to N, March 9, 1915, p. 61
14. MA's Diary, April 10, 1915
15. Polovtsov, p. 138
16. Gushchik, pp. 22–3
17. *Ibid*, pp. 28–9
18. MA's Diary, April 17, 1915
19. *Ibid*, April 19, 1915
20. *Ibid*, May 8, 1915
21. MA to NS, June 5, 1915, GARF 622/20
22. NS to MA, May 24, 1915, GARF 668/78
23. Dimitri to NS, April 28, 1915, GARF 622/28

24. NS to MA, May 29, 1915, GARF 668/78
25. NS to Dimitri, May 21, 1915, GARF 622/28
26. NS to MA, May 29, 1915, GARF 668/78
27. MA to NS, June 5, 1915, GARF 622/20
28. *Ibid*, June 10, 1915
29. NS to MA, June 10, 1915, GARF 668/78
30. MA to NS, June 1, 1915, GARF 622/20
31. *Ibid*, April 7, 1915
32. NS to MA, June 10, 1915, GARF 668/78
33. MA to NS, June 20, 1915, GARF 622/20
34. MA's Diary, June 24, 1915
35. Paléologue, *June 19*, 1915, Vol. II, p. 15
36. NS to MA, June 10, 1915, GARF 668/78
37. MA to NS, June 14, 1915, GARF 622/20
38. *Ibid*, June 20, 1915
39. NS to MA, June 10, 1915, GARF 668/78
40. *Ibid*, March 16, 1915
41. MA to NS, June 10, 1915, GARF 622/20
42. MA's Diary, June 9–20, 1915
43. NS to MA, May 31, 1915, GARF 668/78
44. MA to NS, June 4, 1915, GARF 622/20
45. NS to MA, June 20, 1915, GARF 668/78
46. MA to NS, June 23, 1915, GARF 622/20
47. Stanley Washburn, *The Russian Campaign, 1915*, Andrew Melrose, London, 1916, pp. 261–2
48. *Ibid*
49. NS to MA, June 20, 1915, GARF 668/78
50. *Ibid*
51. MA to NS, June 20, 1915, GARF 622/20
52. NS to MA, June 10, 1915, GARF 668/78
53. MA to NS, June 20, 1915, GARF 622/20
54. *Ibid*
55. *Ibid*
56. NS to MA, May 31, 1915, GARF 668/78
57. *Ibid*
58. *Ibid*, June 20, 1915
59. MA to NS, June 5, 1915, GARF 622/20
60. *Ibid*, June 20, 1915
61. NS to MA, June 30, 1915, GARF 668/78
62. MA to NS, July 7, 1915, GARF 622/20
63. NS to MA, July 10, 1915, GARF 668/78
64. Paléologue, *June 26*, 1916, Vol. II, p. 283
65. NS to MA, July 10, 1915, GARF 668/78
66. *Ibid*
67. MA's Diary, July 15, 1915
68. Dimitri to NS, July 21, 1915, GARF 622/28

SIXTEEN Alexandra the Great

1. Poutiatine
2. Majolier, pp. 83–4
3. MA's Diary, July 22, 1915
4. *Ibid*, July 26, 1915
5. *Ibid*; July 28, 1915
6. *Ibid*, July 30, 1915
7. *Ibid*, August 5, 1915
8. *Ibid*, August 7, 1915
9. *Ibid*, August 15, 1915
10. MA to NS, June 20, 1915, GARF 622/20
11. Grand Duke Andrew's Diary, cited F. A. Golder (ed.), *Documents of Russian History, 1914–1917*, Smith, Gloucester, Mass., 1964 (hereafter: Golder), p. 239
12. Knox, p. 332
13. Paléologue, *August 27*, 1915, Vol. II, p. 60
14. General Alexei Brusilov, *A Soldier's Note-Book*, Macmillan, London, 1936 (hereafter: Brusilov), p. 180
15. AF to N, August 22, 1915, p. 114
16. N to AF, August 25, 1915, pp. 71–2
17. AF to N, August 28, 1915, p. 125

18. Vyrubova, p. 100
19. AF to N, August 27, 1901, cited MM, p. 208
20. Grand Duke Konstantin's Diary, August 25, 1902, *ibid*, p. 219
21. Xenia's Diary, August 19, 1902, *ibid*, p. 217
22. Paléologue, *February 24*, 1915, Vol. I, p. 392
23. *Ibid*, *October 12*, 1915, Vol. II, p. 83
24. *Ibid*, *December 29*, 1914, Vol. I, p. 229
25. R. H. Bruce Lockhart, *Memoirs of a British Agent*, Macmillan, London, 1932 (hereafter: Bruce Lockhart), pp. 128–9
26. Paléologue, *April 15*, 1915, Vol. I, p. 331
27. AF to N, June 22, 1915, p. 105
28. Paléologue, *July 24*, 1915, Vol. II, pp. 35–6
29. AF to N, April 4, 1915, p. 62
30. Knox, p. 334
31. Paléologue, *April 27*, 1915, Vol. I, pp. 333–4
32. *Ibid*, *May 25*, 1915, p. 341
33. *Ibid*, *June 13*, 1915, Vol. II, pp. 12–13
34. AF to N, June 10, 1915, p. 86
35. *Ibid*, June 17, 1915, p. 100
36. *Ibid*, June 25, 1915, p. 110
37. *Ibid*, August 22, 1915, p. 114
38. N to AF, August 25, 1915, p. 70
39. Grand Duke Andrew's Diary, cited Golder, p. 240
40. *Ibid*
41. Buchanan, Sir George, *My Mission to Russia*, Cassell, London, 1923 (hereafter: Buchanan), p. 238
42. N to AF, August 25, 1915, p. 72
43. *Ibid*, August 26, 1915, p. 73
44. Paléologue, *March 13*, 1916, Vol. II, p. 207
45. N to AF, August 27, 1915, p. 74
46. Lincoln, p. 173
47. AF to N, August 31, 1915, p. 132
48. *Ibid*, September 6, 1915, p. 143
49. N to AF, September 11, 1915, p. 87
50. *Ibid*, September 14, 1915, p. 89
51. AF to N, September 16, 1915, p. 168
52. *Ibid*
53. *Ibid*
54. *Ibid*, September 11, 1915, p. 158
55. Princess Paley's title was granted on August 15, 1915
56. AF to N, April 6, 1915, p. 65
57. *Ibid*
58. AF to N, September 11, 1915, p. 158
59. N to AF, September 17, 1915, pp. 90–91
60. AF to N, September 9, 1915, p. 153
61. Yousoupoff, p. 82
62. N's Diary, October 15, 1894, cited MM, p. 98
63. AF to N, September 11, 1915, p. 156
64. *Ibid*, September 8, 1915, p. 152
65. *Ibid*, June 25, 1915, p. 110
66. *Ibid*, August 30, 1915, p. 131
67. Lincoln, p. 159
68. Paléologue, *June 15*, 1916, Vol. II, pp. 13–14
69. AF to N, September 11, 1915, p. 157
70. *Ibid*, September 12, 1915, p. 159
71. *Ibid*, August 23, 1915, p. 117
72. *Ibid*, September 14, 1915, p. 168
73. N to AF, September 16, 1915, p. 90
74. Brusilov, pp. 287–8
75. Paléologue, *September 2*, 1915, Vol. II, pp. 66–7
76. Marie, p. 223
77. Paléologue, *November 11*, 1914, Vol. I, p. 185
78. Abrikossow, p. 236
79. *Ibid*, p. 234
80. AF to N, September 17, 1915, p. 176

SEVENTEEN Rival Courts

1. NS to MA, May 29, 1915, GARF 668/78
2. *Ibid*, June 10, 1915
3. *Ibid*
4. Majolier, p. 69
5. NS to MA, December 20, 1914, GARF 668/77
6. Gushchik, p. 41
7. Majolier, p. 84
8. Gushchik, p. 44
9. Majolier, p. 81
10. *Ibid*, p. 83
11. *Ibid*, p. 54
12. Gushchik, p. 43
13. *Ibid*, p. 29
14. Majolier, p. 83

15. Gushchik, p. 44
16. Knox, pp. 413–14
17. M. V. Rodzyanko, *The Reign of Rasputin*, Philpot, London, 1927 (hereafter: Rodzyanko, *Rasputin*), pp. 164–5
18. Abrikossow, p. 234
19. MA Diary, October–December, 1915
20. *Ibid*, November 19, 1915
21. *Ibid*, August 10, 1915
22. Abrikossow, p. 233
23. *Ibid*
24. *Ibid*, p. 234
25. *Ibid*, p. 236
26. *Ibid*, p. 233
27. *Ibid*, p. 234
28. 'Her Excellency': Address on letters to Gatchina 1914–15, GARF 622/19–20
29. Natasha's Gatchina stationery, 1915 onwards, GARF 668/78
30. MA Diary, October 18, 1915
31. *Ibid*
32. *Ibid*
33. *Ibid*, October 19, 1915
34. *Ibid*, October 24, 1915
35. *Ibid*, November 25, 1915
36. Abrikossow, p. 235
37. Paléologue, *February 10*, 1915, Vol. II, p. 171
38. *Ibid*
39. *Ibid*, p. 173
40. *Ibid*
41. Abrikossow, p. 235
42. *Ibid*, p. 234
43. Paléologue, *February 10*, 1915, Vol. II, p. 172
44. Princess Paley, *Memories of Russia*, Herbert Jenkins, London, 1924 (hereafter: Paley), p. 63
45. Paléologue, *February 10*, 1915, Vol. II, p. 173
46. AF to N, September 2, 1915, p. 135
47. Paléologue, *April 2*, 1916, Vol. II, p. 227
48. Alexander Kerensky, *Memoirs*, Cassell, London, 1966 (hereafter: Kerensky), p. 143
49. *Ibid*, p. 147
50. Abrikossow, p. 236
51. Bruce Lockhart, p. 160
52. Abrikossow, p. 237
53. AF to N, January 7, 1916, p. 256
54. Paléologue, *February 5*, 1916, Vol. II, p. 166
55. MA's Diary, February 9, 1916
56. Rodzyanko, *Rasputin*, p. 175
57. Paléologue, *September 15*, 1915, Vol. II, p. 74
58. *Ibid*, *February 22*, 1916, p. 188
59. MA's Diary, February 9, 1916
60. Rodzyanko, *Rasputin*, pp. 177–8
61. *Ibid*
62. *Ibid*; MA's Diary, February 9, 1916
63. AF to N, February 5, 1916, p. 276
64. Yu. Buranov and V. Khrustalev, *Gibel imperatorskogo doma 1917–1919 gg.*, Progress, Moscow, 1992 (hereafter: Buranov/Khrustalev), p. 46, quoting diary entry for February 21, 1917

EIGHTEEN War on Two Fronts

1. Knox, p. 435
2. MA's Diary, December 11–27, 1915
3. NS to MA, February 29, 1916, GARF 668/79
4. *Ibid*
5. MA to NS, March 7, 1916, GARF 622/21
6. NS to MA, July 9, 1916, GARF 668/79
7. MA to NS, July 20, 1916, GARF 622/21
8. NS to MA, May 9, 1916, GARF 668/79
9. *Ibid*, July 1, 1916
10. *Ibid*, March 11, 1916
11. *Ibid*, June 20, 1916
12. *Ibid*, June 25, 1916
13. *Ibid*, July 9, 1916
14. *Ibid*
15. MA to NS, March 7, 1916, GARF 622/21
16. NS to MA, July 19, 1916, GARF 668/79
17. *Ibid*
18. MA's Diary, August 4, 1916
19. MA to NS, August 5, 1916, GARF 622/21
20. *Ibid*, March 1, 1916

21. NS to MA, March 11, 1916, GARF 668/79
22. *Ibid*, March 21, 1916
23. *Ibid*
24. *Ibid*
25. *Ibid*, March 11, 1916
26. MA to NS, March 20, 1916, GARF 622/21
27. *Ibid*, July 23, 1916, *ibid*
28. NS to MA, July 19, 1916, GARF 668/79
29. MA to NS, August 2, 1916, GARF 622/21
30. *Ibid*, August 12, 1916
31. Dimitri to NS, October 26, 1915, GARF 622/28
32. *Ibid*, January 30, 1916
33. NS to MA, February 29, 1916, GARF 668/79
34. MA to NS, March 20, 1916, GARF 622/21
35. NS to MA, March 1, 1916, GARF 668/79
36. N to AF, April 1, 1916, p. 163
37. *Ibid*, April 4, 1916, p. 166
38. MA's Diary, October 26, 1915
39. AF to N, May 25, 1916, p. 339
40. NS to MA, July 29, 1916, GARF 668/79
41. AF to N, March 26, 1916, p. 307
42. Vorres, p. 150
43. DE to N, May 22, 1916, *Letters*, p. 297
44. Paléologue, *February 15*, 1916, Vol. II, p. 176
45. NS to MA, July 19, 1916, GARF 668/79
46. *Ibid*, July 29, 1916
47. *Ibid*, August 9, 1916
48. *Ibid*, May 1, 1916
49. *Ibid*, March 11, 1916
50. MA to NS, March 4, 1916, GARF 622/21
51. MA's Diary, June 29, 1916
52. MA to NS, June 23, 1916, GARF 622/21
53. Brusilov, cited Lincoln, p. 255
54. MA's Diary, December 1, 1916; the award was made on November 23, citation *Fund for the Museum of the Russian Cavalry*, Hoover Institution archive
55. MA's Diary, August 23, 1916
56. MA to NS, August 28, 1916, GARF 622/21
57. MA's Diary, August 31, 1916
58. MA to NS, August 15, 1916, GARF 622/21
59. MA's Diary, August 31, 1916
60. *Ibid*, September 2, 1916
61. AF to N, September 13, 1916, p. 398
62. NS to MA, March 16, 1915, GARF 668/78
63. *Ibid*, March 11, 1916, GARF 668/79
64. *Ibid*, March 21, 1916
65. *Ibid*, May 1, 1916
66. *Ibid*, March 11, 1916
67. *Ibid*, June 30, 1916
68. *Ibid*
69. MA to NS, July 5, 1916, GARF 622/21
70. *Ibid*, July 7, 1916
71. NS to MA, July 10, 1915, GARF 668/78
72. *Ibid*, June 30, 1916
73. MA to NS, July 5, 1916, GARF 622/21
74. NS to MA, July 19, 1915, GARF 668/78
75. *Ibid*, May 24, 1916
76. *Ibid*, June 10, 1916
77. MA to NS, July 24, 1916, GARF 622/21
78. *Ibid*, August 2, 1916
79. *Ibid*, August 13, 1916
80. *Ibid*
81. *Ibid*, August 28, 1916
82. *Ibid*, February 26, 1916
83. MA's Diary, September 30, 1916
84. *Ibid*, October 3–16, 1916
85. *Ibid*, October 19, 1916
86. MA to N, November 11, 1916, GARF 601/1301
87. MA's Diary, November 17, 1916
88. N to AF, December 9, 1916, p. 303
89. MA's Diary, December 20, 1916

NINETEEN Murder Most Fair

1. AF to N, March 12, 1916, p. 297
2. Knox, p. 412
3. Serge Sazonov, *Fateful Years*, Jonathan Cape, London, 1928, p. 292

4. NS to MA, July 19, 1916, GARF 668/79
5. MA to NS, July 20, 1916, GARF 622/21
6. *Ibid*
7. NS to MA, July 29, 1916, GARF 668/79
8. Grand Duke George Mikhailovich to N, November 24, 1916, cited Golder, p. 248
9. Grand Duke Nicholas Mikhailovich ('Bimbo') to N, *c.* November 1, 1916, cited Golder, pp. 244–5; Sir Bernard Pares, *The Fall of the Russian Monarchy*, Jonathan Cape, London, 1939 (hereafter: Pares), p. 390
10. AF to N, November 4, 1916, p. 433
11. Yousoupoff, p. 187
12. *Ibid*, p. 199
13. *Ibid*, p. 211
14. Paléogue, *November 19*, 1916, Vol. III, p. 96
15. Yousoupoff, p. 205
16. *Ibid*, p. 212
17. *Ibid*, p. 223
18. Meriel Buchanan, *The Dissolution of an Empire*, John Murray, London, 1932 (hereafter: Meriel Buchanan), p. 147
19. Yousoupoff, p. 228
20. *Ibid*, p. 230
21. *Ibid*, p. 232
22. Pares, p. 408
23. *Ibid*, p. 409
24. Vyrubova, p. 178
25. Paléologue, *December 30*, 1916, Vol. III, p. 131
26. Yousoupoff, pp. 241, 246
27. Paléologue, *January 2*, 1917, Vol. III, p. 135
28. Yousoupoff, p. 240
29. *Ibid*, p. 242
30. *Ibid*
31. *Ibid*, p. 245
32. Paley, p. 33
33. Marie, p. 276
34. Paléologue, *January 3*, 1916, Vol. III, p. 136
35. Pares, p. 410
36. Paléologue, *January 5*, 1916, Vol. III, p. 141; Yousoupoff, p. 243
37. Marie, p. 270
38. *Ibid*, p. 272
39. MA's Diary, December 19, 1916
40. Majolier, p. 90
41. Poutiatine
42. Majolier, p. 90
43. AF to N, August 16, 1916, p. 383
44. Poutiatine
45. Majolier, p. 92
46. MA's Diary, December 24, 1916
47. Majolier, p. 92
48. MA's Diary, December 25, 1916
49. Poutiatine
50. Majolier, p. 92
51. Poutiatine

TWENTY Palace Plotters

1. Pares, p. 416
2. Paléologue, *January 12*, 1917, Vol. III, p. 162
3. *Ibid*, *January 9*, 1917, p. 157
4. Paley, p. 38; Marie, p. 279
5. Paléologue, *January 15*, 1917, p. 167
6. *Ibid*, *January 21*, 1917, p. 170
7. Rodzyanko, *Rasputin*, pp. 246–7
8. Paléologue, *January 15*, 1917, Vol. III, pp. 167–8
9. *Ibid*, *January 21*, 1917, pp. 170–71
10. Dimitri to NS, January 16, 1917, GARF 622/28
11. *Ibid*, February 6, 1917
12. MA's Diary, December 31, 1916
13. *Ibid*, January 5, 1917
14. Buchanan, Vol. II, p. 43
15. *Ibid*, pp. 46–9
16. Knox, p. 515
17. Rodzyanko, *Rasputin*, pp. 248–50; *Memoirs*, cited Golder, pp. 117–18
18. Mme Rodzyanko to Prince Yusupov's mother, January 7, 1917, cited C. E. Vulliamy (ed.), *The Red Archives*, Geoffrey Bles, London, 1929 (hereafter: *Red Archives*), p. 122
19. Rodzyanko, *Rasputin*, pp. 253–4; *Memoirs*, cited Golder, pp. 118–19
20. MA's Diary, January 19–23, 1917
21. *Ibid*, January 29, 1917

22. MA to NS, March 20, 1916, GARF 622/21
23. MA's Diary, January 28–9, 1917
24. Brusilov, pp. 287–8
25. *Ibid*
26. MA's Diary, February 3, 1917
27. V. B. Stankevich, *Vospominaniya 1914–1919*, Rossiisky gosudarstvenny gumanitarny universitet, Moscow, 1994, p. 31
28. Pares, p. 428; Pipes, p. 269
29. 'Aleksandr Ivanovich Guchkov rasskazyvaet . . .', *Voprosy istorii*, Moscow, 7–8, 1991 (hereafter: Guchkov), p. 205
30. *Ibid*, p. 206
31. *Ibid*
32. Pipes, p. 269; George Katkov, *Russia 1917: The February Revolution*, Longmans, Green, London, 1967 (hereafter: Katkov), p. 215
33. Chavchavadze, p. 277
34. Rodzyanko, pp. 244–5
35. *Ibid*, quoting Shingarev
36. Pares, p. 428

TWENTY-ONE 'Make Yourself Regent'

1. Alexander, p. 312
2. Vyrubova, cited MM, p. 530
3. Alexander, p. 316
4. Rodzyanko, *Rasputin*, p. 259
5. *Ibid*, p. 260
6. Grand Duke Alexander to his brother Nicholas Mikhailovich, February 14, 1917, cited MM, p. 530
7. AF to N, February 22, 1917, cited MM, p. 536
8. N to AF, February 23, 1917, *ibid*, p. 537
9. Okhrana report, February 24, 1917, BK, Doc. 9, p. 34
10. Pares, p. 436
11. MA's Diary, February 25, 1917
12. BK, Doc. 7, p. 32
13. Pares, p. 442
14. MA's Diary, February 26, 1917
15. Okhrana report, February 26, 1917, BK, Doc. 9, pp. 36–7
16. Rodzyanko to N, February 26, 1917, *ibid*, Doc. 11, p. 40
17. Pares, p. 443
18. Paléologue, *March 11*, 1917, Vol. III, p. 217
19. *Ibid*, *March 12*, 1917, p. 221
20. Okhrana report, February 27, 1917, BK, Doc. 9, p. 39
21. Knox, p. 516
22. Pares, p. 444
23. MA's Diary, February 27, 1917
24. AF to N, February 26, 1917, GARF 601/1151, cited SK, Doc. 7, pp. 78–9
25. N to AF, February 26, 1917, GARF 640/115, cited SK, Doc. 8, p. 80
26. *Ibid*, February 27, 1917, Doc. 11, p. 83
27. Belyaev to N, February 27, 1917, cited SK, Doc. 9, p. 81
28. Pares, p. 441, BK, Doc. 15, p. 41
29. Rodzyanko to N, February 27, 1917, BK, Doc. 16, p. 42
30. V. V. Shulgin, *Dni*, Novoe Vremya, Belgrade, 1925 (hereafter: Shulgin), pp. 178–9
31. *Ibid*, p. 171
32. A. S. Matveev, 'Vel. knyaz Mikhail Aleksandrovich v dni perevorota', *Vozrozhdenie*, Paris, 24, 1952 (hereafter: Matveev's Diary), February 27, 1917
33. MA's Diary, February 27, 1917
34. *Ibid*
35. Matveev's Diary, February 27, 1917
36. Pares, p. 451
37. MA's Diary, February 27, 1917
38. Rodzyanko, cited BK, Doc. 17, p. 42
39. *Ibid*, p. 43
40. Milyukov, *Vospominaniya*, Vol. II, p. 275, cited Katkov, p. 292
41. MA to Gen. Alekseev, BK, Doc. 72, Vol. I, p. 86–7
42. *Ibid*
43. Matveev's Diary, February 27, 1917
44. MA to Gen. Alekseev, BK, Doc. 72, Vol. I, pp. 86–7
45. MA's Diary, February 27, 1917
46. N to Prince Golitsin, February 27, 1917, GARF 601/2089, cited SK, Doc. 10, p. 81
47. MA's Diary, February 27, 1917
48. *Ibid*, Pares, p. 452
49. Katkov, p. 283
50. Paley, p. 62

51. Katkov, p. 283
52. MA's Diary, February 27, 1917
53. *Ibid*
54. *Ibid*
55. Matveev's Diary, February 28, 1917
56. Poutiatine
57. *Ibid*
58. *Ibid*

TWENTY-TWO Address Unknown

1. Katkov, p. 310
2. N's Diary, February 28, 1917, cited MM, p. 541
3. Gen. Alekseev to Pskov, February 27, 1917, BK, Doc. 70, p. 85
4. Gen. Alekseev to army commanders, February 28, 1917, BK, Doc. 73, p. 89
5. N to AF, telegram, February 28, 1917, GARF 640/108, cited SK, Doc. 15, p. 85
6. Pares, p. 456
7. Lili Dehn, *The Real Tsaritsa*, Thornton Butterworth, London, 1922 (hereafter: Dehn), p. 172
8. Count Paul Benckendorff, *Last Days at Tsarskoe Selo*, Heinemann, London, 1927 (hereafter: Benckendorff), pp. 2–3
9. *Ibid*, pp. 14–15
10. Buxhoeveden, p. 255
11. Dehn, p. 156
12. Katkov, p. 312
13. Pares, p. 459
14. N's Diary, March 1, 1917, cited MM, p. 541
15. Vyrubova, p. 209; P. M. Bykov, *The Last Days of Tsardom*, Martin Lawrence, London, 1934 (hereafter: Bykov), p. 32
16. *Nabokov*, pp. 45–6
17. Shulgin, p. 160
18. *Ibid*, pp. 170–71
19. Alexander Kerensky, *The Catastrophe*, Appleton, N.Y., 1927 (hereafter: Kerensky, *Catastrophe*), p. 18, and *Memoirs*, p. 168
20. Kerensky, *Catastrophe*, p. 38
21. Paléologue, *December 21*, 1916, Vol. III, p. 119
22. Shulgin, pp. 189–91, Pares, p. 454
23. Kerensky, *Catastrophe*, pp. 36–7
24. *Ibid*, p. 21
25. *Nabokov*, p. 43
26. *Izvestia*, No. 3, March 1, 1917, BK, Doc. 31, p. 52; Pares, p. 453
27. Meriel Buchanan, p. 168
28. Paléologue, *March 13*, 1917, Vol. III, pp. 229–30
29. Kschessinska, p. 164
30. MA's Diary, February 28, 1917
31. MA to NS, February 28, 1917, GARF 622/22
32. MA's Diary, February 28, 1917
33. Poutiatine
34. *Ibid*
35. Matveev's Diary, March 1, 1917; Putyatina remembered a guard of 40 officer cadets.
36. Matveev's Diary, *ibid*
37. Poutiatine
38. Grand Dukes' manifesto, March 1, 1917, GARF 5881/367, cited SK, Doc. 18, pp. 86–7
39. AF to N, March 2, 1917, SK, Doc. 24, p. 94
40. Buchanan, Vol. III, p. 68
41. MA to NS, March 1, 1917, GARF 622/22
42. Buchanan to Foreign Office, London, *March 14*, 1917, PRO/FO 371/2495
43. Buchanan, Vol. II, p. 68
44. *Ibid*
45. Alexander Kerensky and Paul Bulygin, *The Murder of the Romanovs*, Hutchinson, London, 1935 (hereafter: Kerensky, *Murder*), p. 88
46. Paléologue, *March 22*, 1917, Vol. III, p. 259
47. Polovtsov, pp. 151–2
48. Cyril, p. 209
49. Grand Duke Paul to Kirill, March 2, 1917, Paley, pp. 55–6
50. Kirill to Paul, March 2, 1917, *ibid*, p. 56
51. Matveev's Diary, March 1, 1917
52. Paley, p. 53
53. Rodzyanko to Ruzsky, cited Katkov, p. 318
54. MA's Diary, March 1, 1917
55. General Dubensky, cited Lincoln, p. 337
56. Shulgin, p. 269

57. Telegram from Alekseev to Tsar, March 1, 1917, BK, Doc. 76, p. 91; Katkov, p. 324
58. Ruzsky, March 7, 1917, BK, Doc. 89, p. 102
59. Rodzyanko to Ruzsky, March 2, 1917, BK, Doc. 78, pp. 92–3
60. *Ibid*

TWENTY-THREE A Father's Feelings

1. Gen. Alekseev to Pskov, March 2, 1917, BK, Doc. 79, p. 94
2. Alekseev to army commanders, March 2, 1917, BK, Doc. 80, p. 94
3. Ruzsky, cited Lincoln, p. 340
4. Grand Duchess George (Marie Georgievna), *Memoirs*, Atlantic International Publications, N.Y., 1988 (hereafter: Grand Duchess George), p. 182
5. Alekseev to Nicholas, March 2, 1917, GARF 601/2102, cited SK, Doc. 20, pp. 89–91
6. Lincoln, p. 341
7. N to Rodzyanko, March 2, 1917, BK, Doc. 86 (A), p. 98
8. Ruzsky, in *Russkaia Volia*, Petrograd, March 7, 1917, BK, Doc. No. 89, p. 103
9. *Ibid*
10. Lincoln, p. 341
11. MA's Diary, March 1, 1917
12. Matveev's Diary, March 2, 1917
13. Kerensky, *Catastrophe*, p. 54
14. Alexander, p. 168; Chavchavadze, p. 173
15. George V's Diary, *March 15*, 1917, RA
16. Paléologue, Vol. III: mutiny 2nd Brigade, *September 1*, 1916, p. 17; Petrograd mutiny: *October 16*, *November 9*, 1916, pp. 74–5, 83
17. N. N. Sukhanov, *The Russian Revolution*, Princeton University Press, Princeton, N.J., 1984 (hereafter: Sukhanov), p. 116
18. *Ibid*, pp. 120–2; Paul N. Milyukov, *History of the Russian Revolution*, Academic International Press, Gulf Breeze, Florida, 1978 (hereafter: Milyukov, *Revolution*), p. 34
19. Sukhanov, p. 122
20. *Ibid*
21. *Ibid*, pp. 153–4
22. *Ibid*, p. 154
23. Shulgin, p. 223; Milyukov, *Revolution*, p. 30
24. Sukhanov, p. 155
25. Shulgin, pp. 238–9
26. *Ibid*, pp. 266–77
27. *Ibid*
28. *Ibid*
29. Mossolov, p. 124; Benckendorff, pp. 46–7
30. Nicholas, Protocol of talks, GARF 601/2099, cited SK, Doc. 25, p. 97
31. Guchkov, *ibid*
32. Gen. Boldyrev, *Red Archives*, p. 198
33. Protocol of talks, SK, Doc. 25, p. 99
34. *Ibid*
35. GARF 601/2100, cited SK, Doc. 26, pp. 100–101
36. Katkov, p. 343
37. Gen. Dubensky, cited Lincoln, p. 344
38. N's Diary, March 2, 1917, Pares, p. 469
39. Kerensky, p. 296
40. Milyukov, *Revolution*, p. 36
41. *Ibid*, p. 37
42. Kerensky, p. 214
43. *Ibid*
44. *Ibid*
45. Kerensky, *Catastrophe*, p. 67
46. Rodzyanko to Ruzsky, March 3, 1917, BK, Doc. 95, pp. 109–10
47. Rodzyanko to Alekseev, March 3, 1917, BK, Doc. 96, pp. 110–11
48. Alekseev to army commanders, March 3, 1917, BK, Doc. 97, pp. 112–13
49. *Ibid*, p. 113
50. Kerensky, *Catastrophe*, p. 68
51. Matveev's Diary, March 3, 1917

PART III

TWENTY-FOUR Emperor Michael

1. Melgunov, p. 230
2. Marie, p. 230
3. Princess Cantacuzène, *Revolutionary Days*, Chapman & Hall, London, 1920 (hereafter: Cantacuzène), p. 122
4. E. M. Almedingen, *An Unbroken Unity: A Memoir of Grand Duchess Serge*, Bodley Head, London, 1964, p. 105; the scene was remembered by Princess Marie Obolensky, the last surviving member of the Order
5. *Ibid*
6. V. V. Shulgin, *Dni*, (reprint) Sovremennik, Moscow, 1989 (hereafter: Shulgin II), pp. 263–4
7. *Ibid*, p. 265; Bykov, p. 27
8. *Ibid*, pp. 266–9
9. *Nabokov*, p. 46
10. Matveev's Diary, March 3, 1917
11. Paley, p. 59
12. *Ibid*, p. 60
13. *Ibid*, p. 61
14. Kerensky, *Catastrophe*, p. 68
15. Majolier, p. 99
16. Petrograd telephone directory, 1916
17. Grand Duchess George, p. 177
18. Matveev's Diary, Wednesday, March 1, 1917, records Bimbo arriving that evening at 9 p.m.
19. Poutiatine; Matveev does not record this visit, but Bimbo could not have known about Nicholas's abdication until Friday morning, March 3
20. *Ibid*
21. Shulgin II, p. 277
22. Matveev's Diary, March 3, 1917
23. *Ibid*
24. Milyukov, *Revolution*, p. 39
25. Matveev's Diary, March 3, 1917
26. Kerensky, *Catastrophe*, p. 59

TWENTY-FIVE Playing for Time

1. N's Diary, March 2, 1917, GARF 601/265, cited SK, Doc. 30, p. 107
2. Poutiatine; her reference to 'the latest conversation' MA had with Bimbo places this in the context as early Friday, March 3, 1917
3. Kerensky, *Catastrophe*, p. 69
4. *Nabokov*, p. 49
5. Kerensky, *Memoirs*, p. 207
6. Shulgin II, p. 272
7. *Ibid*, p. 274
8. M. V. Rodzyanko, Gosudarstvennaya Duma I fevral'skaya 1917 goda revolyutsii, from *Arkhiv russkoi revolyutsii* VI, p. 61 (edn. The Hague, 1971)
9. Milyukov, *Revolution*, p. 38
10. Shulgin II, p. 196
11. Milyukov, *Vospominaniya*, Vol. II, p. 17, cited Katkov, p. 408
12. Shulgin II, pp. 263–74
13. *Ibid*, p. 274
14. Paléologue, *March 17*, 1917, Vol. III, p. 240
15. Kerensky, *Catastrophe*, p. 69
16. *Ibid*, p. 70
17. Kerensky, *Memoirs*, p. 216
18. Paléologue, *March 17*, 1917, Vol. III, p. 241
19. Rodzyanko to Alekseev, March 3, 1917, BK, Doc. 96, pp. 111–12
20. *Nabokov*, pp. 35–6
21. Shulgin II, p. 276
22. Baron Nolde, *Nabokov*, p. 19; inadvertently he says 'Michael I' rather than 'Michael II'
23. Poutiatine
24. Shulgin II, p. 277, but neither Matveev nor Putyatina mention Tereshchenko or Nekrasov
25. *Ibid*
26. Nolde, *Nabokov*, p. 19
27. Matveev's Diary, March 3, 1917
28. *Ibid*
29. Bykov, p. 28
30. Wonlar-Larsky, Nadine, *The Russia That I Loved*, MacSwinney, London, 1937 (hereafter: Wonlar-Larsky), pp. 166–7, 171
31. *Nabokov*, p. 47
32. N's Diary, March 3, 1917, cited MM, p. 551

33. A photograph of the telegram appeared in *Illyustrirovannaya Rossiya*, Paris, 3, 1924, LRA MS 1363/141; it is timed at 14.56, March 3, 1917
34. *Nabokov*, pp. 48–9
35. *Ibid*, p. 53
36. *Ibid*, p. 51
37. Baron Nolde, *Nabokov*, p. 27, refers to the 'abdication act', and Nabokov does so on p. 54
38. Nolde, *ibid*, p. 19
39. *Ibid*
40. *Ibid*
41. Paléologue, *March 17*, 1917, Vol. III, p. 241
42. Grand Duke Kirill made that claim when he proclaimed himself Emperor in 1924, Cyril, p. 220
43. GARF 668/131
44. *Nabokov*, p. 53
45. *Ibid*, p. 54
46. Nolde, *Nabokov*, p. 20
47. *Nabokov*, p. 54
48. Quoted by Paléologue, *March 17*, 1917, Vol. III, p. 244
49. *Nabokov*, p. 53
50. Nolde, *Nabokov*, p. 20
51. Shulgin II, p. 279
52. Paléologue, *March 17*, 1917, Vol. III, p. 241
53. Nolde, *Nabokov*, p. 20
54. Lomonosov, quoted by Melgunov, p. 236
55. *Ibid*, p. 237
56. Cantacuzène, p. 122
57. *The Times*, London, *March 19*, 1917
58. N's Diary, March 3, 1917, cited MM, p. 551
59. Alexander, p. 320
60. MA's Diary, March 3, 1917

TWENTY-SIX Retreat to Gatchina

1. MA to NS, March 3, 1917, GARF 622/22
2. Poutiatine
3. Petrograd Soviet Executive Committee, March 3, 1917, BK, Doc. 142, p. 177
4. MA's Diary, March 4, 1917
5. *Ibid*
6. Poutiatine
7. Grand Duchess George, p. 179
8. Melgunov, p. 232
9. MA's Diary, March 4, 1917
10. *Ibid*, March 5, 1917
11. Russian newspapers: LRA MS 1000/5
12. Paléologue, *March 17*, 1917, Vol. III, p. 243
13. Buchanan, Vol. II, p. 71
14. Grand Duchess George, p. 180
15. Maklakov, cited Katkov, p. 411
16. Paley, pp. 60, 67
17. Mossolov, p. 69
18. Dimitri to Yusupov, April 23, 1917, *Red Archives*, p. 127
19. Grand Duchess George, p. 182
20. MA's Diary, April 5, 1917
21. *Ibid*, April 10, 1917
22. Grand Duchess George, p. 183
23. Pipes, p. 307
24. Sukhanov, p. 113
25. Major-General Sir John Hanbury-Williams, *The Emperor Nicholas As I Knew Him*, Arthur Humphreys, London, 1922, p. 179; Chavchavadze, p. 165
26. Paléologue, *April 30*, 1917, Vol. III, p. 322
27. Knox, p. 613
28. MA to Major Simpson, May 5, 1917, LRA MS 1407 (Vinogradoff Collection)
29. Kournakoff, p. 317
30. Grand Duchess George, p. 180
31. *Ibid*, pp. 184–5
32. *Ibid*, p. 185
33. *Ibid*
34. Majolier, p. 100
35. Grand Duchess George, p. 182
36. Pipes, p. 747
37. MA's Diary, May 5, 1917
38. MA to Major Simpson, LRA MS 1407 (Vinogradoff Collection)
39. MA's Diary, May 5–14, 1917
40. Majolier, p. 83
41. N's Diary, March 9, 1917, GARF 601/265
42. Petrograd Soviet Executive Committee meeting, March 9, 1917, SK, Doc. 41, p. 130; BK, Doc. 150, p. 181

43. Pierre Gilliard, *Thirteen Years at the Russian Court*, Doran, N.Y., 1921, pp. 217–18
44. Buchanan, Vol. II, p. 104; Kenneth Rose, *King George V*, Weidenfeld & Nicolson, London, 1983 (hereafter: Rose), p. 210
45. Buchanan's cable re MA and Grand Duke George, *April 5*, 1917, Rose, p. 212
46. Rose, p. 212
47. *Ibid*, pp. 212–13, letter dated *April 6*, 1917
48. *June 4*, 1917, cited Rose, p. 216
49. Rose, p. 215
50. Buchanan, Vol. II, p. 103; Soviet Executive Session of March 9, 1918, SK, Doc. 41. p. 130; BK, Doc. 150, p. 181
51. Polovtsov, pp. 207–8
52. Kerensky, p. 120
53. MA's Diary, July 31, 1917
54. Polovtsov, p. 292
55. MA's Diary, July 31, 1917
56. Robert Wilton, *The Last Days of the Romanovs*, Thornton Butterworth, London, 1920 (hereafter: Wilton), p. 184 (Kobylinsky deposition)
57. Benckendorff, p. 107
58. Kerensky, *Catastrophe*, p. 275
59. Benckendorff, p. 107
60. MA's Diary, July 31, 1917

TWENTY-SEVEN Citizen Michael

1. MA's Diary, August 21, 1917
2. *Ibid*, August 22, 1917
3. Pipes, p. 447
4. Polovtsov, p. 298
5. Paley, p. 94
6. Kerensky, *Murder*, p. 138
7. Kerensky, *Catastrophe*, pp. 137–9; *Murder*, p. 195
8. MA's Diary, August 25, 1917
9. *Ibid*, August 29, 1917
10. Pipes, p. 441
11. Lincoln, p. 415
12. Luckett, Richard, *The White Generals*, Routledge & Kegan Paul, London, 1971, p. 66
13. Kerensky, *Catastrophe*, p. 318
14. Pipes, p. 450
15. *Ibid*, p. 467
16. *Ibid*, p. 460
17. *Ibid*, p. 461
18. Lincoln, p. 423
19. MA's Diary, August 29, 1917
20. *Ibid*
21. *Ibid*, August 31, 1917
22. *Ibid*, September 4, 1917
23. Buchanan to Lord Stamfordham, September 7, 1917, RA GV P 284 A/26
24. MA's Diary, September 6, 1917
25. *September 5*, telegram cited by Buchanan, RA GV P 284 A/26
26. Telegram to Balfour, PRO FO/371/3015, circulated to 'King and Cabinet'
27. MA's Diary, September 13 and 15, 1917
28. *Ibid*, September 2, 1917
29. Wonlar-Larsky, p. 171; Poutiatine
30. Chavchavadze, p. 254
31. Dimitri's Diary, October 1917, Houghton Library, Harvard University
32. Kerensky, *Catastrophe*, pp. 333–4
33. Pipes, p. 489
34. MA's Diary, October 19 and 25, 1917
35. *Ibid*, October 26, 1917
36. *Ibid*, October 27, 1917
37. *Ibid*
38. Kerensky, *Memoirs*, pp. 442–4
39. MA's Diary, October 30, 1917
40. Majolier, p. 118
41. MA's Diary, October 31, 1917
42. Wonlar-Larsky, pp. 172–3; in Russian her married name was Vonlyarlyarskaya, but later, in exile, she used the form Wonlar-Larsky.
43. *Ibid*
44. MA's Diary, November 1, 1917
45. *Ibid*, November 4, 1917
46. Poutiatine
47. MA's Diary, November 5, 1917
48. Poutiatine
49. MA's Diary, November 7, 1917
50. *Ibid*, November 13, 1917
51. *Ibid*, Diary, November 15, 1917

52. MA to NS, November 16, 1917, GARF 622/22
53. Majolier, p. 112
54. MA's Diary, November 15, 1917
55. Yu. Buranov and V. Khrustalev, *Gibel imperatorskogo doma 1917–1919 gg.*, Progress, Moscow, 1992 (hereafter: Buranov/Khrustalev), p. 91
56. Gushchik, p. 22
57. *Ibid*
58. *Ibid*
59. MA's Diary, December 25 and 31, 1917
60. Oliver H. Radkey, *The Election to the Russian Constituent Assembly*, Harvard University Press, Cambridge, Mass., 1950, pp. 20–21
61. Miss Neame, letter to her family, May 16, 1918 (hereafter: Miss Neame letter), private collection
62. MA's Diary, December 5, 1917
63. Miss Neame letter
64. MA's Diary, March 6, 1917
65. Miss Neame letter
66. *Ibid*
67. GARF 130/10, cited Buranov/Khrustalev, p. 92
68. Poutiatine
69. *Ibid*
70. GARF 130/10, cited Buranov/Khrustalev, p. 93
71. *Ibid*
72. Poutiatine
73. MA to NS, March 10, 1918, LRA MS 1363/36–4
74. Poutiatine

TWENTY-EIGHT Prisoner of Perm

1. MA to NS, telegram, March 14, 1918, LRA MS 1363/37–1
2. Letter from Johnson, cited Poutiatine
3. V. M. Khrustalev and L. A. Lykov, *Skorbnyi put Mikhaila Romanova: Ot prestola do Golgofy*, Pushka, Perm, 1996 (hereafter Khrustalev/Lykov), p. 89
4. Letter from Johnson, Poutiatine
5. MA to NS, March 10, 1918, LRA MS 1363/36–4
6. MA to NS, telegram, March 14, 1918, *ibid*
7. Johnson to Lenin, telegram, March 15, 1918, GARF 130/1109, cited Buranov/Khrustalev, p. 94
8. MA to NS, telegram, March 19, 1918, LRA MS 1363/37–2; 'Hermitage Hotel', Chelyshev statement, cited Khrustalev/Lykov, p. 109
9. *The Times*, London, March 22, 1918
10. MA to NS, telegram, March 19, 1918, LRA MS 1363/37–3
11. MA to Bonch-Bruevich, March 20, 1918, GARF 130/1109, cited Buranov/Khrustalev, p. 94
12. Chelyshev to NS, March 26, 1918, LRA MS 1363/37–4
13. MA to NS, telegram, March 19, 1918, LRA MS 1363/37–3
14. *The Times*, London, April 6, 1918
15. MA to NS, April 10, 1918, LRA MS 1363/36
16 I. A. Mirkina and V. M. Khrustalev, 'Sudba Mikhaila Romanova', *Voprosy istorii*, Moscow, 9, 1990 (hereafter: Mirkina/Khrustalev), p. 153; 'Hotel No. 1' appears as the name on photographs of the hotel in 1918
17. S. A. Toropov, 'Samosud', *Vechernyaya Perm*, Perm, January 15, 1990, pp. 37–41
18. Khrustalev/Lykov, pp. 108–9
19. MA to NS, April 10, 1918, LRA MS 1363/36
20. *Ibid*
21. Poutiatine
22. Miss Neame letter
23. *Ibid*
24. Majolier, p. 132
25. March 25, 1918, GARF 130/1109, cited Buranov/Khrustalev, p. 94
26. 'Beard': written by MA on back of the photograph of the 'Prisoner of Perm': LRA MS 1363/268
27. MA's Diary, May 20, 1918, cited Mirkina/Khrustalev, p. 160
28. Krumnis; cited Mirkina/Khrustalev, p. 153
29. *Ibid*

30. Wilton, p. 120
31. Poutiatine
32. MA to NS, telegram, April 19, 1918, LRA MS 1363/37–6
33. *Ibid*, April 25, 1918, LRA MS 1363/26
34. MA's Diary, May 16, 1918, cited Mirkina/Khrustalev, p. 159
35. *Ibid*, May 11, 1918
36. *Ibid*, May 12–17, 1918
37. *Ibid*, May 17, 1918
38. *Ibid*, May 18, 1918
39. Robert Payne, *The Life and Death of Lenin*, Allen, London, 1964, p. 459
40. Victor Alexandrov, *The End of the Romanovs*, Hutchinson, London, 1966 (hereafter: Alexandrov), p. 221
41. Poutiatine
42. Wilton, p. 121
43. The order to report to the Cheka was dated May 20, 1918, Russian Centre for the Preservation and Study of Modern Historical Documents (*RTsKhIDNI*) 588/17, cited Khrustalev/Lykov, p. 92
44. Buranov/Khrustalev, p. 96
45. MA's Diary, May 21, 1918, cited Mirkina/Khrustalev, p. 160
46. MA to NS, June 3, 1918, LRA MS 1363/31
47. MA's Diary, May 19–23, 1918, cited Mirkina/Khrustalev, pp. 160–61
48. Krumnis, GARF 5881/414, cited Mirkina/Khrustalev, p. 153
49. MA's Diary, May 25, 1918, cited Mirkina/Khrustalev, p. 161
50. Wilton, p. 121
51. Unsigned and undated note, LRA MS 1363/22
52. MA's Diary, May 29, 1918, cited Mirkina/Khrustalev, p. 161
53. MA to NS, June 3, 1918, LRA MS 1363/22
54. *RTsKhIDNI*, cited Khrustalev/Lykov, pp. 92–3
55. MA to NS, June 3, 1918, LRA MS 1363/22
56. MA's Diary, June 7, 1918, cited Mirkina/Khrustalev, p. 163
57. G. Myasnikov, 'Filosofiya ubiistva, ili pochemu i kak ya ubil Mikhaila Romanova', *Minuvshee*, Atheneum & Feniks, Moscow & St Petersburg, 18, 1995 (hereafter: Myasnikov), p. 63; Perm archives 630/1–3
58. Biographical note, Myasnikov
59. Wilton, p. 120
60. Shamarin, GARF 539/2765, cited Mirkina/Khrustalev, p. 156
61. Myasnikov, p. 83
62. Kerensky, *Murder*, p. 255
63. Myasnikov, p. 31
64. *Ibid*, pp. 69–70
65. MA's Diary, June 7, 1918, cited Mirkina/Khrustalev
66. *Ibid*, June 8–9, 1918
67. *Ibid*, June 10–11, 1918

TWENTY-NINE Death in the Woods

1. General I. S. Sinolin, *The Alapaevsk Tragedy*, Hoover Institution (hereafter: Sinolin)
2. N's Diary, May 14 and 15, 1918, GARF 601/266
3. Myasnikov, p. 116
4. Malkov statement, GAPO 90/M-60
5. Mikov, GAPO 90/2/M-22b
6. *Ibid*
7. Alexandrov, p. 81
8. *Ibid*, p. 77
9. Myasnikov, p. 59
10. *Ibid*
11. *Ibid*, pp. 82–4
12. Clocks were advanced two hours in Perm on June 2, 1918, MA to NS, June 3, 1918, LRA MS 1363/31
13. British Meteorological Office library, Bracknell, Berkshire
14. In Markov's description of the journey to the murder site, the distance was ten 'versts' – equivalent to 6.5 miles.
15. Myasnikov, p. 59
16. *Ibid*, p. 87
17. *Ibid*, pp. 94–5
18. *Ibid*, p. 95
19. Biographical note, Introduction, Myasnikov
20. Malkov also appears to have diminished the role of Myasnikov

21. Myasnikov, p. 95
22. Khrustalev/Lykov, p. 118
23. Statement by Znamerovsky, Khrustalev/Lykov, pp 118–19
24. Statement by Chelyshev, *ibid*, p. 109
25. Krumnis, cited Mirkina/Khrustalev, pp. 152–3
26. Statement by kitchen maid Yelizaveta Mashirina, cited Khrustalev/Lykov, pp. 114–15
27. Statement by Chelyshev, *ibid*, p. 109
28. Markov, Mirkina/Khrustalev, pp. 152–3
29. *Ibid*
30. Wilton, p. 123
31. *Ibid*
32. Krumnis, cited Mirkina/Khrustalev, p. 153
33. *Ibid* and Myasnikov, p. 97
34. Chelyshev statement, Khrustalev/Lykov, p. 109; Markov, Mirkina/Khrustalev, pp. 152–3
35. Myasnikov, p. 98
36. *Ibid*, pp. 98–100
37. *Ibid*, p. 105
38. *Ibid*, pp. 105–8
39. *Ibid*, p. 111
40. Markov, Mirkina/Khrustalev, pp. 152–3
41. *Ibid*
42. Myasnikov, p. 112
43. Markov, Mirkina/Khrustalev, pp. 152–3
44. Myasnikov, p. 113
45. *Ibid*
46. *Ibid*
47. GARF 130/1109, Mirkina/Khrustalev, p. 152
48. Resolution of Perm Provincial Executive Committee, June 13, 1918, Khrustalev/Lykov, p. 90
49. Wilton, p. 240
50. *Izvestya*, Perm, July 15, 1918; Mirkina/Khrustalev, p. 149
51. V. F. Sivkov, Perm Provincial Executive Committee, cited Buranov/Khrustalev, p. 107
52. Vera Karnaukhova in evidence to Sokolov, *RTsKhIDNI* 588/8, cited Khrustalev/Lykov, pp. 138–40
53. Krumnis, cited Mirkina/Khrustalev, pp. 152–3
54. Myasnikov, p. 116
55. *Ibid*, p. 119
56. N. A. Alina, head of Perm Region Party Archives, quoting Markov, 1965, cited Buranov/Khrustalev, p. 109
57. Myasnikov, p. 114
58. Alexandrov, pp. 81–3
59. *Ibid*

THIRTY Long Live Michael

1. Majolier, p. 129
2. GARF 539/8780, cited Mirkina/Khrustalev, p. 156
3. Poutiatine
4. Majolier, p. 132
5. *Ibid*, p. 131
6. *Ibid*, p. 136
7. *Ibid*
8. Bruce Lockhart, p. 268
9. Telegram no. 551, June 29, 1918, PRO/ADM 137/883
10. *The Times*, London, July 3, 1918
11. July 6, 1918, PRO/GFM 6/139 A33969
12. July 3, 1918, *ibid*, A248
13. July 3, 1918, *ibid*, A28438
14. *The Times*, London, June 27, July 3, 1918
15. July 8, 1918, PRO WO 106/1220/44
16. Moscow to Berlin, July 17, 1918, PRO GFM 6/139 A30977
17. *Nasha rodina*, Moscow, July 21, 1918; Mirkina/Khrustalev, p. 141
18. Dimitri's Diaries, 1918, Houghton Library Harvard University
19. LRA MS 1363/116
20. *Ibid*, 1363/119
21. Stockholm, August 26, 1918, PRO WO 106/1219/815
22. July 17, 1918, PRO GFM 6/139 A30977
23. July 22, 1918, *ibid*, A31268
24. Kiev, August 23, 1918, *ibid* GFM 6/140 AS 4034
25. Investigations which established the essentials of the murder were begun after the Whites captured Ekaterinburg on July 25, 1918

26. Sinolin; it was Sinolin who recovered the bodies and carried out the first investigation of the murders
27. Pipes, pp. 780–3
28. Bruce Lockhart, p. 304
29. Majolier, p. 134
30. *Ibid*, p. 137
31. *Ibid*, p. 145; the evidence dates her arrest as September 7
32. *Ibid*, p. 153
33. *Ibid*
34. *Ibid*, pp. 158–60
35. *Ibid*, p. 142
36. Pipes, pp. 818–19
37. Bruce Lockhart, p. 321, 'hung out of the window', Paley, p. 244
38. *Izvestia*, Perm, cited Mirkina/Khrustalev, p. 156
39. Russian Telegraph Agency, September 20, 1918, cited Mirkina/Khrustalev, p. 156
40. John F. O'Conor (ed.), *The Sokolov Investigation*, Souvenir Press, London, 1972, p. 256
41. August 21, 1918, GARF 1235/36, Mirkina/Khrustalev, p. 156
42. Mirkina/Khrustalev, p. 156
43. Wilton, p. 129
44. September 21, 1918, PRO GFM 6/140 A39669
45. September 29, 1918, *ibid*, A408134
46. October 21, 1918, *ibid*, A44463
47. June 15, 1918, *ibid*, GFM 6/139 A29471
48. *Ibid*
49. LRA MS 1363/82
50. Majolier, p. 142
51. *Ibid*, p. 161
52. *Ibid*
53. *Ibid*, p. 170
54. *Ibid*, pp. 166–9
55. *Ibid*, p. 174
56. GARF 391/161, cited Buranov/Khrustalev, p. 111
57. Kiev, October 21, 1918, PRO GFM 16/140 A44463
58. Kiev, October 24, 1918, *ibid*, A45122
59. Copenhagen, November 2, 1918, *ibid*, A46412
60. Berlin, October 30, 1918, *ibid*, A45995
61. LRA MS 1326/84
62. Majolier, p. 175
63. *Ibid*, p. 176
64. Admiralty Library, Ministry of Defence, London
65. Majolier, p. 177
66. *Ibid*, p. 179
67. *Ibid*, p. 180
68. Admiralty Library, Ministry of Defence, London
69. Majolier, p. 180

PART IV

THIRTY-ONE A Woman Alone

1. Majolier, pp. 181–90
2. *Ibid*, p. 191
3. *Ibid*, p. 190
4. Chavchavadze, p. 254
5. *Ibid*, Grand Duchess George, p. 239
6. Marie, pp. 319–20, 331–2
7. Chavchavadze, p. 254
8. Yousoupoff, p. 256
9. Marie, pp. 263–5
10. Majolier, p. 192
11. *Ibid*
12. *Ibid*
13. *Ibid*, p. 195
14. Gray, p. 135
15. General Biryukov is mentioned in 1916 letters between Michael and Natasha
16. LRA MS 1363/69
17. LRA MS 1363/101, cited Gray, p. 138
18. Majolier, p. 191
19. Gray, p. 136
20. NS to Litchfield-Speer, August 2, 1919, LRA MS 1363/103–3
21. *Ibid*
22. *Ibid*
23. Kolchak telegram, September 15, 1919, LRA MS 1363/98
24. *Ibid*
25. NS to Litchfield-Speer, October 10, 1919, LRA MS 1363/103–4
26. Gray, p. 137
27. *Ibid*, pp. 138–9
28. *Ibid*, p. 135
29. *Ibid*, p. 136

30. MA's Diary, January 3, 1918
31. Gray, p. 139
32. NS to Litchfield-Speer, May 9, 1920, LRA MS 1363/103–7
33. Harrow School records
34. Majolier, p. 199
35. *Ibid*, p. 203
36. *Ibid*, p. 202
37. *Ibid*, p. 204
38. *Ibid*
39. *The Times*, London, July 6, 1924
40. Chavchavadze, p. 231
41. *Ibid*
42. Cyril, p. 220
43. *Ibid*, p. 248
44. *Ibid*, p. 247
45. *Ibid*, pp. 222, 248
46. The letter from the Dowager Empress to Nikolasha was written on October 4, 1924, from Hvidore; the original is in the possession of Prince Nicholas Romanov, Nikolasha's great-nephew, who provided a copy of it to the authors
47. Cyril, p. 222
48. *Ibid*, p. 165
49. *Ibid*, p. 232
50. *Ibid*
51. *Ibid*, p. 248
52. *Almanac de Gotha*, 1936
53. Clarke, pp. 114–15; Majolier, p. 231
54. Majolier, pp. 231–2
55. Gray, p. 139
56. Clarke, p. 130
57. *Ibid*
58. NS to Litchfield-Speer, cited Gray, p. 145
59. Gray, p. 145
60. Harrow School report
61. Gray, p. 146
62. *Ibid*, p. 147
63. Majolier, p. 226
64. *Ibid*, p. 225
65. Clarke, p. 162
66. Majolier, p. 230
67. *Ibid*
68. 5 rue Copernic is the address stated on George's death certificate (Sens, 1931, No. 230), Michael Huberty, *L'Allemagne Dynastique*, Tome 7, Paris, 1964 (hereafter: Huberty), p. 345
69. Press cuttings LRA MS 1363/120–122
70. 11.30 a.m. is the time stated on his death certificate, cited Hubert, p. 345; Majolier, p. 230
71. *Ilyustrirovannaya Rossiya*, Paris, August 1, 1931, LRA MS 1363/123
72. Majolier, p. 230
73. Gray, p. 154
74. *Ibid*
75. Majolier, p. 233
76. NS to Tata, November 14, 1934, LRA MS 1363/106
77. LRA MS 1363/88
78. Majolier, p. 236
79. *Ibid*, pp. 231, 236; Clarke, p. 115
80. Clarke, p. 130
81. *Ibid*
82. *Ibid*
83. *Ibid*
84. Majolier, pp. 238–9
85. *The Times*, London, December 28, 1938
86. Majolier, p. 242
87. *Ibid*, p. 240
88. *Ibid*, p. 243
89. *Ibid*
90. *The Times*, London, December 12, 1938
91. Majolier, pp. 243–4
92. *Ibid*, p. 245
93. *Ibid*
94. *Ibid*, p. 247
95. *Ibid*, p. 246
96. Gray, p. 162
97. Pauline Gray to authors
98. Gray, p. 159
99. *Ibid*, p. 160
100. *Ibid*, p. 163
101. *Ibid*, pp. 163–4
102. Grand Duke Alexander (Mikhailovich): *Always A Grand Duke*, Farrar and Rinehart Inc., p. 9
103. Paris death certificate for Nathalie Sheremetevsky; copy supplied by Alexandra Majolier Smith
104. Authors' visit
105. Gushchik, p. 46

BIBLIOGRAPHY

SOURCES & WORKS CITED

ORIGINAL SOURCES

MICHAEL ALEKSANDROVICH, GRAND DUKE, EMPEROR MICHAEL II:
– *Letters*, 1908–1918: State Archive of the Russian Federation, Moscow
– *Letters*, 1909–1910: Russian State Historical Archive, St Petersburg
– *Diaries*, 1915–1918: Forbes Collection, New York
– *Letters and telegrams*, 1918: Leeds Russian Archive, University of Leeds
– *Legal papers and miscellanea*: Knebworth House archive, England
– *Personal photograph albums*, 1909–1913: School of Slavonic and East European Studies, University of London

NATHALIE SERGEYEVNA BRASOVA ('NATASHA'):
– *Letters*, 1909–1916: State Archive of the Russian Federation, Moscow
– *Telegrams*, 1909–1913; *letters, financial papers, miscellanea*, 1919–1934: Leeds Russian Archive, University of Leeds

GEORGE MIKHAILOVICH, COUNT BRASOV:
– *Letters*, 1918: Leeds Russian Archive, University of Leeds

KOSSIKOVSKAYA, ALEKSANDRA VLADIMIROVNA ('DINA'):
– *Miscellaneous documents*: Hoover Institution, Stanford University, California

DIMITRI PAVLOVICH, GRAND DUKE:
– *Diaries*, Houghton Library, Harvard University
– *Letters*, 1915–1917: State Archive of the Russian Federation, Moscow

BARON FREDERIKS:
– *Letters, telegrams, reports*, 1909–1910: Russian State Historical Archive, St Petersburg

OTHER ARCHIVES CONSULTED:
Moscow Historical Archive
Moscow Archive of Scientific and Technical Documentation
Public Record Office, London (PRO)
Royal Archives, Windsor (RA)
Royal Archives, Copenhagen
State Archive of the Moscow District
State Archive of the Perm District (GAPO)
Wiener Stadt- und Landesarchiv

WORKS CITED

ENGLISH

The Secret Letters of the Last Tsar: The Confidential Correspondence between Nicholas II and His

Mother, Dowager Empress Marie Feodorovna, (ed.) Edward J. Bing, Nicholson & Watson, London, 1937
Letters of the Tsar to the Tsaritsa, 1914–1917, Bodley Head, London, 1929
Letters of the Tsaritsa to the Tsar, 1914–1916, Duckworth, London, 1923
Anon., *Russian Court Memoirs*, Herbert Jenkins, London, 1917
Abrikossow, Dimitri I., *Revelations of a Russian Diplomat*, University of Washington, Seattle, 1964
Alexander (Mikhailovich), Grand Duke, *Once a Grand Duke*, Cassell, London, 1932
Alexander (Mikhailovich), Grand Duke, *Always a Grand Duke*, Farrar and Rinehart Inc., New York, 1933
Alexandrov, Victor, *The End of the Romanovs*, Hutchinson, London, 1966
Almedingen, E. M., *An Unbroken Unity: A Memoir of Grand Duchess Serge*, Bodley Head, London, 1964
Benckendorff, Count Paul, *Last Days at Tsarskoe Selo*, Heinemann, London, 1927
Bertensson, Sergei and Leyda, Jay, *Sergei Rachmaninov*, Allen & Unwin, London, 1965
Browder, R. P. and Kerensky, A. F., *The Russian Provisional Government 1917*, Stanford University Press, Stanford, California, 1961
Brusilov, General Alexei, *A Soldier's Note-Book*, Macmillan, London, 1936
Buchanan, Sir George, *My Mission to Russia*, Cassell, London, 1923
Buchanan, Meriel, *The Dissolution of an Empire*, John Murray, London, 1932
Bruce Lockhart, R. H., *Memoirs of a British Agent*, Macmillan, London, 1932
Buxhoeveden, Baroness Sophie, *The Life and Tragedy of Alexandra Feodorovna, Empress of Russia*, Longmans, London, 1928
Bykov, P. M., *The Last Days of Tsardom*, Martin Lawrence, London, 1934
Cantacuzène, Princess, *Revolutionary Days*, Chapman & Hall, London, 1920
Chavchavadze, Prince David, *The Grand Dukes*, Atlantic International Publications, N.Y., 1990
Clarke, William, *The Lost Fortune of the Tsars*, Weidenfeld & Nicolson, London, 1994
Cyril (Vladimirovich), Grand Duke, *My Life in Russia's Service*, Selwyn & Blount, London, 1939
Dehn, Lili, *The Real Tsaritsa*, Thornton Butterworth, London, 1922
Dillon, E. J., *Eclipse of Russia*, Dent, London, 1918
Dobson, Christopher, *Prince Felix Yusupov*, Harrap, London, 1989
Fischer, Louis, *The Life of Lenin*, Weidenfeld & Nicolson, London, 1965
Freeman, Gillian and Thorpe, Edward, *Ballet Genius*, Thorsons, Wellingborough, England, 1988
Fitzlyon, Kyril and Browning, Tatiana, *Before the Revolution*, Allen Lane, London, 1977
George, Grand Duchess (Marie Georgievna), *Memoirs*, Atlantic International Publications, N.Y., 1988
Gilliard, Pierre, *Thirteen Years at the Russian Court*, Doran, N.Y., 1921
Golder, F. A. (ed.), *Documents of Russian History, 1914–1917*, Smith, Gloucester, Mass., 1964
Gray, Pauline, *The Grand Duke's Woman*, Macdonald, London, 1976
Katkov, George, *Russia 1917: The February Revolution*, Longmans, Green, London, 1967
Kerensky, Alexander, *The Catastrophe*, Appleton, N.Y., 1927
– *Memoirs*, Cassell, London, 1966
– and Bulygin, Paul, *The Murder of the Romanovs*, Hutchinson, London, 1935
Kleinmichel, Countess, *Memoirs of a Shipwrecked World*, Brentano's, London, 1923
Knox, Major-General Sir Alfred, *With the Russian Army*, Hutchinson, London, 1921
Kobylinsky, Colonel Eugene, *Deposition*, cited Wilton, below
Kournakoff, Sergei, *Savage Squadrons*, Harrap, London, 1936
(Kschessinska, Mathilde) Romanovsky-Krassinsky, Princess, *Dancing in Petersburg*, Victor Gollancz, London, 1961

Lincoln, W. Bruce, *Passage Through Armageddon*, Simon & Schuster, N.Y., 1986
Luckett, Richard, *The White Generals*, Routledge & Kegan Paul, London, 1971
Magnus, Sir Philip, *King Edward VII*, John Murray, London, 1964
Majolier, Natalie, *Stepdaughter to Imperial Russia*, Stanley Paul, London, 1940
Marie (Pavlovna), Grand Duchess, *Education of a Princess*, Viking, N.Y., 1931
Maylunas, Andrei and Mironenko, Sergei, *A Lifelong Passion*, Weidenfeld & Nicolson, London, 1996
Milyukov, Paul N., *History of the Russian Revolution*, Academic International Press, Gulf Breeze, Florida, 1978
Mossolov, A. A., *At the Court of the Last Tsar*, Methuen, London, 1935
(Nabokov, V. D.) *V. D. Nabokov and the Russian Provisional Government, 1917*, Yale University Press, New Haven, 1976
Nicholas, Prince of Greece, *My Fifty Years*, Hutchinson, London, 1926
Nicolson, Harold, *King George the Fifth*, Constable, London, 1952
Paléologue, Maurice, *An Ambassador's Memoirs*, Doran, N.Y., 1925
Paley, Princess, *Memories of Russia*, Herbert Jenkins, London, 1924
Pares, Sir Bernard, *The Fall of the Russian Monarchy*, Jonathan Cape, London, 1939
Payne, Robert, *The Life and Death of Lenin*, W. H. Allen, London, 1964
Pipes, Richard, *The Russian Revolution, 1899–1919*, Collins Harvill, London, 1990
Polovtsov, General P. A., *Glory and Downfall*, Bell, London, 1935
Radkey, Oliver H., *The Election to the Russian Constituent Assembly*, Harvard University Press, Cambridge, Mass., 1950
Radziwill, Princess Catherine, *Secrets of Dethroned Royalty*, Cassell, London, 1920
– *Nicholas II: The Last of the Tsars*, Cassell, London, 1931
Rimsky-Korsakov, Nikolay, *My Musical Life*, Knopf, N.Y., 1923
Rodzyanko, M. V., *The Reign of Rasputin*, Philpot, London, 1927
Rodzyanko, Colonel Paul, *Tattered Banners*, Seeley Service, London, 1938
Rose, Kenneth, *King George V*, Weidenfeld & Nicolson, London, 1983
Sazonov, Serge, *Fateful Years*, Jonathan Cape, London, 1928
Steinberg, Mark D. and Khrustalev, Vladimir M., *The Fall of the Romanovs*, Yale University Press, New Haven, 1995
Stites, Richard, *The Women's Liberation Movement in Russia*, Princeton University Press, Princeton, N.J., 1978
(Sokolov, Nicholas A.), (ed.) John F. O'Conor, *The Sokolov Investigation*, Souvenir Press, London, 1972
Sukhanov, N. N., *The Russian Revolution*, Princeton University Press, Princeton, N.J., 1984
Vassili, Count Paul, *Behind the Veil at the Russian Court*, Cassell, London, 1913
Vorres, Ian, *The Last Grand Duchess*, Scribner, N.Y., 1965
Vulliamy, C. E. (ed.), *The Red Archives*, Geoffrey Bles, London, 1929
Vyrubova, Anna, *Memoirs of the Russian Court*, Macmillan, London, 1923
Walker, Robert, *Rachmaninov: His Life and Times*, Pitman Press, London, 1980
Washburn, Stanley, *The Russian Campaign, 1915*, Andrew Melrose, London, 1916
Wilton, Robert, *The Last Days of the Romanovs*, Thornton Butterworth, London, 1920
Witte, Count Sergei, *Memoirs*, Doubleday, Page, Garden City, N.Y., 1921
Wonlar-Larsky, Nadine, *The Russia That I Loved*, MacSwinney, London, 1937
Wrangel, General Peter, *Memoirs*, Williams & Norgate, London, 1929
Youssoupoff, Prince Felix, *Rasputin: His Malignant Influence*, Jonathan Cape, London, 1927
– *Lost Splendour*, Jonathan Cape, London, 1953

RUSSIAN

Artemov, S., 'Mikhail Romanov: "Pobeg" i ego posledstviya', *Zerkalo*, 9 & 12, 1990
Buranov, Yu. and Khrustalev, V., *Gibel imperatorskogo doma 1917–1919 gg.*, Progress, Moscow, 1992

Denikin, General A. I., *Ocherki russkoi smuty*, Povolozky, Paris, 1921
(Guchkov, A. I.) 'Aleksandr Ivanovich Guchkov rasskazyvaet . . .', *Voprosy istorii*, Moscow, 7–8, 1991
Gushchik, Vladimir, *Taina Gatchinskogo dvortsa*, Literatura, Riga, 1927
Isakov, S. G., *Russkie v Estonii, 1918–1940*, Kompu, Tartu, Estonia, 1996
Khrustalev, V. M. and Lykov, L. A., *Skorbnyi put Mikhaila Romanova: Ot prestola do Golgofy*, Pushka, Perm, 1996
Kratkii ocherk Brasovskogo imeniya ego Imperatorskogo Vysochestva . . . Georgiya Aleksandrovicha, Orlovsky vestnik, Orel, 1895
Krylov, A., 'Istoricheskie miniatyury', Moscow, 3, 1990
Matveev, A. S., 'Vel. knyaz Mikhail Aleksandrovich v dni perevorota', *Vozrozhdenie*, Paris, 24, 1952
Melgunov, S. P., *Martovskie dni 1917 goda*, Editeurs réunis, Paris, 1961
Milyukov, P. N., *Istoriya vtoroi russkoi revolyutsii*, Rossiisko-bolgarskoe izdatelstvo, Sofia, 1921
Myasnikov, G., 'Filosofiya ubiistva, ili pochemu i kak ya ubil Mikhaila Romanova', *Minuvshee*, Atheneum & Feniks, Moscow & St Petersburg, 18, 1995
Mirkina, I. A. and Khrustalev, V. M., 'Sudba Mikhaila Romanova', *Voprosy istorii*, Moscow, 9, 1990
Platonov, Oleg, 'Tsareubiitsy', *Literaturnaya Rossiya*, Moscow, 38, 21 September 1990
Rodzyanko, M. V., 'Godsudarstvennaya Duma i fevralskaya 1917 goda revolyutsiya', *Arkhiv russkoi revolyutsii*, Berlin, 6, 1922
Shulgin, V. V., *Dni*, Novoe Vremya, Belgrade, 1925 (reprinted: Sovremennik, Moscow, 1989)
Stankevich, V. B., *Vospominaniya 1914–1919*, Ladyzhnikov, Berlin, 1920 (reprinted: Rossiisky gosudarstvenny gumanitarny universitet, Moscow, 1994)
Toropov, S. A., 'Samosud', *Vechernyaya Perm*, Perm, January 15, 1990
Trubetskoi, V., 'Zapiski kirasira', *Nashe nasledie*, Moscow, 2–4, 1991

FRENCH

Journal intime de Nicolas II, Payot, Paris, 1925
Enache, Nicolas, *La Descendance de Pierre le Grand*, Sedopols, Paris, 1983
Poutiatine, Princesse Olga, 'Les Derniers Jours du Grand-Duc Michel Alexandrovitch', *Revue des Deux Mondes*, Paris, November 1 & 15, 1923

REFERENCE WORKS

Almanac de Gotha, 1900–1936
Baedeker: London, 1908; *Berlin*, 1909; *Paris*, 1913; *Russia*, 1914
Burke's Royal Families of the World, (ed.) Hugh Montgomery-Massingberd, Burke's Peerage, London, 1977
May, Robin, *A Companion to the Opera*, Lutterworth Press, London, 1977
Werlich, Robert, *Russian Orders, Decorations, and Medals*, Quaker Press, Washington, D.C., 1981
Petrograd Telephone Directory, 1916
Moscow Telephone Directory, 1905–1909

GENERAL WORKS

The Willy–Nicky Correspondence, (ed.) Herman Bernstein, Knopf, N.Y., 1918
Almedingen, E. M., *The Empress Alexandra*, Hutchinson, London, 1961
– *The Romanovs*, Bodley Head, London, 1936
Bailey, Geoffrey, *The Conspirators*, Victor Gollancz, London, 1961
Balfour, Michael, *The Kaiser and His Times*, Cresset Press, London, 1964

Battiscombe, Georgina, *Queen Alexandra*, Constable, London, 1969
Benois, Alexandre, *Reminiscences of the Russian Ballet*, Putnam, London, 1941
Bergamini, John, *The Tragic Dynasty*, Constable, London, 1970
Buchanan, Meriel, *Petrograd: The City of Trouble, 1915–1916*, Collins, London, 1918
Bunyon, J. and Fisher, H. (eds.), *The Bolshevik Revolution, 1917–1918*, Stanford University Press, Stanford, California, 1961
Charques, Richard, *The Twilight of Imperial Russia*, Oxford University Press, Oxford, 1955
Cowles, Virginia, *The Last Tsar and Tsarina*, Weidenfeld & Nicolson, London, 1977
Crankshaw, Edward, *The Shadow of the Winter Palace*, Macmillan, London, 1976
Duff, David, *Hessian Tapestry*, David & Charles, Newton Abbot, 1967
Fleming, Peter, *The Fate of Admiral Kolchak*, Rupert Hart-Davis, London, 1963
Florinsky, Michael T., *The End of the Russian Empire*, Collier, N.Y., 1961
Golovine, Lieutenant-General Nicholas, *The Russian Army in the World War*, Yale & Oxford University Presses, New Haven & Oxford, 1931
von Grabbe, Paul and Beatrice, *The Private World of the Last Tsar*, Little Brown, Boston, 1984
Grey, Ian, *The Romanovs*, Doubleday, N.Y., 1970
Grigoriev, S. L., *The Diaghilev Ballet, 1909–1928*, Constable, London, 1953
Hanbury-Williams, Major-General Sir John, *The Emperor Nicholas As I Knew Him*, Arthur Humphreys, London, 1922
Harcave, Sidney, *Years of the Golden Cockerel*, Hale, London, 1970
Harmer, Michael, *The Forgotten Hospital*, Springwood, Chichester, 1982
Hodgetts, E. A. Brayley, *The Court of Russia in the Nineteenth Century*, Methuen, London, 1908
Karsavina, Tamara, *Theatre Street*, Heinemann, London, 1930
Keep, John L. H., *The Russian Revolution*, Weidenfeld & Nicolson, London, 1976
Kochan, Lionel, *Russia in Revolution*, Weidenfeld & Nicolson, London, 1966
Lieven, Dominic, *Nicholas II*, John Murray, London, 1993
Lincoln, W. Bruce, *The Romanovs*, Weidenfeld & Nicolson, London, 1981
Massie, Robert K., *Nicholas and Alexandra*, Victor Gollancz, London, 1972
Moorehead, Alan, *The Russian Revolution*, Collins, London, 1958
Occleshaw, Michael, *The Romanov Conspiracies*, Chapmans, London, 1993
Oldenburg, S. S., *Last Tsar*, Academic International Press, Gulf Breeze, Florida, 1978
Palmer, Alan, *The Kaiser*, Weidenfeld & Nicolson, London, 1978
Pitcher, Harvey, *When Miss Emmie was in Russia*, John Murray, London, 1977
Pridham, Francis, *Close of a Dynasty*, Wingate, London, 1956
Radzinsky, Edvard, *The Last Tsar*, Hodder & Stoughton, London, 1992
Salisbury, Harrison, *Black Knight, White Snow*, Doubleday, N.Y., 1977
Seton-Watson, Hugh, *The Decline of Imperial Russia*, Methuen, London, 1952
Shulgin, V. V., *The Years*, Hippocrene Books, N.Y., 1991
Stone, Norman, *The Eastern Front, 1914–1917*, Hodder & Stoughton, London, 1975
Tarsaidze, Alexandre, *Czars and Presidents*, McDowell, Obolensky, N.Y., 1958
Wilson, Colin, *Rasputin and the Fall of the Romanovs*, Arthur Barker, London, 1964

Index

'M' indicates Michael Aleksandrovich; 'N' indicates Natasha

Abakanovich, Koka, 93, 104, 171, 180
Abakanovich, Maggie, 93, 104, 171, 180, 339, 346, 364, 365
Abrikosov, Dimitri, 37, 140; opinions of M and N, 212–18
Adlon Hotel, Berlin, *see Hotels*
Admiralty, Petrograd, 265, 266, 273
Agamemnon, HMS, 381, 383n, 392
Ai-Todor, near Yalta, 236, 243
Alapaevsk, 353, 370
Albany, Duke of (later Duke of Saxe-Coburg-Gotha), 8
Albert, Prince Consort, 8
Alekseev, General Mikhail, 202, 253, 259, 263–4, 268, 277, 279–81, 290–91, 314, 319
Alexander II, 31, 389; assassination, 17, 20, 28, 29n; constitutional order, 21; morganatic marriage, 20, 29n, 287; 'Tsar-Liberator', 21
Alexander III (*M's father*), 7, 12, 27, 30, 124, 147–8, 208, 257, 325, 388; appearance, 19, 21, 53; personality, 21, 27–8; austerity, 18, 22–3; in Gatchina, 17–18, 21; and Marie Fedorovna, 19; and Queen Victoria, 6; death 18, 21–3;
Alexander Mikhailovich, Grand Duke ('Sandro'), (*M's brother-in-law*), 146–7, 155, 240, 300n; on M, 5; on N, 395; marriage to Xenia, 23, 143–4; on Nicholas's relationship with uncles, 24; with M confronts Nicholas, 255–6; on M's manifesto, 314; acknowledges Kirill as Tsar, 387
Alexander Palace, Tsarskoe Selo, *see Tsarskoe Selo*
Alexandra, Queen of England, 155, 321n, 383; as sister of Dowager Empress, 13, 24; and Hvidore, 54, 78; matchmaking, 13–14; views on divorce, 34; and M's visits to London, 55–7, 146; death 390
Alexandra, Empress of Russia (*M's sister-in-law*), 8, 129, 136, 156, 160, 168, 192, 227, 268, 272, 302, 366; birth of children, 10, 25–6, 44; coronation, 53; marriage, 23; on divorce, 34; and Dr Philippe, 198, 205–6; and Rasputin, 197–201, 207, 219, 228, 237, 240, 241, 244–5, 259; domination over Nicholas, 201, 205, 240, 256; as *de facto* Regent 197; belief in autocracy, 206–7, 208, 237; dismissal of Grand Duke Nicholas, 199–201; denigrated, 137, 200, 237; efforts to remove from politics, 248, 250–51; enmity towards Guchkov, 216; towards ministers, 206, 237; towards Witte, 26; interference by, 205–7; opposes the Duma, 206, 216–17, 241; on Paul's manifesto, 275; in revolution, 268–71; after Nicholas's abdication, 298; 'criminal lunatic', 323; on M's gallantry award, 179; on his being at Stavka, 203, 208; removing him from N's influence, 179, 220; on meeting him, 227; on hostility to, 223–4; opposition in 1900 to his succession, 25–6; on his being Emperor, 298; on denying N a title, 203–4; on N being at Mogilev, 231; on N's son George, 170; and Bimbo, 240; Boris, 30; Dimitri, 168, 204, 243, 245, 318; Dowager Empress, 208, 228; Ella, 240; Kirill, 30; sister-in-law Olga, 228; Marie Pavlovna snr, 247–8; Sandro, 255–6; murder of, 370; estate of 392–3
Alexandra, Princess of Greece, 168
Alexandra, Princess of Hohenlohe-Langenburg, 8
Alexandra Villa, Peterhof, 73
Alexis Aleksandrovich, Grand Duke (*M's uncle*), 27, 31, 166
Alexis Nikolaevich (*Tsarevich*), 217, 259, 277–9, 318; birth, 28; haemophilia, 29–30, 130–31, 197–8, 286–7, 307; and Rasputin, 197, 199; and M's marriage, 130–3, 135; plots to make Emperor, 248, 253; proposed abdication in favour of 277–80, 284–9; first abdication in favour of 281; removed from succession, 286–8, 302, 307, 309, 316; last sight of M, 325; death of, 370
Alfonso, Don, Infante of Spain, 10n
Alfonso XIII of Spain, 10n, 394

Alfred, Duke of Edinburgh, 7
All-Russian Congress, 362
Amalienborg Palace, 78
Ambassador's Theatre, London, 152
'Anastasia' (imposter), 393
Anastasia Nikolaevna, Grand Duchess, (*Nicholas's youngest dau.*) 26, 370, 393; death, 370
Andrew Vladimirovich, Grand Duke (*M's cousin*), 212, 215, 244, 247, 388; and Kschessinska, 11, 30, 152, 214; and their illegitimate son, 30; and M, 143–4, 152, 225; and N, 226; on Nicholas as Supreme Commander, 197, 201
Andronik, Archbishop of Perm, 364
Anichkov Palace, 48, 51, 87, 98, 149, 161, 186, 212, 309, 318–19; described, 19; and Dowager Empress, 20, 24
Annenkova, Mlle, 294–5
Apolant, Hans, 114, 123, 125, 127–8
Arbat City School, Moscow, 36
Arthur, Duke of Connaught, 12
Artsybushev, P. M., 108
Austro-Hungarian Army in first world war, 171–2, 176–7, 179, 229, 347
Ayuna (*N's maid*), 76–7, 209

Baby-Bee, *see Beatrice, Princess*
Bad Kissingen, 114, 116, 123–8, 145, 148
Badmaev (*quack doctor*), 241
Bakhrushin, Michael, 63, 107
Balfour, Arthur, 332
Balkan crisis (1914), 22, 155, 160
Ballets Russes, 153–4
Balmoral, 6
'Baltic Barons', 40
Baranovichi, 169, 186, 202
Batovo, 335
Battenberg, Princess Victoria, *see Milford Haven*
Beatrice, Princess ('Baby Bee'), 6, 7–10, 12
Beauregard (*French actress*), 347
Beecham, Sir Joseph, 154
Beecham, Sir Thomas, 154n
Beloborodov, Aleksandr, 354–5, 362–3
Belyaev, General Mikhail, 259, 265, 272, 298
Benckendorff, Count, 40
Bennett, Mr S. (*head groom*), 150, 152, 159–60
Beringer, Guy, 13
Berlin, 66–8, 76, 79, 122, 125, 140, 154, 161–2, 345
Bernov, General, 45, 59–61, 81
Bernstorff, 78
Bimbo, *see Nicholas Mikhailovich*
Bint, Senior Agent, 122–6
Biryukov General, 382
Birzhevye Vedomosti, 317
'Bloody Sunday', 39, 43, 265
Blue Cuirassiers, *see Russian Army*
Bogdanovich, Colonel, 258
Boissonnas & Eggler, 176, 223, 225
Bologoe, 88, 270
Bolsheviks, 324–5, 329, 334, 336–7, 345; at Motovilikha, 349; and the Czechs, 347; and Constituent Assembly, 338; in Gatchina, 335; and Germany, 365; Kerensky arms, 330, 333; Bolshevik Revolution, 333–5; elections for Constituent Assembly, and closure of, 338; and N's escape, 376; and M's murder, 354; German peace negotiations, 338; in Perm, 343, 347–8, 351–2, 354; and Red Terror, 372; and Social Revolutionaries, 367n; and White Russians, 388
Bolshoi Opera, 40, 96, 100
Bonch-Bruevich, Vladimir, 337, 340, 342, 345
Boris Vladimirovich, Grand Duke (*M's cousin*), 30–31, 113, 189, 213–15, 225–6, 244, 247, 258, 325, 387–8; meets N for first time, 212
Borunov (*chauffeur*), 342, 346, 358, 361, 364, 373
Brasov, George Mikhailovich (*M's son*), 122, 135, 146, 148, 182, 308, 344, 377, 389; appearance, 390; birth and christening, 104–5, 163; and 'doctoring' certificates, 106–8, 109, 125, 129, 163; in Cannes, 128; legitimisation, 164–5, 170, 182; and M, 115, 142, 210, 249; escape to Denmark, 344–5, 368, 376–7; schooling, 382, 384–5, 391; and Dowager Empress, 383; legacy, 390–91; death and burial, 391–2
Brasova, Nathalie Sergeyevna (Natasha), 305, 352; appearance, v, 2, 33, 36–7, 39, 56, 167, 169, 212–15, 375–7, 383, 391–2; birth, 36; childhood; 36–7; education, 37, 53; intelligence, 33, 35, 56, 215, 220; social position, 34–7; personality, 33, 56, 167, 213, 215; extravagance, 54, 66, 68, 140–41, 149; presents from M, 141, 145, 149; marriage to Mamontov 37–40; birth of daughter, 38; and divorce, 40; meets Wulfert, 39; and marriage to, 40, 42, 47, 53; quarrels with, 53–4; his rape and violence, 66, 68, 71; marriage breakdown, 65–73; and his threats of suicide, 71; to force her return, 90; and to murder her, 90–91, 93; and to take away her child, 94–8, 106; Wulfert agrees divorce, 97–8; and renounces father's rights, 107; and meets M, 7, 16; and at regimental ball, 44–5; association in Gatchina, 46–7, 49–50, 52–3, 59–61, 64–6; in Berlin (1909), 67; and in Switzerland, 68–73, 75–6, 82–3; and with

Brasova, Nathalie Sergeyevna (Natasha) – *cont.* M in Copenhagen, 77–9; fears about return, 83–4; in Moscow 84; and renting house, 85–6, 89; and M's ignorance about money, 86–7; and becomes pregnant, 94; difficulties in obtaining separate residency, 91–4; birth of son George, 104; before divorce finalised, 104–6; allowed to go to Brasovo, 111–13; and granted name of, 111; postnatal depression, 106; in Bad Kissingen sanatorium, 114–16, 123; travels abroad (*in 1910*), 109–10, (*in 1911*) 117–18; and objects to 'governesses', 110, 116; in St Petersburg, 118; moves to Gatchina, 118–19; and humiliated, 119–20; and Blue Cuirassiers, 42, 44–6, 59, 81, 101, 120–21; and Chevalier Gardes, 119; and marriage to M, 128; adjudged 'criminal' and banished 133–4; in exile at Cannes, 128, 142, 153–4; in Paris, 144, 149; in Chexbres, 145; in London, and meets Dowager Empress, 146; at Knebworth, 149, 149–52; and Countess Torby, 148, 151; allowed (1914) to return to Russia, 151; and Gatchina, 161; on living there, 180, 183, 209, 231–2; and Nikolaevskaya Street, 183, 209; death of sister Olga, 173; and Vera, 181; in Lvov, 167, 179; in Brasovo, 224, 234, 236, 245–6; at Ai-Todor, 234; and Dimitri, first meeting with, 168–9; his passion for, 170–71, 174–5, 177, 180, 186–7, 192–3, 225–6; on M's character, 95, 97, 101, 184, 188–90, 211, 223–4, 232; worries about M, 167, 171, 175, 177, 188, 195, 225, 232; complaints about, 183, 188–91, 211, 233; love for, 167, 177, 193, 233; compliments about, 167, 184, 212, 214; vanity of; 184, 213, 214, 383; disapproval of, 180, 215, 236; humiliation of, 213, 222–4; views on war, 172, 187–8; and Moscow pogrom, 191–2; political views of, 216; political reputation of, 215–18, 220, 276, 290, 305; and M's manifesto, 316; question of title, 204, 213; as 'Countess Brasova', 108, 212; as Princess, 1, 389, 392; on Nicholas, 227; and Nicholas on, 109, 133, 135; on Alexandra, 223; and Alexandra, 179, 203–4, 220, 231; on Mordvinov, 93, 105, 116, 232; and Mordvinov on, 92–3, 134–5, 203; on Dowager Empress, 229; and Dowager Empress on, 146, 383; and Andrew 143, 152, 215, 226; Boris, 189, 212–15, 226; Kirill, 389; and George Mikhailovich, 299, 318, 320; and Grand Duchess Olga, 50, 52–3, 55, 61, 64; and Abrikosov 37, 212–18; arrested by Kerensky, 327, 331; in Bolshevik revolution, 334, 336–7; and on M's arrest, 339; confronts Lenin, 340, 348–9; efforts to release M, 342; and smuggles George to safety, 344; in Perm, 346–8; arrested, 364–5; and escapes, 371–2; to Ukraine, 376; and German help for, 374–7; and British evacuation of, 377–8; in England, 381–6; fears for M, 383–4; and accepts his death, 386; financial worries and monies, 382, 389, 392–4; death of George, 390–2; poverty of; 394–5; death of, 1–2, 395
Brasovo estate, near Orel, 14, 48–9, 82, 107, 116, 139, 149, 183, 221, 224, 234, 236, 321; described, 111–12, 245–6
Bratolyubov (*an 'inventor'*), 211, 221
Breshko-Breshkovsky, Nikolai, 78
Brest-Litovsk, 186, 196
Brest-Litovsk, Treaty of, 338, 365–6
British embassy, Petrograd, 365, 370, 372
British government, and denying asylum to Nicholas, 322–4; to M and Grand Dukes, 323–4, 332–3, 381
British royals, and changing names, 323
Bruce Lockhart, Robert, 199, 218, 370
Brusilov, General Aleksandr, 176, 178, 197, 252, 254, 280, 328, 368–9
'Brusilov Offensive', 229
Bublikov, 296–7, 308
Buchanan, Sir George, 137, 201, 249–50, 274–5, 282, 317, 320, 323, 331–2
Buckingham Palace, 12–13, 55–7, 98, 113, 151–2, 155–6, 160, 322–3, 394
Budberg, Baron Aleksei, 92–3

Cannes, 9, 117, 123–5, 128, 139–40, 142–4, 148, 153–4, 161
Cantacuzène, Princess, 295, 313–14
Carpathian mountains, 165, 171–2, 178, 183, 229
Catherine the Great, 17, 160
Caucasus, 24–5, 162–3, 174, 201, 280
Caucasian Native Cavalry (Savage Division), *see Russian Army*
Chaliapin, Fedor, 33, 35, 38, 139, 154
'champagne plot', 252
Charlottenlund Palace, 78
Chavchavadze, Prince David, 321n
Cheka, 339–40, 355–6, 358–9, 364, 367n, 371–2
Cheltenham Ladies College, 385–6
Chelyabinsk, 347–9, 351
Chelyshev, Vasily, 342–3, 346, 357–9, 361, 364, 373
Chernigov Hussars, Chevalier Gardes, *see Russian army*

Chernovitsy, 176
Chexbres, 72, 83, 144–5, 148
Chkheidze, Nikolai, 283
Christian X, King of Denmark, 344–5, 368, 376
Chudow Abbey, Moscow, 295
Church of St Basil of Caesarea in Cappadocia, Moscow, 104
Church of St Savva, Vienna, 126–8, 131
Clarke, Captain Henry J. L., 15
Coburg, 7–8
Connaught, Duke and Duchess of, 7; family, 13
Constantinople, 381
Constituent Assembly, 284, 311–15, 317–18, 321, 330, 332–3, 338
Copenhagen, 75–80, 84, 89, 92, 112, 144, 345, 376, 382
Cossacks, 39, 164, 221, 257, 270, 329, 333–4, 368
Council of Ministers, 297, 314
Council of St George, 178
Council of State, 26–7, 219–20, 236, 254
Court Circular (London), 13, 57, 148, 151–2
Cowdray, Lord, 159
Cowes Regatta, 155, 160
Cramer, Colonel, 344
Crimea, 236, 241, 243, 245, 253, 256, 295, 298; Alexander III dies in, 21; M in, 7, 15, 235–6; Dina arrested in, 14; Nicholas in, 21, 25; Alexandra in, 205; M's permit for, 332–3; N escapes to, 377–8
Cromie, Captain Francis, 365–7, 372
Cumberland, Duke of, 5
Czech Legion, 347–9, 351, 354, 366

Daily Telegraph, London, 28
Dalton, Dr Hugh, 381n
Danish embassy, Petrograd, 344, 371
Davidson, Colonel, 384
Dehn, Lili, 270
Den, 317
Denmark, 5, 12, 15, 49, 53–6, 72, 75–80, 161, 368, 382
Diaghilev, Sergei, 154, 342
Dillon, Dr E. J., 28
Dimitri Konstantinovich, Grand Duke, 382n
Dimitri Pavlovich, Grand Duke (*M's cousin*), 182, 189, 212, 240, 251, 353, 368; appearance, 169, 174; childhood, 129, 168; health, 174, 390n; decorated for gallantry, 168; rakish behaviour, 168; and N meets, 169–71; confesses love for, 173–75; relationship with, 177, 180, 186–7, 192, 225–6, 248–9, 333; and in England, 382; and M, 182, 194, 202, 207; and Alexandra, 204, 207, 318; and Rasputin's murder, 31, 241–3; arrest and banishment, 31, 236, 243–5, 247; family petition for, 247–8; in exile, 333; in London, 381; on Kirill declaring himself Tsar, 387; in Paris, 390; marriage, 390; birth of son 390n; at George's funeral, 391; death, 390n
Dimitri Palace, Petrograd, 243
Dina, *see Alexandra Kossikovskaya*
divorce in Russia, 33–4, 82, 94
Dno, 333
Dolgorukaya, Catherine (Princess Yourievskaya), 20, 29n, 287
Drokin, Vasily, 359
Ducky, *see Victoria Melita*
Duma, 39n, 199, 236, 248, 250, 256, 260–61, 277, 311; and Alexandra, 204, 206, 216–17, 241; composition of, 206; reopening 1916 of, 218–19, 221; M and N present at, 218–19; suspension of, 206, 216, 259–60; Grand Dukes' manifesto on recall, 275; *see also Tauride Palace*
Duma, Temporary Committee of, 260, 271, 276, 281–2, 288–9, 291; Kirill acknowledges, 275; regiments proclaim loyalty to, 283; creation of provisional government, 283–5
Dyer, Miss (*governess*), 150
Dzerzhinsky, Feliks (*Cheka supremo*), 361
Dzhunkovsky, General, 199

École des Roches, Verneuil, 390
Eden, Sir Anthony, 155n
Edward VII ('Uncle Bertie'), 7, 12, 58, 148, 393; coronation, 26; funeral, 98; and *HMS Minerva*, 15; honours M, 26; mistresses, 138
Edward VIII, later Duke of Windsor, 138
Ekaterinburg, 342, 346, 351, 353–5, 362, 363n, 370, 383
Ella (Elizabeth), Grand Duchess, 28, 129, 168, 191; last meeting with sister Alexandra, 240; on M's succession as Emperor, 295–6; imprisonment, 353, 366; and Kaiser, 369; murder of, 370
Emery, Audrey, 390
Eristova, Princess Tamira, 391
Ernst, Grand Duke of Hesse-Darmstadt, 8, 30, 191, 393
Evert, General Aleksei, 280

'F'. Prince, 144, 146
Fabergé, 43, 189
'February Revolution' (1917), disorder in Petrograd, 256–9, 273–4; Duma suspended, 259–60; formation of Temporary

'February Revolution' (1917) – *cont.* Committee, 260; and Soviet, 271; garrison troops mutiny, 257–8, 261, 265–6, 273–4; Grand Dukes' manifesto, 275–7; ministers arrested, 271–2; N's journey from Mogilev, 268–71; and return, 302, 314; Alexandra at Tsarskoe Selo, 268, 270–71; Temporary Committee and Soviet, 282–5; Guchkov and Shulgin go to Pskov, 285; N's abdication, 279–81, 285–8; proclamation of M as Emperor, 295–7; meeting at Millionnaya Street, 297–314
Fedorov, M. M., 216–17
Fedorov, Professor Sergei, 285
Finland, 159, 161, 324, 332, 387, 389; M's permit for, 324, 332, 334
First World War, 22, 156, 159; assassination of Archduke Franz Ferdinand, 155; opening battles, 162; Russian victories against Austrians, 162; Carpathian campaign, 171–2, 176; Nicholas's 'victory tour', 184; Russian retreat (1915), 187, 196; Moscow riots, 191–2, 200–2; dismissal of Grand Duke Nicholas, 196, 199–201; Nicholas as Supreme Commander, 197; Brusilov Offensive (1916), 229–30; casualties, 172, 196, 229–30, 237; collapse of discipline 319–20; Kerensky Offensive (1917), 328; Kornilov 'rebellion', 328–30; peace treaty with Germans, 338, 365–6
Fisher, Sir John, 15
Fokine, Michael, 154
Ford, Lionel, 385
Franklin, Elizabeth, 22–3
Franz Ferdinand, Archduke of Austria, 127, 155
Frederick, King of Denmark, 112
Frederiks, Baron, 40, 91–3, 118, 236, 286; and files on N, 88; helps M, 69, 83, 90; and N's divorce, 97, 99, 102; and reaction to M's marriage, 133; and regency question (1900), 25–6; talks to Wulfert, 70–71, 81, 90
Frolova, Katya, 66, 76
Fundamental Laws, 287, 308–9

Galicia, 162, 184
Garrick Theatre, London, 57
Gatchina (town), 16, 69, 82, 128, 164, 180, 235, 245, 265, 274, 299, 324, 330, 385n; described, 17–18; as a garrison town, 33–5, 47; hospital in, 166, 222–3; M's attitude towards, 17, 24, 119, 149, 170, 209, 224, 336; N arrives, 33; and her attitudes towards, 183, 209, 231–2; Tata in, 33, 42, 370–2, 375; capture by Bolsheviks, 335; Nikolaevskaya Street villa, 129, 149, 161, 168, 204, 212, 217, 229, 231, 299, 321, 327, 337–8, 345; and description of, 119, 166, 183–4, 209–10; destruction of, 385; M's other property in, 321–2; Wulfert apartment, 42, 47, 49; Gatchina Palace, 7, 63, 149, 198, 209–10, 227, 298, 325, 371; Alexander III in, 17–18, 21; described, 17–18; M's quarters in, 47–8; childhood there, 22–3; game reserve, 171, 316, 334; palace church, 180, 210, 232, 234, 316; park, 51, 186, 209; Pavilion of Venus, 48
George I, King of Greece, 320
George V, King of England, 150, 160, 249, 275, 390; appearance, 24; coronation, 113; and M's marriage, 135–6; and Miche-Miche, 148; blames Alexandra for abdication, 282; unwillingness to admit Romanovs, 322–3
George Mikhailovich, Grand Duke, warns Nicholas, 240; in Gatchina, 299, 316, 318–19; views on N, 320; attempts to go to England, 320–3; murder of, 382n
George Mikhailovich (Marie Georgieevna), Grand Duchess, 155, 320–21
George Aleksandrovich, Grand Duke (*M's brother*), 23–4, 104, 112; death, 25
George, Prince of Prussia ('Grand Duke Georgy'), 389n
Gerasimov, Major-General Aleksandr, 117–18, 122, 124
German embassy, Moscow, 365
German Ukraine Delegation, 369
Germany, declares war on Russia, 159; signs peace treaty, 338; support for Bolsheviks, 369; concern for fate of Romanovs, 366, 370; hopes for M as Emperor, 366–9; safe passage for George and Miss Neame, 344–5; smuggling N out of Russia, 374–7; territory controlled after peace treaty, 365; and comparison with Bolshevik Russia, 375–6
Gielgud, Sir John, 386n
Gielgud, Val, 386, 392
Gilliard, Pierre, 322
Girard, Baron, 180–81
Golitsin, Prince, 256, 259, 261, 263, 265, 272
Goloshchekin, Filipp, 362, 363n
Gomel, 376
Gorchakov, Prince, 100
Goremykin, Ivan, 206, 217–18, 272
Granitza, 84
Grant, General Ulysses, 295
Gray, Cecil, 392
Gray, Pauline, 38, 45, 392, 394–5
Great Northern War, 41
Grey, Sir Edward, 137

Grigorev (*Kerensky ADC*), 331
Guchkov, Aleksandr, 184n, 216, 276, 281, 296–301, 319, 325; 'Guchkov conspiracy', 253–4, 329; at Pskov, 285–8; at Millionnaya Street, 303–5
Gushchik, Vladimir, 210, 337, 371, 395

Habsburgs, 394
Halida, Finland, 389
Hans, Prince of Denmark, 78–9
Harrow School, 385, 390
Heath, Mr (*tutor*), 23
Henry, Prince of Prussia, 8, 156, 160, 366, 374
Hermitage, Petrograd, 266
Hohenfelsen, Countess, *see Princess Paley*
Hohenlohe-Langenburg, Prince of, 8
Holstein-Gottorp-Romanov, 55n
Holy Synod, 97, 102, 205, 274
HOTELS
- Adlon, Berlin, 76, 122
- Amerika, Ekaterinburg, 362
- Astoria, Paris, 148–9
- Astoria, Petrograd, 166, 169, 180, 189, 214–16, 225–6, 273
- Bristol, Mogilev, 231
- Bristol, Vienna, 83, 109–10
- Cimiez, Nice, 6
- Claridges, London, 155
- d'Angleterre, Copenhagen, 75, 77–9
- d'Angleterre, Vevey, 68, 72
- de l'Europe, 87, 101, 116, 161, 166
- de Londres, Odessa, 377
- du Parc, Cannes, 124, 128, 135, 139, 141–2, 153
- du Signal, Chexbres, 144–5
- Esplanade, Berlin, 122–3, 125
- Grand, Chexbres, 72, 83
- Hermitage, Perm, 342
- Korolev Rooms, Perm, 343, 345–6, 350, 352, 357
- Mirabeau, Paris, 141, 144
- National, Moscow, 84, 87, 173, 235, 249
- Piccadilly, London, 155
- Quirinale, Rome, 110
- Ritz, London, 126n, 146, 151
- Tegetthof, Vienna, 127–8
- Tramontana, Sorrento, 15
- Westminster, Berlin, 67

House of Windsor, 323
Hvidore, Denmark, 54, 78, 129, 390

Ignateva, Countess Ekaterina, 147
Ilyinsky, Paul (*Dimitri's son*), 390n
Imperial Russian Historical Society, 5–6
Imperial theatres, 11n, 213
Ipatev, Nikolai, 353, 369
Irene, Princess of Prussia, 8, 366, 392
Irving, H. B., 57
Ivanchenko, Vasily, 355, 357, 360
Ivanov, General, 264, 268, 270
Ivanov, Nikolai (*lawyer*), 275

Johnson, Mme, 141, 160, 381, 383
Johnson, Nicholas, 141, 149, 160, 169, 180, 209–10, 226, 245, 266–7, 274, 297, 299, 307, 315, 331, 336–7, 357, 364, 373; on Gatchina, 183; meets Kerensky at Winter Palace, 325; arrested 327, 330, 339; asks Buchanan for help, 331; exiled to Perm, 340–3, 345–6; murder of; 358–60

Kadet party, 317n
Kamenets-Podolsky, 227, 252
Kapnist, Count Dimitri, 183–4, 216, 219–20
Kapnist, Countess, 183–4, 226
Karsavina, Tamara, 154
Kasvin, 244
Kaushin, battle of, 168
Kenwood, Hampstead, London, 148, 151
Keppel, Mrs Alice, 138
Kerensky, Aleksandr, 252, 283, 288, 291, 298–9, 316, 389; and 1915 approach by M re succession, 217; role in February revolution, 271–3, 290; theatrical postures, 272–3, 303, 305, 312; Millionnaya Street, 291, 297, 301–2, 304–5, 307, 314; Minister of Justice, 285; prime minister, and moves into Winter Palace, 325; arranges meeting between M and Nicholas, 325–6; transfers Nicholas and family to Tobolsk, 324–5; arrests M, 327–8, 335; complaints to about M's treatment, 331; M's permit for Finland, 324; Kornilov affair, 329–30; Supreme Commander, 330; arms Bolsheviks, 330, 333; declares Russia to be republic, 330, 332; defeated, 334; and flees Bolsheviks, 335
'Kerensky Offensive', 328
Khabalov, General Sergei, 257, 265–6
Khan-Erivansky, Lieutenant, 120
Kharkov, 39
Khitrovo, Margarita, 328
Khludov, Aleksei (*N's godfather*), 36–7
Kiev, 75, 251, 266, 369, 376–7; hospital funded by N, 222–3, 227
Kirill Vladimirovich, Grand Duke, 31, 244, 247, 270, 281–2, 311, 317; banished after marriage to 'Ducky', 30–31, 34, 387; Grand Dukes' manifesto, 275; marches troops to Tauride Palace, 275–6; complains about M, 276; proclaims himself Emperor, 387–9

Knebworth House, England, 209; described, 149; M's rental, 149–53, 159, 160–61, 213; and *Ballets Russes*, 154–5
Knox, Col later Major-General Sir Alfred, 164, 197, 237, 258
Kobylinsky, Colonel Eugen, 325
Kokoshkin, F. F., 338
Kolchak, Admiral Aleksandr, 384
Kolpashchikov, Ivan, 355–60
Konstantin Konstantinovich, Grand Duke, 27, 188–9, 198, 353
'Kornilov affair', 328–30, 332
Kornilov, General Lavr, 327; and 'rebellion', 328–30, 333
Kosmin, Captain Andrei, 327, 331–2
Kossikovskaya, Alexandra ('Dina'), 29, 52, 55, 58, 62, 82; appearance and personality, 10; affair with M, 10–12, 89; Grand Duchess Olga's lady-in-waiting, 6; and dismissed, 12; arrested Odessa, 14; leaves Russia, 15–16; seen as threat in London, 55–7; dies destitute in Berlin, 16n
Kossikovsky, Vladimir, 6, 10–12, 14
Koton, Dr, Gatchina, 195, 246
Kovno, 196
Kozlovsky (*chauffeur*), 263–4
Krasilnikov, A., 124
Krasnoe Selo, 104, 121
Krasnov, General Peter, 295, 334
Kremlin, 36, 348
Kresty prison, 283, 334
Krestyanov (*palace administrator*), 180, 232
Krivoshein, A. V., 205
Krumnis (*Perm witness*), 357–8, 361
Krylov (*police inspector*), 257
Krymov, General Aleksandr, 253–4, 329–30, 333–4
Kschessinska, Mathilde, 11, 30, 143, 152–3, 214, 226, 273, 353
Kulikovsky, Captain Nikolai, affair with Grand Duchess Olga, 50–3, 59–60, 64–5; marriage, 228; and Wulfert, 71
Kuzmenko (*boatswain*), 249

Laënnec hospital, Paris, 1, 395
Lamsdorff, Count Vladimir, 26
Langtry, Lillie, 138
Laslikevich, Captain, 258
Latvians, 341, 353
Lazovert, Dr, 241
Lebedeva, Maria, and daughter Irina, 246
Lechitsky, General, 188, 374
Legge, Colonel the Hon H. C., 56–8
Legnani, Pierina, 11n
Lemberg, 167
Lena, Miss, 102–4
Lenin, Vladimir Ilyich (Ulyanov), 21n, 36, 39, 324, 355, 363, 369; N confronts in Petrograd, 339–40; and in Moscow, 348–9; M cables 341–2; knowledge of M's murder, 362; wounding of, 372
Lesnaya, battle of, 41
Lisino, 119
Litchfield-Speer, John, 385
Litchfield-Speer, Captain Shirley, 383–4
Livadia, 21, 241, 253, 256, 295
Lloyd-George, David, 322
Lomna, 171
Lomonosov, Professor, 312–13
London, M in at funeral of Queen Victoria, and coronation of Edward VII, 26; and visits (1908), 55–8; at funeral of Edward VII, 98–9; with N meets Dowager Empress (1913), 146; at theatre, 152, 154; business investment, 152; M meets George V, 160; Miche-Miche resident in, 147–8; *Ballets Russes* season in, 153–4; Romanov family gathering in (1914), 155; N in (1919–27), 385–6; Dimitri and sister Marie in, 381
Longchamps, 117
Louis XVI of France, 18
Luga, 330
Lukoyanov F. N., 352, 361
Lunarcharsky, A. V., 342, 351n
Luxembourg, Grand Duke of, 148
Lvov, 167, 171, 176–7, 179, 184, 187, 305
Lvov, Prince Georgy, 253, 262–3, 277, 284–5, 287, 297, 300–1, 303, 306–8, 316, 325, 389
Lytton, Earl of, 149

Majolier, Alexandra, 392
Majolier, Michael, 392
Maklakov Vasily, 248, 317
Malaya Vishera, 270
Malaya Yazovaya, 356, 361
Malkov, Pavel, 354, 356–9, 361, 373
Malta, 381, 383n, 392
Maly Theatre, 214
Mamontov family, 35, 390, 395
Sergei, 108; appearance and personality, 37–8; career, 38, 40, 386; marriage to N, 35, 38; and divorce, 33, 40, 47; death, 386n
Nathalie (Natasha), *see Brasova*
Nathalie ('Tata'), 122, 160, 167, 246, 249, 335, 344; birth, 38; childhood in Moscow, 39–40; in Gatchina, 33, 42, 61–2, 64–5; education 102–3, 382, 385; hears quarrels between N and Mamontov 40; and Wulfert 65–6; and behaviour affected by, 71; abroad (1909) with N, 66, 76; in Moscow, 89; in

Udinka, 102–4; in Brasovo, 111–12; in Cannes, 128, 139; and at Knebworth, 149–50; and N, 210, 386, 391–2; and Mamontov, 39–40, 386; and Wulfert, 49; and M, 49–50, 61, 64–5, 113, 145, 234, 384; on his health and fitness, 141–2, 195; on his kindness, 142, 210; and his murder, 384; and half-brother George, 104, 142, 390; and Grand Duchess Olga, 50, 61; and Dimitri, 169, 245, 382; and Rachmaninovs, 100; and Bolshevik revolution, 370–2, 375; visits N in prison, 365; arrest and imprisonment of, 365, 371–2; escape from Russia, 375–8; marriages, 385–6, 392; attempted sale of M's chivalric orders, 393–4; death, 392n

Mamontov Savva, 35

Manikin, General, 308

Mansfield, Earl of, 148

Maria Vladimirovich, 'Grand Duchess', 389n

Marie, Queen of Rumania, 8

Marie Aleksandrovna, Empress, 20

Marie Fedorovna, Dowager Empress, 34–5, 53, 60–61, 119, 137, 154, 212, 232, 332, 389; appearance and character, 19–20, 24, 34, 51; and Alexander III, 19; and engaged to Grand Duke Nicholas, 124n; in Gatchina, 18–19, 48; at Anichkov Palace, 19, 161; in Denmark, 12–14, 53–4, 76, 78–80, 129, 390; in England, 145–6, 155; in wartime Germany, 161; in Kiev 227–8; as colonel-in-chief of Blue Cuirassiers, 34–5, 60–61, 119; and of Chevalier Gardes, 119, 137; on her preference for M, 131; on his affair with Dina, 12, 14–16, 29–30; and his 'betrothal' to Princess Patricia, 12–14, 55, 57; and on N, 109; and M's marriage, 129–32, 136, 145–7, 161; on his reconciliation with Olga, 228; meets N, 144, 146, 383; and Olga's affair with Kulikovsky, 52; and her marriage to, 228; and criticism of Alexandra, 201, 203, 228; and Rasputin, 203; refusal to believe sons murdered, 387; dismay at Kirill proclaiming himself Emperor, 387–8; death 390

Marie Georgieevna, Grand Duchess, *see George Mikhailovich, Grand Duchess*

Marie Nikolaevna, Grand Duchess (*Nicholas's third dau.*), 25, 353n; murder of, 370

Marie Palace, St Petersburg, 26–7, 262–5

Marie Pavlovna, snr, Grand Duchess (Vladimir), banished, 30; social attitudes, 34; hatred for Alexandra, 228, 247–8, 254, and linked to N, 220

Marie Pavlovna jr, Grand Duchess (*Dimitri's sister*), 129, 147, 154, 168, 244, 295, 381

Markov Andrei, 355–60, 362

Marlborough House, London, 146, 151, 155, 383

Marling, Sir Charles, 333, 381

Maryinski Theatre, 213–14, 258, 347

Masurian Lakes, 162

Matveev, Aleksei (*N's brother-in-law*), 90, 104, 113, 116, 168, 182, 225, 325; as legal advisor to M in leasing Moscow house, 85; and in Wulfert divorce, 107–8; in advising N, 92–3; role in arranging marriage, 125–7, 129; widowed, 173; appointed M's executive secretary, 225n; at Ai-Todor, 236; in February revolution, 260, 263–4; at Millionnaya Street, 274, 297–301, 307; role in drafting Michael's manifesto, 308–10; M and N under arrest at his apartment, 331; and children there, 336; and Tata there, 371–2; in Odessa, 377; in Paris, 383, 390

Meck, Nikolai von, 40

Michael I, first Romanov Tsar, 313

Michael Aleksandrovich, Grand Duke (Michael II), 2, 220; appearance, 5, 24, 50, 139–40, 163, 167, 189–90, 345–6; apartment in Gatchina palace, 47–8; assets, 5, 48–9, 136, 153, 164, 182–3, 221–2, 389; character of, 5, 6, 13, 27, 142, 184, 190, 210–11, 213, 252, 337; interest in cars, 48, 154, 235; in military history, 5; in music, 5, 141, 210, 245; photography, 62, 103, 128, 141, 142–3; sport, 5, 13, 24, 164–5; likes and dislikes, 141; health: diphtheria, 194–6, 202–3, 209–10, 212; and gastric ulcers, 112–13, 141, 195, 224, 235, 322, 331, 338, 351; birth, 20; childhood at Gatchina, 22–3, 27–8; relations with father, 27–8; joins Horse Guards Artillery, 24; and after transfer to Blue Cuirassiers, 5, 17, 24, 35, 44, 51, 59, 68; comes of age, 24–5; as heir presumptive, 7, 25–8, 53; as successor to Nicholas, 25–6, 28–9; appointed putative regent, 28; Witte's opinion of as a young man, 26–8; and others, 5–6; meets Queen Victoria at Nice and Balmoral, 6; and at her funeral, 26; at coronation of Edward VII, 26; and his funeral, 98; foreign Orders of, 26, 393–4; and Baby-Bee, 7–9; and affair with Dina, 10–12, 14–16, 29, 55–6; 'matched' with Princess Patricia, 12–14, 57–8; meets N, 7, 16; and at regimental ball, 44–5; and association in Gatchina, 46–7, 49–50, 52–3, 59–61, 64–6; fears about Wulfert, 63–4, 69–71; and challenged by him, 73–4, 82; resigns from Blue Cuirassiers, 74, 76, 81, 121; and as colonel of Chernigov Hussars, 116, 161; and Copenhagen with N, 77–80, 84, 89; and

Michael Aleksandrovich, Grand Duke – *cont.* in Moscow, 84–7, 89–92; and rents house, 85, 89–90; and is criticised by superiors, 91–2; and protests about Wulfert, 90; and demands residency permit for N, 93; and Wulfert divorce, 95, 97–9, 102, 104–7, 109; at Udinka, 100, 102–3; birth of George, and christening, 104; 'doctoring' of his birth and baptism certificates, 106–8; travels abroad (*in 1910*), 109–10, (*in 1911*) 117–18; appointed to and in command of Chevalier Gardes, 118–19, 121, 132, 134, 137, 161, 224; in St Petersburg with N, 118–19; transfers money abroad, 133; and runaway marriage, 112–28; and informs Nicholas and Dowager Empress 128–30; and punishment as 'madman', 131–5, 136, 143, 164; in exile in Cannes, 138–44; in Chexbres, 144–5; in London, and meets Dowager Empress, 146; takes up residence at Knebworth House, 149, 150–4, 160–61; rents Paddockhurst, 159–60; meets George V 160; returns to Russia, and Gatchina, 161; in command of Savage Division, 162–5, 167–8, 171–2, 175–7, 185–90; and of 2nd Cavalry Corps, 221, 224–6, 229–30, 251–2; gallantry awards, 177–9, 189–90, 223, 230, 303; promoted lieutenant-general, 225; adjutant-general, 231; and Inspector-General of Cavalry, 251; pays farewell visit to Brusilov, 252; and N's relationship with Dimitri, 170–71, 173, 175, 177, 182, 192–4, 207, 226; his love for N, 172–3, 177, 180, 186, 191, 224, 233–4; as a family man, 142, 170, 210, 249; legitimisation of son, 164–5, 182; financial problems, 153, 183, 221, 222; 'inventor' scandal, 211, 221; hospitals, 166, 170, 183, 222–3; views on war, 172, 187, 196, 230; and sense of duty 189–91, 225; with Nicholas at Mogilev, 164, 203–8, 230–31; at reopening of Duma, 219–20; at Kamenets-Podolsky, 227; at Tsarskoe Selo, 170, 186, 212, 249, 256; and last meeting, 325–6; warns Nicholas of the need for concessions, 208; and writes to him, 235–6; meets Alexandra, 227; and concerns about, 218, 256; and Rasputin, 218, 240; and Olga, 22–3, 52, 143, 184, 227–8; in favour of constitutional monarchy, 208, 217; seen as Regent, 252–3, 276, 279, 280–2, 284, 288–9; at Marie Palace conference, 260–3; and urged to seize power, 261; and negotiates with Nicholas, and offers to act as Regent, 263–5; at Winter Palace, 265–6; at Millionnaya Street, 266, 273–5, 281–2, 302–11; Nicholas abdicates in his favour, 286–9; proclaimed Emperor, 295–7; objections to, 287, 290, 296; and manifesto, 311–13; and interpretation, 311–14, 316–17; motives for decision, 316; telegram from Nicholas to Emperor Michael, 308–9; and reaction of to M's manifesto, 314; return to Gatchina, 315–16; discharged from army, 318, 321; hopes to visit England, 320–24; obtains permit for Finland, 324; and for Crimea, 332; arrested by Kerensky, 327–8, 330–2; and by Bolsheviks, 335–6; and imprisoned, 338–40; exiled to Perm, 340–2; imprisoned, 342; in Korolev Rooms, 343–52, 357–8; public support, 345, 351, 374; abducted and murdered, 357–61; reports of his escape, 361; and public reaction to, 367; and belief that he was leading counter-revolution, 366–9, 374, 376; 'recapture', 372; rumours of sightings, 282–3; officially dead, 386; memorial to, 395

Michael Mikhailovich, Grand Duke ('Miche-Miche'), 155, 387; morganatic marriage and banishment, 147; ambitions for wife, 148

Michael Nikolaevich, Grand Duke (*Sandro's father*), 26

Michael Theatre, Petrograd, 214, 243

Mikov, A. A., 354

Milford Haven, Marchioness of, 323, 392

Military Revolutionary Committee, 334–5

Millionnaya Street (*Putyatin apartment*), 266, 268, 273–5, 277, 281, 288, 291, 297–300, 309, 312, 315–16, 318, 325, 336

Milyukov, Pavel, 219, 262, 284–5, 288–9, 290, 296, 301, 303–6, 313, 317, 319n, 325

Min, General George, 29

Minerva, HMS, 15

Mirbach, Count Joachim von, 365, 367

Misha, *see Michael Aleksandrovich*

Misitsch, Father, 126–8

Mogilev 202–5, 207–8, 230–31, 234, 257, 259, 262–4, 268, 288, 290, 295, 299, 314, 327, 330, 359, 376

Moltke, Count Carl, 345

Moneanaar, Edgar, 391

Monte Carlo, 142, 154

Montreux, 72, 145

Mordvinov, Captain, later Colonel, A. A., 77, 92–3, 105, 109–10, 116–17, 134–5, 141, 153, 184, 203, 232

Morning Post, London, 13, 148

Moscow, industrial wealth, 33; appearance, 37; and contrasted with St Petersburg, 42–3; Sheremetevsky homes in, 36–7; in 1905 revolution, 39–40; 1915 pogroms in,

191–2, 200; in February revolution, 295; N in, 36–40, 173, 179, 182; with Wulfert, 61, 63; with Wulfert and M, 62–3; with M, 84–7, 89–99, 104, 106, 110, 182, 234–5; with Dimitri, 173–4; and to confront Lenin, 348–9
Moscow City Duma, 36
Moscow Ecclesiastical Authority, 108
Moscow Ecclesiastical Consistory, 97–8, 102
Moscow Private Opera Company, 35
Mossolov, A. A., 317
Motovilikha, 349–51, 355, 359–61
Motovilikha Soviet, 351
Myasnikov, Gavriil, 351–2, 354–63
Mysore, Maharajah of, 145

Nabokov, family,
  Vladimir, 271–3, 297, 308–13, 334–5
  Vladimir (*son*), 312n
  Nadine (*sister*), *see Nadine Vonlyarlarskaya*
Nagorsky (*M's godson*), 352
Napoleonic War, 5, 41
Napolnaya school, Alapaevsk, 353
Naryshkina, Mme, 220
Natasha, *see Brasova*
Neame, Margaret, 140, 209, 330–31, 335–6, 338–9, 371, 381
Nekrasov, Nikolai, 253, 302, 307–8, 325
Neratov, A., 117
Nereide, HMS, 377–8, 381
New International Theatre, London, 152
New Palace, later Alexander Palace, *see Tsarskoe Selo*
Nicholas Aleksandrovich, Grand Duke (*Alexander III's brother*), engaged to Princess Dagmar (Dowager Empress), death, church at Nice, 124
Nicholas I, Emperor, 147
Nicholas II, Emperor, 2, 5, 7, 13, 18, 44, 95, 164, 168; appearance, 24, 53; as a Hussar, 24; and Kschessinska, 11; becomes Emperor, 21; and unreadiness to be, 22; and uncle's browbeating, 24, 27; and marriage, 23; and coronation, 53; birth of children, 25–6; and of heir, 10, 28; appointment of M as putative Regent, 28; illness in Crimea, 25–6; and 1905 revolution, 39; and Witte, 22n, 26–7; attempts to assassinate, 28–9; worries about Romanov scandals, 30–31; belief in autocracy, 208, 287; prohibits M's marriage to Baby-Bee, 8–9; to Dina, 12, 14–15; and continuing concern about, 55–6; banishes M to Chernigov Hussars, 74; M protests to, 91; acknowledges George as M's son, 107; and legitimises him, 182; and N's divorce, 98–9; grants N name of Brasova, 111; orders Okhrana to trail M abroad, 117; and M's marriage, 128, 130–6, 143; guardianship order, 136–7; and lifts it, 221; allows M and N to return to Russia, 159; M's gallantry 179; 'victory tour', 184–5, 187, 200; becomes Supreme Commander, 197, 201–2; at Mogilev with M, 202–5, 207–8; suspends Duma, 206, 216, 259–60; at Duma, 218–20; and Rasputin, 199, 207, 217, 228, 240–41; influenced by drugs, 241; banishes Dimitri, 244; 'exiles' Bimbo, Kirill, Andrew, 247; plots against, 248, 252–3; meets Buchanan, 249–50; and Rodzyanko, 250–51; M and Sandro, 255–6; returns to Mogilev, 256; refuses to appoint M Regent in Petrograd, 264; train to Pskov, 268–71, 274, 277, 286; and return, 302, 314; abdication, 278, 281–2, 284–6, 297, 307, 311; and manifesto, 287–9, 290–91, 295–9, 302, 304, 308, 313, 316; and reaction to M's manifesto, 314; imprisonment at Tsarskoe Selo, 322, 324; and George V's unwillingness to grant asylum, 322–3; transfer to Tobolsk, and last meeting with M, 325–6; transfer to Ekaterinburg, 353; indifference to report of his death, 366–7; murder of, 363, 369–70; assets, 392–3
Nicholas, Prince of Greece, on M, 5
Nicholas Konstantinovich, Grand Duke (*nephew of Alexander II*), 31, 354n
Nicholas Mikhailovich ('Bimbo'), Grand Duke, 145, 316; warns Nicholas 240; and banished, 247; at Duma, 282; at Millionnaya Street 299–300, 302, 317; murder of, 382n
Nicholas Nikolaevich ('Nikolasha'), Grand Duke, 24; dismissal as Supreme Commander, 196–7, 199–201, 207; and Rasputin, 200–1; on Nicholas's abdication, 280; reappointed Supreme Commander, 287; and dismissed by Lvov, 319; opposes Kirill as Emperor, 387
Nijinsky, Vaslav, 154
Nikitin, Colonel Boris, 316
Nikolaevskaya Palace, Moscow, 191
Nikolasha, *see Nicholas Nikolaevich*
Nolde, Baron, 309–12
Norway, 54, 159, 161
Novo-Georgievsk, 196
Novoe Vremya, 39

Obolensky, Prince, 223–4
Observer, London, 13
'October Manifesto', 39, 206
Octobrists, 184, 253
Odessa, 14, 39, 377–8

Odoevsky-Maslov, Prince, 70, 92
Official Messenger, 136–7
Okhrana, 76, 88, 132; and Dina, 6, 14, 55–6; and N, 7, 115–16; ordered to prevent marriage, 117–18; trails M and N, 122–8; in revolution, 257–8
Oldenburg, Alexander, Duke of, 201
Oldenburg, Peter, Duke of, 15, 51, 65, 76, 78; marriage to Olga, 51; gambling and homosexuality, 51; appoints Kulikovsky ADC and accepts *ménage à trois*, 52; divorce, 228
Olga Aleksandrovna, (*M's sister*), 76, 78, 203; childhood with M, 22–3; and Dina, 6, 12, 14–15; on the Romanovs, 31; on her mother, 20, 51; marriage to Duke Peter, 51; affair with Kulikovsky, 51–3, 59, 64; and marriage to, 228; relationship with M, 22, 52, 92, 143, 184, 227–8; Tata on, 50, 61; legacy, 390
Olga Nikolaevna, Grand Duchess (*Nicholas's eldest dau.*), 203, 259; proposal to make her co-Regent, 133–4; suggestion of marrying Dimitri, 168; death of, 370
Olga, Grand Duchess (*mother of Miche-Miche*), 147
Omsk, 368, 374, 384
Order No 1, 319
Orel, 74, 82, 85, 90, 93, 101, 111, 113, 118, 121, 246
Orlov, Grigory, 17
Orsha, 375

Paddockhurst, Sussex, 159–60, 183, 222, 381
Page, Walter Hines, 152
Paléologue Maurice, 1–2, 55n; on N, 40; and her marriage, 126; and her beauty, 214; and her political intrigues, 215; on M, 216; on Russian women, 65, 108, 193; on Alexandra, 198–9; on Dimitri, 207; on Nicholas, 219, 241; on Rasputin, 198–9; and murder, 243; on 'champagne plot', 247; on February revolution, 258, 275; on Millionnaya Street meeting, 305, 312; on army deserters, 319
Paley, Princess (Olga Pistolkors), 31, 129, 168, 204, 216, 298, 317
Paley, Vladimir, 353
Paris, 154; Russian *èmigres* in, 1; Grand Dukes banished to, 31; M and N in, 110, 116–17, 140–41, 144, 149; and M transfers money to, 133, 153; summoned there by Paul, 143; and meets Xenia in, 144; N moves to (1927), 390; funeral of George in, 391; N's last days in, 394–5
Patricia (Patsy), Princess of Connaught, 6, 12–14, 57–8
Paul Aleksandrovich, Grand Duke, 204, 247, 275, 317; banishment, 31, 129, 143, 168; and M, 143; and Alexandra, 248; mishandles Guards corps, 230; and constitutional manifesto, 275; and Nicholas's abdication, 298; execution 382n
Paul I, Emperor, 25, 286
Percy Lodge, near Richmond, Surrey, 385–6
Perm, 340–2, 356, 373, 386, 395; M memorial cross, 395
Perm Cheka, 349–52, 354–5, 359, 361–2, 373
Perm City Soviet, 354, 372–3
Perm *Izvestiya*, 361
Peter Nikolaevich, Grand Duke (*Nikolasha's brother*), 387
Peter the Great, 41, 43
Peterhof, 29, 65, 73, 104, 186
Petrograd, 168, 170, 224, 287, 295, 316, 330, 334; St Petersburg renamed as, 161; M and N return to, 161; M's hospitals in, 166, 170, 223; N and society, 183–4, 213; funeral of Grand Duke Konstantin, 188; M 'detests', 211–12, 218; and 'scum', 224; with N at theatres, 213–14; February revolution in, 256–67, 271–6, 281–5, 288–90; reaction to M's succession, 296; and to M's manifesto, 316–17; Bolsheviks attempt coup, 324–5; Kerensky defence against Kornilov, 330; M under arrest in, 330–2; and imprisoned in, 338–40; falls to Bolsheviks, 333–4; Bolshevik HQ (Smolny), 335, 339; Bolshevik government moves to Moscow, 340; N imprisoned in, 364–5; and escapes, 371–2; British embassy stormed, 372; execution of Grand Dukes in, 382n, *see also St Petersburg*
Petrograd Cheka, 339–40, 364–5, 371–2
Petrograd Soviet of Workers' and Soldiers' Deputies ('Soviet'), 276, 290, 300, 303, 310, 318–19, 321; formed, 271; and composition of, 283; and Kerensky, 271, 273, 285, 305; garrison and, 283–4; wants democratic republic, 282; suspicions, 281; and fears of, 283, 289; sets out agenda for new government, 283–4; and M's manifesto, 312, 315; demands M's arrest, 315; and Nicholas's imprisonment, 322–3; domination of new government, and Order No 1, 319–21, 324; and Kornilov 329–3; and first (1905) Soviet, 39, 271
Petrograd State Bank, 336–7
Petrogradskaya Gazeta, and *Petrogradskaya Listok*, 317
Petrovsky Park, 85, 91, 104, 106, 199

Petukhov (Moscow merchant), 107
Philippe, Dr (Philippe Nizier-Vachod), 198, 205–6
Pistolkors, Olga, *see Princess Paley*
Plehve, General Pavel, 90–91
Poland, M's assets in, 48, 389
Polar Star 76, 78–9
Politiken, Copenhagen, 78
Polivanov, A. A., 237
Pollock, Sir Frederick, 152
Polovtsov A. A., 5–6
Polovtsov Colonel, later General Peter, 163–4, 276, 324, 332
Pospelov Father Peter, 104, 108, 163
Progressive Bloc, 216, 219, 252
Protopopov, Aleksandr, 237, 243, 247–9, 261, 272
Provisional Government, 301, 304, 306, 311–14, 317–20, 322–5, 330, 335, 389; formation of, and named as, 281
Przemysl, 184, 187
Pskov 270, 275, 277, 279, 281, 285, 287–8, 290, 295, 297–9, 302, 307, 345
Purishkevich, Vladimir, 241–4
Pushkin, Aleksandr, 147
Pushkino, near Moscow, 37, 44
Putilov arsenal, Petrograd, 206, 257
Putyatin family, 344, 390
 Prince Pavel, 166, 266, 344, 346, 381
 Princess Olga, 171, 226, 309, 336; meets M, and N, and her description of, 166–7; at Brasova, 244–6; shelters M, 266–7, 273, 291; on M meeting Bimbo, 299–300; luncheon at Millionnaya Street, 307; on M's motives, 316; on British offer of passports, 333; with N at Smolny, 339–40
 Nathalie (*daughter*), 167, 246
Putyatin, Prince Sergei, marries Grand Duchess Marie Pavlovna jr, 381; and son Roman

Rachmaninov family, 113
 Sergei, 33, 35, 38, 100, 113, 179; *and his wife* Natalya, 100, 113, 179; *and their daughter* Irina, 100
Radziwill, Princess Leon, 258
Rakhmanov, Dr, 104, 106
Ramsey, Admiral Sir Alexander, 58n
Rasputin, Grigory, 211, 217, 219; and Alexis's haemophilia, 197; appearance, 198; outrageous conduct, 199; as hated figure, 197, 200, 237; role in dismissal of Nikolasha, 200–1; influence over Alexandra, 197–9, 207; Dowager Empress on, 203, 228; and Guchkov 216; and M, 218, 240; and N, 240; temporary removal of, 199; murder of, 241–5, 247–8, 381; and burial 244, 259; Protopopov and ghost, 247
Rata, Miss (*nanny*), 139, 150, 152, 159–61, 209, 386
Rech, 317n
Red Army, 368n
Red Guards, 339, 355, 357, 366, 370
Red Terror, 372–3
Repin, Ilya Efimovich, 27n
Reuters, 13
Reyer, Armin von, 374
Riezler (*German embassy official*), 365
Riga, Treaty of (1921), 392
Rimsky-Korsakov, Nikolai, 11, 154
Rinaldi, Antonio, 17
Robinson, Williams and Burnands, 149
Rodzyanko, Mikhail, 121n, 270, 272, 279–80, 282, 284–5, 287, 291, 304, 316; with M at Duma reopening, 219; 'peculiar interview' with Marie Pavlovna, 247–8, 254; M consults, 250; and Nicholas, 250–51, 256–8; and Krymov plot, 254; Duma suspension, 260; calls M to help, and urges Regency, 260–2; sends guards to Millionnaya Street, 274; role in Grand Dukes' manifesto, 275–6; Nicholas proposes as prime minister, 277; attempts to suppress Nicholas's abdication manifesto, 290; and Ruzsky, 277, 279, 290, 298; and Alekseev 290; M's offer to help, 281; terror of; 289–90, 295, 303–4; at Millionnaya Street, 300–1, 303–7; and communicates outcome to Mogilev, 314
Rodzyanko, Pavel, 121
Romania, 377, 381
Romanov family, 21, 24, 39, 69, 216, 313, 317–18, 320–1, 344, 353, 367, 393; Queen Victoria's dislike of, 6; and British royals, 13; and palaces, 17; M on, 6; and marital scandals, 30–2; and 1905 revolution, 40; in England, 155; and George V's unwillingness to give them asylum, 322–3; and 'champagne plot', 252; Soviet resolution to arrest, 315; and Ural Soviet decision to execute, 362–3, 369; divisions over Kirill proclaiming himself Emperor, 387
Rome, 110, 154
Roosevelt, Theodore, 27
Roshal, Semen, 335–6
Royal Ascot, 155
Royal Opera House, London, 154
Rubinstein, D. L., 240
Rudolf, Crown Prince of Austria, 19
Russia, industrial power, 33; Russo-Japanese war, 22, 27; 'Bloody Sunday', 39, 43, 265;

Russia – *cont.*
and 1905 Revolution, 39–40; 'October Manifesto' and first Duma, 39; legal 'Estates', 35–6; divorce in, 33–4, 82, 94; husbands' rights, 82; influence of 'Baltic barons', 40; first world war begins, 159; and casualties in, 172, 196; strikes (1916), 217; end of Fourth Duma, *see February Revolution and Provisional Government*; Kerensky declares republic, 330, 332; Bolshevik Revolution, 333–5; elections for Constituent Assembly, and closure of, 338; Treaty of Brest-Litovsk, 338; and civil war, 347–8, 354, 367–9, 384; Germany backs monarchy in, 366–7
RUSSIAN ARMY
Bessarabian Regiment, 75
Blue Cuirassiers, history of, 41; uniforms, 41–2; etiquette, 34–5, 44; Dowager Empress as colonel-in-chief; 34–5, 60–61, 119; Bernov as commander of, 45, 60; von Schweder as colonel of, 40, 120–21; M joins 24, as squadron commander, 5, 7, 16, 44–5; resigns, 74, 76; attitudes towards N, 81, 101, 120–21; and Wulfert, 34, 40–41, 68, 71, 81; and duel, 74; Kulikovsky in, 51–2, 59–60
Chernigov Hussars, 74, 116, 161
Chevalier Gardes, 163, 166, 282; Bernov and, 60, 81; M as colonel, 118–19, 121, 132, 134, 137, 161, 224
Don Cossacks, 21, 221
Garde Equipage, 260
Horse Guards, 168
Horse Guards Artillery, 24
Hussar Life Guards, 197
Litovsky Regiment, 258
Pavlovsk Guards, 257
Preobrazhensky Guards, 258, 266
Semenovsky Guards, 29, 39–40
Volynsky Guards, 258
Yellow Cuirassiers, 41
Zemstvos Hussars, 300
23rd Artillery Brigade, 210
Caucasian Native Cavalry ('Savage Division'), 162–5, 167, 170–71, 175–6, 179, 185–6, 188–9, 221, 230, 251, 276, 316, 320, 328–9, 332–3
Fourth Cavalry Division, 295
Second Cavalry Corps, 165, 221, 224–6, 229–30, 251–2
Third Cavalry Corps, 329, 330, 334
Guards Army, 230; Second Army, 162; Seventh Army, 221; Eighth Army, 176, 178; Ninth Army, 188, 374
Russian Embassy, Berlin, 76, 122
Russian Orthodox Church, 8, 107–8
Russian revolution (1905), 43–4, 259; 'Bloody Sunday', 39, 43–4, 265
Russian Telegraph Agency, 373, 376
Russo-Japanese war, 22, 27
Russo-Turkish war (1877–8), 187n
Ruzsky, General Nikolai, 270, 277, 279–81, 286–7, 290, 295
Rybinsk, 374

St Briac, Brittany, 387
St Leonards-in-Sea College, 382
St Moritz, 152
St Peter and St Paul Fortress, 188, 266, 273, 322–3, 382n
St Petersburg, 18, 142; renamed as Petrograd, 161; assassination of Alexander II, 17; as the capital of imperial Russia, and described, 42–4; compared with Moscow, 42–3; M and N in, 62, 87, 118–21; reaction to M's marriage, 138–9; 'Bloody Sunday', 39; *see also Petrograd*
St Petersburg-Cannes express, 43
Samsonov, General Aleksandr, 162
Sandringham, 56–7, 135, 146
Sandro, *see Alexander Mikhailovich*
Sapozhnikov, Ilya, 357
'Savage Division', *see Russian Army*
Savinkov, Boris, 327, 329
Saxe-Coburg-Gotha, 156; Duke of, 7, 8; Duchess of, 6
Sazonov, Sergei, 205, 237
Scavenius, George, 344
Schlieffer family, 159–60, 166, 171, 214; Maria (*mother*), 113; Marina and Tania, 169
Schweder, Colonel Eduard von, 40, 81, 120
secret police, *see Okhrana*
Serbian Orthodox Church, 126
Serbs, 125–6
Serge Aleksandrovich, Grand Duke (*M's uncle*), 27, 129, 168, 243n; assassination, 28
Serge Mikhailovich, Grand Duke, 11, 30–31, 353, 370
Sergei (*Brasovo majordomo*), 113
Serov (*of Cheka*), 371
Seven Years War, 41
Shaftesbury Theatre, London, 57
Shamarin, A. A., 351
Sharya, 341
Shcheglovitv, Ivan, 271
Shcherbachev, General, 221
Shcherbatov, Prince, 205
Sheremetevsky family, 37
Sergei Aleksandrovich (*father*), 128; as lawyer, 35–7; and M, 101; 'nobility', 36

Julia Vladislavovna (*mother*), 37, 128
Nathalie (Natasha), *see Brasova*
Olga, later Matveev, intelligence, 35, 38; and Wulfert, 71–2, 84; at Brasovo, 113; on Riviera, 116; in Cannes, 128; at Knebworth, 152; death, 173, 179, 182, 225n
Vera (*eldest daughter*), 38, 174; illness and death, 179–80, 181–2, 231
Shidlovsky, Serge, 219
Shingarev, Aleksandr, 338
Shulgin, Vasily, 281, 285–8, 296–7, 299–301, 304, 307–9
Siberia, 199, 215, 342, 368, 374
Simpson, Major, 171, 320–21
Simpson, Mrs Wallis (later Duchess of Windsor), 138
Sipyagin, Dimitri, 26
Sirotino, 308
Skirmisher HMS, 378
Skodsborg, 75
Smolny, Petrograd, 339–40
'Snape', Wadhurst, England, 381–2, 384–5
Socialist Revolutionaries, 338n, 367n
Somme, battle of the, 229
Sorbonne, Paris, 390–91
Sorensen, Captain, 345
Sorokin (*Perm Cheka*), 356, 359
Sorrento, 14–15
Sotheby's, London, 393–4
Soviet, *see Petrograd Soviet of Workers' and Soldiers' Deputies*
Soviet Embassy, Paris, 362
Soviet of People's Commissars, 340, 361
Spala, Poland, 49, 130
ST12 (*British agent*), 368
Staekelberg, Baron, 274
Stakhovich, General, 90–91
Stalin, Joseph, 340, 385n
Stamfordham, Lord, 323, 331–2
Stanislavov 176, 179
Stankevich, Vladimir, 252–3
State Council, 275
Stavka (*Supreme HQ*), 164, 169, 186, 189, 194, 197, 200, 202, 207, 211–12, 227, 230, 234, 236–7, 241, 253, 257, 259, 287, 302
Stockholm Olympics (1912), 121, 168
Stolypin, Nikolai, 266–7
Stolypin, Peter, 29, 92, 266
Stravinsky, Igo, 154
Stryj, 176
Stürmer, Boris, 218–19, 237, 240, 272
Sudeikin (*sculptor*), 154
Sukhomlinov, Vladimir, 91, 196
Sukhotin, Captain Serge, 241
Sukin, 384
Supreme Monarchist Council, 388
Sverdlov, Yacob, 349, 355, 362, 373
Sweden, 159, 161
Switzerland, 66, 68, 79, 89

Tannenberg, East Prussia, 162
Tartars, 165, 177
Tata, *see Mamontov, Nathalie ('Tata')*
Tatiana Nikolaevna, Grand Duchess (*Nicholas's second dau.*), 259, 354n; death of, 370
Tauride Palace, 218–19, 259, 271–3, 275–6, 281–3, 288, 291, 299–302, 312–13
Tchaikovsky 37, 212, 214
Tereshchenko, Mikhail, 253, 304, 307, 325, 331–2
Theatre Royal, Drury Lane, 154–5
Thormeyer M. (*tutor*), 23
Tiflis, Caucasus, 163
The Times, London, 13, 148, 151, 314, 342, 349, 367, 394
Tobolsk, Urals, 324–5, 328, 353, 354n
Tolstoy, Count Leo, 152
Tolstoy, Count Pavel, 195, 217
Torby, Countess, 148, 151, 155; and marriage to Miche-Miche, 147, 151
Trans-Siberian railway, 347
Trevelyan, Miss, 370
Troitsky, Mr (*tutor*), 23
Troitsky Gate, Moscow, 348
Trotsk, as name for Gatchina, 385n
Trotsky, Leon, 39, 324, 349, 361, 385n
Tsarskoe Selo (later Pushkin), 18, 44, 55, 69, 79, 81, 202, 224, 231, 250, 258, 263, 274; M at, 170, 186, 212, 227, 249, 256, 265; and last meeting with Nicholas, 325–6; and Alexandra, 201, 220, 223, 227–8, 240, 251, 255–6, 268, 270–71, 298, 318; and Rasputin, 197–8, 200, 219, 240, 243–4; and Grand Duke Paul, 204, 248; as garrison, 287, 330, 334; imprisonment at, 322, 324
Tupitsin, Olga and Sergei, 347, 350, 357
Turkestan, 367
Turkin, M. P., 362

Udinka, near Moscow, 100–4, 111
Ukraine, 48, 321, 365–6, 374–7, 381, 389
Ukraine (destroyer), 76
Ulyanov, Aleksandr, 21n
Uncle Bertie, *see Edward VII*
Ural Regional Cheka, 352
Ural Regional Soviet, 354–5, 361–3, 366
Urals, 340, 384
Uritsky, Moisei, 339–42, 345, 364–5, 372, 385
Ustse-Zelena, 234

Valdai, 88–9
Vedikhov (*chauffeur*), 328
Venice, 110, 128
Venus, s.s., 159, 161
Verdun, battle of, 230
Victoria, Princess ('Toria') (*Queen Alexandra's dau.*), 56–8
Victoria, Queen, 12, 13; and Alexander III, 6; and M, 6; and Saxe-Coburg-Gotha, 7–8; funeral, 26, 127
Victoria Melita ('Ducky'), Grand Duchess, 6; and marriage to Grand Duke Ernst of Hesse-Darmstadt, 8, 30; and second marriage to Grand Duke Kirill, 30–31, 34, 387; on M and Baby-Bee, 6, 9
Vienna, 124–8, 140, 154, 229
Vitebsk, 375
Vladimir Aleksandrovich, Grand Duke (*M's uncle*), 27, 30, 34
Vladimir Kirillovich, Prince (later 'Grand Duke'), 388–9
Vladimir palace, 252
Vladivostok, 347
Volkov, Aleksandr, 361
Vologda, 341
Vonlyarlarskaya, Nadine, 308, 334–5; and daughter Sophie, 335
'Vova' (*Grand Duke Andrew's illegitimate son*), 30
Vyatka, 368
Vyazemsky, Prince Dimitri, 253
Vyazemsky family, 171, 244–5, 390
  Prince Vladimir, 163, 210, 234, 245, 253n, 325
  Princess, 163, 365, 370, 372, 376–8, 384
Vyazma, 268
Vyrubova, Anna, 132, 198–9, 243–4, 259

War Office, London, 160
Warsaw, 84, 196
Washburn, Stanley, 190
'Whites', 354–6, 369–70, 382, 388
Wilhelm II, Kaiser, 162, 345, 366
William, Prince, of Sweden, 381
Wilson, Woodrow, 322
Wilton, Robert, 314, 342, 346, 349, 351
Windsor Castle, 26, 155
Winter Palace, 18, 19, 44, 218, 259, 265, 274; Alexander II dies in, 20; 'Bloody Sunday', 39, 265; M arrives and orders evacuation, 265–6, 273; Kerensky in, 325, 330; Bolsheviks capture, 333–4; M sees damage, 336
Witte, Sergei, as tutor to M, 26; and preference for him over Nicholas, 26–8; enmity of Alexandra, 26; and 'October Manifesto', 39; opposition to Russo-Japanese war, 27; and to first world war, 22n; dismissed as prime minister, 22n, 26, 39n; and succeeded by Goremykin, 206
'Women's Battalion', 333–4
Wrangel, Baroness, 274–5
Wrangel, Baron Nikolai, 109–10, 116, 274
Wulfert, Natasha, *see Brasova*
Wulfert, Vladimir Vladimirovich, family, 40, 101; and appearance, 41–2, 96; finances, 40–41, 66, 68, 107; N meets, 39; and marries, 33, 34–5, 40; and Tata, 42, 49, 61, 71; in Blue Cuirassiers, 34, 40–41, 64, 68, 71; and removed from 81; and Kremlin post, 70, 81–2, 84, 107; tolerates M's relationship with N, 49, 53, 61–2, 64–5; quarrels with N, 53–4; and marriage breakdown, 65–72; 'marital rape', 66, 71; challenges M, 74, 82; threatens suicide, 71; and to force N to return to him, 90; to murder her, 90–91, 93; and to take her child, 94–8, 106; agrees divorce, 97–8; renounces father's rights, 107; remarries, 107
Würzburg, 128
Wyld, Lieut-Commander, 377

Xenia Aleksandrovna, Grand Duchess (*M's sister*), 132, 147, 155, 184, 241, 383; and Baby-Bee, 9; and Dina, 14–15; marriage to Sandro, 5, 23, 143–4; and her lover, 144, 146; reconciliation with M, 143–4; and on M's meeting with Dowager Empress, 145–6; legacy, 390

Yakhontova, Mme, 375
Yalta, 26, 295
Yar restaurant, Moscow, 199
Yavorska, Lydia (Princess Baryatinskaya), 152
Yusopov family, 44, 240–41
  Prince Felix, 155, 168; and Rasputin's murder, 241–4; in England, 381–2; and N, 385
  Princess Irina, 155, 241–2
Yuzefovich, General, 315

Zankevich, General, 265
Zarnitsa, 48–9, 65, 76, 78–80, 135, 249
Zemstvos, 262
Zhuzhgov, Nikolai, 355–60, 364
Znamerovsky, Colonel Peter, 347–8, 350–2, 357, 364
Znamerovsky, Mme, 373